AN INTERNATIONAL HANDBOOK OF TOURISM EDUCATION

ADVANCES IN TOURISM RESEARCH

Series Editor: Professor Stephen J. Page
University of Stirling, U.K.
s.j.page@stir.ac.uk

Advances in Tourism Research series publishes monographs and edited volumes that comprise state-of-the-art research findings, written and edited by leading researchers working in the wider field of tourism studies. The series has been designed to provide a cutting edge focus for researchers interested in tourism, particularly the management issues now facing decision-makers, policy analysts and the public sector. The audience is much wider than just academics and each book seeks to make a significant contribution to the literature in the field of study by not only reviewing the state of knowledge relating to each topic but also questioning some of the prevailing assumptions and research paradigms which currently exist in tourism research. The series also aims to provide a platform for further studies in each area by highlighting key research agendas which will stimulate further debate and interest in the expanding area of tourism research. The series is always willing to consider new ideas for innovative and scholarly books, inquiries should be made directly to the Series Editor.

Recent published titles in this series include:

PIKE
Destination Marketing Organisations

THOMAS
Small Firms in Tourism: International Perspectives

LUMSDON & PAGE
Tourism and Transport

KERR
Tourism Public Policy and the Strategic Management of Failure

WILKS & PAGE
Managing Tourist Health and Safety in the New Millennium

Forthcoming titles include:

RYAN & AICKEN
Indigenous Tourism

RYAN, PAGE & AICKEN
Taking Tourism to the Limits

WILKS, PENDERGAST & LEGGAT
Tourism in Turbulent Times

LENNON, SMITH, COCKEREL & TREW
Benchmarking National Tourism Organisations and Agencies

BALDACCHINO
Cold Water Tourism

Related Elsevier Journals — sample copies available on request
Annals of Tourism Research
International Journal of Hospitality Management
Tourism Management
World Development

AN INTERNATIONAL HANDBOOK OF TOURISM EDUCATION

EDITED BY

DAVID AIREY and JOHN TRIBE

University of Surrey, U.K.

2005

ELSEVIER

Amsterdam – Boston – Heidelberg – London – New York – Oxford
Paris – San Diego – San Francisco – Singapore – Sydney – Tokyo

ELSEVIER B.V.
Radarweg 29
P.O. Box 211, 1000 AE
Amsterdam, The Netherlands

ELSEVIER Inc.
525 B Street, Suite 1900
San Diego, CA 92101-4495
USA

ELSEVIER Ltd
The Boulevard, Langford Lane
Kidlington, Oxford OX5 1GB
UK

ELSEVIER Ltd
84 Theobalds Road
London WC1X 8RR
UK

First edition 2005

British Library Cataloguing in Publication Data
A catalogue record is available from the British Library.

ISBN: 0-08-044667-1

♾ The paper used in this publication meets the requirements of ANSI/NISO Z39.48-1992 (Permanence of Paper).
Printed in The Netherlands.

Contents

Teaching, Learning and Assessment

Resources, Progression and Quality

Postscript

Contributors

David Airey
University of Surrey, Guildford, Surrey, UK

Paul Barron
School of Tourism and Leisure Management, The University of Queensland, Australia

Nina Becket
Higher Education Academy Network for Hospitality, Leisure, Sport and Tourism, Oxford Brookes University, Oxford, UK

Lyn Bibbings
Department of Hospitality, Leisure and Tourism Management, Oxford Brookes University, Oxford, UK

David Botterill
Welsh School of Hospitality Tourism and Leisure Management, University of Wales Institute Cardiff, Cardiff, UK

Graham Busby
Plymouth Business School, University of Plymouth, Plymouth, UK

Stroma Cole
Faculty of Leisure & Tourism, Buckinghamshire Chilterns University College, High Wycombe, UK

Stephen Craig-Smith
The University of Queensland, Ipswich, Queensland, Australia

Sheryl Elliot
Department of Tourism and Hospitality Management, School of Business, The George Washington University, Washington, DC, USA

Xixia Fan
School of Tourism Management, Beijing International Studies University, Beijing, PR China

Alastair Forbes
Faculty of Leisure & Tourism, Buckinghamshire Chilterns University College, High Wycombe, UK

Walter Freyer
Department of Tourism Economics and Management, Technical University of Dresden, Dresden, Germany

Tim Gale
University of the West of England, Bristol, UK

Michael Hammer
Chair of Tourism Economics and Management, Technical University of Dresden, Dresden, Germany

Lisa Hodgkins
Learning Resources Centre, Buckinghamshire Chilterns University College, High Wycombe, UK

Simon Hudson
Haskayne School of Business, Calgary, Alberta, Canada

Fiona Jordan
University of Gloucestershire, Gloucester, UK

Brian King
School of Hospitality, Tourism and Marketing, Faculty of Business & Law, Victoria University, Melbourne, Victoria, Australia

Adele Ladkin
Bournemouth University, Fern Barrow, Poole, Dorset, UK

Sérgio Leal
University of Surrey, Guildford, Surrey, UK and Faculdades Integradas da Vitória de Santo Antão, Pernambuco, Brazil

Acolla Lewis
Department of Management Studies, University of the West Indies, St. Augustine, Trinidad

Melphon Mayaka
Department of Hospitality and Tourism Management, Kenyatta University, Nairobi, Kenya

Tanja Mihalič
Faculty of Economics, University of Ljubljana, Ljubljana, Slovenia

Miriam Moir
Faculty of Leisure & Tourism, Buckinghamshire Chilterns University College, High Wycombe, UK

Maria Auxiliadora Padilha
Faculdades Integradas da Vitória de Santo Antão, Pernambuco, Brazil

Astrid Piermeier
University of Regensburg, Regensburg, Germany

Derek Robbins
School of Services Management, Bournemouth University, Poole, Dorset, UK

Melville Saayman
Institute for Tourism and Leisure Studies, North West University, Potchefstroom, South Africa

Marianna Sigala
The Business School, University of the Aegean, Chios, Greece

Shalini Singh
Brock University, St. Catharines, Ontario, Canada

Tej Vir Singh
Centre for Tourism Research & Development, Indira Nagar, Lucknow, India

Ginger Smith
Department of Tourism and Hospitality Management, School of Business, The George Washington University, Washington, DC, USA

Karen A. Smith
Victoria Management School, Victoria University of Wellington, Wellington, New Zealand

Dimitrios Stergiou
Technological Educational Institute of Patras, Patras, Greece

Marion Stuart-Hoyle
Canterbury Christ Church University College, Canterbury, Kent, UK

John Tribe
School of Management, University of Surrey, Guildford, UK

Magiel Venema
NHTV, Breda University for Professional Education, Breda, Netherlands

Brian Wheeller
NHTV, Breda University for Professional Education, Breda, Netherlands

Eugenia Wickens
Faculty of Leisure & Tourism, Buckinghamshire Chilterns University College, High Wycombe, UK

Wen Zhang
School of Tourism Management, Beijing International Studies University, Beijing, PR China

INTRODUCTION

Chapter 1

Introduction

John Tribe and David Airey

Rationale and Aims

For some observers, "tourism higher education" might appear to be a term containing mutually exclusive words. Surely tourism cannot merit study at a higher level of education? Indeed in the UK, tourism degrees are sometimes bundled (particularly by opportunist politicians) into a category of deep disdain under the heading of Mickey Mouse Degrees. But new courses have often struggled for due recognition in the academy which is inherently conservative and traditional. For example Silver (1990, p. 131) reports that the UK CNAA (Council for National Academic Awards) board expressed considerable angst about new degree proposals:

> I remember housing studies for example, was one of the crunch points as to whether you could actually make a degree of something of that kind. And then people would point to odd things like paper technology that some of the universities had had for years and said, well what's odd about housing studies.

Housing studies is now an established part of higher education, but the question as to whether tourism is a serious or worthy area for study still hangs in the air. It is this question that provides an initial impetus for this book. With regard to the maturity of the subject, Hall and Page (2002) note that social science scholarship on tourism can be traced back to the 1920s in the USA and Europe while in Chapter 2 of this book Airey finds an example of individual scholarship on tourism dating back to 1891. However, the major growth in the subject has occurred relatively recently since the mid-1980s and this provides the second impetus for the book. The time is ripe for a comprehensive description, analysis and evaluation of the state of tourism education at the international level. The final rationale for the book is to provide those involved in tourism education with guidance on how other people are approaching the task as well as offering some practical tips on design, delivery and review of courses.

An International Handbook of Tourism Education
Copyright © 2005 by Elsevier Ltd.
All rights of reproduction in any form reserved
ISBN: 0-08-044667-1

The aims of the book are captured in the section headings. First, the introduction offers a detailed account of the growth and development of the tourism studies and a review of the literature on tourism education. Second, the crucial issue of curriculum for tourism is unpacked. Third, authors from around the world provide the basis for a comparative analysis of tourism education by providing commentaries from a variety of national and/or regional contexts. Fourth, the "chalk-face" issues of teaching, learning and assessment in tourism are reviewed. Fifth, issues surrounding resources, progression and quality are discussed and finally the state of the art of tourism education is evaluated and key issues for the future are identified.

The rest of this chapter will provide a more detailed introduction to, and overview of, the issues discussed in the various headings.

Introduction

The remainder of the introduction starts with Chapter 2, where David Airey initially charts the development of tourism as a distinct area of study and notes three significant developments. First, there has been a massive increase in the numbers of students, institutions and teachers of tourism. Second, the curriculum has broadened beyond the vocational and tourism has emerged as a subject for study at many different levels of education. Third, this growth and change has led to tensions in the development of the curriculum. On the one hand, Airey sees the danger of excess vocationalism where tourism education does little more than provide a reflection of the world of work. On the other, he cautions against tourism education turning its back on its industry connections as this would jeopardise one of its key *raisons d'etre*.

In Chapter 3, John Tribe evaluates the literature on tourism education. He initially identifies the size of, and trends in, tourism education research and argues that the growing literature on tourism education (at least 302 articles up to 2001) and the existence of three educational journals specific to the field are important indicators of the growing maturity of tourism as an academic subject. Second, he finds that tourism education research has particularly focussed on curriculum issues which have accounted for 86 per cent of the total. Tribe concludes that, for the future a greater attention to methodological issues is required and more research into effective learning and assessment is needed. Additionally he notes that progression into tourism education and issues of widening participation are under-researched and that there is a lack of evaluative and prescriptive literature on resources and quality.

Curriculum

The starting point for this section is the critical analysis of the tourism curriculum provided by John Tribe in Chapter 4. He argues that since curriculum design involves framing in curriculum space, and therefore choice, then any curriculum must be contestable. The main contest is about what knowledge should be included, so Tribe analyses the relationship

between tourism, knowledge and the curriculum. He subsequently considers the basic principles of curriculum design and explores a number of theoretical positions in order to evaluate a number of proposals that have been made for a tourism curriculum. A recurrent theme
in the chapter is that of the schisms that exist in each of the areas of tourism, knowledge and
the curriculum. On the one hand, Tribe notes that tourism, knowledge and the curriculum
may be bounded by a business and vocationalist view of things. But he also holds out the
prospect for tourism education as a means for understanding and responsible action in more
widely drawn, complex world of tourism.

Chapters 5 and 6 provide case studies in curriculum development. In Chapter 5, Sheryl
Elliott and Ginger Smith offer a case study on online education that illustrates curriculum
theory and practice. Their case study describes the establishment of the Accelerated
Master's of Tourism Administration (AMTA) by the Department of Tourism and
Hospitality Management at George Washington University, Washington, DC. Here they
describe how the degree programme was brought fully online and includes a multimedia
animated audio/visual lecture component. In Chapter 6, John Tribe presents a case study,
which examines the process and products of a tourism curriculum development and innovation project for a University in Moldova. Tribe elaborates a method for curriculum
design and development based on strategic management techniques. Specifically he
describes three aspects of situational analysis that were used — a needs analysis, a capability analysis and a force field analysis — and outlines the curriculum that was agreed
based on this analysis. However, Tribe also offsets this "success" of the project with a critical evaluation and offers an alternative "failure" reading of the outcomes. On this latter
view, the influence of Western hegemony and neo-colonial development is surfaced and
flagged as a particularly poignant issue for countries such as Moldova who have only
recently escaped the grip of a strict regime of Soviet ideology. Indeed this chapter can also
offer an interesting critical–reflexive insight into the use of the term "international" in the
title of this text. It reminds us that although this text is international in its content, its overall outlook is heavily saturated by the situatedness of its editors (country, ethnicity, university, gender, class, etc.).

Finally, work placement (sandwich year, internship) is a common feature of the curriculum in tourism programmes and Graham Busby investigates this topic in Chapter 7. Busby
reviews the concept and its implementation and identifies the key attributes and aspects of
good practice that make for a successful work experience programme. The discussion is
illustrated with students' accounts of their experiences during their placements.

International Tourism Education

The section on international tourism education offers insights into provision in 12 countries and regions representing a range of different contexts. These chapters consider issues
such as size and development, government policy and structures, curriculum, teaching and
learning, assessment, research and quality issues.

In Chapter 8, Brian King and Stephen Craig-Smith assess the situation in Australasia.
Here they offer a picture of a rise in tourism education in both Australia and New Zealand
to a position where the majority of public universities in the two countries now offer

tourism and/hospitality degree programmes. The development and funding of the Sustainable Tourism Co-operative Research Centre, a partnership between universities, governments and tourism enterprises is identified as a key factor that has enabled Australia to compete strongly in the international arena in tourism research. King and Craig-Smith also note that international tourism student enrolments have grown rapidly in both countries largely due to the proximity of the expanding Asian student market and the attractiveness of Australasia as a place to study. An interesting point of comparison arises here with the situation in North America (see Chapter 16), where Simon Hudson describes a decline in international post-graduate enrolment.

Chapter 9 provides a contrast where Sérgio Leal and Maria Auxiliadora Padilha examine the situation in Brazil and Latin America. They find tourism education and research in this region to be in its early stages of development. There is little attention paid to the development of qualified professionals working in the sector and only a modest participation of scholars from the region in the international academic community. In Brazil however they find that tourism education and research have rapidly expanded, encouraged by the fast growth of the industry and enabled by the liberalisation of the education sector. The authors note a concomitant growth in the number of specialised publications and research degree programmes but point to the lack of a subject association that would support the development of tourism education.

For the Caribbean, as Acolla Lewis reminds us in Chapter 10, tourism is the "lifeblood" of the majority of the islands. Despite this, Lewis notes that tourism education and training has come under intense criticism with respect to the governance and operation of the institutions as well as the quality of the programmes. However, she sees grounds for optimism with initiatives such as the creation of the Association of Caribbean Tertiary Institutions (ACTI) and the Caribbean Tourism Human Resource Council (CTHRC). The latter encourages development of tourism education in the region through its annual Tourism Educators Forum, the Scholarship Foundation Programme and the establishment of a Caribbean Tourism Learning System (CTLS), which underwrites a unified core curriculum for different levels of certification, a system for transfer of credits between institutions and student exchange programmes. Finally, Lewis also notes that the University of the West Indies (UWI) is set to assume a more active role in tourism education in the region.

In Chapter 11, Wen Zhang and Xixia Fan offer an introduction to the development of tourism education on the Chinese mainland. They identify the three development stages of China's tourism education. The first phase from the founding of New China (in 1949) to the implementation of reform and opening-up (in 1978) was mainly on-job training to front-line employees, such as hotel attendants, coach drivers, interpreters and guides. The second phase from 1978 to the mid-1990s saw a strong growth of China's tourism education and the formation of the tourism educational system. In the third phase, from the mid-1990s to the present, education in tourism schools and colleges has entered the stage of quality development. Attention is being paid not only to the improvement of quality, facilities for running programmes and educational reform, but also to research on the establishment of the tourism discipline, the scientific setup of programmes, co-operation and exchanges with tourism institutions abroad and integration with international practice. Zhang and Fan also point out the areas that need improvement.

Melphon Mayaka considers tourism education in East Africa in Chapter 12. Mayaka argues that the case for co-operation in the East African sub-region is particularly strong since the structure and nature of tourism systems is fundamentally similar in the three countries of Kenya, Uganda and Tanzania. In the chapter current progress in tourism and training and education is examined and the prospects discussed. Mayaka advocates greater involvement at the institutional level based around a range of co-operative arrangements including harmonisation of qualifications, collaborative curriculum development; research; discussions and exchange of ideas; joint publications; information dissemination; as well as technical and student exchanges.

In Chapter 13, Walter Freyer, Michael Hammer and Astrid Piermeier report on the range of educational programmes in tourism, in Germany. They note that vocational training programmes are well established but that tourism education as an academic subject is relatively new. Academic provision currently is dominated by courses at *fachhochschulen*, which aim to integrate practical and theoretical content. But the authors note that there is still no independent study programme or degree for tourism at universities. However they suggest that this is likely to change with increased integration of higher education courses in the European Union.

Shalini Singh and Tej Vir Singh present us with a fascinating picture of tourism education in India in Chapter 14. They examine the historical influences of higher education in India, the effects of colonialism and the distinctive Indian educational philosophy of mind, body and soul. Their starting point is an understanding that education and culture are intimately intertwined so that the cultural patterns of a society shape its educational system. In this way, the philosophy of Indian education emphasises the holistic development of an individual's potentials for the benefit of the society and the nation. Singh and Singh note that recent shifts in political thinking have made way for the introduction of vocational education in Indian universities and educational institutes yet tourism education/training stands out as a classic example in the conflict between conventional ideology of education and the modern interpretation of vocational training. Their critical examination of three tourism curricula explores their fit with conventional education philosophy, on the one hand, and the training of manpower for the industry on the other, and reveals the ideological conflict in tourism education in India.

Magiel Venema gives an historical account and broad overview of the Dutch education system in Chapter 15. Venema includes an account of vocational education, at the secondary and higher levels as well as university education. The chapter also considers the significance of international links, links with industry and competency-based learning.

In Chapter 16, Simon Hudson charts the progress of tourism education in North America from its beginnings in 1963 at Michigan State University to its current state. He finds that tourism continues to enjoy a growing rate of popularity in educational institutions, both as an area of instruction and as a field of investigation. He produces data which shows that there are currently a total number of 55,781 students enrolled in tourism and hospitality courses at 176 different institutions in North America. In addition, 28 universities offer post-graduate courses relating to tourism. It is instructive to note with Hudson the support which tourism education in North America finds from well-established professional associations such as the Travel and Tourism Research Association (TTRA) — the world's largest travel research organisation — and the International Council on Hotel, Restaurant and Institutional Education (CHRIE), as well as newer associations such as the International Society of Travel and Tourism Educators (ISTTE) and the International Academy for the Study of Tourism.

In Chapter 17, Tanja Mihalič describes tourism studies that are offered in Slovenian post-secondary educational institutions. A particular issue here is their growth and development as Slovenia has undergone transition becoming an independent, market-oriented state and a new member of the European Union. This prompts an analysis of the role of students and society in creating tourism programmes. In the course of her chapter, Mihalič poses and answers a number of key questions. First, how do Slovenian tourism education institutions use different kinds of tourism knowledge? Second, how important is the role of academic knowledge and how important is the role of industry? Third, do these factors change according to the time and level of tourism education? Fourth, in which way should it change and finally, how will the Bologna Accord (A European Union initiative to integrate higher education in member states) affect tourism education?

In Chapter 18, Melville Saayman examines tourism education in South Africa. Saayman explains that tourism in South Africa is growing rapidly and that this growth has led to demand for qualified staff exceeding that which training institutions could supply. A major bottleneck here has been a capacity problem with a lack of skills of the trainers at all the various training institutions. But Saayman reports that this problem has been dealt with by the accreditation of courses and trainers. Saayman concludes that while much has been done in the past 10 years to develop quality tourism qualifications, some problems still exist.

Finally, David Airey concludes this section on comparative tourism education in Chapter 19, where he discusses the case of the United Kingdom. Airey estimates that nearly 50,000 students are currently studying tourism-related programmes, a number which has grown substantially from the 20 or so students enrolled on the first two programmes in 1972. Airey finds that while there is great diversity, many of the programmes on offer have a clear vocational intention and that tensions exist between the vocational and more academic approaches to studying tourism. Airey observes a growth in the support structures for tourism including written material, associations, organisations and conferences and notes that tourism programmes have generally been found to offer good quality. Finally, he notes that the level and quality of research has come into greater prominence as a result of government research assessment.

Teaching, Learning and Assessment

This section opens with Chapter 20, where Dimitrios Stergiou offers an evaluation of tourism teaching in higher education. Stergiou devises a framework for the evaluation of teaching and then provides empirical evidence about the main factors that are associated with good teaching in tourism. His findings are summarised under two main headings. The first is teaching ability where Stergiou suggests that a good teacher should encourage "Person-Oriented Intellectual Reinforcement" by exploring with students new approaches and meanings, developing students' capacity to think for themselves and stimulating their intellectual curiosity. A good teacher should also pay attention to the "Structural Organization of Knowledge" by announcing the objectives of the lecture at the beginning, explaining to students how their work will be assessed and connecting lectures to reading. The second of Stergiou's headings encompasses teacher knowledge. Here, a good teacher should have a secure base of up-to-date knowledge. This would be demonstrated for example by being abreast of new developments in the field using journals and examples from the tourism industry, inviting questions in class, applying concepts and techniques appropriately and having the confidence to discard themes that are merely fashionable.

In Chapter 21, Eugenia Wickens and Alastair Forbes investigate the student experience as voiced by a group of first year students through semi-structured interviews. Their findings include evidence that students drawn from lower social groups may be disadvantaged. Additionally, many students felt unprepared by their previous educational and social experience for what was to come in higher education. The fact that peer-group networks are perceived by students to be of particular importance suggests that peer-support mechanisms should be further developed and exploited as part of student support and guidance.

In Chapter 22, Brian Wheeller paints a vivid picture of teaching under attack. Wheeller presents a powerful argument that ideals in teaching are being eroded by the clamour for funding, resource constraints, the rigours of assessment, promotion, the demands of the "immediate" and intense competition with research. Wheeller thereby sees a regrettable transformation from teaching as an educative, liberal and expansive project to a more limited utilitarian and functional one. Offering an antidote to this he concludes by re-iterating the case for the deployment of contextualisation, imagery and the visual in revitalising and enhancing the teaching and learning experience.

Chapters 23 and 24 turn our attention to assessment. In Chapter 23, Nina Becket provides an overview of the key issues and challenges including the use of formative assessment, improving feedback to students, the pressure on staff in assessing large classes, minimising plagiarism, assessing groupwork, and the marking and grading of student work. The chapter is full of useful practical tips and advice. It includes recommendations for development and provides sources for the reader to follow-up. In Chapter 24, Karen Smith investigates the dissertation research project. Smith evaluates the challenges that the dissertation presents to students, educators and institutions and finds that the dissertation exerts high demands on both staff and student resources. Smith argues that support for dissertations should be given to both staff and students. For students, research methods training and support in the use of resources are crucial. For staff, supervisory training and staff development in assessment are important. Smith believes that the dissertation project has a central role to play in the undergraduate curriculum with its emphasis on independent and deep learning.

In Chapter 25, Paul Barron considers cultural issues in learning. Based on research that analysed the learning style preferences of international students studying hospitality and tourism management in Australia, Baron suggests that a large sub-group of international students have learning style preferences that are different to those of other international and domestic students. From this, Baron raises the question whether such students should fit into a system which is very different to their prior experience or whether the system should be more sensitive and accommodating to their needs.

Marianna Sigala reviews the theory, practice, evidence and trends in e-learning and e-assessment in Chapter 26. Her starting point is that e-learning's benefits in tourism education are widely agreed. However, Sigala points out that e-learning models mainly replicate conventional instruction models rather than transforming and extending them. She therefore reviews the literature and discusses best practices in order to explain how knowledge is acquired and how online learning occurs. Additionally, Sigala illustrates how e-learning pedagogy should be designed, considers how e-assessment that can support the curriculum and identifies the factors that influence the effectiveness of e-learning.

In Chapter 27, Fiona Jordan explores the challenges in linking tourism research and teaching for the benefit of student learning. While Wheeller (Chapter 22) argued that research often overshadows teaching Jordan suggests that that there are significant benefits to be realised by both staff and students from linking teaching and research. These benefits stem from staff enthusiasm and their contribution of up-to-date, industry-related knowledge in the context of vocational and/or professional programmes. The practicalities of improving the research/teaching nexus include encouraging staff to integrate their research interests into curriculum design and provision of information about the research and scholarship activities of staff to students.

Stroma Cole concludes this section in Chapter 28 by inviting us to consider community education. Cole notes that large numbers of villagers in remote communities of less-developed countries are in the tourism frontline but they have no access to formal education and training. At the same time while there exists much educational research on tourism training and undergraduate programmes, there is a dearth of literature about community education programmes. Using a case study of villagers in Ngadha, Cole argues the need for community-wide esteem building, cross-cultural understanding as well as education about tourism development and what tourists want. She also suggests that specific education about product development, marketing, finance and food and hygiene would help communities to develop local tourism. Cole concludes that further research is needed on the methods appropriate to deliver informal community tourism education.

Resources, Progression and Quality

In Chapter 29, Marion Stuart-Hoyle points out that tourism teachers are arguably the most valuable resource in tourism education. After all she says, it is they that develop, deliver, assess and review the subject. Her chapter, based on research in the U.K., evaluates the key factors that have influenced the motivation and commitment of tourism teachers. Stuart-Hoyle initially explores the nature of tourism lecturers in terms of characteristics and traits, motivations and "defining features" and then makes observations about the pressured environment within which tourism lecturers operate. She concludes on an optimistic note that despite the increasing demands of the job (to recruit, teach, assess, manage, research and review) lecturers maintain high levels of commitment and enthusiasm.

Lyn Bibbings provides an evaluative guide to learning resources for tourism education in Chapter 30. Bibbings begins by describing the change in emphasis in higher education in the U.K. which has moved towards rewarding excellent teaching and has encouraged a surge in the development of learning resources for the subject area. Bibbings emphasises the role in the UK of the Higher Education Academy subject network in supporting lecturers by developing, promoting and disseminating resources, and how this has been enabled by technological developments. A number of useful links for resources are included in the chapter.

On the employment front, Adele Ladkin reminds us in Chapter 31 of the claims made for the significance of the tourism industry in generating employment globally. She quotes figures, which estimate world travel and tourism employment to be 241,697,000 jobs, representing 8.1% of total world employment for 2004. Figures for 2014 estimate a rise in the total number of jobs to 259,930,000, which will represent 8.6% of total world employment.

Ladkin's chapter investigates issues of career development and employment in the tourism industry. She outlines the characteristics of tourism labour markets and tourism jobs and offers a review of the current understanding of tourism careers and employment. Ladkin evaluates the contribution of tourism education to the development of human capital and the provision of a trained workforce with appropriate skills for tourism jobs and professions. While she notes the popularity of tourism courses, Ladkin draws attention to two key issues. First, she questions how the skills of tourism graduates are used and valued by the tourism industry and second, she notes a lack of career development and the unattractiveness of some occupations in tourism.

In Chapter 32, Derek Robbins considers quality assurance with a particular focus on the U.K. Robbins explores the meaning of quality assurance, why it is required and why there is a need for external independent verification of quality in addition to an institution's internal monitoring systems. Robbins reviews the process of internal monitoring and evaluates the largest scale independent assessment of tourism education that took place in England — subject review. In the light of lessons learned from this he describes recent developments in the external review process.

Finally in this section, postgraduate and Ph.D. education are reviewed by David Botterill and Tim Gale in Chapter 33. Botterill and Gale provide a description of the dimensions and profile of postgraduate study in tourism and demonstrate a strong growth in provision. They also note the continued growth in Ph.D. completions related to tourism in the UK rising from 4 in 1990 to 22 in 1999 and 34 in 2002. Botterill and Gale's analysis of Ph.D.s completed since 2000 finds the topics of tourist behaviour, motivation and demand, and tourism impacts to be the most popular. The authors also raise important questions about capacity, quality and internationalisation.

Postscript

The final part of the book is divided into two chapters. Chapter 34 offers practical advice on the design, delivery; evaluation and resourcing of courses. It is divided into two parts. In the first part, Miriam Moir provides frameworks for procedures for three areas of provision based on her experience as a registrar. The three areas are programme approval from the initial idea through to institutional endorsement; running a module on a course from preparation of assessment to evaluation of the module's operation, and the annual monitoring process used to evaluate quality and standards. In the second part, Lisa Hodgkins offers advice for the effective management of learning resources for tourism students based on her experience as a librarian.

The book concludes with Chapter 35, where the editors offer a review of the state of play of tourism education and identify key issues for further development and research.

References

Hall, C. M., & Page, S. (2002). *The geography of tourism and recreation: Space, place and environment*. London: Routledge.

Silver, H. (1990). *A higher education*. Brighton: The Falmer Press.

Chapter 2

Growth and Development

David Airey

Introduction

The purpose of this chapter is to explore the origins of tourism as a subject of study and to examine and explain the ways in which it has developed over the last 40 years or so. The chapter draws particularly on the experience of the UK, which is where some of the earliest programmes developed and to that extent it provides a national perspective. However, the issues and patterns that it presents are replicated, often with different timescales, in many other parts of the world.

Background to Development

It is now more than 40 years since tourism first appeared as a distinct area of study. Arguably its history goes back far longer than this in that the study of some of its component sectors, notably hotel operations and catering, or component activities such as leisure and recreation can trace their origins to before World War II. Also those specialising in academic disciplines, notably geographers and economists have paid attention to the role of tourism in, for example, regional studies or foreign trade studies over an even longer period. The works of Brunner (1945) and Norval (1936) Ogilvie (1933) and Pimlott (1947) provide some early examples of serious scholarship in tourism and even earlier Rae (1891) had provided an account of the burgeoning travel trade of Victorian England. However, these earlier developments are relatively fragmented either by sector or by individual scholars. It really awaited the 1960s and a number of key changes in tourism, in higher education and in society more generally for tourism to emerge both as a clear area of study in its own right and as a subject for study up to diploma and degree level and for research. The difference between the changes brought by the 1960s and what had happened previously is that the basis was established for a new and fairly discrete subject and an associated community of scholars. One outcome of this change has been a fairly phenomenal rate of growth. In the UK, for example, from about 20 students of tourism in higher education

An International Handbook of Tourism Education
Copyright © 2005 by Elsevier Ltd.
ISBN: 0-08-044667-1

in 1972 the figure had reached more than 4,000 new student enrolments each year by the end of the century (Airey, 2002). There are also many tens of thousands of such students in the UK in further, technical and school education (Airey & Johnson, 1999).

In some ways the driver behind this change is fairly obvious. Tourism as an activity has shown almost continuous growth since 1945. World Tourism Organization (2004) tables indicate 25 million international arrivals worldwide in 1950 growing to 700 million in 2002. At the same time, the organisations involved in meeting the needs of tourists have expanded with the emergence of some major companies, from airlines to hotel corporations to tour operators. This growth, combined with the increasing professionalisation of the tourism suppliers, has played its part in prompting educational institutions to meet the demands and opportunities created by tourism employers. The strong vocational emphasis of the early programmes in tourism bear witness to the extent to which they were brought into being in response to employment opportunities. Also this level of tourism growth has brought with it a complex array of issues from economic benefits to social and environmental problems. These challenges presented by tourism have added and fuelled the sustained interest by scholars, particularly in higher education, in their attempts to understand and explain aspects of an important worldwide phenomenon.

Yet the growth of tourism itself does not provide the complete explanation for the expansion of tourism education programmes. Annual growth in international tourism arrivals worldwide from the early 1970s to 2000 has averaged about 5%. Over the same period the growth of new enrolments onto tourism programmes at university level in the UK has been more than 700%. Similar rapid rates of growth, albeit with different starting dates, are evident at other levels of education and in other parts of the world. For example, in Italy all the 14 tourism courses in universities up to 1996 had been introduced since 1992 (Dipartimento del Turismo, 1996). Clearly, there are a range of other factors that have fuelled this remarkable expansion. Airey (1995) has suggested other drivers. He points to the substantial expansion in the numbers enrolling for further and higher education programmes generally. As evidence for this Dearing (National Committee of Enquiry into Higher Education, 1997) referred to the number of students in higher education in the UK doubling between 1977 and 1997, and for the participation rate for the under-30s rising from 30% to more than 45%. Tourism programmes have also developed within the context of the general development of vocational education. This has been one of the key themes underlying educational developments throughout the Western World during the past 50 years. It has been prompted, in particular, by the high costs of labour, the changes in the world of work, where brainpower has overtaken muscle power as the key ingredient in effective labour use, and the need to maintain competitive advantage. With these influences it is not surprising that governments have also encouraged vocational education. This started with the emergence of successful business schools but has extended to particular sectors as diverse as journalism, housing studies, leisure management and tourism. Further, prompted in part by periods of high unemployment and in part by changes in the system whereby they are made responsible for at least a part of their own study fees, students have become much more aware of employment potential in making their choice of subject of study. This has been a further driver for vocationalism and as a growing sector of activity tourism has been considered to offer good employment opportunities. Finally, Airey (2002, p. 14) has pointed to:

> changes in the funding and regulation of higher education whereby institutions have been free to compete with each other for student demand and the income that it brings; and a recognition by colleges and universities that tourism represents a way of expanding student numbers more reliably and cheaply than many other subject areas.

Combined with the underlying growth of tourism, these together represent a fairly potent set of influences. Of course, they operate at different levels and in different ways in different countries but all of them have at least some resonance in all countries. The important thing here is that they point in the same direction, to growth in tourism education.

Patterns of Development

Vocational Origins in Higher Education

As a subject for study as a whole, as distinct from study and training related to its component parts such as food production and service or airline ticketing, one of the characteristics of the development of tourism is that it first emerged at the higher education level. The very earliest provision, in the mid-1960s, was in the form of optional components in other programmes. In the UK tourism was offered within undergraduate diploma and degree programmes in Hotel and Catering Administration. These were followed in the UK by two Higher National Diploma (HND) (Tourism) programmes started at the end of the 1960s (Airey, 1979). In these, tourism was an "add-on" to provide a specific vocational focus to an essentially business studies course for 18-year-old school leavers.

In many ways more influential than these on the future development of tourism as a field of study were the two postgraduate master degree programmes started in 1972 at the Universities of Strathclyde and Surrey. With these, for the first time, tourism was considered as a domain of study in its own right treated as a multi-sector activity and as a multi-disciplinary subject. One of the important influences on this development was Medlik's (1966) report on the position of tourism studies in Western Europe, but of crucial importance also was the location of these programmes in university departments of hotel and catering management. Hotel and catering management had been accepted as a subject of degree level study earlier in the 1960s during the period of university expansion. Influence on this had in turn come from similar and earlier developments in the United States notably at Cornell University. In many ways this represented a new departure for higher education in the UK, to provide programmes with a fairly tight focus on a relatively confined area of economic activity. The resulting degree programmes were highly vocationally oriented, with close links with industry and employers and with a focus on the practice and operation of the industry. When tourism was established in this environment, and given the influences that had led to its creation as a distinct area of study, it is not surprising that it followed this highly vocational route. This was then further fostered by some early and influential textbooks (McIntosh, 1972, Burkart & Medlik, 1974) that effectively set the boundaries of the curriculum for a decade or more. The other main strand of development, from the HND in Business Studies, further buttressed the position of tourism as a highly vocational area of study.

Paralleling these developments of course, tourism remained a subject for study by those in other academic disciplines, notably geographers; and study areas such as leisure and recreation continued their growth. But, up to and well beyond the creation of the first two undergraduate degree programmes in 1986, the early highly vocational influences remained strong. This can clearly be seen in the curricula of these new undergraduate degree programmes. Table 1 provides an example of one of these programmes which has a heavy emphasis on business, management and links with industry.

Similarly this focus of the provision is clearly reflected in the aims of the programmes on offer. Table 2 indicates that for 99 programmes surveyed in 1998, the first eight aims were specifically vocational. Wider objectives in the form of "sound education/academic understanding" only appear at number 9 with only one-third the number of mentions of the first placed aim.

Broadening of the Curriculum

From this development, and particularly from about 1990 there have been two significant shifts in the development of tourism education. First at University level the curriculum has tended to broaden outwards from its essentially business-oriented vocational origins. This has found expression in the development of a few new tourism programmes which were non-vocational from the start. An example in the UK was the master programme in the *Anthropology of Tourism*. There are other examples around the world. However, more typically it has taken the form of the existing and additional programmes introducing wider issues not specifically related to the operation of the tourism industry and in this sense,

Table 1: Tourism course — BA (Hons) Tourism.

Year 1
Introduction to Tourism; Tourism Environments; Tourism Economics; People, Work and Tourism; Law; Accounting and Finance; Information; Residential Field Trip

Year 2
Economics and Finance of Tourism Ops; Human Resource Mngt; Tourism Marketing; Law related to Tourism; Administration of Tourism; Assessment of Tourism Resources; Research Methods; Residential Field Trip

Year 3
Industrial placement

Year 4
Tourists and Destinations; Business and Tourism; Options; Dissertation

Source: Her Majesty's Inspectorate (1992).

Table 2: Top twenty 'Aims and Objectives' of tourism degree courses.

Aims and Objectives	Mentions $n = 99$
1. Career opportunities	76
2. Employment/employer links/work	53
3. Tourism industry: large/important/global/growth	50
4. Vocational/"reality" skills/theory into practice	48
5. Tourism industry: international opportunities	45
6. Management/business skills	36
7. Private/public sector opportunities	31
8. Transferable relevant skills for other industries	28
9. Sound education/academic understanding	25
10. Broad foundation/wide range/thorough grounding	22
11. To meet the needs of the tourism industry	21
12. Decision making/analysis/judgement	20
12. European context/opportunities	20
14. Social context/sustainable tourism	19
15. Professional/professionalism	17
15. Quality excellence	17
17. Flexibility	14
17. Service delivery/service sector/customer service	14
19. Successful/succeed	10
20. Competitive/compete	7

Source: Airey and Johnson (1999).

non-vocational. In other words, tourism was starting to break out from what Tribe (1999) refers to as the *Vocational/Action* curriculum (see Chapter 4). By the end of the 1990s this broader approach could be clearly seen in the so-called "Subject Benchmark" for tourism. This was agreed with the tourism education community in the UK and promulgated by the UK Quality Assurance Agency (QAA) for Higher Education as providing a guide to the content of tourism courses. Details are provided in Table 3. One of the four broad headings refers to the tourism industry. The others are concerned with the wider issues raised by tourism both in terms of its impacts and in terms of the nature of tourism as a human activity. Of course, to the extent to which these wideissues provide a stronger background in good-stewardship to the world's scarce resources for those progressing to employment in tourism they can been seen as vocational. But the important point is that they are not rooted in day-to-day current operational practice.

The reasons for this broadening of the curriculum can be related to two significant changes. The continuing growth of tourism as a world activity meant that the wider consequences of its development were coming under closer scrutiny. Inevitably for those involved in tourism education it became essential to deal with these issues. But at the same time, as tourism programmes were being created and expanding and as tourism was becoming a dynamic part of education provision, so it attracted scholars and researchers from a wider range of disciplines who in turn all left their mark on the curriculum. The

Table 3: QAA subject benchmark for tourism.

Concepts and characteristics of tourism as an area of study
Products, structure and interactions in the tourism industry
Role of tourism in communities and environments
Nature and characteristics of tourists

Source: Quality Assurance Agency for Higher Education (2000).

result was a much stronger underpinning of tourism studies not only by economists and geographers but also anthropologists, psychologists, archaeologists and many more. This is reflected, perhaps most starkly, in the growth in the number of textbooks and academic journals with content devoted to many different aspects of tourism.

Tourism Education at All Levels

The second important shift from about 1990 is the appearance of tourism as a distinct subject of study at lower levels, in what in the UK is referred to as "Further Education (FE)" (typically for 16–18 year olds) and in the period of compulsory schooling up to 16 years. The first developments in this field in the UK were in the 1980s and were prompted by the tourism industry in the form of American Express who encouraged and supported the creation of a qualification for 16 year olds. This was followed by the creation of what has now become a series of General National Vocational Qualifications at two levels in Leisure and Tourism with a third, at the top level, in Travel and Tourism. These are provided both in FE colleges and in schools and have proved extraordinarily popular. By the early 2000s there were approximately 30,000 students following these programmes. As the name suggests they are ostensibly vocational in focus as is born out by the subject content of one of the advanced programmes provided in Table 4. Students are required to take 6 or 12 of these modules depending on their award.

Table 4: Subject content of advanced vocational certificate of education.

Investigating travel and tourism	Tourism geography
Tourism development	Health, safety and security in the travel
Worldwide travel destinations	and tourism industry
Marketing travel and tourism	Investigating heritage tourism in the UK
Customer service in travel and tourism	Sports tourism
Travel and tourism in action	Countryside recreation
Business systems in the travel and	Resort representatives
tourism industry	Conference and event planning
Human resources in the travel and	The UK retail travel industry
tourism industry	UK tour operations
Financial planning in travel and tourism	
Overseas tourism markets	

Source: AQA (2004).

Developments and Tensions

Criticisms of Growth and Novelty

Not surprisingly, given its rapid growth, the development of tourism has brought with it a number of problems and tensions. Initially these stemmed from the fact that tourism programmes were new and rapidly expanding and as a consequence little understood. For example, programmes have been criticised as lacking in serious content or academic rigour (The Observer, 1995). The growth of programmes has been considered to be far greater than perceived employment opportunities (Airey et al., 1993) and they have been blamed for not providing sufficient skills training. Yet against this, when they have been scrutinised, tourism programmes have fairly consistently been seen to provide the students with a good education leading to appropriate employment prospects (Further Education Funding Council, 1998; HM Inspectorate, 1992). Indeed, HM Inspectorate (1992, p. 25) commented on:

> well-designed programmes which are vocationally relevant, provide a good balance of theory and practice and offer the students adequate academic challenge.

More recently, and based on a total of 109 institutions, a report by the QAA reaffirmed the overall quality of the student experience on programmes in higher education in the related areas of hospitality, leisure, recreation sport and tourism (QAA, 2001). Noteworthy comments include:

> Curricula are multidisciplinary, flexible and coherent with impressive links to industry and the professions. (p. 1)

> The interrelationship between theory and practice is a consistently strong feature… (p. 1)

> The quality of teaching is consistently high. It is characterised by a rich diversity of approaches, including many industry-supported initiatives. (p. 1)

> The progression of diplomates and graduates to employment and further study is satisfactory overall, and an impressive feature of some of the provision. (p. 5)

Clearly, from these comments, some of the initial unease about the development of this aspect of education provision is no longer a cause for concern. However, the same report does pick up on one issue which is a reflection of the relative newness of the subject and suggests an important area for further work:

> …there is a general need to strengthen staff research and scholarly activity in support of the subjects.

The Curriculum Debate

Perhaps more interesting and in many ways of more fundamental importance than the criticisms associated with growth and newness, has been the debate about the tourism curriculum. For more than the first decade of its existence there seemed to be a fairly general agreement about the curriculum. As already noted, the boundaries of the tourism curriculum were strongly influenced by its origins and the early textbooks confirmed the vocational, business-oriented focus of the provision. This is reflected in the chapter titles for one of the early textbooks (Burkart & Medlik, 1974) shown in Table 5. However, as tourism programmes grew and developed and particularly as a wider range of academics entered the field there was increasing unease that there was no real agreement about the curriculum. As Cooper, Scales and Westlake (1992, p. 236) expressed it, tourism programmes "tend to take on the character of the particular expertise of its faculty". Or commenting on the situation in the United States, Koh (1994, p. 853) commented that "several studies found that most of the tourism curricula were designed by educators (influenced by their individual biases) with little/no representation from the tourism industry". This was clearly part of the development of the subject as new academic perspectives and insights were developed. However, Middleton, in the CNAA Report (1993), warned of the dangers if tourism was simply allowed to mean what academics wanted it to mean. In his view this would lead to confusion on the part of applicants to courses, students and potential employers and with no common agreement about what tourism means the development of the subject would be limited. Further Middleton and Ladkin (1996, p. 10) commented that "we believe a key issue for tourism studies over the next few years is likely to focus on how far the subject can not only retain, but also develop its coherence against powerful pressures for diversification and fragmentation…"

This provided the background to a number of initiatives in the mid-1990s to establish a common curriculum for tourism. Holloway (1995), with virtually unanimous support from UK Universities, gave an outline core curriculum for the National Liaison Group for Higher Education in Tourism (NLG). This identified the minimum tourism content for a tourism degree programme. An outline is given here in Table 5. Also, during 1996 and

Table 5: Body of knowledge for tourism.

Burkart and Medlik (1974)	National Liaison Group (1995)
Historical development	The meaning and nature of tourism
Anatomy of tourism	The structure of the industry
Statistics of tourism	The dimensions of tourism and issues
Passenger transport	of measurement
Accommodation	The significance and impact of tourism
Tours and agencies	The marketing of tourism
Marketing in tourism	Tourism planning and management
Planning and development	Policy and management in tourism
Organization and finance	
Future of tourism	

Source: Burkart and Medlik (1974) and Holloway (1995).

1997 The Association for Tourism, and Leisure Education (ATLAS), built upon the NLG work in a project spanning the countries of the European Union. Based on a wide-spread consultation involving universities and the tourist industry across Europe, this identified a similar draft core curriculum (Richards & Onderwater, 1998). A further project by the World Tourism Organization at about the same time set out a range of tourism competencies. The fact that all these attempts have a core curriculum in common that is focused primarily on the vocational and business aspects of tourism provides an indication of the extent to which there was agreement about the position of the tourism curriculum, despite concerns about fragmentation.

To a large extent the work in the 1990s of Tribe (1997) and Airey and Johnson (1999) confirmed this. The latter demonstrated the extent to which the tourism programmes in the UK reflected the core curriculum set out by the NLG. Indeed they comment that there is a great deal of similarity among the programmes in higher education. Tribe drew a distinction between the programmes that have what he calls a "business interdisciplinary approach" and those which do not. The first have a commonality that crystallises around "business" but as he says "there is no comprehensive aggregation of non-business tourism knowledge" (p. 654). In other words, the fears about fragmentation appear to have been unfounded. Most tourism programmes are basically very similar. It is in the small minority where the diversity and lack of curricular agreement are found. Stuart-Hoyle (2003, p. 53) reached similar conclusions, commenting that:

> the most common purpose of tourism undergraduate programmes is to prepare student to work in the tourism industry

The Developing Knowledge Base

For those involved in teaching tourism, one of the big changes over the past decade or so has been the rapid development of the knowledge base. This has found expression in the increase in the numbers of scholarly journals as well as in textbooks and manuals. But perhaps more importantly it has provided new and more traditional areas of knowledge on which to draw for an understanding of tourism. Tribe's work (see Chapter 4) provides a basis for understanding these changes in the knowledge about tourism. For the first years of its development tourism relied on what Tribe (1999, p. 103) refers to as *extradisciplinary* knowledge from "industry, government, think tanks, interest groups, research institutes and consultancies". Given its newness and its vocational origins this is not surprising. It is clearly demonstrated in the very comprehensive reference list of Burkart and Medlik's (1974) early textbook, which is dominated by government and other official reports and studies. As the provision of tourism programmes expanded and as more scholars started examining tourism, the more traditional, discipline-based forms of knowledge were developed. Tribe (1999, p. 103) has suggested that for such knowledge "disciplinary based methodology and peer review are the hallmarks of quality control". This is the type of knowledge that normally underpins higher education. In the case of tourism it provided a rich source of knowledge from many different disciplines as academics skilled in the contributing disciplines have brought in their knowledge and methodologies. In this way, tourism has become *multidisciplinary* in that it draws from different disciplines. A third potential step in this development is the creation of *interdisciplinary* knowledge whereby scholars draw upon more than one discipline to explain a specific tourism problem. As Airey (2002, p. 16) has commented:

> It is this type of knowledge that provides the rationale for tourism as a self-standing area of academic endeavour as distinct from a field of enquiry and experimentation by academics from other communities

An early example of this type of knowledge came in 1980 with Butler's Tourism Area Life Cycle (1980) which to quote Airey (2002, p. 16):

> springs from geography, biology and marketing but is ultimately located centrally within tourism and addresses a specific tourism issue.

A key challenge for tourism now as a distinct academic field lies in the extent to which it can add to this *interdisciplinary* knowledge and thereby move to become a distinct academic field of study that relies as much for its identity on its own knowledge as it does on its vocational links.

Coming of Age

A report published by the Council for National Academic Awards (1993) suggested that tourism as a subject of study had "come of age" by the early 1990s. It has certainly come a long way from its beginnings in the mid-1960s. Worldwide there are thousands of students and teachers involved in tourism studies. One source (Morrison, 2004) suggests that there are now 40 specialist academic journals in tourism in English and there are many hundreds of tourism textbooks in many different languages. Indicators also suggest overall continued growth in student enrolments and in recruitment of tourism scholars. However, against this apparent maturity needs to be set the continuing tensions and uncertainties over the curriculum. Tourism course provision remains strongly vocational and business oriented. Indeed it is from this that it garners much of its strength in terms of student recruitment and hence financial viability and beyond this in its ability to support a community of scholars. Yet if it is to become a truly distinct area of scholarship its knowledge base needs to progress beyond the *extradisciplinary* and even beyond the *multidisciplinary* into *interdisciplinary* work. In being able to draw on extradisciplinary, multidisciplinary as well as interdisciplinary knowledge tourism is in a position to offer much more than precise vocationalism. It can both give a depth and breadth of knowledge and insight as well as vocational relevance that can make a contribution both to the knowledge base and to the future employees of the tourism sector. The danger for tourism education comes from two directions. One is that it remains tied too closely to vocationalism and in this sense does little more than provide a reflection of the world of work. The other is that it turns its back on its industry connections thereby jeopardising one of its key *raisons d'etre*. Somewhere between the two it can provide a model of the way in which academia can make a real contribution to the world of the 21st century.

References

Airey, D. (1979). Tourism education in the United Kingdom. *Revue de Tourisme, 2/79*, 13–15.

Airey, D. (1995). *Tourism degrees — past present and future*. Inaugural lecture, 31 January 1995, Nottingham: Nottingham Business School.

Airey, D. (2002). Growth and change in tourism education. In: B. Vukonic & N. Cavlek (Eds), *Rethinking of education and training for tourism* (pp. 13–22). Zagreb: University of Zagreb, Graduate School of Economics and Business.

Airey, D., & Johnson, S. (1999). The content of tourism degree courses in the UK. *Tourism Management, 20*(2), 229–235.

Airey, D., Ladkin, A., & Middleton, V. T. C. (1993). *The profile of tourism studies degree courses in the UK 1993*. London: National Liaison Group, for the Tourism Society.

AQA. (2004). *Advanced vocational certificate of education, travel and tourism advanced 2005*. Manchester: AQA.

Brunner, E. (1945). *Holidaymaking and the holiday trades*. London: Oxford University Press.

Burkart, A. J., & Medlik, S. (1974). *Tourism, past present and future*. London: Heinemann.

Butler, R. W. (1980). The concept of a tourism area cycle of evolution: Implications for management and resources. *Canadian Geographer, 24*(1), 5–12.

Cooper, C., Scales, R., & Westlake, J. (1992). The anatomy of tourism and hospitality educators in the UK. *Tourism Management, 13*(2), 234–247.

Council for National Academic Awards. (1993). *Review of tourism studies degree courses*. London: CNAA.

Dipartimento del Turismo. (1996). *Sixth report on italian tourism — International Edition*. Florence: Mercury.

Further Education Funding Council. (1998). *Hotel and catering (including leisure, tourism and travel) curriculum area survey report*. Coventry: FEFC.

Her Majesty's Inspectorate. (1992). *Higher education in the polytechnics and colleges, hotel, catering and tourism management*. London: HMSO.

Holloway, C. (1995). *Towards a core curriculum for tourism: A discussion paper*. London: National Liaison Group for Tourism in Higher Education.

Koh, K. (1994). Tourism education for the 1990s. *Annals of Tourism Research, 21*(4), 853–854.

McIntosh, R. W. (1972). *Tourism principles, practices and philosophies*. OH: Grid.

Medlik, S. (1966). *Higher education and research in tourism in western Europe*. London: University of Surrey.

Middleton, V. T. C., & Ladkin, A. (1996). *The profile of tourism studies degree courses in the UK: 1995/1996*. London: National Liaison Group for Tourism in Higher Education.

Morrison, A. (2004). http://omni.cc.purdue.edu/~alltson/journals_1.htm (accessed 13 July 2004).

National Committee of Enquiry into Higher Education. (1997*). Higher education in the learning society*. London: Stationary Office.

Norval, A. J. (1936). *The tourist industry: A National and International survey*. London: Pitman.

Observer Newspaper. (1995). New focus, second class citizens, p. 15, 3 September.

Ogilvie, F. W. (1933). *The tourist movement*. London: Staples Press.

Pimlott, J. A. R. (1947). *The Englishman's holiday*. London: Faber and Faber.

QAA. (2000). *Hospitality, leisure, sport and tourism, subject benchmark*. Gloucester: Quality Assurance Agency for Higher Education.

QAA. (2001). *Hospitality, leisure, recreation, sport and tourism, subject overview report 2000–2001*. Gloucester: Quality Assurance Agency for Higher Education.

Rae, W. F. (1891). *The business of travel*. London: Thos Cook and Son.

Richards, G., & Onderwater, L. (1998). *Towards a european body of knowledge for tourism.* Tilburg: ATLAS.

Stuart-Hoyle, M. (2003). The purpose of undergraduate tourism programmes in the UK. *Journal of Hospitality, Leisure, Sport and Tourism Education, 2*(1), 49–74.

Tribe, J. (1997). The indiscipline of tourism. *Annals of Tourism Research, 24*(3), 638–657.

Tribe, J. (1999). *The philosophic practitioner: Tourism knowledge and the curriculum.* Unpublished doctoral dissertation, University of London, London.

World Tourism Organization. (2004). *Compendium of tourism statistics.* Madrid: WTO.

Chapter 3

Overview of Research

John Tribe

Introduction

Tourism education is of growing significance and attracting a growing body of research. Indeed there are no less than three journals dedicated solely to research in tourism education. These are The Journal of Hospitality and Tourism Education, The Journal of Teaching in Travel and Tourism and The Journal of Hospitality, Leisure, Sport and Tourism Education. A further sign of the maturity is the 29 North American doctoral dissertations related to tourism education listed in Dissertation Abstracts International between 1987 and 2000.

Back in 1981, Ritchie guest edited a special issue of Annals of Tourism Research devoted entirely to tourism education. In that issue Jafari and Ritchie (1981) pointed to some key issues. First, they addressed the question of what is tourism. Second, they considered the important issue of tourism knowledge and provided a framework for understanding this (Jafari and Ritchie's wheel). Third, they noted "the need to develop a body of knowledge in tourism" (p. 29). Fourth, they made some useful observations about perceived weaknesses in tourism education. These include a "lack of empirical research on which to base the design of tourism curricula" (p. 31), the relative isolation of course designers and the "highly vocational nature of material received from North American sources" (p. 31). They also signalled a particular gap in the literature, noting:

> The inclusion of [Blanton's] article which emphasises the social and cultural differences in training needs of developing countries, is made in the hope of stimulating greater interest and concern for this neglected and important area of tourism education. (p. 30)

The aim of this chapter is to describe and evaluate research into tourism education in the period up to the end of 2001. Its structure is as follows. Initially, the methodology of the enquiry is set out. The findings of the enquiry are then discussed under a number of sections. The general findings reflect on some of the quantitative aspects of tourism education research. Thereafter, qualitative aspects of tourism education research are considered under a number of headings — the curriculum, teaching, learning and assessment; student progression and achievement; learning resources and quality management and enhancement. The chapter concludes by revisiting Jafari and Ritchie to determine to what extent their agenda for tourism research has been met and to consider the key challenges for tourism education research for the next 21 years.

Methodology

Initially, a list of research articles was generated by the following technique. The primary database of literature was generated from the author's research interests in tourism education. Mainstream bibliographic abstracting services (e.g. BIDS etc.) included very few specific tourism education entries and in the absence of dedicated databases, a quite basic and laborious technique was used. This entailed building a bibliography by following up the reference list of every article that was encountered. Subsequently this database was expanded using expert opinion. The literature database was then updated using two key abstracting services. The first is the abstracts database operated by CABI publishing (www.leisure-tourism.com). This comprises over 50,000 international bibliographic references originally published in Leisure, Recreation and Tourism Abstracts and includes published research since 1974. The second is Articles in Hospitality and Tourism (AHT). The AHT database (www.surrey.ac.uk/Library/cdaht.htm) provides details of English language articles selected from academic and trade journals published worldwide from 1984. It is produced by the libraries of Oxford Brookes University and the University of Surrey. Some difficulty was encountered in searching the CABI database since the general search using the phrase "tourism education" based on keywords and/or abstract yielded too many results including literature, which had no direct relevance to the field. To narrow down the search it was necessary to limit the search to the title, using the following search words (where * stands for any character or string of characters): tourism educat*, teaching, manpower, human resourc*, education, curriculum, learning and student*. This method also encountered some problems. First, not every journal that includes tourism education is abstracted. Second, some education literature has an enigmatic title that does not include the terms searched for. Third, some spurious literature was still generated although this was eliminated by a visual check. The full database included 302 literature references up to 2001.

Reading and analysis of the literature initially generated 47 different separate areas of interest. These were subsequently grouped together into main themes and subthemes. Classification into the main categories followed the general approach set by the UK Quality Assurance Agency for Higher Education (QAA). The QAA 'aspects of provision' are Curriculum Design, Content and Organisation; Teaching, Learning and Assessment; Student Progression and Achievement; Student Support and Guidance; Learning Resources and Quality Management and Enhancement (QAA, 2000, p. 7). Student Support and Guidance was not used as it was mainly concerned with the general welfare of students (e.g. induction, tutorial support) rather than subject-specific issues. The 47 categories were subsequently rationalised to a total of 16 categories and subcategories. The literature was then sorted into these categories. Table 1 illustrates this categorisation and sorting.

Table 1: Categories of research in tourism education (to 2001).

	Total	%	Total	%
(1) Curriculum	**261**	**86**		
(a) Curriculum planning models			16	5
(b) Critical reviews of the curriculum			49	16
(c) Descriptive profile of provision (UK)			12	4
(d) Comparative tourism education			69	23*
(e) Globalisation			8	3
(f) Community/stakeholder input			3	1
(g) Curriculum and knowledge			14	5
(h) Industry issues and training needs			37	12
(i) Qualifications issues			5	2
(j) Specific subjects in the curriculum			48	16
(2) Teaching, Learning and Assessment	**8**	**3**		
(3) Student Progression and Achievement	**22**	**7**		
(4) Learning Resources	**3**	**1**		
(5) Quality Management and Enhancement	**9**	**3**		
(6) Other	**1**	**—**		

$n=304$. *16.4% covers developing countries and 6.3% covers developed countries.

If a piece of literature covered more than one category then it was included in each, hence the number of entries exceeded the number of literature references. Additionally (although not included in Table 1), a division was made between pre- and post-1995 literature to ascertain whether there were any changes apparent in terms of volume or subject of research.

Findings

General

Medlik (1965) was an early pioneer of research into Tourism Education with his unpublished report into *Higher Education and Research in Tourism in Western Europe*. Subsequently, Lawson (1974) was one of the first to get into print in a similar research area covering tourism education and training in Western Europe. The 1970s saw two further contributions. Airey (1979), who has maintained a strong presence in this area to date, reviewed tourism education in the United Kingdom and Christie-Mill (1978) also considered its development and status. Thereafter, research outputs developed a steady momentum. Fifty-one outputs are counted during the 1980s, a number that was certainly given an extra fillip by the special issue of Annals of Tourism Research (1981). Additionally in 1988, the *International Conference for Tourism Educators*, hosted at the University of Surrey attracted a broad range of research papers. The 1990s saw another large increase in outputs to at least 206. There can be little doubt that the formation of ATLAS — The (European) Association for Tourism and Leisure Education — has influenced this, particularly with its organisation of two major conferences *Tourism and Leisure Education in Europe: Trends and Prospects* in 1994 and *Tourism in Central and Eastern Europe: Educating for Quality* in 1995.

The growth in tourism education research also reflects the extraordinary growth in tourism education itself (Airey & Johnson, 1998, 1999). However one other general feature of note that comes from analysis of the data is the imbalance of the focus of the research. The overwhelming majority of research (86%) is in curriculum-related matters. Against this, the rest of the research fades into insignificance. Seven per cent of research concerns student progression and achievement, 3% is on quality, 3% relates to teaching and learning and 1% is on learning resources.

Curriculum

Curriculum research can be roughly divided into two parts. First, that which is concerned with the curriculum in general and second, that which covers specific aspects of the curriculum. The literature devoted to general issues of the curriculum accounts for 70% of the total and can be divided into a number of sub-categories.

Curriculum planning models   A logical starting point in examining these is the 5% of the total research, which investigates curriculum planning issues. It is useful here to recall Jafari and Ritchie's (1981) criticism of lack of empirical research in curriculum design and planning. There are two things here to be examined. First, is the criticism still valid? Second, is this is a correct diagnosis of the problem?

Koh's (1995) study was prompted by the very fact that "most … tourism management programs in the United States were designed by educators with very little or no empirical input from industry" (p. 68). Koh therefore undertook a two-stage Delphi empirical study using industrialists and educators as respondents. His conclusions identified 15 subjects to be very important for the curriculum forming four main educational clusters. In the same year, Holloway (1995) published a curriculum paper on behalf of the UK National Liaison Group for Higher Education in Tourism (NLG) (now ATHE — The Association for Tourism in Higher Education). Holloway's method was to seek "some consensus on the body of knowledge which would be acceptable to both academics and practitioners in the tourism industry" (p. 2), and this was done by discussion of proposals drafted by an expert group at a conference of industrialists and educators. The result of this exercise was the mapping of seven areas of knowledge deemed to represent the core curriculum for tourism.

Botterill and Tribe (2000) reported on the most recent UK advances in this area where the NLG undertook an exercise on behalf of the UK government's Quality Assurance Agency to provide subject-specific guidelines for tourism higher education. The empirical aspect of this exercise was a substantial national consultation exercise in 1999 using regional panels of academics and the guidelines resulted in the identification of four key areas of the curriculum divided into 17 substatements. More recently, Lewis and Tribe (2001) reported on the results of an empirical study, which generated the key issues for curriculum development using a stakeholder approach in three Caribbean islands. It can be seen from this discussion that empirical studies have provided an improved basis for curriculum planning but a contemporary analysis of education and training needs related to tourism occupations on the lines of Airey and Nightingale (1981) is overdue.

Let us now move onto whether lack of empirical research is the correct diagnosis of the problem. It turns out to be an incomplete diagnosis because it is necessary to have more than just empirical research. Tribe (2001) investigates the impact of research paradigms on curriculum planning. He classifies the Koh and Holloway studies as scientific-positivist approaches and argues that such studies are necessary but not sufficient because of their lack of attention to meaning and values. Tribe explains that

> Data collection methods deployed by Koh were undoubtedly value-free. But an initial value position is imposed by seeking empirical input from industry. The value imposed is that of industry values. (p. 444)

Therefore, conceptual research is necessary to develop models for curriculum design and philosophical and critical research is needed to consider the range of possible aims of tourism education.

Several researchers have analysed curriculum models. Cooper, Shepherd, and Westlake (1994, 1996) devote a whole chapter for this, drawing on the wider literature of the higher education curriculum and Cooper (1997) re-emphasises the need to consider "general principles of curriculum planning" (p. 24). Earlier, Vroom (1983) proposed a model for tourism education based on a study of courses at different institutions in different geographical locations. Murphy (1981) examined social science considerations and Ritchie (1995) reviewed a number of curriculum models including the hotel school model, the general management with a tourism focus model, and the liberal arts programme with a tourism focus model. He then proposed an alternative hybrid model of tourism/hospitality education.

Critical reviews of the curriculum   The heading of philosophical and critical research describes the second most popular area for tourism education research, covering 16% of the total and showing a fairly even distribution before and after 1995. Within this area several themes emerge. First, under policy and practice, Amoah and Baum (1997) describe the formulation and implementation of tourism education in the UK as *ad hoc*. They advocate the development of a tourism education policy, to bring tourism education closer in line with national tourism policies. Interestingly for the UK there has been some move towards a policy of subject benchmarks but no effort to align these to any national tourism policy.

Oversupply of courses provides a second heading for critical review. The UK Council for National Academic Awards (CNAA, 1993) raised this issue which was subsequently developed by Evans (1993). He cites evidence from Cardiff showing only 46% of students in tourism-related employment 1 year after graduating and also points to excess demand for work placement. Ryan (1995) rejects this emphasis on immediate employment in tourism as "a partial argument" (p. 97) pointing out that tourism courses can be justified for a range of reasons including "study which [students] enjoy" (p. 100).

More general critical reviews include that of McIntosh, van Weenen, and Shafer (1983), who reviewed the structure and content of courses and emphasised the need to concentrate on marketing and communication skills. Pirjevec (1990) advocated an 'Alternative' tourism education to match emerging 'alternative' forms of tourism and suggested that the disciplines necessary to cope with developments in modern tourism comprised aspects of sociology and ecology. Gamble (1992) concluded that "the new model for hospitality and tourism education … requires a recognition of the growing importance of know how in terms of obtaining and sustaining competitive advantage" (p. 10). In the UK, the CNAA (1993) reviewed provision. Its findings included questions about academic validity and quality, concerns about a lack of data about provision and staff development and "a very high level of support for the concept of a 'common core curriculum'" (p. 28). Go (1994) identified three periods in the evolution of tourism education. First, the pre-1970s were characterised by concerns for career preparation. Second, the 1980s witnessed a shift from the pragmatic to the academic, emphasising research and methods of enquiry. Finally, the challenges for the 1990s were identified as social change, concern for the environment, the global economy and rapid advancements in technology. Airey (1997) in reviewing 25 years of tourism education concluded that there was a strong move towards coherence in the curriculum and that quality and rigour remained priorities.

But the critical literature often just leaves us with a list of conflicting demands. In order to make sense of these conflicts, a more philosophical approach is needed to consider the underlying aims, values and meanings in tourism education. Under this heading, Busby (1994) highlighted the difference between tourism education and training, a theme taken up by Holloway (1998) who reassessed aims in terms of earning and learning and makes a case for the study of philosophy and ethics in tourism. These two papers point out the different ideologies of vocationalism and liberalism. Walle (1997) contributes to this argument by consideration of generic as opposed to specialised approaches to tourism and hospitality education. Tribe extends the discussion initially by elaborating the theory and practice of liberal education in tourism as an antidote to vocationalism (Tribe, 2000a). Subsequently, he undertakes a comprehensive mapping of what he terms "curriculum space" in terms of competing aims and values and presents a curriculum to educate "Philosophical Practitioners" which develops of vocational and liberal education through reflection and action (Tribe, 2002).

Descriptive profile of provision Descriptive research on the curriculum (4% of total) has provided a number of snapshots of curriculum configurations as well as some valuable longitudinal data on quantitative aspects. The snapshots of provision include Airey (1979), McIntosh and Walther (1981), Airey and Middleton (1984), Swarbrooke (1995) and culminate in Airey and Johnson's (1999) analysis of the content of UK tourism degrees which found that "the aims of the courses are substantially vocational and business orientated" (p. 229). The extraordinary expansion in course provision and student numbers has been recorded by a series of profile studies in the UK (Airey, Ladkin, & Middleton, 1993; Middleton & Ladkin, 1996; Airey & Johnson, 1998).

Comparative tourism education A substantial part of the literature (23%) offers a specific view of tourism education in specific countries, and here it is useful to divide the discussion into developed and developing countries. As well as covering the UK and USA the literature for developed countries includes studies on Ireland (Walsh, 1992), Italy (Formica, 1997), Australia (Hobson, 1995; Wells, 1996; Sims, 1999) and Japan

(Koshizucha, Umemura, Mori, Horiuchi, & Shishido, 1998). Comparative studies here include Cooper and Messenger's (1991) evaluation of tourism education in Europe and Formica's (1996) Euro/American study.

Jafari and Ritchie (1981) should be pleased that tourism education in developing countries is no longer neglected since the database indicates an extraordinary 16% of research outputs in this area. Much of this activity (39%) has been focussed former-communist states of Europe stimulated by the EU's Tempus programme of financial assistance and a dedicated ATLAS conference. Examples here include Croatia (Persic, 1998), Poland (Airey, 1994) and Russia (Petroune & Voskoboinikov, 1998). Elsewhere, studies have included China (Chen, 1990; Zhao, 1991; Xiao & Liu, 1995; Xiao, 2000), the Caribbean (Conlin, 1991; Charles, 1997), Vietnam (Cooper, 1997), Hong Kong (Go & Mok, 1995) and India (Singh, 1997). But what of Jafari and Ritchie's concerns that education be responsive to social and cultural differences?

Globalisation   To a great extent this can be linked to current concerns about globalisation and here the literature (8% of total) tends to divide into two camps. On the one hand, globalisation is seen as a development that tourism education has to adapt to, and serve. The definition of globalisation used by Smith and Cooper (1999, p. 43, 2000) illustrates this. "Globalisation means more destinations competing in the same market niche for the same leisure budget … increasing world-wide competition very sharply". Here globalisation's problem of increased competition represents the challenge for tourism education. A similar conceptualisation of globalisation is found in Go's model where "understanding global industry strategy is fundamental to the development and delivery of Global Education programmes" (Go, 1998, p. 1). Indeed, this stance is recurrent in Go's work on the global curriculum. Although he mentions the safeguarding of national cultures, continual references to "Global Education *for* a Global Industry" (Go, 1998, p. 3, italics added) depict education as subservient to globalisation. Specifically, Go (1998, pp. 12–13) articulates the 10 "I"s of globalisation which include interdependence, innovation, information technology and interaction and explains in detail how a global curriculum can help achieve these. For Chon (1990) and Samenfink (1998), globalisation requires a curriculum response to include the appreciation of internationalisation, the international economy and foreign cultures as well as international networking among institutions. Similarly, Burns in reviewing training in Bulgaria emphasises the need "for above all cultural shifts in business attitudes" (1995, p. 61) particularly to deliver customer service in the newly marketised economy.

The alternative view of globalisation sees it as a threat to local autonomy and culture, particularly in developing countries and one that tourism education should problematise. Here, Theuns and Go (1992, p. 293) note that

> …Western models [of tourism education] have been imported throughout the third world. As a consequence none of these predominantly business study and technician courses fully meets the needs of the hospitality and tourism sector in the Third World, let alone the society at large.

They advocate a 'need led' as opposed to the traditionally practised 'market led' approach to tourism education. This 'need led' approach stresses that the tourism curriculum should be developed in the social, cultural and economic context of the destination. Burns, in reviewing the tourism curriculum in Papua New Guinea argued for "putting local people and the impacts of tourism, rather than industry and business at the centre of concern" (1992, p. 8). Similarly, King (1994) emphasises the need to assess "the cultural needs of participating students" (1994, p. 267) as well as those of the industry. This is echoed by Lewis and Tribe (2002) who examine wider implications of globalisation for the curricula of developing countries and find the need for "a distinct tourism curriculum that reflects their uniqueness, culture and history".

Community/stakeholder input   The issue of community and stakeholder input is significant for curriculum development and particularly so in developing countries. Murphy (1992) was an early advocate for community partnerships in education whilst Tribe (1998) identified the uneven contest between community and commercial interests in tourism education. The practical side of community inclusion has been developed by Shepherd and Cooper (1995) and Cooper and Westlake (1998), who have developed the use of stakeholder input in curriculum planning, a model which has been tested in the field by Lewis and Tribe (2001).

Curriculum and knowledge   Five per cent of the literature examined the relationship between curriculum and knowledge. In an early paper on this topic, Leiper (1981) concluded that "to overcome the defects stemming from a fundamentally fragmented curriculum, a new discipline needs to be created to form the core strand in comprehensive programmes" (p. 71). He went on to propose "tourology … as a suitable name for the scientific study of tourism" (p. 81). Goeldner (1988), Pearce (1991) and Gunn (1992) also contributed to this debate. More recently, Echtner and Jamal (1997) advocate a multidisciplinary approach to tourism and Tribe (1997) refuted Leiper's claim of disciplinary status for tourism, conceptualising it rather as two fields studied through multi-, inter- and transdisciplinary approaches. This controversy has subsequently been revisited (Leiper, 2000; Tribe, 2000b). These epistemological analyses are important since they examine the production of tourism knowledge from which the curriculum is drawn.

Industry issues and training needs   Twelve per cent of the outputs cover industry and training issues. The two main clusters identified are first relationships between education and the industry and second industry needs. Industry participation in tourism education has been a consistent challenge to tourism education as illustrated by Bernthall's (1988) paper which specifically asks "will industry participate?". Burton (1988) saw the need for building bridges by including work experience and the involvement of professional tourism organisations and Hawes (1988) wrote about industry and education meeting the challenge together. Similarly, Goodenough and Page (1993) investigate bridging the gap between industry and education. They advocate good practice steps including student visits to industry, industry speakers and co-operation with industry. Similarly, Cassels (1994) considers harnessing employers' contributions through partnerships, Botterill (1996) deliberates on making connections between industry and higher education and Airey (1998) explores the links between education and industry. The relationship between education and the industry is analysed by Haywood and Maki (1992), Shepherd (1993), Cooper (1993) and Shepherd and Cooper (1997). Haywood and Maki found poor levels of collaboration between industry and industry and Shepherd and Cooper stress the need "that industry and education work together as partners" (p. 47). Interestingly, the role of government in planning tourism education for industry receives scant attention with the exception of Baum, Amoah, and Spivack (1997) who investigated the policy dimensions of human resource management.

The specific needs of industry are addressed by several researchers. In early works, Airey and Nightingale (1981) analysed tourism occupations, career profiles and knowledge, Parsons (1987) analysed jobs in tourism and Sheldon and Gee (1987) undertook a "training needs assessment in the travel industry". Becton and Graetz (2001) investigated the specific needs of small businesses. Bernier (1997) has mapped occupational job titles. Berry-Lound, Batersby, and Parsons (1991) reviewed the labour market for the British Tourism Authority. Collins, Sweeney, and Green (1994) investigated the specific training needs of the UK tour-operating industry. Both Koh (1995) and Yale and Cooke (1995) used the Delphi technique to elicit industry views on the curriculum.

Qualifications issues   A small number of outputs consider issues of qualifications. For example, Bosselman (1996) investigates accreditation issues. Swedlove and Dowler (1992) consider competency-based occupational standards and certification and a World Tourism Organisation (WTO) initiative has tried to encourage world standards for tourism education through its TEDQUAL programme (Fayos-Sola, 1997).

Specific subjects in the curriculum   Around 16% of the research focused on the specific subjects within the curriculum. Of this, the majority of work has been on managerial and professional aspects of tourism education. The question of what to teach specifically for tourism management has been posed by Litteljohn and Watson (1990) and Richards (1992) among others. Typical replies include Parsons' (1991) comparative study which identified a lack of labour market credibility in tourism management courses and the need for "a more constructive synergy" (p. 206) between education and industry. Similarly, Kaplan (1982) argued for more specialisation in courses to meet changes in industry organisation, a theme also visited by Weiermair (1995). However in an empirical study in Hawaii, Sheldon (1989) was positive about the degree of professionalism to be found in the industry. Godau's (1991) case study explains in general terms, how tourism managers are developed at the Friedrcih List Hochscule in Germany. Moscardo (1997) brought a different angle to this issue by analysing creative and flexible thinking in management training.

However there has been a clear change in emphasis in issues over time and since 1995, education for sustainable tourism has assumed increased significance and claims a total of 3% of total research. For example, Bramwell (1996) and Bramwell, Goytia, and Henry (1996) examined the character of sustainable tourism management and reported on the development of educational resources in a series of case studies from European countries. Richards (1998b) describes a consultation exercise on sustainable tourism management education and Henry, Jackson, and Larrauri (1998) produced curriculum guidelines which emerged from this exercise. Similarly, Howie (1996) has analysed the skills, understanding and knowledge required in education for sustainable tourism.

Sustainability is closely tied to ethics which represents the next most important research topic with 2% of the total entries (albeit mainly pre-1995). Enghagen (1990) found that most undergraduate hospitality programmes included ethics in the curriculum. However, Hultsman (1995) suggested that tourism educational materials do not appear to deal adequately with ethical issues. He therefore proposes a framework based on ecological impacts, marketing, sustainable development, humanistic and social concerns to inform programmes for teaching ethics on tourism courses.

Given its pervasive growth it is perhaps surprising that only 1% of the outputs have covered I.T. in the curriculum. Buhalis (1998) has examined the implications of information technologies for the tourism curriculum, while Daniele and Mistilis (1999) sought an industry view of information technology skills required in tourism graduates in Australia. Subsequently, Mistilis and Daniele (2000) interpreted the impact of their findings for Australian government policy. Finally, 5% of the total articles have covered an array of other curriculum components including subjects such as tourism economics (Tribe, 1995), human resource management (Baum & Nickson, 1998), the gaming industry (Cummings & Brewer, 1996), language skills (Davies, 1999) and entrepreneurialism (Echtner, 1994).

Teaching, Learning and Assessment

Burke's (1988) observation that tourism education is "fun and games and fluff" (p. 30) is not one which is substantiated by evidence nor found elsewhere in the scant literature in this area (3% of total). Pointers to successful teaching and learning techniques are few and far between. An exception is Enghagen (1990), who discusses the teaching of ethics in hospitality and tourism education and concludes that case studies provide an excellent method of instruction. The managing of industrial placements does receive some scrutiny in the literature. Busby, Brunt, and Baber (1997) consider their benefits to students particularly in terms of their skills development and Cave (1997, 1999) provides best practice suggestions based on a case study of the Lancashire Business School, UK.

Rafferty (1990) studied the effects of instruction in geography on college students' perception of world regions as tourism destinations and found that despite a very significant improvement in students' knowledge of world geography, the effects on students' perception of world regions as tourism destinations was modest. Spears, Boger, and Gould (1999) discussed the use of a collaborative web-based project on tourism and marketing. Haywood (1989) was an early advocate of students taking responsibility for their own learning and developing capabilities to cope with uncertain conditions and changing needs in the industry.

There has been little work on teachers or their qualifications although Cooper, Scales, and Westlake (1992) examine the staffing of tourism and hospitality in the UK. Their results showed a considerable depth of industry experience among educators at all levels. The only discernible research on assessment is that of Sivan, Yan, and Kember (1995), who investigated the use of peer assessment.

Student Progression and Achievement

Seven per cent of the literature covered an aspect of student progression and achievement. For example Khwaja and Bosselman (1990) investigated the problems of cultural adjustment of international graduate students in American hospitality and tourism programmes. Shepherd (1997) discusses the graduate tourism aptitude test (GTAT) as an attempt to develop an international benchmark of student achievement and Crompton (1991) profiled students on doctoral programmes at US universities. But most of the literature under this heading concentrated on careers. Ross (1997) provided one of several pieces that examined attitudes to careers in the industry. Others included Airey and Frontistis (1997) who made an Anglo Greek comparison and national studies were authored by Charles (1992) (the Caribbean), Chen, Chu, and Wu (2000) (Taiwan), Getz (1994) (Scotland), and Kusluvan and Kusluvan (2000) (Turkey). Further along the progression route McKercher, Williams, and Coghlan (1995) reported on the career progress of recent tourism graduates.

Learning Resources

Less than 1% of the literature examined issues of learning resources and this comprised two articles by Richards (1997, 1998a) on developing networks for tourism educators.

Quality Management and Enhancement

Around 3% of the literature was on quality management and enhancement. This included Fayos-Sola (1997), who described the WTO TEDQUAL initiative and methodology for quality in tourism education and training and Tan and Morgan (2001) who examined relevance and quality in Australian tourism higher education. In terms of quality enhancement, the key literature is on staff development which includes Ritchie's (1993) guidelines for educating tourism educators and Busby's (1995) consideration of the changing role of staff development for travel and tourism lecturers. Finally, Cooper et al. (1994, 1996) produced a manual of tourism and hospitality education.

Conclusion

Jafari and Ritchie's (1981) comments provide a useful starting point for concluding comments. They were "pleasantly surprised" (p. 31) by the 22 manuscripts received for their special edition of *Annals*. Perhaps the first most significant conclusion is the sheer weight of literature that now exists in this area with a stock of some 300 articles by the end of 2001. Second, there were concerns about tourism, knowledge and the curriculum. Researchers have made considerable advances in each of these areas bringing more conceptual clarity to their inter-relationships. Curriculum studies has received particular attention and especially the notion of a core curriculum. Third, concerns were voiced about the vocational nature of material received from North America. In overall terms, tourism education research now embraces a wider concept of tourism so that is no longer so heavily skewed towards the vocational. Fourth, the lack of empirical research on which to base curriculum planning has to some extent been addressed at a general level, but the specific needs of industry remain largely uncharted. Fifth, the educational needs of developing countries are no longer a "neglected … dimension of tourism education" (p. 31). Sixth, the proliferation of tourism educational research, specific journals, internet groups, regular conferences and established professional networks mean that that the time has passed when "most academics in the field are forced to conceptualise and design tourism courses … in a setting of relative isolation"

(p. 31). Seventh, while in 1981 "very few institutions attempt transdisciplinary studies in tourism" (p. 25) which "would imply the establishment of Faculties of Tourism Studies" (p. 24), in the UK at least such Faculties are now more commonplace. In short, most of the concerns of Jafari and Ritchie have been addressed. Additionally, there is no longer a problem of lack of data about provision (CNAA, 1993).

Does this mean that research into tourism education has done its job? Far from it — rather a new set of imperatives emerge for the future. First, a greater attention to methodological issues is required. Here an appeal is made to extend curriculum research from the empirical (Jafari & Ritchie, 1981) to include the philosophical. This is because the curriculum is a contested construct and therefore the purposes of tourism education need careful consideration. Second, research should include critical methods as well as empirical studies. There are a range of interests and stakeholders involved in tourism education and this raises important issues of power and influence. Empirical methods which are ostensibly value free may assemble evidence on behalf of a particular interest group and unwittingly endorse the legitimacy of that group.

The other main group of concerns stem from the imbalance in research evident from Table 1. For example, just 2% of research has analysed teaching, learning and assessment. How to teach has been overshadowed by what to teach and issues of effective learning and assessment have been overlooked. Next, the literature on student progression and achievement has focussed on careers and progression from higher education. Progression into tourism education and its fit with feeder layers in the educational system is uncharted. In the UK, widening participation is a particular issue here. Additionally, resources and their use and effectiveness have received scant attention and moves towards virtual learning environments remain undocumented and lacking evaluative studies. Finally, quality is an issue that is fundamental to all aspects of tourism education. Indeed, how does tourism higher education match up to other degree programmes? The lack of evaluative and prescriptive literature in this area is of prime concern.

Acknowledgement

This chapter is based upon an article which first appeared in *Acta Turistica, 14*(1), 61–81.

References

Airey, D. (1979). Tourism education in the United Kingdom. *The Tourist Review, 34*(3), 13–15.
Airey, D. (1994). Education for tourism in Poland: The Phare programme. *Tourism Management, 15*(6), 467–471.
Airey, D. (1997). After 25 years of development: A view of the state of tourism education in the UK. In: E. Laws (Ed.), *The ATTT tourism education handbook* (pp. 9–12). London: Tourism Society.
Airey, D. (1998). Exploring the links between education and industry. Paper delivered to *Tourism education exchange,* University of Westminster.
Airey, D., & Frontistis, A. (1997). Attitudes to careers in tourism: An Anglo Greek comparison. *Tourism Management, 18*(3), 149–158.
Airey, D., & Johnson, S. (1998). *The profile of tourism studies degree courses in the UK: 1997/98.* London: The National Liaison Group for Higher Education in Tourism.

Airey, D., & Johnson, S. (1999). The content of degree courses in the UK. *Tourism Management*, *20*(2), 229–235.

Airey, D., Ladkin, A., & Middleton, V. (1993). *The profile of tourism studies degree courses in the UK 1993*. London: The National Liaison Group for Higher Education in Tourism.

Airey, D., & Middleton, V. (1984). Tourism education course syllabuses in the UK: A review. *Tourism Management*, *5*(1), 57–62.

Airey, D., & Nightingale, M. (1981). Tourism occupations, career profile and knowledge. *Annals of Tourism Research*, *8*(1), 52–68.

Amoah, V., & Baum, T. (1997). Tourism education: Policy vs. practice. *International Journal of Contemporary Hospitality Management*, *9*(1), 5–12.

Baum, T., Amoah, V., & Spivack, S. (1997). Policy dimensions of human resource management in the tourism and hospitality industries. *International Journal of Contemporary Hospitality Management*, *9*(4/6), 221–229.

Baum, T., & Nickson, D. (1998). Teaching human resource management in hospitality and tourism: A critique. *International Journal of Contemporary Hospitality Management*, *10*, 75–79.

Becton, S., & Graetz, B. (2001). Small business — small minded? Training attitudes and needs of the tourism and hospitality industry. *International Journal of Tourism Research*, *3*(2), 105–113.

Bernier, C. (1997). Occupational map of tourism and leisure job titles. In: E. Laws (Ed.), *The ATTT tourism education handbook* (pp. 56–60). London: Tourism Society.

Bernthall, R. (1988). Designing curriculum: Will industry participate? Paper presented at International conference for tourism educators, Guildford, University of Surrey.

Berry-Lound, D., Batersby, D., & Parsons, D. (1991). *Jobs in tourism and leisure: A labour market review*. London: British Tourist Authority.

Bosselman, R. H. (1996). Issues of accreditation in hospitality and tourism education: The value controversy. *Tourism Recreation Research*, *21*(2), 31–35.

Botterill, D. (1996). *Making connections between industry and higher education in tourism*. London: The National Liaison Group for Higher Education in Tourism.

Botterill, D., & Tribe, J. (2000). *Guideline 9: Benchmarking and the higher education curriculum*. London: National Liaison Group for Higher Education in Tourism.

Bramwell, B. (1996). Sustainable tourism management education in Europe. *Tourism Management*, *17*(4), 307–308.

Bramwell, B., Goytia, A., & Henry, I. (1996). Developing sustainable tourism management education. In: G. Richards (Ed.), *Tourism in central and eastern Europe: Educating for quality* (pp. 207–224). Tilberg: Tilberg University Press.

Buhalis, D. (1998). Information technologies in tourism: Implications for the tourism curriculum. Paper presented at ENTER — international conference on information and communication technologies in tourism, Istanbul, Turkey.

Burke, J. F. (1988). Teaching tourism in the USA. Paper presented at International conference for tourism educators, Guildford, University of Surrey.

Burns, P. (1992). Going against conventional wisdom. *Tourism Concern*, *3*, 8.

Burns, P. (1995). Hotel management training in Eastern Europe. *Progress in Tourism and Hospitality Research*, *1*(1), 53–62.

Burton, P. (1988). Building bridges between industry and education. Paper presented at International conference for tourism educators, Guildford, University of Surrey.

Busby, G. (1994). Tourism education or tourism training for the 1990s? *Journal of Further and Higher Education*, *18*(2), 3–9.

Busby, G. (1995). The changing role of staff development for travel and tourism lecturers. *Journal of the National Association for Staff Development in Further and Higher Education*, *33*, 19–26.

Busby, G., Brunt, P., & Baber, S. (1997). Tourism sandwich placements: An appraisal. *Tourism Management, 18*(2), 105–110.

Cassels, D. (1994). Employer/educator partnerships: Harnessing employers' contributions. Paper presented at NLG conference, London.

Cave, P. (1997). *Placements in industry — experience in the Lancashire Business School.* London: The National Liaison Group for Higher Education in Tourism.

Cave, P. (1999). *Best practice in tourism placements.* London: The National Liaison Group for Higher Education in Tourism.

Charles, K. (1992). Career influences, expectations, and perceptions of Caribbean hospitality and tourism students: A Third World perspective. *Hospitality and Tourism Educator, 4*(3), 9–14.

Charles, K. (1997). Tourism education and training in the Caribbean: Preparing for the 21st century. *Progress in Tourism and Hospitality Research, 3*, 189–197.

Chen, S. C. (1990). The outline of higher level education in tourism in China. *Revue de Tourisme, 45*(4), 24–27.

Chen, J. S., Chu, H. L. K., & Wu, WuChung. (2000). Tourism students' perceptions of work values: A case of Taiwanese universities. *International Journal of Contemporary Hospitality Management, 12*(6), 360–365.

Chon, K. (1990). Toward a global perspective of hospitality education. *Hospitality and Tourism Educator, 2*(3), 10–11.

Christie-Mill, R. (1978). *Tourism education: Its development and current status with special reference to selected segments of tourism-related industries in Michigan.* East Lancing: Michigan State University.

CNAA (Council for National Academic Awards). (1993). *Review of tourism studies degree courses.* London: CNAA.

Collins, S., Sweeney, A., & Green, A. (1994). Training for the UK tour operating industry: Advancing current practice. *Tourism Management, 15*(1), 5–8.

Conlin, M. V. (1991). Credible higher education in tourism: A Caribbean example. *Tourism: Building credibility for a credible industry. Proceedings of the Travel and Tourism Research Association twenty-second annual conference* (pp. 227–232). Hyatt Regency Hotel, Long Beach, CA, June 9–13.

Cooper, C. (1993). An analysis of the relationship between industry and education in travel and tourism. *Teoros International, 1*(1), 65–75.

Cooper, C. (1997). A framework for curriculum planning in tourism and hospitality. In: E. Laws (Ed.), *The ATTT tourism education handbook* (pp. 24–27). London: Tourism Society.

Cooper, M. (1997). Tourism planning and education in Vietnam: A profile 1995–2010. *Pacific Tourism Review, 1*(1), 57–63.

Cooper, C., & Messenger, S. (1991). Tourism education and training for tourism in Europe: A comparative framework. Paper presented at the international congress for education and training in tourism professions, Milan, Italy.

Cooper, C., & Westlake, J. (1998). Stakeholders and tourism education: Curriculum planning using a quality management framework. *Industry and Higher Education*, 1292, 93–100.

Cooper, C., Scales, R., & Westlake, J. (1992). The anatomy of tourism and hospitality educators in the UK. *Tourism Management, 13*(2), 234–242.

Cooper, C., Shepherd, R., & Westlake, J. (1994). *Tourism and hospitality education.* Guildford: University of Surrey.

Cooper, C., Shepherd, R., & Westlake, J. (1996). *Educating the educators: A manual of tourism and hospitality education.* Madrid: WTO.

Crompton, J. L. (1991). A profile of students in recreation, park, and tourism doctoral programs at eight major US universities. *Journal of Park and Recreation Administration, 9*(1), 1–12.

Cummings, L. E., & Brewer, K. P. (1996). Issues facing education in an emerging aspect of tourism: The gaming industry. *Tourism Recreation Research, 21*(2), 63–68.

Daniele, R., & Mistilis, N. (1999). Information technology and tourism education in Australia: An industry view of skills and qualities required in graduates. In: D. Buhalis & W. Schertler (Eds), *Information and communication technologies* (pp. 140–150). Vienna: Springer.

Davies, J. (1999). Language skills in the leisure and tourism industry. *Tourism, 102,* 20.

Echtner, C. (1994). Entrepreneurial training in developing countries. *Annals of Tourism Research, 22*(1), 119–134.

Echtner, C., & Jamal, T. (1997). The disciplinary dilemma of tourism studies. *Annals of Tourism Research, 24*(4), 869–883.

Enghagen, L. K. (1990). Teaching ethics in hospitality and tourism education. *Hospitality Research Journal, 14*(2), 467–474.

Evans, J. (1993). Tourism graduates: A case of over production? *Tourism Management, 14*(4), 243–246.

Fayos-Sola, E. (1997). *An introduction to TEDQUAL: A methodology for quality in tourism education and training.* Madrid: WTO.

Formica, S. (1996). European hospitality and tourism education: Differences with the American model and future trends. *International Journal of Hospitality Management, 15*(4), 317–323.

Formica, S. (1997). The development of hospitality and tourism education in Italy. *Journal of Hospitality and Tourism Education, 9*(3), 48–54.

Gamble, P. R. (1992). The educational challenge for hospitality and tourism studies. *Tourism Management, 13*(1), 6–10.

Getz, D. (1994). Students' work experiences, perceptions and attitudes towards careers in hospitality and tourism: A longitudinal case study in Spey Valley, Scotland. *International Journal of Hospitality Management, 13*(1), 25–37.

Go, F. (1994). Emerging issues in tourism education. In: W. Theobald (Ed.), *Global tourism: The next decade.* London: Butterworth Heinemann .

Go, F. (1998). Globalization and emerging tourism education issues. Paper delivered to *Tourism Education Exchange, University of Westminster.*

Go, F., & Mok, C. (1995). Hotel and tourism management education: Building a centre of excellence in Hong Kong. *Tourism Recreation Research, 20*(2), 46–57.

Godau, A. (1991). Developing tourism managers — the Friedrich List Hoschule in Dresden. *Tourism Management, 12*(3), 257–258.

Goeldner, C. R. (1988). The evaluation of tourism as an industry and a discipline. Paper presented at International conference for tourism educators, Guildford, University of Surrey.

Goodenough, R., & Page, S. (1993). Planning for tourism education and training in the 1990s: Bridging the gap between industry and education. *Journal of Geography in Higher Education, 17*(1), 57–72.

Gunn, C. (1992). The need for multi-disciplinary tourism education. *World Travel and Tourism Review, 2,* 265–271.

Hawes, B. (1988). *Education and the tourism industry: Meeting the challenge together.* London: English Tourist Board.

Haywood, K. M. (1989). A radical proposal for hospitality and tourism education. *International Journal of Hospitality Management, 8*(4), 259–264.

Haywood, K. M., & Maki, K. (1992). A conceptual model of the education employment interface for the tourism industry. *World Travel and Tourism Review, 2,* 237–248.

Henry, I., Jackson, G., & Larrauri, M. (1998). Curriculum guidelines for sustainable tourism management education. In: B. Bramwell, I. Henry, G. Jackson, A. Goytia Prat, G. Richards & J. van der Straaten (Eds), *Sustainable tourism management: Principles and practice* (pp. 243–250). Tilberg: ATLAS.

Hobson, J. (1995). The development of hospitality and tourism education in Australia. *Hospitality and Tourism Educator, 7*(4), 25–29.

Holloway, C. (1998). Learning and earning: Reassessing the aims and purposes of a tourism degree. In: G. Richards (Ed.), *Developments in the European tourism curriculum* (pp. 7–18). Tilberg: ATLAS.

Holloway, J. C. (1995). *Towards a core curriculum for tourism: A discussion paper.* London: The National Liaison Group for Higher Education in Tourism.

Howie, F. (1996). Skills, understanding and knowledge for sustainable tourism. In: G. Richards (Ed.), *Tourism in central and eastern Europe: Educating for quality* (pp. 183–206). Tilberg: Tilberg University Press.

Hultsman, J. (1995). Just tourism. An ethical framework. *Annals of Tourism Research, 22*(3), 553–567.

Jafari, J., & Ritchie, J. R. B. (1981). Towards a framework for tourism education. *Annals of Tourism Research, 8*(1), 14–34.

Kaplan, A. (1982). A management approach to hospitality and tourism education. *International Journal of Hospitality Management, 1*(1), 11–17.

Khwaja, H. S., & Bosselman, R. H. (1990). Cultural adjustment of international graduate students in American hospitality and tourism programs. *Hospitality Research Journal, 14*(2), 75–82.

King, B. (1994). Tourism higher education in island microstates. *Tourism Management, 15*(4), 267–272.

Koh, K. (1995). Designing the four-year tourism management curriculum: A marketing approach. *Journal of Travel Research, 24*(1), 68–72.

Koshizucha, M., Umemura, M., Mori, M., Horiuchi, M., & Shishido, M. (1998). Tourism education at four-year universities in Japan. In: B. Faulkner et al. (Eds), *Progress in tourism and hospitality research 1998. Proceedings of the 8th Australian tourism and hospitality research conference* (pp. 577–578). Canberra: Bureau of Tourism Research.

Kusluvan, S., & Kusluvan, K. (2000). Perceptions and attitudes of undergraduate tourism students towards working in the tourism industry in Turkey. *Tourism Management, 21*(3), 251–269.

Lawson, M. (1974). *Teaching tourism: Education and training in western Europe: A comparative study.* London: Tourism International Press.

Leiper, N. (1981). Towards a cohesive curriculum in tourism: The case for a distinct discipline. *Annals of Tourism Research, 8*(1), 69–83.

Leiper, N. (2000). An emerging discipline. *Annals of Tourism Research, 27*(3), 805–808.

Lewis, A., & Tribe, J. (2001). A stakeholder-informed approach to tourism education in developing countries: Case studies in the Caribbean. Paper presented at international conference on tourism development and management in developing countries, Guilin, China.

Lewis, A., & Tribe, J. (2002). Critical issues in the globalisation of tourism education. *Tourism Recreation Research, 27*(1), 13–20.

Litteljohn, D., & Watson, S. (1990). Management development for hospitality and tourism: Management development approaches for the 1990s. *International Journal of Contemporary Hospitality Management (Supplement), 2*(2), 36–42.

McIntosh, R., & Walther, C. (1981). Teaching tourism in 4-year degree program. *Annals of Tourism Research, 8*(1), 134–135.

McIntosh, R., van Weenen, I., & Shafer, E. (1983). Tourism education. *Tourism Management, 4*(2), 134–139.

McKercher, B., Williams, A., & Coghlan, I. (1995). Career progress of recent tourism graduates. *Tourism Management, 16*(7), 541–545.

Medlik, S. (1965). *Higher education and research in tourism in western Europe, study tour report,* unpublished.

Middleton, V., & Ladkin, A. (1996). *The profile of tourism studies degree courses in the UK 1995/96.* London: The National Liaison Group for Higher Education in Tourism.

Mistilis, N., & Daniele, R. (2000). Education and Australian government policy: Delivering information technology outcomes for tourism businesses? *Information Technology and Tourism, 3*(1), 3–14.

Moscardo, G. (1997). Making mindful managers. *The Journal of Tourism Studies, 8*(1), 16–24.

Murphy, P. (1981). Tourism course proposal for a social science curriculum. *Annals of Tourism Research*, *8*(1), 96–105.

Murphy, P. (1992). Community partnerships: The need for mutual education. *World Travel and Tourism Review*, *2*, 273–281.

Parsons, D. (1987). Jobs in tourism. *Employment Gazette*, *95*(7), 336–346.

Parsons, D. (1991). The making of managers. Lessons from an international review of tourism management education programmes. *Tourism Management*, *12*(3), 197–207.

Pearce, P. (1991). Locating tourism studies in the landscape of knowledge. *New horizons conference proceedings*. Calgary, University of Calgary.

Persic, M. (1998). Training of tourism professionals in Croatia. *World Leisure and Recreation*, *40*(3), 19–25.

Petroune, I., & Voskoboinikov, S. (1998). Globalisation, localisation and identity of tourism higher education: A Russian perspective. In: G. Richards (Ed.), *Developments in the European tourism curriculum* (pp. 49–60). Tilberg: ATLAS.

Pirjevec, B. (1990). 'Alternative' tourism education and training. *Acta Turistica*, *2*(2), 140–145.

Quality Assurance Agency for Higher Education (2000). *Subject review handbook*. Gloucester: QAA.

Rafferty, M. D. (1990). The effects of instruction in geography on college students' perception of world regions as tourism destinations. *Tourism Recreation Research*, *15*(2), 30–40.

Richards, G. (1992). What are we teaching tomorrow's professionals? *Proceedings of tourism society conference* (pp. 1–8). *London, May 1992*.

Richards, G. (1997). ATLAS: A European network for tourism education and research. In: E. Laws (Ed.), *The ATTT tourism education handbook* (pp. 49–55). London: Tourism Society.

Richards, G. (1998a). A European network for tourism education. *Tourism Management*, *19*(1), 1–4.

Richards, G. (1998b). Sustainable tourism management education: Educational, environmental and industry perspectives. In: B. Bramwell, I. Henry, G. Jackson, A. Goytia Prat, G. Richards & J. van der Straaten (Eds), *Sustainable tourism management: Principles and practice* (pp. 7–22). Tilberg: ATLAS.

Ritchie, J. R. B. (1993). Educating the tourism educators: Guidelines for policy and programme development. *Teoros International*, *1*(1), 9–24.

Ritchie, J. R. B. (1995). Design and development of the tourism and hospitality management curriculum. *Tourism Recreation Research*, *20*(2), 7–13.

Ross, G. (1997). Hospitality and tourism job applications and educational expectation. *International Journal of Contemporary Hospitality Management*, *1*, 24–127.

Ryan, C. (1995). Tourism courses: A new concern for new times? *Tourism Management*, *16*(2), 97–100.

Samenfink, W. (1998). Preparing students to function in the international hospitality industry: A new approach. *Journal of Hospitality and Tourism Education*, *10*, 37–41.

Sheldon, P. J. (1989). Professionalism in tourism and hospitality. *Annals of Tourism Research*, *16*, 492–503.

Sheldon, P. J., & Gee, C. Y. (1987). Training needs assessment in the travel industry. *Annals of Tourism Research*, *14*(2), 173–182.

Shepherd, R. (1993). Dimensions of the education–industry interface for tourism. *Proceedings of research and academic papers 5*. USA: Society of Travel and Tourism Educators.

Shepherd, R. (1997). The graduate tourism aptitude test (GTAT). In: E. Laws (Ed.), *The ATTT tourism education handbook*. London: The Tourism Society.

Shepherd, R., & Cooper, C. (1995). Innovations in tourism education and training. *Tourism Recreation Research*, *20*(2), 14–24.

Shepherd, R., & Cooper, C. (1997). The relationship between tourism education and the tourism industry: Implications for tourism education. *Tourism Recreation Research*, *22*(1), 35–48.

Sims, W. (1999). Tourism and hospitality education in Australia: An overview. In: K. Chon (Ed.), *Conference proceedings of the first Pan-American conference: Latin American tourism in the next millennium: Education, Investment and Sustainability* (pp. 95–100).

Singh, S. (1997). Developing human resources for the tourism industry with reference to India. *Tourism Management, 18*(5), 299–306.

Sivan, A., Yan, L., & Kember, D. (1995). Peer assessment in hospitality and tourism. *Hospitality and Tourism Educator, 7*(4), 17–20.

Smith, G., & Cooper, C. (1999). The challenge of globalization from theory to practice: Competitive approaches to tourism and hospitality curriculum design: The case of the International School of Tourism and Hotel Management, Puerto Rico. In: K. Chon (Ed.), *Conference proceedings of the first Pan-American conference: Latin American tourism in the next millennium: Education, investment and sustainability* (pp. 43–57).

Smith, G., & Cooper, C. (2000). Competitive approaches to tourism and hospitality Curriculum design. *Journal of Travel Research, 39*, 90–95.

Spears, D., Boger, C., & Gould, R. (1999). Collaborative web-based project on tourism and marketing. *Journal of Hospitality and Tourism Education, 10*(4), 38–41.

Swarbrooke, J. (1995). Tourism and leisure education in the United Kingdom. In: G. Richards (Ed.), *European tourism and leisure education: Trends and prospects.* Tilberg, Netherlands: Tilberg University Press.

Swedlove, W., & Dowler, S. (1992). Competency-based occupational standards and certification for the tourism industry. *World Travel and Tourism Review, 2*, 283–286.

Tan, J., & Morgan, D. (2001). Relevance and quality in Australian tourism higher education: Educator and professional views. *Journal of Teaching in Travel and Tourism, 1*(1), 59–78.

Theuns, H. L., & Go, F. (1992). Need led priorities in hospitality education for the third world. In: J. Brent Ritchie, D. Hawkins, F. Go & D. Frechtling (Eds), *World travel and tourism review indicators.* Wallingford: CAB International.

Tribe, J. (1995). Tourism economics: Life after death? *Tourism Economics, 1*(4), 329–340.

Tribe, J. (1997). The indiscipline of tourism. *Annals of Tourism Research, 24*(3), 638–657.

Tribe, J. (1998). Community and commercial interests in tourism: Whose world is it anyway? In: G. Richards (Ed.), *Developments in the European tourism curriculum* (pp. 19–30). Tilberg: ATLAS.

Tribe, J. (2000a). Balancing the vocational: The theory and practice of liberal education in tourism. *The International Journal of Tourism and Hospitality Research (The Surrey Quarterly Review), 2*(1), 9–26.

Tribe, J. (2000b). Indisciplined and unsubstantiated: Reply to Leiper. *Annals of Tourism Research, 27*(3), 809–813.

Tribe, J. (2001). Research paradigms and the tourism curriculum. *Journal of Travel Research, 39*(4), 442–448.

Tribe, J. (2002). The philosophic practitioner. *Annals of Tourism Research, 29*(2), 338–357.

Vroom, J. A. (1983). Tourism education: A model program. *Tourist Review, 38*(2), 6–9.

Walle, A. H. (1997). Hospitality and tourism education: Generic vs. specialised perspectives. *Journal of Hospitality and Tourism Education, 9*(1), 73–76.

Walsh, M. E. (1992). Some recent innovations in tourism education in Ireland. *Tourism Management, 13*(1), 130–133.

Weiermair, K. (1995). Structural changes in the tourism industry and adaptation of professional training systems. *Espaces, 13*, 109–114.

Wells, J. (1996). The tourism curriculum in higher education in Australia: 1989–1995. *The Journal of Tourism Studies, 7*(1), 20–30.

Xiao, HongGen (2000). China's tourism education into the 21st century. *Annals of Tourism Research, 27*(4), 1053–1054.

Xiao, Q. H., & Liu, Z. J. (1995). Tourism and hospitality education in China. In: A. Lew & L. Yu (Eds), *Tourism in China: Geographic, political, and economic perspectives.* Boulder, CO: Westview Press.

Yale, L. J., & Cooke, R. A. (1995). Content of tourism curricula: An industry delphi panel. In: K. Chon (Ed.), *New frontiers in tourism research. Proceedings of research and academic papers Volume VII* (pp. 98–113). USA: Society of Travel and Tourism Educators.

Zhao, J. L. (1991). A current look at hospitality and tourism education in China's colleges and universities. *International Journal of Hospitality Management, 10*(4), 357–367.

CURRICULUM

Chapter 4

Tourism, Knowledge and the Curriculum

John Tribe

Introduction

The aim of this chapter is to offer a critical analysis of the tourism curriculum. It initially discusses definitions of curriculum by reference to a number of studies on the subject and introduces the idea that any curriculum involves framing in curriculum space. Hence, the notions of choice and contestability are introduced.

Since a curriculum involves choice of what knowledge is to be included and knowledge itself represents a particular way of looking at a target phenomenon it is important next to understand the relationship between tourism knowledge and the curriculum.

Having done this some basic principles of curriculum design are considered before introducing and evaluating a number of curriculum proposals that have been proffered for tourism. Finally, a number of theorists are assembled to offer a more deep critique of curriculum emphasising the role of ideology in their construction.

The issue that arises throughout the chapter is that of the schisms that exist in each of the areas of tourism, knowledge and the curriculum. On the one hand, tourism, knowledge and the curriculum may be bounded by a business and vocationalist view of things. On the other, tourism education may be seen as a quest for understanding and acting in a more widely drawn complex world of tourism.

Curriculum

A simple definition of the curriculum can be found in Taylor and Richards (1985) who define the curriculum as that which is taught. More complex definitions include that used by Kerr (1968) which embraces a much wider experience capturing all the learning which is guided by an institution. There is also a literature which unearths a hidden side to the curriculum (Snyder, 1971; Cornbleth, 1984; Graves, 1983). Here, the spotlight falls not just on the explicit aims and objectives of the curriculum, but also on the implicit values that accompany it. Exponents of the hidden curriculum point to the significance of what is left out of the curriculum as well as what is put in.

For the purposes of this chapter, the curriculum is defined as a whole programme of educational experiences that is packaged as a degree programme. Its constituent parts are a number of modules or courses, which in turn may be specified as a series of syllabi or course contents. Alongside this, a wider concept of curriculum space is proposed to capture not just what is taught, but what is excluded.

The term curriculum is more widely used and accepted in compulsory education, than in higher education. For in many older universities and traditional single honours degrees, the canon of the discipline represents what is to be taught. But for newer universities and newer courses, curriculum has more relevance. The expansion of higher education and a proliferation of new courses (including tourism) has given the concept of the curriculum more significance since there is no simple disciplinary structure to form a core for many of the new courses. Therefore, the question of what to teach is thrown into sharper focus. Indeed, emerging worries about chaotic or accidental curricula (and "Mickey Mouse" degrees) have prompted some calls for a government-regulated national curriculum for higher education.

The term curriculum space (Tribe, 2000b) enables us to visualise some important steps in curriculum construction. The term denotes the expanse or area that contains the range of possible contents of a curriculum (the what could be). Curriculum space is populated with a large array of possible knowledge, skills and attitudes. The idea of framing (Bernstein, 1971) is useful to understand the point of curriculum space. The construction of any particular curriculum will entail framing, where some areas of curriculum space will be included, and others excluded. When a framed curriculum is identified within curriculum space, what is left outside the curriculum becomes evident. The idea of curriculum space also enables the concept of curriculum as a contested construction to emerge as illustrated in Figure 1.

The inside rectangle of Figure 1 illustrates curriculum space for tourism. The circles inside the rectangle (X and Y) each represent a particular framing of the curriculum. Around the outside boxes represent the various interests which may influence a particular framing. The actual content of the framed curriculum will depend upon the power exerted by these interests. So, for example, circle X illustrates an outcome where the government exerts a strong central control on the curriculum. Circle Y illustrates a curriculum influenced by the interests of lecturers in critical subjects.

Tourism Knowledge and the Curriculum

Since the curriculum is a packaging of knowledge and knowledge is our way of understanding the phenomenon of tourism this gives rise to the need to distinguish between the terms tourism, knowledge and the curriculum and examine their inter-relationship. Tourism is a practice or performance which exists in the external world. It is what people are engaged in when they visit friends and relatives, or go skiing or visit Venice. The phenomenon of tourism (particularly because of its rapid growth) has generated interest among academics whose investigations into the phenomenon result in a growing body of knowledge of tourism. Tourism education and the tourism curriculum offer packages of knowledge in

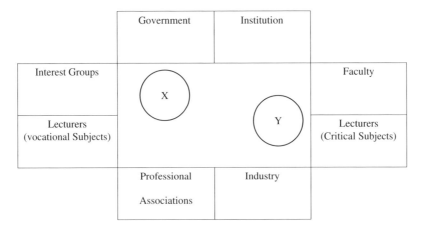

Figure 1: Curriculum space.

order to better understand the phenomenon of tourism. So what is the relationship between tourism as a phenomenon, tourism knowledge and the tourism curriculum?

Tourism as a phenomenon is that part of the external world where humans go about the business of being tourists and that part of the external world which is affected by tourism. It is large, messy, complex and dynamic. It encompasses a range of possible practices and outcomes. It is not the same world as the study of tourism. The latter consists of a tourism research community and a symbolic record of tourism knowledge. It is an attempt by humans to capture, to represent, to describe, to explain and to predict the phenomenon of tourism. The study of tourism uncovers new ways of seeing tourism, maps out new concepts, elaborates new theories and builds up a body of knowledge. Tourism knowledge is however essentially much less than the activity that it describes. It is essentially in the business of making generalisations about the phenomenal world of tourism and the packaging of theories.

Tourism knowledge can therefore offer only an incomplete account of tourism. Indeed, there may well be interesting aspects of tourism which are not as yet revealed or discovered by the study of tourism. The relationship between the study of tourism and the phenomenon of tourism also points up the important issue of the knowledge gaze. Our knowledge gaze determines what parts of the phenomenon of tourism are studied in tourism studies and how these parts are known and conceptualised.

Moving to education we should avoid the temptation to elide the terms curriculum and knowledge. They only coincide in limited cases — mainly in traditional universities, and for traditional courses where curriculum would appear to be a redundant term. The undergraduate programme here represents a process of induction of students into a particular discipline.

But for tourism higher education, any move to define the curriculum in terms of induction into a discipline, or body of knowledge is a problematic one. Tourism studies may be conceived of as being pre-paradigmatic (Kuhn, 1970). It has not yet settled into "normal tourism". The pattern of research activity and puzzle solving is not settled nor is the direction for future activities agreed by those operating in the field. Because tourism studies is in a pre-paradigmatic state, there exists a variety of different knowledge systems in operation.

Since the concept of tourism knowledge is problematic, the curriculum cannot be reduced to an induction into a discipline. A knowledge choice has to be made.

So two key issues for the tourism curriculum are first, a choice of which aspects of the tourism phenomenon are to be studied and second, a choice of which types of tourism knowledge are used to approach to these phenomena. The curriculum for tourism education itself represents several steps of removal from the phenomenal world of tourism and encompasses a smaller domain. This is because the curriculum has necessary limits. There is after all only a certain amount that can be incorporated into a curriculum. For tourism degrees, the curriculum typically spans a period of 3 academic years. Just as tourism knowledge occupies a smaller space than that of the tourism phenomenon, the tourism curriculum can only incorporate a limited amount of what is offered by tourism knowledge. These domains of phenomenon, knowledge and curriculum are illustrated in Figure 2.

Some important points emerge from Figure 2. First it may be noted that the tourism curriculum is smaller than the larger domain of tourism knowledge. In turn, tourism knowledge represents an incomplete insight into the phenomenon of tourism. Additionally, since the curriculum is not only constructed from tourism knowledge its circle straddles the non-tourism world. Note that there is a flow from the phenomenon of tourism, through tourism knowledge to tourism education and the curriculum, which illustrates the refining and selection process in action. However, the flows are not uni-directional. For example, there is a flow from both tourism knowledge and the tourism curriculum back to the phenomenon of tourism. This captures the important point that tourism knowledge and tourism education have the possibility of influencing and changing the phenomenon of tourism itself. So for example, the elaboration of theories of socio-cultural impacts of tourism and the transmission of such theories into the wider world through tourism education may lead to pressure to amend tourism to take more account of its socio-cultural impacts.

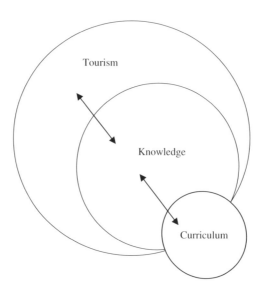

Figure 2: Tourism, knowledge and the curriculum.

Having explored the concept of the curriculum and mapped its relationships with tourism and knowledge the latter concepts are now examined more fully.

Tribe (1999, p. 80) defines tourism as:

> The sum of the phenomena and relationships arising from the interaction in generating and host regions, of tourists, business suppliers, economies, governments, communities and environments.

His definition reveals the key dimensions of a comprehensive tourism world namely:

- those related to the tourist (including motivation, experience, demand, choice, satisfaction and interaction);
- those related to business (including profit, marketing, human resourcing and corporate planning of transport, hospitality and recreation organisations);
- those relating to the host community (including perceptions, economic, social and cultural impacts);
- those relating to the host environment (including ecological and aesthetic impacts);
- those relating to host governments (including measurement of tourism, policy and planning);
- those relating to the generating country (including economic, environmental, aesthetic and socio-cultural effects) (Tribe, 1999, p. 80).

In offering this definition, Tribe seeks to allow the concept of tourism room to celebrate its full complexity. That is not only tourism that represents consumer and business activities but also tourism that reflects environmental, aesthetic, ethical and cultural issues. Crudely speaking then, the phenomenon of tourism can be roughly split between the business of tourism and non-business aspects.

Turning to tourism knowledge, Tribe (1997) suggests that knowledge about tourism is organised through the established disciplines (e.g. economics, anthropology), through interdisciplinary approaches (e.g. environmental studies, marketing) and through extra-disciplinary approaches (e.g. customer service). Tribe further postulated that a coalition of approaches (mainly interdisciplinary and extra-disciplinary) under the banner of tourism business studies had established a substantial inroad and major presence in the study of tourism. However, things have changed somewhat since Tribe's 1997 analysis. First there has been an extraordinary burst of research activity and articles relating to sustainable tourism. Second a new wave of tourism research is gathering momentum concentrating on "studies" rather than "business". The increasing interest in such approaches is signalled by new journal titles such as *Tourist Studies* and the *Journal of Tourism and Cultural Change* and new approaches include those using interpretivist and critical methodologies by researchers working in for example gender studies and cultural theory.

Figure 3 aligns these different levels of the tourism phenomenon, tourism knowledge, and the tourism curriculum one above the other, dividing each level into two key constituent domains. The diagram illustrates a fundamental rift evident between two camps. On the one side is the view of tourism as a business phenomenon to be investigated through business knowledge and giving rise to curricula for vocational ends. On the other,

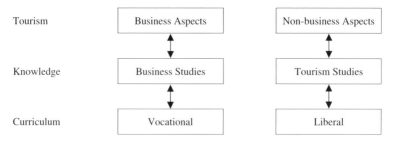

Figure 3: Tourism, knowledge and the curriculum.

the view of tourism is as an unrestricted phenomenon, to be investigated by a range of knowledge approaches and giving rise to curricula for liberal ends.

These ideas of liberal and vocational education are taken up later in this chapter but the following examples show how the different approaches to tourism education are illustrated in the curricula of different universities. University A demonstrates a curriculum with vocational aims:

> to prepare [students] for a management career within the travel and tourism industry through a sound education in the principles and practices of management in the industry and to develop a set of personal skills and management competences appropriate for managerial careers in the travel and tourism industry.

On the other hand, University B demonstrates a curriculum that encompasses a more liberal approach:

> The key areas of study in this course are Introduction to the Sociology and Anthropology of Travel and Tourism; Tourism and the Global Culture; Thesis Writing; Tourism, Heritage & Environment; Space, Place and Society; Tourism, Myth and Pilgrimage; Travel Writing and Media Representations; Dissertation.

The diagram also demonstrates that these levels of phenomenon, knowledge and curriculum are not independent of each other, but each is interconnected so that the emergence of a particular type of tourism, knowledge and curriculum reinforces, and is reinforced by, developments at the different levels.

Approaches to Curriculum Design for Tourism

A number of writers including Tyler (1949), Eraut et al. (1975), Rowntree (1982) and Manwaring and Elton (1984) propose models for curriculum design. Each of these suggest that curriculum design is preceded by consideration of the aims and purposes of the planned course. Indeed, a typical sequence of curriculum design is shown as follows:

- Establish rationale;
- Conduct market research/consultation;

- Define aims and objectives;
- Establish modular structure including progression between levels and compulsory/elective elements;
- Choose modules;
- Establish learning outcomes for modules;
- Determine assessment strategy;
- Determine teaching and learning strategy;
- Develop a system for validation, evaluation, review and improvement.

In terms of evaluation issues that should be addressed are for example

- does the curriculum deliver its stated aims?
- is it coherent (i.e. does it avoid duplication, does it have a framework that connects the various modules, do the parts add up to a meaningful whole?)
- does it offer breadth (i.e. does it avoid over narrow specialisation?)
- is it balanced (i.e. does it include functional and critical elements?)
- integration (i.e. are there attempts to integrate themes across modules and to bring together theory and practice?)
- progression (i.e. do modules lead on to each other in a sequential way and does the intellectual content demonstrate a progression in difficulty over the length of the course?)

An early contribution to the debate about what should constitute the tourism curriculum was initiated by the UK National Liaison Group for Higher Education in Tourism (NLG) (Holloway, 1995). The NLG aim was to seek "some consensus on the body of knowledge which would be acceptable to both academics and practitioners in the tourism industry" (Holloway, 1995, p. 2). This consensus was sought at a national conference attended by academics and industrialists that was held in London in December 1994. However, the conference was not provided with a *tabula rasa*, but rather with a set of "seven 'areas of knowledge' on which the committee members of the NLG were agreed" (Holloway, 1995, p. 2).

Reference to an earlier review by the UK Council for National Academic Awards (CNAA, 1993, p. 32) enables the genealogy of the NLG project to be traced and there can be found seven similar subject areas. The CNAA review is more explicit on how these seven areas have been identified. They are based upon Airey and Middleton's (1984) review of the curriculum of tourism courses, which was based on Burkart and Medlik's (1981) 'Body of Knowledge', and, "information supplied by academic institutions for this review" (CNAA, 1993, p. 32).

The NLG core comprised:

- The meaning and nature of tourism;
- The structure of the industry;
- The dimensions of tourism and issues of measurement;
- The significance and impacts of tourism;
- The marketing of tourism;
- Tourism planning and development;
- Policy and management in tourism.

The NLG core articulated key aspects of a vocational tourism curriculum but it was uncritical in that it avoided philosophical issues of alternative ends of tourism education. A key omission of the NLG core was its lack of articulation of ethical elements of tourism or the accommodation of disciplinary, critical or non-business approaches to the field. A significant area of the possible curriculum for tourism was therefore omitted.

The rationale for Koh's (1995) study entitled "Designing the four year tourism management curriculum" was that hitherto there had been "little or no empirical input from industry" (Koh, 1995, p. 68) on current U.S. programmes. This was a deficiency that Koh sought to redress. He used a combination of survey and Delphi technique with respondents from the academic and business worlds. The key elements for the tourism curriculum according to Koh were:

- Theories of human resource management;
- Written communication skills;
- Theories of marketing;
- Hotel & restaurant operations;
- Managerial accounting;
- The travel & tourism industry;
- Microcomputer literacy;
- Ethics & social responsibility;
- Entrepreneurship & innovation.
- Managing service quality;
- Interpersonal relation skills;
- Practicum after year 3;
- Practicum after year 2;
- Principles of tourism development;
- Practicum after year 1;

It is notable that the Koh curriculum included ethics and social responsibility but, like the NLG core it is still essentially dominated by vocationalist thinking — a curriculum for the industry with a quite narrow view of tourism.

The year 2000 saw the publication of benchmark statements in the U.K. to "provide a means for the academic community to describe the nature and characteristics of programmes in a specific subject" (Botterill & Tribe, 2000, p. 13). For tourism, the NLG undertook the drafting of benchmark statements and held a series of consultative meetings to validate them with the tourism subject community. The core areas of study were agreed as:

- The concepts and characteristics of tourism as an area of academic and applied study;
- The nature and characteristics of tourists;
- The structure of and interactions in the tourism industry;
- The role of tourism in the communities and environments that it affects;
- The nature and characteristics of tourists.

Benchmarking therefore represents the staking out of a compulsory zone within curriculum space. Tribe (2000b, pp. 9–10) discussed the main strengths and weaknesses of this approach.

The main strengths are as follows: The draft statements have avoided the pitfalls of the earlier NLG core and the Koh curriculum which over-focussed on the vocational. They offer a recipe for a balanced curriculum which avoids the narrow confines of vocationalism and operationalism or academicism and idealism. Disciplinary knowledge, communities, environments and the ethical are all given due weight. They offer coverage of a key middle ground of curriculum space and represent something of a Blairite "Big Tent" within which most tourism academics can probably operate. Benchmarking is stimulating a critical review of the tourism curriculum. It offers protection against accidental and chaotic curricula.

The main weaknesses can also be examined: The exercise is a-theoretical. The theory and methodology of curriculum design are not foregrounded. Benchmarking may be interpreted as a definitive and comprehensive curriculum statement. Some departments may attempt to teach it as is. The full richness of curriculum space may become obscured. Benchmarking may impose closure where the freedom to construct a curriculum in any part of curriculum space is lost. It may cause a homogenisation of the tourism degree product and a curbing of the curriculum dynamism of this sector. It may herald a move towards a safe middle ground and institutional aims and objectives for QAA subject review may show this. They may represent the start of a more comprehensive project, where incrementally the detail is filled in and the curriculum becomes tightly specified. They may constrain curriculum development: Would tourism higher education have developed if benchmarking had existed 20 years ago?

Critical Models of the Curriculum

This section illustrates how different writers have surfaced a number of taken for granted issues that are not always obvious when discussing the curriculum. The ideas contained in this section are summarised in Table 1 and may help curriculum authors to ask more critical questions about their proposals.

For example, Scrimshaw's (1983) framework effectively divides curriculum space into eight underlying ideologies. An ideology (Barnett, 2003) is a coherent set of ideas. Ideologies can involve closure and blindness when they are deeply embedded and saturate our ways of thinking so that we are not aware of their operation but rather see the ideas expressed within them as common sense. Scrimshaw identified the ideologies of progressivism, romanticism, humanism, academicism, traditionalism, vocationalism, technicism and reconstructionism. His purpose was to reveal ideologies implicit in curricula. In situating curricula in relation to ideological typologies, he provided an insight into the full extent of curriculum space and what may be missed by an over narrow framing. For example, a technicist and vocationalist curriculum may preclude humanist or progressivist aspects.

Silver and Brennan (1988) analyse the vocational curriculum as a continuum along a vocational–liberal axis. A vocational curriculum is a curriculum for employment. It is a curriculum to equip students to engage in the vocational world and to participate in it. A liberal curriculum is a curriculum for thinking and reflection. Indeed in some cases it consciously seeks refuge from the world of action in order that its deliberations may proceed without being tainted by the world of the here and now. Youll and Brennan (in Boys et al., 1988, p. 196) utilise an academic–vocational axis where academic programmes induct students into the principles of a discipline, and vocational programmes concentrate on the employability of graduates.

Lawton's (1989, 1996) cultural analysis model constructs the curriculum as a selection from culture. Lawton's work concentrates on the compulsory curriculum and subdivides culture into nine systems — the socio-political system, the economic system, the communications system, the rationality system, the technology system, the morality system, the belief system, the aesthetic system and the maturation system. Lawton's analysis exposes the cultural features common to all societies. His view was that the compulsory curriculum should ensure that these aspects of culture are transmitted. Lawton's nine cultural systems

Table 1: Comparison of curriculum frameworks.

Framework	Purpose	Components
Scrimshaw (1983)	To describe the ideologies implicit in curricula	Progressivism Romanticism Humanism Academicism Traditionalism Vocationalism Technicism Reconstructionism
Silver and Brennan (1988)	To describe the nature of vocational education	Liberal Vocational
Lawton (1989)	To describe the essentials of culture for transmission by the compulsory curriculum	Socio-political system Economic system Communications system Rationality system Technology system Morality system Belief system Aesthetic system Maturation system
Squires (1990)	To describe the undergraduate curriculum	Knowledge Culture Student development
Goodlad (1995)	To prescribe the essential elements of a curriculum for the nourishment of persons	Theory Practice Society Individual
Tribe (2002)	To prescribe the essential elements of a curriculum for good thought and action in a tourism world which is a conjunction of the liberal and the vocational (Philosophic Practitioner)	Vocational Liberal Reflection Action

do help to develop the full extent of possible curriculum space and indicate what may be missed by over specialisation. For example, a vocationalist curriculum would concentrate on the economic and technical systems lacking any analysis of what is right or good which might be informed by, for example, the morality or aesthetic system.

Squires notes "the need for some kind of frame of reference for thinking about the curriculum, and asking what is and should be taught" (1990, p. 29) and offers a framework built around three dimensions of the curriculum. These dimensions are first the curriculum as knowledge, second the curriculum and culture and third, the curriculum and student development. Squires also offers a useful way of looking at knowledge using the terms 'object', 'mode' and 'stance' (1990, p. 53). Squires uses the term 'object' to describe "what the course is about" (1990, p. 52). Here, the classification is in terms of subjects and groups of subjects. Squires uses the term 'mode' to grapple with what he calls "the problem of philosophy" (1990, p. 56). He distinguishes between normal, reflexive and philosophical approaches to any discipline which is the object of the curriculum. This dimension examines the degree of critical engagement that a student makes with the discipline. It encompasses at one end a passive learning of the facts of a discipline and at the other end, a critical appraisal of knowledge creation in the discipline. Squires also uses the term 'stance' which is used to "distinguish broadly between the intention of knowing and the intention of doing" (1990, p. 54).

Goodlad (1995) constructs a model to enable him "to propose a position concerning the nourishment of persons" (1995, p. 1). For him, curriculum space is conceptualised in four possible dimensions under the headings of theory, practice, society and the individual. These he describes as "the institutional correlatives of the social, personal, intellectual and practical dimensions of the person" (1995, p. 21). His argument exposes what he terms heresies which arise when there is imbalance between these dimensions. It is the development of students that is the curriculum imperative for Goodlad.

Stenhouse (1975) advocated a process approach whereby the curriculum evolves from negotiations between lecturers, students and their environment. This approach did not specify any particular components of curriculum space. Rather it saw education as a relatively unconstrained, negotiated journey through curriculum space, without any compulsory elements.

Most recently, Tribe (2002) — largely as a response to the a-theoretical approaches of previous curriculum proposals in tourism — developed principles for the ordering of the curriculum for tourism higher education. The framework proposed comprises four key domains of vocational action, vocational reflection, liberal reflection and liberal action as illustrated in Figure 4. His framework enables the problems of curricula that are over-focused in one

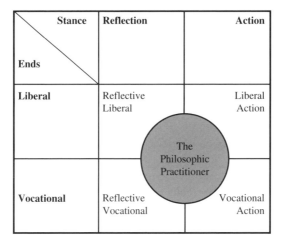

Figure 4: A Curriculum for the Philosophic Practitioner.

part of curriculum space to be surfaced. It also enables the case to be made, and the content outlined, for a tourism higher education which educates *philosophic practitioners*. These would be graduates who deliver efficient and effective tourism services, attempt a comprehensive understanding of the tourism phenomenon while at the same discharging, the role of stewardship for the development of the wider tourism world in which these services are delivered. The curriculum for philosophic practice covers all four of the domains illustrated in Tribe's model and thus represents a synthesis of the dichotomy described previously in Figure 3.

Vocational action refers to the actions of those employed in the tourism industry. So, for example, the marketing of a destination or an attraction, the management of a hotel or restaurant involve vocational actions. The aims and objectives of vocational action are simply defined as preparation for effectiveness at work. In the reflective vocational part of Tribe's curriculum space there is an emphasis on reflection, evaluation and modification of tourism industry skills and knowledge. The development of individual or personal knowledge is encouraged. This is knowledge that is developed from experience and action in the world. Vocational reflection draws fully on Schön's (1983) concept of the reflective practitioner.

The three philosophical activities of attempting to uncover "the truth", a sustained scepticism about things and the search for "the good life" are central to most definitions of liberal education (Tribe, 2000a) and these are all encompassed in the idea of the reflective liberal curriculum. However, liberal *action* requires the extra step of translating better understanding and critiques of the wider world of tourism into action. Here, ethical and just treatment of people (Apple, 1990) and place affected by tourism are essential. This action may herald changes at the individual level, but may also be changes at a societal level in the form of collaborative action with others. The discourse of this quadrant of curriculum space therefore includes notions of world-making, emancipation and liberation.

Conclusion

This chapter has examined a number of aspects of the curriculum in tourism higher education. It has unpacked the concept of the curriculum, considered basic approaches to curriculum design and evaluation and given examples of expositions of curricula both at the general level and at the institutional level. Beyond this it has offered a number of avenues for the critical evaluation of the tourism curriculum.

Initially it has outlined the idea of curriculum space as a concept which delivers three important insights. First it demonstrates that when curricula are framed, some things are contained inside the frame and others excluded since any curriculum can offer only a selection from knowledge. Second it illustrates the potential power of the various influences on the curriculum. Bringing these two ideas together means that any curriculum will be a contested construct.

The important differences and interconnections between tourism, knowledge and the curriculum have also been analysed and a rough dichotomy has been established between two camps. In curriculum terms these are represented by one the one hand courses relating to vocational studies of tourism and on the other, those relating to liberal studies of tourism.

Finally, a number of theorists have provided pointers for critiquing the curriculum. These include the significance of the transmission of culture: knowing and doing: student development: social development: criticality: philosophy and the influence of ideology on the curriculum. Ideology offers a way of identifying ways in which the curriculum may be skewed by sets of ideas which are deeply embedded in our ways of thinking so that they are taken for granted. The critical insights here demonstrate that ideologies come in many guises, but the main battle lines may be summarised as follows. On the one hand, Tapper and Salter (1978) warn us of the dangers of vocationalist courses and Apple (1990) alerts us to the risk of technicism where higher education becomes narrowly obsessed with the demands of employability and technique, respectively. In doing so, the critical and transformative possibilities of higher education are lost. But on the other, Birch (1988) warns us of the threats of liberalist curricula and Goodlad (1995) describes the perils of academicism. Here, thinking becomes an end in itself so that any notion of having to work or act in the real world is lost to debilitating ivory tower mentality.

Of course there is nothing necessarily wrong about designing courses which are mainly vocational or mainly liberal. But decisions to frame courses in a narrow part of curriculum space need to be made conscious of the situatedness of course designers in particular ideological streams and mindful of the consequences of narrow specialisation.

References

Airey, D., & Middleton, V. (1984). Tourism education course syllabuses in the UK: A review. *Tourism Management, 5*(1), 57–62.

Apple, M. (1990). *Ideology and the curriculum.* London: Routledge and Kegan Paul.

Barnett, R. (2003). *Beyond all reason. Living with ideology in the university.* Buckingham: Open University Press.

Bernstein, B. (1971). Classification and framing. In: M. Young (Ed.), *Knowledge and control.* London: Collier Macmillan.

Birch, W. (1988). *The Challenge to higher education.* Buckingham: Open University Press.

Botterill, D., & Tribe, J. (Eds). (2000). *Guideline 9: Benchmarking and the higher education curriculum.* London: National Liaison Group for Higher Education in Tourism.

Boys, C., Brennan, J., Henkel, M., Kirkland, J., Kogan, M., & Youl, P. (1988). *Higher education and the preparation for work.* London: Jessica Kingsley.

Burkart, A., & Medlik, S. (1981). *Tourism, past, present and future.* London: Heinemann.

Cornbleth, C. (1984). Beyond hidden curriculum. *Journal of Curriculum Studies, 16*(1), 29–36.

Council for National Academic Awards (CNAA). (1993). *Review of tourism studies degree courses.* London: CNAA.

Eraut, M., Goad, L., & Smith, G. (1975). *The analysis of curriculum materials, Occasional Paper 2.* Brighton: University of Sussex.

Goodlad, S. (1995). *The quest for quality.* Buckingham: Open University Press.

Graves, D. (Ed.) (1983). *The hidden curriculum in business studies.* Chichester: Higher Education Foundation.

Holloway, J. C. (1995). *Towards a core curriculum for tourism: A discussion paper.* London: The National Liaison Group for Higher Education in Tourism.

Kerr, L. (Ed.) (1968). *Changing the curriculum.* London: University of London Press.

Koh, K. (1995). Designing the four-year tourism management curriculum: A marketing approach. *Journal of Travel Research, 33*, 68–72.

Kuhn, T. S. (1970). *The structure of scientific revolutions.* Chicago: University of Chicago Press.

Lawton, D. (1989). *Education, culture and the national curriculum.* London: Hodder and Stoughton.

Lawton, D. (1996). *Beyond the national curriculum.* London: Hodder and Stoughton.

Manwaring, G., & Elton, L. (1984). Workshop on course design. In: P. Cryer (Ed.), *Training activities for teachers in higher education (Vol. 2)*. Windsor: NFER-Nelson.

Rowntree, D. (1982). *Educational technology in curriculum development.* London: Harper & Row/Paul Chapman.

Schön, D. A. (1983). *The reflective practitioner.* London: Maurice Temple Smith.

Scrimshaw, P. (1983). *Educational ideologies (Unit 2, E204) purpose and planning in the curriculum.* Milton Keynes: Open University Press.

Silver, H., & Brennan, L. (1988). *A liberal vocationalism.* London: Hodder and Stoughton.

Snyder, B. (1971). *The hidden curriculum.* Cambridge, MA and London: MIT Press.

Squires, G. (1990). *First degree: The undergraduate curriculum.* Buckingham: Open University Press.

Stenhouse, L. (1975). *Introduction to curriculum research and development.* London: Heinemann Educational.

Tapper, T., & Salter, B. (1978). *Education and the political order.* London: Macmillan Education.

Taylor, P., & Richards, C. (1985). *An introduction to curriculum studies.* Windsor: NFER-Nelson.

Tribe, J. (1997). The indiscipline of tourism. *Annals of Tourism Research, 24*(3), 638–657.

Tribe, J. (1999). The concept of tourism: Framing a wide tourism world and broad tourism society. *Tourism Recreation Research, 22*(2), 75–81.

Tribe, J. (2000a). Balancing the vocational: The theory and practice of liberal education in tourism. *The International Journal of Tourism and Hospitality Research (The Surrey Quarterly Review), 2*, 9–26.

Tribe, J. (2000b). The national curriculum for tourism higher education. In: D. Botterill & J. Tribe (Eds), *Guideline 9: Benchmarking and the Higher Education Curriculum* (pp. 2–12). London: National Liaison Group for Higher Education in Tourism.

Tribe, J. (2002). The philosophic practitioner: A curriculum for tourism stewardship. *Annals of Tourism Research, 29*(2), 338–357.

Tyler, R. (1949). *Basic principles of curriculum and instruction.* Chicago: University of Chicago Press.

Chapter 5

Curriculum Theory and Practice:
A Case in Online Education

Sheryl Elliott and Ginger Smith

1. Introduction and Background

The Accelerated Master of Tourism Administration degree (AMTA) program at The George Washington University (GW) emerged in 1997 out of a concern among Department of Tourism and Hospitality Management (DTHM) faculty members that there were few programs for tourism professionals equivalent to the executive MBA programs flourishing at universities throughout the country. To help create equity in higher education for tourism professionals, GW's DTHM began researching methods for delivering a master's degree program through distance education.

2. Literature Review

Distance education had its beginnings in "correspondence schools", which date back over a hundred years in both Europe and the US (Sherry, 1996, p. 337). The University of Chicago offered its first correspondence course in the late 1800s (McIsaac, 1996). Although technology has greatly changed the landscape for distance education, the basic concept remains intact: the delivery of instruction when teacher and student are separated by physical distance. Recent studies have reported that a large and growing number of people are making use of distance learning resources. In Europe, it is estimated that 2.25 million people are involved in distance learning programs every year. (Economics of Distance Education, 1993). In the US, several states have been particularly aggressive in embarking on state-funded distance learning programs, notably Colorado, where distance education has been introduced statewide through the Extended Studies Program. More than 10,000 courses are offered annually in Colorado, with a total annual enrollment of over 125,000 (Colorado Annual Report of the Statewide Extended Campus, 1993–1994).

An International Handbook of Tourism Education
Copyright © 2005 by Elsevier Ltd.
All rights of reproduction in any form reserved
ISBN: 0-08-044667-1

In the preparatory stages of developing a graduate degree in tourism and hospitality management delivered through distance education, a review of literature was conducted to identify the problems and issues most often encountered in the distribution of various forms of education.

The major benefit of distance education is, recognizably, its ability to reach remote and special population groups who do not have access to "live" instructional settings. Examples of such populations include working professionals, students and teachers in rural communities, the physically disadvantaged, senior citizens, and individuals in correctional institutions (National Network of Regional Educational Laboratories, 1995; Williams, 1995; Luetke-Stahlman, 1995; Noor-Al-Dean, 1994). Though considerable criticism of distance education has waged throughout history, four professors at Crichton College in Tennessee suggest in a study examining the pluses and minuses of online education that high-quality education is, in fact, highly attainable through new types of delivery systems. They maintain that online courses: necessitate "active learning" as students interact with course material, promote interaction with professors and collaboration with other students, and lend themselves to the use of writing as a tool for learning (Knowlton, 2001). While AMTA desired to optimize these positive aspects and benefits of distance education, there were other issues and obstacles documented in literature to overcome.

Distance education can be resource intensive and costly. A cost study by Caffarella (1992) compared four telecommunications systems for delivering university courses to remote locations against live instruction, with the teacher traveling to the remote site for compressed instruction. The four systems were compressed video, vertical blanking interval video, satellite video, and audiographic systems. The least costly alternative was live instruction, and the most costly was satellite video (Caffarella, 1992). Rumble, who developed a mathematical model for calculating the costs of distance education, found "that distance systems have a high absolute cost and that it is cheaper to use conventional methods where student numbers are restricted" (Rumble, 1988, p. 255). In a later study, Rumble observed that while costs of online courses depend on the nature of the materials and their associated development costs, the courses they analyzed varied from US$6000 to $1,000,000 for a three-unit Internet course (Rumble, 2001, p. 84). In fact, Rumble suggests that the costs of online education may actually be driving up the costs of overall distance education (Rumble, 2001, p. 91). Possible solutions offered to this problem include obtaining grants for technology funding from state agencies and private foundations, cash awards, business partnerships, and the use of discarded materials, such as computers, from corporations (Schroth, 1995). In sum, keeping distance education affordable for both the producer and the receiving student is an ongoing challenge.

The second most prevalent issue to emerge focused on the service provider — the instructor. Radically changing technologies require instructors who are on the "cutting edge". Finding and training teachers to accommodate these new technologies may be a significant problem, as more institutions incorporate this mode of education (Pietras, 1995). There is often resistance of instructors to adapt to a distance education environment, viewing it as inferior or substandard to the conventional classroom delivery system. In a paper, *Why Teach Teachers to Teach Online*, Levine-Elman comments, "The prospect of teaching courses online is generating anxiety among educators for many reasons. They are being overwhelmed by the rapid release of new versions of software and hardware products".

She contends that professors are also concerned that once online their lectures can be duplicated ad infinitum, and in the end may be replaced by an electronic duplication of themselves (Levine, 1997).

An additional challenge in distance learning is dealing with student assessment and evaluation. In an exaggerated instance, assignments and course work could be completed and delivered by a paid or sympathetic third party. This suggests the possibility of degrees being bought and sold rather than attained by genuine scholarship and academic merit, and raises the specter of a "diploma mill". A two-year study by Middle States Tennessee University examined the problem of student cheating in online courses and proposed several solutions: change assignments each semester; use multiple forms of assessment (online-timed tests, mini-essays and assignments, individual research projects); use discussion boards; make an online student's work more application-oriented; use an honor code where students pledge they did not cheat on an assignment (Saunders, 2002).

The use of intellectual property likewise appeared as an issue in the development of distance education programs. The Copyright Law of 1976 in the US was established to provide special provisions for the education environment. Essentially, a "fair use" provision within the law provides copyrighted materials for use without express permission when the purpose is for educational use. Since the rapid advancement in technology for distance education occurred after the copyright law, it is not altogether clear how the law applies in the distance education classroom (Guide #13: Copyright and Distance Education, 1996). The question is: can copyrighted materials (including print matter, videos, and multi-media materials) be placed in closed circuits for use in a particular class without express permission?

AMTA carefully considered how to resolve the foregoing issues before launching its first distance education course.

3. Dimensions and Profile

AMTA began as a weekend, classroom-based executive management program at GW's Hampton Roads (VA) Center in 1997. After 18 months, it was transformed into a program delivered totally online. There were several reasons for this. First, in 1998, a DTHM professor developed the first online course at the University to include a multimedia lecture component. This course was unique in that it used off-the-shelf technology, thus giving it a built-in affordability factor for both the producer and the learner. Students would not have to travel to a GW campus for weekend classes (as was the case in Hampton Roads) or to a video-conferencing center (a popular distance education technology at the time). The University did not have to invest in expensive video-conferencing or satellite broadcasting systems, and all development software was either open source or off-the-shelf at reasonable consumer prices.

The first online course was developed as standard HTML pages, with multi-media elements developed in Macromedia Director (Figure 1). It was designed with 16 learning units, each having six component parts: (1) a multi-media lecture (where the pace of the lecture could be controlled by the student — "start again", "pause", and "continue"), (2) downloadable lecture slides for note-taking, (3) one or more reading assignments (many downloadable electronically), (4) a unit graded assignment, (5) a discussion room for

Figure 1: First online course.

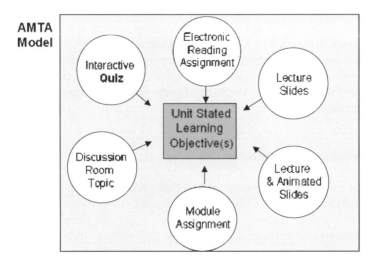

Figure 2: The AMTA model.

weekly discussion of topics, and (6) a non-graded quiz for learner reinforcement of materials covered in that unit.

The model developed for the first online course was an important step, as it served then as the model for all graduate courses to be developed in the AMTA program (Figure 2).

The second reason the AMTA program turned to an online environment was GW's willingness to support the development of an online classroom management system (CMS) called Prometheus. This was a School of Business student incubator CMS project that soon became available to all professors at the University. At the time of Prometheus' development, there were several small commercial online course development companies in existence, but no one vendor holding the predominant market share, as is the case today with Blackboard and WEB CT. As such, an early CMS was in place where professors could easily post their syllabi, course outlines, course files, course assignments, etc. in a template, without knowing HTML, and most importantly, all of this was free of charge. The University later sold Prometheus to Blackboard, and now Blackboard is the CMS licensed by the University.

The third reason the AMTA embraced an online delivery system for their master's degree program was clearly business-based — the geographic market potential for students would be exponentially increased through an online delivery system. In the new online format, AMTA would maintain the same admission criteria that it had for its classroom-based Hampton Roads weekend program, as well as the concept of admitting a "cohort" or group of students at different intervals during the year. The AMTA admission criteria remain today the same as at its inception: a bachelor's degree from a regionally accredited institution, an acceptable cumulative grade point average and 5 years of experience in the tourism industry. If prior professional and educational experience does not meet accepted standards, applicants are required to take the Graduate Record Examination (GRE). As Table 1 indicates, in a period of 5 years, AMTA has successfully enrolled 166 students.

3.1. Creating a Virtual Learning Community

All distance education programs encounter the challenge of how to minimize the psychological "distance" in distance education. The DTHM faculty engaged in many long and sometimes contentious discussions of how to create a virtual "learning community", concluding that it was not possible for all faculty members to agree on a program that would be 100% virtual. However, a compromise was achieved, utilizing a "blended learning" approach. Students would be required to attend a 1-week residency at the beginning of the program (referred to as the "inaugural" residency) and one at the end of the program (the "graduation" residency), during which students would experience multiple modes of learning. It was readily apparent how important it was for each incoming cohort to bond as a group, since they would advance through the program together and work with one another on team projects. Therefore, team-building skills were introduced, as well as social events at which students could become acquainted among themselves and with their professors, whom they would "see" only in the virtual classroom after the initial residency week.

A critical component of the inaugural residency was computer literacy and training. In adult learners, the range of computer skill sets can be enormous. The DTHM master's degree program faculty had already adopted an "IT Across the Curriculum" approach and had in place one course that would teach information systems technology in tourism and hospitality management not only in a theoretical context but in a practical one as well. It was obvious that a portion of this course should be a fundamental part of the inaugural residency. One half of the inaugural residency is held in a computer lab. Students receive three 8-hour days of hands-on tourism information technologies education (three units of an 8-unit course that they will later complete online for credit toward their degrees). This contributes to the "blended learning" approach advocated in the AMTA program.

Table 1: Total AMTA program — number of domestic and international students admitted and enrolled by cohort group.

	Cohort group 1 Mar 1998	Cohort group 2 Jan 1999	Cohort group 3 Sept 2000	Cohort group 4 Jan 2001	Cohort group 5 May 2001	Cohort group 6 Sept 2001	Cohort group 7 Jan 2002	Cohort group 8 May 2002	Cohort group 9 Sept 2002	Cohort group 10 Jan 2003	Cohort group 11 May 2003	Cohort group 12 Sept 2003	Total and %
Metro area	17			8	2	4	6	3	9	10	7	4	53 32%
Other states		22	16	4	3	3	7	2	5	8	5	4	96 59%
Other country				0	4	1	2	3	1	1	1	2	15 9%
Total	17	22	16	12	9	8	15	8	15	19	13	12	166

4. Theory, Concepts, and Practice

4.1. Calculating Seat-Time

"Seat-time" is an issue that cannot be ignored in online program development, particularly, since student loan programs do not always recognize distance education courses as qualifying for assistance. A common problem of all distance education and online education degree programs is how to create and justify an equivalency for the seat-time clock hours of a traditional on-campus course. The seat-time equivalency for the AMTA program is presented in Table 2. The accuracy of the calculation, formulated at the time the AMTA course model was developed, has since been validated through a series of interviews with students enrolled in the program (Figure 3).

4.2. Traditional Course Changes: Grade Weighting and Exams

It was observed during the program's development stage, that it may be necessary to adjust course grade weightings in a distance education course to reflect the unique environment of its students. For example, in keeping the student motivated and on-track, it is generally better to give a greater weight to weekly assignments and discussions over exams or the final project. If the distance education program is geared toward professionals, as in the case of AMTA, an adult learner entering the program, may fear final exams more than a traditional on-campus student who is conditioned to the exam process. There is also value in enabling distance education students to see their weekly progress; assignments are graded weekly, with feedback from the professor. Students frequently log on to their Blackboard account to see if their grades have been posted - again, keeping them connected to the learning community.

Table 2: Seat-time equivalency for an online 3 credit hour course.

	Seat-time lecture clock hours	Online multi-media lecture clock hours	Interactive discussion room	Weekly unit assign-ment	Course project	Total hours
Distance education 3 credit hours **online course**	6.5	5.5	8	12	Equivalent	32
Conventional education 3 credit hours **on-campus course**	24.6	0	0	0	Equivalent	24.6

Explanation of Calculation

A. Seat-time Lecture Clock Hours-Online Graduate 3 Credit Hours Course

$$\frac{80 \text{ hours*}}{12 \text{ courses}} = 6 \text{ hours and 40 minutes}$$

*40 hour one-week inaugural residency
*40 hour one-week concluding residency

*Seat-time Lecture Clock Hours-*Traditional *On-Campus Graduate 3 Credit Hours Course*

(14 weeks)(1 hour and 50 minutes) = 25 hours and 40 minutes

B. Online Lectures (listening, viewing, reviewing)

(40 minutes)(8 units) = 5 hours and 20 minutes

C. Weekly Interactive Discussion Room (includes reading the professor's explanation of the topic, researching the topic, responding to the topic in writing, reading other students' comments and interacting, reading professor's summary comments on the discussion).

(1 hour)(8 units) = 8 hours

D. Weekly Written Assignment (includes research by student, written response, and feedback from the professor).

(1 hour and 30 minutes)(8 units) = 12 hours

Figure 3: Explanation of "Seat-time".

Table 3: Grade weighting for a traditional versus online course.

	Weekly assignment	Discussion (participation)	Project	Exam
Online course	40% (8)	15%	20%	25% (1 exam)
Traditional course	15%	5%	35%	45% (2 exams)

Table 3 shows a sample grade weight for an online versus traditional course.

Exams in AMTA courses are conducted in an "open book" format, but in a specific time window. Within the Blackboard exam functionality, an instructor sets an exam to open and close at a specific time. Once students open the exam, they must complete it. They cannot use the back-arrow key to re-enter the exam at a later period. Recognizably, there are no guarantees that the person taking the exam is the actual student enrolled. At the same time, there are no assurances that a paper submitted in a traditional on-campus course or an online course is the work of its purported author.

4.3. Course Roll-Out Challenge and the Merry-Go-Round Model

While the costs associated with AMTA's development were considered manageable, they were "front-end loaded", consisting largely of the vendor costs of multi-media lecture presentations and the development fee paid to the instructor. There was no built-in system at the University to amortize these costs over the reasonable life of the course, and the AMTA program had to absorb the costs in its first year of operation. While the online program broke even in its first year, and showed some surplus in years three through five, it did not meet its targeted 30% surplus until the fiscal year 2002–2003. Budgetary considerations made it impossible to offer all courses in the curriculum online each semester, for students to elect the courses they wanted to take. A "merry-go-round" course delivery model, combined with a cohort group intake system, was adopted for AMTA, in which three to four courses are offered each semester (Figure 4). Critical to this model's success is that there are no prerequisites for any course. Continuing students cycle through the merry-go-round to completion of their degrees, with new cohort groups entering the "merry-go-round" at the time of their admission into the program. Thus, at any one given time, a course may have students from several cohorts enrolled. Though these courses may have as many as 50 students, students stay within their cohort groups in terms of projects and the discussion room. If a student needs to take a semester off for personal or professional reasons (and this occurs with some frequency), he or she can re-enter when the needed courses are offered again, as the merry-go-round recycles every 18 months.

4.4. Developing Online Lectures

Developing lectures for online multi-media delivery requires much organization on the part of the instructor. The instructor typically must condense a 1–2 h classroom lecture to between 20 and 30 min. This is not an impossible undertaking, considering that much class time involving a traditional lecture may include extraneous content: questions, discussions, instructors' anecdotes, etc. In most cases, when a lecture was stripped of extraneous content and the substantive content organized and rewritten for narration, it was found to last an intensive 15–20 min. Thus, the "pause", "replay", and "advance" functions of the multi-media lecture are an important feature to students (see Figure 5).

Participating instructors have indicated that meeting the online development requirements has improved their classroom lectures. There is also anecdotal evidence from students who are enrolled both online and on-campus: that the classroom courses taught by professors with online experience are better and certainly more organized.

The AMTA program requires instructors to prepare their lectures as scripts. The instructors may include or suggest graphics, models, and bulleted points that they wish included in the presentation. Generally, most instructors use Microsoft PowerPoint to prepare such lectures, using the "View"/"Note Page" option.

The presentation is then given to the contracted multi-media vendor who records the narration and creates the animated, synchronized visual lecture enhancements, utilizing a multimedia software program, Macromedia Flash. This software has been found to be the best for compressing graphics and audio for high-quality streaming at both low and high bandwidth. The lectures are also made downloadable as printable slides for note-taking by the students. Students can also purchase the lectures on CD-ROMs for a nominal charge (currently $10 per course). This is particularly helpful for students who desire to work off-line, e.g. they can view and listen to the lectures while traveling on an airplane. The ability to

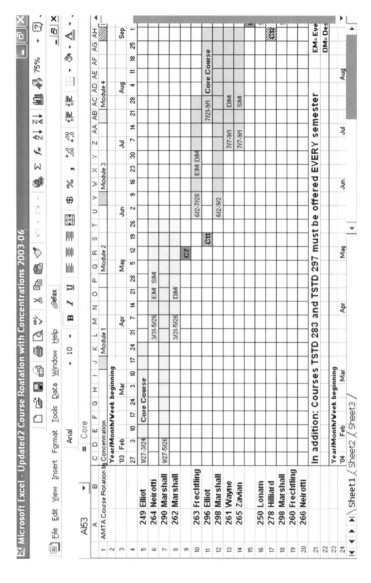

Figure 4: The merry-go-round model for course delivery.

Figure 5: Pause and play functions of a multi-media lecture.

work off-line using the CD-ROMs is also important for those students who live in countries where telecommunication costs are high.

There are a number of reasons why instructors agree to develop their courses for online delivery and teaching: (1) they receive an additional fee for the first time development of the course; (2) they may not be able to teach in a conventional campus setting, owing to other professional commitments or travel; (3) they find that developing a course for online delivery helps to organize and improve their lecture content for in-class courses, and (4) they enjoy the convenience and efficiency of working from home.

At one time it was thought that online education offered the opportunity to have classes with an unlimited number of students. AMTA has found that the "critical mass" for any course with one instructor and one facilitator is no more than 50 students. This is due to the fact that online distance education actually requires more contact between the instructor and student than traditional classroom teaching. Most online instructors will readily admit that teaching online requires more hours each week than teaching in a conventionally delivered course.

4.5. Quality Management and Online Education

Building a quality management system for the AMTA program became the primary responsibility of a faculty and staff appointed by the AMTA Quality Management Committee. This committee was charged not only with addressing program quality issues, but also with budget oversight, as well as developing a marketing plan for the program. At the end of the first year, the committee conducted a quality audit of each course in the program. To minimize student frustration with technical aspects of how the courses were delivered, the committee tried to achieve uniformity in the layout and design of all courses, so that they have similar navigation menu bars, similar structure in the learning modules and the content of those modules, and generally a "similar feel" for students.

The first audit included a matrix checklist to ascertain whether all module components were present in each course, all external links within courses worked, all file links worked, and that documents could be downloaded (Table 4). The lectures for all courses were also reviewed by the committee, in order to identify any content problems, such as excessive duplication of content among courses, mistakes, outdated content, etc.

Once an audit is completed, the report is given to the AMTA Program Director, who can then meet with each instructor to discuss necessary changes and modifications. To assist instructors in acclimating to an online environment, a training manual was developed that presented instruction in the best method for converting traditional courses to a Prometheus and later to a Blackboard environment. The manual contained technical information on CMS functionality, as well as hints on how to prepare lecture scripts, how to locate and integrate graphics into a course, how to prepare a lecture for a recording session, etc. A mentoring system was also developed and proved particularly helpful to first time online instructors.

Course facilitators, who work with instructors in a way similar to a teaching assistant, were provided with support as well. Each instructor chooses his or her own course facilitator, and to date, most of the facilitators are actual graduates of the program. This has been fortuitous, as AMTA graduate facilitators, having had the experience of being a student in an online program, are knowledgeable about the curriculum as well as the frustrations and problems that arise in that context.

Also part of the quality management process is providing a system for course and program assessment and evaluation by the students. In AMTA, at the conclusion of each

Table 4: Matrix checklist for quality audit of courses.

TSTD ———	Navigation Menu	8 Learning Modules or Units	Discussion Room	Exam	Directed Study Project(s)	Unit Lecture and Downloadable Lecture Slides	Unit Assignment	Unit Quiz	Unit Downloadable Articles/Links
Course									
Unit 1									
Unit 2									
Unit 3									
Unit 4									
Unit 5									
Unit 6									
Unit 7									
Unit 8									
Extra Unit for Exam, etc.									

AMTA course, an electronic evaluation survey is conducted, using the same course evaluation instrument in general use by the department, with slight modifications appropriate to online courses. There are 28 objective, multiple-choice questions and three subjective questions: What did you like most about this course? What did you like least? What would you do differently? Most instructors find that the subjective questions provide the most useful feedback in terms of what may be needed to improve a course in the future.

A focus group at each graduation residency of the program also provides valuable data for analyzing which parts of the program or the courses require improvement and change. In addition, all graduating students participate in an exit survey that is administered by the department and school.

5. Main Issues and Challenges

5.1. Students and Computer Literacy

Success in an online program is not possible if the student does not have adequate keyboard skills. This may present a problem in countries where keyboard skills are considered only part of the curriculum for clerical jobs.

5.1.1. Academic Integrity   In the information age, it is difficult, at best, to manage academic integrity in a traditional campus setting, and it is even more difficult to manage in an online environment. Rethinking higher education in competency-based terms renders a different model that may be more applicable for the learning environment today. Focusing on course objectives and student deliverables (team projects, team presentations, projects that cannot be duplicated elsewhere, weekly assignments, and weekly discussions) create a system that moves away from final and "one-time" assessment, to one of continuous assessment.

5.1.2. Student Motivation   Success in a distance education program depends upon maintaining individual motivation. Most online programs are designed to attract those in the workplace — people who may have extended personal and professional commitments. This requires flexibility on the part of program administrators, who need to recognize such commitments and adjust the program accordingly so that such individuals are not lost or discouraged in the process.

5.1.3. Attrition and Advising   To minimize attrition, which is linked to motivational issues, a well-thought-out program of advising becomes paramount. Past experience has shown that there is a direct correlation between personal contact with students and the attrition rate. AMTA requires advising each semester, and students are blocked from registering for a course if they have not met with an advisor. The advising periods are conducted by telephone, e-mail, chat-room, and instant messaging.

5.1.4. Emphasis on Educators   Not all instructors are equipped by temperament and technical know-how to succeed in online teaching. Online and distance education instructors must be as committed to their role as educators as they are to being scholars in their particular disciplines.

5.1.5. Marketing Issues Countless universities and higher education proprietary schools have turned to the business of distance education to reach revenue goals. The distance education waters are currently very difficult for potential students to wade through and be confident that they are selecting quality programs.

5.1.6. DE and Development Costs Converting traditional curricula to online formats is a business proposition; there are real risks and real costs. Most programs that go online will have a large development cost in the first year of operation. Amortizing these costs over a three-to-five year period would make sense, but many institutions of higher education do not have such business models in place to allow this to happen. Green suggests, "Amortization — virtually unknown in the campus community but well understood in the corporate environment — must become a critical financial tool for managing real costs [of online education]".

5.2. Copyright — Intellectual Property and Fair Use

One issue all institutions must face as they commit to online education, is the question of who owns courseware materials developed by an instructor. "Just hiring a person is not enough to make a copyright belong to someone other than the author of a work" (Harper, 2001). The author is the owner unless the course is created by the instructor within the scope of his/her work, or where an agreement commissioning the course was signed before the work began. AMTA requires all online instructors to sign such an agreement before a course begins development.

As to the use of published materials such as uploaded digitized articles, portions of a book, etc. educational institutions have considerable latitude under the U.S. doctrine of fair use of the U.S. Copyright Statute (found in Title 17 of the United States Code). Understandably, there are limits imposed, such as the number of chapters that may be transposed from a published book. In assessing intellectual property and fair use of published materials, it is prudent for any institution to seek legal guidance in this matter.

5.3. Distance Education and Federal Student Loans

There are federal policies that "limit the extent to which schools can deliver distance education courses and still qualify to participate in the federal student aid programs" (Government Accounting Office (GAO), 2004). Generally, the "50% rule" exists where an institution that offers more than half of its courses through distance education is not able to qualify for participation in federal student aid programs.

5.4. Standards

Online distance education has become a part of the higher education landscape faster than certifying boards and accrediting associations can be organized to monitor their progress. To date, there is little substantive information available to potential students on the relative quality of the different programs. This issue was also addressed in the GAO report cited above. Current federal policy limits some schools that offer distance education from participating in federal student aid programs. The GAO reviewed the policies of seven accrediting agencies as to the extent they reviewed distance education programs. They found that the accrediting agencies "differed considerably in when and how they included reviews of distance education" (GAO, 2004).

6. Conclusion

The AMTA program has been and continues to be a challenging undertaking; however, an early well-thought-out plan for its development and implementation has contributed to it's being a leader and success story for the business school and University as well as a model for other programs to follow. First, researching distance education options, and then, developing a model for course development and curriculum delivery proved essential to the process of converting an on-campus program to an online format. Second, the development and delivery of distance education courses required a team approach — including faculty, faculty mentors, technical specialists, administers, and others. Third, a thought-out model prior to the beginning of the program was most essential, as opposed to those programs that start with an idea of "we must get on the distance education bandwagon today" and then hastily assemble a course for an online delivery with a disconnected array of content and technical "bells and whistles". This is not to say that any distance education model should remain static and unchanging. Rather, a good model allows for continual technical and quality improvements, and if the process is in place to allow this to occur, there will be real winners in higher education for the long term — for both the producer and receiver alike.

Acknowledgments

Dr. Elliott and Dr. Smith wish to convey their deep appreciation to the faculty of the Department of Tourism and Hospitality Management and to the Dean and administration of the School of Business for their long-standing engagement in and support of the AMTA program at The George Washington University, Washington, DC.

References

Caffarella, E., Azama, A., Gregg, J., Persichitte, K., Riddle, F., & Zvacek, S. (1992). *An analysis of the cost effectiveness of various electronic alternatives for delivering distance education compared to the travel costs for live instruction.* Greeley, CO: University of Northern Colorado, Western Institution for Higher Learning. (ERIC Document Reproduction Service No. ED 380 127).

Colorado Annual Report on the Statewide Extended Campus., (1993–1994). Colorado State University.

Economics of Distance Education. (1993). *Proceedings of the AAOU Annual Conference*, Hong Kong, November.

Government Accounting Office. (2004). *Distance education: Improved data on program costs and guidelines on quality assessments needed to inform federal policy.* GAO-04-279, February 26. http://www.gao.gov/atext/d04279.txt.

Green, K. (1997). Think twice — and businesslike — about distance education. *American Association of Higher Education Bulletin, 83,* 3–6 October.

Guide #13: Copyright and Distance Education (1996). http://uidaho.edu/dist1.html.

Harper, G. (2001). *The copyright crash course.* copyright 2001 Georgia K. Harper. http://www.utsystem.edu/ogc/IntellectualProperty/cprtindx.htm.

Knowlton, D. (2001). Why online education: The view of four practitioners. *CyberPeer Newsletter.* http://www.crichton.edu/cdealt/cyber_peer/why-online-classes.htm.

Levin-Elman, L. (1997). Why teach teachers to teach online. *Second annual virtual conference on trends and issues in online instruction: Teaching in the community college.* Kapi'olani Community College, Honolulu, HI, April.

Luetke-Stahlman, B. (1995). *Deaf education in Kansas public schools.* Kansas: University of Kansas. http://www.sign-lang.uni-hamburg.de/BibWeb/LiDat.acgi?ID=37900.

McIsaac, M. S., & Gunawardena, C. N. (1996). Distance Education. In: D. H. Jonassen (Ed.), Handbook of *research for educational communications and technology*: A project of the Association for Educational Communications and Technology (pp. 403–437). New York: Simon & Schuster Macmillan.

National Network of Regional Educational Laboratories. (1995). Pulling together: R & D resources for rural schools. http://www.ncrel.org/rural/dochome.htm.

Noor-Al-Dean, H. S. (1994). Education moves into high gear on the information highway. *Educational Media International, 31*(1), 46–52.

Olivas, J. (2002). Retooling skills for online teaching. *American Association of Higher Education Online Bulletin,* December. http://aahebulletin.com/member/articles/online_instruction.asp.

Rumble, G. (2001). The costs and costing of network learning. *JALN, 5*(2), 75–91. http://216.109.117.135/search/cache?p=%22economics+of+distance+education%22&ei=UTF8&fl=0&u=www.aln.org/publications/jaln/v5n2/pdf/v5n2_rumble.pdf&w=%22economics+of+distance+edu-cation%22&d=A958008204&icp=1&.intl=us.

Rumble, G. (1988). The costs and costing of distance/open education. In: J. Jenkins (Ed.), *Commonwealth co-operation in open learning: Background papers.* London: Commonwealth Secretariat (pp. 255–258, 264–266).

Saunders, J., & Haulser, J. (2002). A comparison of problems encountered teaching online courses at Middle Tennessee State University (MTSU) and the Tennessee Board of Regents (TBR) Online Degree Program (RODP). *Mid-South Instructional Technology Conference,* April 7–9. http://www.mtsu.edu/~jhausler/arkpaper.htm.

Schroth, G. (1995). Implementing technology without breaking the bank. *Proceedings of the American council on rural special education.* March. http://extension.usu.edu/acres/conference/

Sherry, L. (1996). Issues in distance learning. *International Journal of Distance Education, 1*(4), 337–365.

Twig, C. (2001). *Quality assurance for whom? Providers and consumers in today's distributed learning environment* (pp. 3–4). Monograph, Center for Academic Transformation, Rensselaer Polytechnic Institute, Troy, NY.

Williams, E. (1995). Distance education as a future trend for pre and inservice education. Reaching to the future: Boldly facing challenges in rural communities. *Conference proceedings of the American Council on Rural Special Education (ACRES),* Las Vegas, NV, March 15–18.

Chapter 6

Curriculum, Development and Conflict: A Case Study of Moldova

John Tribe

Introduction

Moldova faces multiple problems. It is economically dependent on Russia. Its economy is focussed on primary production in agriculture. It has suffered from serious falls in output — GDP fell by 8.6% in 1998 and a further 4.4% in 1999. Its population is among the poorest in Europe with a per capita income of some $353 per annum in 2000 (United Nations Development Programme, 2000). Innovation and development are thus crucial to future prosperity, but difficult to achieve. Moldova's long association with the Soviet bloc meant that relationships with other countries have been slow to develop and that its institutions tend to be bureaucratic in structure and conservative in outlook. The Moldovan economy has found it difficult to adapt to free market conditions.

This chapter examines the THEME project (Tourism and Higher Education in Moldova with the European Union (EU)), which is part of an EU policy initiative to promote innovation and development. The innovation aspects relate to the tourism curriculum while the development aspects relate to both tourism and higher education in Moldova. The chapter is divided into four parts. Initially, consideration is given to context factors. A brief analysis of the situation facing Moldova is undertaken together with a description of the EU Tempus Tacis programme. Next, the methodology of the project is described. The results of the project are then discussed. Finally, a section titled "critique" reflects on the product and process and this is followed by a brief conclusion. The chapter examines specific issues of curriculum design theory and reviews the use of these within a framework of competing methodological paradigms.

Context

Moldova

Moldova is situated in Eastern Europe, bordering Romania and the Ukraine. It has been classified as a Newly Independent State (NIS) since 1991 when it secured its independence from the USSR. It has a territory of 33,700 sq. km and a population of 4.3 million, of which 64.5% speak Romanian, 14% Ukranian and 13% Russian.

In the period after Moldovan independence in 1991, the economy suffered a severe downturn. Indeed, most of the post-1991 period has witnessed negative growth, for example – 6.5% in 1998, and with the exception only of 1997 with growth of 1.6% and 2000 with 1.9%, Moldova ranks 104th in human development (UNDEP, 2000). It has one of the lowest per capita income in Europe and is second lowest of all East European and NIS economies. Over the last few years, industry and agriculture, the two largest sectors, have faced a collapse in traditional markets, a sharp increase in costs of raw materials and problems with availability. Much of its industry is large scale and dependent on markets throughout the former Soviet Union. Although industrial output has recovered, agriculture continues to decline in production. There is widespread hidden unemployment in Moldova, mainly ex-industrial workers with two-thirds being women. Half of the unemployed are less than 30 years old.

Tourism has a role to play in the economic restructuring of Moldova. Tourism as an industry has the capability to generate high economic multipliers in developing countries if introduced in a sustainable manner. The country has the physical resources to attract independent, low impact tourism that will bring economic benefits to the heart of the community. Small and medium sized tourism companies could make use of locally produced products to cater for visitors, and this could also be a method to inject money into the local economy. However, tourism activity declined in the 1990s and a skills shortage is inhibiting the full exploitation of the potential of this area.

Small and medium enterprises (Echtner, 1994) are crucial for Moldova to maximise potential economic development from tourism. The development of these will depend to a great extent on the training of the local population in the application of business skills, marketing, environmental management and technology to the tourism industry. But capacity here is currently limited: The Soviet educational system under which Moldova has been operating for the last 50 years placed its emphasis on theory rather than the more technical applications of vocational courses. At present, tourism is studied as a specialisation but there are few opportunities in the country to take complete and comprehensive programmes focused on tourism.

Tempus Tacis

The Tempus programme was launched by the EU in 1990. Its goals include the development of the higher education systems in target countries and co-operation between higher education institutions in the partner countries. The target countries in the initial "Phare" phase was on 11 Central and Eastern European (CEE) partner countries (Richards, 1996a) such as Poland (Airey, 1994; Golembski, 1991) and Romania (Cristureanu, 1996), which were seeking closer links with the EU (Airey, 1999). Following the collapse of the USSR, the programme was subsequently extended to include the countries of the former Soviet bloc (the "Tacis" phase). Indeed, recent programmes have concentrated on Armenia, Azerbaijan, Belarus, Georgia,

Kazakstan, Kyrgyzstan, Moldova, the Russian Federation, Tajikistan, Turkmenistan, Ukraine, Uzbekistan and Mongolia. The specific areas addressed by recent programmes include

- curriculum development and renewal in priority areas;
- the reform of higher education structures and institutions and their management;
- the development of skill-related training to address skill shortages.

While the Tempus programme offers an overall macro-policy framework for innovation and development, Tempus is a "bottom-up" programme in that it consists of a number of microprojects selected to be responsive to the specific needs of individual institutions.

THEME was one such project. The overall objective of the THEME project was "to develop university courses in Moldova focused on employability in tourism". The project partners were Buckinghamshire Chilterns University College (BCUC, UK), the University of the Balearic Islands (UBI, Spain) and the National Institute of Physical Education and Sport (NIPES, Moldova).

Method

Cooper, Shepherd, and Westlake (1994) discuss a number of theoretical models for curriculum design. A common feature of many of these models is that the aims and objectives of a curriculum need to be determined prior to curriculum design. Koh (1995) has shown at a macro level how aims and objectives may be derived in tourism. However, at the micro (institutional) level, constraints are an important consideration for curriculum design (Rowntree, 1982). There has been much discussion of the tourism curriculum specifically in developing countries (Charles, 1997; Cooper, 1997; Echtner, 1995; Ogorelc, 1999; King, 1994; Singh, 1997; Zhao, 1991), but there are few instances where the practicalities of curriculum development have been addressed. This chapter offers elaboration of how aims and objectives for a tourism curriculum were derived in a practical setting.

The method used for the project is as follows. Initially, an overall research group was formed from academics of each of the partner institutions with responsibility for curriculum design. A scoping exercise was undertaken to agree the extent, the responsibilities and a timetable for the project. Next, researchers from each of the partner institutions compiled reports for the initial situational analysis of the problem. The reports were then discussed by the full research group. In the light of these discussions, members of the research group were asked to prepare aims, objectives and module outlines for the THEME curriculum. These were tabled and discussed at a subsequent series of meetings where the framework of the THEME curriculum was agreed. The next stage of the project involved the setting up of working groups consisting of relevant academics from the partner institutions to flesh out the learning objectives, teaching and learning strategies, booklists and assessments for each of the modules. These working groups involved East–West and West–East mobility movements. The final stage of the project involved validation of the new course. Figure 1 illustrates the model used for curriculum development.

The first element of this process, the situational analysis, was designed to take place before the curriculum development to enable the curriculum constructed to fit well with the particular circumstances in Moldova. It is based on methods used in strategic management (Tribe, 1997). It comprised three activities and outcomes. The first was a needs

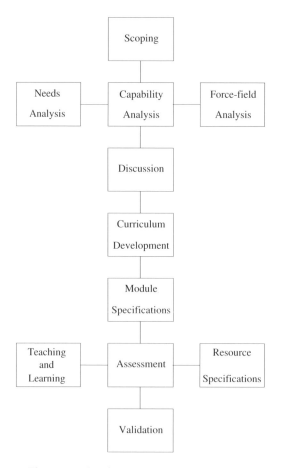

Figure 1: Curriculum development model.

analysis (Theuns & Rasheed, 1983; Theuns & Go, 1992) and report, the purpose of which was to investigate the specific needs in Moldova that the tourism curriculum will respond to. The second element was a capability analysis and report. Its aim was to investigate and summarise the resources available in each institution to best meet the project needs. It uses resource auditing as its model (Buchele, 1962). The third element was a force field analysis report (Lewin, 1935; Nutt, 1989) to identify the main drivers and inhibitors acting on the planned changes with a view to enabling an easier implementation.

Results

Needs Analysis

The needs analysis focussed on two main issues — those relating to tourism itself and those relating to higher education.

In terms of tourism, recent trends showed a considerable decline of tourism in Moldova. Data indicate that inbound visitor numbers dropped drastically between 1991 and 1994 although there was a small recovery in 1995 (World Tourism Organisation, 1997). The collapse of the USSR and the emergence of the NIS countries led to a considerable decline in travel between the former Soviet bloc countries. The Moldovan tourist market is nearly exclusively European with the exception of a few visitors from South Asia.

Visitors to Moldova mainly arrive by rail followed by road. It is interesting to note that while the majority of visitors in 1991 were visiting for leisure purposes, since 1994 the main purpose of visit has switched to business and professional. Nights stayed follow a similar pattern to that of overall visits having fallen sixfold between 1991 and 1994 and again showing some recovery in 1995. The number of hotel rooms and bed spaces in hotels rose slightly between 1991 and 1995. However, the occupancy rate fell by over 60% in line with the decline in visitor numbers. Outbound tourism increased in 1995 to twice its 1994 level but by then it was still only half of its 1991 level. International tourism receipts and tourism expenditure both rose sharply in 1995.

The needs analysis noted the following features of tourism support and infrastructure in Moldova. In the hospitality sector, accommodation is mainly in the form of hotels. These are predominantly located in the capital, Chisinau. For both hotels and food, the quality of services often falls short of international standards and there is no necessary relationship between price paid and quality of service. In common with many other ex-communist countries the culture of customer service is not well developed (Burns, 1998). This is summed up by the Moldovan research group:

> Tourism services offered in Moldova have not yet fully adjusted to the demands of a market system. In many cases services are not yet analysed and developed sufficiently and do not yet correspond to the requirements and standards suggested by their marketing.

The Moldovan researchers also noted that

> Tourism along with most other activities in the ex-Soviet Socialist Republic of Moldova was organised in a framework of State and Trade Union structures. This operated through a strict hierarchic, regularised and centralised management. The effects of this are still apparent in the conservatism of the tourism industry and personnel in the field.

Additionally, training of tourism professionals was not geared towards consumer satisfaction, marketing, efficiency or profitability. This problem is shared by many CEE countries, as Airey (1996, p. 22) noted in Poland:

> Particular gaps include those areas of the curriculum concerned with successful business operation, particularly finance, economics, marketing, management and customer care

There are also many barriers to tourism in terms of pre-travel, arriving in the country and transportation within the country. There is a lack of government provision of information or marketing of the country to foreign visitors. The high visa cost (US$80) is a significant disincentive to tourists, and travel within the country is difficult, compounded by the fact that most tourist agencies provide facilities for outbound tourism with only a small number dealing with inbound and internal tourists.

The needs analysis noted that Moldova has yet to be fully discovered by the western tourist. As a destination, Moldova appeals currently to those tourists who want to venture off the beaten track and discover something different to the western world. It has a number of natural features which are relevant to tourism. Its natural environment includes forests of beech, oak and hornbeam, located in the central regions although the majority of its land is utilised for farmland. Native fauna include Wolves, Wild boar, Roe Deer, Spotted Deer, Badgers, Foxes, Martins and many other small mammals. However, vineyards and cultivated fields have displaced much of their natural habitat. There are number of large watercourses holding fish that include, carp, bream, pike and perch.

In terms of its cultural heritage, Moldova has numerous monasteries, ancient fortresses, wooden churches and war memorials. Literature, art, music and dancing are all important in Moldova. Folk music and the costumes that accompany it are potential tourist attractions. Moldovan food is based on a Russian menu and the country is reputed for its wine production.

The needs analysis demonstrated that the following types of tourism have potential in Moldova:

- Activity tourism;
- Religious tourism;
- Business tourism;
- Nature tourism;
- Spa and health-related tourism;
- Cultural tourism;
- Heritage tourism;
- Educational tourism;
- Wine tourism;
- Festival tourism;
- Urban tourism.

Additionally, a survey of managers of Moldavian tourist agencies undertaken in the needs analysis identified that that the personnel of the tourist agencies need more training in the following fields:

- Tourism marketing;
- Management in tourism;
- Management of quality;
- Business administration in tourism;
- Informational technologies in tourism;
- Modern languages;
- Cultural tourism.

The tourism aspects of the needs analysis thus resulted in an understanding of the strengths, weaknesses and opportunities for tourism in Moldova. Consideration of these enabled the aims and objectives of the THEME curriculum to be clarified.

The other aspect of the needs analysis was to understand the strengths and weaknesses of higher education institutions in Moldova, and specifically those of NIPES. Many of the observations about tourism and the higher education system in Moldova are similar to those found in accounts elsewhere in CEE. Like most public sector institutions in Moldova, the Higher Education sector has suffered from an acute lack of current and capital funding. An indication of the severity of this problem is the frequent absence of heating in university buildings in winter. Similarly, telephone and postal communications are often interrupted. Academic salaries are low in comparison to those that are achievable in the new economy.

Richards' observation about the meanings and roots of tourism and its development as a subject of academic study in CEE countries has parallels in Moldova:

> In CEE the predominance of social tourism in the domestic market led to a view of tourism as a social phenomenon, rather than a commercial "industry". Whereas tourism courses in the West can trace their origins to hotels schools or management departments, in CEE developments have stemmed from geography and physical education. (Richards, 1996b, p. 301)

The Moldovan partner institution in the THEME project was an Institute of Sport and Physical Education and throughout discussion between the research groups it became apparent that there was not a common understanding of the term "tourism". For example, the Moldovan group often referred to activities such as "recuperation" and "outdoor activities" as tourism and these were subjects that they wanted to feature in the curriculum. This echoes experience from Poland where Jung and Mierzejewska (1996, p. 65) reported that "the academies of Physical Education … view tourism from an extremely broad perspective" and that the tradition of tourism education "was activity-oriented (preparation for 'animators' of social and qualified tourism)" (p. 67).

Many of the other issues of curriculum, learning resources, teaching and learning and assessment are linked together and describe a situation of tradition and conservatism in higher education in Moldova. Many observations that had been made in previous studies of tourism education development in CEE were equally true for Moldova. For example, Richards (1996c, p. 12) had noted "resistance to change within many of the more traditional institutions of higher education" and in Bulgaria, Bachvarov (1996, p. 36) found "conservatism, inertia, and opposition to practical forms of education".

The traditional didactic teaching methods noted by Airey (1996) in Poland were common. Theory and theory-mastery is central to Moldovan higher education in a similar fashion the situation noted by Bacharov in Bulgaria:

> teaching … is old fashioned stressing mainly the memorising and reproduction of theoretical knowledge (1996, pp. 36–37).

An international dimension (Cross, 1998) has been neglected in the Moldovan tourism curriculum. External links and staff and student mobilities had been traditionally extended within the USSR with a particular focussed on Russia and Moscow. This meant that wider external links were underdeveloped. Bacharov found a linked problem in Bulgaria where "the weakest link … is industrial placements" (1996, p. 37), and this represents another challenge for the development of tourism higher education in Moldova.

The combination of lack of financial resources, a localised view of the meaning of tourism and the need to provide resources for a newly developed course meant that text-books were a priority. Again, this is a similar situation to that found elsewhere in CEE. For example, Vukonić (1996, p. 45) noted a need for tourism education in Croatia "to ensure sufficient number of high quality textbooks" and Airey (1996, p. 23) noted "important gaps in resources, particularly textbooks and computers" in Poland.

Capability Analysis

The purpose of the capability analysis was to categorise the resources that existed within the project consortium and identify any significant gaps that existed. Each partner reported on its capabilities.

The UK team's analysis included the following factors. First, tourism education takes place in a specialised faculty (i.e. it is not an offshoot of a management faculty), which includes a relatively large group of specialist staff. The faculty offers courses at under-graduate and postgraduate levels based on a modular scheme and this means that there exists a ready stock of diverse modules at different levels in tourism. Second, the UK group is part of research centre specialising in tourism higher education. Third, as in many UK universities, comprehensive systems of course development, and validation have been developed along with the associated documents. Finally, the UK group identi-fied the importance of its learning resources — particularly its library facilities and computer suites.

The Spanish group was identified as one of the leading institutions of tourism education in Spain with 1400 students. It offers a suite of undergraduate and postgraduate courses in tourism in state-of-the-art buildings. The courses are underpinned by a philosophy that emphasises an international and strategic approach to tourism. The courses have the support and collaboration of both the public and private sectors and a clear strength is links with the tourism industry and policy makers. The academic staff have experience of developing and teaching on a range of tourism courses including distance learning and also of working on cross-cultural projects.

The Moldovan team reported extensive resources in terms of "108 specialists in all the tourism spheres including 48% with a scientific degree". It also noted the possibility of co-opting specialists from other institutions. Physical resources identified for specialist train-ing in tourism, included "a special methodic auditorium, a sport base on the bank of the Black Sea, ground for training the technique of tourism, stadium, swimming-pool, etc.". The Moldovan team also expressed confidence in their learning resources noting that the "informational potential of the Institute (library, computer class, and laboratory of techni-cal means) permit study at a high level".

Force Field Analysis

The Moldovan team undertook a force-field analysis designed to identify the main driving and resisting factors related to the project implementation.

The following are the main resisting factors. One significant factor noted was the "previous experience of centralised stereotype of the field". In other words, the conceptualisation of tourism was potentially idiosyncratic but deeply embedded. Richards noted a similar barrier in CEE countries where

> the focus of tourism education was often on spatial planning or economics, and did not have [a] management focus (1996c, p. 12).

The issue of conservatism was extended to cover the general culture of faculty staff summarised by an observation about the "conservative stereotype of the field's staff". Development of this area of the curriculum was also felt to be constrained by the absence of any existing initiatives — the "lack of elaboration of new programmes aimed at Moldavian specialists' training in the field of Tourism". Additionally, the conservatism of students was noted as a challenge:

> Whilst university graduate students are becoming accustomed to seeking work in areas of the new economy such as tourism, many of them are not well-prepared to understand or work within the changed the conditions of a market economy.

The economic and political environment of the country was also seen to present significant hurdles. There was an overall concern about the "low level of the country's economy" and "difficulties of the period of transition to a market economy" and the inhibiting effects of these on the development of tourism. One particular difficulty identified was that resulting from "political and administrative, state and interstate reorganisation in the ex-Soviet countries". These general observations gave way to some specific issues related to tourism. It was observed that while there was a "readjustment of touristic objectives" this had not yet translated itself into very tangible results. This resulted in a "lack of normative acts in the framework of legislation on the development of Tourism in the Republic of Moldova". The lack of a credible plan for tourism development signalled problems for manpower development and it was noted that "at present, the structure and the content of the professional training of future specialists as well as their readjustment to the demands of tourism market requirements is not established".

The following were identified as driving factors. First it was noted that there was support for the project at a high level with "interest and support of the project on behalf of NIPES Rector's personnel and [the] Ministry of Education of the Republic of Moldova". It was also felt that the "establishment of partnership relations with corresponding institutions from European countries under the aspect of long term collaboration" was favourable.

On the demand side for the course it was noted that "currently there is a lack of highly qualified specialists in Tourism". There was also a favourable response towards such a course from potential students:

> The results of a survey show that the majority of graduates from the faculties of physical culture and sports (that is 80% from a population of 150)

are interested in taking conversion qualifications to allow them to enter the field of tourism. A majority consider that tourism possesses a favourable potential for development.

It was also noted that there was a base of research outputs in the field of tourism. "This includes methodological and scientific research, monographs, methodological guidance and other publications that analyse the issue of tourism". Finally, it was noted that there had been some advances in the support of tourism by central government and that "in 2000 the Parliament of the Republic of Moldova adopted the Law on Tourism and also created the Department of Tourism".

The Curriculum

The THEME curriculum was formulated following a series of meetings of the project group. The agenda of the preparatory curriculum development meeting considered the situational analysis reports from each team. As a result of this meeting, team members were asked to produce further reports which considered the aims and objectives of the curriculum and produce brief descriptions of modules that were to be proposed for inclusion in the curriculum. The second meeting discussed these reports and modules. There was considerable discussion which highlighted the different traditions and conceptions of tourism. Because of this it was not possible to reach an agreement on a single THEME curriculum. This is interesting because it shows that it was not possible to produce a workable single synthesis, which accommodated the desires of the different groups. The UK/Spain axis remained unconvinced of the concept of tourism offered by the Moldovans. Equally, the Moldovans did not want their understanding of tourism to be swamped by an alien concept. Therefore, it was agreed to develop two streams with a common core. The two streams that emerged were a Tourism Administration course and a Tourism Activity Management course and the elements of these may be found in Figure 2.

The curriculum is a modular 2 year masters' programme with seven modules taken each year. The core elements, in year 1 lay the ground for students converting to this field of study, with modules such as Principles of Tourism and Sustainable Tourism (Bramwell, Goytia, & Henry, 1996; Howie, 1996). The inclusion of cultural tourism in the core responds to the needs analysis, which found this to be a potential growth area. Similarly, Small Business Management supports the fact that small- and medium-sized enterprises are such an important contributor to tourism development. It also introduces students to the culture of management for profit in contrast to management for State enterprise. Language skills are also seen as an essential (Davies, 1999). The Research Methods and Dissertation modules are also core, but designated as integrated as they seek to bring together other aspects of the core. The Tourism Administration route also responds to some key findings in the needs analyses. Quality Management offers techniques for driving up service quality. Strategic Management encourages longer term planning and development against organisational aims and Marketing offers techniques for defining, communicating and improving tourism services.

The Tourism Activity Management route was driven by two main considerations. First it responded to a strongly held Moldovan view of tourism as outdoor recreational activities.

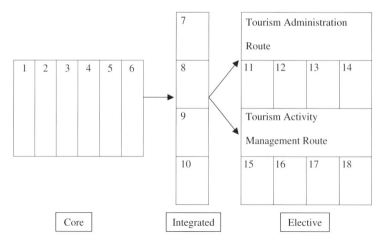

Figure 2: The THEME curriculum. Modules: 1. Principles of tourism; 2. Sustainable tourism; 3. Cultural tourism; 4. Information technology; 5. Small business; 6. English language; 7. Research methods; 8. Dissertation; 9. Dissertation; 10. Dissertation; 11. Strategic management; 12. Marketing; 13. Quality Management; 14. Organisation and resource management; 15. Active tourism; 16. Recreational and recuperational tourism; 17. Ecological tourism; 18. Sport tourism.

Second it responded to the expertise available at the Moldovan institution that was evident from the capability analysis and a desire to continue to exploit this expertise.

Critique: Success or Failure?

Success

There are many grounds for claiming the THEME project a success. First, the project concluded despite the inefficiencies and blockages created at the bureaucratic level by the Tempus office of the EU. Second, international collaborative projects often fail due to cultural differences. The THEME project encountered many of these and there were many moments of disagreement, which sometimes became sufficiently profound to threaten the continuation of the project. All of these were surmounted — largely because of the underlying project values of respect for differences and openness to debate.

Third, the model devised for this project has proved to be a useful and robust one and could usefully be deployed elsewhere in developing specialist curricula. Particular effort was made to stimulate innovation while maintaining a sensitivity to the constraints and traditions of a particular situation. It was designed to minimise aspects of cultural imperialism that can arise from the use of "foreign experts". Another consideration was to avoid the pitfalls of exporting a ready made, off the shelf product, which might be impossible to implement in its new context. This philosophy is based on the problems encountered in early agricultural development projects which offered technological solutions (e.g. new tractors), which failed because they were inappropriate to local conditions (e.g. excess labour force, little money for running costs, lack of expertise for maintenance etc.). Hence, the importance not only of the needs analysis, the capability analysis and the force-field analysis but also of the discussion meetings to allow feasibility of ideas to be tested, cultural differences to be aired and ownership encouraged. This helped to overcome cultural differences in the definition and scope of tourism. These were clearly evident in some of the resources that the Moldovan team highlighted in their capability analysis. To overcome the problem of incommensurable (Kuhn, 1962) definitions of tourism, two strands of tourism are now in place in the curriculum and this offers an opportunity for adjustments to be made as innovation becomes embedded.

Failure

The THEME project developed a method based on a strategic management approach to curriculum design. In the reflective educational literature, criticisms have been levelled at such an approach. For example, Ball (1990, p. 156) drawing on Foucauldian analysis notes that:

> Management is a professional, professionalizing discourse which allows its speakers to lay exclusive claims to certain sorts of expertise … that casts others, subordinates as objects of those procedures.

In other words, as a discourse it lays claim to being *the* way of doing things (i.e. it excludes other ways) and often carries the implicit assumption that it is "the one best method" (Ball, 1990, p. 156). This thinking can be applied to the THEME project where the UK/Spanish partners are the insiders and experts of such a discourse and it is a discourse which is largely alien to the culture of an ex-Soviet country. In this view, the Moldovian Institute is easily cast as the object of management of the project, its role become subordinate, its views downgraded. In other words, management discourse supports a number of dichotomies (the us/the other: the expert/the amateur: the developed/the underdeveloped: the successful/the failed: the UK and Spain/Moldova) all of which are encouraged by an insider, technical specialist language.

   To avoid this charge the project methodology was designed to incorporate important elements of the interpretive paradigm. Tribe (2001, p. 445) explains that "the interpretive approach to curriculum design seeks understanding and meaning". To achieve this in curriculum design all the participants in the project need to be given a voice so that the curriculum is written collaboratively. Practically, in the THEME project this involved a co-operative approach to scoping the project, the assignment of situational analysis reports to each team to encourage competing views and the use of cross-team discussion workshops not only to discuss the findings, but also to construct the curriculum on the basis of dialogue. In the terminology of Habermas (1989, 1991), the project attempted to complement technical rationality with communicative rationality. But this move was limited in its effect. Interpretive methodology does not offer much beyond a post-modern cacophony of multiple understandings. It does not offer a way of judging between different understandings. In the event, the tyranny of managerial rationality reasserted itself — wide ranging discussions with no clear agreement were not acceptable outcomes. We needed project deliverables.

It is here that power relations (Foucault, 1980) assume significance. In terms of power relations in the project, the project co-ordinating institution in the UK was able to wield most power because of a number of factors. First it was the author of the research project and therefore brought its preferred methodology to the project, which once accepted by the EU became largely a given. Second, as co-ordinating institution it had prime responsibility for allocating project funds. Third, the operating language of the project was English. Fourth, both the cultural values of the UK and Spain were quite closely aligned with the possible result that the Moldovan view was seen as marginal or "the other", or to put it another way its practices were to become those to be changed or amended. For example, a key cultural division emerged from the capability analyses. While each group judged their own capability to be high, the UK and Spain groups were not convinced of the suitability of the Moldovan resources to deliver the tourism education they envisaged. Of course the Moldovan resources were seen as appropriate to deliver their understanding of the key activities of tourism. Fifth, the UK was responsible for setting meeting agendas, chairing meetings and writing minutes. So while aspects of an interpretive methodology were used, management of the understandings that resulted from it was subject to unequal power relations.

Indeed, criticism of the methodology may be extended by consideration of critical paradigms. Critical theory foregrounds the problems of ideology and hegemony in research.

> The job of critical theory is initially to identify which particular ideological influences are at work. Ideology critique then asks whose interests are being served by a particular ideology (Tribe, 2001, p. 446).

We can think of ideology as being a regime of beliefs that directs the thought and practices of those that inhabit it. Hegemony, as developed by Gramsci (1971), offers an account of how particular ideas dominate thinking in society:

> It refers to an organised assemblage of meanings and practices, the central, effective and dominant system of meanings, values and actions which are *lived* (Apple, 1990, p. 5, italics in original).

What is of particular significance in hegemony is how it "saturates our very consciousness" (Apple, 1990, p. 5) so that it becomes the taken for granted way of thinking and doing. A critical theorist's view of the project might be twofold. First, it might be noted that even its interpretive quest for understanding is operating within a dominant ideology. Understanding and meanings outside of the dominant ideology may not surface since interpretive methods do not necessarily sensitise researchers to the operation of ideology. A second observation might be that far from being a neutral exercise in curriculum development, the project is saturated with "taken for granted" meanings and values. This in turn undermines the notion of meaningful "bottom up" participation and contribution. Rather the project is open to criticisms that its implicit values and meanings — its ideological baggage — facilitate the process where a developing country — Moldova — may be subsumed into Western hegemony and neocolonialism.

Conclusion

This chapter has presented and reviewed both the process and product of tourism curriculum development in Moldova. On one level it has described the use of strategic management theory, and situational analysis as a method for curriculum development. It is suggested that within the paradigm of management discourse this method is appropriate and the resulting curriculum will be an effective measure in helping to provide modernisation of the target institution, educate a workforce to develop tourism and contribute to the development of the emerging market economy of Moldova. On this basis the use of situational analysis is commended as a useful way of approaching curriculum development sensitive to the particular conditions and variety of contexts found in developing countries.

On another level, the chapter has subjected the method of strategic management to the scrutiny of critical theory. On this view the sensitivity to condition and context claimed for this method is revealed as the benign aspect of a Trojan Horse concealing the onward march of Western hegemony and neocolonial development. This is perhaps a particularly poignant issue for NIS countries such as Moldova who have only recently escaped the grip of a strict regime of Soviet ideology.

These two conflicting conclusions illustrate the paradoxes and problems submerged in the process of globalisation as it extends its influence across the developing world and ex-communist states.

Acknowledgements

This chapter is based upon an article originally published as:

Tribe, J. (2003). Curriculum, development and conflict: A case study of Moldova. *Journal of Teaching in Travel and Tourism, 3*(1) and is reproduced by kind permission of the publisher — The Haworth Press Inc, West Hazleton, PA, USA — with whom copyright resides. Articles copies are available form The Haworth Document Delivery Service: 1-800-HAWORTH, email: docdelivery@haworthpress.com.

The author would like to thank all of the members of the project team for their various contributions to this chapter, in particular, Richard Vickery (formerly of BCUC, UK), Julio Batle (UIB, Spain), Pavel Tolmaciov and Boris Risneac (NIPES, Moldova) and Elena Turcova (AES, Moldova).

References

Airey, D. (1994). Education for tourism in Poland: The phare programme. *Tourism Management, 15*(6), 467–471.

Airey, D. (1996). Tourism education and manpower development in Central and Eastern Europe. In: G. Richards (Ed.), *Tourism in Central and Eastern Europe: Educating for quality* (pp. 15–26). Tilberg: Tilberg University Press.

Airey, D. (1999). Education for tourism — East meets West. *International Journal of Tourism and Hospitality Research, 1*, 7–18.

Apple, M. (1990). *Ideology and curriculum*. London: Routledge.

Bachvarov, M. (1996). The current state of tourism and tourism education in Bulgaria. In: G. Richards (Ed.), *Tourism in Central and Eastern Europe: Educating for quality* (pp. 27–40). Tilberg: Tilberg University Press.

Ball, S. (1990). Management as moral technology. In: S. Ball (Ed.), *Foucault and education* (pp. 153–166). London: Routledge.

Bramwell, B., Goytia, A., & Henry, I. (1996). Developing sustainable tourism management education: A European project. In: G. Richards (Ed.), *Tourism in Central and Eastern Europe: Educating for quality* (pp. 207–224). Tilberg: Tilberg University Press.

Buchele, R. (1962). How to evaluate a firm. *California Management Review, (Fall)*, 5(1), 5–16.

Burns, P. (1998). From communist to common-weal: Reflections on tourism training in Romania. *Tourism Recreation Research*, 23(2), 45–52.

Charles, K. (1997). Tourism education and training in the Caribbean: Preparing for the 21st century. *Progress in Tourism and Hospitality Research*, 3, 189–197.

Cooper, C., Shepherd, R., & Westlake, J. (1994). *Tourism and hospitality education*. Guildford: University of Surrey.

Cooper, M. (1997). Tourism planning and education in Vietnam: A profile 1995–2010. *Pacific Tourism Review*, 1(1), 57–63.

Cristureanu, C. (1996). The current state of tourism and tourism education in Romania. In: G. Richards (Ed.), *Tourism in Central and Eastern Europe: Educating for quality* (pp. 75–92). Tilberg: Tilberg University Press.

Cross, J. (1998). Tourism education: The international dimension. *Tourism*, 97, 16–17.

Davies, J. (1999). Language skills in the leisure and tourism industry. *Tourism*, 102, 20.

Echtner, C. (1994). Entrepreneurial training in developing countries. *Annals of Tourism Research*, 22(1), 119–134.

Echtner, C. (1995). Tourism education in developing nations: A three pronged approach. *Tourism Recreation Research*, 20(2), 32–41.

Foucault, M. (1980). *Two lectures on power*. In: C. Gordon (Ed.), *Power/Knowledge*. London: Harvester.

Gramsci, A. (1971). In: Q. Hoare & G. Smith (Trans.), *Selections from the prison notebooks*. New York: International Publishers.

Golembski, G. (1991). The needs of a higher level education in tourism in post-communist countries of Middle-Eastern Europe (as illustrated by Poland). *Tourist Review*, No. 1, 3–5.

Habermas, J. (1989). *The theory of communicative action* (Vol. 2). Cambridge: Polity.

Habermas, J. (1991). *The theory of communicative action* (Vol. 1). Cambridge: Polity.

Howie, F. (1996). Skills, understanding and knowledge for sustainable tourism. In: G. Richards (Ed.), *Tourism in Central and Eastern Europe: Educating for quality* (pp. 183–206). Tilberg: Tilberg University Press.

Jung, B., & Mierzejewska, B. (1996). Tourism education in Poland: An overview. In: G. Richards (Ed.), *Tourism in Central and Eastern Europe: Educating for quality* (pp. 57–68). Tilberg: Tilberg University Press.

King, B. (1994). Tourism higher education in island microstates. *Tourism Management*, 15(4), 267–272.

Koh, K. (1995). Designing the four-year tourism management curriculum: A marketing approach. *Journal of Travel Research (Summer)*, 34(1), 68–72.

Kuhn, T. (1962). *The structure of scientific revolutions*. Chicago: University of Chicago Press.

Lewin, K. (1935). *A dynamic theory of personality*. New York: McGraw-Hill.

Nutt, P. (1989). Selecting tactics to implement strategic plans. *Strategic Management Journal*, 10(2), 145–161.

Ogorelc, A. (1999). Higher education in tourism; an entrepreneurial approach. *Tourist Review*, 54(1), 51–60.

Richards, G. (Ed.). (1996a). *Tourism in Central and Eastern Europe: Educating for quality.* Tilberg: Tilberg University Press.

Richards, G. (1996b). Developing tourism education in Central and Eastern Europe. In: G. Richards (Ed.), *Tourism in Central and Eastern Europe: Educating for quality* (pp. 301–305). Tilberg: Tilberg University Press.

Richards, G. (1996c). The development of tourism in Central and Eastern Europe. In: G. Richards (Ed.), *Tourism in Central and Eastern Europe: Educating for quality* (pp. 1–14). Tilberg: Tilberg University Press.

Rowntree, D. (1982). *Educational technology in curriculum development.* London: Harper and Row/Paul Chapman.

Singh, S. (1997). Developing human resources for the tourism industry with reference to India. *Tourism Management, 18*(5), 299–306.

Theuns, H. L., & Go, F. (1992). Need led priorities in hospitality education for the Third World. In: J. Brent Ritchie, D. Hawkins, F. Go & D. Frechtling (Eds), *World travel and tourism review indicators.* Wallingford: CAB International.

Theuns, H. L., & Rasheed, A. (1983). Alternative approaches to tertiary tourism education with special reference to developing countries. *Tourism Management (March), 4*(1), 42–51.

Tribe, J. (1997). *Corporate strategy for tourism.* London: Thomson Learning.

Tribe, J. (2001). Research paradigms and the tourism curriculum. *Journal of Travel Research, 39*(4), 442–448.

United Nations Development Programme (UNDEP). (2000). *The human development report CD ROM: Human development statistical database 1999.* New York: United Nations Development Programme.

Vukonić, B. (1996). Tourism education in Croatia. In: G. Richards (Ed.), *Tourism in Central and Eastern Europe: Educating for quality* (pp. 41–46). Tilberg: Tilberg University Press.

World Tourism Organisation. (1997). *Compendium of tourism statistics.* Madrid: WTO.

Zhao, J. L. (1991). A current look at hospitality and tourism education in China's colleges and universities. *International Journal of Hospitality Management, 10*(4), 357–367.

Chapter 7

Work Experience and Industrial Links

Graham Busby

Introduction

Many tourism programmes in higher education are based in business schools, or at least grounded in the business studies vocational area, and, as a result, tend to incorporate a range of links with industry (Cooper & Westlake, 1998; Evans, 2001; Tribe, 1997). Higher education — industry links occur through supervised work experience (SWE), comprising both short and long placements (Busby, Brunt, & Baber, 1997), involvement with programme validation (Morgan, 2004), through guest speakers and via field trips. There are other forms of involvement although these are the principal ones. This chapter focuses chiefly on the period of supervised work experience for this appears to be probably the single most important link; certainly it is the activity emphasised by Dearing (1997) and Harvey, Moon, Geall, and Bower (1997) in their extensive reviews. In Britain, the most frequently used term for the period of SWE is sandwich placement; elsewhere the terms 'internship' and 'cooperative education' are used (Busby, 2003a; Leslie & Richardson, 2000; Waryszak, 1997).

The Centre for Higher Education Research and Information and the Centre for Research into Quality (CHERI/CRQ, 2002) have commented on the limitations of Higher Education Statistics Agency data with respect to estimating numbers of students undertaking SWE in Britain. Brewer (1995) estimated that there were, in the academic year 1994–1995, a total of 231,146 higher-education students on work placements of some form. Within the Business and Administrative Studies domain, there were a total of 36,163 students on placement in 1997/98 (HESA, 1999). There are difficulties in attempting to calculate the numbers from tourism programmes. As Cooper, Shepherd, and Westlake (1994) and Dale and Robinson (2001) observe, there is more than one type of tourism degree: the single honours, such as Tourism Management and other 'themed' awards, and those which use tourism to enhance combined awards, such as Tourism and Biology. It is not easy, therefore, to estimate the number of potential placement students because of the range of major and minor pathways containing tourism in the award title; for example, over 950 programmes with Autumn 2003 entry, to British institutions, contained 'tourism'

An International Handbook of Tourism Education
Copyright © 2005 by Elsevier Ltd.
All rights of reproduction in any form reserved
ISBN: 0-08-044667-1

Table 1: Aims of the tourism placement.

- To experience employment and, where appropriate, accept responsibility for the completion of tasks and the supervision of others
- To develop key graduate attributes and skills
- To acquire further practical skills and experience
- To obtain an insight into management and management methods
- To gain greater maturity and self-confidence
- To be involved in the diagnosis and analysis of problems
- To develop attitudes and standards appropriate to career objectives

in their title (Busby, 2003a). Nonetheless, it seems unlikely that there are more than 600 or 700, from 'tourism management' degrees, in the UK, on placement at any one time, especially in light of the introduction of tuition fees (Busby, 2003a).

The inclusion of work experience is intended to provide an appropriate vocational aspect to what might be a predominantly academic curriculum (Richards, 1995; Cooper & Shepherd, 1997). In Britain, work experience on tourism degree programmes varies from 12 weeks to 12 months in duration and is to be found in those based around the social sciences as well as business management courses (Busby et al., 1997). A study of British tourism degrees, with admissions in 2001, identified 23% providing a full 12-month placement (Busby & Fiedel, 2001); a few institutions, such as Bournemouth University, provide a compulsory placement (Linzner, 2004). While Table 1 illustrates the aims of the 12-month tourism placement for University of Plymouth students, it is considered that these apply to most programmes in the UK and, indeed, internationally; they certainly accord with those of the University of Ulster (Neill & Mulholland, 2003).

The commercial imperative, implied by these aims, is critical in many placements, as Collins (2002) has observed; the aims are intended to inculcate essential vocational skills or what Tribe (2001, p. 444) terms "implicit adherence to business values". According to Duignan (2003), placements also provide familiarity with professional practices and are intended to raise graduate labour-market value. From another perspective, placements undoubtedly provide the balance between theory and practice advocated by Go (1994) and Airey (1996).

Concepts and Practice

Concepts

It appears, *prima facie*, as though there are three stakeholders in the tourism higher education — industry relationship: the student, the institution and the employer (Dale & Robinson, 2001; Leslie & Richardson, 2000). In their review of the benefits for students, industry and institutions, Leslie and Richardson (2000) observe that a simple count of the advantages does not show the benefits residing primarily with any one of the stakeholders because of the difficulty of measuring the 'weight' of each. However, it is worth noting that they identify six advantages for students, eight for industry and three for institutions.

Ellis and Moon (1998a,b) argue that the professions, the state and the community at large should also be considered stakeholders, as Figure 1 illustrates. Given that the tourism industry comprises such a diverse range of sectors, identification of the professions creates difficulties; however, as an example, Busby (2001) has drawn attention to the increasing number of local government tourism vacancies which request possession of a tourism degree — indeed, in Britain, the Tourism Management Institute has been established (www.tmi.org.uk), a proto-professional body.

From the perspective of the state as stakeholder, Ellis and Moon (1998a) draw attention to the student placement as "especially beneficial to the nation", based on findings from the Research into Sandwich Education Report (RISE, 1985), the inference presumably being that the student has become both more employable and responsible as a result of the SWE. Certainly, findings in the UK government Dearing Report (1997) indicate this, and the National Council for Work Experience (NCWE) was established as a response to Dearing Report. The aims of the NCWE are to:

> improve the quality and increase the quantity of work experience, raise the academic value of work experience, become recognised as independent and authoritative by the business and academic communities, become a one stop shop of expertise and advice on all aspects of work experience (NCWE, 2004).

With regard to the local community, as a stakeholder, there are important connections if, for example, well-qualified students are retained in the area rather than undertaking economic migration. Universities play an important role in the cultural life of towns and cities, leading to regeneration in some cases, and to employment through 'spin off' businesses (DfES, 2003); in this two-way interaction, the student is critical. Knowledge transfer between universities, business and the wider community produces economic returns (Lambert Review, 2003). One way in which this has been identified, in the UK, is through 'clusters', whereby areas have a number of business sectors with strong links with their local universities; in both South West England and Wales, there are 'deep' links between tourism businesses and Higher Education Institutions (Lambert Review, 2003).

Despite the range of stakeholders, it is apparent that good relations need to be maintained between higher-education institutions and employers, in particular (Ellis & Moon,

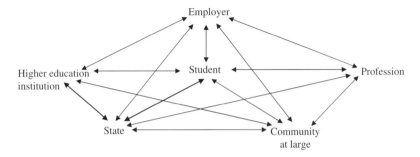

Figure 1: Tourism higher-education stakeholders.

1998a,b). As Teixeira and Baum (2001) and Collins (2002) observe, good placements are expensive and difficult to acquire and monitor; however, perception of a university by industry may be influenced by the interaction with the placement service provided. Based on their research, Ellis and Moon (1998a, p. 188) assert that the use by employers of a placement service permits them to "judge the university as a whole". To that extent, getting it 'right' should be a priority for the institution.

In reviewing employer-course involvement in higher education, Cassells (1994), from the University of Northumbria, identified three levels: arms length relationships, partnerships and strategic alliances. It is argued that institutions will not possess many strategic alliances

> if only because the dynamic nature of the industry can mean that budgets preclude recruiting a student one year and not the next (Busby, 2002, p. 224).

An example of one strategic alliance is illustrated through the BSc Cruise Operations Management award, at the University of Plymouth, whereby Cunard were involved in the curriculum design and, as a result, take a number of students on placement as trainee pursers every year. Themed tourism education, such as this, encourages closer stakeholder links, by default (Dale & Robinson, 2001).

Undoubtedly, there are partnerships "where employers and educators really want to develop the relationship to the benefit of both" (Cassells, 1994, p. 3). Almost certainly, this sums up the arrangement of most sandwich placements in the UK and, it is argued, this allows for a break of one or two years' placement offer before coming back to the institution when conditions permit recruitment again. A variation on this level has been observed over the last decade, namely, what might be termed the personality-based, non-corporate relationship. This will occur when key personnel move to a new organisation and begin to recruit students, for placement, from the same university because they are familiar with the average student performance, institutional procedures and academic staff. One example, of a North American tour operator, can be cited: a senior member of staff joined in 1998, having recruited University of Plymouth students at her previous company. Students were recruited and satisfaction has grown to the extent that nine have been employed for 2004 and more would have been taken if possible — all because the tour operator knows the type of students and background they will secure.

However, it is argued that many placements are based on an "arms length relationship", almost an economic transaction, whereby the university supplies students for vacancies which may be difficult to fill with dependable, locally sourced labour. The employer knows the student is likely to stay in order to achieve the certificate or requisite credits. Before leaving consideration of the arms length relationship, it is argued that there are two types: those which work satisfactorily, albeit without much of a challenge, and those whereby the students are "exploited by their employers" (McMahon & Quinn, 1995, p. 15).

Practice

Whether a placement office is being established for the first time, in a university, or an existing one is under review, a number of elements for each of the three key stakeholders need to be checked. Table 2 identifies a number of these minimum elements, or standards,

Table 2: Key stakeholder elements.

Employer	Student	University
Awareness of responsibilities (QAA, 2001)	Awareness of rights and responsibilities (QAA, 2001)	Responsibilities of all parties defined (QAA, 2001)
Awareness of insurance, health & safety and equal opportunities requirements (NCWE, 2004)	Awareness of expectations (Garavan & Murphy, 2001; QAA, 2001; Schaafsma, 1996)	Guidelines re-expecta tions (QAA, 2001; Schaafsma, 1996)
Recognition of role of mentor (Garavan & Murphy, 2001; Schaafsma, 1996)	Involvement in company meetings (Reeve, 2001)	Support before, during and post-placement (QAA, 2001)
Awareness of expectations (QAA, 2001; Schaafsma, 1996)	Reflection on experience (Tribe, 2001)	Competent staff involved (QAA, 2001)
Publication of job descriptions (Garavan & Murphy, 2001)		Complaints procedures in place (QAA, 2001)
Outcomes identified and feedback frequent (NCWE, 2004)		Procedure monitoring (QAA, 2001)
		Frequent contact with student (Bourner & Ellerker, 1998a,b)

based on the work of Bourner and Ellerker (1998a,b), Garavan and Murphy (2001), NCWE (2004), QAA (2001), Reeve (2001), Schaafsma (1996) and Tribe (2001).

A few of these elements will be considered. Awareness of responsibilities cannot be underestimated — and this applies to the student as much as the employer and university. Publication of a job description aids awareness and yet this frequently does not occur despite the fact that it helps demarcate responsibilities; it also helps appraisal and relevant feedback. Ryan, Toohey, and Hughes (1996) have remarked on poorly supervised placements generating negative outcomes. Negative outcomes are much less likely to occur if the individual has a job description from the outset. Allied to identification of responsibilities is an understanding of the remuneration package. The student needs to clearly understand whether there is a bonus element, or other benefits, besides the salary. Some tourism placement students have received £300 per month in bonus payments (Busby, 2003a) and others free or subsidised accommodation.

In terms of placement assessment, the experience may be credit-rated, for academic purposes, or result in a separate certificated award. The key issue here is 'weighting': if the SWE contributes to the honours classification, can it be worth more than 10%? In any event, there is the issue of ensuring parity of assessment across a wide range of both employer and sectoral types. The aspect of comparability/consistency has been remarked on by Fowler and Tietze (1996) who point out that it is not just organisational size that can affect the experience; the type of work allocated and rotation from department to department within the organisation can make comparability of placements difficult. Furthermore, Duignan (2003, p. 344) has suggested that if the placement is to be credit-rated, "conventional measures of attainment will need to become unconventional in academic terms"; however, he does not provide any examples. If this is to be performance-related (Church & Watson, 2002), the issue of consistency becomes critically important and also very time-consuming (Gray, 2001; Ottewill & Wall, 1996).

A common method of assessment for the academic component is production of a project, frequently related to the business the student is engaged in. In this scenario,

> the placement experience provides a practical foundation for the fourth…
> year of study, which attempts to find solutions to real business problems

as Evans (2001, p. 28) observes for those enrolled at the University of Northumbria, UK. Ideally, students can utilise the placement project as a practice run for the honours dissertation frequently found in the final year of under-graduate programmes. In both cases, the student is working alone and needs to be creative in terms of data collection and use of resources. The project will show some element of reflection on the process besides content related to what was taught in the university.

Drawing on the work of Robson (1993), Gray (2001) emphasises that the concepts of validity, reliability and authenticity are of paramount importance in any measurement of work-based learning assessment. The three forms of validity — construct, content and predictive — all relate to SWE. Arguably, they become much more important if the experience is credit-rated. For example, content validity may be secured if the student is expected to be able to work with spreadsheets but construct validity cannot be said to apply if an abstract concept has not been operationalised in the assessment. Similarly, if a student is being sponsored, as some on Plymouth's BSc Cruise Operations Management are, it is essential that the assessment possesses predictive validity, that is, identification of those likely to be high performers in the near future. In his Briefing for the Learning and Teaching Support Network, Gray (2001) provides guidelines for improving the reliability of marking related to work-based learning. The reader is recommended to view this document at the following internet address: www.ltsn.ac.uk/genericcentre.

A number of aspects to good practice have been raised highlighting the need for a clear definition of roles within the HEI itself. Table 3 illustrates those functions which need to be allocated to either the academic tutor or a placement administrator, based on the author's experience and the work of Neill and Mulholland (2003).

Implicit within the functions identified in Table 3 are a number of sub-components. For example, use and regular updating of placement notice-boards is recommended: not just for the notification of vacancies but also for posting vignettes of individuals currently 'out' and their achievements. The value of vignettes cannot be over-emphasised for they provide illustrations of the 'real world' pros and cons of a particular employer. Importantly, they also indicate sectoral employment proportions: it is very difficult to secure a placement with an airline, as Cave (1997) has observed, and yet the pre-placement student seldom accepts this. One University of Plymouth student contacted 126 airlines before securing a position with a ground transport operator at London Heathrow airport.

Table 3: Placement functions allocation.

Employer database maintenance
Marketplace monitoring
Plan and monitor securing placements
Deal with major complaints on placement
Monitoring national initiatives
Pre-placement student database
Placement preparation sessions throughout the year
Organising final year mentors for second year students
Presentation on cultural issues
Vacancies notification
Collation and mailing of student CVs
Organisation of interviews
Individual placement details confirmed
Placement responsibilities briefing
Health and Safety briefing
Approval of job descriptions and authority to commence placement
Confirm employers' insurance liability
Students on placement database
Contact with students on placement
Organising tutors' visits
Monitoring of visit report forms
Coordination of assessed work, employer reports
Distribution of assessments to academic staff
Placement de-briefing
Student feedback, when available
Review process

In the pre-placement stage, talks by 'returned' students can be of invaluable help (Neill, Mulholland, Ross, & Leckey, 2004) as well as contact with those currently on placement, the latter being aware of the organisational position at that point in time. An adjunct to this is that students should be seen on a one-to-one basis when discussing whether to undertake a placement or not: both anecdotal evidence and research (Duignan, 2003) suggests self-selection, that is, those undertaking a placement may well be academically more capable. Individual discussions provide scope for staff to emphasise the value of a placement to students looking to take the easy option of avoiding application and interview.

The issue of contact with students on placement is one which requires serious attention; increased use of e-mail can help to address those occasions when the student cannot contact the academic by telephone and vice versa. Distribution lists, by e-mail, can also help maintain a sense of placement cohort identity with the Higher Education Institution. While the Higher Education Funding Council for England recommends at least two visits (Church & Watson, 2002), it is argued that the norm is one. This does not mean that the placement "is insufficiently valued" as Church and Watson (2002, p. 26) suggest, rather it is a reflection of the various costs involved. Furthermore, with the state of technology today, a placement in most parts of the world can be monitored by e-mail and telephone. For readers interested in a model placement system, based on the Quality Assurance Agency for Higher Education's Precepts, the following internet site is recommended: www.placenet.org.uk/docs/doc.pdf

Global Aspects

Founded in 1983, by a group of universities, colleges and employers, the World Association for Cooperative Education (WACE) is the only body promoting cooperative education on an international level (WACE, 2004). WACE is:

> an international non-profit organization dedicated to helping interested individuals and institutions forge close ties between the classroom and the workplace. It actively advocates cooperative education (also known as work-integrated learning or co-op) around the world. It also provides technical information and assistance to schools, businesses, and governments that want to establish or strengthen cooperative education programs (WACE, 2004).

Affiliated to WACE are a number of national bodies including the Canadian Association for Co-operative Education (CAFCE), Britain's Association for Sandwich Education and Training (ASET), the China Association for Cooperative Education (CASE) and the Southern African Society for Cooperative Education (SASCE).

While the literature concerning cooperative education research can be said to be international, remarkably little has reviewed the tourism perspective. Hospitality Management SWE has been considered and there are, undoubtedly, significant overlapping areas of concern. However, it is surprising that international cross-sectional research, such as Waryszak's (1999) on the hospitality curriculum at Melbourne, Oxford Brookes, Strathclyde and The Hague has not been matched for Tourism.

At a time of increased graduate numbers in the United Kingdom, it might be expected that students would perceive completion of a 12-month sandwich placement as one means of differentiating themselves in the job market; in other words, providing a competitive advantage. Studies of graduates indicate that placement experience is, undoubtedly, a key factor in securing relevant employment (Harvey et al., 1997; Kiely & Ruhnke, 1998; Purcell, Pitcher, & Simm, 1999); in fact, it has been shown that for Business Studies graduates, work experience does, undoubtedly, result in higher earnings (CHERI, 2002).

Nonetheless, interest is certainly declining — sharply, according to Fell and Kuit (2003). It is worth examining the position at the University of Plymouth: the placement was made an optional component of the degree in 1998 and numbers participating plummeted (Busby, 2003a) despite abundant evidence of the relationship between certain types of graduate job and possession of placement experience (Busby, 2001). The introduction of tuition fees, whereby half the normal amount being payable when on placement, has undoubtedly affected this, an observation also made by Fell and Kuit (2003). However, to provide a comparison, numbers on placement (compulsory) from Bournemouth University remain approximately level with 5 years ago, at about 70 per annum (Linzner, 2004), whereas those at University of Wales Institute Cardiff (UWIC) have followed the Plymouth pattern (Tresidder, 2004).

There is also the issue of working for a large, possibly international, organisation versus a small or medium-sized enterprise. In the former, the placement is more likely to be demarcated than in a small business where a wider range of tasks and responsibilities may occur (Lambert Review, 2003); this has been the experience of many students at Plymouth University. What is not axiomatically related to the scale of organisation is students' experience, during placement, of sustainable tourism practices. With increasing emphasis on sustainability and development, the concept of tourism employee as "philosophical practitioner" (Tribe, 2002) can be greatly influenced by the placement year.

Student Accounts of SWE

Longitudinal study of those on placement from the University of Plymouth over the last 10 years has generated a wealth of verbatim accounts. Several are recorded here in order to illustrate a number of points raised in the chapter. The first account indicates how the experience accords with the stated aims for the sandwich placement. In this case, the student was employed by CITP (Conference and Incentive Travel Partnership, now defunct) in west London. The individual is currently an Account Manager with Principal Promotions, having graduated in 2000.

> My experience at CITP was a very good one — I liked the fact that I was thrown right into it from the day I started. I felt like a valuable member of the team as I wasn't so much concerned with making coffee but was involved in writing numerous client proposals and went on site with the client on several occasions. On my commencing the placement I went on site for the football World Cup in France where I worked extremely long hours but enjoyed the perks of watching the semi-final as well as the final (!) of the tournament.

> Generally, I worked very hard and very long hours for most of my time there but I still refer back to my 'training' at CITP for a lot of the work I do today. Many skills that I attribute to having learned during my placement (such as an eye for detail, painstaking planning and organisation, time management etc.) still apply in my current job (perhaps it helps that I am still in the same line of business). I still consider creative proposal-writing one of my strengths. Just this weekend, I was discussing CITP with a friend who also worked there at the time and we both agreed that while it was extremely hard work, it gave both of us an excellent grounding.

Reflecting on the aims listed in Table 1, this individual certainly experienced the real world of work, acquiring a number of skills and gaining an in-depth knowledge of that particular sector of the tourism industry. The attitudes and standards appropriate to career development appear to have been inculcated.

Given the passage of several years since her experience, a graduate from 1999 was asked to reflect on her tour operator placement undertaken in Canada. The following good and bad points were identified in February 2004 — a British national, she returned to Canada and has been working there ever since. The importance of the placement project, referred to above, can be seen in this graduate's statement.

Good Points

1. Application of theory into practice was priceless, e.g. working for the 'wholesaler' rather than reading about it made the whole distribution channel model much more understandable;
2. Character building;
3. Detection of areas of which you wouldn't wish to work while exploring areas that interest you. However, I distinctly remember telling Network that I would under no conditions go and work in the accounting department as I was a travel student, not a finance student: Just goes to show how things change;
4. After studying the travel industry in the UK, a placement in an International country such as Canada allowed for a more 'Global perspective';
5. The placement project was a great way of studying further the company you were on placement with;
6. A great introduction to the working world especially for those who had never previously worked full-time, particularly in the areas of authority, i.e. who you answer to and the degree of responsibility placed on you.

Bad Points

1. The pay was rather poor but to be expected, especially in my case, the student loan was critical to fulfill the cost of living in Canada.
2. I had a really bad experience with the person who originally arranged my accommodation in Canada . . . I survived however, and am probably better off for it.

It is interesting to note that, totally unsolicited, the graduate made her first good point one that relates to the integration of the placement with the curriculum: an excellent example of the placement being the vehicle for delivery of the subject. However, the extent to which this happens is variable in the extreme. Perhaps, Gray's overview is important here: he suggests that while acquiring knowledge and technical skills is what a placement is about, it is also "a case of reviewing and learning from experience" (Gray, 2001, p. 4). This individual is now a qualified accountant in the cold storage industry (!); however, the experience of a Canadian placement was the cause of her permanent emigration to that country.

The importance of the sandwich placement to long-term career-planning, identified by Ottewill and Wall (1996) amongst others, is further exemplified by the following account from a German graduate. While the human resource staff do not appear to have structured circulation around a number of departments, this individual was not deterred: she made contact herself and this has proved beneficial since graduation.

> In summary, the industrial placement at Thomas Cook (former C&N AG) was a very good experience as it gave me the opportunity to work in a variety of

different departments. I learned about the processes and tasks and managed to built (*sic*) up a personal network throughout the company which is now of great help for my current job at Thomas Cook as Planning and Marketing Manager. Furthermore, this placement served as a first orientation in order to find out my strengths and weaknesses on the job and which area of work I wanted to focus on after my degree.

The only drawback I encountered during the placement was the fact that I had to establish the contact with the departments I was interested in myself and did not receive a lot of support from the human resource department in that respect. However, overall the placement was a very good opportunity to establish a contact with a potential later employer and to get an insight into the processes of a tour operator.

Given that the placement will almost certainly influence the individual's future employment, one aspect of increasing importance relates to perception and practice concerning sustainability. The following verbatim quotes from two students are in response to being asked what they learned during their airline placements:

Importance of a sustainable business plan. Defining sustainable development and stating its importance for airlines. Environmental concerns i.e. built, natural and social.

Because of the current economic climate of the airline industry today (i.e. rising fuel costs, carrying capacity well exceeding demand, reduction in premium passengers etc), particularly in the larger airlines with many aircraft, the need for effective/sustainable business planning…(Busby, 2003b).

Whatever the level of knowledge acquired, the placement experience will directly or indirectly feed into the final year of the degree programme when the student returns to the home institution (Morgan, 2004). It will, undoubtedly, also influence the individual for years beyond graduation.

Industrial Links

Clearly, the SWE is the exemplar of links between higher education and industry. However, there are a number of other connections; for example, local authority involvement with higher education is manifest during the consultation phase of tourism strategy preparation, when academics are invited to contribute, and with guest speaker programmes. This is not just a British phenomenon or a 'one-way' practice; for example, in Canada, tourism development officers are invited to the University of Guelph for specialist lectures to MBA students (Joppe, 2004). Industry is also involved in course design, although this can lead to the development of links with one sector alienating another (Ladkin, 2002); for example, overt emphasis on retail travel and tour operation may be at the expense of public sector consideration. On-going input, from organisations, may continue after degree validation via industry advisory panels.

At Nottingham University, the philanthropic Christel de Haan, co-founder of Resort Condominiums International, donated £2 million for the establishment of a Travel and Tourism Research Institute, now named after her (Anon, 2004a). Similarly, Glasgow Caledonian University has the Moffat Centre, established in 1998, with an endowment from the founders of the A.T. Mays travel agency chain (Anon, 2004b). Professorships, such as the QANTAS Chair, at the University of New South Wales, currently held by Larry Dwyer, are also endowed by industry.

Allied to the example cited above with Cunard and Plymouth University, Princess Cruises have hosted a careers day linked to the BSc Cruise Operations Management, onboard the Royal Princess, for final year under-graduates. To whet their appetite, Princess Cruises also provided a 4-day Barcelona-to-Naples cruise, in June 2004, in order to familiarise them with the type of work and for them to find out more about the organisation.

Consultancy and commissioned research abounds in higher education although it is questioned just how much of this informs the curriculum. Nonetheless, it is valuable staff development. Employers may also be involved, on campus, in the assessment of student work — this does require clear explanation of academic scoring criteria, based on anecdotal evidence.

Conclusion

The range of links between industry and higher education is both diverse and variable. As discussed, the commercial imperative influences continuity of some of these links although, it is argued, there is a certain durability of personal contacts between individuals in industry and education which continues despite switching organisations. Cassells' three levels do encompass the types of SWE relationship and emphasise the need for caution when students are placed with 'arms length' organisations for the duty of care is paramount.

The stakeholder elements, identified in Table 2, are by no means definitive, they highlight the minimum standards which should be operationalised and built into action plans. Assessment, when credit-rated, requires careful planning; as Gray (2001) observes, the issues of validity, reliability and authenticity are important. Implicit within the university staff functions, identified in Table 3, is frequent contact. The significance of this aspect can be illustrated by the experiences of summer 2004 when students on placement with employers in Florida experienced not one or two but three hurricanes within a short period of time. The duty of care in ascertaining their safety within a short period of time was critical.

Students undertaking SWE should, axiomatically, secure a competitive advantage over their peers who have taken a purely academic route to graduation; the experience is also highly likely to introduce some aspect of the sustainability debate, critical to a 21st century world-view. The vignettes from Plymouth University students, over a number of years, emphasise how placements help the acquisition of knowledge, skills and attributes — indeed, they illustrate the formative nature of the experience.

References

Airey, D. (1996). Tourism education and manpower development in Central and Eastern Europe. In: G. Richards (Ed.), *Tourism in Central and Eastern Europe: Educating for quality* (pp. 15–25). Tilburg: Tilburg University Press.

Anon. (2004a). http://www.moffatcentre.com/about.htm viewed 10 March.

Anon. (2004b). http://www.nottingham.ac.uk/ttri/ viewed 10 March.

Bourner, T., & Ellerker, M. (1998a). Sandwich placements: Improving the learning experience — part 1. *Education and Training, 40*(6/7), 283–287.

Bourner, T., & Ellerker, M. (1998b). Sandwich placements: Improving the learning experience — part 2. *Education and Training, 40*(6/7), 288–295.

Brewer, J. (1995). Work based learning — an overview. In *Proceedings of The Management of Placements Conference*, ASET, University of York, cited in Ellis & Moon, op.cit.

Busby, G. (2001). Vocationalism in higher level tourism courses: The British perspective. *Journal of Further and Higher Education, 25*(1), 29–43.

Busby, G. (2002). Tourism sandwich placements revisited. In: B. Vukonić & N. Čavlek (Eds), *Rethinking of education and training for tourism* (pp. 213–230). Zagreb: University of Zagreb.

Busby, G. (2003a). Tourism degree internships: A longitudinal study. *Journal of Vocational Education and Training, 55*(3), 319–334.

Busby, G. (2003b). The concept of sustainable tourism within the higher education curriculum: A British case study. *Journal of Hospitality, Leisure, Sport and Tourism Education, 2*(2), 48–58.

Busby, G. D., Brunt, P., & Baber, S. (1997). Tourism sandwich placements: An appraisal. *Tourism Management, 18*(2), 105–110.

Busby, G., & Fiedel, D. (2001). A contemporary review of tourism degrees in the UK. *Journal of Vocational Education and Training, 53*(4), 501–522.

Cassells, D. (1994). Employer/educator partnerships: Harnessing employers' contributions. Paper presented at the NLG Conference, London, 2 December.

Cave, P. (1997). *Placements in industry — experience in the Lancashire Business School*, Guideline No. 6. London: The National Liaison Group for Higher Education in Tourism.

CHERI (2002). *UK graduates and the impact of work experience*. A report to the HEFCE by the Centre for Higher Education Research and Information. London: CHERI.

CHERI/CRQ (2002). *Nature and extent of undergraduates' work experience*. A report to the HEFCE by the Centre for Higher Education Research and Information and the Centre for Research into Quality. London: CHERI and Birmingham: CRQ.

Church, A., & Watson, J. (2002). *Research award for business sector skills development — tourism*. A report to Higher Education South East (HESE) and South East England Development Agency (SEEDA). Brighton: University of Brighton.

Collins, A. B. (2002). Gateway to the real world, industrial training: Dilemmas and problems. *Tourism Management, 23*(1), 93–96.

Cooper, C., Shepherd, R., & Westlake, J. (1994). *Tourism and hospitality education*. Guildford: University of Surrey.

Cooper, C., & Shepherd, R. (1997). The relationship between tourism education and the tourism industry: Implications for tourism education. *Tourism Recreation Research, 22*(1), 34–47.

Cooper, C., & Westlake, J. (1998). Stakeholders and tourism education. *Industry and Higher Education, 12*(2), 93–100.

Dale, C., & Robinson, N. (2001). The theming of tourism education: A three-domain approach. *International Journal of Contemporary Hospitality Management, 13*(1), 30–34.

Dearing Report (1997). *Higher education in the learning society*. Report of the National Committee. London: National Committee of Inquiry into Higher Education.

DfES (2003). *The future of higher education*. CM 5735. Norwich: HMSO.

Duignan, J. (2003). Placement and adding value to the academic performance of undergraduates: Reconfiguring the architecture — an empirical investigation. *Journal of Vocational Education and Training, 55*(3), 335–350.

Ellis, N., & Moon, S. (1998a). Business and HE links: The search for meaningful relationships in the placement marketplace — part one. *Education and Training, 40*(5), 185–193.

Ellis, N., & Moon, S. (1998b). Business and HE links: The search for meaningful relationships in the placement marketplace — part two. *Education and Training, 40*(9), 390–397.

Evans, N. (2001). The development and positioning of business related university tourism education: A UK perspective. *Journal of Teaching in Travel and Tourism, 1*(1), 17–36.

Fell, A., & Kuit, J. A. (2003). Placement learning and the Code of Practice — rhetoric or reality? *Active learning in higher education, 4*(3), 214–225.

Fowler, G., & Tietze, S. (1996). A competence approach to the assessment of student placements. *Education and Training, 38*(1), 30–36.

Garavan, T. N., & Murphy, C. (2001). The co-operative education process and organisational socialisation: A qualitative study of student perceptions of its effectiveness. *Education and Training, 43*(6), 281–302.

Go, F. (1994). Emerging issues in tourism education. In: W. F. Theobald (Ed.), *Global tourism — the next decade* (pp. 330–346). Oxford: Butterworth-Heinemann.

Gray, D. (2001). *A briefing on work-based learning*. Assessment Series No.11, York: LTSN Generic Centre.

Harvey, L., Moon, S., Geall, V., & Bower, R. (1997). *Graduates' Work: Organisational change and students' attributes*. Centre for Research into Quality, Birmingham: University of Central England.

HESA (1999). Students in Higher Education Institutions 1997/98, Higher Education Statistics Agency web-site: www.hesa.ac.uk/acuk/publications/student_1997-98_table_7.pdf viewed on 23 February 2004.

Joppe, M. (2004). Director, School of Hospitality & Tourism Management, University of Guelph, Canada, Personal Communication, 7 March.

Kiely, J. A., & Ruhnke, J. (1998). BA Business Studies Degree: Employment experiences of 'sandwich' degree graduates versus 1-year 'conversion' programme graduates. *Journal of Vocational Education and Training, 50*(4), 487–501.

Ladkin, A. (2002). The relationship between employment and tourism education: Issues for debate. In: B. Vukonić & N. Čavlek (Eds), *Rethinking of education and training for Tourism* (pp. 45–56). Zagreb: University of Zagreb.

Lambert Review (2003). *Business–university collaboration*. Norwich: HMSO.

Leslie, D., & Richardson, A. (2000). Tourism and cooperative education in UK undergraduate courses: Are the benefits being realised? *Tourism Management, 21*(5), 489–498.

Linzner, D. (2004). Senior Lecturer, Bournemouth University. Personal Communication, 26 February.

McMahon, U., & Quinn, U. (1995). Maximising the hospitality management student work placement experience: A case study. *Education and Training, 37*(4), 13–17.

Morgan, M. (2004). From production line to drama school: Higher education for the future of tourism. *International Journal of Contemporary Hospitality Management, 16*(2), 91–99.

NCWE (2004). www.prospects.ac.uk/cms/ShowPage/Home_page/The_value_of_work_experience/p!ejiagi viewed on 13 February 2004.

Neill, N. T., & Mulholland, G. E. (2003). Student placement — structure, skills and e-support. *Education and Training, 45*(2), 89–99.

Neill, N., Mulholland, G., Ross, V., & Leckey, J. (2004). The influence of part-time work on student placement. *Journal of Further and Higher Education, 28*(2), 123–137.

Ottewill, R., & Wall, A. (1996). Sandwich education — preparing students for placement, *Capability*, 2 (2), displayed at http://www.lle.mdx.ac.uk/hec/journal/2-2/2-1.htm.

Purcell, K., Pitcher, J., & Simm, C. (1999). *Working Out? — graduates' early experiences of the labour market*. Short Report, Warwick: Institute for Employment Research.

QAA (2001). *Code of practice: Placement learning*. Gloucester: Quality Assurance Agency.

Reeve, R. S. (2001). *Employers' guide to work-integrated learning*. Boston, MA: World Association for Cooperative Education.

Richards, G. (1995). Introduction. In: G. Richards (Ed.), *European tourism and leisure education: Trends and prospects* (pp. 3–13). Tilburg: Tilburg University Press.

RISE Committee (1985). *An assessment of the costs and benefits of sandwich education*. London: HMSO.

Robson, C. (1993). *Real world research*. Oxford: Blackwell.

Ryan, G., Toohey, S., & Hughes, C. (1996). The purpose, value and structure of the placement in higher education: A literature review. *Higher Education*, *31*, 355–377.

Schaafsma, H. (1996). Back to the real world: Work placements revisited. *Education and Training*, *38*(1), 5–13.

Teixeira, R. M., & Baum, T. (2001). Tourism education in the UK: Lesson drawing in educational policy. *Anatolia*, *12*(2), 85–109.

Tresidder, K. (2004). Senior Lecturer, University of Wales Institute Cardiff. Personal Communication, 27 February.

Tribe, J. (1997). The indiscipline of tourism. *Annals of Tourism Research*, *24*(3), 638–657.

Tribe, J. (2001). Research paradigms and the tourism curriculum. *Journal of Travel Research*, *39*(4), 442–448.

Tribe, J. (2002). The philosophic practitioner. *Annals of Tourism Research*, *29*(2), 338–357.

WACE (2004). World Association for Cooperative Education, http://www.waceinc.org/what_is_wace.shtml viewed on 12 February 2004.

Waryszak, R. Z. (1997). Student perceptions of the cooperative education work environment in service industries. *Progress in Tourism and Hospitality Research*, *3*, 249–256.

Waryszak, R. Z. (1999). Students' expectations from their cooperative education placements in the hospitality industry: An international perspective. *Education and Training*, *41*(1), 33–40.

INTERNATIONAL TOURISM EDUCATION

Chapter 8

Australasia

Brian King and Stephen Craig-Smith

Introduction

Tourism education in Australasia is offered by a wide range of providers and at a number of levels; high schools and secondary colleges, colleges of further education (vocational education and training or VET), universities, private colleges (e.g. hotel schools) and 'in house' industry training. This chapter provides some commentary on provision across these various sectors with a particular focus on Australia.

The different levels of provision originated at different times. Vocational courses, focusing initially on food and beverage studies and commercial catering and later travel agency training originated in Australia in the mid-1960s. Courses and programmes at higher education level did not start until the mid-1970s, initially in Victoria and Queensland and subsequently during the late 1980s and early 1990s in other states and territories (Craig-Smith, Davidson, & French, 1994). Most postgraduate programmes have come about only in the late 1990s.

In New Zealand, degree programmes were developed at Massey University in the 1980s, building upon the first tourism subjects that were introduced at the University in 1978 (King, 1990). The levels of programme provision range from training modules and sections of the curriculum in the high school sector, to training modules in the VET sector, to degree and postgraduate programmes in the university sector.

The nomenclature used varies across the various educational establishments and sectors. For most providers, a period of study leading to an educational award such as a Bachelor of Tourism Management or a Diploma of Hospitality is called a programme. The individual building blocks making up a programme are typically described as courses in higher education and modules in further education, although such practices are not universal, and some university courses are further sub-divided into modules. A variety of providers offer their own discrete courses and programmes. There are many instances of joint provision. Secondary schools regularly cooperate with further education (VET) providers and many universities also collaborate with the VET sector. Within the provision of a degree programme, VET may be involved in the delivery of the practical components.

Providers in both the VET and higher education sectors are also involved in active engagement with industry. Some universities also work in close cooperation with private educational providers. A small number of universities are classed as 'dual sector' and incorporate both a VET division and a higher education division; examples include Charles Darwin University (in the Northern Territory) and Victoria University in Melbourne. These institutions combine the functions of what are commonly known as community colleges in the US-system, as well as the more established University model. In these institutions, there is a particular emphasis on providing students with opportunities to progress 'seamlessly' from vocational certificates and diplomas into degree programmes.

Education for the tourism sector can be broadly divided into two sub sectors. Programmes focusing primarily on hotel, restaurant and catering management were the first to be established (Goodman & Sprague, 1991). These are variously called either hotel or hospitality programmes. Although the curriculum of these programmes often incorporates consideration of other aspects of tourism, this extra material is usually offered to students on an elective basis. Such programmes are primarily focused on accommodation and related services. In recent years, a number of hospitality education providers have segmented their offerings into the provision of programmes in event management, club management and gaming management. In most cases, these have been off-shoots or variants of hospitality, though the recent expansion of freestanding degrees in event management may result in the development of a discrete sector of educational provision. The other broad sub-section of programmes focuses primarily on travel and tourism activities and on the planning and management of tourism. These are typically known as tourism or (less frequently) travel programmes. Like the provision of programmes for the hospitality sector, these too have proliferated and have in due course given rise to more specialist programmes in cultural tourism, indigenous tourism, ecotourism, and recreation and sports tourism. All are essentially more specialised variants of tourism. Some providers have coupled event management with a specialisation in tourism. A number of programmes set out to encompass both the hospitality and tourism sectors and as such usually include reference to both descriptors in their names. The Bachelor of International Tourism and Hotel Management at the University of Queensland is an example of this phenomenon. The present chapter includes an examination of both sub categories — hospitality and tourism.

Programmes for the tourism industry come in a variety of forms and structure (Airey, 1990). Those targeted very explicitly at the industry or at tourism as an academic study in its own right are most commonly offered as dedicated degrees or diplomas in hospitality or tourism (Leiper, 1981). Other programmes take a more generic approach. These include degrees or diplomas in fields such as business or commerce, environmental management or services management, and typically offer hospitality or tourism in the form of a 'major', 'minor', 'specialisation' or 'field of study'. The more generic programmes often feature a smaller element of hospitality or tourism content than the more specialised ones. The naming of a programme in Australia commonly has as much to do with faculty politics or with the status afforded to cognate disciplines, rather than the level of content (Craig-Smith, 1998). In a survey of the tourism programme content prevailing in the mid-1990s, Wells (1996) discovered that specific tourism content varied from a high of around 60% of total programme content, to a low of around 15%. Determining the proportion accounted for by specific tourism or hospitality content is not without its problems. The categorisation of curriculum into tourism or hospitality material is often fairly arbitrary. Should a course on human resource management, for instance, be precluded from classification as hospitality content because the word hospitality does not occur in the course title? Similarly, should a course in research methods only be classified as tourism content in instances where tourism is specifically included in the course title? What about combined degrees? Intense competition has led to the proliferation of double majors such as Accounting/Hospitality Management and Marketing/Tourism Management. Are these types of programmes better thought of as belonging to the generic business discipline (in these cases accounting and marketing) or to hospitality and tourism?

Although vocational education courses and programmes started in the 1960s, tourism higher education programmes took off only in the late 1980s to early 1990s, some years later than the equivalent developments in North America and Western Europe (McIntosh, 1992). There are a number of reasons for this. Until the advent of cheap long-haul air travel in the 1980s, both Australia and New Zealand were too distant and too costly for the majority of mass leisure travellers to visit, who at that time originated overwhelmingly in Western Europe and North America. Until the mid-1980s, the majority of visitors to the region were business travellers who clustered around the major cities or else those who were visiting the region mainly to see relatives and friends who had previously migrated. The presence of ties with family and friends were sufficient inducements to overcome the influence of distance, cost and time as inhibitors to long-haul travel. As such, the vast majority of early visitors made limited use of commercial tourism infrastructure and services. This held back the need for the development of a sophisticated and developed system of tourism and hospitality training.

Circumstances began to change in the early 1980s. Some of the rapidly industrialising countries of Asia, such as Japan, then followed by South Korea, Singapore, Malaysia and Thailand emerged as the world's third major tourism-generating region. Unlike North America and Europe, South East Asia is located adjacent to Australia and New Zealand, and not on the other side of the planet. The emerging group of Asian tourists had fewer family ties with Australasia and were visiting overwhelmingly for leisure purposes. For this group, the provision of commercial tourism services such as hotels and visitor attractions was the order of the day, as they could not rely on the support of family and friends. The emerging tourist groups were accustomed to formal modes of service provision and expected to be provided with high quality standards in terms of both infrastructure and service. The expenditure of these tourists increased the demand for tourism services, particularly for higher quality experiences than had previously been acceptable. The level of tourism growth to Australia is evident from the visitation data. After the Second World War, it took 40 years for annual visitation to Australia to reach the magical 1 million mark in 1984. To reach 2 million took only a further 4 years!

To capitalise on the emerging growth markets, the region went into overdrive in terms of both providing additional tourism infrastructure, and bringing the tourism workforce up to international standards of quality and reliability (King, 1996). This required a rapid expansion of tourism education provision and a rapid increase in the availability of qualified tourism teachers and university academics (Airey & Nightingale, 1981). This latter need was met by the recruitment of significant numbers of trainers, teachers and academics from Europe and North America. The influx of staff was particularly prominent at the

higher education level. While many Australians had the relevant industry and travel experiences and some educational qualifications, few had specific Masters or Doctoral qualification in tourism or hospitality. Over the past 20 years, the situation has been transformed
and Australian-trained academics now occupy positions in other countries, indicative of a
shift from importing qualified staff to exporting them.

Tourism Education at High School and Secondary College Level

Largely, as a consequence of the unitary political system that prevails in New Zealand, secondary education is fairly uniform across the country. In Australia by contrast, education
provision is the responsibility of the six states and two territories. As a result, there are
many variants in the system of provision. The introduction of both hospitality and tourism
education at this level has occurred for a number of reasons.

Recently, the provision of vocationally focused courses undertaken during the advanced
years of the secondary school curriculum, has accelerated. This trend has been prompted
by a desire to increase the employment prospects of school leavers, especially among those
less suited to further study. Subjects in both hospitality and tourism have been introduced.
With a few exceptions, these courses have tended to focus on the type of knowledge and
skills most immediately relevant to the industry. To this end, many schools offering these
courses have formed a close association with the vocational education sector. The programmes offered are sometimes referred to as 'VET in Schools'. Courses at this level often
serve a dual function, as a constituent component of the secondary school curriculum and
as a formal credential (further education certificate) within the VET sector. The bulk of
provision has been in hospitality and has been associated with the study areas of food technology and home economics. The employment outcomes are viewed as very positive, particularly in the light of the expansion of the hotel and café sector.

Provision of tourism vocational education at high school level has been more modest.
Employment outcomes such as tour guiding have been commonly viewed by the various
state industry training boards as being less well suited for teenagers. Tourism education
provision is more commonly linked with social sciences and is less clearly identified with
clearly defined vocational outcomes. The decline of employment in the retail travel sector,
in the face of online distribution and industry rationalisation, has largely removed this
employment outcome, which has historically held some appeal among school leavers. This
has constrained the development of vocationally focused travel and tourism courses at
secondary level.

Though there have been many examples of successful tourism education offered at high
school level, a number of difficulties have been encountered. One of the greatest challenges
has been that teachers of courses at this level must be both qualified and registered secondary school teachers and in addition have the requisite knowledge, skills and relevant industry experience to satisfy the requirements of the VET sector and the industry. A second
difficulty has been that these courses tend to attract students with an orientation that is more
vocational than theoretical. In some states, such vocationally focused courses are not recognised for the purposes of university entry. Notwithstanding such challenges, there are
increasing examples of closer formal links between schools offering tourism education and

local university departments of tourism. The tourism courses taught in high schools may lead to advanced standing for students who are successful in gaining entry to university.

Tourism Education in the VET Sector

As is the case with secondary education, VET in Australia is also the responsibility of the respective states and territories. This has led to a diversity of applicable systems and procedures. Partly to overcome the difficulties associated with eight different systems across the country, the Federal Government has introduced a national framework (the Australian Qualifications Framework or AQF) with a view to giving equivalence to certificates, diplomas and advanced diplomas. The structure of the various qualifications and the programmes that align to different levels are endorsed as being of equivalent standard and meaning by key parties including industry.

Australia-wide, the system of VET is directed by the Australian National Training Authority (ANTA) under a board composed predominantly of industry representatives. Programme delivery is based around what are known as 'workplace competencies'. Programmes to achieve these competencies may be delivered either in a college or in a workplace setting. As part of the expansion of delivering recognised qualifications in the workplace, a wide range of private sector providers have been designated as Registered Training Organisations (RTOs) and now compete with public sector providers to deliver training outcomes.

The Provision of Undergraduate Tourism Education

Undergraduate tourism education started in Australia in the early 1970s in Melbourne (Victoria) and near Brisbane (Queensland) (Wise, 1978). These two developments were a response to identified local (state-based) education and training needs. For the rest of the 1970s, however, the two providers (the former Footscray Institute of Technology and the former Queensland Agricultural College) were the dominant providers of such education in Australia and enjoyed national as well as local recognition. Growth in the provision of programmes was slow in the 1970s, doubling from only two to four by the end of that decade. The pace of expansion was still fairly modest during the 1980s with the four programmes on offer in 1980 expanding to five in 1985, six in 1987 and seven in 1988. It was the boost to international tourism generated by Australia's Bicentenary Celebrations, which had the greatest impact. By 1989, 15 programmes were on offer across Australia and by 1990 this had increased to 19. From 1990, the number of programmes escalated with 21 in 1993, 32 in 1995, 44 in 1997 and a staggering 95 in 2004. Even this figure hides the true growth rate, since a number of the 95 programmes include fields of specialism, which are not readily classified as hospitality and tourism, but are of direct relevance. According to data from a national survey being undertaken at the time of writing, there are a total of 112 undergraduate programme offerings if all options are taken into account.

Prior to 1990, higher education in Australia was characterised by the so-called binary system made up of two distinct sectors. These consisted respectively of universities, which specialised in the more established disciplines and exhibited a degree of research intensivity and Colleges of Advanced Education (equivalent to the former polytechnics found in a number of European countries), which specialised in more vocationally orientated programmes and in consultancy-focused research. The two sectors were merged in 1990 as part of a rationalisation of higher education in Australia. Many of the former colleges had been the pioneers of tourism education provision at the undergraduate level. A number of the top research-focused universities remain conspicuously absent from the long list of university providers at the undergraduate level.

In New Zealand, the number of universities has expanded much more gradually than has been the case in Australia. Some of the so-called 'polytechnics' have expanded modestly from diplomas into degree provision but research activity has remained the domain predominantly of the universities. A notable exception to this general rule has been Auckland Institute of Technology, which was granted university status in the 1990s (as Auckland University of Technology) and has actively expanded its research capability.

The geographical dispersal of the various programmes in Australia follows the population distribution to a greater extent than the distribution of the major holiday destination areas. As of mid-2004 there were 33 programmes offered in Queensland, 29 in New South Wales, 22 in Victoria, 10 in Western Australia, eight in South Australia, three each in Tasmania, the Northern Territory and the Australian Capital Territory and one programme offered by the one university in Australia that is federal rather than state based. Of the 112 programme offerings, 13 combine tourism and hospitality (up from three in 1996) (Craig-Smith, 1998). A further 43 specialise in tourism and 15 in particular components of tourism such as eco or cultural tourism. The total provision of tourism courses is 58, up from 27 in 1996. A further 32 are in hospitality together with a further nine in club or event management amounting to a total of 41 (up from 14 in 1996).

Growth of this magnitude is unlikely to be sustainable in the long run and it appears as if the period of rapid growth is finally coming to an end. Bond University in Queensland has already ceased to offer a degree in hospitality management. Two other universities with relatively long established programmes in tourism and hospitality (RMIT University in Victoria and Central Queensland University) have announced that they will be discontinuing their dedicated degree programmes in these fields as of 2005. Possibly in anticipation of an imminent shakeout, much of the more recent development has been in niche areas such as cultural tourism, sport tourism, event management, club management and environmental tourism. This trend is reflective of a view that the market for 'conventional' tourism or hospitality degrees is either already saturated or is approaching saturation point. While enrolments have been growing, there was a marked softening of demand for tourism programmes in the wake of 9/11 and SARS and there is a likelihood of future rationalisation.

Given that most graduates from the various tourism and hospitality degree programmes intend to join the tourism industry following graduation, it is not surprising that most programmes are offered in the domain of either business or commerce. Of the 112 programme options, almost half (about 60) are incorporated within programmes of business or commerce. Some of the hospitality programmes and 12 tourism programmes (mainly those in the eco or environmental tourism areas) are however offered in science faculties. While there is considerable variety in programme content, some system-wide observations may be made, based upon an analysis of recent programme content data. Hospitality programmes typically have a leaning towards specific hospitality functions, particularly food and beverage management, accommodation, hospitality operations and the range of attendant business functions (Briester & Clements, 1996). Tourism programmes, on the other hand, focus more on investigating the nature of the tourism phenomenon and on tourism behaviour, as well as including components of tourism planning and policy (Jafari, 1990). This approach tends to be less specifically targeted at industry employment needs. Although most tourism degrees contain an important element of business skills development, this aspect is less concentrated or prominent (King, McKercher, & Waryszak, 2003). For example, they typically include a smaller component of financial management than their hospitality counterparts. The extent of direct industry applicability is highlighted when the incidence of industrial attachments is taken into account. Whereas, approximately two-thirds of all hospitality programmes have a compulsory industry placement component, only one-third of tourism programmes have the same requirement.

Undergraduate programmes in New Zealand are less prolific than is the case in Australia, but there has recently been a growth of both supply and demand. In New Zealand, there are currently eight degree programmes on offer in tourism and two in hotel management. Four of the ten programmes are on offer in the North Island and six in the South island reflective more of the major tourism receiving areas rather than areas of high population concentration.

The Provision of Postgraduate Tourism Education

Programmes in tourism and hospitality at the postgraduate coursework level are the most recent in origin, having been introduced predominantly over the last 5 or 6 years. The expansion has occurred at a time when Australian domestic students have been expected by Government to pay upfront fees for coursework postgraduate education. Few stipend-based scholarships have been available and this has been a deterrent to enrolments on any significant scale. With the recent introduction of a government-managed postgraduate loans schedule (PELS), it is expected that programmes at this level will experience some expansion, albeit not as fast or as extensively as has been the case with the undergraduate sector. To date, entry into postgraduate coursework programmes has been dominated by overseas students and (to a lesser degree) by industry personnel wishing to upgrade their qualifications. In an environment where high numbers of students are completing undergraduate qualifications in hospitality and tourism, students appear somewhat reluctant to embark on postgraduate programmes. Data provided in the Good Universities Guide also indicate that starting salaries for those who have completed postgraduate qualifications in hospitality and tourism are lower than is the case in other industries and that employment rates are poorer (Aschenden & Milligan, 2004). This has probably had the impact of constraining demand for programmes offered at this level.

Universities are generally able to exercise considerable discretion over who is eligible to enter postgraduate coursework programmes. Many are offered as conversion programmes designed to prepare students from a variety of disciplines for careers in the tourism and/or hospitality fields. At this level, programmes are very often 'nested' with a Graduate Certificate being granted after one semester of successful study, a Graduate

Diploma after two semesters and a Masters Degree being granted after three semesters of study. In some cases, the final stage involves a thesis component, although the rapid expansion of international student numbers has reduced the incidence of a formalised thesis component; smaller-scale project type subjects have emerged as a surrogate for the thesis. A recent trend has been the award of masters degrees after 12 months of concentrated study rather than over three semesters. Government visa restrictions imposed on overseas students may, however, work in the opposite direction prompting universities to extend masters programmes to two calendar years rather than the present 18 months. The nesting type arrangements are useful because the academic requirements are typically less stringent for entry onto a certificate or diploma programme. Flexible entry into the lower levels allows students to progress into higher awards on the basis of their current academic performance rather than what they accomplished prior to enrolment. This approach is particularly useful for attracting industry managers who might otherwise miss out entirely on a university education.

In New Zealand, Otago, Lincoln and Waikato Universities have all been active in postgraduate tourism education. As has been the case in Australia, international students have accounted for an increasing share of total enrolments.

Tourism Research

Tourism research in Australia is undertaken by a wide range of organisations, with the university sector playing a significant role. Most university tourism departments and schools offer research Masters and doctorates in addition to undergraduate degrees. For the most part, Australia has generally adhered to the UK approach towards PhD enrolments, whereby there is minimal compulsory coursework and the award is determined exclusively on the basis of a final thesis examination. Within some Australian Universities, discussions are currently under way to consider a stronger alignment towards the North American doctoral model, with a substantial amount of coursework incorporated at the early stages of enrolment. In some Australian institutions, students may undertake studies in tourism and hospitality research as the thesis component of a Doctor of Business Administration. To date, this has not yet led to any proposals for a professional Doctorate of Tourism or Hospitality, though this prospect cannot be ruled out since the number of professional doctorates in areas such as education and psychology has grown recently.

The tourism research environment in Australia has been transformed as a result of the establishment and development of the Sustainable Tourism Co-operative Research Centre (STCRC). The STCRC is the largest of the CRCs established by the Commonwealth Government to provide strategic research capacity as a result of partnerships between government, the private sector and universities. Established in 1997, the STCRC has progressively expanded from its original base in Queensland and Northern New South Wales to each of the states and territories. All states and territories now have at least one university partner, as well as the participation of the relevant state or territory tourism commission and some private sector partnerships. Panels incorporating representatives from each sector are involved in the determination of initial research parameters and in the subsequent decisions about which specific projects merit funding. The system has provided substantial funding into the research sector and has enhanced the capacity of tourism academics to attract competitive funding. Typically, the success rate for applications to the STCRC is higher than is the case with the more mainstream sources of government funding such as the Australian Research Council (ARC). The other benefit for tourism education and research has been the integral involvement of key private and public sector stakeholders. This has enhanced the perceived relevance and applicability of the research outputs. The availability of funds has also stimulated collaboration between academics employed by the 15 member universities. This has helped the research agenda to progress beyond state and territorial boundaries, and to address issues of national (and increasingly international) importance. The STCRC has also provided a significant stimulus to the establishment of professorships of tourism at the various member universities, including in the less populous states and territories (e.g. Australian Capital Territory (ACT) and Tasmania). Intellectual property issues have been an emerging concern for the STCRC with some of the models that have been produced exhibiting considerable potential for commercialisation. The so-called *Decipher* model has received strong financial backing from the Commonwealth Government because of its potential for small- and medium-sized enterprises.

A recent initiative, which brings into focus the potential impact of STCRC on educational provision, has been the establishment by the Commonwealth Government of the International Centre of Excellence in Tourism and Hospitality Education (ICE-THE). Auspiced by the STCRC with the approval of Government, ICE-THE is a 4-year programme involving a collaboration between the 15 University STCRC members and Tertiary and Further Education (TAFE) New South Wales. It aims to enhance the credibility of Australia as an international centre of educational excellence for tourism and hospitality. The initiative will encompass a range of activities including visiting scholars to and from Australia, promotional activity, student exchange and programme development. It is likely that ICE-THE will capitalise on Australia's success in attracting international students to undertake tourism and hospitality programmes. McKercher (2001) has previously identified the emergence of a group of leading tourism and hospitality higher education providers, based on reputation, scale of operation and resources. The translation of STCRC into the programme development and provision areas is likely to accelerate this process. While non-STCRC members will be able to participate in ICE-THE, it is likely that there will be a barrier to entry, which will certainly act as a deterrent for participation by the smaller-scale public sector providers.

The expansion of higher education provision in hospitality and tourism has been accompanied by increasing collaboration between the various providers. In Australia, the higher education sector is represented by the Council of Australian Universities Tourism and Hospitality Education (CAUTHE). CAUTHE hosts an annual conference and meets twice a year. Networks also exist for provision at the secondary, VET and private providers sectors, respectively. Of the various groupings, the private sector and higher education providers exhibit the greatest collaboration at national level. Being state funded and administered, secondary school and VET providers have a stronger focus on collaboration at the state level. A tourism education and research conference is held in New Zealand, usually every second year. While smaller in scale than their Australian counterparts, these conferences are reflective of the diverse research being undertaken by New Zealand researchers and scholars.

The Future

The outlook for the tourism sector in Australia remains bright. Despite some over-provision of educational programmes, the combined prospects for the ongoing expansion of inbound tourism and the proximity of key Asian markets suggest that opportunities will still exist for trained tourism personnel. The success of the Australian tourism educational exports sector, reinforced by government (and to a lesser extent industry) support for research (through the STCRC) and for education (through ICE-THE) will enhance Australia's emerging reputation as a leader in the field. The implementation of the new 'Brand Australia', campaign by Australia's recently re-named National Tourism Organisation, Tourism Australia is an indication that Australia's appeal as a place to visit will be increasingly coupled with Australia's reputation as a place to learn and study tourism and hospitality. Across the Tasman Sea, the success of the '100% Pure New Zealand' brand is reflective of a similar dynamic, and indicative of an optimistic future for New Zealand as an education destination.

As a region of the world, which enjoys an appealing climate and sought-after lifestyle, Australasia generally and Australia in particular are poised to capitalise on the connection between youth travel and study. The importance of pursuing high standards of professionalism in the service industries is now widely recognised. Australia's reputation as a leader in tourism and hospitality education and research appears likely to continue for the foreseeable future.

References

Airey, D. (1990). Tourism education — a UK perspective of tourism education. *National tourism conference papers* (pp. 15–22). Canberra: Bureau of Tourism Research.

Airey, D., & Nightingale, M. (1981). Tourism occupations, career profiles and knowledge. *Annals of Tourism Research*, 8(1), 52–68.

Aschenden, D., & Milligan, S. (2004). *The good universities guide 2005 edition*. Melbourne: Hobsons Australia.

Briester, D., & Clements, C. (1996). Hospitality management curriculum for the 21st century. *Hospitality Education*, 8(1), 57–60.

Craig-Smith, S. (1998). *Degree programs for the tourism industry: Their development, evolution and future direction*. Unpublished Master of Education thesis, University of Queensland.

Craig-Smith, S., & French, C. (1990). Selected issues in Australian tourism and hospitality education. In: *Proceedings of the Australian Tourism Education Conference*, Canberra, Bureau of Tourism Research (pp. 144–150).

Craig-Smith, S., Davidson, M., & French, C. (1994). Hospitality and tourism education in Australia: Challenges and opportunities. In: W. Faulkner, M. Fagence, M. Davidson & S. Craig-Smith (Eds), *Tourism research and education in Australia conference* (pp. 311–320). Canberra: Bureau of Tourism Research.

Goodman, R., & Sprague, L. (1991). The future of hospitality education: Meeting the industry needs. *The Cornell Hotel and Restaurant Administration Quarterly*, 32(1), 66–70.

Jafari, J. (1990). Research and scholarship: The basis of tourism education. *Journal of Tourism Studies*, 1(1), 33–41.

King, B. E. M. (1990). Higher education in tourism, the UK, Australia and New Zealand experience. *Massey Journal of Asian and Pacific Business*, 2(3), 7–9.

King, B. E. M. (1996). A regional approach to tourism education and training in Oceania: Progress and prospects. *Progress in Tourism and Hospitality Research*, 2, 87–100.

King, B. E. M., McKercher, B., & Waryszak, R. (2003). A comparative study of hospitality and tourism graduates in Australia and Hong Kong. *International Journal of Tourism Research*, 5(6), 409–420.

Leiper, N. (1981). Towards a cohesive curriculum in tourism — the case of a distinct discipline. *Annals of Tourism Research*, 8(1), 69–84.

McIntosh, R. (1992). Early tourism education in the United States. *Journal of Tourism Studies*, 3(1), 2–7.

McKercher, B. (2001). The future of tourism education: An Australian scenario? *Tourism and Hospitality Research*, 3(3), 199–212.

Wells, J. (1996). The tourism curriculum in higher education in Australia 1989 to 1995. *Journal of Tourism Studies*, 7(1), 20–30.

Wise, B. (1978). *The development of higher education for the catering industry in the United Kingdom and Australia.* Unpublished Masters thesis, Strathclyde University (Scottish Hotel School).

Chapter 9

Brazil and Latin America

Sérgio Leal and Maria Auxiliadora Padilha

Introduction

Since a long time, tourism education has been a topic of debate in academia and numerous studies have been published about the theme in some of the major international specialised journals (see e.g. Jafari & Ritchie, 1981; Airey & Johnson, 1999; Tribe, 2002). Some parts of the world, however, have been left out of the discussion for several years, as is the case of Latin America, only more recently addressed by Pizam (1999). Also, only a limited number of researchers have approached the topic of tourism education provision in countries of the region, such as Charles (1997), who wrote about the past and future development of tourism and hospitality education and training in the Caribbean region and Knowles, Teixeira, and Egan (2003) who presented a comparison of tourism and hospitality education in Brazil and in the United Kingdom (UK).

Similarly, tourism research has become a very much-examined topic in specialised publications, academic conferences and discussions worldwide (see e.g. Van Doren, Koh, & McCahill, 1994; Botterill, Haven & Gale, 2002; Page, 2003). Once again, Latin America has not been a focal point of attention of researchers and no major international publication has dealt with the topic in the region to date.

Brazil is used in this chapter to highlight the major concerns and indicate some of the tendencies of education and research in tourism in Latin America. Initially, an overview of tourism education and research in the Latin American context is given. Then, a description of the Brazilian education system is offered, followed by a discussion of the main issues regarding Tourism Higher Education (THE) and research in the country. Finally, conclusions about the development of tourism as a subject in higher education in Latin America are drawn out.

The Context — Tourism Education and Research in Latin America

The development of tourism education in Latin America is still in its early stages. Pizam (1999), in one of the few papers about the topic published to date, brings out some of the major concerns and perceptions of key tourism 'industry' stakeholders from the region, including businesses and government bodies, on the topic of human resources in the tourism sector. The study shows that the private sector perceives a shortage of qualified labour force in the 'industry' at all levels, especially with regard to the very much-needed skills of foreign languages, information technology and marketing. Tourism education is seen as a problematic issue in the region and as one of the major reasons for the lack of qualified human resources in the sector. Both, employers and National Tourism Organisations, perceive the material taught in tourism education in institutions from their own countries as irrelevant to the real needs of the 'industry'. Also, the lack of dialogue between education providers and businesses is reported by the two sets of respondents as a point of concern.

According to Schlüter (2003), Latin American studies on tourism research have been greatly influenced by Jafari and Aaser's paper on the development of doctoral dissertations with tourism as a subject of investigation. Analogous studies have been developed in countries such as Cuba and Brazil, where, according to Schlüter, the most significant and complete study of the topic in the region (Rejowski, 1996) has been done to date.

The existence of refereed tourism journals in the region since the early 1990s is an indication of the growing maturity of the subject in some Latin American countries, such as Argentine and Brazil. Also, the publication of some articles of the Argentinean *Estudios y Perspectivas en Turismo* (Tourism Studies and Perspectives) in English and the bilingual publication of all issues of the Brazilian *Turismo: Visão e Ação* (Tourism: Vision and Action), in Portuguese and English, give an opportunity to researchers from the region to disseminate their studies to the international academic community. However, it is noteworthy that such journals still reach domestic academics much more than their international peers.

Tourism Education and Research in Brazil

The Brazilian Education System

To understand fully the provision of THE in Brazil, it is necessary to comprehend the Brazilian education system. Brazilian provision of education is highly regulated by the government through the Ministry of Education and the Federal Council of Education. The government is the main pre-university education provider, with only a small share of the provision of this level of education in the hands of private institutions. At the tertiary level, on the other hand, the number of private Higher Education Institutions has increased significantly since the New Education Principles and Guidelines Act (*Lei de Diretrizes e Bases*), which sets out the structure of the Brazilian education system (Brazil, 1996). The liberalisation of the education sector in Brazil and other Latin American countries was a result of the subordination to multilateral agencies, such as the World Bank, the International Monetary Fund and the World Trade Organization, which sponsor projects and programmes in the country and directly influence the education policies according to their own interests (Antunes, 2002; Santos, 2002). Even with a significant increase in the supply of higher education in the country, the percentage of youngsters aged between 18 and 24 that get to university education is only 12%, that is, the smallest in Latin America (Gomes, 2004).

In comparison to the UK, higher education in Brazil is a lot more didactic, with more modules and course hours. A bachelor degree in tourism, for instance, has to have at least 3000 course hours spread over a minimum of 4 years (Ansarah, 2002). Besides the traditional route to higher education (4-year programmes), industry-oriented 2-year programmes are a recent addition to the provision. All undergraduate curricula are fixed and specified by government bodies and have a similar core curriculum in each subject area, which facilitates the organisation and standardisation of programmes. This approach, however, generally overlooks the regional needs of some parts of the country.

At the postgraduate level, there are two main routes available to students, the *lato sensu* programmes and the *stricto sensu* ones. The former encompasses taught programmes with a minimum of 360 course hours. Such programmes do not award degree titles, just certificates, and are vocational in essence, directed to the development of professional skills. The *stricto sensu* programmes are the equivalent to MPhil programmes and the doctorates, with a minimum of 2–4 years, respectively. Their objectives are mainly academic and scientific. There is also the vocational masters' degree (*Mestrado Profissionalizante*), which attempts to research and apply specific knowledge to the context of the professional world.

Teacher qualification is a very important aspect for programmes and institutions in the country because of the value given by the government during the authorisation process and periodic evaluation of programmes (CEETur/SESu/MEC, 2001). Because of the rapid increase in the supply of higher education in the country over the last 10 years, there is currently a shortage of qualified teachers to serve all new undergraduate programmes.

Tourism Higher Education in Brazil

The provision of THE in Brazil was initiated in 1971 with the launch of the earliest bachelor degree in tourism in the country, at *Faculdade de Turismo do Morumbi*, in Brazil's largest city — Sao Paulo. This institution is now part of one of the leading private universities in the country in the areas of tourism and hospitality. The Brazilian experience with the provision of THE is different from the North American and European ones, where the offering of tourism-related modules in other subject area programmes took place before the creation of tourism degree programmes. Also, Brazilian hospitality and hotel management programmes were only created subsequently to tourism ones, with the first hotel management programme launched in 1978 (Rejowski, 1996).

According to Ansarah (2002), the provision of THE in Brazil can be divided into four distinct phases. The earliest one, the 1970s, was marked by the creation of the country's first programmes. The second phase, the 1980s, was affected by the impacts of the economic crises that most Latin American countries were facing and few new programmes were created during this decade. The 1990s, on the other hand, represented a milestone in the provision of higher education in Brazil. During this period, the number of tourism programmes increased considerably — more than 900% according to Teixeira (2001). The fourth phase, according to Ansarah (2002), will be marked by a search for a balance between quantity and quality of programmes. Alternative curricula will be developed and unconventional programme titles (e.g. Events Management, Eco-tourism, Recreation, etc.) will be created in order to meet the particular needs of each region of the country.

The evolution of the growth in the number of tourism programmes in higher education in Brazil is presented in Table 1. Due to the difficulties in obtaining official data about the provision, different sources are used and there are some discrepancies among the discrete sources. Such inconsistencies, whenever different numbers were available, are identified throughout Table 1. Data about the period prior to 1994 were not available, restricting the examination to the 1994–2005 period.

From the nearly 3.5 million students enrolled in higher education programmes in Brazil in 2000, almost 70,000 were in travel, tourism and/or leisure education, roughly 2% of all

Table 1: The growth in number of tourism undergraduate bachelor degree programmes in Brazil (1994–2005).

Year	Number of programmes
1994	32^a
1995	$36^{b,*}$
1996	40^c
1997	$53^{d,***}$
1998	$89^{d,***}, 119^{e,**}, 73^{f,*}$
1999	$156^{e,**}$
2000	$230^{d,***}, 225^{e,**}, 204^f$
2001	$322^{d,***}, 250^{g,****}$
2002	463^h
2003	510^h
2004	Not available
2005	$834^{i,**,*****}$

[a] Ansarah and Rejowski (1994, cited in Ansarah, 2002).
[b] Silva, F. (2002). *Hotelaria e turismo trazem muitas opções de atuação*. Available at http://www1.folha.uol.com.br/folha/educacao/ult305u9304.shtml, retrieved January 18, 2005.
[c] Ansarah and Rejowski (1996, cited in Ansarah, 2002).
[d] Official data of the Ministry of Science and Technology, available at http://www.mct.gov.br/estat/ascavpp/portugues/3_Recursos_Humanos/tabelas/tab3_3_2.htm, retrieved January 24, 2005.
[e] Ministry of Education (cited in Teixeira, 2001).
[f] Rejowski (2000, cited in Ansarah, 2002).
[g] Brazilian Association of Tourism and Hotel Management Schools' Managers (cited in Teixeira, 2001).
[h] Mota (2003).
[i] Data available at http://www.educacaosuperior.inep.gov.br, retrieved before the beginning of the 2005 academic year, January 26, 2005.

[*] Number of tourism, hotel management and business administration (with emphasis in tourism) programmes altogether.
[**] Number of bachelor degrees and 2-year technology degrees altogether.
[***] Number of travel, tourism and leisure programmes altogether.
[****] Number of institutions, not programmes. The same institution may offer several programmes.
[*****] The number includes distance learning programmes. Each location where a programme is offered is counted as a different one.

tertiary-level enrolments in the country.[1] This figure, however, is likely to have increased significantly over the last 5 years, since the number of programmes almost tripled from 2000. According to Silveira (2001, p. 52):

> Lamentably the number of technical courses is not very significant and the reality is that with an oversupply of undergraduate courses the market for this kind of human resources is being filled with overqualified profession-als that lack in terms of basic skills.

At the postgraduate level, tourism-taught programmes are becoming increasingly more popular in Brazil. However, the number of research degree programmes is still far lower than the country's needs, especially when it comes to the need for qualified lecturers for the numerous undergraduate programmes. In 2004, there were only four programmes that were the equivalent to the UK's MPhil and only two doctorate programmes (Lohmann, 2004). These numbers are better understood when contrasted with the bigger picture. In 2000, there were a total of 1490 research masters' programmes and 821 doctorate pro-grammes available in the country.[2] Although tourism has been the subject of postgraduate research in several programmes, the first postgraduate tourism degree programme was only created in 1993 (Rejowski, 1996).

Taught masters' programmes, 'industry'-oriented, on the other hand, have grown con-siderably over the last years. Most private institutions offering tourism education at the undergraduate level see postgraduate taught programmes as a market opportunity to attract more students. However, supply is becoming greater than demand and several programmes do not have a sufficient number of students to start off a group. Table 2 presents the num-ber of tourism postgraduate programmes in the country.

According to Lohmann (2004), an undesirable lack of balance was generated in the country by the high number of undergraduate courses in contrast with the low number

Table 2: Number of tourism postgraduate programmes in Brazil in 2003–2004.

Level of programme	Number of programmes
Taught Masters (specialisation)	Not available[a]
Research Masters*	4[b], 5[c]
Doctorate*	2[b,c]

[a] Although the number is not available, it is believed to be by far larger than the others once the legal and aca-demic requirements are more flexible, and no institution needs to have their programmes authorised beforehand.
[b] Lohmann (2004).
[c] Panosso Netto (2003).
* Different from the structure adopted in countries such as the UK, where programmes are research-based only, both programmes in Brazil have an initial taught phase followed by a research one.

[1] Data available at the website of the Brazilian Ministry of Science and Technology, http://www.mct.gov.br, retrieved January 24, 2005.
[2] Data available at the website of the Brazilian Ministry of Science and Technology, http://www.mct.gov.br, retrieved January 24, 2005.

of research degree programmes. The need for qualified teachers, in particular, is deeply affected by this situation, where, at the same time, the number of undergraduate programmes increases, very few opportunities for research degrees are available to prospective lecturers.

The sustainability of the tourism education sector in the country might be under threat because of the high number of institutions and graduates (Mota, 2003) in a market that, as Pizam (1999) highlights, perceives low standards of quality and irrelevance of what is being taught in the programmes to the real needs of the 'industry'. Mota (2003) believes tourism education in Brazil may be facing the maturity stage of its life cycle and planning is the only way to prolong this stage and avoid an early decline of the sector. She proposes a major study to estimate the actual growth of the tourism 'industry' and measure the amount of human resources needed to fulfil the real needs of the sector.

The links between THE providers and the industry are virtually non-existent in most cases. As in most countries, the balance between entrepreneurial, professional, academic and vocational skills is an extremely difficult matter for most Brazilian institutions (Silveira, 2001). The lack of recognition of the importance of tourism education and training in formal institutions by most 'industry' stakeholders is an immense obstacle for further partnerships in the creation of new programmes and adaptation of existing ones. It also means that graduates are not highly valued by the 'industry'.

Regarding the quality of programmes, the Ministry of Education, pressured by the growing recognition tourism education was gaining in the academy and the increase in the number of programmes, decided to create a commission of tourism experts (Ansarah, 2002). The founding members of this commission were responsible for preparing a set of benchmark standards for the evaluation of quality of tourism undergraduate programmes in the country (CEETur/SESu/MEC, 2001). Such benchmarks are used by committees visiting institutions for authorising the opening of new programmes as well as for validating existing ones after the first group graduates.

Tourism Research in Brazil

Rejowski (1996) made an important study of the development of tourism research in the country. In this study, the author presents a list of all 55 dissertations and theses related to tourism that led to an academic award at the postgraduate level in Brazilian institutions from 1975 to 1992. She highlights that such research was developed in different faculties, departments and programmes (e.g. geography, communications, business, urban and regional planning, etc.), especially because the first institution to offer a tourism research degree programme, the *Universidade de São Paulo* (USP), only initiated its programme in 1993.

From the creation of the first Brazilian postgraduate programmes in the 1960s to the first tourism research degree programme in 1993, tourism has received the attention of academics from different subjects (Rejowski, 1996). The creation of the country's first tourism programme at the postgraduate level, however, was a milestone for the further development of tourism research. In addition to the offering of tourism research degree programmes, the establishment of academic journals and the publication of tourism-related books also helped Brazilian tourism research to grow. According to Panosso Netto (2003), knowledge development in Brazil faces several limitations and, as a result, cutting-edge research is generally outdated when compared to the state of the art internationally. He notes that the epistemology of tourism, for instance, has been seriously discussed by international researchers for over 40 years, whereas the topic has only been the focus of attention in Brazil for a decade or so.

One important aspect restricting the development of cutting-edge tourism research in the country in the past was the fact that most researchers did not have access to international publications, first, because of the costs involved in subscribing to them, and second, because of the language barrier. The government's agency for human resources development in higher education (*Coordenação de Aperfeiçoamento de Pessoal de Nível Superior — CAPES*) has recently invested a large amount of money to provide electronic access to the major international journals in all subject areas for every single public Higher Education Institution and for private universities offering at least one doctorate programme that has achieved a positive evaluation (five or more in a seven-point scale).[3] However, the language barrier is still a problem to be overcome.

The growth of tourism education during the 1990s stimulated the creation of institutional journals (but many were more similar to newsletters than to refereed journals) and a few nationally recognised refereed ones. Currently, there are only four refereed journals in the country acknowledged by most members of the tourism academic community. *Turismo em Análise* (Tourism Analysis), first published in 1990 by *Universidade de São Paulo*, is not only Brazil's earliest tourism journal but also the most traditional and well-known. It took almost a decade to have the second tourism journal in the country launched, *Turismo: Visão e Ação* (Tourism: Vision and Action), published by the *Universidade do Vale do Itajaí* from 1998. In 2002, the *Revista Eletrônica de Turismo* (Electronic Tourism Journal), freely available on the internet,[4] was launched by the *Faculdade Cenecista Presidente Kennedy*. Finally, in 2003, the first issue of the *Boletim de Estudos em Hotelaria e Turismo* (Journal of Tourism and Hotel Management Studies) was published by the *Faculdades Integradas da Vitória de Santo Antão*.

The growing number of tourism education providers and tourism journals in Brazil, in addition to the increasing interest about it in the academy and the easier access to international cutting-edge research, may lead to the consolidation of a knowledge base of tourism as a research topic. It is argued, however, that the majority of Brazilian tourism research may still lack conceptual, theoretical and methodological maturity.

Lohmann (2004), while making a comparison between tourism research in Brazil and Australia, argues that there is no Brazilian similar to the Council for Australian University Tourism and Hospitality Education (CAUTHE). As a result, there is no academic conference in the country directed to tourism experts and no outlet for cutting-edge research. However, he also notes that the recent creation of the National Association of Postgraduate Tourism Programmes (ANPTUR in the Portuguese acronym), is expected to help promote tourism research in Brazil while giving researchers the opportunity for networking. It is also important to note that several other initiatives, such as the Tourism Research Seminar of MERCOSUR[5] (the Southern Cone Common Market), organised by the *Universidade de*

---

[3] Information available at the portal from where researchers within the institutions' networks access the journals (http://www.periodicos.capes.gov.br/).

[4] http://www.presidentekennedy.br/retur.

[5] MERCOSUR is a free-trade organisation founded by Argentine, Brazil, Paraguay and Uruguay in the 1990s. Integration of education systems throughout its member states is among the priorities of the organisation.

Caxias do Sul, have developed over the last few years and some events are getting more popular among the members of the tourism academic community. These recent initiatives are likely to help improve the quality of tourism research in the region.

Final Comments

Although tourism education and research in Latin America is still in its infancy, it seems to be taking its first steps into maturity with the explosion in the number of undergraduate programmes and with the consolidation of some postgraduate research degree programmes and refereed journals across the region.

Important episodes throughout the world over the last few years (e.g. foot and mouth disease in the UK, terrorist attacks in the United States. Severe Acute Respiratory Syndrome (SARS) in Asia and other parts of the world and, more recently, the Asian Tsunami) have deeply impacted on the tourism sector and regions not directly affected have the opportunity for attracting a larger number of international tourists than ever. Therefore, tourism is expected to grow in most Latin American countries and the perceived need for quality education and training for the sector, highlighted in Pizam's (1999) work, will also grow.

The possible strengthening of the links between 'industry' and education providers may lead to the further development of applied research. Besides, improved communications, offered by recent technological developments, especially the internet, have facilitated the access to international cutting-edge research and Latin American researchers are starting to take part in the international tourism academic community, by both keeping abreast in terms of scholarship of developments in tourism and publishing their own work.

Acknowledgements

Sérgio Leal would like to thank the Programme Alβan (the European Union Programme of High Level Scholarships for Latin America, scholarship no. E04D049282BR) and *Faculdades Integradas da Vitória de Santo Antão* for the support given for his Ph.D. studies in the UK. Maria Auxiliadora Padilha would also like to thank *Faculdades Integradas da Vitória de Santo Antão*.

References

Airey, D., & Johnson, S. (1999). The content of tourism degree courses in the UK. *Tourism Management, 20*(2), 229–235.

Ansarah, M. G. dos R. (2002). *Formação e capacitação do profissional em turismo e hotelaria: Reflexões e cadastro das instituições educacionais no Brasil*. Sao Paulo: Aleph.

Antunes, R. (2002). *Os sentidos do trabalho: ensaio sobre a afirmação e a negação do trabalho* (6th ed.). Sao Paulo: Boitempo editorial.

Botterill, D., Haven, C., & Gale, T. (2002). A survey of doctoral theses accepted by universities in the UK and Ireland for studies related to tourism, 1990–1999. *Tourism Studies, 2*(3), 283–311.

Brazil (1996). Lei nº 9.394, de 20/12/1996. Estabelece as diretrizes e bases da educação nacional. *Diário Oficial da União*. Brasília: Gráfica do Senado, year CXXXIV, nl. 248, 23/12/1996.

CEETur/SESu/MEC (2001). *Manual de Orientação para Verificação 'In Loco' das Condições de Reconhecimento*. Brasília: MEC.

Charles, K. R. (1997). Tourism education and training in the Caribbean: Preparing for the 21st century. *Progress in Tourism and Hospitality Research*, *3*(3), 189–197.

Gomes, A. M. (2004). *Relação governo e educação superior nas décadas de 1980 e 1990: um olhar comparativo*. Available at http://www2.uerj.br/%7Eanped11/26/trab1.rtf. Retrieved January 14, 2005.

Jafari, J., & Ritchie, J. R. B. (1981). Towards a framework for tourism education. *Annals of Tourism Research*, *8*(1), 14–34.

Knowles, T., Teixeira, R. M., & Egan, D. (2003). Tourism and hospitality education in Brazil and the UK: A comparison. *International Journal of Contemporary Hospitality Management*, *15*(1), 45–51.

Lohmann, G. (2004). Cauthe 2004: Pesquisa em turismo e hotelaria na Austrália. E o Brasil com isso? *Turismo em Análise*, *15*(2), 250–253.

Mota, K. C. (2003). Concepção de um Planejamento Sustentável da Educação Superior em Turismo e Hotelaria no Brasil. *Turismo em Análise*, *14*(2), 103–126.

Page, S. J. (2003). Evaluating research performance in tourism: The UK experience. *Tourism Management*, *24*(6), 607–622.

Panosso Netto, A. (2003). O Problema Espistemológico no Turismo: Uma Discussão Teórica. In: L. G. G. Trigo & A. Panosso Netto (Eds), *Reflexões Sobre um Novo Turismo: Política, Ciência e Sociedade*. Sao Paulo: Aleph.

Pizam, A. (1999). The state of travel and tourism human resources in Latin America. *Tourism Management*, *20*(5), 575–586.

Rejowski, M. (1996). *Turismo e pesquisa científica: pensamento internacional X situação brasileira*. Campinas, SP: Papirus.

Santos, B. de S. (2002). Os processos da globalização. In: B. de S. Santos (Ed.), *A globalização e as Ciências Sociais*. Sao Paulo: Cortez.

Schlüter, R. G. (2003). *Metodologia da Pesquisa em Turismo e Hotelaria*. Sao Paulo: Aleph.

Silveira, C. E. (2001). *An appraisal of the higher education system for tourism in Brazil, having the World Tourism Organization's framework as benchmark*. Unpublished Master Thesis. University of Strathclyde, Glasgow.

Teixeira, R. M. (2001). Ensino Superior em Turismo e Hotelaria no Brasil: Um estudo exploratório. *Turismo em Análise*, *12*(2), 7–31.

Tribe, J. (2002). Rethinking of education and training for tourism. *Acta Turistica*, *14*(1), 61–81.

Van Doren, C. S., Koh, K., & McCahill, A. (1994). Tourism research: A state-of-the-art citation analysis (1971–1990). In: A. V. Seaton (Ed.), *Tourism: The state of the art* (pp. 308–315). West Sussex: Wiley.

Chapter 10

The Caribbean

Acolla Lewis

Introduction

Tourism has emerged as a major force in the global economy, with most countries, whether developed or developing, having increasing opportunities to participate, as both host and guest, in this socio-economic phenomenon. The tourism sector in the Caribbean has assumed prominence as a result of consistent stagnation in the traditional economic sectors. The region has become so dependent on tourism that the governments and leaders of the Caribbean have finally and almost unanimously come to the view that tourism is anything from *an important*, to *the most important*, to *the only* means of economic survival for their states (Pattullo, 1996).

Conventional mass tourism has dominated the region over the past 30 years. This form of tourism can largely be characterised as undifferentiated products, origin-packaged holidays and a heavy reliance upon developed markets such as the United States, Canada and Britain. During the last decade in particular, there have been a number of technological, environmental and political changes that have affected tourism in the region that have initiated a move towards a more sustainable approach to tourism development. Education has been identified as an integral component in ensuring the sustainability of tourism in the region. It is for this reason that these changes have challenged academia to reassess their approach to tourism education and training in the Caribbean.

It is against this background that this chapter seeks to critically examine tourism education provision in the Caribbean. The chapter begins with a discussion on the Caribbean tourism environment for which tourism graduates must be adequately prepared. This is followed by an evaluation of the development of tourism education in the region focusing on curriculum development and quality assurance in tourism programmes. The chapter continues with an analysis of government policy and structures and research on Caribbean tourism. The discussion concludes with an examination of the major challenges faced by tourism educators and the prospects for the further development of tourism education in the region.

An International Handbook of Tourism Education
Copyright © 2005 by Elsevier Ltd.
All rights of reproduction in any form reserved
ISBN: 0-08-044667-1

The Caribbean Environment

At the outset, it is important to set forward a geographic definition of the Caribbean that will be followed throughout this chapter. In a general sense, it has been considered as any country, region or island, which is either in the Caribbean Sea or which touches upon it. For the purposes of this chapter, the term "Caribbean" is used to identify 33 destinations that are members of the umbrella organization of the region's tourism industry, the Caribbean Tourism Organisation (CTO). In this definition, the Caribbean region includes the Dutch-speaking territories of Aruba, the Netherlands Antilles and Suriname; Haiti; the 17 English-speaking countries that identify themselves as the Commonwealth Caribbean; a few countries on the mainland in South and Central America. Table 1 lists the CTO membership countries.

These countries vary tremendously in terrain, size, population, culture and economic prosperity. Notably, these islands suffer from restricted natural resource endowments, with few exceptions, Jamaica with bauxite and Trinidad with petroleum. As a result, these island states are continuously struggling to identify activities which will contribute to the goals of long-term economic development. According to Hall and Page (1996, p. 2),

> virtually the only resources where there may be some comparative advantage in favour of [island microstates] are clean beaches, unpolluted seas and warm weather and water, and at least vestiges of distinctive cultures.

It is primarily for this reason that many Caribbean island states have found it comparatively easy to attract tourists, and thus, the tourism industry has become the cornerstone of the majority of these island economies.

Table 1: Caribbean Tourism Organisation member countries.

Anguilla	Antigua and Barbuda
Aruba	The Bahamas
Barbados	Belize
Bermuda	Bonaire
British Virgin Islands	Cayman Islands
Cuba	Curacao
Dominica	Grenada
Guadeloupe	St. Barts
St. Maarten	St. Martin
Guyana	Haiti
Jamaica	Martinique
Monsterrat	Puerto Rico
St. Eustatius	St. Kitts and Nevis
St. Lucia	St. Vincent and Grenadines
Suriname	Trinidad and Tobago
Turks and Caicos Islands	US Virgin Islands
Venezuela	

Source: CTO (2004).

Since the initial rush to develop tourism in the islands in the late 1950s, tourism in the Caribbean has experienced exponential growth and this trend is set to continue. While worldwide visitor arrival growth between 1990 and 2000 increased an average of 4.3%, average annual growth in arrivals to the Caribbean increased 4.7% (CTO, 2002). The Caribbean currently leads all other regions worldwide as having the largest relative dependency on travel and tourism in its output, employment and investment. In the region today, the industry represents 21% of GDP compared to 12% worldwide. In employment terms, one in every six jobs is travel and tourism related and is expected to grow to one in every 5.8 jobs by 2011 (CTO, 2002). These statistics serve to confirm Mather and Todd's (1993, p. 11) view that

> there is probably no other region in the world in which tourism as a source of income, employment, hard currency earnings and economic growth has greater importance than in the Caribbean.

What is noteworthy is that Caribbean tourism is critical for the future development of the region. Concomitantly, the development of human resources within the industry is crucial for the continued success of Caribbean tourism within a competitive global marketplace. It is within this context that tourism education provision is vital to the development and sustainability of the tourism industry in the region on two levels. On the one hand, tourism is a great generator of employment in the region. It creates direct employment in hotels, restaurants, airlines, tour operations, and also generates a significant amount of indirect employment in the wholesale, retail and distributive trades. To this end,

> the increase in world tourism (and tourism to the region), the tourist demand for quality goods and services and the increasing capacity of tourism enterprises require professionally trained and educated personnel for the variety of jobs that will be created in the industry during the next decade (Brathwaite, Charles, Hall, & O'Reilly, 1990).

Moreover, as Baum and Conlin (1995, p. 6) observed,

> the influx of large numbers of tourists to an island destination is likely to have a more profound effect on the destination in cultural, social and environmental terms because of the destination's small scale.

As the tourism industry continues to expand, so too the negative impacts of tourism development are multiplied. Economically, the industry is dominated by foreign ownership, high leakage and expatriate domination of management at high levels (Hall & Page, 1996). The industry thrives on a fragile resource base, the natural environment, which is highly susceptible to natural disasters. The attitude of the locals towards tourism development is significantly influenced by their colonial history that manifests itself in the host guest interactions. The tourism environment in these Caribbean islands is such that tourism education is crucial not only in terms of supporting the industry by way of maintaining a stable work force, but also in terms of responding to the broader issues with tourism development that affect the wider society.

Tourism Education in the Caribbean

Early Beginnings

It was an understanding of this dynamic Caribbean tourism environment that prompted a move towards the provision of tertiary tourism education and training in the region, which is the focus of this chapter. The majority of educational contribution to the industry is at the tertiary level and the limited education at the primary and secondary levels are confined primarily to the Social Studies curriculum which is not consistent between countries. Seward and Spinrad (1982) observed that the decade of the 1960s was characterised by great optimism towards the potential for a viable tourism industry in the region. In the initial rush to capitalise on rapid expansion of tourist demand, local governments therefore provided generous financial incentives to attract foreign investors willing to develop hotels and related projects. It was during this time that the governments of Barbados and Jamaica, two of the more developed tourist destinations, saw the need to train their nationals for entry-level positions in hotels. To this end, the Barbados Hotel School was established in 1966 as a culinary school. The Jamaica Hotel School started its operations soon after in 1968 with a focus on equipping individuals with skills in the front office, housekeeping, dining room and kitchen departments (O'Reilly, 2002). These two hotel schools were the prototype for other schools in the region such as the Trinidad and Tobago Hotel School (1970s) and the Bahamas Hotel Training College (1975).

As a number of destinations began to approach the development stage in their life cycle in the 1970s, there was an urgent need for the education and training of local managers for the regional hotel and tourism industry. In response to this need, the University of the West Indies (UWI), Department of Management Studies established in Jamaica a Hotel Management degree programme in 1977. UWI's degree programme was designed to educate, train and generally prepare Caribbean students to assume future leadership roles in the region's hospitality and tourism industry. As the name suggests, the programme focused specifically on hotel management and thus there was limited or no attention given to the wider socio-economic and cultural issues arising from tourism development in the region. It was not until 1983 that a Bachelor's degree in Tourism Management was introduced to address some of these key issues. Both programmes were then transferred to Nassau, Bahamas where the Centre for Hotel and Tourism Management (CHTM) was established, as this island was viewed as having the best-developed tourism plant for effective university–industry interface.

Current Provision

As tourism continues to develop in the region, so have the schools and programmes within schools that have hospitality and tourism studies as their major concentration expanded. These schools and programmes range widely in their focus, length of study and type of award. According to CTO's membership reports, in the Caribbean there are currently 52 tertiary institutions offering programmes in hospitality and tourism education. This represents a 100% increase in the number of schools as there were 24 institutions recorded in 1994. See Table 2 for a complete listing of the destinations, the number of institutions and the programmes offered.

Table 2: Tertiary hospitality and tourism training programmes.

Destination/ No. of institutions	Hospitality programmes				Tourism programmes			
	Cert	Dip	Ass. Degree	B.Sc.	Cert	Dip	Ass. Degree	B.Sc.
Antigua and Barbuda (2)	3	2					1	
Aruba (1)			1					
Bahamas (3)	7	4		1	3		1	
Barbados (2)	4		1				2	1
Belize (2)			1				1	1
Bermuda (1)	3		2					
B.V.I. (1)	2		1					
Cayman Islands (2)	1		1				1	
Cuba (3)	6	1			1	2		
Grenada (3)	4			1	3			
Guadeloupe (1)	5				3			
Jamaica (8)	14		1	4			2	4
Puerto Rico (11)								
St. Kitts and Nevis (1)	2							
St. Lucia (1)		1	1					
Trinidad and Tobago (4)	4		4		2		1	1
Turks and Caicos (1)	1	1						
U.S. Virgin Islands (1)			1					
Venezuela (5)			4	1			2	2
TOTAL	56	9	18	7	12	2	11	9

It is important to note that of the 52 institutions offering hospitality and tourism programmes, 13 are universities and the others are community colleges. Two noteworthy observations can be made from the above table. First, the majority of educational contribution to the industry is limited to the Associate Degree level with a focus on preparing graduates for entry-level positions within the hotel and tourism sector. Second, instruction at the tertiary level is skewed towards Food and Beverage, Hotel Operations and other hotel/restaurant courses. This was an observation previously noted by Brathwaite et al. (1990) in their research on the status of tourism education in the Caribbean. More than a decade on, the provision of hospitality programmes continues to grow at a much faster rate than the tourism offerings. In addition to this, of the nine Bachelor Degrees in Tourism in the above table, only the two programmes offered in Venezuela focus primarily on Tourism. The other seven programmes are degrees in Hospitality and Tourism. This raises the question as to whether this is in response to a demand by industry and potential students or simply what the institutions are offering. There is no doubt that the hotel sector, which generally hires the largest number of employees in the industry in the region (O'Reilly & Charles, 1990), demands highly skilled, trained and motivated graduates. However, there is an urgent need for other areas of instruction, notably tourism and tourism-related courses, which institutions are at present not addressing fully.

The UWI has been identified as the primary institution in the region with the responsibility of contributing towards meeting the tourism human resource needs by preparing graduates to assume management roles in the industry. The Office of the Board for Undergraduate Studies (OBUS) is spearheading this initiative. In view of this, the UWI has positioned itself to forge ties through the Association of Caribbean Tertiary Institutions (ACTI) with other regional colleges and universities. One of the outputs of this association is to make new product offerings in tourism education and training by way of the introduction of four-year Joint B.Sc. degrees in Hospitality and Tourism Management. To date, the UWI has established five such associations with tertiary institutions in Jamaica, Barbados, Bahamas, Antigua and Trinidad. These associations are commonly referred to as a 2+2 arrangement whereby students are required to complete 2 years at the partnering institution after which they receive an Associate Degree in Hospitality and Tourism Management. The students then have the choice to complete the final 2 years at any one of the three UWI campuses. The first joint degree was launched in 1998 in Jamaica between the UWI and the University of Technology. Other collaborative initiatives have since been undertaken by the UWI with the Barbados Community College, Antigua State College, College of the Bahamas and the Trinidad and Tobago Hospitality and Tourism Institute.

The introduction of this 2+2 arrangement has facilitated the development of areas of specialisation. The pioneering Bachelor's degree in Tourism Management offered at the CHTM since the 1980s has recently been discontinued as of the 2004–2005 academic year. The rationale for this decision lies in the recognition that tourism has now become a much more multifaceted discipline than it was during the 1980s. Based on the Strategic Plan for the CHTM in Nassau, it has been noted that the social, cultural, environmental, economic and technological aspects of tourism must be explored and formally incorporated into the tourism product. Tourism management education should facilitate this integration. The CHTM is ill-equipped to meet this mandate and therefore there is a need to draw on the expertise and resources of all Faculties across the three campuses of the UWI. To this end, the UWI offers five areas of specialisation for students in their final 2 years of the Joint Hospitality and Tourism Management programme to be completed at the requisite campus:

- Hotel and Restaurant Management (Bahamas);
- Food, Beverage and Catering Management (Bahamas);
- Events and Entertainment Management (Trinidad);
- Tourism Product Management (Jamaica and Barbados);
- Eco-tourism Site Management (Trinidad).

In addition to the undergraduate offerings, there are three postgraduate programmes in hospitality and tourism. The UWI Institute of Business in Trinidad offers an MBA with concentration in Tourism Management with around 20% tourism-related courses. In September 1999, the UWI in Jamaica launched the first Masters degree in Tourism and Hospitality Management in the English-speaking Caribbean funded by the European Union. The Universidad de Oriente is the only other tertiary institution in the region with a Master's degree in Tourism Planning/Tourism Marketing/Hotel Management. To date, there are no PhD programmes and no plans are presently afoot to develop such. As indicated earlier in the discussion, the Caribbean region is the most tourism-dependent region in the world (Jayawardena, 2000). Although the provision of hospitality and tourism education and training in general has expanded over the last decade, postgraduate offerings in tourism education in particular have not kept apace with the development of the industry. If the industry is to be released from the strangle hold of foreign dominance then education and training at the postgraduate level must be provided to empower the locals to successfully usher the industry into the future. Equally critical to the industry's success is the hospitality and tourism curricula, which directly impacts on the quality of graduates in terms of knowledge and experiences.

Curriculum Development

In considering the tourism curriculum in Caribbean islands it is the wider socio-cultural, political and economic contexts that take centre stage. Given the critical importance of tourism to these island economies, tourism educators are faced with the challenge of ensuring that the curriculum prepares students to plan, manage and develop tourism in the islands, as well as, responds to the key global and local issues that affect the wider society. In other words, attention must be placed on how the socio-cultural, political and economic issues can be reflected in the vocational and liberal agenda of the tourism curriculum.

In research conducted in the region, Lewis (2002) observed that a number of educational institutes created and designed tourism programmes simply by copying popular programmes from developed countries without taking sufficient account of the needs of the local tourism sector. In agreement, Jayawardena & Cooke (2002) further noted that in so doing, most of these institutions took shortcuts in introducing academically accepted programmes, but as a consequence they lacked industry and market orientation. The pioneering B.Sc. in Tourism Management at the CHTM has come under significant criticism for its ineffectiveness in mirroring the industry's concerns. In a review of the CHTM conducted by the OBUS (2000, p. 4), it was indicated that

> the existing degree and diploma programmes lack distinctiveness and do not play a major leadership role in tourism and hotel management in the region.

The report further noted that although the programme aspires to provide students with a learning experience that will prepare them for leadership positions within Caribbean tourism and hospitality, scrutiny of the existing curriculum does not suggest that this objective can be met through the courses that are offered.

With the introduction of the 2+2 arrangement, which is the new direction for hospitality and tourism education in the region, a number of important lessons have been learnt from the experiences of the CHTM. Chief among them is the pivotal role that an understanding of the needs of the industry and the issues in the wider society play in informing the tourism curriculum. It is with this understanding that in implementing the first Tourism and Hospitality Joint Degree between the UWI and the University of Technology in Jamaica, the needs of the industry in Jamaica and the wider Caribbean was of paramount importance. Quality Consultants, a regional consulting firm was commissioned by the

CTO to conduct a study of tourism training needs in 25 Caribbean countries. The findings of the study revealed that there was a training deficiency in the areas of marketing, leadership, human resource management, finance and accounting, communications, computer literacy and customer relations (Quality Consultants, 1999). These findings as well as other research conducted in the region informed the aims and objectives of the programme in Jamaica and subsequently in Barbados and Trinidad.

In general, the 2+2 programme is designed to meet the needs of the hospitality and tourism market and aim at producing graduates who have:

- Immediate functional competencies;
- An entrepreneurial and innovative attitude to work;
- A good overall knowledge of the business and competitive environments in the industry;
- Strong people skills;
- Language and cultural sophistication, awareness and appreciation;
- A strong sense of social obligations and environmental responsibilities of the industry;
- Strong self-learning orientation;
- Respect for vocational work;
- A self-conscious identification with the industry (problems and solutions) (Jayawardena & Cooke, 2002, p. 53).

The aims of the curriculum clearly emphasise the business and technical skills needed for a career in the industry. This is facilitated in part by the involvement of industry professionals in the programme and the provision of practical training through the internship programme. Minimal attention is given to the liberal aspect of the curriculum where the wider issues in the society become paramount. The consensus among a number of stakeholders that were interviewed in the region is that tourism knowledge in the curriculum for the Caribbean should embrace the whole field of tourism studies, both tourism business studies and non-tourism business studies. The rationale here is that this balance in knowledge enables students to better analyse the tourism phenomenon in the islands and places them in a better position to make informed decisions as potential leaders regarding the growth of tourism. However, non-tourism business studies are not well-represented in the curriculum, which is an issue that needs to be addressed. The course offerings, as itemised in Table 3, reflect the vocational emphasis of the curriculum. The pure management courses are the same at all three UWI campuses but the tourism courses vary from campus to campus.

Quality Assurance in Tourism Programmes

There are several types of institutes in the region offering hospitality and tourism programmes from Community Colleges to Hospitality Institutes to Universities. The quality of the wide-ranging programmes is highly dependent on both the internal and external measures that are put in place. Currently, some institutions have formal quality assurance frameworks that were developed over the last few years. Others are still operating with traditional academic controls such as the use of external examiners. Very few institutions relate to an external quality assurance (QA) agency. This is partly due to the absence of such QA agencies in the Caribbean.

Table 3: Hospitality and Tourism Joint Degree core course offerings.

Year I (Partner institution)		**Year II (Partner institution)**	
HTM100	Introduction to hospitality and tourism	HTM200	Principles of hospitality management
HTM101	Sanitation and nutrition	HTM201	Business communications
HTM104	Culinary arts I	HTM210	Food and beverage management
HTM101	Introduction to computers	HTM212	A la Carte I
		HTM213	Baking I
	English for academic purposes	HTM220	Hotel operations
	Introduction to microeconomics	HTM230	Tourism management
	Introduction to macroeconomics		
	Foreign languages I and II		Introduction to statistics
	Maths for the management sciences		Introduction to psychology
	Sociology for the Caribbean		Introduction to financial accounting
			Foreign language III and IV

Year III (UWI)		**Year IV (UWI)**	
MS 22A	Organizational behaviour	MS 32A	Human resource management
MS 23C	Quantitative methods in management	MS 32B	Industrial relations
MS 20D	Contemporary hospitality and tourism trends	TR 31A	Integrated service management
		TR31C	Tourism planning and policy development
MS 30C	Marketing research	MS 33B	Business strategy and policy
FD course	Foundation course	MS 30D	Marketing planning
MS 26A	Managerial economics	MS 33C	Entrepreneurial studies
MS 28D	Financial management I	TR31B	Tourism destination marketing
MS 21B	Management information systems I		
TR21C	Transportation and travel		
FD course	Foundation course		

According to a report by London and Paul (2003) on QA and Articulation in Hospitality and Tourism Programmes in the Caribbean, it was noted that only seven colleges and two universities in the region have implemented formal quality assurance mechanisms. The common components in the respective quality assurance frameworks include Mission and Purpose, Governance and Administration, Programmes, Human Resources, Student Services, Libraries, Equipment and Supplies. With the 2+2 joint degree programme, in addition to the internal inputs, a few key semi-external inputs are ensured periodically from:

- Joint University Committee;
- Board of Advisors;
- Student Bodies;
- Accreditation Bodies.

The report pointed to three systems that are currently available for the certification of education and training in Hospitality and Tourism including City and Guilds, The American Hotel and Lodging Association Institute (AHLA) and Tourism Education Quality (TEDQUAL). The City and Guilds is an organisation that franchises its curriculum to organisations interested in providing training or education in a wide range of occupations. The AHLA offers professional certifications to individuals who meet specified combinations of formal training, occupational and/or professional experience. The TEDQUAL Certification System of the World Tourism Organisation (WTO) offers tourism education institutions the opportunity to obtain a WTO Certification affirming the validity of their tourism education.

The challenge for the region is the absence of a QA system to ensure and assure quality and efficiency in Hospitality and Tourism programmes. With the introduction of the Caribbean Single Market and Economy and the free movement of skilled persons this quality assurance is an imperative. In view of this, London and Paul (2003) have recommended institutional policy guidelines for quality assurance in hospitality and tourism programmes in the region. They propose that each institution shall develop a set of policy guidelines that respond to both institutional and programmatic standards. Within an institutional context, the standards focus on legal authority; mission, goals and objectives; planning; institutional resources; governance and administration; relations to the public; and institutional assessment. The programme effectiveness revolves around the training staff; training curricula; student support services; training facilities; internships and on-the-job training; and related educational activities. The recommendation is that the Caribbean Tourism Human Resource Council (CTHRC), the training and education arm of the CTO, assumes general oversight of the QA system. The rationale is that such a system will allow for some measure of standardisation and benchmarking, thus facilitating programme articulation and the mobility of persons in the industry throughout the region.

Research in Caribbean Tourism

Despite the importance of tourism to the region, academic research on the industry in the Caribbean is still in its infancy. A recently compiled bibliography on tourism research in the Caribbean shows that more than 80% of research on the sector has been done by private consultants (Boxill & Martin, 1998). Most of this research has either been conducted by or commissioned by the CTO, as one of their principal functions is the collection and dissemination of research and data on the development of the regional industry. The focus of much of this research is statistical in nature with the exception of specially identified areas of research resulting from the needs of industry.

Where academic research is concerned there is a visible lack of intellectual leadership. In the review of the academic staff at the CHTM, the OBUS (2000) noted that scholarly activity does take place and research publications from most staff are at an acceptable level. However, the CHTM staff does not play a leadership role in Caribbean tourism and hospitality research. Boxill (2002, p. 329) observed from his work that Caribbean academics have conducted little systematic research on the sector. One of the reasons he cited for this is that until recently,

> many Carribeanists have been reluctant to see tourism studies as a legitimate discipline, worthy of a place in a regional university.

This sentiment was echoed by other researchers addressing the area of sustainable development in the region who argued,

> researchers have not thought that tourism was sexy or interesting enough to put in the sweat equity to determine whether the policy context is appropriate (Harrison, Jayawardena, & Clayton, 2003, p. 297).

The academic research that has been done on the region has been conducted primarily by international researchers and has tended to focus on the environment and the impacts of tourism development on the culture and the economy. Unlike areas such as agriculture, mining and manufacturing in the region, there is very little scholarship on what Boxill (2002, p. 335) refers to as the "*meta-theoretical issues of tourism*" as the basis for a development strategy in the Caribbean. He goes on further to state that what is needed is

> a body of research on tourism in the Caribbean which focuses on the empirical, theoretical and developmental aspects of tourism as a single development strategy, or part of such a strategy.

The CTO concurs with this suggestion and is currently spearheading the coordination of research activities in tourism among Caribbean social scientists. Some research needs identified by Harrison et al. (2003, p. 297) in their research include:

- Understanding the socioeconomic implications of enclave tourism compared to community tourism;
- Identifying impediments to participation in tourism policy, planning and development and investment on the part of local peoples as well as determining incentives and other means to encourage greater participation in the future;
- Developing case studies of best practices in responsible tourism policy, planning and development.

Government Policy and Structures

One of the fundamental challenges faced by tourism education in the region is the lack of recognition among industry, governments, funding agencies and educational institutions of the strategic importance of human resource development for the long-term success of the region's tourism industry. This is evidenced by the lack of funding and support structures to support the development of tourism education in the region. As John Bell stated in discussing the state of the region's tertiary institutions:

> despite the labour intensive nature of the hotel and tourism sector, and the many technical and practical skills involved, those hotel training schools, invariably government-owned, that do exist within the region are horribly under funded, under-established and in general treated like low grade technical schools for the students who cannot make it into other careers (Bell, 1991).

To date, there is an ongoing need in the region for institutional strengthening in order to allow the schools and programmes to command the respect of their institutions and governments in order to access the necessary resources they need to upgrade their physical plants, their programmes and their faculties.

Notwithstanding this, there are a number of regional organisations that have a vested interest in promoting tourism education and training including the Caribbean Regional Hotel Training Program (CRHTP), which is a training initiative of the Caribbean Hotel Association (CHA). Two regional tertiary educational organisations exist. One, the Association of Caribbean Tertiary Institutions (ACTI) that focuses on regional institutional accreditation among colleges and universities in the region. Second, the Council of Caribbean Hospitality Schools (CHOCHS), which also focuses on a regional programme accreditation scheme and a regional occupational standards and certification scheme.

While there are a number of organisations that play an instrumental role in tourism education in the region, it was noted that there was no one organisation that was appropriate to oversee and coordinate tourism education in the region. With the full endorsement of the CARICOM Heads of government and the support of the regional private sector, the Caribbean Tourism Human Resource Council (CTHRC) was established in 1998. The council's mission is to

> develop and promote a systematic and coordinated approach to human resources planning, research, education and training in Caribbean tourism to meet the demands of a globally competitive tourism environment (Morgan, 2003).

Since its inception, the council has been and continues to be an invaluable support mechanism for both industry and academia and it has been the cornerstone for the continued advancement of tourism education in the region.

Challenges and Future Prospects for Caribbean Tourism Education

As clearly established at the outset of this chapter, the provision of high-quality education and training is the most critical component in the future growth and development of the tourism industry in the Caribbean. Over the years, tourism education and training has come under intense criticism with respect to the governance and operation of the institutions as well as the quality of the programmes. Conlin and Titcombe (1995, p. 67) characterised education in the region as "fragmented, unco-ordinated, and occasionally redundant." The perpetual lack of funding and adequately trained staff has plagued the regional institutions for decades. This has been exacerbated by the failure of the public sector to invest sufficiently in physical facilities. Tertiary tourism educational establishments in the region have also been criticised by a Barbadian accommodation manager as having

> lost touch with the industry that they have been training people for…The industry itself holds many, if not all those establishments almost in disdain….You mean you qualified in UWI, well that doesn't mean you qualified in anything (Lewis, 2002).

The underlying concern here, which is echoed by other researchers (Conlin & Titcombe, 1995; Baum & Conlin, 1994) is the notion that the programmes are not relevant to what the industry requires. In the assessment of the programmes at the CHTM it was noted

> the current curricula are relatively dated and there is little evidence that it has evolved significantly in response to changes in the industry, technological or student environment since 1978 (OBUS, 2000, p. 7).

Notwithstanding the challenges besetting tourism education in the region, there is cause for optimism. Significant progress has been made in addressing several of the challenges identified since the CARICOM Heads of State Summit in 1992. What is particularly encouraging is the extent to which recent developments have been strategic in their scope. The current approach taken to tourism education and training can now be considered a reflection of the degree of importance attached to the industry by regional governments. Initiatives such as the creation of the ACTI and the CTHRC are steps in the right direction. The latter represents a critical milestone in the development and coordination of tourism education in the region as the council continues to support tourism human resource development through its annual Tourism Educators Forum, the Scholarship Foundation Programme and recently, the establishment of a Caribbean Tourism Learning System (CTLS). Some of the key elements of the CTLS include a unified core curriculum for different levels of certification, system for transfer of credits between institutions and student exchange programmes. The UWI has also expressed the desire and demonstrated the ability and will to assume a more active role in tourism education in the region. This is evidenced by the introduction of the 2+2 programme, the greater emphasis on area specialisation in the various campus territories, the change from the CHTM to the Centre for Hospitality Management and moreover, the establishment of an

Institute of Hospitality and Tourism in Mona Jamaica to spearhead and coordinate tourism research activity among social scientists in the region.

Underlying these initiatives is the apparent and timely move towards a seamless system for training and education in the region. For insular, small island states bound by the Caribbean Sea, this is indeed a step in the right direction. Importantly,

> a seamless system for education and training must have at its core accommodation for the diversity of backgrounds, experiences and desires of people from separate yet similar cultures (Hayle, 2002, p. 368).

Moreover, if education is in fact an essential element in the sustainability drive of the tourism industry in the region, then stakeholder involvement in institutional strengthening as well as in the design and improvement in tourism programme curricula is critical (Hing, 1997; Hayle, 2002; Lewis, 2002). Different stakeholder groups in the society indicate the values and needs of the society, they speak for the culture of the destinations and they reveal the general attitude of the locals towards tourism development. Given the importance of tourism to the future development of the Caribbean, academia can no longer adopt a "laidback" attitude to the industry's development. Educational institutions must employ a more creative and proactive approach to tourism education to lead and not follow the industry. This approach hinges on three fundamental actions — greater coordination between educational institutions in the region; more visible intellectual leadership in the form of relevant academic research and; greater stakeholder involvement in decision-making.

References

Baum, T., & Conlin, M. V. (Eds) (1995). *Island tourism: Management principles and practice.* Chichester: Wiley.

Baum, T., & Conlin, M. V. (1994). Comprehensive human resource planning: An essential key to sustainable tourism in island settings. *Progress in Tourism, Recreation and Hospitality Management, 6*, 259–272.

Bell, J. (1991). Caribbean tourism realities. *World Travel and Tourism Review, 1*, 111–114.

Boxill, I. (2002). Challenges of academic research in Caribbean tourism. In: C. Jayawardena (Ed.), *Tourism and hospitality education and training in the Caribbean.* Jamaica: University of the West Indies Press.

Boxill, I., & Martin, P. (1998). *Select Bibliography of Tourism Research in the Caribbean.* Report prepared for the World Bank, Washington DC.

Brathwaite, R. D., Charles, K. R., Hall, J. A., & O'Reilly, A. M. (1990). The status of tourism education in the Caribbean — primary, secondary and tertiary. In: J. A. Hall et al. (Eds) *Tourism education and human resource development for the decade of the 90s: Proceedings of the 1st Caribbean conference on tourism education*, University of the West Indies, Mona, Jamaica.

Caribbean Tourism Organisation (2002). *Caribbean tourism statistical report.* Barbados: Caribbean Tourism Organisation.

Caribbean Tourism Organisation (2004). *List of CTO country members.* Barbados: Caribbean Tourism Organisation.

Conlin, M. V., & Titcombe, J. A. (1995). Human resources: A strategic impertaive for Caribbean tourism. In: M. V. Conlin & T. Baum (Eds), *Island tourism: Management principles and practice*. Chichester: Wiley.

Hall, M., & Page, S. (Eds) (1996). *Tourism in the Pacific: Issues and cases*. London: International Thomson Business Press.

Harrison, L., Jayawardena, C., & Clayton, A. (2003). Sustainable tourism development in the Caribbean: Practical challenges. *International Journal of Contemporary Hospitality Management, 15*(5), 294–298.

Hayle, C. (2002). A seamless education and training system for Caribbean tourism human resource development. In: C. Jayawardena (Ed.), *Tourism and hospitality education and training in the Caribbean*. Jamaica: University of the West Indies Press.

Hing, N. (1997). A review of hospitality research in the Asia Pacific: A thematic perspective. *International Journal of Contemporary Hospitality Management, 9*(1), 5–12.

Jayawardena, C. (2000). An analysis of tourism in the Caribbean. *Worldwide Hospitality and Tourism Trends, 1*(3), 122–136.

Jayawardena, C., & Cooke, M. T. (2002). Challenges in implementing tourism and hospitality joint degrees: The case of the University of the West Indies and University of Technology, Jamaica. In: C. Jayawardena (Ed.), *Tourism and hospitality education and training in the Caribbean*. Jamaica: University of the West Indies Press.

Lewis, A. (forthcoming). Rationalising a Tourism Curriculum for Sustainable Tourism Development in Small Island States: *A stakeholder Perspective, Journal of Hospitality, Sport and Tourism Education*.

London, E., & Paul, D. (2003). *Quality assurance and articulation in hospitality and tourism programmes in the Caribbean*. Barbados: Caribbean Tourism Organisation.

Mather, S., & Todd, G. (1993). *Tourism in the Caribbean*. Special Report No. 455, London: Economist Intelligence Unit.

Morgan, B. (2003). *CTHRC'S goals and objectives*. Barbados: Caribbean Tourism Organisation.

Office for the Board of Undergraduate Studies (OBUS) (2000). *Review of the Centre for Hotel and Tourism Management, Nassau, Bahamas*. University of the West Indies, Mona, Jamaica: Office for the Board of Undergraduate Studies.

O'Reilly, A. M., & Charles, K. R. (1990). Creating a hotel and tourism management programme in a developing country: The case of the University of the West Indies. *Hospitality and Tourism Educator, 18*, 47–49.

O'Reilly, A. M. (2002). Past, present and future of tourism and hospitality education in the West Indies. In: C. Jayawardena (Ed.), *Tourism and hospitality education and training in the Caribbean*. Jamaica: University of the West Indies Press.

Pattullo, P. (1996). *Last Resorts: The cost of tourism in the Caribbean*. London: Cassell.

Quality Consultants Ltd. (1999). *Tourism training for the new millennium*. Barbados: Caribbean Tourism Organisation.

Seward, S., & Spinrad, B. (1982). *Tourism in the Caribbean: The economic impact*. Ottawa: International Development Research Centre.

Chapter 11

China

Wen Zhang and Xixia Fan

Introduction

In China, leisure tourism in modern sense began after China's implementation of economic reform and opening-up in 1978. China's tourism education has developed with the sustained growth of China's tourism industry. Full-time tourism education at schools started in 1978. Before, there was only on-job training with no tourism schools and colleges at all in China. In October 1978, Jiangsu Tourism Technical School (now Nanjing Tourism School), a secondary vocational school, was founded, and in October 1979 China's first tourism institution of higher learning – Shanghai Institute of Tourism – was established. The founding of the two schools was the prelude of the development of full-time tourism education in China. Since then tourism schools and colleges mushroomed throughout the country, such as Sichun Tourism School, Guilin Specialized Tourism Institute, and the Beijing Institute of Tourism. In 1980, the Beijing Second Foreign Language University (now Beijing International Studies University) was transferred to the direct administration of the China National Tourism Administration (CNTA). Since the beginning of 1980s, CNTA appropriated funds for several universities across the country, such as Dalian Foreign Language Institute, Nankai University, and Northwest University, to help establish tourism programs in order to meet the urgent needs for tourism professionals with higher educational background. Entering the 1990s, with the deepening of reform in general higher education of the country, and the growing demand for professionals with higher tourism educational background due to the rapid growth of China's tourism industry, many institutions of higher learning across the country established tourism specialties or programs on the basis of existing relevant programs. China's tourism education entered a period of fast development in the 1990s. Table 1 shows the growth of number of tourism schools and colleges and students from 1990 to 2003.

China's tourism vocational training has also developed from the initial stage of adaptive training of the basic skills for a particular job to a nation-wide network of tourism vocational training and a system managed by three levels, namely the state, local authorities and enterprises. In 2003, 1929.6000 tourism employees attended various kinds of

An International Handbook of Tourism Education
Copyright © 2005 by Elsevier Ltd.
All rights of reproduction in any form reserved
ISBN: 0-08-044667-1

Table 1: Growth of tourism schools & colleges and number of students 1990–2003.

Year	Schools		Students (hundred)	
	No.	**Growth (%)**	**No.**	**Growth (%)**
1990	215		490	
1991	266	23.7	581	18.6
1992	258	−3.0	614	5.7
1993	354	37.2	827	34.7
1994	399	12.7	1021	23.5
1995	622	55.9	1393	36.4
1996	845	35.9	2043	46.7
1997	936	10.8	2215	8.4
1998	909	−2.9	2338	5.6
1999	1187	30.6	2764	18.2
2000	1195	0.7	3279	18.6
2001	1152	−3.6	3428	4.5
2002	1113	−3.4	4170	21.6
2003	1207	8.4	4590	10.1

Source: China National Tourism Administration (1990–2003) Made according to the Yearbook of China Tourism 1991–2003 and China National Tourism Administration (2003) CNTA Statistical Report on China's Tourism Education in 2003.

training courses offered by various levels of tourism education and training institutions, which accounted for 27.9% of the total number of direct employees of the tourism industry in China in 2003 (CNTA, 2003).

Development of Tourism Education in China

Owing to China's reform of its economic system, the development of its tourism education can be divided into three phases.

The first phase was from the founding of New China (in 1949) to the implementation of reform and opening-up (in 1978). In 1950s, in order to meet the needs of friendly exchanges with foreign countries and visits by overseas Chinese, China established two travel services: the Overseas Travel Service (the predecessor of today's China Travel Service) and the China International Travel Service (CITS) to take care of transportation, sightseeing, accommodation and food of foreign visitors and overseas Chinese. During this period, tourism education was mainly on-job training to the front-line employees, such as hotel attendants, coach drivers, interpreters, and guides. The type of training was adaptive training of the basic skills for a particular job given by individual enterprises or organizations (Tao, 1997). At that time, travel and tourism service in China was considered as a part of the reception work of foreign affairs.

The second phase was from 1978 to the mid-1990s. This period saw a strong growth of China's tourism education and the formation of the tourism educational system. During this time, China's tourism was transforming from reception work of foreign affairs to an industry generating economic returns. Both the number of inbound visitors and the income of foreign currency increased substantially. The urgent needs for qualified professionals of the tourism industry because of its development and transformation promoted the rapid growth of tourism education in China. From 1978 when the first tourism secondary school – the Nanjing Tourism School – was founded to 1995, the number of schools and colleges that offered full-time tourism education reached 622, of which 138 were institutions of higher learning and 484 were secondary vocational schools. These schools and colleges had a student body of nearly 140 thousand and offered more that 20 programs which fell into four categories: tour-guiding, management, techniques, and teacher-training (CNTA, 1996). Some of the universities began to offer graduate programs. The quality of tourism education was being improved with the growth of the number of tourism schools and colleges.

Along with the development of full-time tourism education at schools and colleges, part-time education and on-job training also took a big step forward. Television University, night schools, and employee's colleges started to offer tourism programs to grant diplomas or bachelor degrees. Some certified examinations run by local educational departments also included tourism specialities. Besides, a large number of tourism employees were trained every year. On-job training was planned and organized by the state and local tourism administrations and tourism enterprises, and implemented by tourism schools and colleges, training institutions, and human recourse departments of tourism enterprises. Taking 1995 for example, the number of tourism employees who took various training courses amounted to more that 160,000, taking up 15% of the total direct employment of the tourism industry in that year (CNTA, 1996). By 1995, basically all the technical workers, service staff members, and managerial staffs of tourism enterprises had received one kind of training or another. In specific terms, 80,000 employees received before- and on-job training; about 70% of the managerial staff of tourism administrative departments and enterprises (nearly 150,000) received various level of training. Since the adoption of tour-guide certificates, a total of 80,000 tour-guides received training and took examinations, of whom 50,000 were granted certificates (Tao, 1997).

In order to learn from the advanced technologies and management experiences of tourism in developed countries, the state government, local governments, and tourism enterprises sent many people abroad to further their studies since 1980. These people, after they came back, became a key force in tourism education, enterprise operation, and management in China.

The features of this phase were: (1) tourism education and human recourse development became managed according to plans and projections; (2) a nation-wide tourism educational system was formed (see Table 2); (3) a three-level system of tourism part-time education and on-job training system was established with CNTA in charge of policies and regulations concerning training and qualifications of general managers of large tourism enterprises, tourism bureaus of provinces, autonomous regions, and municipalities taking care of the implementation of local training programs and supervising qualifications of medium-level managers of large enterprises and managers of medium and small

Table 2: Structure of tourism education in China.

Tourism Education in China		
Tourism schools and colleges	Secondary tourism education	Secondary vocational school Technical school Secondary school
	Higher tourism education	Diploma Undergraduate Post-graduate
Vocational tourism education	On-job training	Training for certificate Job training
	Part-time education	Secondary Diploma Undergraduate
	Further studies abroad	Degree Non-degree

Source: Revised according to Tao (1997).

enterprises (MSEs), and tourism enterprises carrying out training of their employees; and (4) the educational objectives and graduate placement of tourism schools and colleges were placed in line with the projections and management of the state and local tourism authorities.

The third phase is from the mid-1990s to the present. During this period, China's transformation from a planned economy to a market economy has sped up and China has entered the rank of big tourist countries in the world. In 1996, the inbound tourist arrivals reached five million, foreign exchange income amounted to US$10 billion, and China became one of the top 10 largest tourism destination countries in the world (CNTA, 1997). A system of tourism training has been formed with standardization and institutionalization; training policies and regulations have been well implemented; the scale of training has been enlarged; the contents and methods of training have been innovated with new concepts, skills, and facilities becoming more and more popularly used, such as multimedia facilities, experiential training; and market-oriented management of training are taking shape (Yu, 2003). Since 1995, China has formulated some national and industrial standards, such as the National Standard of Tour-Guiding and the Industrial Standard of Tourist Coach Service. CNTA had designed instructive curricula and syllabuses for training courses of key positions such as general manager and section manager. These national and industrial standards have raised the requirements of standardization for tourism education and training. Education in tourism schools and colleges has entered the stage of quality development since 1995. Tourism schools and colleges are paying more and more attention not only to the improvement of quality, facilities of running programs, and educational reform, but also to researches on the establishment of the system of the tourism discipline, the scientific setup of programs, cooperation and exchanges with tourism institutions abroad, and integration with international practice.

Today's Tourism Education in China

The Profile

By the end of 2003, the number of tourism schools and colleges reached 1207 and the total number of students was 459,000, while in 1990 the number was 215,000 and 49,000 respectively. The annual average increase rate from 1990 to 2003 is 15.6% and 19.4% respectively. From Table 1, we can see that the scale of tourism education has been increasing from 1990. However, the rate of increase has been going down since 1997. This may explain why the expansion of China's tourism education has slowed down as the focus has been shifted to quality improvement and market needs. Besides, every year many people get diplomas or degrees from tourist programs offered by the Television University, night schools, employee's colleges, and certified examinations. It is a pity that up to now there is no official statistics of the number of these people. In 2003, 1,929,600 tourism employees from various parts and sectors of China's tourism industry attended on-job training courses (see Table 3), which accounted for 27.9% of the total number of direct employees of the industry in the same year (CNTA, 2003).

Level and Structure

By 2003, there were 1207 tourism schools and colleges with a student body of 459,000. Of the schools and colleges, 494 were institutions of higher learning with 199,682 students, and 713 were secondary tourism schools with 259,322 students. According to statistics those having diploma programs take up about 70%; those offering undergraduate program account for 35%, and those running postgraduate and doctoral programs occupy 10% (Yang, 2003). Now China's tourism education has formed a pyramid-type program system: from bottom to top are secondary education, diploma programs, undergraduate programs, postgraduate programs, and doctoral programs.

Since the issue of the Regulations on Post Training of Tourist Enterprises by CNTA in 1990, China has established a rationally structured training system of three levels, namely the state, local authorities, and training institutions or tourist enterprises. Each level performs

Table 3: Number of employees in China's tourism industry who took part in training courses in 2003.

Total	1,929,646
Hotels	1,325,440
Travel services	348,808
Tourist attractions	160,248
Tourist coaches	58,366
Administrative departments	19,843
Others	16,941

Source: China National Tourism Administration (2003) CNTA Statistical Report on China's Tourism Education in 2003.

different functions in tourism training, with the national tourism administration in charge of macro management and GM training, local tourism bureaus in charge of local management and the training of medium-level managers, and tourist enterprises in charge of the training of employees. The training of the trainers and the application and operation of training courses are given more attention than before. However, the emphasis of tourism training today is still, generally speaking, on the front-line employees instead of the management.

Regional Distribution

At present, there are tourism schools and colleges and training institutions in all the provinces, autonomous regions, and municipalities (not including Taiwan, Hong Kong, and Macau) in China. The regional distribution of tourism education, in general, complies with the development of tourism in the regions with only a few exceptions. That is, the more developed the regional tourism industry is, the more tourism schools and training institutions are, and the larger the number of students at school and the number of employees trained are in the region. In the western part of China, tourism development is relatively slower than the eastern part. Therefore, the development of tourism education is slower. There is a gap in educational input, teaching force, facilities, and quality between East and West.

Figure 1 shows the proportion of tourism employees, schools and colleges, students at schools and tourism employees trained of each of the 31 provinces, autonomous regions and municipalities in 2002. From Figure 1 we can see that the ups-and-downs of the four lines are, in general, in the same trends with only a few exceptions. The exceptions indicate the lack of co-ordination of tourism education and development of the tourism industry there.

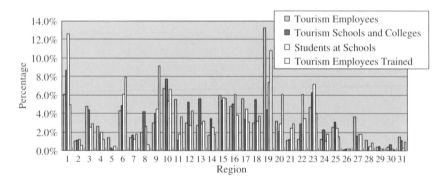

Figure 1: Proportion of tourism employees, schools, students at schools, and tourism employees trained of each of the 31 provinces, autonomous regions, and municipalities in 2002. *Source:* Made according to the Yearbook of China Tourism 2003. 1=Beijing; 2=Tianjin; 3=Hebei; 4=Shanxi; 5=Inner Mongolia; 6=Liaoning; 7=Jilin; 8=Heilongjiang; 9=Shanghai; 10=Jiangsu; 11=Zhejing; 12=Anhui; 13=Fujian; 14=Jiangxi; 15=Shandong; 16=Henan; 17=Hubei; 18=Hunan; 19=Guangdong; 20=Guangxi; 21=Hainan; 22=Chongqing; 23=Sichuan; 24=Guizhou; 25=Yunnan; 26=Tibet; 27=Shaanxi; 28=Gansu; 29=Qinghai; 30=Ningxia; 31=Xinjian.

Program Setup

Tourism schools and colleges in China now offer more than 30 tourism programs at various levels, which cover almost all the areas of the tourism industry. Tourism management and hotel management are two major programs, and new programs have recently been added, such as Property management, convention and event management, design and development of tourism crafts, e-commerce, environmental science, anthropology of tourism, etc.

Major types of programs of institutions of higher learning are:

- *Tour-guiding*: English, Japanese, French, German, Spanish, Arabic, Russian, Italian, etc.
- *Economics and management*: tourism management, hotel management, tourism accounting, hotel finance and accounting, tourism recourse development and management, travel agency management, marketing, etc.
- *Teacher-training*: hotel management, food and beverage management, ethnic culture and tourism, tourism education, etc.
- *Techniques*: food arts, cookery, hotel engineering, etc.

Major types of programs of secondary vocational schools are:

- *Tour-guiding*: Mandarin, tourism English, tourism Japanese, etc
- *Service and management*: hotel service and management, tourist service, secretarial work, accounting, hotel security, public relation and etiquette, etc.
- *Techniques*: Chinese or Western cookery, cookery and kitchen management, Chinese or Western bakery, beauty salon, bartending, hotel electrician, hotel refrigeration, etc.

Teaching and Research

Besides reform and innovation of contents and methods of teaching, tourism schools and colleges also attach importance to researches on the construction of tourism disciplines and programs, especially the construction of the system of tourism science, and the establishment of the key courses. The achieved research results have provided guidance to the program setup and curriculum design of tourism schools and colleges. There are more and more exchanges and cooperation among tourism schools and colleges, and more conferences and seminars on tourism education, which have greatly improved the level of researches at tourism schools and colleges. Many universities have undertaken various kinds of research projects funded by the state, local authorities and big tourist enterprises. The results of these projects are mostly applicable in the development of the tourism industry.

In China, seminars and forum on tourism training at various levels are held every year. By attending these conferences, training managers and trainers can exchange experiences, share new information and new knowledge. This has indirectly helped the improvement of the quality of tourism training.

International Exchanges and Cooperation

There are now more and more exchanges and collaborations between Chinese tourism schools, colleges and training organizations, and tourism education institutions abroad, such as joint efforts in running programs, students and teachers exchanges, students internship abroad, visiting scholars, guest lecturers, and international conferences and seminars. China's tourism industry and educational system have close ties with international tourism organizations such as the World Tourism Organization (WTO), the World Travel and Tourism Council (WTTC), Asia Pacific Tourism Association (APTA), world famous universities such as Cornell University and the Educational Department of embassies in China.

Areas that Need Improvement

Quality and innovation of tourism education need improvement (Du, 2003; Yu, 2003; Wang & Wang, 2001; Liu & Bi, 2001).   Because of the great demands for tourism talents in China, China's tourism education has adopted a development pattern of quantity expansion since 1980s, especially in the 1990s. However, such expansion has resulted in the duplication of educational input and repeated investment. As a result, efficiency can scarcely be achieved; the limited educational input of the country cannot be fully utilized; and the return of educational investment stays low. The basic level of tourism training remains simple operational training, and the training for the management level is mainly post-qualification training of what should be known. Training that cultivates creativeness, improves overall quality, and provides frontier information is not popular. China lacks influential brand-name schools, programs and training institutions in its tourism educational system.

The objectives of tourism education and training at various levels are not clearly identified (Yu, 2003).   The present problems are: (1) Undergraduate education is too theory-oriented. As the tourism industry is an applied and comprehensive industry, the undergraduate education of tourism management should combine theory with practice, and get closely integrated with the practice of the industry. Teaching based on textbooks and theory can mean that students find it difficult to adapt to the development of the industry. (2) There is not much difference between diploma education and undergraduate education. (3) Vocational education can not be called "vocational", but is more like general education. Vocational education should be centered on training of ability and for job posts. However, teaching at some vocational schools is classroom centered and little attention is paid, so their graduates are not qualified for posts they were trained for. (4) Training programs lack clear objectives. Some training programs are set up not because of what is needed, but because of what teachers/trainers are available. Besides, there is a tendency of "following suit" in tourism training, i.e. setting-up training programs as what others are doing despite what is really needed.

An efficient evaluation system is necessary (Fu & Wu, 2004; Qiu, 2004; Yu, 2003). Efficient evaluation is an important step for the improvement of quality. However, many schools lack efficient evaluation systems, or where these do occur, careful studies of the evaluations and subsequent improvement. Some training institutions do not even conduct evaluations of training courses. This has greatly affected the quality of education and training.

Teaching methods and textbooks need improvement (Yu, 2003; Yang, 2003; Zhang & Gu, 2003; Wang & Wang, 2001; Xu, 1999; Yuan, 1999).   There are quite a number of institutions, and their teachers who still follow the traditional "classroom-centered" teaching method, i.e. teachers give lectures and students take down notes. There is not much interaction between the trainer and trainees, and there are few applications of modern facilities. Examinations are based on the content of textbooks and notes. This kind of teaching method may result in students' good memorization of theories, but does not encourage competence in solving problems or creativeness and originality. However, the development of the tourism industry needs its employees to acquire skills such as information processing, interpersonal communication, problem-solving, etc.

Every year there are now large numbers of imported, translated, and domestically compiled textbooks published in China. However, duplications are often seen in imported and translated textbooks, while some domestically compiled textbooks can hardly reflect the recent theoretical innovation and development in the tourism industry or practices and operation in tourism management. To some extent, the lack of quality textbooks and reference materials has restricted the improvement of the educational level of the tourism programs. Furthermore, the textbooks of some tourism schools and colleges have remained unchanged for many years, and the contents are already out-of-date. Some of the textbooks for training courses have not reflected new features in training and consist mainly of theories without case analysis, interactions, or workshops. The widely used teaching methods of distance education and internet education are not popular in tourism education and training.

Generally speaking, in curriculum design of tourism education, there is a tendency to emphasize enterprise management while neglecting industrial management; emphasize hotel management while neglecting attraction management; emphasize operation while neglecting marketing and promotion; emphasize technology while neglecting culture, and emphasize theory while neglecting practice. There is no systematic consistency between before- and after-job education in terms of objectives, curricula, and textbooks.

Qualified teachers are needed (Qiu, 2004; Yu, 2003; Wang & Wang, 2001). Because of the short history and rapid growth of China's tourism education, lack of qualified teachers for both school education and training has become an obvious issue. The majority of the teachers and trainers currently involved in tourism education come from other disciplines (foreign languages, economics, history, geography, etc.), and their educational background varies greatly. What's more, some of them have no working experiences in the tourism industry or lack understanding of the practice of the industry either at home or abroad. Moreover, compared with the continuing occurrence of new phenomena and issues of the rapid growth of China's tourism industry, the knowledge structure of teachers in tourism education seems obsolete, the contents of teaching out-of-date and method of education outmoded. Therefore, the improvement of the expertise of tourism educational professionals is a big challenge of China's tourism education.

Student internship needs to be enhanced and close ties with the industry need to established (Zhong, 2004; Zhang & Gu, 2003; Du, 2003). The aim of tourism education is to train high-quality professionals for the industry, so tourism education should attach great importance to practical training. Currently, in China's tourism education, the proportion of practical training and internship in the curriculum is relatively larger in secondary vocational schools because their main objectives are training front-line employees for the industry. In most of the tourism institutions of higher learning, the proportion is far from adequate. Some schools only arrange 1 or 2 months of internship for 4-year undergraduate programs and 3-year master programs, while some have no arrangement for students' internship. Therefore, their graduates can hardly meet the requirements of the industry. The digression of tourism education and the practice of the industry has led to the situation that tourism enterprises are not willing to hire college graduates for they can hardly fit into the posts after graduation. Owing to tight budgets, most tourism schools are unable to construct teaching labs and internship bases on the one hand, and have no close connection with the industry to provide enough opportunities for students to do internship on the other hand.

Development Trends and Prospects of Tourism Education in China

According to the prediction of WTTC, the number of employees of China's tourism industry will increase at a speed of 3.2% per year recently, with an annual average growth of more than one million (Wang & Wang, 2001). Beijing Tourism Administration (2001) has projected that in 2010 the total number of employees of the Beijing tourism industry will reach 650,000 (currently, 346,000), and managerial personnel of medium and advanced levels will come up to 70,000 (currently about 30,000). These figures show that China's tourism education has an arduous task in fostering tourism professionals for the 21st century. China's entry into the WTO has brought about both opportunities and challenges. The new situation has set up new and higher qualifications to tourism professionals and talents. Now there is still a big gap between China's tourism education and the world level. In order to get integrated with the world practice, China needs to import advanced teaching methods and textbooks from abroad and to create more opportunities to send more people to study abroad.

At present, the mechanism of running tourism schools in China is uniform. Currently, the majority of the tourism schools and colleges in China are public. China's integration with world practice and its tourism development needs a diversified system of running tourism schools. The central government should enact policies to encourage tourist enterprises, public organizations, international and domestic investors to run tourism schools or programs. Tourism schools and training institutions should make efforts to run joint programs and training courses with tourist enterprises and international organizations. The development of China's tourism needs tourism institutions to get a close connection with the practice of the industry by offering tailor-made training programs, participating in consultation, and management of tourism enterprises. In turn, institutions can gain financial support from the industry and to form a win-win relationship with the business (Du, 2003). In addition, reform is necessary for China's tourism education to establish a more rational teaching mode of an integration of education as the core base, technical training as the practical link and research as the development direction. Such an educational system can optimize the allocation of resources and adapt to the law of market (Ma & Shu, 1997).

Now the mode of teaching of China's higher tourism education is transforming from "knowledge-imparting" to "ability-cultivating", and will ultimately get to "quality-training" (Yuan, 1999). The present program setup and curriculum system will be adjusted according to the educational goal of "solid foundation and high adaptability". Tourism

schools should speed up their reform in teaching methods and contents, increase the proportion of courses teaching practical skills, promote case method of teaching, and popu-
larize modern technologies in teaching. Emphases should be given to cultivate students'
creativity. Great development will be seen in areas like continuing education, multimedia
education, internet education, and distance education.

The certifying of qualifications is an important measure for human recourse development in many countries. Since 1989 and the introduction of tour-guide certificates, China
has implemented certifying hotel front-line employees and tourist enterprise managers.
Now over 60% of the employees of these posts have certificates. However, with the arrival
of the information economy and the popularization of technologies, the period of renew-
ing knowledge is getting shorter and shorter. From the perspective of industrial needs and
personal growth, continuing and lifelong education will be an important part of China's
tourism education (Chen & Yu, 2004).

With the rapid growth of China's tourism, the development trend of its tourism education is to establish a talent-fostering mechanism integrated with world practice and adapting to Chinese characteristics and market needs: to set up a tourism education and training
system of school and college education: certifying of qualifications, for after-job training
and technical appraisement, and to develop lifelong, tailor-made and brand-name education. China's tourism education should provide a solid foundation of human recourse for
the development of its tourism industry.

To be in line with China's position as a big tourist country, tourism education on a
national-wide scale is needed. A comprehensive tourism education network should be
established to promote education of awareness, knowledge and aesthetics of tourism, to
guide tourism, and to create a good environment for travel and tourism.

The founding of the Tourism Education Association subordinated to the China Tourism
Association will promote the improvement of the quality of tourism education, research
and textbooks, enhance exchanges between tourism institutions, enterprises and government departments, and create a favorable environment for the upgrading of the academic
position of the tourism discipline.

References

Beijing Tourism Administration (2001). *Projection of the development of Beijing tourism human
    resource*. Beijing: China Travel and Tourism Press.
Chen, Z., & Yu, C., (2004). Ten relations between development and management of tourism talents,
    Tourism Tribune. 2004 Special Issue of Tourism Education, 6–9.
China National Tourism Administration (2003). *CNTA statistical report on China's tourism educa-
    tion in 2003*. Unpublished government document.
China National Tourism Administration (1990–2003). *The yearbook of China tourism 1990–2003*.
    Beijing: China Travel and Tourism Press.
Du, J., (2003). Reforms and development of higher tourism education in China. In: G. Zhang, X. Wei &
    D. Liu (Eds), *Green book of China's tourism development 2002–2004* (pp. 221–230). Beijing:
    Social Scientific Literature Press.
Fu, H., & Wu, Y., (2004). Views on the course contents of tourism programs, *Tourism Tribune*. 2004
    Special Issue of Tourism Education, 31–34.

Liu, M., & Bi, D. D., (2001). Problems and measures of China's tourism education and training. *Journal of Adult Education of Hubei University, 19*(5), 9–12.

Ma, Y., & Shu, B., (1997). A research on the 'trinity' model for tourism education, *Tourism Tribune.* 1997 Special Issue of Tourism Education, 42–45.

Qiu, Y., (2004). A summary of researches on tourism education in China, *Tourism Tribune.* 2004 Special Issue of Tourism Education, 173–175.

Tao, H., (1997). On the development stages of tourism education in China, *Tourism Tribune.* 1997 Special Issue of Tourism Education, 6–9.

Wang, W., & Wang, Y., (2001). On the development of China's higher tourism education. *Journal of Jinggangshan Normal Institute, 22*(6), 51–54.

Xu, C., (1999). A discussion on the curriculum of undergraduate tourism program. *Journal of Guilin Tourism Institute*. 1999 Supplementary Issue of Tourism Education, 143–145.

Yang, Z., (2003). On China's higher tourism education, www.cthy.com, 2003-4-9.

Yu, C., (2003). *Development of tourism human resource*. Beijing: China Travel and Tourism Press.

Yuan, S., (1999). Development and reform of China's tourism education in the 21st century. *Tourism Tribune*. 1999 Special Issue of Tourism Education, 39–42.

Zhang, W., & Gu, H., (2003). Rethink of China's tourism education and research, *China Tourism Hotel, 15*(6), 53–55.

Zhong, Z., (2004). Establishing an educational bi-system and fostering 'applied' tourism management talents. *Tourism Tribune*. 2004 Special Issue of Tourism Education, 22–26.

Chapter 12

East Africa

Melphon Mayaka

Introduction

The 20th and the early part of the 21st century have been associated with very rapid changes in virtually all aspects of life. Internationalisation of trade and, therefore, gradually the labour markets are trends that seem to affect all economic sectors and tourism is no exception. Consequently, there are numerous challenges confronting the human resource development landscape be it at national or regional level. Tourism training and education in particular thrives in a global context where traditional priorities of predictability and stability (in line with Newtonian–Cartesian paradigm) seem to give way to greater flexibility, adaptability and a high demand for transferability of skills across borders and across sectors.

Tourism is by its very nature a global phenomenon. There therefore needs to be co-operation and collaborative initiatives if tourism training and education systems are to remain relevant in meeting the needs of both industry and the student. Co-operation is necessary both in the sourcing of students and the provision of training and education. In the case of developing countries, co-operation and collaboration among institutions and governments may help to achieve economies of scale and are potentially efficient ways of utilising meagre economic resources. Consequently, the Economic Commission for Africa (ECA), in its outline of policy objectives, recognises the need for regional co-operation to ensure efficient utilisation of the continent's tourism resources. This emphasises the salient need for co-operation among African countries at all levels in the development of attractions, capital infrastructure, natural and human resources to serve the needs of the domestic and international inter-regional and intra-regional tourism sectors. For this regionalism goal to be realised, the small sub-regional groupings are vital. Regional integration presents great opportunities for partnerships and linkages both at inter-government and institutional levels.

The case for co-operation in the East African sub-region is particularly strong for a number of reasons: the three countries namely Kenya, Uganda and Tanzania have had very strong historical ties since the colonial period; they rely very heavily on nature-based tourism; and their tourism is inbound. Thus, the structure and nature of tourism systems are

An International Handbook of Tourism Education
Copyright © 2005 by Elsevier Ltd.
All rights of reproduction in any form reserved
ISBN: 0-08-044667-1

fundamentally similar. In addition, domestic and intra-regional tourism movements are necessary to cushion the sub-region from the turbulence that has characterised the traditional source markets of Europe and North America in recent years. In this chapter, the progress in tourism and training and education within East Africa is examined and the prospects for co-operation discussed. A number of co-operative arrangements are proposed including harmonisation of qualifications, collaborative curriculum development, research, discussions and exchange of ideas, joint publications, information dissemination, as well as technical and student exchanges. The chapter recognises the different levels of co-operation and collaboration and strongly advocates greater involvement at the institutional level.

The historical experience of the countries of East Africa can perhaps provide lessons for regional integration and co-operation in the African continent as a whole (Sindiga, 1999). The East African Community (EAC), bringing together Kenya, Uganda and Tanzania, was formed soon after the independence of the three countries around 1963 and became the most promising community in sub-Saharan Africa boasting a common currency, well-coordinated infrastructure, harmonised economic policies, common institutions and labour mobility (World Bank, 1989). Consequently, there was easy tourism flow within the region. The EAC, however, collapsed in 1977, largely due to ideological and political differences between leaders of the member countries and mistrust resulting from perceived imbalance in the share of economic benefits.

Co-operation in tourism in East Africa can be traced back to about 1938 when a common tourism policy within the region began to emerge (Sindiga, 1999). This led to the formation of the East African Publicity Association (EAPA). A Governors' conference that took keen interest in developing tourism followed. It is this conference that paved the way for a regional tourism conference in 1947. This chain of events culminated in the formation of a quasi-government organization with the role of developing and promoting tourism to the region, the East African Tourist Travel Association (EATTA) incorporated in 1948. Tour operators and others were able to operate tours freely in any of the three countries as a result of this framework. Soon after the independence of the three countries, however, cracks began to appear in the system with some members complaining of gaining less (Dieke, 1998). This was soon followed by the collapse of EATTA in 1965. All collaborative efforts and all forms of co-operation in tourism came to an end following the EAC's collapse in 1977. Tanzania even closed its borders with Kenya. There are now deliberate measures in place aimed at reviving the EAC albeit with new understanding between members.

The treaty for the reestablishment of the EAC was signed on 30th November 1999. This provides new challenges and great opportunities for the region in as far as regional co-operation is concerned (Kamar, 2003). Article 115 (1) of the treaty on tourism, in particular, outlines (in part) the undertaking of the member states to develop a collective and co-ordinated approach to the promotion and marketing of quality tourism into and within the EAC. Kamar further cites the need to establish a regional framework for co-operation in such areas as education and human resources development. In fact, section (2) of the same article is even more specific in suggesting that the member countries 'harmonise professional standards of agents in the tourism and travel industry within the community' (EAC, 2002, p. 86). Within this policy framework, three 'centres of excellence' for tourism training and education have been identified: Soroti Flying School in Uganda, Kenya Utalii

College in Kenya (KUC) and College of African Wildlife Management (CAWM), Mweka, in Tanzania (Kamar, 2003).

A major lesson to be learned from the East African experience of co-operation is that co-operation at the inter-governmental level relies very heavily on the political will of the governments of the day. It is the view of the author that there are regional socio-anthropological factors, the discussion of which is beyond the scope of this chapter, that impact upon the politics of the region and, indeed, sub-Saharan Africa (see Hofstede, 1980). Given these anthropological and political contexts, co-operation between institutions provides a quicker means for realising common goals for tourism. Such co-operation, and in the context of the present chapter, among tourism training and educations institutions, may hasten and inspire greater co-operation at the intergovernmental level. Metaphorically, this may be likened to friendly relationships which often develop between parents of children whose sense of camaraderie is developed either at play or at school.

In order for meaningful regional cooperation in tourism to take place, there has to be recognition of two equally important levels (Figure 1): intergovernmental co-operation and sectoral-technical co-operation at institutional level (Dieke, 1998). Sectoral co-operation can be realised through existing professional associations and bodies such as African Hotel Association (AHA), Association of Hotel Schools in Sub-Saharan Africa (AHSSA), African Tourist Training Centre Association (ATTCA), African Travel and Tour Operations Association (ATTOA) and, as is being proposed in the current chapter, through institutions of learning such as colleges and universities. As has been stated previously, co-operation at one level can easily lead others. As depicted in Figure 1 there is a likelihood of closer bonds and ties between two institutions than say two states. The bonds so formed can strengthen the relationship at the intergovernmental level. The result is a network of institutions and other stakeholders.

The lesson from the EAC is that the strong intergovernmental commitment can only exist in an environment of even stronger ties and linkages at the institutional level. Lack of these strong ties at institutional level may have contributed to EAC's failure.

Regional co-operation in tourism education and training can be a means of gaining competitive advantage for the entire sub-region through the development of the appropriate human resource pool. Arguably, a competent workforce could be a means of achieving resilience in the wake of region-specific turbulence in international inbound tourism as has

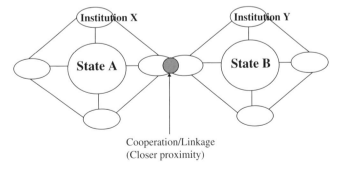

Figure 1: Regional co-operation in tourism at two levels.

been experienced in recent times (Mayaka & King, 2002). It has to be borne in mind that the tourism industry in Kenya, for example, has in the past attributed its success to strong private sector participation (Ikiara, 2001). Co-operation at institutional level could also be a means of forming linkages with other regions as well as enhancing existing ones. Without ignoring competition of individual countries for the tourist dollar, it is reasonable to think that emergence of the EAC as a trading block also engenders a vibrant local market that individual firms and enterprises could tap into. Regional tourism is not only desirable but also necessary for Africa (Dieke, 1998, p. 30). Currently, there is no co-operation on the ground in tourism, let alone tourism training and education.

Global Context for Co-operation in Tourism Training and Education

There is debate currently going on about the nature of tourism education and the emerging trans-national content of curriculum and the global distribution of graduates (Richards, 1998). Within this context, the European Union (EU) sponsored ERASMUS educational exchange, for example, has seen student exchanges between participating universities and exchange agreements between them. The SOCRATES programme initiated through ATLAS in 1996 shifted from small subject networks to contracts between institutions. However, within this institutional understanding there were created European Thematic Networks (ETN) bringing together groups of academics single subject areas together on a European-wide basis to discuss issues of common interest.

The stated aims of the ETNs were 'to define and develop a European dimension' within a given academic discipline through co-operation between university facilities or departments and academic associations (Richards, 1998). Such co-operation could lead to curriculum development which will have lasting impact across a range of institutions. Within the 1996–1997 academic year there were over 400 expressions of interest in the first call for proposals for ETNs. The process of co-operation and collaboration first began with discussions between educational institutions in consultations with industry. The addition of the 'European dimension' to the body of knowledge not only illustrates the similarities in tourism supply and demand within the region but also highlights the differences. This European experience could provide a model for co-operation and collaboration between institutions within the East African region.

Holloway has observed that there is increasing collaboration between industry and educationalists (in Richards, 1998). In addition, governing bodies of colleges are increasingly dominated by representatives from industry. There is also technology transfer from industry, e.g. in the case of small island nations' institutions in the Pacific benefiting from relationships with international airlines, e.g. Qantas Airlines (King, 1996). The biggest challenge in this scenario is the tendency for industry to have less concern for general skills that are transferable between organisations than job-specific skills serving the technical needs of individual tourism sectors. More importantly, however, this collaboration with industry would bring about much greater benefits through the synergy created in regions from resulting networks and partnerships.

An education system must be relevant to the needs and contexts of its learners. Accordingly, a regional approach to co-operation in tourism training and education has two key advantages. First, it achieves an important goal of being international (thus ensuring mobility of the learner). Second, such co-operation is likely to ensure that the curriculum is context-related (Cooper, 2000). Internationalisation of the industry and the related training and education is only a dream if the learners cannot realise the key goal of being able to find the relevant employment. It is, thus, easy to see how a student from the South East Asia region is likely to find a job from within any country in the sub-region (international nature) since the nature and structure of the tourism industry within the region bears resemblance (a regional context). This is more feasible than say a tourism student from East Africa (having studied all his life in the same region) finding a job in Europe (a somewhat alien context).

In the East African region, linkages between industry, educationalists and community would be in line with the sustainable tourism initiatives aimed at ensuring that tourism benefits local communities (Kamar, 2003). Moi University's 'Division of Tourism' (which brings together three departments of Hospitality, Travel and Tour Operations Management and Tourism Management) for example, has recently made attempts to work with local operators and communities in Western Kenya to identify and revive pro-poor tourism projects (27 have been identified). This form of linkage with the local economy is one of the best ways to enhance local economic benefits. From a systems' perspective, a co-operative arrangement between Moi and another university, for example, is likely to have a flow on effect to linked local communities.

In this age of knowledge-based economies, local community links with universities are vital. These communities are likely to benefit from collaborative research and through technical assistance offered by the latter. Success of collaborative initiatives where local communities work closely with university departments have been observed to be effective means of community capacity building (Jeffries, 2001; Aisensen, Bezanson, Frank, & Reardon, 2002). Jeffries cites relevant examples of local university/community collaboration in UK, France and USA. In one such example, Coventry Warwickshire Promotions is a not-for-profit destination marketing company whose board has representatives from three universities, the local chamber of commerce and tourist trade interests. These sorts of linkages are in line with the vision of regional integration in East Africa aimed at creating wealth, alleviating poverty and raising the living standards and quality of life of its people (Kamar, 2003).

Kenya

Up to the 1960s there was no tourism education policy in Kenya (Sindiga, 1999). The tourism businesses were hitherto run by expatriates. Tourism and hospitality education had its debut in Kenya in 1969 through the introduction of a hotel management course at the Kenya Polytechnic. The hotel management focus of this course was obviously narrow and so there was still need for broader training and education to cover other areas in tourism. This led to the establishment of KUC as a joint project between the Swiss and Kenyan governments in 1975.

KUC now offers courses for the accommodation, travel and tour operating sectors. The college admits both local students and students from 40 other countries (Sindiga, 1994). Due to its limited capacity, KUC has not been able to meet all training needs. This has led to the proliferation of middle level institutions both public and private which now number up to 119 in the whole country (Mayaka, 1999; Mayaka & King, 2002; Sindiga, 1996). Unfortunately, the private provision seems to be so heavily commercialised that there have been calls for regulation and a harmonisation of both curricula and qualifications (Sindiga, 1994; Mayaka, 1999; Mayaka & King, 2002). Efforts are underway to establish some mechanism for standardisation and harmonisation. Tourism training and education is the only major means of indigenisation of the management and ownership of tourism businesses. Such indigenisation, it is argued, will increase employment within the industry by reducing the level of foreign exchange leakage (Mayaka, 1999; Sindiga, 1999).

Continuing training and education in tourism is lacking and is currently limited to refresher and management development courses normally run over 2-week periods at KUC. This is a matter of great concern, especially since a vast majority of those working in the industry (including high-level managers) still remain untrained (Mayaka & King, 2002).

Tourism training and education at university level was initiated at Moi University's Chepkoilel Campus in 1992 following a presidential committee report that decried a lack of conceptual and high-level management skills in the existing training and education (Republic of Kenya, 1991). Other universities such as Maseno University, Kenyatta University, Nairobi University and now Egerton University have followed suit with introduction of either departments in tourism and related areas (e.g. hospitality and institutional management) or tourism subjects within traditional discipline-based departments such as Geography, Business, History, etc. The African Virtual University based at Kenyatta University also offers some tourism subjects via distance education while United States International University (USIU) has a department of hospitality and tourism within the Faculty of Business. Moi University is the foremost institution, having three specialised departments namely Tourism (policy and planning), Travel and Tour Operations Management and Hospitality and Hotel Management and now offers degrees up to master level and is in the process of developing a Ph.D. programme. There is potential for establishing a school of tourism, travel and hospitality studies at Moi University.

Despite the apparent advancement in tourism training and education in Kenya, there are still big gaps in a number of areas. Tourism training and education is uncoordinated as there is still no one body that oversees all the activities. Each institution offers what it deems fit for the industry sometimes in a parochial way. In addition, it is a matter of concern that there may not be enough qualified staff in many of the institutions. Educate the educator programmes such as the one developed by the World Tourism Organization (WTO) (WTO/Surrey, 1996) would be of great benefit. A national tourism training and education strategy in line with national tourism policies has been proposed (Mayaka, 1999).

Tourism research is still lacking, partly due to lack of focus, motivation and even funding. There is room for collaboration of institutions of higher learning through research and exchanges in seminars and conferences. Similar initiatives elsewhere, for example the Council of Australian University Tourism and Hospitality Educators (CAUTHE), could provide models for the East African region (King, 1996). The only conference that brings scholars and researchers in tourism together is one annually organised by Moi University's Department of Tourism (MUDOT), which is yet to acquire greater publicity and gain status as a national or regional event. It is the author's view that institutions could mutually benefit through exchanges even on methods of delivery. The application of problem-based learning (PBL) which has taken root in MUDOT and its sister departments is, for example, unique in tourism-related studies. Its effectiveness and challenges could provide useful insights to other institutions through such exchanges.

In countries that attach a lot of importance to tourism, education is not only offered at colleges and universities, but in schools (especially at high school level) (see King, 1996). This component is lacking in Kenya. Teaching tourism and hospitality in school would have an added advantage of increasing general public awareness, especially of its benefits and impacts and the role of the host community in the inbound tourism systems. This would also increase the prospects of students developing early interest in tourism as a field of study. The end result may be the attraction of the best brains into this field of study and, therefore, the enhancement of research and scholarship in tourism and hospitality. Coupled with this, is the need to extend basic education to include skills that are beyond numeracy and literacy skills (which are important but not the only ones relevant in modern society) as a means of capacity building (Esbin, 2002). Given the role that basic education plays in an individual's life, it is important and in the best interest of any nation to consider tourism-related skills in this formative pedagogic experience in its education system.

Tanzania

Tourism training and education in Tanzania is relatively less developed (when compared with her northern neighbour Kenya). The National College of Tourism in Dar-es-Salaam, established in 1969, offers certificate courses in the areas of hospitality namely: food production, front office operations, food and beverage sales and services as well as house-keeping and laundry. Plans are underway to expand the college through a donor-funded project. The Hotel and Tourism Training Institute at Arusha also offers technical training under a UNDP/ILO assisted project. Management training and education in tourism and related areas is hitherto obtained in Kenya or in Europe (URT/ NOVIJVP, 1995). There have also been proposals to the University of Dar-es-Salaam to develop management modules in tourism and hospitality but this has not happened yet.

Tanzania's success story has been the CAWM at Mweka. The story of this college (popularly known as Mweka College) is particularly important as it depicts just what partnerships and collaborations can achieve. It is to be noted that, although this is not a tourism or hospitality college, it fits into 'related areas' and so is included in the current chapter since tourism in East Africa is predominantly wildlife based.

The CAWM was established in 1963 after the chief game wardens and directors of national parks from Tanzania and Kenya along with representatives of ministries concerned with wildlife management, a representative from the then East African Common Services Organisation (EACSO, a precursor of EAC) and a senior game warden from the then Northern Rhodesia (Zambia) laid down the necessary formal framework (CAWM, 1995). The college received substantial funding from donor governments and agencies including: USAID, Frankfurt Zoological Society, African Wildlife Leadership Foundation, Federal Republic of Germany, British Government, Rockefeller Brothers Fund and Ford Foundation. The Government of Tanzania provided the land and buildings among other things. The most remarkable feature of Mweka College is that its composition is very evidently regional and includes states and institutions. EACSO and later the EAC, the East

African University (the only one at the time) were represented. Kenya and Uganda still have representation in the 15 member Governing Board by virtue of having students studying in the college.

Mweka College has maintained a regional outlook both in its organisation and approaches to curriculum development and delivery. Apart from receiving 47% of its students from the sub-region it deliberately recruits teaching staff from the other East African countries. It also hosts conferences and seminars that are regional in nature. An interesting observation is the fact that the Principal is also a member of the Governing Board of the National College of Tourism.

Uganda

Of the three East African countries, Uganda is a relative newcomer in tourism training and education, which could be attributed to its turbulent political history, particularly in the 1970s and the 1980s. The Crested Crane Hotel & Tourism Training Institute in Jinja (Uganda's second largest and most industrial town) was established by government statute in 1994 to offer the highest level of professional qualifications and standards for the tourism industry in Uganda. Another public college, Buganda Royal Institute offers diplomas in Tourism Management and in Hotel and Institutional Catering. There are now several private colleges.

The first tourism and related course at university level was offered at Nkuba University in Makerere in 1994. Makerere University's Faculty of Business Management also offers diplomas in leisure and hospitality management which includes modules in tourism while Kampala International University offers diplomas in both tourism and catering and hotel management. There is a growing interest in tourism and hospitality studies as a whole.

Prospects, Directions and Issues

The foregoing analysis of the development of tourism training and education in the three East African countries underlines the fact that the three countries are at different levels of economic progress and hence tourism development. According to the World Bank, Kenya is designated as 'developing country' while Tanzania and Uganda are 'least developed' (WTO, 2002). There are prospects of each benefiting from each other's experiences. This could, for example, be easily facilitated through exchanges of academics, students and flow of knowledge across the region. The prospects of such exchanges have even been made easier by changes in the political landscape brought about by the realisation of the need to form a regional economic block.

The absence of travel restrictions for citizens of the three countries, for example, means that students from Tanzania can have access to higher, yet cheaper education in Kenya and not Europe or North America as has been the case. Flow of knowledge could also be facilitated through conferences and institutional networks. Harmonisation of qualifications and collaborative curriculum development could be achieved through subject and thematic networks cited above. This is particularly important if quality standards in tourism products and services have to be harmonised across the three member countries. The differences (e.g. cultural) should also be highlighted in this context. A tourist on a circuit that includes Kenya and Uganda should not realise disparity in the level of service quality across the border. Labour mobility within the region is desirable and could be realised as a result of such collaborative initiatives.

It is also clear from the above that tourism training and education, except perhaps in Kenya's case, has been dominated by craft/technician and middle level colleges. However, as the industry in the three countries is maturing, there is increasing need for managers at strategic level for the industry and its component sectors. There is still little integration in the individual countries between industry and training providers. This integration has to be sought along with the establishment of linkages and other collaborative initiatives between institutions. There are also prospects of co-operation in forming the body of knowledge as well as delivery of visitor education, especially since the countries share similar natural as well as cultural and historical heritage.

Tourism training and education has always attracted international organizations such as WTO, ILO and the donor community interest. There are prospects of exploring this further in order to raise the level and quality of tourism training and education in the region. Raising the quality of training and education increases the possibility of exporting the same by way of receiving students from other parts of the continent if not other parts of the world.

There are issues that have to be addressed in each country and ultimately in the entire region. The issue of supply versus demand (e.g. graduate and post graduate) has to be addressed. There is no simple way to deal with this except through careful manpower planning in each country. However, the issue strengthens the case for co-operation and collaboration as there may not be, for example, a need for duplication of courses that are offered by another institution across the border if capacity exists. The issue of narrowing the gap between industry and providers is critical. Given the different levels of development, there are different expectations in co-operation and collaboration initiatives. There is need for harmonising policies and legislation to avoid mistrust and to provide the necessary broader legal and policy framework for co-operation and collaboration. Institutions entering into collaboration and co-operation have to have well thought through agreements, contracts or memoranda of understanding to avoid misunderstandings.

Conclusion

The chapter has highlighted the need for co-operation and collaboration in the teaching of tourism within the East African region. This is in view of the fact that the countries share a common cultural, natural and historical heritage. There have been attempts to foster such co-operation before but this succumbed to various challenges, particularly at the political, inter-governmental level. It has been noted that there is now a new political landscape emerging and this is favourable for co-operation in tourism. The chapter, however, argues that strong and sustainable co-operation can only be achieved through strong institutional networks and linkages.

Collaborative and co-operation efforts can be directed in the areas of exchanges: exchange of knowledge; student exchanges; staff and technical exchanges as well as exchange of ideas through conferences, discussions and even joint publication. There is a need for harmonisation of standards and curricula in order to achieve harmony in the level of quality of tourism products and services in the region. This harmonisation can be at subject and theme levels and should highlight differences in the countries as each is unique. Harmonisation would reduce waste through duplication, since there is no point in starting a course that is being offered in another institution which has enough capacity to accommodate students from the region. Linkages between institutions of learning have the potential to integrate with local communities and, therefore, to impact on local economies.

Improving the level of quality of tourism training and education in the region has the potential of being of economic benefit by way of attracting students from other parts of the continent and even the world. In addition, there is the likelihood of achieving the dream of establishing an economic block (EAC) through improved intra-regional tourism. Intra-regional tourism has the potential of cushioning the region from the effects of volatility of international tourism originating from traditional European and North American countries. This chapter acknowledges that there are issues and challenges that have to be overcome in cooperating in the area of tourism training and education. These should be addressed if such co-operation and collaboration is to be sustainable. The position taken in this chapter is that, with the current moves towards integration of the East African region as an economic block, co-operation and collaboration is in the long-term interests of the region and is achievable.

References

Aisensen, D., Bezanson, L., Frank, F., & Reardon, P. (2002). Building community capacity. In: *Technical and vocational education and training in the twenty-first century, new challenges in guidance and counselling*. Paris: UNESCO.

College of African Wildlife Management (CAWM). (1995). *A success story of collaboration and cooperation*. Mweka: College of African Wildlife Management.

Cooper, C. (2000). Curriculum planning for tourism education: From theory to practice. Paper presented in CAUTHE peak performance in tourism and hospitality research conference. Mt. Buller, Victoria, Australia. February 2000.

Dieke, P. U. C. (1998). Regional tourism in Africa. In: E. Laws, B. Faulkner & G. Moscardo (Eds), *Embracing and managing change in tourism: International case studies* (pp. 29–48). London: Routledge.

East African Community (EAC). (2002). *Treaty for establishment of the East African Community*. Arusha: EAC.

Esbin, H. B. (2002). Basic education and TVET in UNESCO, *Technical and vocational education and training in the twenty-first century, new challenges and guidance and counselling*. Paris: UNESCO.

Hofstede, G. (1980). *Culture's consequences: International differences in work related values*. CA: Sage Publications.

Ikiara, M. (2001). *Policy framework of Kenya's tourism sector since independence and emerging policy concerns*. Nairobi: KIPPRA.

Jeffries, D. (2001). *Government and tourism*. London: Butterworth Heinemann.

Kamar, M. J. (2003). The role of East African community in the promotion of sustainable development of community-based tourism in the region. Keynote Speech in *Atlas Africa Conference* 20–22 February 2003, Arusha, Tanzania.

King, B. E. M. (1996). A regional approach to tourism education and training in Oceania: Progress and prospects. *Progress in Tourism and Hospitality Research*, 2, 87–101.

Mayaka, M. A. (1999). *Assessing tourism industry of training and education: The case of the tour operating sector in Kenya.* A Master of Business in Tourism Dissertation, Victoria University of Technology, Melbourne, Australia.

Mayaka, M. A., & King, B. E. M. (2002). Quality assessment of training and education for Kenya's tour operating sector. *Current Issues in Tourism*, 5(2), 112–133.

Republic of Kenya. (1991). *Development and employment in Kenya: A strategy for the transformation of the economy. Report of the Presidential Committee on Employment.* Nairobi: Government Printer.

Richards, G. (1998). European network for tourism education. *Tourism Management*, 19(1), 1–4.

Sindiga, I. (1994). Employment and training in tourism in Kenya. *Journal of Tourism Studies,* 5(2), 45–52.

Sindiga, I. (1996) Tourism Education in Kenya. *Journal of Tourism Research*, 23(3), 698–701.

Sindiga, I. (1999). *Tourism and African development: Change and challenge of tourism in Kenya.* Hampshire: Ashgate Publishing.

United Republic of Tanzania. (URT), Nicholas O'Dwyer Vermos International Joint Venture Partnership (NOVIJVP). (1995). *Tourism Infrastructure Project (ITP) Feasibility Study Final Report Part I*, pp. 52–55.

World Bank. (1989). *Sub-Saharan Africa: From crisis to sustainable growth, a long-term perspective study.* Washington DC: World Bank.

WTO. (2002). *Tourism and poverty alleviation.* Madrid: World Tourism Organization.

WTO and University of Surrey. (1996). *Educating the educators in tourism: A manual of tourism and hospitality education.* Tourism Education and Training Series. Madrid: World Tourism Organization.

Chapter 13

Germany

Walter Freyer, Michael Hammer and Astrid Piermeier

Introduction

The development of tourism in Germany was well established by the mid-19th century and has continued rapidly since the end of the Second World War. Actually German tourists are the largest single group in the total number of international tourists. By way of contrast, the tourism education system is relatively new. The first courses to include tourism were established in the 1960s. To date there is no single university course leading to a degree that exclusively deals with tourism. But the outstanding importance of the tourism industry in Germany (a contribution of around 6–8% to the GNP) as well as its growing impacts and the growth of the tourism professions are having the effect of changing this.

Tourism as an integral and interdisciplinary phenomenon is influenced by a wide range of other subsystems such as the economy, society, ecology, politics and others. For that reason the aspect of interdisciplinary thinking becomes more and more significant in the tourism labour market. Particularly managers in leading positions have to meet higher requirements in a market determined by increasing competition. Basic skills such as knowledge of economics, transportation or geography are no longer sufficient and switching from other branches into the field of tourism is increasingly presenting challenges, at least on upper and higher management levels. For this reason, a specific tourism education becomes essential. Besides fundamental knowledge of tourism economics and politics, tourism managers have to know about the above-mentioned areas too. As illustrated in Figure 1 they are more generalists than specialists. At the same time a division of tasks between various tourism training centres is important.

Establishments for vocational education (e.g. technical colleges for hotel and catering) are particularly engaged in the transmission of professional skills. Establishments for the academic sector (universities, *Fachhochschulen*,[1] *Berufsakademien* [academies of cooperative education]) are engaged in the transmission of interdisciplinary skills. Despite the continuing

---

[1] In the 1960s a new sector of higher education emerged in Europe due to changed basic conditions within the educational system. One of the first facilities was the German *Fachhochschule* (university of applied sciences), which is similar to the English "polytechnics" and the French *Instituts Universitaires Technologie* (IUT) (Teichler, 2004).

An International Handbook of Tourism Education
Copyright © 2005 by Elsevier Ltd.
All rights of reproduction in any form reserved
ISBN: 0-08-044667-1

Figure 1: Professionalism versus interdisciplinarism.
Source: after Freyer (1999, p. 109) and Kaspar (1990, p. 22).

crisis in the tourism industry the demand for tourism programmes particularly in the academic sector is still growing. Two or three applicants apply for every available university place (Jürs, 2003, pp. 160–162).

The supply of educational services in Germany has reacted to this development and offers a wide range of educational programmes concerned with tourism, both in vocational education and academic education. The latter can currently be found at 16 universities and 22 *Fachhochschulen* (see Figures 5 and 7). Generally, the flood of these programmes has resulted in an industry without transparent structure and degrees that are not precisely comparable to those in other European or in countries elsewhere in the world. But driven by increasing internationalisation, standardised degree programmes are becoming more and more evident. For that reason the AJT (*Fachverband für touristische Aus- und Weiterbildung e. V.* = German professional association for further education in tourism) has called for a standardised education and a consolidation of the existing tracks of professional training and educational programmes in tourism. More transparency will be helpful for both school-leavers and students to make their decision about the intended track of education, and for tourism companies and institutions in their staff recruitment (AJT, 2004).

The following chapter gives an overall view of the existing nature of tourism education in Germany and describes new developments that tourism education will face in the coming years (cf. Donhauser (2004); DWIF (1991); Freyer (2000); klemm (1998); Steinecke & klemm (1998)).

Vocational Education in Tourism

Initial Vocational Training in Tourism

Vocational training in tourism is a highly specific, well-established activity in Germany, which concentrates on the detailed application of lower level, often practical skills. It is generally sector-specific and seeks to equip the apprentice with clearly defined skills, such as ticketing or waiting and customer contact skills. Apprentice training in Germany is primarily based on a dual system of education (*Duales System der Berufsausbildung*) as shown in Figure 2.

The dual system of education is a combined training, which usually takes 3 years. It is undertaken in the training enterprise (on-the-job-training) supported by off-the-job-training at a compulsory vocational school (*Berufsschule*). Vocational school education is either held once a week or periodically as full-time instruction depending on the individual arrangement

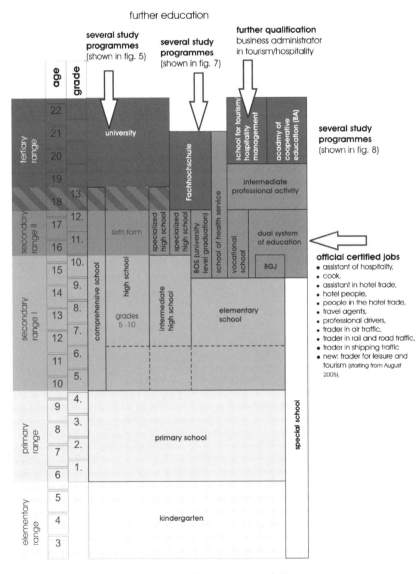

Figure 2: Educational system of Germany.
Source: after Anweiler (1996, p. 52).

of the responsible school. The minimum requirement for an apprenticeship in the tourism sector is generally a *Hauptschulabschluss* (elementary school grade) or a *Realschulabschluss* (intermediate high school certificate), or even in some cases the *Abitur* or *Fachabitur* (matriculation standard). Under certain conditions a reduction of this 3-year training period is possible, as for example with a higher general graduation (*Abitur*). Apprentices get an education grant according to official standards; working time is also regulated by a wage agreement.

Apprentices have to pass an intermediate examination after 1 year and a final one supervised by the IHK (*Industrie- und Handelskammer* = Chamber of Commerce), consisting of both a theoretical and a practical part. The final examination which primarily focuses on practical skills is carried out by examiners with several years' professional experience and detailed knowledge about practical requirements of the job market. Depending on the initial vocational training and after five to seven years working experience it is possible to take an examination in order to get the *master craftsman's certificate* (*Küchenmeister, Restaurantmeister, Hotelmeister*). A precondition for this mastership is not only that the employee has reached the minimum age of 24, but also that he or she has acquired the permission to train apprentices independently.

Vocational Training in the Hospitality Industry

The German hospitality industry currently offers more than 60,000 training places and more than 1.2 million jobs in about 200,000 enterprises, within which there are different working areas, for example restaurant service, kitchen, housekeeping, reception and administration, depending on the size of the establishment. The majority of the employees in the hospitality industry have passed an initial vocational training. Most of them work as cooks (more than 30%) or as hotel staff (30%).

For the officially certified jobs in hospitality *Fachgehilfe im Gastgewerbe* (assistant of hospitality), *Hotelfachmann/-frau* (professional hotel people), *Restaurantfachmann/-frau* or *Fachmann/-frau für Systemgastronomie* (trained waiters), *Koch* (cook), *Hotelkaufmann/-frau* (people in the hotel trade), *Kaufmannsgehilfe im Hotel- und Gaststättengewerbe* (assistant in hotel trade) combined training in an enterprise supported by off-the-job-training at a vocational school is compulsory. These apprenticeships usually take three years except *Fachgehilfen im Gastgewerbe*, who pass the examination after a 2-year training period. The apprenticeship for *Fachgehilfen im Gastgewerbe* is multifaceted but less specialised and includes job rotation within the training enterprise, containing working areas like industrial safety and hygiene, housekeeping, basic work in the office, in the service, in the kitchen and at the buffet and communication skills in foreign languages.

After passing the examination it is possible to add a third year of vocational training to become a *Hotelfachmann/-frau, Fachmann/-frau für Systemgastronomie* or *Restaurantfachmann/-frau*. Most of the tasks and duties of a *Restaurantfachmann/-frau* are similar to those of the assistants (*Fachgehilfen im Gastgewerbe*) but they are more specific and deeper. Professional hotel people (*Hotelfachmann/-frau*), people in the hotel trade (*Hotelkaufleute*) and assistants in the hotel trade (*Kaufmannsgehilfen im Hotel- und Gaststättengewerbe*) are especially assigned to work in the front and back office and in the commercial department. While certain soft skills (e.g. customer contact skills) are expected for vocational training in the hospitality sector, craft-based skills and operational areas vary depending on the particular training establishment. The course content is fairly standard although the emphasis may vary slightly between institutions. Pressure from industry since the late 1970s has led to the adoption of management and business economics elements into the courses (WTO, 1996, p. 142). Characteristically in Germany it is also possible to take another way of professional training in the hospitality industry. One possibility for school leavers is to attend a vocational school for hospitality (*Hotelberufsfachschule*) followed by a 1-year theoretical training (*Berufsgrundbildungsjahr*). This training gives a review of various fields of the tourism industry and establishes the basis for the succeeding shortened vocational training. The other possibility is to pass a 3-year training period at a vocational school for hospitality. Then the theoretical off-the-job-training is supplemented by practical courses in hotels, because acquisition of practical experience and skills is essential as well as in the dual system of education.

Vocational Education with Tour Operators, Travel Intermediaries, Associations and Tourist Boards

Travel agents can follow their vocational training (as *Reiseverkehrskaufmann/-frau*) in various establishments within the tourism industry. With tour operators, travel intermediaries, associations and tourist boards, travel agents consult customers and tourists in their decision-making process and arrange transportation and accommodation services as well as complete packages (Schöpp, 1999, p. 343). The set of duties also includes administration, ticketing, sales, marketing and controlling. Off-the-job-training for travel agents takes place at a commercial vocational school (*kaufmännische Berufsschule*). According to the multifarious job requirements of travel agents, establishments generally either expect an intermediate high school certificate (*Realschulabschluss*) or a matriculation standard (*Abitur* or *Fachabitur*).

Vocational Education in Tourist Transportation

Some of the 136,000 employees working in passenger traffic in Germany are *Berufskraftfahrer für Personenverkehr* (professional drivers), who are specialised in customer and guest service, tour management and travel marketing. That is why they can be seen as a part of the tourism sector, although strictly speaking this vocational training belongs to the transport sector. Special requirements for the 2-year vocational training are a suitable driving license (*Führerscheinklasse* 2) and a minimum age of 21.

Furthermore, there are also three different kinds of apprenticeships in the commercial sector for air, rail and shipping traffic in tourist transportation: *Luftverkehrskaufmann/-frau* (air traffic), *Kaufmann/-frau im Eisenbahn- und Straßenverkehr* (rail and road traffic), *Schifffahrtskaufmann/-frau* (shipping traffic). Apprentices are given detailed training in commercial and business economics, technical knowledge, personnel and financial concerns. Due to the large spectrum of theoretical and practical issues, applicants need to have a matriculation standard (*Abitur* or *Fachabitur*) and must not be older than 24 years. For air stewards and hostesses there is no official certified vocational training at the moment but serious consideration is being given to establish this as soon as possible.

Educational Professions in Tourism

About 2000 guest hosts and about 3000 tour guides are employed in German tourism companies, and although there are high demands on them concerning both soft skills (customer communication) and hard skills (foreign languages, knowledge in history, etc.), there is no adequate professional training for this occupational group. Only for children and youth hosting and for teaching some kinds of sports, do employees require a certificate. Couriers generally take further education courses.

After passing an initial vocational training and a certain period in the hospitality or tourism sector, employees can get a further qualification at the school for hospitality/tourism management (*Hotelfachschule*). These institutions provide intermediate, sub-degree level business skills and management education in form of 2-year full-time courses offering the qualifications required for access to higher education.

Depending on the specialisation in tourism or hospitality management, graduates get the title *Staatlich geprüfte/r Betriebswirt/-in* (business administrator in hospitality) or *Staatlich geprüfte/r Touristikassistent/-in* (business administrator in tourism). As shown in this chapter, initial and further vocational training at assistant and craft-level in Germany is various and wellestablished. The needs for initial and further training nevertheless are high in some segments of the tourism-related job-market. Details are provided in Figure 3.

Tourism Education as an Academic Subject

Tourism as an academic subject is relatively young and even by generous estimates, it is only a maximum of 50 years old (WTO, 1996, p. 46). Before the Second World War only a few universities, teachers and scientists in Germany were concerned with tourism as a field of research and education. For the first time in the 1960s, corresponding to the growth of international tourism and to the German travel boom, advanced courses for tourism managers were developed and made available at universities (first sector of higher education) and *Fachhochschulen* (second sector of higher education) within the disciplines of business economics, political economics and geography. Most of these institutions are publicly financed. Only a few private schools demand tuition fees. The profile of tourism training and education has been increased as a result of growing recognition in government and a booming tourism industry. Courses were established at several university-level institutions and these still form the basis for tourism education at higher level today (cf. Freyer (2000); klemm (1998); Nahrstedt et al. (1994)). But, in reality, until now tourism was not wellestablished as an area for serious academic study: it lacks the history and evolution of some more mature fields of study, which possess the theoretical underpinning. In addition to this, tourism as an area of academic study still has an image problem which is based on the prejudice, that it is somewhat "soft" and "smells of laziness!" (Romeiß-Stracke, 1998, p. 8).

Because tourism is a cross-sectional industry, tourism education has to be multidisciplinary in its approach and it possesses elements which are attractive to other disciplines. The human dimensions of tourism are particularly interesting to geographers, historians

	Number of jobs	Need for Initial Education	Need for Further Education
Segment of Tourism Industry			
Hospitality	1.000.000	high	high
Tourist Transportation (Road)	40.000 - 60.000	medium	high
Tourist Transportation (Air Traffic)	100.000	high	high
Tourist Transportation (Shipping)	10.000	low	low
Tourist Transportation (Rail Road)	240.000	medium	medium
Tour Operators, Travel Intermediaries	65.000	medium	medium
Travel Management	not reported	high	high
Health Resorts and Facilities	250.000	medium	high
Associations and Tourist Boards	12.000	medium	high
Convention Service	850.000	high	low
Exhibitions	5.600	medium	low
Camping	65.000	low	high
Supplementing Industry			
Guest Hosting/Tour Guiding	not reported	high	low
Computer Reservation Systems	not reported	high	low
Leasing	not reported	high	high
Initial and Further Training	not reported	high	high
Border Areas of Tourism Industry			
Catering Trade	not reported	high	high
Sports	not reported	high	low
Culture	not reported	high	medium

Figure 3: Needs for initial and further education within the tourism industry.
Source: Becker (2002).

and behavioural scientists, while the commercial activity associated with tourism is important for economists, financiers and those involved with business studies. So tourism education is often seen as simply contributing case study material to add interest to and enrich
other disciplines such as economics and geography (WTO, 1996, p. 46). Institutions and
teachers which develop curricula and offer tourism education are affected by this problem.

In 1971, the *Fachhochschule* of Munich (*FH München*) established the first curriculum for
tourism in Germany within the discipline of business economics. Several more followed. At
the beginning of its history, traditional tourism education only took place in *Fachhochschulen*,
which aimed at a practical approach. The programmes were designed for students who had
completed vocational training without a matriculation standard and who wanted to get further
qualifications through a different educational route (in Germany: *Zweiter Bildungsweg*). Also

in the 1970s and at the beginning of the 1980s, universities and *Fachhochschulen* developed integral courses linked with geography, sociology and education science.

Tourism education at an academic level in Germany currently is provided through a combination of full-time and part-time courses that are provided by universities, *Fachhochschulen* and academies of cooperative education. First, there are 4-year (eight semesters) courses and 1-year post-graduate programmes with a tourism specialisation at universities. Secondly, there are *Fachhochschulen* providing 3- or 4-year business courses with a tourism, travel and hotel management specialisation. And finally, there are academies of cooperative education (*Berufsakademien*) and professional institutions offering courses on a 1-year full-time or 3-year part-time basis. While most of these institutions are publicly financed, some private ones (P) offer programmes with tuition fees. (see Figures 5 and 7).

Figure 4 provides an outline of the educational structure for German *Universities* and *Fachhochschulen* in comparison with institutions of higher education outside continental Europe.

The right-hand side shows the traditional German educational structure, which is characterised by single-staged programmes that normally run for 4 years at *Fachhochschulen* or up to 5 years at universities, respectively. Both types of institution confer the traditional degree: *Diplom* (indicated by the abbreviation "FH" if obtained at a *Fachhochschule*). Driven by the Declaration of Bologna, German universities are also engaged in establishing consecutive Bachelor and Master courses. Currently, these programmes make up only 15% of the total number of courses offered by German universities (Schwarz-Hahn & Rehburg, 2004, p. 13).

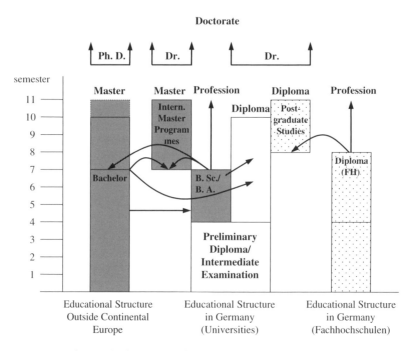

Figure 4: Structure of higher education in Germany.

Appropriately qualified graduates of universities have the opportunity to take a doctorate. A degree awarded by *Fachhochschulen* is not sufficient for this. Currently there are no independent doctoral studies in tourism. Usually, graduate students studying for a doctorate are employed as research assistants to support lecturers or professors in activities concerned with teaching and research. Their doctoral studies take place within this framework. A second possibility is to get a grant for doctoral studies from a foundation or from private institutions outside the universities ("external graduations").

Tourism Education at Universities

One implication of the relative immaturity of the subject area is that there is no independent study programme and no degree specifically for tourism education in Germany. German universities provide tourism education as a compulsory subject, optional subject or specialisation subject within a range of different study programmes and disciplines: geography (nine universities), business studies (six universities), cultural studies (two universities), transportation economy (one university), sociology (one university), environmental sciences (one university) and education science (one university). These universities and their tourism specialisations are given in Figure 5. Depending on the parent discipline, the balance between the included core elements varies substantially between the universities.

The tourism courses offered at university are linked to study programmes of particular disciplines, which generally take nine semesters. The duration of study varies slightly, depending on the aspired degree, diploma or M.A. (*Magister Artium*). After four semesters of basic study, in most cases the students have to pass an intermediate examination to enter the five semester main study period which includes the final examination and a diploma thesis.

Tourism education within the context of geography emphasises an interdisciplinary approach, which combines natural and spatial sciences with economics and social sciences. Some universities have developed tourism-related curricula and provide special tourism programmes ("tourism geography") others have avoided a complete specialisation in this area and offer courses without a specified recurring curriculum. In certain cases business economics is a compulsory optional subject alongside other optional subjects, such as sociology, regional studies, spatial planning, politics, public law, etc. According to Klemm (1998, p. 929) courses within geography meet the interdisciplinary requirements of tourism-related study if there is an adequate emphasis on tourism-related content and if the contents are embedded in a transparent structure. Regarding the job-market requirements the interdisciplinary approach of tourism education within the context of geography is advantageous. The graduates (*Diplom-Geograph/-in*) primarily are in employment with tourism boards, tourism associations and, to a minor degree, with tour operators and travel intermediaries. Despite this, however, graduates of business studies have better professional prospects, as was shown by a study of the authors of job-market requirements of the German tourism industry in 2001 (Figure 6) (cf. also Nahrstedt et al. (1994); Kirstges (2003)).

Students who are enrolled in business economics also have the opportunity to specialise in tourism studies at some German universities. The existing programmes show different strategies: courses in "tourism economics" or "tourism management" are provided both as an independent optional subject, which can be followed by students of several economic studies or as an optional subject formally embedded in the main study of business economics. Beside

Institution	Study Programme	Degree
Aachen, RWTH	Geography	Dipl.-Geograph/-in, M.A.
Berlin, Freie Universität	Regional Tourism Planning and Management	certificate
Bielefeld, Universität	Education Sciences	Dipl.Pädagoge/-in
Bielefeld, Universität	Tourism Economics	certificate
Cologne Business School (P)	Business Studies	Bachelor Tourism/ Tourismus-Betriebswirt/-in
Dresden, Technical University	Transportation Economy	Dipl.-Verkehrswirt/-in
Dresden, Technical University	Business Studies	Dipl.-Kaufmann/-frau
Dresden, International University (P)	Tourism Management & Mobility	Master (MBA)
Eichstätt, Katholische Universität	Geography	Dipl-Geograph/-in
Göttingen, Georg-August-Universität	Geography	Dipl-Geograph/-in
Greifswald, Ernst-Moritz-Arndt-Universität	Geography	Dipl-Geograph/-in
Lüneburg, Universität	Business Studies	Dipl.-Betriebswirt/-in
Lüneburg, Universität	Applied Cultural Studies	M.A.
Lüncburg, Universität	Environmental Sciences	Dipl.-Umweltwissenschaftler/-in
München, LMU	Economic Geography	Dipl.-Wirtschaftsgeograph/-in
München, LMU	Business Studies	Dipl.-Kaufmann/-frau
Münster, Westfälische Wilhelms-Universität	Geography	Dipl-Geograph/-in
Paderborn, Universität-Gesamthochschule	Geography	Dipl.-Geograph/-in, M.A.
Passau, Universität	Economic and Cultural Space Studies	Dipl.-Kulturwirt/-in
Regensburg, Universität	Geography	Dipl.-Geograph/-in
Rostock, Universität	Business Studies	Dipl.-Kaufmann/-frau
Trier, Universität	Geography	Dipl-Geograph/-in
Trier, Universität	Business Studies	Dipl.-Kaufmann/-frau
Trier, Universität	Sociology	Dipl.-Soziologe/-in

Figure 5: Tourism education at German universities.

general economics which takes first priority, tourism courses are combined with business and financial management, taxation, marketing, personnel management, etc. While the volume of tourism-related contents of the programmes varies slightly between the different universities, it is worth emphasising that it is certainly less extensive and less vocationally oriented compared with *Fachhochschulen*. At this university-level graduates are awarded the academic title *Diplom-Kaufmann/-frau* (similar to a master of business administration).

While geography is concentrated on location research and economics, ecological and social impacts of tourism and economics emphasises economic effects resulting from tourist activities, further disciplines have developed tourism programmes with a focus on the leisure sector and professional skills like administration of leisure facilities, guest hosting, tour guiding and

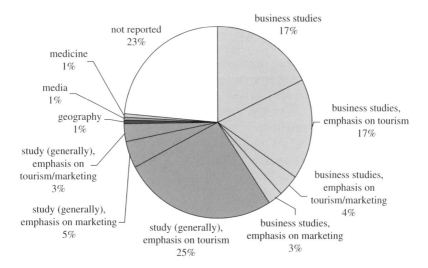

Figure 6: Courses of study required in job advertisements for graduates in Germany in 2001.
Source: Authors.

entertainment. Cultural studies, sociology and education science offer courses included in diploma and master programmes. A unique programme including tourism courses is being offered by the Dresden University of Technology. Its programme "Transportation Economy" combines economic and transportation aspects and includes the course "Tourism Economics and Management" as an optional subject. Above all the close connection between tourism on the one hand as well as mobility and economics respectively on the other hand is to be stressed.

Finally, some universities provide post-graduate programmes to qualify graduates of different subjects for a higher management level and to improve their professional prospects. The vocational requirements of these programmes follow an interdisciplinary approach and they are focused on tourism management, tourism research, law, facility planning and development, product development, scientific based tour guiding etc. After the 1-year programme, which is divided into a basic and a main course, students have to do a thesis and pass a final examination to get certification. This certification now has official status.

Also some *Fachhochschulen* offer such programmes. These include for example the "Post-graduate Diploma in European Tourism Management" at the FH Heilbronn, which is characterised by an international approach. Unlike the university programmes, this programme enables graduates to acquire the master degree after doing an additional master thesis.

Tourism Education at Fachhochschulen

In line with their relatively long history, *Fachhochschulen* offer the largest supply of tourism-related programmes within the German system of higher education. Most tourism courses offered at *Fachhochschulen* are embedded in business economic subjects and, to a minor degree, within educational studies. Tourism education especially is provided through

4-year diploma or a 3-year bachelor (plus 2-year master) programmes. Master and bachelor programmes are comparatively new in Germany compared to the well-established diploma programmes.

Diploma programmes are generally divided into four semesters of basic study and four semesters of main study, which include the final examination and a diploma thesis. The basic study emphasises the core elements of business and political economics, propaedeutics and foreign languages and ends with an intermediate examination. Generally, only the main study offers the opportunity of specialisation in tourism. The main focus of tourism-related courses varies between the institutions and is oriented towards the professional requirements of the hospitality industry, tour operators, travel intermediaries, local and regional associations and tourist boards. The courses within the main study are primarily concentrated on tourism management, tourism marketing, law and some institutions additionally offer courses in transportation management. *Fachhochschulen* offer an intense vocational orientation. Considering this fact, it is not surprising that the institutions require practical courses before or during the programme. Work experiences in several companies within the tourism industry take about 25% of the duration of study (i.e. about two semesters). At this level graduates are awarded the academic title *Diplom-Betriebswirt/-in (FH)* (similar to a master of business administration). According to Klemm (1998, p. 927), tourism education within business studies at *Fachhochschulen* primarily focus on general economic subjects, tourism subjects are subordinate. As a result many graduates take jobs outside the tourism industry. Within educational studies, courses are concentrated on the leisure sector and convey professional skills like administration of leisure and cultural facilities, guest hosting, tour guiding and entertainment. Graduates in this subject are awarded the academic title *Diplom-Sozialpädagoge/-in (FH)*. Figure 7 gives a list of existing programmes.

Tourism Education at Academies of Cooperative Education (*Berufsakademie*)

Tourism education at *Berufsakademien* or BA (academy of cooperative education) is also based on a dual system of education (*Duales System der Berufsausbildung*). It is a 3-year combined training which takes place both at the academy and at the training place. Theoretical and practical knowledge alternate in half-year periods. So the students receive an education, which closely connects theoretical knowledge with practical skills. Entry requirements are the matriculation standard and a contractually fixed training relationship with a company in the tourism industry. These academies of cooperative education provide tourism education in Germany with three different emphases: tour operators and travel intermediaries; hospitality; public administration of tourism including the cure and spa business.

The theoretical studies are based on general business and public economics, accounting, statistics, data processing, law, foreign languages and special business economic courses. These special courses, like hospitality and travel management, destination management, tourism geography, hotel marketing, personnel management, food and beverage management, vary between the institutions according to the particular emphasis of the academy. The academies of cooperative education providing tourism education in Germany are shown in Figure 8.

The programme contains a 1-year period of professional placement in the tourism industry during which students pass through different departments of the training company. After

Institution	Study Programme	Degree
Bad Honnef, Internationale FH (P)	International Hospitality & Tourism Management	Bachelor
Bad Honnef, Internationale FH (P)	Tourism Management, Hospitality Management	Dual Degree Bachelor/Dipl.-Betriebswirt/-in (FH)
Bergisch Gladbach, FH der Wirtschaft	Business Studies	Dipl.-Kaufmann/frau (FH)
Braunschweig/Wolfenbüttel-Salzgitter, FH	Tourism Management	Dipl.-Kaufmann/-frau (FH)
Bremen, FH	Nautics and International Economics	Bachelor/Master international Tourism Management
Bremen, Hochschule FH (P)	Social Studies	Diplom-Freizeitwissenschaftler/-in (FH)
Deggendorf, FH	Tourism Management	Dipl.-Betriebswirt/-in (FH)
Dortmund, ISM – International School of Management (P)	Tourism-, Event- and Hospitality Management	Dipl.-Kaufmann/-frau (FH)
Eberswalde, FH	Sustainable Tourism Management	Master
Gelsenkirchen/Abt. Bocholt, FH	Economics	Dipl.-Betriebswirt/-in (FH)
Göttingen, Private FH (P)	Tourism and Travel Management	Dipl.-Kaufmann/-frau (FH)
Heide, FH Westküste	International Tourism Management	Master, Bachelor
Heilbronn, FH	European Tourism Management	Master
Heilbronn, FH	Tourism Business Studies	Dipl.-Betriebswirt/-in (FH), Bachelor
Kempten, FH	Tourism Management	Dipl.-Betriebswirt/-in (FH)
Lahr, Süddeutsche Hochschule für Berufstätige (P)	Economics	Dipl.Betriebswirt (FH)
München, FH	Tourism Management	Dipl.-Betriebswirt/-in (FH)
Nordhessen, FH	Business Studies	Dipl.-Betriebswirt/-in (FH)
Rendsburg, Norddeutsche Hochschule für Berufstätige (P)	Economics	Dipl.Betriebswirt (FH)
Schmalkalden, FH	Business Studies	Dipl.-Betriebswirt/-in (FH)
Stralsund, FH	Leisure and Tourism Management	Bachelor (BA)
Wernigerode, FH Harz	Tourism Management	Bachelor
Wernigerode, FH Harz	International Tourism Studies	Dual Degree Bachelor
Wilhelmshaven, FH	Tourism Economics	Dipl.-Kaufmann/-frau (FH)
Worms, FH	Transportation/Tourism	Dipl.-Betriebswirt/-in (FH)
Zittau/Görlitz, FH	Tourism	M.A. or Bachelor

Figure 7: Tourism education at German *Fachhochschulen.* P = Private, FH = Fachhochschule, BA = Berufsakademie.

a 2-year phase of practical and theoretical education and passing a certified examination, students get the title *Wirtschaftsassistent/-in (BA)* (assistant of business administration). After a further year the academic title *Diplom Betriebswirt/-in (BA)* (similar to a master of business administration) is awarded to the graduates.

Institution	Study Programme/Emphasis	Degree
Berlin, BA	Business Economies/Tourism Economies	Dipl.-Betriebswirt/-in (BA)
Breitenbrunn, BA Sachsen	Business Economies/Tourism Management	Dipl.-Betriebswirt/-in (BA)
Eisenach, BA Thüringen	Business Economies/Tourism Management	Dipl.-Betriebswirt/-in (BA)
Hannover, BA (Leibniz-Akademie)	Business Economies/Travel Management	Dipl.-Betriebswirt/-in (BA)
Ravensburg, BA	Business Economies/Tourism Management	Dipl.-Betriebswirt/-in (BA)
Schleswig-Holstein, Wirtschaftsakademie	Business Economies/Tourism	Dipl.-Betriebswirt/-in (BA)
Stuttgart, BA	Business Economies/Industrial and Service Management	Dipl.-Betriebswirt/-in (BA)

Figure 8: Tourism education at academies of cooperative education.
(BA = Berufsakademie).

New Trends within Academic Tourism Education in Germany

Studying tourism has developed into a very attractive subject for school-leavers intending to take up studies at an institution of higher education. Some universities receive many more applications than there are places available. So they are forced to set up selection procedures. (Jürs, 2003, p. 162). But apart from the negative effects (e.g. higher administrative expenses, disadvantageous staff/student ratio) this fact offers a chance for the establishment of new and, if desired, more specific tourism programmes at institutions of higher education.

Another recent development will support activities of that kind and will cause fundamental structural changes in academic tourism education at the same time. In 1999, the Ministers responsible for higher education from 29 European countries signed the "Bologna Declaration". The main objective of this is the realisation of the so-called *European Higher Education Area* by the year 2010. The process aims at creating convergence rather than standardisation or uniformity of European higher education. The main principles of the declaration are:

- the creation of a consecutive structure of education (Bachelor and Master);
- assessment of results by using a credit point scheme (analogous to the European Credit Transfer System);
- structuring courses into thematic blocks (modularisation);
- internationalisation of the curriculum;
- defining rules for the recognition of programmes (accreditation).

Major benefits of this development will be:

- students will be able to move freely across European higher education institutions. Results and degrees will be recognised in all participating countries;

- the process will lead to a greater student and staff mobility and will produce students with transnational experience, cultural maturity, and not least, language ability: all these are experiences and skills, which are increasingly required by employers in the European labour market;
- movement away from long courses (eight to 12 semesters) to shorter bachelor degrees (six semesters) with an option of attending a subsequent master programme (four additional semesters), which are increasingly offered in English. This will mean that European higher education becomes more attractive worldwide.

At the conference of Berlin (September 2003), one of the follow-up conferences to Bologna, all ministers committed themselves to starting the implementation of a two-cycle system by the year 2005.

The development towards a consecutive system in academic education started earlier in Germany. The first academic institutions offered Bachelor and Master courses in addition to their traditional *Diplom* and *Magister* courses in the mid-1990s. The legal basis for the establishment of these courses followed the amendment of the German Framework Act on Universities (*Hochschulrahmengesetz*) in August 1998.

Consecutive Structure in Tourism Education

In the area of tourism education, several academic institutions in Germany have already adopted this model and started Bachelor and Master courses with different priorities (Figures 5 and 7) or they intend to do so. Generally, Bachelor and Master programmes can be offered in three different ways: independent Bachelor courses, independent Master courses or both can be part of consecutive programmes. Currently, at the beginning of the reform process most German universities with subjects in travel and tourism have "Single Bachelors" or "Single Masters". The latter is often used for post-graduate studies (usually in form of commercial courses).

In addition to the comprehensive theoretical and methodical knowledge it is intended to introduce more practical content (integrated workshops, traineeships, foreign experience, lecturers from tourism companies) to prepare students for positions at upper and higher management levels so as to ensure employability. Accordingly, the existing programmes reveal two significant characteristics: a strong emphasis on management elements as well as an international orientation. Both of these are also expressed by the course titles (Loderstedt, 2004, p. 191). Furthermore, two different strategies are pursued. On the one hand, new tourism-specific courses are created, normally alongside the traditional *Diplom* or *Magister* courses. This is a positive development in that it permits tourism subjects, formally embedded into higher courses of study, to acquire greater independence and their own degree title. It also allows greater depth of coverage in tourism studies. In the winter term 2004–2005, for instance, the *Fachhochschule* in Heide (FH Westküste) started its course International Tourism Management. It is concerned mainly with tour operator management, destination management, hospitality management and sport tourism management. Lectures are partly given in English. Practical terms will be integrated as well as one term in a foreign country. Besides this course tourism studies are integrated within the traditional business management course (*Diplom* degree). Also the University of Eichstätt as well as the *Fachhochschule* Munich are pursuing this "dual" model (Jürs, 2003, p. 162). As all courses in the area are still relatively new, no evaluation of their quality and acceptance among students and tourism companies has yet been carried out.

On the other hand there are higher education institutions that are going completely to substitute their traditional *Diplom* and *Magister* courses by the new Bachelor and Master programmes, without any transitional phase. The University of Lüneburg for instance plans a complete rearrangement at the beginning of the winter term 2005–2006. Students, enrolled in *Diplom* courses will have the opportunity to join the new Master courses (e.g. M.A. Tourism). At the same time the University of Lüneburg will merge with the local *Fachhochschule*, which probably will positively affect the quality and extent of tourism education. Also the *Fachhochschule* Heilbronn has replaced its *Diplom* course Tourism Management by an equivalent Bachelor course from the winter term 2004–2005. A Master level course will follow in 2006.

It is often argued that apart from a change of the course title and the transition into a modularised system no fundamental changes in the structure and the content of these courses will take place. There is also a concern that *Fachhochschulen* will simply try to be like the more scientifically orientated universities. The traditional distinguishing mark shown by the abbreviation "FH" after the degree (e.g. *Diplom-Betriebswirt [FH]*) will not be adopted for the new titles.

The quality of these programmes will be ensured by an accreditation procedure, which defines minimum standards and is compulsory for courses established after 01/01/2003. Authorised by the German Accreditation Council (est. in 1999) there are actually six accreditation agencies in Germany: ZEvA, FIBAA, ASIIN, ACQUIN, AHPGS, AQAS.[2] The agency, usually used for the accreditation of tourism programmes is FIBAA, as it gives priority to economic based subjects.

Developments in Post-Graduate Studies

Post-graduate studies in tourism mainly focus on those already working in the tourism industry. Their objective is to gain further qualifications for reaching higher management levels or to get the opportunity to take a doctorate (Figure 4). Actually there are only a few post-graduate courses at German universities that are concerned with tourism. The University of Bielefeld ("Tourism Science") and the FU Berlin ("Tourism with the focus on Management and Regional Tourism Planning") offer courses that emphasise the interdisciplinary character of tourism. Above all the programmes combine economic, geographical, cultural, ecological and social content, which are significant for a profession in the area of tourism. Both programmes last two semesters and lead to the award of a certificate. A specific title (e.g. *Diplom, Master*) will not be conferred on participants.

---

[2] ZevA (Zentrale Evaluations- und Akkreditierungsagentur), FIBAA (Foundation for International Business Administration Accreditation), ASIIN (Akkreditierungsagentur für Studiengänge der Ingenieurwissenschaften, der Informatik, der Naturwissenschaften und der Mathematik), ACQUIN (Akkreditierungs-, Certifizierungs- und Qualitätssicherungs-Institut), AHPGS (Akkreditierungsagentur für Studiengänge im Bereich Heilpädagogik, Pflege, Gesundheit und Soziale Arbeit e.V.), AQAS (Agentur für Qualitätssicherung durch Akkreditierung von Studiengängen).

In the course of the rearrangement of the higher educational structure in Europe, internationally oriented courses, which lead to an internationally recognised degree will be increasingly in demand. For several years graduates have had the opportunity to attend the programme "European Tourism Management" (one of the first in Germany), which is offered by the *Fachhochschule* Heilbronn in co-operation with another five European universities.[3] This three semester full-time Master programme (at least two semesters) seeks not only to develop the existing knowledge base of tourism graduates, but also to develop multinational strategic and operational tourism management skills.

Further examples for post-graduate studies in tourism are the courses "M.A. Sustainable Tourism" (FH Eberswalde), "MBA International Tourism Management" (*Hochschule* Bremen) as well as the Master programme "Tourism and Mobility," which is intended to be introduced by the Dresden International University in 2005.

Introduction of Study Fees

In accordance with the German Framework Act on Universities (*Hochschulrahmengesetz*) the elementary education at institutions of higher education actually is free of charge (laid down in § 27 (4) HRG). Most universities are publicly financed and students just have to pay fees of around 100 Euro per semester. There are only a few institutions of higher education offering tourism programmes that are financed via study fees. Examples are the Cologne Business School and the International School of Management in Dortmund (see Figures 5 and 7). But recent developments have started a new discussion. Several federal states have instituted proceedings against the regulation on the basis that as matters concerning institutions of higher education such as financing are in the jurisdiction of the federal states.

Also a range of officials representing universities in Germany as well as representatives of the private economy support this development. By charging study fees universities will establish a stronger financial basis for their activities in both teaching and research. At the same time the state and federal states will benefit. At the plenum of the German Rectors' Conference (*Hochschulrektorenkonferenz*) held on June 2004 the German rectors claimed that universities should be enabled to charge study fees. Under continuing state sponsorship they suggest an amount of approximately 500 Euro per term. In the end Germany's federal states will probably be in position to decide over the introduction of study fees. Although it is often argued that students belonging to lower social classes will be discriminated against this will be a chance to enhance quality in tourism education as universities have to offer attractive programmes for attracting students.

References

AJT – Fachverband für touristische Aus- und Weiterbildung e. V. (2004). Chaos im touristischen Aus- und Weiterbildungsangebot. http://www.ajt-fachverband.de/presse/ pm_040604.php, 20/09/2004.

---

[3] Bournemouth University (GB), Högskolan Dalarna, Borlänge (S), Nationale Hogeschool voor Toerisme en Verkeer, Breda (NL), Université de Savoie, Chambéry (F), Universidad Rey Juan Carlos, Madrid (E).

Anweiler, O. (1996). Deutschland. In: O. Anweiler, et al. *Bildungssysteme in Europa* (pp. 31–56). Weinheim/Basel: Beltz Verlag.

Becker, P. (2002). Neue Berufe im Tourismus. Manuskript zu den Tegernseer Tourismustagen 2002. Unpublished.

Donhauser, A. (2004). *Trendbranche Tourismus — Ausbildung und Studium in Deutschland, Österreich und der Schweiz.* Nürnberg: Bildung und Wissen Verlag.

DWIF (1991). *Strukturanalyse des touristischen Arbeitsmarktes — Grundlagenuntersuchung im Auftrag des Bundesministers für Wirtschaft.* München: DWIF.

Europäische Kommission (1997). *Beschäftigung und Tourismus: Handlungsmaximen für Maßnahmen,* Schlussbericht. Luxemburg: EC.

Freyer, W. (1999). Reisebüro-Management: Allgemeine Grundlagen. In: W. Freyer & W. Pompl (Eds), *Reisebüro-Management* (pp. 99–140). München/Wien: Oldenbourg.

Freyer, W. (2000). Steigender Bedarf an touristischen Akademikern. In: Tourismus Interessen Kreis (TIK) (Ed.), *Tourismus-Ausbildungs-Analyse 2000* (pp. 47–49). Dresden: TIK, TU Dresden.

Jürs, M. (2003). In den Hörsälen herrscht Hochbetrieb, Zahl der Touristikstudenten steigt trotz Branchenkrise — neue Strukturen für schnellere Abschlüsse. *FVW International, 37,* 160–162.

Kaspar, C. (1990). Requirements of Higher Level Education in Tourism — Introduction to the general theme of the 40th AIEST Congress. In: *AIEST, Requirements of Higher Level Education in Tourism* (pp. 21–26). St. Gallen: AIEST.

Kirstges, T. (2003). Analyse des Stellenmarktes "Tourismus" 2002, http://www.fvw.de/_pdf/ KIRSTGES_MTI_2004.pdf, 20/09/2004.

Klemm, K. (1998). Die akademische Tourismusaus- und -weiterbildung in der Bundesrepublik Deutschland. In: G. Haedrich, et al. (ed.), *Tourismus-Management — Tourismus-Marketing und Fremdenverkehrsplanung* (pp. 925–936). Berlin, NewYork: Walter de Gruyter.

Loderstedt, K. (2004). Das Tourismusstudium in Deutschland: Die Auswirkungen der Internationalisierung auf Forschung und Lehre. In: M. Groß & A. Dreyer (Eds), *Tourismus 2015 — Tatsachen und Trends im Tourismusmanagement* (pp. 185–198). Hamburg: ITD-Verlag.

Nahrstedt, W., Stehr, I., Schmidt, M., & Brinkmann, D. (1994). *Tourismusberufe für Hochschulabsolventen. Untersuchung zur Sicherung und Effizienz und Qualität der Aus- und Weiterbildung von Tourismusexperten an den deutschen Hochschulen unter besonderer Berücksichtigung der Differenzierung nach Universitäten und Fachhochschulen.* IFKA-Dokumentation, Vol. 14. Bielefeld: IFKA.

Romeiß-Stracke, F. (1998). *Tourismus — gegen den Strich gebürstet. Essays.* München: Profilverlag.

Schöpp, U. (1999). Aus- und Weiterbildung für Reisebüros. In: W. Freyer & W. Pompl (Eds), *Reisebüro-management* (pp. 341–364). München, Wien: Oldenbourg.

Schwarz-Hahn, S. & Rehburg, M. (2004). *Bachelor und Master in Deutschland, Empirische Befunde zur Studienstrukturreform.* Münster et al: Waxmann.

Steinecke, A. & Klemm, K. (1998): *Blätter zur Berufskunde — Berufe im Tourismus,* Bielefeld: W. Bertelsmann Verlag.

Teichler, U. (2004). Changing patterns of the higher education system and the perennial search of the second sector for stability and identity. http://www.ipv.pt/millenium/Millenium21/21_4.htm, 20/09/2004.

WTO — World Tourism Organization (1996). *Educating the educators in tourism. A manual of tourism and hospitality education.* Madrid: WTO.

Chapter 14

India

Shalini Singh and Tej Vir Singh

Introduction

Tourism and education share an intrinsic commonality — that of internalization. Both possess the capacity to contribute significantly to individual and societal values. Practices in tourism especially those emanating from human, societal and environmental values contribute significantly to socio-cultural evolution. With this premise, tourism has been legitimized as a subject worthy of serious study. Education, on the other hand, is conceived primarily as part of a socio-cultural project of intentionality for future development and progress that societies and groups clarify in the mirror of the other (Schriewer, 2000). Educationists strongly hold that information or knowledge is worthy only if it contributes to the culture of the community (Whitehead, 1951). The learning process links culture and education in a mutually interactive manner, whereby culture prescribes norms, evolves goals and builds beliefs that help us tackle the challenges of existence (Csikszentmihaly, 1990) and is, in turn, informed and modified by the prevailing environments. The prime purpose of planned education, then, is to induct individuals into a culture in such a way that their individuality and creativity may be enhanced (Stenhouse, 1967, p. 7) and that the educated populace, as a collective may be guided by this creative insight to progress (Sankar, 2004) towards 'world citizenship' (Golmohamad, 2004). The need for world citizenry is eminent for globalization, and it calls for responsive mechanisms. Perhaps education can be utilized effectively to deliver the goods.

Integrated Education — Problems and Opportunities

Tynjälä, Välimaa, and Sarja (2003) clearly articulate the problems of higher education and its fractured relationship with the society in current times. The new world order appears to have created new forms of knowledge that have engendered a need for redefining the identity of established systems of higher education. From amongst the numerous aspects of these systems is the prospect of integrating theoretical and practical know-how

An International Handbook of Tourism Education
Copyright © 2005 by Elsevier Ltd.
All rights of reproduction in any form reserved
ISBN: 0-08-044667-1

to create knowledge that could be fruitfully employed to resolve issues for the future. Harris and Alexander (1998) suggest that an integrative approach to education is capable of delivering both social and academic purposes. Now, the challenge is in putting this idea into action.

The issue of integration is not a recent one and has long been debated upon (Langham & Phillips, 2001; Gaskell & Hepburn, 1997; Tynjälä et al., 2003). Educational philosophers such as Dewey (1916) and Whitehead (1951) propound the values of education with whole-some intellectual and social meaning of a vocation. An almost similar ideology has been espoused by Indian thinkers who have expounded their belief in the trinity of body, mind and soul for wholesome education. All thinkers are in unison in proposing a balance between knowledge, wisdom and craft. This is not an easy task, though. Educational psychologists have documented the multi-faceted complexities of integration. While the integration of dis-ciplines (intra and inter) is known to be the most frequently discussed, nevertheless it is real-ized that the integration of theory with practice is eminent (Gaskell & Hepburn, 1997). Välimaa (in Tynjälä et al., 2003, p. 148) observes that 'pragmatic universities' have embraced this mission and achieved a fair measure of success in implementing the idea of amalgamat-ing career goals with academic goals. Composite programmes of such nature have come to be known by various names, such as professional education, career academics, occupational curricula and even practice programmes. Despite conscious efforts to amalgamate these goals, scholars continue to engage themselves with this agenda, largely because the process and philosophy of amalgamated curricula remains to be deciphered in the real world context. Some scholars argue in favour of education through occupations instead of education for occupations (Dewey, 1916), while others consider theoretical knowledge to be of greater rel-evance than practical know-how. The UNESCO Report (Delors, 1996), on *Education for the Twenty-first Century*, asserts the importance of identifying the dilemma of integrated cur-riculum in order to confront and overcome them. The tensions identified in this report relate to conflicts between globalization and localization; universality and individuality; tradition and modernity; long-term and short-term considerations and competition and equity. The bipolar nature of issues concerning integrated curricula is indeed daunting.

Integration in Tourism Studies

Few scholars envisage tourism with a predominant disciplinary interest. From amongst them, Leiper (2000) proposes 'tourology' to encourage research in this 'cross-fertilized discipline', while Tribe (2001) emphasizes practical, emancipatory and technical interests to design a curriculum for non-vocational purposes. Interestingly, a majority of scholars determinedly view tourism studies with professional interest. For them the question is not of defining the scope of tourism as a discipline, but of determining the scope of tourism studies in terms of professionalization. Owing to these precepts and the inseparability of tourism from hospitality, initial phases of tourism education were fraught with significant confusion. With time, tourism studies and hospitality education and training emerged as mutually interdependent fields requiring attention of scholars for the advancement of knowledge, skills and managerial acumen. The acceptance of this complementarity is exhibited in the current status of tourism education, in general.

Presently, tourism education is faced with issues of integrated curricula and it could be a long time before a consensus is achieved. Considering that tourism should serve academic as well as professional purposes, researchers have attempted to develop broad frames of reference for tourism curriculum. Koh (1995) suggests a tourism curriculum within the four clusters of general, business, tourism specific (such as industry dynamics, operations, laws, planning and geography) and experiential education. Churchward and Riley (2002) emphasize the commercial aspects of tourism to design curricula so as to access jobs in both the public and private sectors. For this reason they recommend that conventional disciplines be coordinated with business perspectives to study tourism. In confirmation to this, Airey and Johnson (1999) found that tourism courses were substantially vocational and business orientated. In their study it was revealed that although most courses included common areas of knowledge, yet there existed a range of opinions regarding the need for a common core body of knowledge.

Scholars, such as Jafari (1997), nonetheless caution against sectoralized education in tourism. In order to extend the study of tourism beyond the commercial provisioning of services and products, Smith and Cooper (2000) envisage an integrated objective for tourism education. Their recommendation was based on developing a global pool of human resources for the tourism industry. In all probability, the availability of appropriate human resources is an eminent enigma of tourism and its study (Jafari, 1990; Cohen, 1999). To this end, scholars propose multi- and inter-disciplinary approach to tourism education and training (Przeclawski, 1993; Leiper, 2000).

Indian Education — An Overview

The Background

In general, education in India has a long history that commences from the Vedic times, continuing through the colonial period, to present times. As early as the first five centuries, centres of learning like Nalanda (in Bihar) and Taxila (now in Pakistan), had a paramount influence on scholars from as far as China and Greece, for centuries. Now converted into archaeological sites, these two centres of learning continue to epitomize the best of education in India. Researchers, such as Raina and Vats (1988), claim that Indian education was traditionally multifaceted in as much as it sought to define various states of the mind, understanding, consciousness, perception, memory, intelligence, character, behaviour and conduct. In order to improve upon these human faculties, physiological, psychological and environmental factors of etiological significance were recognized and included in the learning process (Varma, 1965). This approach made classical Indian education a multi-disciplinary concern (Raina & Srivastava, 1997). Furthermore, traditional Indian education system combined formal and informal methods of delivery and learning, for which students spent a large proportion of their time in observing, and working alongside, their mentors (*Gurus*) who assisted them to conceptualize while in practice. These practices evolved and subsequently institutionalized into a hierarchy of occupation-based caste system (*Varnashram Dharma*). Subsequently, the caste signified the vocational acumen of individuals and communities.

However, as the system stratified, the institutions developed parasitic rigidities, that eventually began to eat into its vitals. It was sometime during this process of devolution of values that modern education was introduced in India by the British colonizers. While the missionaries attended to primary education, the colonizers undertook the task of initializing a system of higher education that would accomplish the twin tasks of developing the required manpower for bilateral commerce and administration so as to achieve cultural colonization (Chitnis, 2000). This was in sharp contrast with the conventional system of learning and education. Scholars (Singh, 2001; Chitnis, 2000) decry the rejection of indigenous knowledge that had guided the lives of the common people, particularly because it resulted in the breach of the symbiotic relationship between indigenous systems that were the life and living forces of the people.

In the mid-1940s, Indian thinkers such as Sri Aurobindo, Rabindra Nath Tagore, J. Krishnamurti, Swami Vivekanand and Mahatma Gandhi raised voice against this British system and pleaded for a system that serves best in the society (Sapre & Ranade, 2001, p. 372).

The educational philosophy of these thinkers stressed upon the importance of moral leadership through comprehensive education that would aim at developing the total personality of the individual in harmony with society and nature (Raina & Sibia, 1995). Gandhi had a belief that all learning came from *doing* — from interacting with the physical world in order to meet our basic needs. This approach to learning has been referred to as 'basic' or 'craft-centred' education, since art and craft requires the use of the *hand, head and heart* to make learning a live and dynamic experience. Similarly, Aurobindo, and other seers laid emphasis on 'integrated training' of the body, mind and soul for holistic education. The collective ideologies of these thinkers laid down the corner stone for education in the country.

In Pursuit of Contemporary Needs

The post-independence period (after 1947) witnessed rapid expansion and reforms in higher education to evolve a system of education relevant to the life, living and aspirations of the people. In the wake of educational developments in independent India significant advisory and regulatory bodies specifically for higher education were instituted. Relevant among these being:

- *The University Grants Commission* (*UGC*) set up in 1952, was constituted as a statutory body under an Act of Parliament in 1956. The establishment of the UGC was the first major legislative measure initiated by the Government of India (GOI) under the constitutional provision reserving to it the powers for coordination and determination of standards in universities;
- *The All India Council for Technical Education* (*AICTE*) an advisory body, set up in 1948, to assist the Central Government in the planning and development of technical education at the post-secondary level. Education in engineering and technology, architecture, management and pharmacy lies within the purview of the AICTE. In 1988, the AICTE was constituted as a statutory body under an Act of Parliament;

- *National Council for Teacher Education* (*NCTE*) established in 1973 by a Government resolution, as a national expert body to advise Central and State Governments on all matters pertaining to teacher education. The Council was made a statutory body by an Act of Parliament in 1993.

Systematic efforts, on the part of the government, were made towards the preparation of educational policies for the future that needed 'radical changes' to actualize a national system of education (Indian National Commission for Cooperation, 1998) that would equip the country to 'compete' in the global economy made possible through the modernization of India. In order to implement the new policy, it was decided that higher education needed to be amended so as to produce manpower to facilitate capital growth, as committed by the government. A new culture of vocational (skills oriented) and professional (conduct oriented) education was henceforth initialized through various educational institutions in the country. The expression 'radical changes' thus came to be interpreted as generating manpower for the globalized order. The current 10th Five-Year Plan (2002–2007) has initiated a major programme of vocationalization, at the under-graduate level, in about 35 subjects. Vocational courses need to be designed with job potential in emerging areas such as information technology, biotechnology, biomedicine, genetic engineering, applied psychology, tourism and travel, physical education and sports (GOI, 2004a, b), to name a few. Unlike conventional vocations, the newly identified areas of knowledge allayed with the new world ordering. Educating a generation of intellectuals and workers for participation in a global system now poses a fresh challenge. Future times alone will judge India's prudence in coping with these challenges.

The Case of India

Tourism Education Practices

Although tourism may have been a latecomer to India (Singh, 1997, p. 301), its practice and principles had been in place centuries ago. In this context, the tradition of *Tirtha-yatra* (pilgrimages) was a sophisticated and highly evolved approach to learning and education (Bharadwaj, 1973). Kaur's (1985) treatise on *Himalayan Pilgrimages and the New Tourism* provides sufficient evidence of the elaborate level of documentation and service provisioning. Since then, times have changed and with it modern tourism has captured the attention of the government and businesses for commercial economics.

Tourism research in India commenced in the early 1970s, when the first known authoritative study of tourism as an industry was published (Singh, 1975). Ten years from then, a few other researchers (Kaur, 1985; Singh, 1985) ventured into the phenomenon. These studies were essentially works of geographers whose discipline in integrative approaches could be readily applied to such a disparate and conglomerate field (Singh, 1992). Indian researchers, have by and large, been wary of tourism for reasons of ambiguity and novelty. The few (such as Singh, 1989; Bisht, 1994; Chaudhary, 1996; Singh, 1996; Singh & Singh, 1999; Chaturvedi, 2002; Kuniyal, 2002; Gardner, Sinclair, Berkes & Singh, 2002; Sekhar,

2003; Singh, 2004; Singh & Singh, 2004; Singh, 2004) who have engaged with it have focused on impact studies. To further the cause of tourism education and research in India, the Centre for Tourism Research and Development, Lucknow committed to the publication of the academic journal *Tourism Recreation Research*, in 1976. Its 30 volumes, thus far, have forged new directions to encourage tourism research and education in the country. Few have heeded to the need of tourism studies in the country. The publication, *AN Newsletter* of the EQUATIONS (Equitable Tourism Options) an NGO based in Bangalore, is similarly devoted to research, training and the promotion of holistic tourism in India. Recently, the The Energy and Resource Institute (TERI), New Delhi, has accomplished a few significant projects on tourism and its impacts (see TERI, 2000, 2001). An interesting observation worth noting is that institutions engaged in tourism research in India are largely non-governmental organizations. In comparison to their research activities, relatively little is known of university based researches. One explanation for this perhaps is that the study of tourism in India is largely delivered with a vocational intent rather than academic earnestness.

Singh (1997) and Jithendran and Baum (2000) have investigated and documented the evolution of hospitality and tourism education and training in India. In their accounts, the Centre for Vocational Studies, University of Delhi, was identified as the pioneer institute in initializing a tourism studies programme in 1972. As an employment oriented programme, much of the course work was devoted to training personnel for airline ticketing and tour guiding services. Prior to this, programmes in hospitality were training personnel for manpower needs of the hotel industry, under the aegis of the All India Council of Technical Education (AICTE). The students in these programmes were groomed for the middle management and craft levels of performance. Parallel to this, hotel companies and the government owned Indian Tourism Development Corporation (ITDC) had been quick to set up their own training institutions to meet with the growing demand for skilled and semi-skilled manpower for a promising tourism industry.

The establishment of the Indian Institute of Travel and Tourism Management (IITTM) marks the right beginning of tourism (non-hospitality) education in the country in 1983 (Jithendran & Baum, 2000). In the initial phase the institute developed programmes for the in-service personnel of tourism administration, largely the government employees. Gradually, it expanded this function to service employees of the different sectors of the tourism and travel industry, such as managers, tour operators and travel agents. As an apex body for tourism education in India, the IITTM catalyzed the initiation of tourism courses in Indian universities, largely at the Master's level. Historically, Kurukshetra University was the first to recognize and formally adopt tourism education in 1991. Since the adoption was ratified by the UGC, there are more than 40 universities and affiliated colleges that offer tourism programmes today (IITTM, 2004). In addition to these the AICTE has granted approval to numerous private institutions of management to make a bid for tourism education, either within their MBA course structure or as a stand alone. These programmes are of course subject to stringent periodical reviews and evaluations. Depending upon their capacities, some universities and institutions render tourism programmes through distance education. In this regard, the Indira Gandhi National Open University (IGNOU) has an impressive outreach across the country. Interestingly, although the tourism programmes offered by the three institutions, viz. IITTM, UGC and the IGNOU aim to provide tourism programmes with distinct vocational bearings, they tend to differ considerably in their content and approach to tourism studies.

The Search for Integrated Tourism Curricula

The challenge of an integrated approach to tourism education lies in blending conventional and contemporary disciplines and practices in a manner that may be of use to the society at large. Dale and Robinson (2001) forward a three-domain model of tourism education based on generic, functional, and product/market-based themed degree routes. In a slight deviation from this, Echtner (1995) constructs a three-pronged approach to tourism education — vocational, professional and entrepreneurial. The commonality in the models presented by Dale and Robinson and Echtner is that tourism training and education are seemingly blended. Nonetheless, their conspicuous avoidance of the disciplinary approach to tourism studies could undermine the values of tourism as a disciplinary investigation.

In a comparative study between tourism and hospitality programmes, Chen and Groves (1999) model three basic approaches to philosophical integration of the two (see Table 1). The first type bears heavily on the mutual inclusion of tourism and hospitality philosophies, where the two are seen as combining their individuality in a manner that enhances their ability to achieve more than what could have been achieved separately. The overlaps in content are generally in the process of delivering the two disciplines. Thus, while tourism relates largely to the impact of marketing studies (economic, environmental and social impact studies), hospitality is focused on services, marketing, and management related to travel, hotels, restaurants, commercial recreation and leisure businesses. Perhaps, this model illustrates the ideal blend that appreciates the value of each in a symbiotic balance. This model necessarily includes esoteric research that is aimed at strengthening the discipline. Owing to the evaluative nature of the contents, it is almost impossible to find recognition for this model by business professionals, which is perhaps its major limitation. Following this, the second model is a contraposition to the first, as it seeks to align itself primarily with the industry in receiving inputs for the content and structure of tourism courses. Herein, the contents are hospitality dominated, and tourism is positioned as an adjunct to the service-based industry, thus limiting its scope to the realm of travel. These courses are distinctively flavoured by business management studies in specialized areas of hotels, restaurants, casinos, conventions, clubs and catering. An indispensable component of such courses is professional job training for experiential learning. This ensures that learning is performance oriented and serves the needs of the industry. Advancement of knowledge is sought for through applied researches in operations management and human resources, primarily. Hence, professional affiliation for such courses is indeed obligatory. The third model of tourism courses deviates from the second primarily on account of its focus on employment opportunities in the public and quasi public tourism sectors. For this purpose, tourism is conceptualized as an economic system that includes hospitality as one of its sectors. Here, tourism is contextualized for economic development and hence the course design emphasizes the study of planning and management, economics, geography and the like. Institutions offering these courses must maintain professional affiliations for job placements, as in the second model.

Table 1: Philosophical Relationships between Tourism and Hospitality (t & h) Academic Programmes.

Model — 1	Model — 2	Model — 3
Nature Contemplative, philosophical; abstract; directed towards critical inquiry.	**Nature** Vocational/professional standardized; specific, training	**Nature** Sector directed; focused on public sector
Mutually inclusive Initial socialization is achieved t & h and where one discipline begins to appreciate the value of the other.	**Hospitality dominated** Tourism is encompassed in varying degrees.	**Tourism dominated** Hospitality is a sector
Symbiotic relationship	Tourism is viewed as the travel sector.	Tourism is an important factor to the economic sector
Visible parity (balance)		
Overlaps Can be applied and transferred from one discipline to another	Tourism is an important factor to the economic sector	Tourism is seen as a system
In course contents such as leisure, geography, language, general business management, information systems, marketing, management information systems, and economics.	**Service-based Content** Business management with specialization in areas such as hotels, restaurants, casinos, conventions, catering, clubs.	**Approach** "How to develop a tourism business to replace other industrial or other economic developmental segments that have been lost?"
Identity of each maintained Content-specific and the materials cannot be transferred	**Professional job training** Specialized — chef, casino administrator, waiter(ess)	Tourism programmes are content-based depending on the location within the academic unit.
Focus of tourism in these relationships is the impact of marketing studies (economic, environmental and social impact studies)	**Applied research** In hospitality industry such as travel agencies, resort/casino management, tour organizations, hotel reservations.	**Student** Can select a career based on a large number of direct and support industries. Complain about not being able to find employment, but this may be due to a
Hospitality's focus is service, marketing, and management related to travel, hotels, restaurants, commercial recreation, and leisure businesses	**Affiliations** Professional hospitality associations required	
Combining their uniqueness in their disciplines that gives them the ability to achieve more than can be achieved separately		

Table 1: Continued.

	Model — 1	Model — 2	Model — 3
	Research is esoteric Doctrine oriented **Affiliations** Limited professional involvement with organizations **Students** Ability to problem solve and view the big picture	**Students** Receive skill-specific training	lack of understanding of the multiplicity of industries and how they relate to one another.

Source: Adapted from Chen and Groves (1999).

Comparative Study of Three Tourism Programmes from the Indian Education System

A study of the stipulated Post Graduate (P.G.) course-work for Tourism Studies of three national-level institutions has been carried out to identify the approach to tourism education in India. The primary criteria for selecting these institutions is that all of them have a nationwide influence, in the specific context of programme structure, large-scale operational networks and high student enrollments. All these elements are mutually interdependent. Another interesting fact of the selected tourism programmes is that they have been integrated with management studies. The proposed models have been modified to adapt to a comparison between tourism programmes in the context of management, as opposed to the relationship between hospitality and tourism. Hence the analysis is limited to large nationwide samples, as the programmes (a) are representative of their popularity by high student enrollments, (b) are offered by recognized institutions, (c) are declared to be distinct from hospitality programmes that are within the exclusive purview of the National Council of the Hotel Management and Catering Technology institutions, (d) have had a long-standing existence and (e) offer a wide range of programmes for various levels. For the purpose of uniformity among the samples, tourism programmes at the master's or postgraduate level have been selected for this study. It is pertinent to state that these programmes are offered to all those students who have successfully completed their Bachelor's degree, in tourism studies or any discipline that may potentially contribute to their understanding of these programmes. The three tourism programmes being examined here are those of the UGC, IGNOU and IITTM.

The UGC Course Work on Tourism Administration and Management

By way of a background, the UGC is responsible for setting the standards for education in universities and is directly under the purview of the Government of India. Altogether, 93 subjects have been identified and enlisted by the UGC, of which Tourism Administration and Management is one among them. This programme is conducted in University departments which may be exclusively designated for Tourism Studies or be lodged within other departments such as History, Commerce, Management or any other related disciplines. The completion of the programme culminates into the award of a Masters degree. The tourism programme therefore assessed here is that of the P.G. level. It must be known that the University system in India is an autonomous one and has legislative sanction to maintain and carry out its academic functions with negligible government intervention. The duration of the programme is typically 2 years.

The course content is oriented towards maintaining a balance between administration and management aspects of the tourism industry and the disciplinary conceptualizations of the subject of tourism. Tourism is, therefore, a subject of study and inquiry that interfaces with conventional disciplines. To this end, the course structure and contents are laid out exhaustively. Students must begin to learn about the subject from its foundations, upwards. This translates into understanding the basic concepts, definitions, elements, trends and patterns, followed by intensive studies on the organization and distribution patterns of the industry, in general separate courses are devoted to the hotel industry, transport sector and the travel agencies. In the second year students combine their previous learning with managerial and administrative aspects of the subject matter. These courses relate to planning and policy, tourism marketing research methods, management, and financial management and planning (further details of the course contents are provided in Table 2).

The course material is largely textual and includes a wide variety of ingredients that are conceptual, analytical, integrated, multidisciplinary and interdisciplinary. The contents were specifically geared towards the country's own settings and offerings in the field of tourism practices. A vast course, such as this, is best approached through class-room activities such as instructions and open discussions primarily. This is supported by presentations, problem solving and brain-storming exercises. Learning is largely instructor based and is further facilitated by student enthusiasm and awareness of real world situations gleaned from additional sources from the print media and national television networks, experiences and case studies. A field study is an essential component that is undertaken annually. The field study may or may not be linked to research assignments, although projects and dissertations are compulsory for the successful completion of the programme.

The IGNOU Course Work on Masters in Tourism Management Programme

The IGNOU is especially designed to serve the larger masses of interested learners through their distance education programmes. This was devised in 1985 to democratize education through easy access to learning at all levels. Its tourism programmes target the work force already employed or seeking employment in this area of study or activity. Knowledge is disseminated through innovative multi-media teaching and learning systems as well as printed reading material. As with the Indian University system, the IGNOU, along with its programmes, enjoys an autonomous status with regard to its programme/course offerings and in its functioning. This facet enables it to retain exclusivity without having to rely on professional organizations, academic or industrial. Since its system is developed essentially for distance education, the university has a nationwide network of administrative units. Additionally, it utilizes the facilities of existing academic services and structures.

Table 2: Comparison of Three Tourism Programmes Offered in India.

Institutions & Title of Tourism Programme → Variables ↓	UGC Tourism Administration & Management Model — 1 Programme	IITTM P.G. Diploma in Tourism Management Model — 2	IGNOU Masters in Tourism Management Model — 3
Influential	Tourism and hospitality are mutually inclusive	Hospitality dominated	Tourism dominated
Affiliations	Negligible government intervention	Professional/ institutional — national/international travel agencies and Asia-Pacific (regional) education network	Autonomous
Learning objectives	Intellectual development and understanding, critical thinking, problem solving abilities	Practice oriented learning; skill development; hands-on training	Development of rational and logical understanding
Research	Conceptual and discipline-oriented	Negligible	Project work
Course content	**Year 1** Understanding tourism — the basic concepts, definitions, elements, trends and patterns. Organization and distribution patterns of the industry. Functions and inter-relationships between local, regional, national and international organizations in tourism, travel and hospitality. Provisioning of products and services and the horizontal and vertical flow of information are examined. Fundamentals of tourism studies — the types and uses of tourism resources,	Travel and tourism — tourism concepts and impacts, travel agency and tour operations, geography and international tourism, tourism products of India and transport. Management — general concepts of management and organizational behaviour; quantitative analysis and events	**Year 1** **Module 1** — Management concepts — professionalism, management processes and skills, communication, organization culture and managerial ethos, planning process, interpersonal relations, leadership and group dynamics are clustered into one module. **Module 2** — Planning and development of human resources that

Table 2: Continued.

Institutions & Title of Tourism Programme → Variables ↓	UGC Tourism Administration & Management Model — 1 Programme	IITTM P.G. Diploma in Tourism Management Model — 2	IGNOU Masters in Tourism Management Model — 3
	the nature, culture and heritage resources of the country, along with the issues related with the use of these. The hotel industry — linkage with the tourism industry, the structure of the industry; different types of accommodations found in India; hotel operations in the public and the private sectors; HRD; fiscal and non-fiscal incentives and ethical and legal regulations. The transport sector — types of transport systems available in India and their future prospects Travel agency — tour operations business such as air ticketing, packaging, cargo handling, aspects of entrepreneurship in the travel business. **Year 2** Tourism planning and policy perspectives — levels, types, sectoral plans and life-cycles of India's tourism policies and planning mechanism. Feasibility studies, master plans, ethics and sustainability	management; marketing for travel and tourism Computer and information technology — computing and information systems in tourism. In the second half of the programme students study tourism policy, planning and development; contemporary issues; accounting and finance for management; business communication and personality development, advanced computing and information system in tourism. A foreign language Specializations (in any five of the elective offerings) in airfares	include planning, forecasting methods and techniques, job evaluation, task analysis HR information systems, HR auditing, HR accounting, HR and the service industry. **Module 3** — Training for the tourism industry — recruitment, selection, motivation, appraisal, career planning, monitoring, counseling, discipline, grievance handling, compensation and salary administration, and legal aspects. **Module 4** — Information systems in India — information management, MIS, computers, MIS and decision making, social and legal dimensions in computerization. **Module 5** — Accounting/finance/working capital —

Table 2: Continued.

Institutions & Title of Tourism Programme →	UGC Tourism Administration & Management Model — 1 Programme	IITTM P.G. Diploma in Tourism Management Model — 2	IGNOU Masters in Tourism Management Model — 3
Variables ↓			
	Tourism marketing — concepts, processes, components, marketing services and communication strategies. Research methods — field techniques, trends, methodology, statistical analysis, probability, standard deviation, testing and sampling are taught through practical assignments. Management — concept, nature, business orientation to monitoring, organizing, planning, MIS, controlling and computer networking for CRS. Financial management and planning in tourism — importance of financial management, budgeting, structure of financial plans and their analysis, the management of earnings, accounting and policy and the functioning of the Tourism Finance Corporation of India.	and ticketing tour package operations air cargo operations hospitality and resort management information technology in tourism services marketing	divided into five major sub-sections titled: accounting framework, financial statements, cost management, financial and investment analysis and financial decisions **Module 6** — Marketing — principles of marketing (4Ps), planning, distribution and strategizing. **Module 7** — Sales and product management — aspects of selling, promotion, communication and the like. **Module 8** — Entrepreneurship and small scale enterprises — aspects of business entrepreneurship in tourism. **Year 2** **Module 1** — Tourism markets — national and international types and characteristics.

Table 2: Continued.

Institutions & Title of Tourism Programme → Variables ↓	UGC Tourism Administration & Management Model — 1 Programme	IITTM P.G. Diploma in Tourism Management Model — 2	IGNOU Masters in Tourism Management Model — 3
			Module 2 — Tourism impacts — social, environmental, economic, political, legal and global environment. Module 3 — Tourism planning and development Module 4 — Tourism product — design and development Module 5 — Business and management of tour and travel agency operations Module 6 — Transport system operations (road specifically) Module 7 — The MICE (meetings, incentives, conferences and expositions) industry Module 8 — Dissertation

The IGNOU offers four basic programmes in the area of tourism studies, namely a 6-month certificate, a 1-year diploma, a 3-year Bachelors and a 2-year Master's course. Of these, the course work for the 'Masters' programme is examined here to maintain congruency among the samples for the study. This programme enrolls students who will have completed a Bachelors degree programme successfully. An alternative eligibility criterion admits diploma holders of the Hotel Management programme — a 3-year study legitimized by the National Council of Hotel Management and Catering Technology. These students will, nonetheless, be expected to study and qualify in four additional courses on the fundamentals of tourism, its development, management and marketing, before undertaking Masters level studies.

The Masters level course comprises 16 modules, in all. The first half of the programme is developed along the fundamentals of management studies, with specific bearing on tourism. General aspects of management, planning and development of human resources, training for the tourism industry, information systems in India, accounting/finance/working capital and marketing, entrepreneurship, national and international tourism markets impact issues, tourism planning and development, and tourism product design and development, the business and management of tour/travel agency operations and transport (road specifically) system operations and the MICE industry (further details of the course contents are provided in Table 2). The entire course is concluded with the completion of a dissertation work, for which a separate guide booklet is made available besides designating supervisors.

This programme is delivered in modules (16 in all), largely in the form of printed text for study and limited contact classes. The contact classes and counselling sessions are announced well in advance and are valuable for students who need initiation into distance learning. A variety of resources have been mobilized to assist students in the learning process. Thus, books and related reading materials are supplemented by audio–video resources. Nationwide teaching programmes are telecasted via national television network for convenient access to students. In order to successfully accomplish the programme, students are evaluated on their assignments, on a regular basis, although term end exams and the dissertation constitute a major proportion of final grade. This distance education programme seeks to reach out to a large proportion of the working population, who may be keen learners either for self-education or for career/self-development. With this presumption, the approach to education is largely self-learning and/or work-based learning which is provided through conceptualization and analytical thinking. The approach employed in the dissertation component underlines these aspects of the programme, as the students are directed to evaluate and research on tourism-related themes emerging from their work or local environments. Thus far, programmes offered by IGNOU have proved to be successful in their agenda of democratizing education in general. This programme seems to have attempted to socialize tourism studies to some extent by incorporating and adapting to the country's social, natural, cultural and economic settings.

The IITTM Course Work in P.G. Diploma in Tourism Management Programme

In contrast to the previous two autonomous academic institutions, the IITTM is a government owned and operated establishment. It operates directly under the Ministry of Tourism, Government of India, and enjoys the reputation of a national institution. Although its outreach is not as expansive as those of the UGC and the IGNOU, it does exert a nationwide presence through its headquarters at Gwalior, nine chapters and one regional centre. This institution was set up in 1983 with the primary objective of meeting the manpower needs of the Indian tourism industry. In this regard, the IITTM appropriately fits within the Professional Institution category of institutions of Higher education in India. For this reason, the institution maintains professional affiliations with the Indian Association of Tour Operators (IATO), Travel Agents Association of India (TAAI), International Federation of Freight Forwarders Association (FFFAI), Association of Domestic Tour Operators of India (ADTOI), and Network of Asia-Pacific Education and Training Institutes in Tourism (APETIT).

IITTM offers four programmes in tourism education specifically; namely, P.G. Diploma in Tourism Management (PGDTM), Diploma in Destination Management, Diploma in Travel and Tourism Industry Management and Bachelor (with Honors) in Management. The institution has recently introduced a Business Management programme which offers three specialization electives in services marketing, tourism management and IT in tourism. The PGDTM course work has been selected for examining here. The programme is of year long duration and is a full time course for students who have successfully completed their Bachelors studies with any discipline. The primary objective of the programme is to train potential professionals in the management of travel, tourism and air cargo management, by enhancing their skills, knowledge and analytical acumen.

The course work is partitioned into two semesters of 6 months each. The first set of the modules are further sub-divided into three major components — Travel and Tourism; Management and Computer and Information Technology essentially (further details of the course contents are provided in Table 2). Evaluations for the course work and student learning are based on class participation, home assignments, projects, mid-term tests and term end examinations. Upon the successful completion of this course the students are assisted with job placement and supported through on-the-job training guidance. The course structure is clearly geared towards employment. The study of tourism is largely knowledge and skills oriented and also incorporate a work-based component.

Discussion

Integrated studies usually combine practice-oriented course structures with those that are generalized and principle based. While the former contributes directly to the development of human capital, the latter is aimed at developing intellectual capital. Hence, the importance of neither can be ignored in the context of contemporary education needs. Educationists continue to grapple with creating a perfect balance between concept and practice inputs in higher education, though with little success. Perhaps the quest is likely to continue, since it is difficult to find consensus on an ideally balanced course structure. Tourism courses, too, tend to be inclined towards one or the other. Assuming that variable orientations exists in course construction for tourism studies, three tourism programmes were selected from the Indian higher education system for a closer examination of their bearings. In general, it was observed that these courses were fairly similar in the sense that they are contingent on the subject of management in varying measures. However, each of them was found to maintain a certain level of uniqueness, in their content and approach to tourism studies. An attempt is made to juxtapose these cases with the conceptual framework of Chen and Groves (1999) (refer Table 1) although it was found that none of the case examples made a perfect fit with the descriptions offered in the models. The outstanding rationale for this blurring is attributed to the fact that courses in hospitality were excluded from this study, as the investigation was aimed at understanding the philosophies enshrined in tourism programmes alone. Differences in national education policy thrust, and standards between countries, could have also contributed to the indistinctness of boundaries in model reconstruction. Nonetheless the model proved useful in identifying the philosophical approaches adopted by the three tourism programmes.

In the first case (*The UGC Course Work on Tourism Administration and Management*), the nature of the course adopts a liberal, abstract, contemplative, philosophical/critical inquiry approach. Such an approach to the study of tourism requires imaginative inputs necessary for the acceptance of tourism as a discipline. This programme seemed to belong to the category of Model 1 within which intellectual development is intended. Students of this programme are given a broad understanding of tourism as a phenomenon and are then trained to think critically and solve problems that threaten it. The absence of professional ties between the industry and the institution may be perceived as a structural weakness of the programme. In this context the third case (*The IITTM Course Work in P.G. Diploma in Tourism Management Programme*) appears to have an advantage over the first, since the IITTM was not merely a professional institution but maintained ties with a set of travel and tourism agencies, of national and international importance. Besides this the IITTM's P.G. programme has distinct practice-related inputs in the course structure such as language skills, technical (ticketing) skills and on-the-job training. In this regard the course was found to bear towards management in tourism with some aspects of vocational/professional training that are globally standardized and job specific. In all possibility the IITTM course work for P.G. Diploma in Tourism Management matches with Model 2 of Chen and Groves (1999). The third model, proposed by Chen and Groves, indicates heavy leanings towards management and commerce so to aid in career development opportunities in the public and/or the private sectors. *The IGNOU Course Work on Masters in Tourism Management Programme* is laden with studies in marketing, entrepreneurship and human resources, information technology and the tourism industry. Hence, while the course structure is fairly expansive, it does not seek to train for potential employment nor does it contribute to the understanding of tourism as a phenomenon. By and large, the course presents tourism as an industry where employment opportunities may exist.

In brief, the tourism programmes of the UGC and the IGNOU seem to challenge student's reasoning and acumen for thoughtful action. Despite this basic similarity, the two were found to differ on the purpose of education. In the latter case (IGNOU), the course clearly demonstrated an industrial context, as there is an explicit emphasis on the growth and development of tourism business at the entrepreneurial and corporate levels. The tourism programme of the UGC, on the other hand, has a wide scope that includes an understanding of tourism through its myriad sectors and related issues. In the absence of internships and practicum, and due to the predominant presence of a focus on concepts and principles, this programme provides a general knowledge base of the philosophies and practices in tourism. Perhaps, it would be worthwhile to investigate the details of course contents and the delivery process, of the UGC's tourism programme, to determine the extent to which it contributes to intellectual development of its learners. The third programme, that of the IITTM is typically vocation oriented which makes it essentially a workforce generating programme rather than one that arouses inquisition.

Conclusion

It is pertinent to state that the purpose of this study was not to advocate the relevance and utility of one course over the other. Instead it is interesting to note that the three major tourism programmes, at the post graduate levels, have varying philosophical perspectives that reflect the complexities of integrated studies/learning. These are not unique to India. In fact it is typical of countries struggling with economic restructuring to grapple with issues concerning the integration of academic and occupational curricula (Gaskell & Hepburn, 1997). Nonetheless, India, with its own history of philosophical thought on education, progress and development has recently been confronted with these issues. The issues become even more so complicated owing to the structure and processes in higher education system.

India is one among numerous other countries undergoing economic re-structuring. This has had an immediate impact on its education policies, due to which manpower development programmes are beginning to occupy a centre stage in the Indian higher education system. Regrettably, this responsiveness has occurred with little planning for the nation's needs for intellectual capital as well as its needs for human resources. This is more so evident in the case of tourism that had to contend long for recognition as an industry, which is rather ironic as it has yet to gain the respectability of an academic discipline, as well. Perhaps, this explains for the near absence of conceptualization of tourism as a discipline. Through an examination of three tourism courses, it is evidenced that so far the study of tourism is by and large perceived within a managerial domain for which it is embraced by educational institutions. With this context, the three cases corroborate a future for tourism education towards professionalization. Apparently, tourism courses fail to ascribe to the Indian education philosophies laid down by its visionaries. Furthermore, it is observed that the philosophies that guide higher education in India presently have been geared towards accommodating the emergent needs for manpower development largely. The recent workshop held by the IITTM (see Singh, 2001) showcases the institution's primary engagement with tourism and hospitality trade. It is at this juncture, that 'need' develops a dichotomous meaning. Hence, it is worthwhile to question the nature of the need — viz. is it the need of the times to remain steadfast on the ideological path for national education upon which the current system has developed or should the system be flexed to accommodate the need of contemporary times of competition and economic growth? The basic problem is in identifying this 'need' — both for the short term and the long run. This is most certainly a debatable issue — one that calls for visionary decision making on whether to flow with the current trends or toil against the current to chart new trends towards an integrated curriculum in tourism education.

References

Airey, D., & Johnson, S. (1999). The content of tourism degree courses in the UK. *Tourism Management, 20*, 229–235.

Bharadwaj, S. M. (1973). *Hindu places of pilgrimages in India*. New Delhi: Thompson Press Ltd.

Bisht, H. (1994). *Tourism in Garhwal Himalaya with special reference to mountaineering and trekking*. New Delhi: Indus Publishing House.

Chaturvedi, G. (2002). Ecotourism in Gangotri region of the Garhwal Himalayas. *Tourism Recreation Research, 27*(3), 41–51.

Chaudhary, M. (1996). India's tourism: A paradoxical product. *Tourism Management, 17*(8), 616–619.

Chen, K. -C., & Groves, D. (1999). The importance of examining philosophical relationships between tourism and hospitality curricula. *International Journal of Contemporary Hospitality Management, 11*(1), 37–42.

Chitnis, S. (2000). The challenge of access in Indian higher education. *Liberal Education, 86*(4), 10–17.

Churchward, J., & Riley, M. (2002). Tourism occupations and education: An exploration study. *International Journal of Tourism Research, 4*, 77–86.

Cohen, E. (1999). Towards an agenda for tourism research in Southeast Asia. *Asia Pacific Journal of Tourism Research, 4*(2), 79–89.

Csikszentmihaly, M. (1990). *Flow: The psychology of optimal experience*. Harper Perennial: New York.

Dale, C., & Robinson, N. (2001). The theming of tourism education: A three-domain approach. *International Journal of Contemporary Hospitality Management, 13*(1), 30–34.

Delors, J. (1996). *Learning: The treasure within*. Report to UNESCO of the International Commission on Education for the Twenty-first Century. Paris: UNESCO.

Dewey, J. (1916). *Democracy and education: An introduction to the philosophy of education*. New York: Macmillan.

Echtner, C. (1995). Tourism education in developing nations: A three pronged approach. *Tourism Recreation Research, 20*(2), 32–41.

Gardner, J., Sinclair, J., Berkes, F., & Singh, R. B. (2002). Accelerated tourism development and its impacts in Kullu-Manali, H.P., India. *Tourism Recreation Research, 27*(3), 9–20.

Gaskell, P. J., & Hepburn, G. (1997). Integration of academic and occupational curricula in science and technology education. *Science Education, 81*(4), 469–481.

GOI. (2004a). Approach Paper on Education for Inclusion in 10th Plan — 2002–2007. http://www.education.nic.in. Accessed April 13, 2004.

GOI. (2004b). Professional education — Comprehensive information on Indian Education on the occasion of the celebrations of the 50th year of Indian independence. http://shikshanic.nic.in/cd50years/n/75/7Y/757Y0801.htm. Accessed June 30, 2004.

Golmohamad, M. (2004). World citizenship, identity and the notion of an integrated self. *Studies in Philosophy and Education, 23*, 131–148.

Harris, K. R., & Alexander, P. A. (1998). Integrated, constructivist education: Challenge and reality. *Educational Psychology Review, 10*(2), 115–127.

IITTM. (2004). *Directory — Education and training institutes of tourism and travel in India*. Indian Institutes of Tourism and Travel Management, Gwalior.

Indian National Commission for Cooperation. (1998). Higher education in India — vision and action. UNESCO world conference on higher education in the twenty-first century. Paris, 5–9 October 1998.

Jafari, J. (1990). Research and scholarship — The basis of tourism education. *Journal of Tourism Studies, 1*(1), 33–41.

Jafari, J. (1997). Tourismification of the profession: Chameleon job names across the industry. *Progress in Tourism and Hospitality Research, 3*, 175–181.

Jithendran, K. J., & Baum, T. (2000). Human resources development and sustainability — The case of Indian tourism. *International Journal of Tourism Research, 2*, 403–421.

Kaur, J. (1985). *Himalayan pilgrimages and the new tourism*. New Delhi: Himalayan Books.

Koh, K. (1995). Designing the four-year tourism management curriculum. *Journal of Travel Research, 34*(1), 68–72.

Kuniyal, J. C. (2002). Mountain expeditions: Minimising the impact. *Environmental Impact Assessment Review, 22*, 561–581.

Langham, T. C., & Phillips, C. L. (2001). Developing a program in sociological practice: Program structure, curriculum design, and professional culture. *Sociological Practice: A Journal of Clinical and Applied Sociology, 3*(1), 55–74.

Leiper, N. (2000). An emerging discipline. *Annals of Tourism Research, 27*(3), 805–809.

Przeclawski, K. (1993). Tourism as a subject of interdisciplinary research. In: D. G. Pearce & R. W. Butler (Eds). *Tourism research — Critiques and challenges* (pp. 175–200). London: Routledge.

Raina, M. K., & Sibia, A. (1995). Schooling in Mirambika — A case study. Unpublished manuscript, Department of Educational Psychology and Foundations of Education. New Delhi: NCERT.

Raina, M. K., & Srivastava, A. K. (1997). Educational psychology in India: Its present status and future concerns. *International Journal of Group Tensions, 27*(4), 309–340.

Raina, M. K., & Vats, A. (1988). Neuropsychological perspectives in the school-age child in India. *School Psychology International, 9*, 33–37.

Sankar, Y. (2004). Education in crisis: A value-based model of education provides some guidance. *Interchange, 35*(1), 127–151.

Sapre, P. M., & Ranade, M. D. (2001). Moral leadership in education: An Indian perspective. *International Journal of Leadership in Education, 4*(4), 367–381.

Schriewer, J. (2000). Forms of externalisation in educational knowledge. *Seminar at Oxford University Day Conference on 'Theory, method and practice in comparative education'*, 9 February.

Sekhar, N. U. (2003). Local people's attitudes towards conservation and wildlife tourism around Sariska Tiger Reserve, India. *Journal of Environmental Management, 69*, 339–347.

Singh, M. (2001). Reflections on colonial legacy and dependency in Indian vocational education and training (VET): A societal and cultural perspective. *Journal of Education and Work, 14*(2), 209–225.

Singh, S. (1992). Geographers on tourism geography. *Tourism Recreation Research, 17*(1), 60–67.

Singh, S. (Ed.) (1996). *Profiles of Indian tourism.* New Delhi: APH Publishing Corporation.

Singh, S. (1997). Developing human resources for the tourism industry with reference to India. *Tourism Management, 18*(5), 299–306.

Singh, S. (2001). National seminar on tourism education and training in India. *Tourism Recreation Research, 26*(1), 126–127.

Singh, S. (2004). Domestic tourism in India: Chaos/crisis/challenge. *Tourism Recreation Research, 29*(2), 35–46.

Singh, S. (2004). Shades of green: Ecotourism for sustainability. New Delhi: TERI.

Singh, S. N. (1985). *Geography of tourism and recreation.* New Delhi: Inter India.

Singh, T. V. (1975). *Tourism and tourist industry of U.P.* New Delhi: New Heights.

Singh, T. V. (1989). *The Kulu Valley: Impact of tourism development in mountain areas.* New Delhi: Himalayan Books.

Singh, T. V., & Singh, S. (1999). Coastal tourism, conservation and the community: Case of Goa. In: T. V. Singh & S. Singh (Eds). *Tourism in the critical environments* (pp. 65–76). New York: Cognizant Communication Corp.

Singh, T. V., & Singh, S. (2004). On bringing people and park together through ecotourism: The Nanda Devi National Park, India. *Asia Pacific Journal of Tourism Research, 9*(1), 43–55.

Smith, G., & Cooper, C. (2000). Competitive approaches to tourism and hospitality curriculum design. *Journal of Travel Research, 39*(1), 90–95.

Stenhouse, L. (1967). *Culture and education.* London: Thomas Nelson.

TERI. (2000). http://www.teriin.org/reports/rep16/rep16.htm.

TERI. (2001). http://www.teriin.org/reports/rep17/rep17.htm.

Tribe, J. (2001). Research paradigms and the tourism curriculum. *Journal of Travel Research, 39*(4), 442–448.

Tynjälä, P., Välimaa, J., & Sarja, A. (2003). Pedagogical perspectives on the relationships between higher education and working life. *Higher Education, 46*(2), 147–166.

Varma, L. P. (1965). Psychiatry in ayurveda. *Indian Journal of Psychiatry, 7*, 293–312.

Whitehead, A. N. (1951). *The aims of education.* New York: North American Libraries Mentor Books.

Chapter 15

The Netherlands

Magiel Venema

Introduction

The aim of this chapter is to provide an overview of travel and tourism education in the Netherlands. In this it focuses particularly on the institutes preparing mainly young people for jobs in the travel and tourism industry at secondary and higher levels of vocational education. The chapter starts with a brief overview of the Dutch educational system. This is followed by a short description of the first institute for tourism and leisure education in the country and a broad description of tourism education at secondary vocational and higher vocational levels, as well in the universities. Attention is also given to the new models of competency-based learning, both at the secondary and higher levels; to the relations with the industry and the organisations who regulate this involvement; and to teacher training and teacher organisations. The chapter also includes some comments on the related study areas of hotel and restaurant education, leisure education and those institutes preparing for media and entertainment management.

Vocational Education in the Netherlands

The School Level

In the Netherlands there are two main types of educational institutes public and private (not for profit). The private, not for profit, schools comprise mainly those with a religious denomination. Both types are, by constitution, treated equally by the government, receive the same funding and have to adhere to the same standards. This equality is an important feature of the Dutch educational system. It dates formally from 1917 and was achieved after a long political dispute between Catholics and Protestants who each wanted their own primary schools, with equal state funding. In 1917, this was achieved and extended also to secondary and higher education. In vocational education there are also private schools, which offer different types of courses on a commercial basis. These operate for profit and

An International Handbook of Tourism Education
Copyright © 2005 by Elsevier Ltd.
All rights of reproduction in any form reserved
ISBN: 0-08-044667-1

receive no support from the government although if they prepare for the same awards as the government subsidized forms of education, they have to adhere to the same standards.

Education is compulsory in the Netherlands from the age of four for 12 years or until the year in which the age of 16 is reached. Primary education starts at the age of four and lasts for eight years. After that there are two options for secondary education. The first is a theoretical/academic type of education of five-years at *Hoger Algemeen Vormend Onderwijs* (HAVO) (General Secondary Education) or six-years at *Voorbereidend Wetenschappelijk Onderwijs* (VWO) (Pre-University Education). The HAVO offers direct access to the Dutch system of *Hoger Beroeps Onderwijs* (HBO) (Higher Professional Education, colleges with a 4-year Higher Vocational Education Programme, leading to a Bachelor degree). VWO gives access both to these Colleges and to the Universities (four years, leading to a Master degree). The second option is to enter the system of vocational education. After four years of initial vocational education at a junior secondary school, pupils can enter the system of secondary vocational education *Middelbaar Beroeps Onderwijs* (MBO) (Vocational education at secondary level). The MBO offers participants from the age of 16 a choice of over 700 courses, four training levels and two routes towards the final qualification for all kinds of professions. There is a full-time college-based route that includes work placements and there is a part-time work-based route, which combines part-time education with an internship in the industry.

Secondary Vocational Education

The secondary vocational education programmes are organised on the basis of the four main sectors of the economy: Engineering and Technology, Care and Welfare, Business and Agriculture. National bodies represent the different sectors of the economy and act as centres of knowledge and expertise responsible for the content and relevance of the courses. The provision is concentrated in more than 40 *Reginale Onderwijs Centra* (ROC) (Regional Training Centres) that cater for the needs for both students and adults wishing to gain a qualification. The ROCs and the national bodies are responsible for the education for a profession in practice. The national bodies ensure that approved learning establishments offer sufficient good quality placements. The colleges are required to offer courses to participants and work practice, and are responsible for coaching the participants. They arrange the rights and obligations of all involved in a practice agreement, drawn up between the parties. The work experience is made compulsory by the Adult and Vocational Education Act so as to guarantee the relevance of the courses to industry practice, and thus strengthen the ties between education and the labour market.

The ROCs are required to schedule 1,600 study hours and 850 hours of teaching per course per year. The courses offered are organised along a qualification structure, which comprises four levels of training:

- *Level 1*: Courses at assistant level. Students should be able to perform simple executive tasks;
- *Level 2*: Basic Vocational Training. Students should be able to perform executive tasks at a higher level. This level equals the minimum qualification that everyone in the field should possess;

- *Level 3*: Holders of Professional Training Diploma. Should be able to carry out tasks completely independently;
- *Level 4*: Middle Management or Specialist Training. Should be able to carry out tasks completely independently, combined with the ability to perform a broad-range of tasks in a particular field. They must also demonstrate that they possess non-job-specific skills, such as tactical and strategic thinking. They are expected to take up posts in which they have hierarchical, formal and organisational responsibilities.

These four levels are established within the European Union structure and make international comparison possible.

Today 700 qualification profiles are already defined. In principle, each of the courses for these awards should be offered in the variants full time or part-time with an apprenticeship. For each of the qualifications, core competencies are defined. In the future the qualification will not only encompass the professional core competencies, but will also include citizen competencies and learning competencies. The exit qualifications describe in abstract terms what is expected of students at each level. However, it is up to the ROCs how to organise their teaching and they are free to devise their own programmes for the courses they offer on the basis of the exit qualifications. To ensure that the qualifications are met, a special body is assigned to produce final examinations that students from all schools have to sit and pass.

Higher Vocational Education

The enrolment into the Colleges of the Higher Vocational Education System (HBO) is open to graduates of HAVO and VWO schools and also to holders of the level-4 qualification in a related field of secondary vocational education (MBO).

The duration of the HBO programmes is four years with a study load of 240 credit points under the European Credit Transfer System (ECTS). Each credit comprises a study load of 28 h. Graduates of the VWO and MBO can complete their studies in three years. MBO students need to possess a diploma in a related field of study. At the end, all students are awarded a Bachelor degree. Students can then continue to pursue a Master degree at a HBO College or at one of the Dutch universities in 3 or 4 semesters. All degree courses need to be accredited by the *Nederlands-Vlaamse Accreditatie Organisatie* (NVAO) (Dutch Flemish Accreditation Organisation).

Under Dutch law, every participant of full-time education aged 18 and over receives a study grant. At higher vocational level students receive a performance-related grant for a maximum of four years.

Education for Tourism

The Origins: NWIT in Breda

Education for tourism in the Netherlands in part owes its origins to an interchange in the early 1960s between the Dutch Secretary of Commerce, aware of the growing importance of tourism for the country, and the Director of the Convention and Visitor Bureau of Breda, a city in the south of the Netherlands. An initial outcome of this interchange was the recognition that there was no formal education for this growing sector. The more substantial outcome was the creation of the first tourism School. Following several reports in 1965, the budget of the Ministry of Education provided the necessary funds to start an institute, which would educate the future 'Tourism Officers'. The city of Breda was happy to provide housing and an old monastery in the city centre was made available for that purpose. The resulting *Nederlands Wetenschappelijk Instituut voor Toerisme* (NWIT) (Dutch Scientific Institute of Tourism) was created to operate with three areas of activity: education and training; research; a meeting place for tourism scholars and researchers from all over the world.

For the education and training activity, in 1966 the first 60 students enrolled on a programme lasting for 2 years and 3 months. The initial focus was very much on tourist attractions worldwide although it quickly became apparent that there was a need for a stronger emphasis on more theoretical subjects — economics, sociology, psychology and managerial skills. As a result, in 1967, the Institute refocused its education provision on more managerial and professional studies and at the same time became an official part of the Dutch higher vocational education system.

The education provision was organised as follows. In the first year the students had a common preparatory programme. After that they could choose from three areas of study: inbound and domestic tourism, outbound tourism; recreation and leisure. The programme included two internships of eight weeks each and the study was concluded with a thesis. Having earlier been extended to three years, in the 1980s the programme was extended to the normal higher vocational education duration of four years.

As far as the other activities of the Institute are concerned, the research department, became independent in 1971 under the name of the Dutch Research Institute of Tourism and Recreation (NRIT) and today still functions under that name. However, the idea of the 'Meeting Place' never really materialised.

From NWIT to NHTV

In 1987, after a merger with the Transport Academy based in the city of Tilburg, NWIT became part of the *Nationale Hogeschool voor Toerisme en Verkeer* (NHTV) (National College for Tourism and Transportation). Currently the NHTV (now named NHTV Breda University for Professional Education) has a student population of around 6,000 students. It is a themed college, where virtually every aspect of tourism and leisure can be studied. It offers the following four-year Bachelor Degree programmes: Tourism Management; Hotel Management; Facility Management; Functional Tourism Management; Leisure Management; Urban Planning; Transportation and Logistics Management; Media and Entertainment Management. It is also a partner in the European Tourism Management Master Degree programme (together with universities in Germany, United Kingdom, France, Spain, Sweden, Italy, and Portugal). In 2004, it was awarded the Tedqual Certification of the World Tourism Organization.

In 1989, together with the teacher-training department of the *Katholieke Leergangen* (Roman Catholic Institute for Education) from Tilburg, the NHTV started an experimental project in which teachers from the tourism departments of *Middelbaar Toeristisch en Recreatief Onderwijs* (MTRO) (Secondary Level Tourism and Leisure Education) of the ROCs were to be trained. The teacher training was part of the geography teacher-training department. The input of the NHTV consisted of the tourism and leisure related subjects (such as Introduction to Travel and Tourism, Travel Agency Operation, Wholesaler Practice), and the *Katholieke Leergangen* contributed geography and general didactic subjects. However, the government was not prepared to issue an official Tourism Teacher Grade Qualification, so after a number of years the project was abandoned.

Tourism Education at the Secondary Vocational Education Level (MBO)

The secondary vocational education for tourism is carried out in the ROCs by the MTROs. The MTROs started in 1978 in four cities in the Netherlands (Leiden, Utrecht, Zwolle and Maastricht). Later this was extended to 10 schools and today, since the Dutch government allowed the ROCs to decide for themselves which types of education they want to offer, there are over 40 ROCs with a MTRO department.

In the MTROs students are educated only for the levels 2–4 of the qualification structure. Typically they offer qualifications in two areas of tourism: Travel (preparation for jobs with travel agencies and wholesalers) and Tourism Information (for jobs at tourism information services). Table 1 shows the content of the programmes leading to these qualifications for the highest level (level 4).

The planning of the study is cumulative. This means that first the student prepares for the level 2 qualifications, at a later stage this is extended to the contents for level 3 and, if applicable, to level 4. In addition to this there is an internship of five months.

Table 1: Subjects qualification structure MTRO*.

Qualification area	Travel	Tourist information
Leisure Travel	*	
Tour Operating/Wholesaling	*	
Tourist Information		*
Basics of Management	*	*
Operational Management Travel	*	
Operational Management Tourist Information		*
Business Plan Travel	*	
Business Plan Information		*
English	*	*
German	*	*
Elective: Spanish, French or Italian	*	*

Source: Nieuwsbrief De Toerist (2003).

Table 2: Enrolments in tourism and Leisure higher vocational education 2003 and 2004*.

Type of studies	Enrolments 2003	Enrolments 2004
Tourism Management	948	981
Leisure Management	1008	968
Hotel Management	927	940
Media and Entertainment Management	777	971

Source: NHTV Breda University for Professional Education (2004).

Tourism Education at the Higher Vocational Education Level (HBO)

As already indicated, the first institute in the Netherlands was founded in 1966 in Breda and until 2000 the NHTV was the only institution of its kind in the Netherlands. However, growing demand meant that other HBOs were also interested in starting a department for tourism and leisure. The Ministry of Education responded to this with the result that there are now four HBOs with a travel and tourism department. Apart from the NHTV the following colleges now offer travel and tourism programmes: *Christelijke Hogeschool Noord Nederland* in Leeuwarden, *Hogeschool Inholland* in Diemen and *Saxion Hogeschool* in Deventer. Other similar institutions have started departments or specialisation areas in recreation, leisure, therapeutic recreation and sports management.

The four specialised Colleges have agreed a common curriculum, based on the same core competencies. The curriculum is for 60% centred on the same topics. The remaining part can be developed according to their preferences. All offer both Travel and Tourism related studies, as well as Leisure Management programmes. Yearly enrolments on the programmes for all colleges are shown in Table 2.

Tourism in the Universities

There are three university departments in the Netherlands with a specialism in travel, tourism and leisure. Since the 1980s, Tilburg University has had an independent department of Leisure Studies. This department is interdisciplinary (Economics, Sociology and Psychology). The core of the curriculum is Leisure Sciences and leads to a Master Degree centred on leisure. Tilburg University is also a member of the Programme in European Leisure Studies (PELS), which offers a one-year Master Degree programme with partner universities from Belgium, United Kingdom and Spain. There is also a chair in Tourism at The Erasmus University of Rotterdam. This was founded and is funded jointly by Holland International (now TUI), American Express, Best Western Hotels, Grenswisselkantoren, KLM Royal Dutch Airlines, the Ministry of Economic Affairs and the Horeca Education Foundation. The specialisation of the department is the economic and business aspects of tourism and leisure and it focuses on research rather than education. Finally Wageningen University (the former agricultural University) offers a programme in recreation management. Initially, its emphasis was mainly on spatial aspects of tourism. Now the focal points are the economic aspects, social and cultural effects and sustainability of tourism. Wageningen is a member of the European Leisure Studies Group (ELSG).

Apart from these, there are many other University-institutes that pay attention to various aspects of tourism, recreation and leisure (among them Groningen University and Nijmegen University).

Private (for profit) Tourism Education in the Netherlands

In the Netherlands there are numerous private institutes offering short travel and tourism courses. Most of these institutes are small and offer short travel and tourism courses for front-office jobs in agencies and tourist information services. Until recently, the government demanded that travel agencies operate under a licence. One of the demands for such a licence was that the owner or one or more staff members possessed certain diplomas, showing their competency in the travel and tourism business. These diplomas (the so-called SEPR diplomas) (*Stichting Examens en Proeven voor het Reisbureaubedrijf*) (Foundation for the Examinations for the Travel Industry) were in great demand by young people wishing to enter tourism. In its heyday a couple of thousand people sat for the diploma each year. When the requirement for a licence was abolished most such private institutes closed. There are, however, two exceptions (*TIO College* and *Instituut Notenboom*). For the past two years it has been possible under Dutch law to offer Bachelor degree programmes in travel and tourism outside the state-funded educational system. These two institutes have made a successful switch from their specialised travel diploma to offering Bachelor degree programmes, in effect becoming private polytechnics, obviously adhering to strict standards set by the government.

European and International Dimensions of Dutch Education

In the Netherlands, priority is given to international co-operation within the European Union (EU) area. Outside Europe, internationalisation focuses on certain countries like Indonesia, China and South Africa. There is also a tendency to forge links with countries that have significant populations in the Netherlands notably Morocco, Turkey and Surinam.

Under EU regulations there are a lot of possibilities for both faculty and staff exchanges. Students can get special funding for exchanges with European partner institutes. Also there is significant progress in the mutual recognition of diplomas and qualifications. This includes support for vocational education for which special funds have been earmarked. The *Socrates-II* Programme for faculty and student exchange and the *Leonardo-II* programme, which aims at a close co-operation between European vocational educational institutes, are particularly important in providing support from cross-EU initiatives. The Declaration of Bologna of 1999 is a start in the creation of an open higher education area in Europe. An aim is to obtain greater transparency in higher education. It is based on a two-cycle undergraduate and graduate system (the so-called Bachelor-Master system). This more transparent system is to enable institutes of higher education to strengthen their position in the international education market and to respond more effectively to international trends.

Today all institutions of higher vocational education and universities offer the possibility to follow most of their courses in the English language as well in Dutch. This has permitted the substantial growth in the numbers of international exchange students including those studying tourism.

Other Organisations

In 1971, the organisation *Stichting Vakopleiding Toerisme en Recreatie* (SVATOR) (Foundation for Vocational Education in Tourism and Recreation) was formed to co-ordinate all initiatives for specialised travel and tourism courses in the Netherlands at a secondary vocational level. Under the umbrella of SVATOR there were three one-year courses. The first was a course for information officers for Convention and Visitor Bureaux, the second, a school of the *Algemeen Nederlands Verbond van Reisondernemingen* (ANVR) (Dutch Travel Agents Society) and the third, *TIO College*, a private initiative, also aimed at both information officers and travel agency employees. It also co-ordinated the efforts of two institutes (*LOI* and *PBNA*) offering correspondence courses in the field of leisure and tourism. With the growth of travel and tourism and, as a result the demand for jobs in that sector, SVATOR developed itself into a kind of officially recognised advisory board for tourism and leisure education. As a result of the work of SVATOR some private institutions became partly funded by the Ministry of Economic Affairs and became therefore more or less recognised as official schools. SVATOR became instrumental in the development of curricula at the secondary vocational level.

SEPR was established to produce and organise the exams for the travel agency industry. The board of SEPR consists of representatives of the industry. Initially there were two diplomas: a diploma for a course about the travel aspects of the travel industry and the other one was about the business aspects. Possessors of both diplomas could apply for a licence to operate a travel agency. Later a third diploma about Business Travel (with an emphasis on Fares, Ticketing and GDS) was added.

SVATOR was renamed *Onderwijscentrum Toerisme en Reizen* (OTR) (Centre for Education in Tourism and Travel) and became more and more the official link between the industry and education. Educational institutes could obtain an official OTR seal of approval. However, when the government abolished the demand for the possession of certain diplomas to operate a travel agency, the number of candidates diminished dramatically and with that the main source of income of OTR. An important task of OTR was the definition of job-profiles, together with the qualification structure for those jobs. They were commissioned to execute this study by the *Fonds voor Opleiding en Ontwikkeling Reisbranche* (FOOR) (Fund for Education and Development of the Travel Industry) established in 1998. Under Dutch law, industry is obliged to spend a percentage of the total amount of wages into a fund for education and training. FOOR was the foundation (which united the industry and the labour unions) to execute activities of that fund. FOOR plays an instrumental role in the promotion of quality in vocational education in tourism, to improve the relations between the industry and the schools and to improve the possibilities for employees to participate in projects of continuing education. One of the latest projects of FOOR is the introduction of a programme aimed at pupils and study advisors of secondary schools, in which they promote working in the tourism sector.

Finally there is *GEOTOER* (The Association of Dutch Teachers of Travel and Tourism). The aim of *GEOTOER*, established in 1988, is to promote contact between teachers and industry and the mutual contact between teachers. *GEOTOER* organises each year a symposium where speakers both from the industry and from the field of education present and discuss topics. There are a little over a 100 members.

Other Related Education

In the Netherlands, at the secondary vocational level, there are numerous schools offering preparation for jobs in the hotel and restaurant industry and at the higher level (HBO) there are five Hotel Management Schools: The Hague, Maastricht, Leeuwarden, Deventer and Breda. A more recent development is the specialisation in Media and Entertainment Management. Media consumption is becoming an important and popular field of study. Not only are people spending more and more time consuming the output of media, but there is also a constant need for new programmes and entertainment.

Competency-Based Learning

In common with many other countries, the approach to setting learning outcomes of programmes is changing. In the Netherlands there is a move, both in secondary and in higher vocational education, to express outcomes in the competencies one should possess after finishing one's education. The Competency Matrix developed an NHTV provides an example. This sets out the core competencies expected of an NHTV student after four years of study. The starting point is the assumption that leisure and tourism is a "people business", where experiences play an important role and where high quality services are paramount. So students have to be able to work on themselves ("me"), work within an organization ("we") and work with clients ("they"). A future manager in tourism has to be able to be innovative, communicative, result-oriented and responsible. In an organisation they should be able to plan, organise, cooperate, guide and evaluate. They also need to be able to initiate plans (marketing, sales, development), to execute those plans and to evaluate them and to reflect upon them. This is translated into a competency matrix as set out in Table 3. This consists of nine cells. The rows contain the activities that graduates probably will be performing in their professional situation; the columns show the three domains in which they will be situated. Each cell then is a result of a specific domain and a specific activity and contains a competency.

Table 3: Competency matrix NHTV University for professional education*.

	Concept developer	Marketeer/ sales manager	Operations manager
To plan, to initiate, entrepreneurial	Development plans for concepts of services and products	Marketing plan, sales plan	Business plan, Policy planning
To manage, execute and exploit	Products and services itself	Communication plan	Implementation of plans
To check, to evaluate and to reflect	Plans for monitoring and evaluation	Profit and loss evaluation, evaluation of market position	Output and efficiency reports

*Source: Werkgroep Competenties MT NHTV (2004) (Translated by author).

These competencies are then translated into a curriculum. The learning process is executed along five learning domains. These are:

1. *Integral domain*. In this domain the field of study is offered in the forms of projects. These projects could be real and/or simulated. Students have to define the problems themselves and to see if they can offer suggestions for solutions and can compare the results, so that the best solution will be chosen;
2. *Conceptual domain*. In this domain students have to master the concept of concepts. They need to learn to talk or reason like professionals in the field. This domain is taught by guest lecturers and in workshops, rather than in a traditional class situation;
3. *Skills domain*. This includes special skills for the trade (like specific computer systems), but also foreign languages and communication skills;
4. *Practical domain*. This will be in the form of internships or in any other way the student can have a contact with practice;
5. *Personal domain*. Students will be coached individually in their years of study. They will be responsible for their own study progress. As proof of their progress a portfolio with results has to be kept.

The content of each of these cells is translated into competencies and each competency is connected with attributes to measure whether the competencies are really gained by the student. This represents a considerable change for the teaching staff in that their role becomes more that of a coach than of the traditional teacher in front of a room full of students.

As already noted above, in secondary tourism vocational education (MTRO) a qualification structure has been developed whereby students are trained at three levels: level 2 (basic skills), level 3 (independent execution of tasks) and level 4 (middle management or specialist training). These levels are performed in three fields of activity: front office, travel services and leisure and recreational services. This leads together to 12 competency fields or job possibilities.

Quality Control

In the Netherlands the so-called 'BaMa' structure has come into operation. This means that students who study at a HBO receive after four years a Bachelor (BA) degree. The HBO institutes are also allowed to offer a Master degree (MA) if they are accredited by the, previously mentioned, NVAO (Dutch and Flemish Accreditation Organization). The HBOs are judged on the following criteria:

1. Aims and goals of the educational institute;
2. The content of the programme;
3. The performance of staff;
4. Facilities;
5. Internal systems of quality management;
6. Results.

For each of these parts, a detailed protocol is devised. Institutes have to be accredited on a regular basis.

Conclusions

Education and training for tourism in the Netherlands has many similarities with that of other countries. It has experienced significant growth at all levels, it has diversified to deal with different sectors of tourism, it has responded to changes in the quality assurance regimes and changes in competency measures. But it also has a number of particular features. One of these relates to its international links. The Netherlands continues to operate programmes across international boundaries and to attract overseas students. The fact that many of its programmes are now provided in English language bears testimony to its continuing position in an international market for tourism education. The Netherlands has also gone a long way towards ensuring that the tourist industry has been involved in the process of development and operation of programmes. But perhaps its most distinctive feature, and one that has now come to an end, has been the extent to which higher level vocational education was concentrated at one particular centre, NHTV Breda University for Professional Technical Education. By providing a focal point for tourism studies in the country this provided the Netherlands with a strong and clear basis for the development of the subject of study as well as a strong international presence. Given the growth in the size and range of tourism studies it is not surprising that provision has now extended beyond NHTV, but this background certainly put the Netherlands in a strong position as a leading centre for tourism studies.

Acknowledgements

Special thanks to Hans Uijterwijk, Dean of the NHTV for his valuable contributions.

Further Reading

Author(s) Unknown. (2001). *Handboek Toerisme en Recreatie,* Kluwer, Deventer.
Beelen, E. (1991). *25 Jaar Nationale Hogeschool voor Toerisme en Verkeer: van NWIT naar NHTV, een avontuur met visie,* NHTV, Breda.
Diepstraten. J. (1981). *NWIT Lustrumboek,* NWIT, Breda.
Kosters, M. J. (1985). *Focus op Toerisme,* VUGA, 's-Gravenhage.
NHTV (2004). *Discover Your World,* NHTV, Breda.
Stichting FOOR. (2003). *Jaarverslag 2002,* Stichting FOOR, De Meern.

Websites

The Education System in the Netherlands (2001/2002) http://www.eurydice.org/Eurybase (September 15, 2004).
NRIT Actueel Database. http://www.dendries.nl/nrit/actueel (September 28, 2004).
Vocational education & training and adult education (VEP). http://www.minocw.nl/english/education/vocational.html (September 28, 2004).

Chapter 16

North America

Simon Hudson

Introduction

Tourism education has expanded rapidly over the last few decades reflecting the growing recognition of tourism (and the travel industry that serves it) as one of the world's most significant economic, social, and environmental forces (Evans, 2000). Education and training has been developed at various levels, ranging from highly vocational courses through to higher research degrees. The growth reflects the widely held belief that one of the major challenges the industry faces is to recruit, develop, and retain employees and managers with appropriate educational backgrounds. Although this rapid growth of university programs in tourism is not without critics (Evans, 1993), the trend is generally recognized for its merits (Ryan, 1995).

Size and Location

Tourism education is provided at many levels in North America. Tourism subjects are taught at high schools, vocational schools produce entry-level employees for the industry, and junior community colleges offer education and training in various skills applicable to the travel industry. Trade associations and professional services are also active in tourism education. Examples of those are the educational programs and home study courses of the American Society of Travel Agents, the Institute of Certified Travel Agents, the Educational Institute of American Hotel and Lodging Association, and the National Restaurant Association Education Foundation. In addition, most public carriers, especially the airlines, provide rigorous training and educational programs for their employees.

Colleges and universities are also active in providing tourism education. In keeping with the diversity of the industry, courses are offered in schools of business, schools of hotel and restaurant administration, colleges of natural resources, and in departments of commercial recreation, sociology, geography, and anthropology. A number of schools offer graduate programs in travel and tourism, with an increasing number of institutions granting doctoral degrees in tourism-related subjects. Finally, land-grant schools provide services through the Cooperative Extension Service, which operates in all 50 states of the U.S. These educational services are available to managers of hotels, motels, restaurants, resorts, clubs, marinas, small business services, and similar enterprises from some state organizations. Short courses and conferences are sometimes held for managers of these businesses to make them more effective and productive.

Formal study of tourism in North America began in the 1940s but the subject area really started to develop in the 1980s (Koh, 1994). In the U.S. and Canada, tourism studies and hospitality management courses are integrated to a large extent, making it hard to classify (all the relevant courses and the range of curricula and modularization make) generalizations difficult. However, over the past few decades tourism education has grown in tandem with the rapidly expanding industry. Given the nature of the tourism industry and the appeal of the exciting career opportunities offered by the industry, tourism programs have achieved substantial popularity among college students. On many campuses, students in other programs take tourism courses to enhance their future employment prospects.

Michigan State University, with its 1963 tourism course, was probably the first U.S. university to offer tourism (Jafari, 2003), and the number of post-secondary institutions offering tourism and hospitality programs has more than quadrupled in the last 25 years. In the early 1970s there were approximately 40 four-year programs in the U.S. that offered degrees in tourism-related subjects. Now there are over 170 programs granting degrees and more than 800 programs offering associate degrees, certificates, or diplomas (McIntosh, 1992; National Tourism Foundation, 2004; CHRIE, 2004). The Council on Hotel, Restaurant and Institutional Education (CHRIE) lists schools that offer 2-year, 4-year, and graduate study programs in North America. The publication (now on CDRom), *A Guide to College Programs in Culinary Arts, Hospitality and Tourism* provides a detailed description of tourism programs (CHRIE, 2004). Programs are grouped by types of degrees awarded (2-year, 4-year, and graduate), by geographic location (United States and International), and by specialization (culinary arts, hotel and lodging management, restaurant and food service management, travel and tourism management).

Table 1 lists the number of institutions, types of qualifications offered, and reported student enrolment. According to CHRIE, there are a total number of 55,781 students

Table 1: Number of institutions offering Tourism & Hospitality Qualifications and number of students Enrolled.

Type of qualification offered	Number of institutions offering each type	Enrollment
Associate degree, certificate and diploma	63	17,105
Undergraduate	115	35,807
Graduate	68	2,869
TOTAL	176 (Different institutions)	55,781

CHRIE (2004).

enrolled in tourism and hospitality courses at 176 different institutions in North America. Most of these (35,807) are studying undergraduate degrees, and about a third are enrolled in associate degrees, certificates, and diplomas. The CHRIE directory lists 28 universities offering post-graduate course relating to tourism. Although the directory does not distinguish between masters and PhD degrees, a study of tourism doctoral degrees by Jafari and Aster (1988) found the leading degree granting institutions in the U.S. to be Texas A&M University and the University of Michigan.

In Canada specifically, 17 universities have tourism/hospitality-related degree programs, whereas approximately 71 colleges have 2-year diploma programs (Reid, 2004). There were 251 tourism-related courses in 2004 and 153 courses related to hospitality (Canadian Tourism Human Resource Council, 2004). While colleges have offered tourism-related diplomas for over 15 years, half of the university programs have been around since 1995. This pattern is consistent with other countries.

Up to September 11, 2001, the growth in student numbers in tourism programs had been fuelled by an increasing number of international students. Universities in North America attract over half a million students a year from a broad range of student markets, with mainland China being the major source for international recruitment (Education Travel, 2004). Other important markets are Germany, France, Japan, and Korea. However, the last few years have seen a significant decline in the number of international applications by prospective graduate international students, especially to the U.S. mainly because of the difficulties faced in securing visas (American Council on Education, 2004).

Government Policy and Regulations Regarding Tourism Education

As a result of the growth and development across the entire range of the employment spectrum in tourism, there have been increasing demands to support the evolution of the industry with an equally sophisticated education and training infrastructure. In Canada, education remains a provincial responsibility, so much of the thinking and progress in this regard has occurred at the provincial level. However, this has been done with the full support of Federal authorities and their direct stimulation. Pollock and Ritchie (1990) reported on the efforts of two provincial governments — Alberta and British Columbia — to formulate an integrated strategy on which to base the planning and development of a tourism education system. The goal of such integration was to ensure a greater degree of interdependence among different levels of the total education system so as to provide well-defined alternative career paths for present and future students. In 1987, Alberta established the Alberta Tourism Education Council (ATEC) and a year later the province of British Columbia established the Pacific Rim Institute of Tourism (PRIT). Both of these institutions had as their primary roles to act as coordinators and catalysts for the development of the many needs to be met in the area of tourism education and training.

Indications are that the establishment of these organizations has had a substantial impact on improving the quantity and quality of tourism-related education. Tourism education and training has gained a new found credibility, considerable progress has been made in the area of developing certification standards for a broad range of professions in the tourism industry, and access to government funding for tourism education and training has been significantly improved. For example, in 1996, British Columbia's Ministry of Education, Skills and Training released a Strategic Plan for colleges calling for the development of 'Block Transfer' agreements allowing transfer of credits between institutions and eliminating the time-consuming process of course-by-course institutional credit assessment. The 'B.C. Tourism Learning System' is part of this mix. The system links high school with college/university programs and is designed to facilitate degree completion.

In 1993, the Canadian Tourism Human Resource Council (CTHRC) was formed, a national organization 'that facilitates the coordination of human resource development activities, which support a globally competitive and sustainable Canadian tourism industry' (Human Resources Development Canada, 2004). Since forming, the Government has provided CTHRC with CDN$40 million in project funding. The industry and other stakeholders have contributed approximately CDN$71 million to the Council. The CTHRC's Board of Directors consists of 6 business representatives, 6 labour representatives, 8 national industry associations, 13 provincial/territorial Tourism Education Councils and 1 representative from the education and training system. The CTHRC offers national training, national occupation standards, professional certifications, and tourism career planning; the Canadian Academy of Travel & Tourism, tourism research and tourism careers for youth. The Academy offers tourism courses, projects, and activities as part of the high school curriculum in selected schools across Canada. Currently, 18 schools in 7 provinces are involved.

The U.S. Government has no direct policy with respect to tourism education. However, because the Government has entered into tourism agreements with countries that do have 'tourism education policies', some attempts have been made to acknowledge tourism education. For example, there is a U.S.–Mexico Tourism agreement whereby both parties pledge to encourage their respective experts to exchange appropriate information in the following fields: (a) systems and methods to prepare teachers and instructors; (b) tourism scholarships for teachers, instructors, and students; and (c) curricular and study programs for tourism and hotel schools.

Curriculum Development and Articulation Agreements

Due to its growing popularity and pervasive presence, tourism education is continuing to move more and more towards the mainstream of post-secondary education. It generally shares degree requirements which are consistent with other university programs. And, like other university programs, graduate and post-graduate degree programs in tourism often coexist with undergraduate curricula. In a 1995 research study, a panel of U.S. tourism industry experts agreed that a 4-year tourism management curriculum should comprise 26 elements classified under four broad educational headings; general education, business education, tourism education, and experiential education (Koh, 1995). The CHRIE more recently said that most hospitality and tourism programs consist of four main areas: the major; general education and advanced learning skills; electives; and work experience (CHRIE, 2004). They highlight the key attributes of tourism and hospitality programs by type or level (see Table 2).

The major is the vehicle that brings practical application to the college curriculum. Making up between 25 and 40 percent of the undergraduate curriculum, the major is the true core of undergraduate studies. Students commit to a major by choice, and the major

Table 2: Key attributes of hospitality and tourism programs by type or level.

Program type	Institutional settings	Curriculum objectives	Completion time	Faculty
Certificate diploma* programs	Business, technical and career institutes	To provide students with specialized skills for specific hospitality and tourism jobs	1–3 years	Primary industry experience and training May also have baccalaureate degrees, and some have graduate degrees
Associate and diploma* programs	Community colleges and technical institutes	To provide training and education necessary for hospitality and tourism management careers Emphasis is on career education and technical skills, but curricula includes general education components. Some degrees can be transferred to baccalaureate programs	2 years	Combination of industry skills and experience with combined undergraduate and, in some cases, graduate training
Baccalaureate degree granting programs	Four-year colleges and universities	To provide career education in combination with a broad general studies components and advanced learning skills Emphasis on developing conceptual abilities and integrating knowledge of hospitality and tourism with other disciplines	4 years	Combination of industry experience and graduate education. Heavy emphasis on graduate education
Graduate degree granting programs	Universities	To provide advanced education for specialized industry positions or for further educators Emphasis on creating an interdisciplinary base for applied and research, policy analysis, planning and theoretical education	1–2 years (master's) 3–5 years (doctorate)	Doctoral education with industry experience Industry experience not always required

* Diplomas at some Canadian community colleges and European technical colleges are awarded for completion of a course of study which meets or exceeds requirements for an associate degree in the United States. (CHRIE, 2004).

department or program becomes their 'home' on campus, because it is a source of social contacts and personal advice, and also because it provides both focus and a sense of purpose for undergraduate life. Given the diversity among hospitality and tourism programs, it is difficult to present a single description of the major, but in general, most will resemble, to one degree or another, one of five broad categories or approaches: craft/skill approaches; tourism approaches; food systems/home economics approaches; business administration approaches; and combined approaches (CHRIE, 2004).

In many respects, the *general education* component of the college curriculum is what is left of a core liberal arts education, at one time the dominant type of American undergraduate education. General education acts to ensure that all students obtain some understanding of the skills which will aid them in advanced studies and lifelong learning. This includes knowledge of cultural heritage as it is expressed in the humanities, the social sciences, the arts, and the natural and physical sciences. General education requirements relate more to the individual than to the major, but that does not lessen their importance in educating the total person. With advances in technology, knowledge, and social responsibility, *advanced learning skills* have been expanded to include mathematical precision, statistics, practical ethics, and computer literacy. These skills relate directly to both the individual and the hospitality and tourism major.

Electives, like the major, are chosen by the student and provide opportunities for broadening the educational experience. For example, electives can be used to acquire additional advanced learning skills that are not part of the required curriculum, and to develop interests or talents in the arts. They may also be used to bolster personal competencies in areas that are part of, or related to, the major area of study.

Many tourism and hospitality programs require that students undertake and complete significant *work experience* in the industry before they graduate. This experience is usually paid by an outside employer and typically ranges between one and three summers (CHRIE, 2004). An increasingly popular way of obtaining work experience in the industry involves students taking a semester off and completing an extended internship, often at a facility away from their home state. Both employers and students like this arrangement. For students, it is an opportunity to get a feel for a company and perhaps try their hand at a variety of jobs. For employers, this arrangement permits longer term staff planning and allows them to evaluate prospective management employees. This work experience goes by a variety of names such as co-op, internship, and practicum.

The study of tourism draws on a host of disciplines including anthropology, business science, psychology, economics, planning, and many others, whereas hospitality tends to focus more heavily on business-oriented sub-disciplines such as marketing, operations, finance, human resource, and information technology. As a result, the philosophical models of tourism and hospitality programs vary from school to school, depending on the overall program emphasis. A recent study of six North American programs (Levy, 2002) shows that tourism and hospitality programs can be located in various schools, although the programs tend to be similar in awarding bachelor degrees in business or hospitality management/ administration (see Table 3). The one exception is Texas A&M which awards a Recreation, Park and Tourism Sciences Degree. However, in all the schools it is possible to receive a concentration in tourism or hospitality management. The concentrations at the University of Las Vegas show how specialized and industry specific modules are becoming.

Table 3: Specifics on six North American programs.

University	School	Bachelors degree awarded	Hospitality/Tourism concentrations offered
George Washington University	Business and Public Management	Business Administration	Hospitality Mgmt., Sport and Event Mgmt.
Purdue University	Consumer and Family Sciences	Hospitality and Tourism Management	Lodging Mgmt., Foodservice Mgmt., Tourism Mgmt.
Texas A&M	Agriculture and Life Sciences	Recreation, Park & Tourism Sciences	Park and Nat. Resources Mgmt, Rec. and Park Admin., Tourism Resource Mgmt.
University of Calgary University of Central Florida	Business Hospitality Management	Bachelor of Commerce Hospitality Management	Tourism, Tourism and Marketing Six Career Tracks including Tourism Management Track
University Nevada-Las Vegas	Hotel Administration	Hotel Admin., Recreation and Leisure Studies	Tourism and six other concentrations*

* Convention, Meeting and Exposition Management, Human Resources, Casino Management, Tourism, Club Management, and Entertainment and Event Management.

The same study analyzed the structure of each program, finding that each can be completed in 4 years with an average of nearly 125 credits (see Table 4). On average, nearly 37 per cent of all coursework, or the equivalent of 15 semester-long courses, is grounded in general education. General education or managerial requirements range from half the total coursework at Texas A&M to 30 per cent at the University of Calgary and University of Central Florida. The subject matter in these courses normally includes mathematics, statistics, economics, English, humanities, and natural and social sciences. Department specific requirements, which average 40 percent of the coursework, depend on the type of program offered. For example, in hospitality programs, modules tend to be focused on business courses integral in the hospitality industry such as hospitality marketing and restaurant operations. Other schools that grant business degrees require more general business courses such as strategy and accounting. The rest of the coursework, averaging nearly of quarter of all required courses, is a blend of department electives and free electives.

Hybrid Programs

It is traditionally accepted that the tourism and hospitality industry requires a large number of employees possessing the technical skills required to service the growing number of visitors that must be lodged, fed, and managed as they visit attractions and pursue other travel

Table 4: Structure of programs in six North American Schools.

University	Credits needed	General Ed. req's		Dept. req's*		Dept. electives		Free electives	
		Number	%	Number	%	Number	%	Number	%
George Washington University	120	39	33	48	40	9	8	24	20
Purdue University[†]	130	48	37	52	40	15	12	15	12
Texas A&M	129	65	50	39	30	15	12	10	8
University of Calgary	120	36	30	54	45	6	5	24	20
University of Central Florida	120	36	30	52	43	18	15	14	12
University Nevada-Las Vegas	128	53	41	46	36	15	12	14	11
Average	*124.5*	*46.2*	*36.9*	*48.5*	*39.1*	*13.0*	*10.4*	*16.8*	*13.6*

* Department requirements also include courses that are tourism-oriented concentration or career-track specified courses.

[†] Estimated.

experiences. More recently, these tourism/hospitality/services sectors have recognized the desirability of hiring employees who also possess a basic business and liberal arts education in addition to their technical skills. While a certain number of technically trained employees have responded to this need by proceeding to obtain university-level degrees in business and the liberal arts, this has been an inefficient and ill-adapted process. Recognizing these difficulties, some institutions have developed hybrid programs especially adapted to students seeking long-term careers rather than simply jobs in the tourism and hospitality sector. One such program in North America is the Bachelor of Hotel and Restaurant Management (BHRM) degree at the University of Calgary in Canada (Ritchie, Hudson, & Sheehan, 2002).

The total learning period of this program is 4 years. During the first 2 years, students follow a traditional 2-year technical program designed to ensure they have the basic entry-level skills required by the industry. The best graduates from such programs may then pursue a further 2 years of management education, specifically designed for the tourism and hospitality industry. The final product is an individual possessing both the specific technical skills and the broader management education that larger firms in the tourism and hospitality sector find highly attractive.

In Canada, it is only in the last decade that block transfers, or the '2+2 model' have become palatable to Canadian universities. They generally take the form of an articulation agreement that allows block transfer credits and typically allows diploma graduates direct entry into year three of a 4-year university degree program. Reid (1999) attributes this slow uptake to the fact that Canadian universities and college systems have different roles and mandates, and that tourism and hospitality as a discipline has seen slow acceptance in Canadian universities.

The articulation agreements typically operate so that individual institutions conduct evaluations of incoming transfer students and set their own standards for course requirements. Many college students are unable to enter university directly, due to academic, monetary, or geographical reasons. Transfer allows student access and opportunities for degree completion. Of the 17 Canadian universities offering tourism/hospitality-related degree programs, nine have variations on this '2+2 model', which would appear encouraging. However, Reid (1999) suggests that transferable programs advertised on university web sites in Canada typically do not provide links to the colleges with which they are affiliated, and students often express dissatisfaction with the way the transfer process is handled. The province of Ontario, for example, has a bleak record where college/university transfer is concerned.

After studying articulation agreements in Canada, Reid concludes that an articulation system needs to be developed whereby block transfer credits are given for related programs. In this ideal model, curriculum for the block is established collaboratively, whereby the outcomes of the sending program are matched to the requirements of the receiving program through an agreed upon set of desired learning outcomes that include the desired knowledge, skills and abilities of students entering the university program. According to Reid there are no examples of this approach to block transfer in Canada.

Monitoring Curriculum and Quality Issues

It has been suggested that a curriculum must be periodically reviewed to maintain its relevance to the needs of its clientele — the industry and students (Koh, 1995), and there is evidence that Universities occasionally conduct research of their own to support program design and evaluation. Milman (2001) presents a case study illustration of a qualitative research approach for enhancing an undergraduate curriculum of a hospitality and tourism management program at the University of Central Florida. Ritchie and Sheehan (2001) also used a qualitative approach at the University of Calgary to evaluate student satisfaction with existing programs and to identify desirable characteristics of future programming. Finally, Gilmore and Hsu (1994) report on a research study that assessed the perceptions of alumni of hospitality programmes to determine the importance of the content of each course to the success of their careers.

Standards for tourism education are also set and evaluated externally. The World Tourism Organization (WTO), for example, is the most widely recognized and leading international organization in the field of travel tourism, and has made significant efforts to set standards for tourism education. The newly developed accreditation program for tourism education institutions (TedQual) has encouraged many institutions in North America to certify their tourism and hospitality courses. Examples of WTO TedQual certified institutions are the University of Quebec, The George Washington University, Johnson & Wales University, and the University of Hawaii at Manoa. The specific aims of this certification system are to establish a quality standard for tourism education and training systems; and to smooth the way towards greater pedagogic productivity in tourism.

Teaching Methods and Assessment

Advances in information technology have brought new delivery methods into tourism education. One significant change is the increased emphasis on multimedia use in the classroom. But learning to design and develop multimedia courseware is a multifaceted and demanding task, and the plethora of skills, time, and equipment required to create multimedia materials for a specific groups of learners often makes the task impossible for most faculty members. McNeil and Chernish (2001) suggest that a multimedia design team can overcome these barriers, and they report on a collaborative multimedia project between the Hilton College of Hotel and Restaurant Management and the College of Education at the University of Houston. Students and faculty members worked collaboratively to develop Internet-based courseware for an actual instructional context in a university undergraduate class in human resource management.

Despite the considerable number of games and simulations available for teaching purposes, the standard lecture format still prevails as the main teaching method. Some authors have discussed how Virtual Enterprises can assist in tourism education (Hill & Schulman, 2001; Marshall, 2001). A Virtual Enterprise (VE) is an inter-disciplinary business simulation, where students use technology to trade products and services through a global e-commerce network of more than 3000 firms. Zapalska, Rudd, and Flanegin (2003) have provided some useful tips on how to design an educational game for learning and how best to tailor it for tourism and hospitality classroom learning. The authors discuss an educational game where players act as travel agents to learn how a travel agency functions. As auctions are increasingly conducted throughout the world, students are placed in an auction scenario. They become travel agents using resources to satisfy their travel agency's needs. Each travel agent develops a business strategy in order to trade the available rooms that he/she owns for any needed rooms in other hotels. As students become active buyers and sellers in the auction market, they observe how their strategic behaviour affects the buying and selling activities of other players and how the strategic behaviour of other players affect their trading activities.

Use of the Internet

Sigala (2002) suggests that although an increasing number of tourism and hospitality educators are incorporating the Internet into their instruction, only a few are fully exploiting the Internet's capabilities to transform and extend their pedagogical models. She calls for further research to investigate how the educational community can adopt and support the design and implementation of effective e-learning models and move on from current educational paradigms. The identification of critical success factors for achieving such a transition is also vitally important.

Despite these concerns North American tourism educators have began to utilize the Internet for teaching purposes. Cai, Morrison, and Ismail (2001) describe the evolution of a Tourism Geography class at a Mid-West American University as it has been continuously redeveloped and enhanced through the use of the information and communication features provided by the Internet. The class designers have found that the Internet has made it possible to achieve traditional objectives more efficiently time wise (i.e. describing major geographic features, locating and identifying destinations, natural wonders, historic sites, and other tourist attractions). This frees up more time to introduce additional relevant topics and to add more higher-level learning activities and objectives. However, the authors acknowledge that while the Web is an effective medium for students to access information, and to gain knowledge, the demonstration of higher levels of learning such as understanding or application require multiple instructional delivery techniques.

Others are using the Internet to create learning opportunities for students around the world. Table 5 lists the number of online tourism and hospitality degrees listed in a directory of online education (WorldWideLearn.com, 2004). Clements, Buergermeister, Holland, and Monteiro (2001) describe the evolution of a distant Global Hospitality Management Master's program at the University of Wisconsin-Stout. The program was the result of a global partnership involving educational institutions in the U.K., Germany, and the U.S. In discussing lessons learned from developing the program, the authors suggest that access to learning needs to be convenient and hassle-free. Learners need to be able to communicate easily with the learning community. This means that institutions need to stay in touch with the latest technologies and maintain sufficient network infrastructure. Also, communication among learning facilitators is critical. While the technology can support relationships, in-person contact is also needed. These meetings are key to building trust and fostering collaborative problem solving in the world of distance learning. Finally, the authors suggest that it is a challenge for many traditional professors to make the paradigm shift from disseminator of information to a facilitator and coordinator of learning. Team teaching can help in overcoming these barriers, but compensation structures need to be adjusted to reward team teaching before a true buy-in takes place.

Table 5: Online degrees in tourism & hospitality management.

Institution	Type of degree offered
Ellis College of New York Institute of Technology	Bachelor of Science in Interdisciplinary Studies/ Hospitality Management
Touro University	Bachelor of Science in Business Administration — Tourism and Hospitality Management MBA in Hospitality Management
The George Washington University	Accelerated Master of Tourism Administration
Herkimer County Community College	Associate in Applied Science in Travel and Tourism
Southern New Hampshire University	Master of Science in Hospitality Administration
Sullivan University	Bachelor of Science in Business Administration degree with a concentration in Hospitality Management
Texas Tech University	Master of Science in Restaurant, Hotel and Institutional Management.
University of Guelph	MBA in Hospitality and Tourism
The University of Houston	Executive Master of Hospitality Management (M.H.M.)
University of Wisconsin-Stout	Master of Science in Hospitality and Tourism

Industry educators are also incorporating the Internet into their teaching methods. In 2004, the Canadian Tourism Human Resource Council (CTHRC) launched 'emerit', an online national brand of tourism training, standards, and professional certification. The program was the result of 3 years of industry consultation, concept design, and product development and enhancement. A Web site was developed to provide on-line training in flexible modularized formats for selected occupations and on-line exams for over 25 occupations, from Front Desk Agent, to Casino Dealer to Food and Beverage Manager. New professional recognition options are also available depending on level of knowledge and experience.

Integration of Research and Teaching

In North America, tourism education and research are often mentioned together because it is necessary for academics to be involved in both activities in many educational institutions. Research in tourism and hospitality marketing has matured over the last few decades, fuelled by a proliferation of texts and journals specifically related to the subject. A veritable explosion of new journals has been introduced as an outlet for academic publication of research in hospitality and tourism. A recent inventory yielded a count of 69 journals (Hudson, 2004). Tourism education can only benefit from these research advances. Research efforts of a growing, but still small, community of researchers, have heightened the status of tourism (Jafari, 2003).

Ritchie (1993) has commented that there are too few programs specifically designed to provide doctoral-level qualifications for individuals seeking a systematic focus on tourism. Similarly, he suggests there are too few short programs that seek to provide a mechanism for upgrading of teaching and research skills in the field. He discusses a number of key policy issues that need to be addressed in order to provide an environment required for the successful long-term development of the tourism education infrastructure. These include providing programs that are industry sensitive; making the educational system know you are serious; focus on developing a limited number of quality centres and programs; and providing dedicated positions for career professionals.

It is questionable whether too much has changed since these proposals were made in the early 1990s. Some suggest that there is still a shortage of suitably qualified tourism educators. Jafari and Aster (1988) proposed that too few Universities offer tourism doctoral degrees because of the persistence of disciplinary inflexibility which allows only the 'traditional' dissertation foci. However, in more recent years, many U.S. Universities have expanded their existing doctoral programs in such fields as education, recreation, and urban/regional planning to include tourism (Jafari, 2003).

Professional Associations

Professional Associations are an important part of establishing tourism's academic presence, and tourism and hospitality educators in North America have several domestic and international associations they can participate in. One of the oldest is the Travel and Tourism Research Association (TTRA). It is the world's largest travel research organization made up of academics and professionals devoted to improving the quality, value, scope and acceptability of travel research, and marketing information. Approximately 20 percent of the TTRA membership are tourism and hospitality educators. The International Society of Travel and Tourism Educators (ISTTE) is a smaller, newer organization made up of universities, colleges, and proprietary schools. It seeks to promote the development and exchange of information related to tourism education and research.

The International Academy for the Study of Tourism is another relatively new organization, and is an international body of multi-disciplinary scholars committed to the advancement of knowledge in the field of tourism. It has a number of North American members. Another influential association referred to earlier in this chapter is the CHRIE, who publish the *Hospitality and Tourism Research Journal*. Finally, the Society of Park and Recreation Educators (SPRE) is a branch of the National Recreation and Park Association (NRPA). The group works on appropriate curriculum and features programs on education and research.

In addition to these organizations, other professional associations are creating sections or special interest groups so that members interested in tourism can network and react. An example is the American Marketing Association's special group in tourism and hospitality.

Interface with the Tourism Industry

Many researchers have focused their attention on the role that tourism studies should play with regard to serving the needs of the travel and tourism industry (Collins, Sweeney, & Green, 1994; Middleton & Ladkin, 1996; Cooper & Shepherd, 1997; Busby, Brunt, & Baber, 1997; Amoah & Baum, 1997; Leslie & Richardson, 2000). Haywood and Maki (1992) suggest that there are differing expectations between employers and the education sector in that employers emphasize practical skills and general transferable skills, whereas educators are developing more conceptual and tourism-specific materials. They contend that this has resulted in a communication gap characterized by poor levels of communication between the two groups; a lack of involvement of educators in the industry; and industry's role in education (through advisory bodies, etc.) often being poorly defined. There have also been criticisms of the tourism industry itself not recognizing the value of tourism research. Rarely does the industry contribute to its application and development (Jafari, 2003).

Pasevic (1993) also suggested that the education system in the early 1990s was not able to meet the tourism industry's need for management trainees. He encouraged the development of partnerships between education and industry that would be helpful in coordinating mutually beneficial employee and management development programs. He also criticized tourism and hospitality programs for being too insular, and suggested that they become less industry-specific and more general and analytical in order to prepare graduates to deal with the demands of the 21st century.

Tourism is multi-faceted and inherently multidisciplinary making it difficult to classify and to design syllabi which are integrated, academically rigorous, and relevant to the changing needs of the employment market (Evans, 2000). Shepherd and Cooper (1994) believe that the diversity of the tourism/hospitality industry makes it difficult for an education system to identify the needs of the industry as a whole, and both Cotton (1991) and Leslie (1991) commented that the actual fit between education provision and demand for employers in tourism and hospitality was a poor one. It was always a mismatch between the expectation of the recruiters and the actual performance of the graduates. Kivela and Li (1998) ascertained that the graduates from such programs should attain competency in the specific areas that would be performed by a manager.

No matter what approach it takes, a hospitality and tourism education program is still no substitute for experience. The industry seldom hires management-level people who lack substantial, varied, and responsible work experience, regardless of a college degree (CHRIE, 2004). It is important that prospective managers have a solid commitment to a career in hospitality and tourism and that they have experiential knowledge of the industry. Therefore, as mentioned previously, many programs now require that students undertake and complete significant work experience in the industry before they graduate.

Conclusion

As for the future, Jafari (2003) predicts that the cumulative process of building a scientific foundation for tourism will continue, with a greater recognition of tourism across campuses and departments. In particular, he foresees a narrowing of the gap between tourism and leisure/recreation communities — a cross-fertilization benefiting both communities.

However, there are some concerns for those involved in tourism education in North America. One is the significant decline in the number of international applications by prospective graduate international students. An increasing number of internationally mobile students are looking for academic opportunities outside the U.S. mainly because of the difficulties they face securing visas (American Council on Education, 2004). The problem is especially serious for Chinese applicants to U.S. graduate programs. Some students are looking to Canada as an alternative for international study, but others consider Canada part of the North American continent and hence just as problematic (Education Travel, 2004). The slowdown in graduate applications could exacerbate the shortage of suitably qualified tourism educators referred to earlier in the chapter.

There are also some who suggest that tourism education should be changing in response to world events that have occurred in this century. Go (2004) discusses the increasing calls for global tourism education in American schools that will foster international knowledge and skills. In addition, he says that the knowledge needed to compete under conditions of complexity is becoming more diverse as the rate of change in tourism markets occurs at an increasingly rapid pace. Dwyer (2004) also suggests that tourism education must prepare students to play a leadership role in an industry that is undergoing rapid changes on both the demand and supply sides. He contends that future industry leaders in tourism will be those who have the knowledge and skills to enhance organizational competitive advantages via strategy formulation and implementation in a difficult, dangerous, dynamic, and diverse world.

Despite these concerns, as this chapter has shown, tourism continues to enjoy a growing rate of popularity in educational institutions throughout North America, both as an area of instruction and as a field of investigation.

References

American Council on Education. (2004). Fewer international grad students applying to study in the United States http://www.acenet.edu, retrieved 22 September.

Amoah, V. A., & Baum, T. (1997). Tourism education: Policy versus practice. *International Journal of Contemporary Hospitality Management, 9*(1), 5–12.

Busby, G., Brunt, P., & Baber, S. (1997). Tourism sandwich placements: An appraisal. *Tourism Management, 18*(2), 105–110.

Cai, L. A., Morrison, A. M., & Ismail, J. (2001). Teaching global tourism geography using the internet: A case study of the paradigm shift in educational technology. *Journal of Teaching in Travel & Tourism, 1*(2/3), 17–38.

Canadian Tourism Human Resource Council. (2004). Tourism related education and training. www.cthrc.ca, retrieved 6 February.

CHRIE. (2004). A guide to college programs in culinary arts, hospitality and tourism. The Council on Hotel, Restaurant and Institutional Education, VA, US.

Clements, C. J., Buergermeister, J., Holland, J., & Monteiro, P. (2001). Creating a virtual community. *Journal of Teaching in Travel & Tourism, 1*(2/3), 73–89.

Collins, S., Sweeney, A. E., & Green, A. G. (1994). Training for the UK tour operator industry: Advancing current practice. *Tourism Management, 15*(1), 5–8.

Cooper, C., & Shepherd, R. (1997). The relationship between tourism education and the tourism industry: Implications for tourism education. *Tourism Recreation Research*, *22*(1), 34–47.

Cotton, B. (1991). Graduates who jump off the ladder. *Caterer and Hotelkeeper*, *182* (5 October), 30.

Dwyer, L. (2004). Trends underpinning global tourism in the coming decade. In: W. Theobold (Ed.), *Global tourism: The next decade* 3rd ed., Oxford: Butterworth-Heinemann.

Education Travel. (2004). Canada's promise. *Education Travel.* http://www.hothousemedia.com, retrieved 9 September.

Evans, J. (1993). Tourism graduates: A case of over production. *Tourism Management*, *14*(4), 243–246.

Evans, N. (2000). Tourism higher education revisited: A business management framework. In: M. Robinson, P. Long, R. Sharpley & J. Swarbrooke (Eds), *Management, marketing and the political economy of travel and tourism* (pp. 103–120), Sunderland: Business Education Publishers Limited.

Gilmore, S. A., & Hsu, C. H. C. (1994). Alumni Perspectives of an undergraduate hospitality curriculum,. *Hospitality and Tourism Educator*, *6*(1), 71–73.

Go, F. M. (2004). Globalization and emerging tourism education issues. In: W. Theobold (Ed.), *Global tourism: The next decade* (3rd ed., pp 482–509). Oxford: Butterworth-Heinemann.

Haywood, K. M., & Maki, K. (1992). A conceptual model of the education/employment interface for the tourism industry. In: J. R. B. Ritchie & D. Hawkins (Eds), *World travel and tourism review*. Oxford: CAB.

Hill, J., & Schulman, J. (2001). The virtual enterprise: Using internet based technology to create a new educational paradigm for the tourism and hospitality industry. *Journal of Teaching in Travel & Tourism*, *1*(2/3), 153–167.

Hudson, S. (2004). *Marketing for tourism and hospitality: A Canadian perspective.* Toronto: Nelson Thomson Learning.

Human Resources Development Canada. (2004). Government of Canada helps tourism industry prosper. Retrieved from http://www.hrdc-drhc.gc.ca, on 6 April.

Jafari, J. (2003). Research and scholarship: The basis of tourism education. *Journal of Tourism Studies*, *14*(1), 6–16.

Jafari J., & Aster, D. (1988). Tourism as the subject of doctoral dissertations. *Annals of Tourism Research*, *15*, 407–429.

Kivela, J. J., & Li, L. (1998). Different perceptions between hotel management and students regarding levels of competency demonstrated by hospitality degree graduates. *Australian Journal of Hospitality Management*, *5*(2), 47–53.

Koh, K. (1995). Designing the four-year tourism management curriculum: A marketing approach. *Journal of Travel Research*, *34*(1), 68–72.

Koh, K. (1994). Tourism education for the 1990s. *Annals of Tourism Research*, *21*(3), 853–854.

Leslie, D. (1991). The hospitality industry, industrial placement and personnel management. *The Service Industry Journal* (Jan), 63–73.

Leslie, D., & Richardson, A. (2000). Tourism and co-operative education in UK undergraduate courses: Are the benefits being realized? *Tourism Management*, *21*(5), 489–498.

Levy, S. (2002). A *comparative study of undergraduate tourism and hospitality programs.* Unpublished paper, University of Calgary.

Marshall, L. A. (2001). Restaurant management and operations: A tourism virtual experience. *Journal of Teaching in Travel & Tourism*, *1*(2/3), 169–182.

McIntosh (1992). Early tourism education in the U.S. *Journal of Tourism Studies*, *3*(1), 2–7.

McNeil, S. G., & Chernish, W. N. (2001). Collaborative approach to multimedia courseware design and development. *Journal of Teaching in Travel & Tourism*, *1*(2/3), 107–123.

Middleton, V. T. C., & Ladkin, A. (1996). *The profile of tourism studies degree courses in the UK 1995/96.* London: National Liaison Group (NLG) for Tourism in Higher Education.

Milman, A. (2001). Hospitality and tourism curriculum development: A qualitative case-study approach. *Journal of Teaching in Travel & Tourism, 1*(4), 65–76.

National Tourism Foundation. (2004). Database of schools offering travel and tourism curriculum. Retrieved from http://www.ntfonline.org, on 7 May.

Pasevic, D. V. (1993). Hospitality education 2005: Curricular and programmatic trends. *Hospitality Research Journal, 17*(1), 285–194.

Pollock, A., & Ritchie, J. R. B. (1990). Integrated strategy for tourism education/training. *Annals of Tourism Research, 17*, 568–585.

Reid, L. (1999). The blocked pathway: A look at tourism/hospitality articulation agreements in canadian universities and colleges. In: C. H. C. Hsu (Ed.), *Proceedings of the new frontiers in tourism research conference* (pp. 1–9). Canada: Vancouver.

Reid, L. (2004). Connecting the dot··· Educational pathways for hospitality & tourism — are they truly connected? Presentation made at the Atlantic tourism educators conference, May 25–27.

Ritchie, J. R. B. (1993). Educating the tourism educators: Guidelines for policy and program development. *Teoros International, 1*(1), 9–23.

Ritchie, J. R. B., Hudson, S., & Sheehan, L. R. (2002). Hybrid programs in tourism and hospitality: A review of strengths, weaknesses and implementation issues. *Acta Turistica, 14*(1), 29–45.

Ritchie, J. R. B., & Sheehan, L. R. (2001). Practicing what we preach in tourism education and research: The use of strategic research methods for program design, implementation and evaluation (Part I — Visioning). *Journal of Teaching in Travel & Tourism, 1*(1), 37–57.

Ryan, C. (1995). Tourism courses: A new concern for new times? *Tourism management, 16*(2), 97–100.

Shepherd, R., & Cooper, C. (1994). Dimensions of the education-industry interface for tourism. *Industry and Higher Education,* (March), 36–45.

Sigala, M. (2002). The evolution of internet pedagogy: Benefits for tourism and hospitality education. *Journal of Hospitality, Leisure, Sport and Tourism Education, 2*(2), 29–45.

WorldWideLearn.com. (2004). *Online degrees in tourism & hospitality management,* Retrieved from WorldWideLearn.com, on 13 September.

Zapalska, A. M., Rudd, D., & Flanegin, F. (2003). An educational games for tourism and hospitality education. *Journal of Teaching in Travel & Tourism, 3*(3), 19–36.

Chapter 17

Slovenia

Tanja Mihalič

Introduction

Around the world the tourism industry is seen as a prospective employer. Growing numbers of trained, educated and competent people are needed to help run the hotels and restaurants, attractions, travel agencies, computer reservation systems, tour operations and transport companies that make up this vibrant industry. Many are needed to conceive, plan and develop the industry (WTO, 1992). In addition, jobs and businesses are also being created in other, "non-tourism" industries and in the public sector and it is imperative that these employees, earning some of their incomes because people travel, also acquire some knowledge and understanding of tourism.

Tourism education as well as training and research should, in principle, take into account the requirements of the industry, as well as its development and trends. It has to be adapted to practical needs, yet the link between education and practice is in many ways dialectical. Simply adapting education to the needs and requirements of the tourism industry has no future (Keller, 1999, p. 10). Education in tourism must also stay one step ahead of the industry with new technologies, new innovations and new developments. These are rarely developed and implemented within the tourism industry without suitable research. The tourism industry needs tourism professionals who are well up-to-date in their education. In the era of the new economy, which is bringing enormous changes to tourism, turning it into an electronic business is truer than ever before. Changing transitional countries, in which economic, social and political transformations continue to accelerate at an even faster pace, must adapt to the international and global dimension of tourism and educational programmes and simply cannot be left out of this process. There is a real need to make tourism education programmes more comparable, to promote exchange and compatibility within Europe and around the world. Transition countries like Slovenia and their education institutions have to catch up and become part of the European (international) tourism exchange education system in order to be able to support the competitiveness of the domestic tourism industry. Since education and training have a strong relationship with competitiveness (Gee, 2000, p. 2), it is vital to develop quality education.

An International Handbook of Tourism Education
Copyright © 2005 by Elsevier Ltd.
All rights of reproduction in any form reserved
ISBN: 0-08-044667-1

The number of tourism education programmes is increasing worldwide. This chapter deals with the growth of such programmes in the relatively new European state of Slovenia. It focuses on the roles of different partners in creating programmes: academia, industry, students and society. International best practice in tourism education, European recommendations delivered through European higher education development support measures and international tourism educational certification systems (such as TEDQUAL) have played important roles in developing the tourism curricula in Slovenia (Mihalič, 2001, p. 8). It could be argued that the future development will follow these European, international and global standards and that academic insiders will be the main force in this process, together with the tourism industry, students and society. While to a certain extent these standards and best-practice models offer guidance for curricula development, the latter is always influenced by the national environment. Important topics surrounding this development can be articulated through a range of relevant questions. What is the role of the growing tourism academic environment in Slovenia? What is the role of industry? How industry and theory-relevant should tourism programmes be? Do the answers to these questions change according to the time and level of tourism education? In what way should they change?

About Slovenia and Slovenian Tourism

Slovenia is a new transitional country located between Italy, Austria, Hungary and Croatia (Figure 1). It was established in 1991 by separation from former Yugoslavia. Although it was a relatively independent republic in the old federal state, the separation brought about an enhanced reorientation towards a more market economy. Slovenia is a small country

Figure 1: Slovenia and its neighbouring countries. *Source:* Polikons (2004).

with a surface area half the size of Switzerland (20,256 km^2), a population one-third that of Switzerland's (2 million) and a GDP per capita of EUR 12,000.

The beginning of Slovenian tourism stretches far back in history. The Lipica stud farm with its famous white horses was founded in 1580. The Rogaška spa is more than 330 years old. Postojna cave — one of UNESCO's world famous natural phenomena — has been open to tourists for 180 years. Coastal tourism in Portorož has been organised for over 120 years and the first gambling licence was given to the Portorož Casino in 1913 by the Austrian crown (Sirše & Mihalič, 1999, p. 34). Nevertheless, in the old Yugoslav times Slovenia was mostly a transit country for European tourist flows heading towards the Adriatic coast. After becoming an independent state, Slovenia has intensified the development of its spa, coastal, Alpine and countryside tourism, including its city tourism. Today, tourism is an important economic sector and represents in total about 9% of Slovenian GDP. Foreign tourism earnings, including an important amount of casinos' foreign currency income, are about EUR 1.1 billion and make up about 10% of Slovenian exports. In 2002 Slovenia recorded more than 2 million tourists and 7.3 million overnight stays; 1.3 million of these were foreign visitors who make 4 million overnight stays (SURS, 2004).

The figures on the Slovenian tourism industry reflect the country's smallness. Slovenia has about 150 hotels, 5 casino companies, 5,000 restaurants, inns, bars and coffee houses. Around 52,500 people are employed in tourism. The concentration of capital among some hotel firms started to take place after 2000. However, majority of the, about 150, Slovenian hotels are medium- and small-sized companies. The travel agent and tour operator sector is dominated by a few big tour operators and many small travel agents. Air transport used to be heavily monopolised by the national air company Adria Airways and a small number of foreign airlines and consequently a share of tourist air traffic took advantage of the cheaper air connections available at neighbouring Austrian and Italian airports. In 2004, Slovenia received its first low-cost connection to London (EasyJet) that substantially increased the number of visitors coming by air. Other low-cost connections are expected to follow to make Slovenia even more easily accessible by air. Slovenia has kept its role as a road transit country for European tourism flows leading towards the Croatian Adriatic coast, which have recovered in recent years following the stabilised political situation in the Balkans.

Post-Secondary Tourism Education in Slovenia

Changes leading towards a more plural society and economy have been reflected in the education system and the speeding up in the process of educational internationalisation. Globalisation and integration into the European Union (EU) are posing additional challenges that will have to be met in terms of increasing the compatibility of education systems, credit-hour transfers and degree recognition across the EU and around the world. Slovenian education institutions are trying to internationalise their programmes, foster student and professor exchanges, develop joint programmes with foreign universities, as well as establish international cooperation in curriculum development and research. At present, Slovenia has three universities (Ljubljana, Maribor and Primorska), along with post-secondary educational institutions that are not part of any university, as well as public and private schools and programmes.

Several tourism-related post-secondary programmes are offered in Slovenia, with the majority established after 1991. For the present study, a tourism programme is defined as one that is officially labelled and known as a tourism or hospitality, catering or hotel programme and in which tourism and hospitality subjects make up at least 25% of the total programme. Beside such programmes, Slovenia's higher education institutions also offer a variety of tourism-related subjects that students with a different, e.g. non-tourism, study orientation are able to take optionally. These subjects are offered at universities and link to the primary expertise of the faculty concerned.

As set out in Table 1, tourism post-secondary education in Slovenia encompasses the following programmes and studies:

- 2-year post-secondary programmes;
- 3- to 4-year post-secondary tourism programmes;
- undergraduate university tourism programmes that are currently confined to individual and optional tourism-related subjects in other non-tourism programmes at universities;
- 1-year postgraduate tourism specialisation programmes;
- 2-year master degree tourism programmes;
- doctoral research studies related to tourism.

Two-Year Post-Secondary Education

Three programmes in Bled, Maribor and Ljubljana offer a 2-year post-secondary tourism education in tourism and catering. At present, more than 400 students enrol in these programmes each year (Table 1). Practical training in the tourism industry represents a substantial part of these programmes, their learning process is very vocational-action oriented and promises good employment prospects to graduates specialising as cooks, waiters, sommeliers or barmen. These schools also offer a tourism specialisation, but these graduates have little chances of finding a job in a tourism agency; so many continue their studies at a higher education level.

Three- to Four-Year Post-Secondary Education (Non-University Level)

Currently, 400 first-year students study tourism at business or tourism colleges (see Table 1) which are an organisational part of three different Slovenian universities, but in Slovenia are considered as non-university programmes (sometimes called applied university programmes). The programmes are primarily in economics and business administration, but also offer more than 25% of tourism-related classes such as Introduction to Tourism, Tourism Management, Tourism Marketing, Environmental Economics in Tourism and Sociology of Tourism (VPŠ, 2004). In Ljubljana and Maribor students acquire more general knowledge in economics and obtain a degree in economics. At the Tourism College in Portorož, the degree is in tourism with several subjects related to tourism and hospitality such as Culinary, Catering Management, Hotel Management, Gambling, etc. (Turistica, 2004). Internships in the tourism industry are part of this programme.

Table 1: Post-secondary tourism education in Slovenia — programmes and optional subjects, 2004.

Education	Institution	Programme	No. of full-time students	No. of part-time students	Optional tourism subjects
1	2	3	4	5	6
Two-year post-secondary programmes	• Vocational College of Catering and Tourism Bled	Catering	70	30	
		Tourism	70	50	
	• Vocational College of Catering Maribor	Catering	70	15	
		Tourism	45	40	
	• Vocational College of Catering and Tourism ZARIS	Catering	0	10	
		Tourism	0	35	
Three- or four-year post-secondary programmes	• Faculty of Economics, UL, Business School	Tourism	40	40	
	• Faculty of Economics and Business, UM	Tourism			
	• Turistica, College of Tourism, UP	Tourism Hotelier Casinos	120	200	
Undergraduate tourism university education	• Faculty of Economics, UL				Tourism Economics, Environmental Economics in Tourism
	• Faculty of Arts, Department of Geography, UL				Tourism Geography
	• Biotechnical Faculty, Department of Landscape Architecture, UL				Tourism and Recreation
	• Faculty of Sport, UL				Recreation in sport

Table 1: Continued.

Education	Institution	Programme	No. of full-time students	No. of part-time students	Optional tourism subjects
1	2	3	4	5	6
Postgraduate one-year specialisation programme	• Faculty of Economics, UL	Tourism		25	
	• Faculty of Economics and Business, UM in Tourism	Marketing Management		5	
Tourism postgraduate two-year master of science programme	• Faculty of Economics, UL	Economics — tourism study field		10	
Doctoral programme	• All faculties of UL, UM, UP	Ph.D. thesis		5	

UL, University of Ljubljana; UM, University of Maribor; UP, University of Primorska.
Source: Research Tourism Education in Slovenia (2004).

Tourism Education at University Level

In Slovenia no undergraduate tourism programme that meets the above definition is offered at the university level. Nevertheless, some university faculties offer optional tourism-related subjects such as Tourism Geography at the Faculty of Arts, Tourism and Recreation at the Faculty of Sports, Tourism Economics at the Faculty of Economics and Tourism and Recreation at the Biotechnical Faculty (Table 1).

Tourism Specialisation Education at Postgraduate Level

Two tourism specialisation programmes are offered to the holders of 3- or 4-year vocational degrees, as well as to university graduates. The tourism specialisation programme at the Faculty of Economics (Podiplomski študij – specialistični študij turizem, 2004) is a multi-disciplinary programme offering tourism-related knowledge from the perspective of many related disciplines. Since some areas are not covered by Slovenian academics, professors from other universities (Croatia, United Kingdom and Finland) act as guest lecturers. Tourism subjects offered at the specialisation level are Research Methods in Tourism, Tourism Microeconomics, Tourism Economics and Tourism Policy, IT in Tourism, Tourism International Operations, Sustainable Tourism, Tourism Geography, Cultural Heritage, Cross-Cultural Communication, Operational Management in Tourism, Tourism Entrepreneurship, Hospitality Management, Tour Operator and Travel Agent Management, Tourism Law, and Tourism Marketing. Beside tourism subjects, a variety of more economic and business related subjects (such as Finance or Accounting) are offered as options to candidates.

The Marketing Management in Tourism specialisation programme at the University of Maribor offers tourism subjects that study marketing and management issues of tourism business, such as Tourism and Development, Tourism Product Management, Strategic Tourism Management, Tourist Behaviour, Tourism Image Management, Research Methods in Tourism, Sustainable Tourism, Recreation and Regional Development, Internet Marketing and Tourism Promotion.

Master Degree Programmes in Tourism

Although there are no university tourism programmes, it is possible to take tourism as the main area of a study at the postgraduate level. At present, there is only one tourism programme at the master degree level. It is offered by the Faculty of Economics of the University of Ljubljana as a sub-programme within programme of Economics. Five tourism-related subjects are offered here: Tourism Economics, Economics for Tourism Enterprises, Management in Tourism, Sociology of Tourism, and Tourism Policy. Students may also choose a tourism-related thesis topic. Such a thesis is also possible at other university faculties in Slovenia. Some offer individual optional tourism-related subjects at master level, and/or send their students to take some of the tourism-related subjects at the Faculty of Economics and promote combined mentorship through two institutions in order to satisfy the multidisciplinary requirements of tourism research. Knowledge from geography, sociology, cultural heritage or spatial planning have been combined with management, economics and marketing in the last few years. At present, master programmes at Slovene universities are academic in focus.

Doctoral Programmes in Tourism

In Slovenia, master programmes normally last for 2 years and require an additional year for the master thesis. Doctoral candidates are required to hold a master degree and earn a doctoral degree by defending their doctoral thesis only. All Slovenian university faculties may allow a PhD thesis that also refers to tourism. In the 30-year period 1960–1991 just four tourism-related PhD degrees were completed, while, after 1991, along with the establishment of more tourism schools and programmes there has been a growing need for more academics holding a doctoral degree. In the last few years Slovenia has seen four individuals completing their PhD research in tourism and currently there are at least five more such theses in preparation. Like at the master level, doctoral research may be monitored by two mentors from two different universities, as in the case of a sport- and tourism-related thesis undertaken through the faculties of economics and sport.

The Future Development of Tourism Programmes in Slovenia

The Bologna Declaration has brought new standards for the duration and architecture of educational degrees across Europe. Following the Bologna process, some Slovenian schools and faculties will implement a 3+2 year formula (3 for the undergraduate level and 2 years for the master level) in the next academic year (2005/2006), while others will do so in later years. Higher school tourism education will be transferred to undergraduate (3 years Bachelor) and postgraduate (2 years Master) programmes. A new curriculum has been developed at each faculty, taking into account the requirements of the tourism industry, society and students.

The Relationship between Tourism Knowledge Development and Education

Tourism studies started in Slovenia at two universities in 1961 (University of Maribor and University of Ljubljana) and thus have a long tradition. Before the transition, two tourism areas had been addressed at both universities throughout that time: Tourism Economics and Management in Tourism. There was a small number of academics and researchers in tourism, academic research did exist but was not extensive. After 1991, more tourism subjects have been offered by both the old and newly established post-secondary schools. The greater number of tourism programmes attracted more students and resources, including more scholars and researchers. In designing tourism programmes, different partners and teaching methods have been taken into account; tourism knowledge has been drawn to education institutions from different areas. The internationalisation of tourism programmes and co-operation with EU educational development schemes and foreign universities have influenced curriculum development, as has the national environment, the Slovenian tourism industry and society as well as the growing number of tourism PhD holders and academics.

Influences on the Curriculum

As in other countries, there have been a range of influences on the development and knowledge and on the tourism curriculum in Slovenia. Tribe (2000) and Airey (2002) refer to knowledge about tourism being developed in a number of areas. First, so-called extra-disciplinary knowledge is developed outside the academic community in industry, government, think tanks, interest groups, research institutes and consultancies. According to Airey (2002, p. 17) much of the early study and education in tourism in the United Kingdom (UK) relied heavily on this type of study and was strongly vocational, having arisen to meet the needs of the growing tourism industry. Such a relationship between extra-disciplinary knowledge and education leads to programmes that focus on what Tribe (2000) has called a "vocational action" learning approach, such as learning by industry placement, including industry-related projects and case studies.

The second type of knowledge identified by Tribe is traditional academic knowledge and is being developed by academia. The number of scholars at higher level study is essential for the growth of tourism research and for the production of academic knowledge (Airey, 2002, p. 16). The number of scholarly journals devoted to tourism and hospitality reflects this development. Academic knowledge requires more liberal thinking (instead of vocational action) and is reflected in educational programmes differently and away from its very vocational roots. A shift from vocational action towards more reflective and liberal areas of learning has been documented in the UK (Airey, 2002, p. 17). Development of the knowledge base has freed up the curriculum from a mainly vocational action approach.

Further, to analyse the development of tourism knowledge and education development, it is also important to distinguish between multi-disciplinary and inter-disciplinary issues of tourism knowledge. First, multi-disciplinary tourism knowledge comes from different disciplines such as geography, sociology, management, marketing, etc. Second, tourism knowledge is also potentially inter-disciplinary in that it can serve as a focal point in which disciplines come together and create new theory. It is obvious that inter-disciplinary knowledge, tourism theories and strong tourism subjects represent the higher level of the development of tourism knowledge and stronger foundations for tourism education.

According to Airey (2002, p. 18), the development of British tourism education faces three main challenges. First, it needs to continue to develop an inter-disciplinary knowledge base; secondly, it has to extend its course provision outside the vocational action areas of the curriculum and, thirdly, it needs to keep its vocational credentials in order to provide students with good employment prospects. How are these challenges being addressed and met by Slovenia's tourism education system?

In the past, tourism curricula in Slovenia were mainly academic-driven, while the employment possibilities of graduates were not specifically addressed by the socialist system. After 1991 educational programmes turned much more towards industry needs in order to offer proper and more marketable education products and more employable diploma holders. Some new tourism programmes are private and students have to pay tuition fees, some are financed by the government and thus are free. Nevertheless, all institutions are competing for students. Partly in order to attract more students and partly due to internationalisation and the international certification of tourism programme requirements institutions are now involving different partners in the creation of programmes: academia, industry, students and society. The international dimension of all tourism programmes is increasing, supported by European student, staff and research mobility cooperation programmes such as Leonardo da Vinci and Socrates (Lebe, 2002, p. 260) and some attempts to develop joint degree tourism and/or double degrees with foreign programmes are currently in process.

The relevant questions in the development of tourism programmes are questions about the role of different partners, questions related to "reflective liberal" versus "vocational action" use of curriculum space and questions about relationship between academic and extra-disciplinary knowledge. To explore this, a small study was conducted in Slovenia in 2004. For this seven interviews were carried out with faculty directors and tourism programme managers and their responses summarised using a 5-point Likert scale. The results are provided in Figures 2, 3 and Tables 3, 4.

Table 2 gives an indication, for programmes at different levels, of the relative role of academia, industry, students and society in the creation of the programmes. Since tourism academics have been partly responsible for initiating all tourism programme developments, their role in developing these programmes has been significant. Table 2 suggests that 2-year tourism programmes have the strongest ties with industry and take their requirements into account. Although the managers of these schools claim they have not taken student groups into account when designing programmes, they are likely to have done so indirectly. By being suitable for industry, they produce employable graduates. For the higher and postgraduate study programmes the students' needs and wishes are ranked higher. Only the postgraduate level has evaluated the role of academics with the highest grade which also implies a less vocational and more liberal thinking approach at the higher levels of tourism studies. Since the tourism specialisation programme is the newest, developed after the Faculty of Economics adopted the international TEDQUAL certification, we expect that all stakeholders will be taken into account more or less equally, as shown in Table 2. In the future we anticipate that the international accreditation of programmes at all tourism education institutions will firm up the roles of all partners.

Table 2: The role of different partners in creating tourism education programmes, evaluated with a 5-point Likert scale.

Partner	Two-year tourism programmes	Three- to four-year undergraduate tourism programmes	Postgraduate tourism specialisation programme	Postgraduate tourism programme at master level
1	2	3	4	5
Academia	5	4.7	5	5
Industry	5	4.0	4	2
Students	1	4.3	5	3
Society	4	3.3	4	3

Note: 1 = low, 5 = high.
Source: Research Tourism Education in Slovenia (2004).

In Figure 2 and Table 3 the use of the curriculum space is explored. Vocational action oriented teaching refers to seminars and practical training in school laboratories, guest lectures, internships and industry-related projects and case studies presented in the classroom. Reflective liberal teaching is based more on class lectures on theory and research presentations and studies. As shown by a linear trend line in Figure 2, such reflective liberal teaching gains importance at the postgraduate level (III and IV) and, it can be assumed that, it will be more strongly represented in the new university tourism programmes, which currently do not exist and were thus not evaluated in the present research. This means that the present 3- to 4-year tourism colleges that will transform into 3+2 programmes may have to develop more reflective liberal subjects and put less stress on vocational action subjects. Some may use the greater curriculum space for theory already in the first 3 years, but it may be imperative to use more curriculum space for tourism theory at the postgraduate level of the new programmes (the last 2 years).

Such trends in the use of academic and extra-disciplinary knowledge can also be seen in Figure 3 and Table 4 where rankings of the importance of research findings and industry requirements for tourism curriculum development are evaluated. The *Y*-axis shows the importance and relevance of academic/basic research and the *X*-axis the same for applied research and industry requirements. The results show that higher educational and postgraduate tourism programmes take academic knowledge into account to the same extent and, on the contrary, the very vocationally oriented 2-year tourism programmes do not depend much on academic findings in the creation of their curricula. Further, requirements of the industry sector have been quite strongly taken into account at all levels, except at master degree level (grade 4 out of 5, Table 4). Applied research seems unpopular at all educational levels, although it would be expected to be important for tourism colleges. The trend line in Figure 2 shows that academic knowledge is important at the higher education level, nevertheless, there is no difference in attributed importance at levels II, III and IV although one would

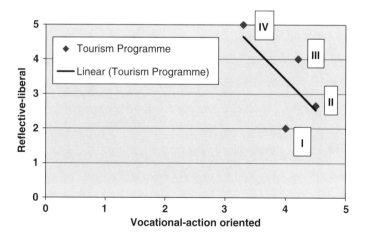

Figure 2: Use of curriculum space, evaluated by 5-point Likert scale. I, 2-Year Tourism Programme; II, 3- to 4-Year Undergraduate Tourism Programme (non-university); III, Postgraduate Tourism Specialisation; IV, Tourism Master. *Source:* Table 3.

Table 3: Use of curriculum space, evaluated with a 5-point Likert scale.

Use of curriculum space	Teaching method	I Two-year tourism programmes	II Three- to four-year undergraduate tourism programmes	III Postgraduate tourism specialisation programme	IV Postgraduate tourism programme at master level
	1	2	3	5	6
Vocational action oriented	Lectures — case studies	4.6	5	5	5
	Seminars, laboratories	4	4.6	5	3
	Guest lectures	4.6	5	5	4
	Internships	5	4	1	1
	Industry projects	5	4.3	5	3
	Applied research	3.3	4.3	4	4
	Average	*4.4*	*4.5*	*4.2*	*3.3*
Reflective-liberal	Lectures – theory	3	3.6	3	5
	Basic research	1	1.7	5	5
	Average	*2*	*2.65*	*4*	*5*

Note: 1 = low, 5 = high.
Source: Research Tourism Education in Slovenia (2004).

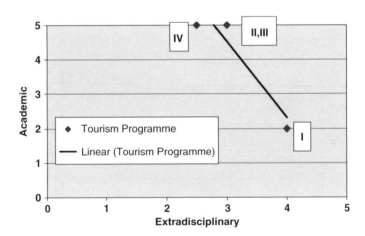

Figure 3: Importance of research findings and industry requirements for tourism curriculum development, evaluated by 5-point Likert scale. I, 2-Year Tourism Programme; II, 3- to 4-Year Undergraduate Tourism Programme (non-university); III, Postgraduate Tourism Specialisation; IV, Tourism Master. *Source:* Table 4.

Table 4: Importance of research findings and industry requirements for tourism curriculum development.

Knowledge	Source	Two-year tourism programmes	Three- to four-year undergraduate tourism programmes	Postgraduate tourism specialisation programme	Postgraduate tourism programmes at master level
1	2	3	4	5	6
Academic	University academic research	2	5	5	5
Extra disciplinary	Applied research/ consultants	3	2	2	3
	Industry	5	4	4	2
	Average	*4*	*3*	*3*	*2.5*

Note: 1 = low, 5 = high.
Source: Research Tourism Education in Slovenia (2004).

expect a slight differentiation. Development towards less extra-disciplinary knowledge is more differentiated according to the level of education. Postgraduate specialisation programmes are in the same position as tourism undergraduate colleges since specialisation programmes are meant to be more industry-oriented. Table 4 shows that industry requirements have been taken into account at the specialisation level quite strongly (grade 4 out of 5) which is to be expected given the nature of these industry-oriented postgraduate programmes.

Conclusion and Discussion

One of the key challenges for tourism education and research is both to pay due regard to the industry's requirements while at the same time staying one step ahead in critical thought and insight (Mihalič, 2002, p. 504). As already noted, the mere adaptation of education to the requirements of the tourism industry has no future (Keller, 1999, p. 10). Above all, the tourism industry needs up-to-date, well-educated tourism professionals who can draw on both practical and academic knowledge. This is as true in the economies in transition as it is in other parts of the world. A distinguishing feature of provision of tourism higher education in these countries is the extent to which by origin it was not particularly close to industry but, in the process of transition, the needs of industry have become more paramount. Slovenia is now at the stage where the achievement of a correct balance between these two is an important issue. In this, quality curriculum development is especially dependent upon international relationships and mobility (Peršić, 2001, p. 71). There is a real need to make the tourism education programmes more comparable so as to promote exchange and compatibility within Europe and across the world. Transition countries, like Slovenia, and their institutions of education have to catch up and become part of the European (international) tourism exchange education system in order to be able to support the competitiveness of the domestic tourism industry.

It is clear in this study that tourism education in Slovenia will continue to develop and there will be even more tourism-related education post-secondary programmes in the near future. The studied pattern of development of the relationship between academic and extra-disciplinary knowledge use in the programmes, as well as the relationship between the vocational and reflective liberal use of the curriculum space and teaching methods have shown that development from levels I to II (from the 2-year to 3- or 4-year post-secondary programmes) have followed the expected pattern. Level III, which refers to the postgraduate tourism specialisation level shows deviation from the expected pattern, being more vocationally and extra-disciplinary oriented compared to level II. This is not surprising as postgraduate specialisation programmes are designed to be "close" to the tourism industry, as opposed to master postgraduate programmes (level IV) which are intended to be more academic.

The Bologna Declaration is bringing new challenges for Slovenia in the development of its future tourism programmes. The existing faculties will adapt to the new standards and it is the common 3+2 formula that has been adopted by the Slovenian government and thus by the current tourism education institutions. This means that new tourism undergraduate programmes will be offered in the near future (3 years), as well as new tourism programmes leading to master degrees (2 years). The existing 2-year vocational programmes are not expected to change much, the 1-year specialisation programmes are expected to cease since 2-year postgraduate master programmes will be opened to 3-year diploma holders. There will be a challenge as to the extent to which new programmes will be willing to move towards an academic and reflective liberal orientation. Calls for more practical tourism studies, presently quite strong in Slovenia, will also have to be considered. Universities seeking to firm up their cooperation with industry in order to be recognised as industry-relevant in order to boost the employability of their diploma holders will certainly listen to voices from praxis. At the same time, current professionally oriented specialisation postgraduates are expected to disappear. In general, master level programmes should fight for both greater academic freedom and use of progressive methods of teaching that is not so vocational or practically-oriented. At the same time, it is also necessary for such programmes to be more entrepreneurial and more industry-oriented, but they should be strategic partners of the industry rather than followers.

The current debate shows, that there might be a need to differentiate between different profiles of master degrees, such as academic versus professional or specialist MBA (Tauch and Rauhvargers, 2002, p. 19). It is expected that in Slovenia different tourism master degree programmes will choose slightly different orientations. More professional programmes are likely to boost the relevance of their graduates for the industry's routine jobs at lower and medium levels, while graduates of more academic master programmes with developed reflective thinking might be more appropriate for jobs in upper management, project leadership, consulting, development, research and academic teaching.

References

Airey, D. (2002). Growth and change in tourism education. In: B. Vukonić & N. Čavlek (Eds), *Rethinking of education and training for tourism* (pp. 13–22). Zagreb: Mikrorad, d.o.o.

Gee, C. Y. (2000). WTO and tourism education in a global economy. Presented at: *Globalisation or Internalization? Challenges and opportunities in tourism education. The strategy of WTO and THEMIS. WTO conference on tourism education and training*, 27 January 2000. Fitur, Madrid: World Tourism Organization.

Keller, P. (1999). Tourism education and training is one of the most important components in the quality and the success of tourism products. Interview with leading tourism figure and academic, *Tedqual,* No 1. Madrid: WTO, pp. 10–13.

Lebe, S. (2002). Tourism education and training programmes regarding the specific needs of the SME sector in Slovenia. In: B. Vukonić & N. Čavlek (Eds), *Rethinking of education and training for tourism* (pp. 259–276). Zagreb: Mikrorad, d.o.o.

Mihalič, T. (2001). Internationalisation of tourism studies at the Faculty of Economics, University of Ljubljana. Constraints and Measures. Paper presented at: *Tourism education: Challenges, trends and European experiences, International Conference*, 2 July 2001. Guildford: University of Surrey.

Mihalič, T. (2002). Internationalisation of tourism education programme — a look at the Faculty of Economics, University of Ljubljana, Slovenia. In: B. Vukonić & N. Čavlek (Eds), *Rethinking of education and training for tourism* (pp. 503–516). Zagreb: Mikrorad, d.o.o.

Peršić, M. (2001). Quality of University's tourism education. *Tourism and Hospitality Management,* 6(1/2), 73–84.

Podiplomski študij – specialistični študij turizem (2004). Faculty of Economics, University of Ljubljana, URL: http://www.ef.uni-lj.si/studij/podiplomskiStudij/specialisticni/Turizem/ (Retrieved 10.08.2004).

Polikons (2004), internal database, Polikons, Ljubljana.

Sirše, J., & Mihalič, T. (1999). Slovenian tourism and tourism policy: A case study. *Tourism Review,* 54(3), 34–47.

SURS (2004). *Statistical Yearbook of the Republic of Slovenia,* SURS, Ljubljana, URL: http://www.stat.si/letopis/index_vsebina.asp?poglavje=27&leto=2003&jezik=si (Retrieved 20.8.2004).

Tauch, C., & Rauhvarges, A. (2002). *Survey on master degrees and joint degrees in Europe.* Brussels: European Commission.

Tribe, J. (2000). Balancing the vocational: The theory and practice of liberal education in tourism, *Tourism and Hospitality Research,* 2(1), 9–25.

Turistica (2004). Turistica, University of Primorska, Portoro, URL: http://suzi.turistica.si/turistica/ (Retrieved 10.08.2004).

VPŠ (2004). Visoka poslovna šola. Faculty of Economics, University of Ljubljana, URL: http://www.ef.uni-lj.si/studij/Vps.asp (Retrieved 10.08.2004).

WTO (1992). *World directory of tourism education and training institutions.* Madrid: World Tourism Organization.

Chapter 18

South Africa

Melville Saayman

Introduction

Since World War II tourism has developed rapidly into one of the largest industries in the world. According to Schulman and Greenberg (1993, p. 57) travel and tourism form a complex global activity involving millions of people. Hudman (1981) and Waters (1976) elaborate by emphasising that it is a significant global socio-economic phenomenon. This phenomenon is brought about by changes in lifestyle, higher incomes, higher levels of education and greatly enhanced mobility (Ritchie & Goeldner, 1987; Mill & Morrison, 1985; Mieczkowski, 1990). According to Hall (1991, p. 3) domestic and international travel expenditures had by 1991 reached a level larger than the gross national product of all but three countries, while a report of the World Tourism Organization (WTO) indicates that tourist arrivals grew by 2.4% in 1998 (WTO, 1998). There can, therefore, be no denying the success of the tourism industry in the last three decades. This tremendous growth of the industry has not been achieved without effort, as tourism has had to meet the challenges of economic uncertainties, political upheavals, deregulation and shifts in the levels of consumer confidence with a remarkable degree of ingenuity, management flexibility, marketing skills, commitment to service quality and a responsibility towards the travelling public. In spite of these challenges tourism will continue to be a growth industry because the factors that have been responsible for its growth during the past decade will continue (Harrison & Husbands, 1996, p. 2; World Bank, 1998; WTO, 1998).

South Africa with its phenomenal tourism resource base has also shown tremendous growth and the first democratic election of the country in 1994 dramatically changed the country's tourism prospects (Msimang, 1995, p. 20). The more favourable political climate has led to an increase of international tourist arrivals (Hicks, 1997, p. 7; Saayman, 1996), although the tourism industry has not been able to reach its full potential (White Paper on Tourism, 1996, p. 4) and one of the reasons is inadequate tourism education and training (White Paper on Tourism, 1996, p. 4; Saayman & Van Der Merwe, 1996; BMI, 1997, p. 1). Various international studies, such as the one conducted by Sheldon and Gee in Hawaii, concluded that the success of the travel industry in any destination is to a large measure dependent on the quality of its staff (Sheldon & Gee, 1997, p. 173). The reason for this is based on the fact that tourism is a peoples' industry. Hence service and specifically quality service plays an important role.

Wood (1995, p. 29) and Croukamp (1996, p. 14) point out that South Africa, like many other countries, relies heavily on tourism for its economic prosperity. In order to maximise the benefits of tourism, South Africa should, however, not rely solely on foreign expertise to meet its skilled labour requirements as this would result in tourism-generated revenue leaking out of the country as management fees and allowances for multinational enterprises and their expatriate personnel, while South African citizens would be left with the low skilled jobs, as has been the case in so many developed countries. To prevent this, the South African government has ensured that training is more accessible and affordable as the future success of the South African tourism industry is closely related to the development of the industry's human resources capacity (White Paper on Tourism, 1996, p. 29). One of the major problems experienced due to the growth of tourism is a "mushrooming effect" on the number of institutions offering tourism studies. This has led to an enormous growth in the number of tourism programmes and more institutions do not necessarily mean better training. Tourism is currently presented at universities, technikons (Universities of Technology), technical colleges and a vast number of private institutions. Another problem is a lack of properly qualified lecturers to present the above-mentioned courses which led to an influx of foreign educators, not only in South Africa, but also in the rest of Africa. In developing countries such a situation is not always seen in a positive light due to cultural, language and many other barriers that are experienced.

This chapter will, however, not dwell on these aspects, but rather give an overview of tourism training in South Africa and the challenges it faces.

The Evolution of Tourism Studies

In order to understand the pressures exerted on tourism as a field of study, it is necessary to establish the exact origins of tourism education. Airey (1988) draws attention to the fact that tourism is a relative newcomer to the education repertoire. This is supported by authors such as Jaspers (1987, p. 580) and Van Der Merwe (1999) who state that tourism courses were only developed in the 1970s, while Pearce, Morrison, and Rutledge (1998, p. 358) conclude that the growth of tourism degree courses has been significant in the 1990s in the Asian Pacific region only. In South Africa, travel courses were introduced in the 1980s and tourism management courses were mainly developed in the early 1990s. Because of the relatively short period of time in which tourism and hospitality courses have been on offer, many challenges have to be met and questions answered when reviewing tourism and hospitality studies. Furthermore, the way tourism has developed as a discipline gives rise to a number of issues (Cooper, Shepherd, & Westlake, 1996, p. 30). According to Jaspers (1987, p. 580) tourism education developed in an ad hoc and unplanned way in many countries. Stephen and Moutinho (1989, p. 119) agree and add that the subject of education and training for careers in tourism has been poorly identified. While tourism education has experienced tremendous growth, it is fragmented like the industry it provides the manpower for and is still emerging as a discipline (Goeldner, 1988).

In tertiary institutions around the world, tourism courses originated in subjects such as geography, anthropology, sociology, history, leisure and recreation while others had their roots in business management, economics, marketing and hospitality management (Cooper et al., 1996). In South Africa many technikons (Universities of Technology as they are currently referred to) accommodated travel courses in their Departments of Secretarial Studies or Communication Studies when they were originally introduced in the early 1980s (Duvenage, 2000). Courses at full-fledged universities in South Africa have evolved from recreation management and/or business and marketing management courses. This resulted in a widespread and varied range of provision of tourism courses, which lack consistency in terms of quality and co-ordination.

In some countries this lack of consistency has led to public sector intervention, in an effort to standardise provision and to control entry. In South Africa, public sector intervention came in the form of the then Hotel Industry Training Board (HITB) currently known as THETA (Tourism Hospitality Education and Training Authority) which controls standards for the Hospitality and Tourism sector and acts as a registered training body (BMI, 1997, p. 111). THETA is currently the institution responsible for setting standards and to do quality assurance. At technikons external quality control is the responsibility of evaluation committees appointed by the Certification Council for Technikons Education (SERTEC). Evaluation is done every 4 years. These committees consist of representatives from technikons and industry. Universities have their own form of evaluation in terms of internal and external evaluation which is done by means of panels of experts. Normally external evaluation would also include specialists from other countries.

Apart from the fact that tourism courses at tertiary institutions originated in different departments, they have developed internationally in three distinct ways (Cooper et al., 1996, p. 30; Geldenhuys, 2000).

1. The development of sector-based vocational courses for the travel trade has had a strong influence on the direction of tourism education. These well-established courses offer a narrow skills training. Examples are South African Airways' (SAA) Fares and Ticket courses, the International Air Transport Association Billing and Settlement Plan Southern Africa (IATABSPZA) course and The Central Reservation Systems (CRS) courses, such as Galileo, Worldspan and Amadeus, which are normally offered by the airlines. Van Der Merwe (1999, p. 27) states that because tourism training was initially linked to operators of intermediaries, or in various craft operations for hospitality, much of tourism training is still confined to these areas;

2. In Business Study courses, a subject such as marketing views tourism as an interesting industry application and lectures offering these subjects use tourism examples to enrich their courses. Because of the economic importance of tourism these courses currently include subjects such as Marketing for Tourism, Tourism Economics and Travel and Tourism Management, which are some of the major subjects in the Bachelor degree: Tourism Management;

3. Traditional disciplines, such as geography, anthropology, sociology, history and communication studies include tourism as an optional specialisation subject. Many South African universities follow this trend due to the fact that tourism draws large numbers of students and integrating tourism as part of their curricula can be regarded as a survival strategy.

When the three main approaches to tourism courses are considered, the historical influences are clearly noticeable:

- Most of the tourism courses offered in South Africa groom students for specific posts within the tourism industry and are purely vocational. This is especially true for the private institutions. Pearce et al. (1998, p. 358) define this as training where a set of highly specific skills are developed which are immediately applicable in targeted occupations;
- According to Lambert (1997, p. 24) the solution to high productivity can come from the simultaneous application of skills and knowledge heavily spiced with commitment. The research by Seward and Gers as in Lambert (1997, p. 25) indicated that new skills and knowledge could easily be transferred into the work place. A great number of product owners follow this approach especially in the hospitality sector;
- Courses that view tourism as an activity worth studying in its own right are the most recent additions to the tourism portfolio and are, according to Van Der Merwe (1999, p. 27), products of the 1980s and 1990s. This is especially true for university training in South Africa. Pearce et al. (1998, p. 358) argue that education, as contrasted to training, seeks to develop an understanding of a phenomenon or issue, and provides instruction so that students may learn a set of generally applicable principles. They conclude that individuals that occupy positions in the tourism industry need both training-based skills and educational insight to function effectively in the industry. They are of the opinion that a combination of training and education, skills development and analytical thinking, is desirable for all tourism staff (Pearce et al., 1998, p. 359);
- Finally, there are courses where students do not necessarily expect to be employed in the tourism industry. Tourism is used as an illustration to enrich traditional disciplines and fields of study. Many departments in Faculties of Economic Science, such as Marketing and Management, use tourism examples as case studies.

According to Van Der Merwe (1999, p. 27) the development of tourism education over the last few decades has grown from being simply an add-on to established disciplines, to courses where tourism is the primary area of study. In reviewing tourism courses offered at traditional tertiary institutions, this also proves to be the case in South Africa (Geldenhuys, 2000). Universities offer tourism courses as a field of specialisation up to doctorate level.

Government Policy

Saayman (1996) indicates that while the tourism industry has tremendous potential to create jobs, the government recognises that appropriate skills and experience are necessary to facilitate employment growth as well as international competitiveness. With the projected staffing needs of the tourism industry and the current lack of physical and financial capacity to deliver education and training, the industry will increasingly be faced by a critical shortage of skills.

The White Paper on Tourism (South Africa, 1996) states that tourism education and training is one of the fundamental pillars of the development of a new responsible tourism in South Africa. The main principles governing the approach to education and training are as follows:

- to promote the involvement of the private sector and private sector institutions in the provision of education and training;

- to encourage the tourism private sector to increase its commitment to training;
- to encourage capacity building between the previously neglected groups and address the specific needs of small, micro and medium-sized businesses and emerging entrepreneurs;
- to make training more accessible to the previously neglected groups of society;
- to promote tourism awareness at all levels of society;
- to develop and invest in an education system that will lead to self-sufficiency and reduce reliance on imported skills;
- to encourage the local media and non-governmental organisations to become partners in the tourism education and awareness process in South Africa;
- to ensure that training is accessible to the previously neglected groups in society in terms of the appropriateness, affordability, location, duration, costs, packaging and language of instruction;
- to execute training as a joint responsibility of the national and provincial governments.

The Government is committed to the promotion of human resources development through the following policy guidelines:

- to support the provision of introductory courses to facilitate entry into the industry by previously neglected groups and others;
- to improve access to training opportunities through a system of scholarships, student revolving loans and incentive schemes;
- to support the improvement of design, marketing, production and packaging skills of craft producers;
- to develop appropriate programmes of skills at the introductory level as well as more specialist shorter courses for accreditation;
- to create a dedicated funding mechanism for training, with a view to strengthening institutional capability and efficiency in delivering the quality and quantity of appropriate education and training required;
- to review and evaluate the existing tourism education and training system with a view to strengthening institutional capability and efficiency in delivering the quality and quantity of appropriate education and training required;
- to ensure the establishment of a tourism education and training data base to facilitate planning, development and co-ordination;
- to assess the current training curricula to ensure that standards comply with industry requirements;
- to establish an effective co-ordination formula for tourism training and education, where all institutions involved in the field are represented;
- to effectively co-ordinate the efforts of government departments involved in tourism training and education, for example departments of Labour, Education and Environmental Affairs and Tourism;
- to develop a series of linked and accredited courses in accordance with the national qualifications framework;
- to support ongoing efforts to ensure that school programmes and curricula are specifically targeted to include sections on tourism;
- to improve skills training at levels including communication skills and the range of languages for tour guides and information officers;

- to institute a system of practical training through summer jobs, interschool and practical attachments within the tourism industry and to develop placement schemes for trainees;
- through consistent and continuous investments in tourism education and training, to create a major new avenue of export earnings through export education and training services.

Tourism as an industry can be developed through education, however, it is important to identify the components within the tourism industry that must be developed and to realise what can be included in the curriculum.

Trends in the Provision

This section focuses on trends in the provision of tourism education and it should be noted that these techniques are not necessarily unique to the study of tourism and hospitality (Geldenhuys, 2000).

Distance Learning

The post-apartheid South Africa has placed tertiary institutions under pressure to address the inequalities of the past and the government of South Africa expects institutions of higher learning to find innovative methods to accommodate more students with a limited infrastructure.

This method might not be effective in South Africa as many students who might opt for a distance learning programme would not be able to utilise this advanced technology. According to Kitching (2000) most of the students from rural communities, have no access to computers, televisions or video players.

Van Aardt (2000) has identified the high dropout rate of students to be one of the main problems associated with distance learning. Her experience is that the absence of traditional face-to-face interaction between students and lecturers leads to a feeling of isolation which many students cannot cope with. Saayman (2003) supports Van Aardt by stating that tourism is an industry where personal contact and communication play a vital role, hence it should not be offered by means of distance learning. Most institutions use this method purely from an economic point of view.

Modularisation

Modularisation refers to the system in which courses are divided into self-contained areas of study, which reflect a clearly defined theme or topic. It is, therefore, possible to study modules on a one-off basis or as part of a formal course or qualification making this method of delivery extremely flexible. The structure of this type of course makes it possible for students to 'pick and mix' the elements or modules which they consider to be most interesting or appropriate. Cooper et al. (1996, pp. 157–158) points out that modular instruction allows students to tailor their courses to their needs and it facilitates selective updating and re-qualifying while it extends the access of students to educational programmes. This is an approach that is also adopted by a number of universities in South Africa.

Credit Accumulation Transfer Schemes (CATS)

CATS is a system designed to facilitate student mobility. This development goes hand in hand with modular instruction.

Since students earn credit for completed modules, CATS makes it possible for students to transfer credits between institutions and courses, getting exemption for credits already earned elsewhere. Although the system for credit transfer is extremely complex, it is already applied in many countries. The South African Qualifications Authority (SAQA) is a specialised organisation that aims to standardise the process of credit accumulation and transfer.

When CATS becomes fully operational in South Africa it will certainly improve mobility between courses and institutions, and reinforce the trend towards student-centered education, despite the difficulties at higher education level (Cooper et al., 1996, pp. 158–159).

Accreditation for Prior Experiential Learning (APEL)/Recognition of Prior Learning (RPL)

APEL/RPL is a concept, which complements modular instruction and permits credits towards a qualification being awarded based on evidence drawn from an individual's past achievements. Modularisation of courses assists APEL as defined content of modules already undertaken by students can be compared to the content of the module for which the student is seeking exemption. In the case of previous relevant experience, the student will be assessed on whether they possess the competencies, which would have been developed, if the student had taken the module. Lower levels of training and education can easily be accommodated in this way (Cooper et al., 1996, pp. 159–160).

Continuing Education (CE)

Continuing education (CE) refers to courses that are offered as part of a professional updating scheme for people in employment. Many educational institutions offer programmes that are designed to update and re-skill individuals in their chosen, specialised fields. Some offer credit which counts towards other recognised industry qualifications.

Although the main delivery mode of CE has traditionally been a face-to-face activity, it is moving towards distance learning. Some argue that attendance at conferences is also a form of CE since these could play a major role in updating skills. Another trend in CE is the accumulation of credits by attending short courses that eventually constitute a recognised qualification. This means that students who work can simultaneously re-skill themselves to gain a recognised qualification.

In-company training refreshes employees' knowledge, assists them in undertaking their jobs more effectively, and can be seen as another type of CE. Cooper et al. (1996, pp. 160–161) explain that these programmes are generally well-structured and of major benefit to the employee. They are seldom accredited on a formal basis and they do not count towards an external qualification.

Computer-Based Training (CBT) and Computer-Assistance Learning (CAL)

Because of the growth in the availability of a wide range of computer software and the minimal cost associated with its purchase, CBT or CAL are starting to exert a greater influence on the delivery of training and education. Some educational departments, which have a large increase in student numbers, have introduced software to communicate the basic skills at entry level.

This allows students to work at their own speed. There is, however, an enormous range in quality of software and it is important that those responsible for purchasing and introducing computer-based schemes are fully conversant with the objectives of the course. They should also be confident enough in the subject area themselves to be able to judge the relative merits and demerits of the various packages.

CBT/CAL is still in its infancy but has the potential to become an important delivery mode in the future, especially where student numbers are expected to rise (Cooper et al., 1996, pp. 161–162).

Most training institutions are currently experimenting with all, or at least a significant number, of these methods.

Key Issues and Opportunities Pertaining to Training in the South African Tourism Environment

Creating a Greater Awareness

One of the greatest challenges facing the tourism industry is to create awareness amongst the greater population. Training institutions also have a role to play here. In terms of growing a greater awareness amongst communities tourism was introduced as a school subject in 2000. This subject was introduced at grade 10 (standard 8) up to grade 12 (standard 10 or matric). One of the great advantages of tourism as a school subject is that it also has an impact on tertiary tourism training because the tertiary education curriculum can now be regarded as an extension of the school curriculum where previously this was not the case. A number of concepts that were dealt with at tertiary level have now been moved to school level.

Accreditation and Communication

A lack of official accreditation is a problem common to many of the sub-sectors within the tourism industry. This is seen by many as the best means of improving general training standards. THETA is the official body for accreditation together with the SAQA. Their greatest barrier is a lack in human resources to assess all the various programmes and courses in South Africa. Not only the institutions, but also the lecturers and course materials used in training are subject to accreditation (Cairns, 2000).

An extensive portion of training within the industry is conducted in-house and this has made the setting of national standards more difficult. The industry has recognised the need for the introduction of a national accreditation system which, if effectively implemented, is envisaged significantly to improve training standards and ultimately levels of service.

There is a lack of communication between the various stakeholders that has resulted in inappropriately trained people who do not satisfy the demands of industry (Geldenhuys, 2003). Effective interaction and better communication among industry, associations and the training providers could solve this problem. An accreditation system should be flexible enough to allow for changes in the industry being structured sufficiently to meet the needs of the latter.

Addressing Training Needs

The BMI Report on Tourism Training Needs and Resources in South Africa (BMI, 1997, p. 112; Geldenhuys, 2000; Van Der Merwe, 1999) identified four core areas.

In-house training   South African tourism employers still have a negative perception of training and perceive it as a resource drain rather than resource development. They have yet to be convinced of the importance of training and the positive impact effective training will have on medium- and long-term profits (BMI, 1997, p. 113).

The need for basic job skills training   Training courses offered by tertiary institutions appear to lack basic job skills for two main reasons:

- basic job skills training is not perceived to be economically viable as the target market for such skills generally draws members from the lower income groups, who in many cases are unable to afford private training and education;
- traditional universities, technikons and hotel schools provide advanced tertiary education aimed at the junior management end of the market.

Owing to their lack of profitability, it is unlikely that private-training bodies will supply basic skills training. Technical colleges and community colleges should be encouraged to liaise with technikons so that a wide range of tourism-related skills can be covered, utilising the technikons' established links with industry while providing market-related basic skills training, with a strong practical component.

Changing to training courses offered by universities and technikons   Tertiary institutions train students to enter tourism at junior management level while private training providers provide a wide range of courses ranging from basic skills to junior management level. While technikons rely on advisory committees to advise them on market demands, feedback from industry appears to be on an ad hoc basis, if at all, for the private colleges.

Most of the universities in South Africa have some or the other tourism course in combination with a variety of subjects. However, only two universities have tourism courses at both graduate and post graduate level specialising fully in the field of tourism studies. As far as technical colleges are concerned, 11 offer courses in travel and tourism, while the THETA lists 10 as offering courses in hotel management.

Traditional tertiary institutions in South Africa have been criticised for:

- not keeping abreast of industry trends — this is particularly true in the case of the technologies utilised in day-to-day job applications;

- providing training focused on specific sectors;
- not focusing enough, in terms of course content, on the importance of service and the potential customer.

The need for sector-specific courses   The area where these courses are applicable includes the travel sector, tour operators and tourist guides. A growth in the demand for especially tourist guides and tour operators necessitates this development. Other areas where there is a growing demand is in the field of ecotourism and game farm management. The skills required with regard to the latter is in terms of the planning of game farms as well as managerial skills and tourism knowledge.

In Service Training

A large number of private employers prefer employing school-leavers and then providing them with on-the-job training. They cite the inappropriateness of training courses offered at institutions as the main reason (BMI, 1997, p. 120). The problem with this approach is mainly from an accreditation and standards point of views.

From the above it is clear that the industry lacks the confidence to invest in graduates from universities and technikons.

Greater Focus on Ethics

There is a lack of a tourism culture, both within the tourism industry and among the South African population. Research also found that tourism courses in general lack a focus on ethics. This becomes very important since South Africa consists of a great number of cultures. All of them have their own views on what is right and wrong and working in an industry that requires greater standardisation, it is important that this aspect be introduced and practised.

Quality Training

Quality training is the foundation of the quality product and remains a challenge. Quality training can be seen as training directed at a specific market, based on specific needs and provided by quality teachers and lecturers alike. A lack of service quality has always been and remains a major challenge. More training is not necessarily better. What needs to be addressed is the level or standard of training methods. As yet, there is no training course for the prospective tourism trainers. There is, however, a growing number of under-qualified or inappropriate trainers entering the tourism industry.

Many of trainers, currently training in industry, have either recently completed a tertiary tourism course, have extensive tourism experience without qualifications or have formal qualifications in the field unrelated to the tourism industry. Both the accreditation bodies of the hospitality and the travel sectors have been criticised for not implementing effective trainer standard control systems.

Suggested solutions to the above problems are the following:

- Stricter and more effectively enforced training accreditation procedures should be put in place;

- All trainers need to pass a training examination before they can officially register as official industry trainers. At technikons and universities, lecturers need to have a higher qualification than the one they offer;
- Tourism, as was mentioned earlier, is also offered as a subject in schools. Teachers offering this subject have had no training. The Department of Education envisages that as soon as the tourism and hospitality subjects become more widely recognised, the teacher-training institutes will introduce appropriate training courses.

Globalisation

This aspect has an enormous impact on training, not only in South Africa but in the rest of the world. One of the results of globalisation is a greater movement of companies across the globe. These companies are looking for specific skills to manage their properties. The same also applies for training institutions, especially from developed countries where there is a huge influx of foreign universities to South Africa. Some of them set high standards while others are just the opposite. But because they are foreign some people are of the view that they are better than South African training institutions, which in most cases is not true. However, this is an aspect that the tourism industry needs to deal with in general (Saayman, 2003).

Affordability and Accessibility of Training

The fees for education, and more specifically tourism education, at almost all tertiary institutions make tourism courses inaccessible to the lower income groups. Many of the players in the formal tourism sector are finding it increasingly difficult to meet their affirmative action goals, as there are few black graduates from the traditional tourism schools. Financial constraints are not the only reason why traditional tertiary institutes cannot meet industry's needs for black graduates. Most black students have never been exposed to tourism when they enrol for tourism courses. They have a limited frame of reference, particularly where destinations are concerned, as very few have had the opportunity to travel. Hence the awareness aspect comes into play again and remains paramount.

Hospitality versus Tourism

In South Africa there is still little integration of the training of hospitality and tourism management. Most courses that attempt to offer these subjects in one course tend to have a definite emphasis on one or the other. This is mainly because from a historical perspective that these two aspects are dealt with as separate sectors, even though both fall into the same industry serving the same people. Hence, this perception has to change if quality assurance is going to be effective.

Conclusion

Tourism training in South Africa is expanding at all levels placing a greater demand on the tertiary infrastructure and relevance of courses. Courses are developed for all aspects of the industry, however, a lack of well-trained lecturers remains a problem. Policies are in place to create the right framework for training to take place. It is up to the relevant institutions to make a success of the training which should lead to effective service delivery. A great number of challenges are facing the South African tourism industry and especially the training sector. The country has grown tremendously in terms of demand (tourist arrivals) and supply (the number of new products). In order to provide a quality service, people with proper skills are required, that led to a significant growth in the number of tourism courses. A great number of problems are associated with a rapid growth in any industry. Luckily systems have now been put in place to deal with those problems, for example accreditation which applies to courses, facilitators and institutions alike.

Acknowledgements

The author would like to give a special thanks to three of his post graduate students who has done tremendous work on this theme, namely Peet Van Der Merwe, Sue Geldenhuys and Mathilda van Niekerk.

References

Airey, D. (1988). Cross cultural approaches to teaching tourism: Teaching tourism into the 1990s. *First international conference for tourism educators*, University of Surrey.

BMI. (1997). *Tourism training needs and resources in South Africa: An institution analysis to assist in the formulation of a tourism training strategy*. Rivonia.

Cairns, C. (2000). Verbal communication with Mr. C. Cairns. Chief Executive of The Travel Education and Training Authority of South Africa (TETASA), 17 May.

Cooper, C., Shepherd, R., & Westlake, J. (1996). Educating the educators in tourism: *Manual of tourism and hospitality education*. SI: World Tourism Organisation and University Of Surrey.

Croukamp, J. (1996). Tourism: Major growth ahead. *Human Resources Management, 12*(4), 14–15, May.

Duvenage, D. C. (2000). Verbal communication with Mr. D. C. Duvenage. Secretary of The Dean, Faculty of Information Science, Technikon Pretoria, 11 October.

Geldenhuys, S. (2000). *Career profiles for the travel sector of the tourism industry*. MCom dissertation, Potchefstroom University for Christian Higher Education, Potchefstroom.

Geldenhuys, S. (2003). *An ecotourism curriculum for Higher education institutions*. Unpublished Ph.D. thesis, Potchefstroom University for Christian Higher Education, Potchefstroom.

Goeldner, C. R. (1988). The evaluation of tourism as an industry and a discipline. *First international conference for tourism educators*, University of Surrey, 14–18 July.

Hall, D. R. (1991). *Tourism and economic development in eastern Europe and the Soviet Union*. New York: Wiley.

Harrison, L. C., & Husbands, W. (1996). *Practicing responsible tourism*. New York: Wiley.

Hicks, R. (1997). Tactics for tourism. *Your Own Business, 3*(9), 7, Dec./Jan.

Hudman, L. E. (1981). *Directory of tourism education programs*. Wheaton, Ill: Merton House.

Jaspers, G. (1987). International harmonisation of tourism education. *Annals of Tourism Research, 14*(4), 580–582.

Kitching, Z. (2000). Verbal communication with Mr. Z. Kitching. Lecturer, Travel and Tourism Practice, Technikon South Africa, 19 May.

Lambert, T. (1997). Global competitiveness: Advantage comes with people development. *Human Resources Management, 12*(10), 24–25, Yearbook.

Mieczkowski, A. (1990). *World trends in tourism and recreation.* New York: Lang.

Mill, R., & Morrison, A. (1985). *The tourism system.* Englewood Cliffs, NJ: Prentice-Hall.

Msimang, M. (1995). New vistas for tourism industry. *R.S.A Review, 8*(4), 20–29, May.

Pearce, P. L., Morrison, A. M., & Rutledge, J. L. (1998). *Tourism: Bridges across continents.* Sydney: McgrawHill.

Ritchie, B., & Goeldner, C. R. (1987). *Travel, tourism and hospitality research.* New York: Wiley.

Saayman, M. (1996). *En route with tourism.* Potchefstroom: Leisure Consultants and Publications.

Saayman, M., & Van Der Merwe, P. (1996). *Manpower analysis of the tourism industry in The North West Province.* Potchefstroom: Leisure Consultants and Publications.

Saayman, M. (2003). *Tourism in South Africa — a future perspective.* Inauguration speech, Potchefstroom University for Christian Higher Education: Potchefstroom.

Schulman, S. A., & Greenberg, J. A. (1993). Review of the literature on tourism education and institutional linkages. *Community College Review, 21*(4), 57–67, Spring.

Sheldon, P. J., & Gee, C. Y. (1997). Training needs assessment in the travel industry. *Annals of Tourism Research, 24,* 173–182.

Stephen, F. W., & Moutinho, L. (1989). *Tourism marketing and management handbook*: Education and training in tourism. New York: Prentice-Hall.

Van Aardt, I. (2000). Verbal communication with Dr. I. Van Aardt. Programme Manager For Tourism, Technikon South Africa, 6 July.

Van Der Merwe, P. (1999). *A training analysis of the tourism industry in the North West Province.* MA dissertation, Potchefstroom: PU vir CHO.

Waters, S. (1976). Educational systems as loosely coupled systems. *Administrative Science Quarterly, 21,* 1–19.

White Paper on Tourism. (1996). *Department of environmental affairs and tourism. White paper on the development and promotion of tourism in South Africa.* Pretoria.

Wood, S. (1995). Tourism takings: Rosy opportunities abound but more government interaction needed, and the investors must avoid over development. *Finance Week, 66*(9), 29–30. 31 August.

World Bank. (1998). World Bank and World Tourism Organisation examine the role of tourism in development. http://www.world-tourism-org/pressure/WBWD. [Date of access 3 December 1998]

WTO. (1998). Results prove strength of tourism. [Online]. Available at: Http://Www.World-Tourism.Org/Pressrel/1997res.

Chapter 19

United Kingdom

David Airey

Introduction

As already explained in Chapter 2, tourism education in the UK can be said to have begun in 1972 with the introduction of two postgraduate programmes at the Universities of Strathclyde and Surrey. Tourism-related programmes existed before this date, notably for the hospitality sector where there were already bachelor degree as well as diploma programmes (Airey & Tribe, 2000). Tourism was studied as optional components of these and other programmes and it was considered as part of more traditional disciplinary studies. But 1972 marked a change in that for the first time tourism was considered in its own right as a distinct field of study. The first two undergraduate programmes were introduced in 1986. From this early, and very small beginning (there were about 20 students on the two first postgraduate programmes) tourism has now come to occupy a major part of UK further and higher education with up to 40,000 students enrolled on tourism programmes. According to one source, there was "an estimated 375 tourism teachers in 1995 [in higher education] and … more than 250 textbooks and 30 journals" (Airey & Johnson, 1999, p. 229) as well as related conferences, organisations and researchers.

Structure of Education in the UK

An outline summary of the structure of educational awards for those over 14 years in England is provided in Figure 1. Arrangements for the other parts of the UK are slightly different although the basics are very similar. Figure 1 identifies eight levels of award up to doctorate plus an entry level. It also suggests the likely age at which candidates start their programmes of study for these awards although, of course, many may commence at later ages. A distinction is made in the middle stages between general education, vocational education and occupational training. This reflects the major choice paths available. For degree level study both vocationally and non-vocationally oriented programmes are offered. Provision of programmes leading to these awards takes place in schools (compulsory to the

An International Handbook of Tourism Education
Copyright © 2005 by Elsevier Ltd.
All rights of reproduction in any form reserved
ISBN: 0-08-044667-1

Level	Normal Minimum age at start	General	Vocational	Occupational
8	21+	Doctor degree (3 years full-time)		
7	21	Master degree (1 year full-time)		
6	18	Bachelor degree (3 years full-time)		
5	18	HND/Foundation Degree (2 years full-time)		NVQ Level 5
4	18	Certificate HE		NVQ Level 4
3 Advanced	16	A level	AVCE (Vocational A level) National Diploma/Certificate	NVQ Level 3
2 Intermediate	16	GCSE	Intermediate GNVQ First Diploma/Certificate	NVQ Level 2
1 Foundation	14	GCSE	Foundation GNVQ Introductory Diploma/Certificate	NVQ Level 1
Entry	14	Certificate		

Figure 1: Structure of UK further and higher education awards. A level, Advanced level General Certificate of Education; AVCE, Advanced Certificate of Vocational Education; GCSE, General Certificate of Secondary Education; GNVQ, General National Vocational Qualification; HE, Higher Education; HND, Higher National Diploma; NVQ, National Vocational Qualification.

age of 16 but with the possibility to stay on until 18 years); in colleges of further education, which normally recruit students at a minimum age of 16, but also recruit 18 year olds as well as mature students to further and higher level programmes; in universities and other higher education institutions;[1] as well as in private institutions and in the work place. There is a range of awarding bodies of which the major ones are the universities for degrees and three major qualifications bodies[2] for the lower level awards. As far as tourism is concerned, it is now represented throughout the education repertoire outlined in the structure given in

---

[1] In 2003, there were 90 universities, 116 university institutions and 55 Colleges of Higher Education (UUK, 2003).
[2] Assessment and Qualifications Alliance (AQA); EDEXCEL; OCR.

Figure 1. Typically it is offered as a discrete subject or linked with leisure studies for the general and vocational qualifications. For the occupational awards, which are primarily competency based, the awards are linked to a range of specific tourism jobs such as tour guides, museum officers, publicity assistants, tourist information officers, travel consultants and travel services. But perhaps the most important point to emphasise is that the provision is widespread at all levels.

Growth and Scale

An estimate of the total number of tourism students at the various levels is given in Table 1. This is based on a number of sources that are not strictly comparable, hence it can only provide a very rough indication. Yet, even if it is a considerable under- or over-estimate it still confirms that tourism is a major activity at both further (Advanced Certificate of Vocational Education (AVCE) and below) and higher (HND and Foundation Degree and above) education. One recent study estimates the total number of students on tourism programmes in higher education at 12,000 (LTSN, 2002). Although this only represents about 1 per cent of total enrolments into higher education it is nevertheless on a similar scale to well-established areas of study such as agriculture, it is about half the size of enrolments to mathematics and about one quarter that of enrolments to medicine.

In some ways more remarkable than the current scale of provision is the rate of growth. Table 2 shows the growth between 1972 and 2003 in numbers of institutions, programmes and

Table 1: Estimate of total numbers of tourism students.

Level	Numbers	Comments
Doctorate	150+	Based on number of research active centres (Botterill & Haven, 2003) with estimate of three Ph.D. enrolments per centre
Master degree	700(1) 1,235(2)	(1) Based on Airey and Johnson (2000) (2) UCAS annual data 2003 entry
Bachelor degree	10,500(1) 7,130(2)	(1) Based on Airey and Johnson (2000) (2) UCAS annual data 2003 entry
HND/Foundation degree	2,700	UCAS annual data 2003 entry
AVCE	9,500	(Based on awards made in 2003. Excludes Scotland. Source: AQA, EDEXCEL, OCR)
Intermediate GNVQ	15,500	(Based on awards made in 2003. Excludes Scotland. Source: AQA, EDEXCEL, OCR)
Foundation GNVQ	5,000	(Based on awards made in 2003. Excludes Scotland. Source: AQA, EDEXCEL, OCR)
GCSE	2,500	Based on awards made in 2003. Excludes Scotland. Source: AQA
Total	approx 45,000	

Table 2: Course provision and enrolments.

	1972	1991	1993	1995	1997	1999	2003
Institutions	2	15	36	43	50	73 67†	55*
Undergraduate (UG) programmes		12	27	42	66	97 75†	n/a
Postgraduate (PG) programmes	2	10	26	33	33	48 59† 81‡	n/a
New student enrolments (UG)		750	1,750	3,600 1,666¶	n/a 2,300¶	3,340 2,363¶	n/a 3,095¶
New student enrolments (PG)	20	250	750	815	n/a	685	n/a

Source: CNAA (1993), Middleton and Ladkin (1996), Airey and Johnson (1998), Airey and Johnson (2000), Stuart-Hoyle (2003); http://www.ucas.co.uk/figures/archive/applications/
* Based on institutions offering undergraduate programmes only.
† Based on LTSN (2002) relating to 2000.
‡ Flohr (2001).
¶ Based on acceptances by the Universities and Colleges Admission Service.

new enrolments in higher education. Again the figures come from more than one source. Some of the major discrepancies are explained by the definition of a "tourism programme" with the widest definitions encompassing all programmes with tourism in the title. Also the Universities and Colleges Admissions Service (UCAS) figures for undergraduates are based on acceptances, whereas the others are based on actual first year enrolments. Notwithstanding these discrepancies there is clearly a pattern of substantial and sustained growth. This is also confirmed by the *Baseline Statement* of the Learning and Teaching Support Network (LTSN) for hospitality, leisure, sport and tourism (LTSN, 2002) which identifies a 142 per cent growth in single honours programmes in tourism from 31 in 1996 to 75 in 2000. By 2003, one half of the higher education institutions in the UK offered a tourism programme. Similarly, both undergraduate and postgraduate programmes and enrolments have continued to expand.

The Main Providers

Tourism is provided by a range of institutions in the UK including schools, colleges and universities. Indeed, nearly all colleges of further education include tourism in their provision and it has already been noted that about one half of higher education institutions offer a tourism programme. It is difficult to identify the main providers. Botterill and Haven's (2003) work, based on the returns from the 2001 Research Assessment Exercise (RAE), provides one way of doing this. They set out both the tourism-related outputs, mainly in the form of papers to academic journals, submitted for the RAE together with the numbers of academic staff submitting these papers. Of course this does not include all academic staff, since only those submitting for the RAE are included and neither does it include all papers since the process was limited to four papers per academic. But it does provide a rough indicator of scale, as set out for the top 10 centres in Table 3.

A key point to note from this list is that with the exception of the Universities of Strathclyde and Surrey, which were granted University status in the 1960s, all the others are former polytechnics or institutes of higher education which became universities in 1992. This provides a reflection of the way in which tourism as a new and substantially vocational field of study fitted well with the vocational orientation of the former polytechnics. Stuart-Holye (2003) confirms this pattern. She found that of the institutions offering undergraduate programmes in 1998–1999 only 14 per cent were universities created before 1992. It should be noted that both Strathclyde and Surrey themselves similarly had strongly vocational origins. It is only much more recently that the older and more traditional universities, such as Nottingham and Exeter, have begun to include tourism in their course offerings.

Programme Titles and Types

With the exception of occupational awards, which have titles related to specific occupations, other awards at the level of further education are largely confined to generic titles "Leisure and Tourism" for General National Vocational Qualification (GNVQ) and "Travel and Tourism" for AVCE. The combination with "Leisure" is a reflection of the broad vocational coverage of studies for these youngest groups whose career choices are unlikely to be made at this stage. There is no such consistency in the names of programmes at the level of higher education. The most popular title (about 20 per cent) according to Airey and Johnson (2000) in 1999/2000

Table 3: Main research centres for tourism.

Institution	Tourism-related outputs	Academics producing tourism-related outputs
University of Surrey	36	14
University of North London (now London Metropolitan University)	36	12
University of Luton	26	7
University of Strathclyde	24	10
Bournemouth University	24	7
Derby University	21	9
Sheffield Hallam University	17	7
Glasgow Caledonian University	15	7
University of Brighton	12	5
Leeds Metropolitan University	12	5

Source: Botterill and Haven (2003).

was "Tourism Management" followed by "Tourism", "Leisure and Tourism Management", "International Tourism Management", "Tourism Studies", "Tourism and Hospitality Management" and "Travel and Tourism Management", all with at least three examples. Beyond these they identified a further 36 different titles reflecting different orientations of the programmes and attempts to gain market differentiation. Examples include "Adventure Tourism", "European Tourism", "Sport, Recreation and Tourism", "Rural Tourism" and "Tourism in Developing Countries". The LTSN (2002) has provided a listing as given in the footnote.[3] More recently, the orientations of some programmes have become even more precise with the introduction of programmes in, for example, "Cruise Operations Management".

Stuart-Hoyle (2003) has also noted a trend for institutions seeking to differentiate themselves from one another by drawing on lecturer's distinct research and other interests and experience. She points to these being translated into new special interest optional courses offered as a part of the programme hence allowing the institution to form a distinct identity within what she calls "an overcrowded market place" (p. 58).

Curricula Issues

However, notwithstanding the attempts at differentiation, in reality the curricula of tourism programmes remain remarkably similar across institutions. An outline of typical curricula and some of the key issues in their development are provided in Chapter 2. The key characteristic is the extent to which curricula both in further education as well as in universities have a strong vocational slant. In undergraduate programmes this finds expression, *inter alia* in programmes containing periods, normally 1 year, of professional placement in the tourism industry (Busby et al., 1997). Airey and Johnson (2000) found that about one half of programmes contained a professional training year. A further reflection on this is given by Stuart-Hoyle (2003) who provides an analysis of the aims and methods relating to undergraduate programmes. These are summarised in Table 4. This shows the overwhelming importance of "preparation for a career in tourism" as well as the significance of business and management skills as a part of the programme. This vocational and business orientation also comes through Stuart-Hoyle's (2003) analysis of content as shown in Table 5. For this she included course titles which featured in 10 or more undergraduate programmes.

This latter point is further reflected in the departmental location of tourism programmes which are overwhelmingly found in departments of business/management or similar. This is shown in Table 6. It is worth noting that even other departments typically include the word "management" in the title, e.g. Leisure and Food Management, Hospitality Management. The information provided in Table 7 relating to the key orientation of undergraduate tourism programmes provides further confirmation of the same pattern.

---

[3] Tourism, Tourism Management, Tourism Studies, Tourism Development Studies, European Tourism, International Tourism, International Tourism Management, Tourism Marketing, Tourism Business Management, Tourism Resource Management, Eco-tourism, Tourism and the Environment, Responsible Tourism, Cultural Tourism, Adventure Tourism, Adventure Tourism Management, Sports Tourism Management, Tourism and Heritage Management, Heritage Management, Heritage Studies, Travel and Tourism, Travel and Tourism Management, Travel and Tourism Administration, International Travel, Transport and Travel and Travel Agency Management.

Table 4: Undergraduate Tourism Programme aims and methods.

Key Programme Aim and Method of Achieving Aim	Percentage $n = 30$
Preparation for a career in tourism (method unstated)	13
Preparation for a career in tourism (predominantly through development of business/management skills)	13
Preparation for a career in tourism (predominantly through development of an intellectual/academic understanding of tourism)	14
Preparation for a career in tourism (through developing an intellectual/academic understanding of, and approach to tourism as well as development of business/management skills)	27
Preparation for a career in general (through skills and knowledge development)	10
Academic/intellectual development (through studying tourism)	23
	100

Source: Stuart-Hoyle (2003).

Table 5: Undergraduate tourism core course titles.

Course	No. of programmes which include course
Business Information Systems/Computing	17
Dissertation/Individual Project	22
Economics/Tourism Economics	16
Financial Accounting/Management	21
Human Resource Management	14
Industrial Placement	14
Introduction to Business	10
Language	13
Management/Tourism Management	12
Marketing/Tourism Marketing	28
Principles of/Introduction to Tourism	18
Research Methods	14
Skills Development Course	11
Strategic Management/Tourism Strategy	12
Tourism Environment/Geography of Tourism	10
Tourism Impacts	10
Tourism Industry Organisations/Business of Tourism/Tourism Operations	21
Tourism Policy and Planning/Development	16

Source: Stuart-Hoyle (2003).

Table 6: Departmental location of Undergraduate Tourism Programmes 1999/2000.

Department	Number
Business/Management	23
Leisure Sport	11
Hospitality/Hotel/Catering	10
Social Sciences/Sociology	7
Environment/Geography/Land Use/Planning	4
Tourism/Tourism Management	6

Source: Airey and Johnson (2000).

Table 7: Key orientation of Undergraduate Tourism Degree Programmes 1999/2000.

Key orientation	Number
Business/Management	45
Social Sciences/Sociologyq	12
Geography/Environmental Planning	9
Leisure/Sport	3
Hospitality/Hotel	3
Other	5

Source: Airey and Johnson (2000).

Support Structures

Alongside and supporting the development of the programmes in tourism has been a rapidly developing range of support including tourism teachers, textbooks, journals, staff development programmes, organisations and conferences. Reference has already been made in Chapter 2 to the 40 or so academic journals relating to tourism that are published in English. There are also hundreds of general and specialist textbooks (Morrison, 2004) for all levels, including many written specifically for GNVQ and AVCE programmes, as well as videos, case studies and other classroom support. As far as academic staff is concerned, two studies have pointed to the extent to which the teachers of tourism are well qualified. Airey and Johnson (2000) noted that more than 80 per cent of the staff they surveyed in higher education had a qualification at master degree level or above (in most cases tourism-related) and of the 20 tourism teams surveyed by Stuart-Hoyle (2003) all had at least one member qualified at master's level in tourism, 16 had one or more member with a PhD and all teams were research active. She also found experience in tourism or other industries to be considerable.

A organisational support structure specifically for the academic community for tourism in the UK emerged fairly early in its development. *The Association for Tourism Teachers* (now the *Association for Tourism Teachers and Trainers* (ATTT)) was formed in 1975 with the simple aim of helping those at all levels to be more effective teachers of tourism. In 1979, it became a specialist group within the *Tourism Society* (TS) (http://www.tourismsociety.org/)

which had been established in 1977 as the professional body for tourism. Unlike existing professional bodies the TS was set up to cover all sectors of tourism and its membership has notably included those working at management levels in the tourism industry, those employed in government bodies at national, regional and local levels, consultants, educators and students. In 2003, 186 of the members were involved in education and training, including many who are also members of ATTT (Tourism Society, 2003). In 1993, a separate group was formed called the *National Liaison Group for Tourism in Higher Education*. Initially, this sought to draw its membership from institutions involved in providing tourism programmes in higher education as well as from the tourism industry. The need for a body specifically to represent tourism in higher education combined with a general lack of success in involving the tourism industry led in 2000 to the organisation confining its membership to educational institutions. At the same time it changed its name to the *Association for Tourism in Higher Education* (ATHE) (http://www.athe.org.uk/). ATHE currently has about 40 members, mainly universities, and its prime role is to act as the subject association for tourism. In this it represents the interests of tourism in higher education, notably to government agencies. For example, it was centrally involved in drawing up the benchmark statements for tourism referred to in Chapter 2. It has also sought to help its members by providing opportunities to meet and by publishing guidelines on matters of interest. Recent guidelines have included commentaries on the tourism curriculum (Botterill & Tribe, 2000), on sustainability issues in tourism education (Eber, 2003), on the RAE (Botterill & Haven, 2003) and the recent developments in tourism education (Stuart-Hoyle, 2004). Earlier guidelines have been brought into a compendium (Airey & Botterill, 2003).

These voluntary support structures were joined in the early 2000s by government funded bodies designed to provide subject support. One of these so-called LTSN, which now forms a part of the government backed Academy for Higher Education is specifically related to Hospitality, Leisure, Sport and Tourism (http://www.hlst.ltsn.ac.uk/). This aims to encourage and broker the sharing of good learning and teaching practice across its subject areas of UK higher education. The resources that it offers include a newsletter, a Guide to Current Practice, Resource Guides and Case Studies. It is also responsible for events and provides an online journal *Journal of Hospitality, Leisure, Sport and Tourism Education* (http://www.hlst.ltsn.ac.uk/johlste/about.html).

Development and Future Issues

Stuart-Hoyle (2004), based in part on earlier work by Airey, has identified three stages in the development of tourism education in the UK. In reality, there is a considerable overlap between these stages but they do independently provide a useful framework for understanding the development. The first stage up to the early 1990s is a period of *Turbulence* marked in particular by rapid growth, already noted above; by Government exhortation for tourism education to expand, partly in response to employment needs; and the abandonment of much of the central control over expansion. In particular, education policy and funding arrangements became far more market-oriented making institutions relatively free to develop their programmes to meet market needs as they thought best. This was complemented by the creation of the new universities and giving these institutions far more freedom to develop their own programmes than the former polytechnics originally possessed. As a popular area with the student market, tourism flourished in this context. The second stage to the end of the 1990s is a period of *Unease*. This is marked by concern about the over-provision of programmes, questions about relevance of programmes to employment needs, lack of agreement about the tourism curriculum (as noted in Chapter 2) and a lack of data about numbers of courses and students.

The final stage is the one marked by an emphasis *on quality assurance and enhancement*. At all levels of education new arrangements have been introduced to provide assurance to the various stakeholders, notably government, students and employers, that the quality of the provision is appropriate. This has taken the form of reviews, assessments and audits of provision, development of frameworks for education qualifications, the introduction of codes of practice and the identification of subject benchmark statements and programme specifications. The outcome has been a much greater level of control, guidance and information about the quality and nature of the provision, even though the basic freedom to make the provision remains. As far as tourism is concerned this has meant, for example, the publication of a benchmark statement (QAA, 2000) which acts as a kind of guide for the curriculum content. It has brought a Subject Overview Report (QAA, 2001), which draws on the main conclusions from the subject review of hospitality, leisure, recreation, sport and tourism. And in the form of the RAE, it has brought a form of grading of research quality for tourism.

The benchmark statement and comments from the subject overview report have already been considered in Chapter 2. The RAE process and results have raised a number of further issues for the subject area of tourism. First, the 2001 exercise records an impressive volume of research. In their study of the results, Botterill and Haven (2003) identified 363 tourism outputs by 146 staff. This supplements a separate study that identified 149 doctoral theses related to tourism accepted by UK and Irish universities between 1990 and 1999 (Botterill, Gale, & Haven, 2002). Secondly, it highlights what Botterill (2002) has referred to as the "invisibility" of tourism research. The invisibility comes in large part from the fact that tourism is not identified as a separate entity within the RAE. Rather, it is subsumed within at least seven other headings to which individual scholars and centres may submit their work. The most common of these are Business and Management, Sports-Related Studies and Geography. As a result tourism simply becomes lost. The final issue to note here is that on the whole tourism research does not receive a high-quality rating. The RAE rates research on a 7-point scale. In the 2001 RAE, of the 43 centres noted by Botterill and Haven (2003) as including tourism in their submission, only two centres were included in the top two categories and only a further eleven were in the third category. The majority were in the bottom four categories.

In many ways, tourism education in the UK is now in a strong position. It certainly appears to be attractive to students and each year recruits a large student population. It is also supported by a large community of teachers and scholars who can draw upon both national and international specialist support in the form of journals, books, conferences, organisations and other resources. Yet behind this apparent success there are still some important uncertainties. As a subject for research it has not yet gained real credibility. Despite the quantity of research from the growing academic community there is still an important need to enhance the quality and the recognition of the research. As a subject for teaching it is still more often than not linked with other related areas such as hospitality, leisure, recreation and sport. Notably for the LTSN, the subject benchmarking as well as the subject review exercise, tourism has always been linked with these related areas, which

Table 8: Applications and acceptances to Tourism Undergraduate Degree Programmes 1995–2003.

Year	Applications	Acceptances	Ratio
1995	18,115	1,666	11:1
1996	14,293	1,924	7:1
1997	14,739	2,300	6:1
1998	14,789	2,350	6:1
1999	13,249	2,363	6:1
2000	12,922	2,388	5:1
2001	13,099	2,716	5:1
2002	14,073	3,109	5:1
2003	14,252	3,095	5:1

Source: Stuart-Hoyle (2004); http://www.ucas.co.uk/figures/archive/applications/

inevitably has an influence on curricular thinking. But the most important uncertainty relates to its popularity as an area of study. As shown in Table 8, figures for applications to undergraduate programmes reveal a worrying trend that they have, at best, reached a plateau. For most of its history tourism has been buoyed by strong and growing student applications. With a large pool of applicants this has allowed growth and allowed programmes to recruit some of the best students. Obviously, growth cannot continue indefinitely. Perhaps the most important thing for tourism education in the UK now is to work further on maintaining the quality of the provision both for teaching and for research.

References

Airey, D., & Botterill, D. (2003). *NLG guidelines 1–9*. Guildford: Association of Tourism in Higher Education.

Airey, D., & Johnson, S. (1998). *The profile of tourism studies degree courses in the UK: 1997/98*. London: National Liaison Group for Higher Education in Tourism.

Airey, D., & Johnson, S. (1999). The content of tourism degree courses in the UK. *Tourism Management, 20*(2), 229–235.

Airey, D., & Johnson, S. (2000). *Tourism degree and postgraduate level courses in the UK 1999/2000 – dimensions, characteristics, contents – a report to the British Travel Education Trust* (unpublished study for the British Travel Educational Trust).

Airey, D., & Tribe, J. (2000). Education for Hospitality. In: C. Lashley & A. Morrison (Eds), *In search of hospitality*. Oxford: Butterworth Heinemann.

Botterill, D. (2002). Tourism studies and research quality assessment. *Journal of Hospitality, Leisure, Sport and Tourism Education, 1*(2), 71–74.

Botterill, D., Gale, T., & Haven, C. (2002). A survey of doctoral theses accepted by Universities in the UK and Ireland for studies related to tourism, 1990–1999. *Tourist Studies, 2*(3), 267–281.

Botterill, D., & Haven, C. (2003). *Tourism studies and the research assessment exercise 2001, (Guidelines No 11)*. Guildford: Association for Tourism in Higher Education.

Botterill, D., & Tribe, J., (2000). *Benchmarking and the higher education curriculum, (Guidelines No 9)*. London: National Liaison Group for Tourism in Higher Education.

Busby, G., Brunt, P., & Barber, S. (1997). Tourism sandwich placements: An appraisal. *Tourism Management, 18*(2), 105–110.

CNAA. (1993). *Review of tourism studies degree courses.* London: Council for National Academic Awards.

Eber, S. (2003). *Integrating sustainability into the undergraduate curriculum: Leisure and tourism, (Guidelines No 10).* Guildford: Association of Tourism in Higher Education.

Flohr, S. (2001). An analysis of British postgraduate courses in tourism: What role does sustainability play in higher education. *Journal of Sustainable Tourism, 9*(6), 505–513.

LTSN, Hospitality, Leisure, Sport and Tourism. (2002). *Baseline statement.* Available from http://www.hlst.ltsn.ac.uk/resources/baseline.pdf.

Middleton, V. T. C., & Ladkin, A. (1996). *The profile of tourism studies degree courses in the UK: 1995/6.* London: National Liaison Group for Tourism in Higher Education.

Morrison, A. (2004). Available from http://omni.cc.purdue.edu/~alltson/books.htm.

QAA. (2000). *Hospitality, leisure, sport and tourism, subject benchmark.* Gloucester: Quality Assurance Agency for Higher Education.

QAA. (2001). *Hospitality, leisure, recreation, sport and tourism, subject overview report 2000–2001.* Gloucester: Quality Assurance Agency for Higher Education.

Stuart-Hoyle, M. (2003). The purpose of undergraduate tourism programmes in the United Kingdom. *Journal of Hospitality, Leisure, Sport and Tourism Education, 2*(1), 49–74.

Stuart-Hoyle, M. (2004). 1993–2003 *Critical incidents: Tourism in higher education, (Guidelines No 12).* Farnham: Association of Tourism in Higher Education.

Tourism Society. (2003). *Membership directory 2004.* London: Tourism Society.

UUK. (2003). *Higher education in facts and figures.* London: UUK.

TEACHING, LEARNING AND ASSESSMENT

Chapter 20

Teaching

Dimitrios Stergiou

Introduction

Although there has been considerable emphasis in current research in tourism on developing a systematic and rigorous body of knowledge about tourism education, it is noteworthy that remarkably little attention has been given to the conduct of teaching itself, particularly teaching evaluation for higher education in tourism. That few researchers participate in codifying what we know about teaching, identifying research agendas, and creating new knowledge presents a problem. The activity of teaching constitutes an integral part of the educational context. It is within the context of teaching that the curriculum is interpreted and acted upon, where the link between students and institutions is almost always created and provided. These fundamental assumptions behind the literature on the general field of education have led most educational researchers to subscribe to the assertion that research on education depends for its advancement most heavily on research about teaching (Winne & Marx, 1977). In the current context, this presumption suggests that by ignoring the significant contributions that knowledge about teaching can make to the field, the body of research on tourism education disenfranchises an integral part of its knowledge base.

This missing element has not gone unnoticed. For example, in his review of research trends in tourism education, Tribe (2002a, p. 73) observes:

> How to teach has been overshadowed by what to teach and issues of effective teaching and assessment have been overlooked.

Stergiou, et.al. (2002, p. 150) make a similar case, observing that:

> The preoccupation of authors and researchers with what is and what ought to be taught — the curriculum — has tended to drive out issues related to the conduct of teaching, to the extent that research on teaching within the field is notable mainly for its absence.

These words were written in 2002. Since then the position has not changed and it is fair to say that the tourism educational world is still short of a properly worked-out examination of the activity of teaching.

Against this background, there seems to be a clear need for research which is focused as directly as possible on tourism teaching and its evaluation, and for theory which is generated from such research. As Tribe (2002a, p. 73) observes, "the lack of evaluative … literature in this area is of prime concern". It is in connection with this last point that this chapter seeks to add a perspective by addressing issues about the nature and the evaluation of teaching tourism. The focus is on tourism in higher education, which is provided in the universities or other higher education institutions. The chapter is not concerned with the management and leadership of institutions, although clearly their structures and processes have an impact upon teaching. Rather, it places the teacher in the centre stage and focuses upon the question "What does it mean to be a good teacher in tourism higher education"? The discussion draws mainly on published sources and these relate mostly to the experience of the UK. However, many of the themes and issues developed are of international interest.

Evaluation of Teaching

Given the abundance of relevant publications available, a comprehensive review of extant literature on teaching seems inappropriate and falls outside the scope of this chapter. However, in the absence of relevant literature in the field of tourism education, it would be an omission not to discuss major topics and resources for tourism students and other readers who are approaching the issues of teaching and its evaluation for the first time. The discussion is structured around the following two propositions:

(1). dimensions of teaching evaluation should be introduced as evaluative elaborations on the generic concept of teaching;
(2). there exists a basic dichotomy in the dimensions on which teachers vary, corresponding generally to (1) a teacher's understanding of what is to be taught and (2) how it is to be taught.

Some brief explanation of the rationale behind these propositions is in order. The more one studies education, the more one becomes convinced of a confusion of the generic meaning of "teaching" with its elaborated forms, such as good teaching and successful teaching. In fact, this issue was one of Jackson's (1986) prime concerns. In his book on the practice of teaching he raises the question as to whether it is possible to define teaching in a way that speaks of its true meaning or essence without also becoming entangled with a definition that involves the meaning of good teaching.

An investigation into the features that are attached to the concept of teaching as a result of the way the term is used in the language of everyday discourse sets forth an analysis that attempts to offer a response to Jackson's question. The main point of this analysis is to present an argument regarding the content, character, and dimensions of teaching that also reveals how easily one can confuse the generic meaning of teaching with its elaborated meanings. The question that focuses the argument is one posed by Hirst (1973) some years ago: How do we distinguish teaching from other activities? This question initiates an onto-logical analysis, the task of which is to tease out the basic meaning of the word "teaching".

The work of Fenstermacher (1986, p. 38) on the different methods for research on teaching provides a helpful way to initiate this analysis. He sets out what he calls "The Generic Conditions" for teaching as follows:

1. There is a person, P, who possesses some;
2. content, c, and who;
3. intends to convey or impart c to;
4. a person, R, who initially lacks c, such that;
5. P and R engage in a relationship for the purpose of R's acquiring c.

Returning to the question that initiated this inquiry (how do we distinguish teaching from other activities?), one answer is that a teacher possesses some knowledge or other content not understood by others, presumably the students, and he or she intends to convey this content to the students, leading to a formation of a relationship between them for this pur-pose. In doing so, the tasks of the teacher include selecting the content to be learned, adapt-ing the material to the level of the students, helping students to get access to the content, serving as a primary source of knowledge so that they become skilled at acquiring content. Therefore, teaching necessarily begins with a teacher's understanding of what is to be taught and how it is to be taught (Shulman, 1987). It proceeds through a series of activi-ties during which the students are provided instruction and opportunities for learning, though it is important to note that learning itself cannot be fully attributed to teaching, but also remains the responsibility of the students.

This last point bears a bit more exploration because some readers may argue that in order for P to be teaching at all, R must acquire what P is teaching. That is, there can be no teaching without learning. If R never learns c as a result of his association with P, can it still be maintained that P is teaching R? The answer is yes. To argue that there is no teaching without learning confuses the generic conditions with what might be called the appraisal conditions of teaching. As Fenstermacher (1986, p. 38) has nicely put it, "it makes no more sense to require learning in order to be teaching than it does to require winning in order to be racing, or finding in order to be looking". Clearly, ideas about teaching must relate to ideas about learning, because the purpose of the former is in some way to enhance the latter (Squires, 1999). However, it is important to remember that learning goes on all the time, whether people are being taught or not. Indeed, there is now widespread evidence from studies of adult learning that the learning that goes on within the confines of formal education is only the visible tip of a much larger iceberg of ubiq-uitous, informal, self-directed learning (Tough, 1971; Brockett & Hiemstra, 1991; Candy, 1991).

The five characteristics listed above constitute a generic meaning of teaching. The generic conditions provide the basis for answering whether or not some activity is teach-ing as opposed to something else. It follows logically that any additions to these conditions are simple elaborations on this generic concept. There are many ways to elaborate on this generic notion depending on the approach adopted by researchers when they study the concept. For example, anthropologists make cultural elaborations, behavioural psycholo-gists make behavioural elaborations, and so it goes for the many different approaches to the study of teaching. In a similar manner, researchers concerned with what might be called the appraisal conditions of the activity make evaluative elaborations.

Having established the relationship between the ontology and the evaluation of teaching, the focus of the discussion returns to the generic conditions of the activity because they suggest two basic and powerful questions that one can ask about all teaching situations. The two questions are: What is to be taught? How is it to be taught?

The first question permits the analysis to consider a key aspect of the teaching process, that of the content of a subject. In education, the word "content" is quite ambiguous. It can refer to everything that the student experiences as part of a course, or it can refer more narrowly to the subject matter (Squires, 1999). It is being used in the latter sense here, because it is important to identify content as an aspect of teaching that needs attention in its own right, and does not simply get subsumed under something else. This point of view is perhaps nowhere stated with more clarity and succinctness than in the work of Dunkin and Biddle. In *The Study of Teaching*, Dunkin and Biddle (1974) set forth their view that the content ought not be viewed as a context variable, comparable to class size or classroom climate, but should rather occupy a prominent position in the agenda of research on teaching.

Central to any discussion of content — the subject matter of a course — is the academic unit responsible for teaching this content. The thrust of the argument is based on the assumption that a teacher should certainly possess a certain minimum facility with, and understanding of, the subject to be taught (Wilson, Shulman, & Richert, 1987). For all its apparent concreteness or obviousness, this argument introduces a new twist in the analysis. Up to this point, the subject matter of a course has been the focal concept, whereas a teacher's subject-knowledge now appears to be an important conception. Within the context of this chapter, this twist in the analysis may be stated in the form of the question: What knowledge is essential for an academic teaching tourism? This inquiry into the nature of teacher knowledge within the confines of tourism higher education, involves some fundamental epistemological questions, which serve as the starting point for analyses dealing with knowledge: How is this knowledge organised? How is it justified? What forms does it take? Which are the sources informing this knowledge?

What is important here is that the teacher has special responsibilities in relation to subject-knowledge, serving as the primary source of student understanding of subject matter (Smith, 1983). This responsibility places special demands not only on the teacher's own depth of subject matter knowledge, but also on the teacher's understanding of how that knowledge should be ordered in ways that will be clear and accessible to the students (Shulman, 1987).

This analysis opens up the wider discussion concerning the methods and techniques of teaching — the "how" of the activity. The point of concern within the context of this chapter is what is actually meant by a teaching method. Within the realm of teaching studies, "method" is a term usually associated with the ways of going about the activity of teaching. It refers to all forms of educational hardware and software that teachers have at their disposal and the methods and techniques for using them (Squires, 1999). It is in this sense that we can speak of teaching methods as procedural, in that a teacher is always concerned with and involved in going about things and doing things.

The word procedural is being used here not only to mean an identifiable, often linear sequence of steps and operations but also to capture the subtler and less explicit ways, styles and approaches that form part of the collective professional wisdom of teachers. As

Squires (1999) argues, the point about teaching methods is that they need to be tailored to situations which are not wholly routine, but in which new problems have to be handled. The implication of this is that although everyday common sense is important, it is insufficient to meet professional demands and the teacher has to acquire some additional kinds of know-how: the capacity to turn intention into effect in a particular context. Methods of teaching thus connote not just a particular technique (for example using group work) but also a whole approach to teaching, and it is in this sense that the term is used here.

While the discussion may seem to have come a long way from the initiation of this analysis, the underlying point is still the same. The means and forms of teaching structure and colour our perception of the whole activity. A teacher's understanding of *what* is to be taught is entangled with *how* they teach it.

Good Teaching

In the first real attempt to look systematically at issues of teaching in tourism higher education, Stergiou (2004) built this basic split in thinking about the activity of teaching into an evaluative study of tourism teaching in the UK, in the form of two major dimensions on which teachers vary: teacher knowledge (the "what" of the activity) and teaching ability (the "how" of the activity). Stergiou asked a large number of tourism teachers and students to specify their views to a bank of statements by which these two dimensions can be evaluated.[1] The methodological procedures of the study have been given elsewhere (Stergiou, 2004; Stergiou et al. 2002, 2003, 2004) and will not be elaborated here except to say that the results of responses to the statements were submitted to factor analysis in an attempt to identify the major factors that are associated with "good" teaching.

The results of this analysis yielded four primary factors underlying perceptions of the desirable traits of tourism teachers (see Table 1). More specifically, what appears to be of key importance, as far as teaching ability is concerned, are the ways in which the teacher stimulates the students' thinking (Person-Oriented Intellectual Reinforcement) and the way in which they organise the classes (Structural Organisation of Knowledge). For the dimension relating to teacher knowledge the important issues are being up-to-date (Up-to-Dateness) and confident in their knowledge (Secure Base of Fundamental Knowledge). Within these it is worth noting a specific tourism characteristic. Specific statements relating to "new developments in the field", "examples from the tourism industry", "key developments in the field" and "sources of information about the industry" all point to an emphasis, among the surveyed respondents, on the vocational aspect of tourism studies.

The results from the responses to teaching reported in Stergiou's study, contain elements that are predicable but at the same time also identify some important messages about teaching in tourism. As far as the predictability is concerned, it is not unexpected that students rely on the teachers to organise their material or look to them to stimulate their thinking. Nor, for what are mainly designed as vocational courses, is it in any way odd that teachers are expected to be current with information about tourism. However, a glance at

---

[1] The statements used in the study are available on request.

Table 1: Factors associated with "good" teaching.

Teaching ability

Person-oriented intellectual reinforcement
The teacher explores with students new approaches and meanings
The teacher develops students' capacity to think for themselves
The teacher stimulates the intellectual curiosity of students

Structural organisation of knowledge
The teacher announces the objectives of the lecture at the beginning
The teacher explains to students how their work will be assessed
The teacher connects lectures to reading

Teacher knowledge

Up-to-dateness
Has main aim of getting up-to-date information out of the journals
Has sufficient confidence in their knowledge to invite and answer questions in class
Reviews and modifies knowledge on the basis of new developments in the field
Uses examples from the tourism industry

Secure base of fundamental knowledge
Reads research reports and more informal studies
Is aware of the key developments in the field
Has a good knowledge of the sources of information about the industry
Is able to set and solve problems by applying concepts and techniques appropriately
Is sufficiently confident to discard many of the themes that are fashionable at the time

the statements included in the factors proposed by Stergiou for each dimension in Table 1, suggest that the students' and teachers' views do extend beyond simple vocationalism. Statements about "connects lectures to reading", "explores … new approaches and meanings", "develops … capacity to think for themselves", "stimulates the intellectual curiosity", "reviews and modifies knowledge", "confidence to discard … themes", all suggest a deeper level of understanding of the purpose of higher education for tourism. Students are clearly not at University solely for vocational relevance but are also seeking a deeper set of experiences, which are also recognised by tourism teachers. This of course clearly links to the debate about the curriculum and the tension between industry and academic aspects of tourism that has tended to dominate the literature in the field.

Mind the Gap

In their contributions to this collection, Airey and Tribe have produced compelling evidence and arguments to suggest that, as far as tourism is concerned, the curriculum is mainly being framed as a vocational one, dominated by business, managerial and instrumental aims.

Indeed empirical evidence in most recent publications support the existence of these partial and incomplete framings of tourism curricula. For example, a study of tourism degree and postgraduate level courses in the UK concludes that:

> As far as orientation is concerned there remains a clear bias towards business and management ... with business studies occupying predominant positions in the content of many courses. (Airey & Johnson, 2000, p. 40)

In part, as Tribe (1999, p. 103) has suggested, this orientation is influenced by a utilitarian ethos of knowledge, which judges success "by its ability to solve a particular problem, its cost effectiveness, and its ability to establish competitive advantage, that is its effectiveness in the real world". For tourism studies in particular, the link with the successful operation of a sector of the economy is perhaps more pronounced than for education in general. The original rational for the study of tourism was prompted in large measure by a desire to meet the perceived needs of a growing tourism industry (Airey, 2002) and, as indicated by the findings of Stergiou's study, the vocational continues to provide a crucial and desirable ingredient to the teaching experience.

Clearly, there are strong arguments in favour of a vocational tourism education. In many ways, at least in the short term, vocationalism closely fits the needs of the key stakeholders in tourism education: the employers, the students and the educators. An emphasis on vocational ends helps meet employers' immediate workforce needs, it provides students with fairly good initial employment prospects and it ensures that the educators have a good demand by students for their programmes of study (Airey, forthcoming).

However, there is another important dimension to this. The focus of a vocational tourism education has a particular discourse and represents a constellation of beliefs that amount to a routinised formula for determining how things should be done. The ends are those of enhancement of tourism business organisations which in turn aim to deliver tourist satisfaction (Tribe, 1999). This implies a short-term, instrumental concern with knowledge — a pursuit of means of technical efficiency rather than the means to a stimulating and penetrating education. Following this, a gap has been unearthed within the context of Stergiou's study between the students' and teachers' understanding of the purpose of higher education for tourism, and the nature of the current provision. Whilst the stated focus of provision remains that of preparing graduates for the world of work in the tourism and other industries, teachers and students in tourism higher education take a broader perspective, seeking a deeper set of experiences. It is argued here that closing, or at least narrowing, this gap represents an outstanding challenge to tourism higher education — a challenge that has meaning at all levels of scale and for most activities in tourism.

In this chapter, the view developed by Tribe (1997, 1999, 2000) and others is shared, that insufficient interaction across such a gap, and therefore between industry and academic aspects of tourism, sets serious limitations to the achievable basic understanding of the wider world of tourism as well as limiting unnecessarily the basis for policy-making and action. Airey (forthcoming) has caught the essence of the problem:

> The sheer growth of tourism has brought with it not just economic benefits but a whole range of other impacts both positive and negative. The outcome is that the successful development of tourism increasingly needs not only

skilled operators of existing procedures but also a cadre who in Tribe's terms pay attention to the good stewardship of the scarce tourism resources. In other words, what tourism increasingly requires is individuals and managers who can take a longer and broader view of tourism both to satisfy societal goals but also to permit the destinations and enterprises to maintain their resources and achieve competitive advantage.

Within this context, the vocational orientation at the core of tourism education provision is not sufficient in itself to meet the needs of the future. It is increasingly important to move beyond the boundaries of vocationalism into an education which encourages vocational competence balanced by competence that seeks better development of the wider tourism world. The important finding to emerge from Stergiou's work in relation to this, is that the need for this aggregative approach to education appears to be realised by students and teaching faculty, in tourism higher education in the UK. In this connection, Tribe's curriculum concept of the philosophic practitioner is especially relevant.

The Curriculum Concept of the Philosophic Practitioner

Over recent years, in the field of tourism education, Tribe (1999, 2002b) in the UK has developed a curriculum concept bearing the name of the "philosophic practitioner". The idea is both powerful and productive, but is in essence simple. It is that if the tourism curriculum is restricted too tightly to the vocational, the education provision does not do justice to the individual students, to the industry, or to the subject area itself. It is as a response to these issues arising from partial framings of the tourism curriculum that the concept of the philosophic practitioner is developed, mapping an education the aim of which is to promote a balance between satisfying the demands of business and the wider aims for the tourism world.

Tribe (2002b, p. 351) points up the challenge for the curriculum for philosophic practitioners:

> This is to develop and seek to reconnect two key roles that have become separated. These are the roles of the occupational person in tourism and the responsible one overseeing and participating in its development.

He goes on to explain that (2002b, p. 354):

> the philosophic practitioner curriculum is designed to satisfy the labour market, to respond to consumer wants, and to promote economic welfare. It is also designed to create a reflective workforce to further the debate about the destiny of the tourism world and an active workforce to create a tourism society that has been deeply thought about.

Clearly, this wider conception of the curriculum for tourism studies provides important ingredients of education. For the students themselves, it is this complementary role of development for occupational competence and responsibility that equips them with the breadth that enables a free analysis of tourism to take place. This synthesis can also make a vital contribution to the tourism industry itself, by producing a workforce that is able to think outside the boundaries of existing paradigms and practices. And as far as the subject itself is concerned, it is only by entering new areas and making a contribution to new knowledge and new insights that it will refresh itself and maintain its relevance, whether for the world of work or beyond (Airey, forthcoming).

The point of mentioning these reflections is not to launch on a digression about the tourism curriculum, important though that is. Their presence here has a different purpose. Following the results of Stergiou's study, the argument of this section amounts to the proposition that every student should be a "philosophic practitioner". The student has his or her subject field with its own corpus of technical expertise and propositional knowledge, and is, it is to be hoped, sufficiently interested to become immersed in it. But tourism education is clearly not just about the provision of technical expertise to fulfil the production purposes of the tourism industry. Nor is it about simply learning existing facts and truths. From the students' and teachers' perspective it goes well beyond this and as suggested by Tribe the concept of the philosophic practitioner provides a basis to counter the development of dualisms in tourism higher education by offering a way of unifying these discrete traditions.

From this perspective, a tourism higher education of the kind envisaged by the respondents in Stergiou's study can only be realised when the student is able to raise him or herself out of the conventions of vocationalism and to engage in discourses of "good thought and action in a world of tourism for vocational and liberal ends" (Tribe, 1999, p. 130). Only through such a position of critical consciousness can the restricted aims and purposes of incomplete framings of tourism curricula, and their possible ideological strains, be recognised for what they are. Only through becoming a continuing "philosophic practitioner" can the student — and the graduate — avoid succumbing naively to conventional "wisdom" about the world of tourism. Of course, as Stergiou's results suggest, the vocational orientation continues to provide a crucial ingredient to the student experience; but expectations about tourism higher education do extend beyond this corner of the curriculum.

Educational Implications

The educational implications of embracing a wider conception of tourism education and the values which it presupposes are considerable. In particular, there are implications for the content of the curriculum and its organisation, for teaching itself, and for the student experience.

For tourism courses, the space — intellectual and practical — which tourism higher education of the kinds envisaged here calls for, points to significant levels of student autonomy and independence in both thought and action. This implies an ethos in which students are encouraged to find their own voices and are invited to claim responsibility for their own learning. It implies that teachers should not teach that x or y is the case as such, but put it forward as a credible hypothesis for students' real consent. This, in turn, suggests that formal didactic teaching should be kept to a minimum, with teaching sessions containing real interaction between teacher and students, and encouraging interaction between the students themselves. Where lectures have to be given in the traditional form of continuous unbroken speech from the teacher (i.e. due to resource constraints), they should be carefully thought through so that they do offer students overviews to tourism topics from a critical standpoint, as well as attempting to challenge the students' thinking.

This broader notion of tourism education can also be supported by the use of simulated or actual professional situations, in which the students' repertoire of technical knowledge can be extended, as well as by offering opportunities to develop critical skills in articulating envisaged possibilities of professional action. But there are also questions to be asked of tourism curricula about the extent to which theory and practice are really integrated; the degree to which they are genuinely interdisciplinary, intertwining (as the demands of professional life in the tourism industry call for) different disciplinary perspectives; and whether there are opportunities for the very real value and ethical questions to be explored (to which the tourism graduate is going shortly to be exposed) or is the professional role simply presented as a technical one, of putting skills and technologies in operation according to a set of well-defined rules (Tribe, 1999, 2002c)?

It will be apparent that a tourism education of the kind argued for here calls for higher order thinking on the part of the student. Whether engaged in propositional thought or in professional action, students should be encouraged to engage in a critical dialogue with themselves in all they think and do. To put it sharply, the outcome to be desired from tourism higher education is the development of "philosophic practitioners".

Beyond Dualism

The chapter ends with one final point about tourism higher education of the kind suggested here. A good deal of the discussions in this collection has been concerned with what might be called the "grand dualisms" of tourism education: theory and practice; propositional and procedural knowledge; the tensions between the vocational/business approach to tourism and the wider perspectives. In one way, this is quite natural. The debate on any issue tends to get polarised so that arguments of the day typically take this antithetical form. But that is no reason to assume that tourism educational issues are inherently dualistic, matters of either/or, and therefore best formulated in these terms.

The findings of Stergiou's study imply a shift from dualism to something more complex and relativistic. They suggest that tourism higher education is clearly not just about education for an industry or education for immediate employment. Nor is it about simply learning existing facts and truths. What teachers and students expect from tourism higher education is a synthesis of vocational relevance and a challenging education in a more traditional sense. Put simply, tourism higher education needs to provide both "tourism" and "higher education". From the perspective of teaching, this can be translated into the suggestion that tourism educators need to disengage from vocationalist teaching approaches and energetically encourage reflection and action away from a narrow business conception of a vocational world towards a richer, more complex conception of a tourism world — all within a clearly structured, stimulating and considerate environment. Teachers ought to provide clear signs to help students appreciate the links and points of separation between parts of the content, and to enable them disentangle insights from examples. They should explain what they are doing and why. Talk should pass between teacher and students, not just from teacher to students. Students should have to do something more stimulating than just listening and note-taking, preferably in cooperation with each other, and they should work on questions and ideas that will enable them to identify different aspects of tourism and forms of tourism knowledge. Developments in enquiry-based learning and peer supported activities, as well as careful use of case studies, group exercises and projects and dissertations provide mechanisms for achieving this. The important point is that the use of these mechanisms needs to be informed by the requirement to provide both "tourism" and "higher education".

This should be a source of excitement for tourism higher education and grasped as a marvellous opportunity to show what it has to offer the individual and the wider world. But this calls for an intellectual and moral confidence that is not always evident within the tourism academe, let alone outside it. Minimally, it implies at its best an ethos, an approach to education and teaching, that is open, responsible and disinterested and that demonstrates an acceptance of obligation to the students, the society and the wider world. No doubt this demands a precarious balancing act, at times hard to recognise or define; but is there a better alternative? In the end, as Barnett (1990) argues, the practice of education (and teaching) cannot be value free.

It will be apparent that tourism higher education of the kind argued for here places definite and considerable responsibilities on tourism teachers. In an education for immediate employment or for the transmission of simple facts and truths, the responsibilities of the teacher are definite but limited: on the one hand, to bring students to a mastery of identified technical skills and, on the other hand, to enable students to live comfortably in disciplinary territories. In a tourism higher education for life, the teacher's responsibilities are expanded.

In essence, the role of the teacher implied by our explorations here is that of turning a cohort of students into a learning community of "philosophic practitioners", by stimulating their intellectual abilities and encouraging them to claim their independence and develop their critical consciousness. In so doing, the teacher has to establish some sense of where the learning is going, in terms of outcomes and priorities. This should help define mutual expectations and purposes. The tourism teacher has also special responsibilities to be fully on the inside of their disciplinary calling: they should have confidence in their knowledge but also keep current with information about tourism.

To put it sharply, being a tourism teacher of the kind envisaged here is a complicated matter. It entails bringing of a set of transactions with, and modes of development in, a group of students, that will enable them to find their own voices, to become more fully themselves, and to develop within frameworks of understanding made available to them that extend beyond the business aspects of tourism. It would be wrong to infer from this that tourism higher education should be dismissive about its vocational elements or the teaching of skills and development of capabilities in response to individual and social requirements in pursuit of learning and knowledge for work effectiveness. But this should not be the totality of its responsibilities or commitments.

Acknowledgements

The author would like to thank Professor David Airey, School of Management, University of Surrey, for comments on this chapter.

References

Airey, D. (2002). Growth and change in tourism education. In: B. Vukonić & N. Čavlek (Eds), *Rethinking of education and training for tourism* (pp. 13–22). Zagreb: University of Zagreb, Graduate School of Economics & Business.

Airey, D. (forthcoming). *Tourism education: From practice to theory*. Paper presented at the WTO 15th General Assembly, Beijing.

Airey, D., & Johnson, S. (forthcoming). *Tourism degree and postgraduate level courses in the UK 1999–2000: Dimensions characteristics, contents — A report to the British travel educational trust*. Unpublished study for the British Travel Educational Trust.

Barnett, R. (1990). *The idea of higher education*. Buckingham: SRHE & Open University Press.

Brockett, R. G., & Hiemstra, R. L. (1991). *Self-direction in adult learning: perspectives on theory, research and practice*. London: Routledge.

Candy, P. (1991). *Self-direction for lifelong learning: A comprehensive guide to theory and practice*. San Francisco: Jossey Bass.

Dunkin, M., & Biddle, B. (1974). *The study of teaching*. New York: Holt, Rinehart & Winston.

Fenstermacher, G. D. (1986). Philosophy of research on teaching: Three aspects. In: M. Wittrock (Ed.), *Handbook of research on teaching* (3rd ed., pp. 37–49). New York: Macmillan.

Hirst, P. H. (1973). What is teaching? In: R. Peters (Ed.), *The philosophy of education* (pp. 163–177). Oxford: Oxford University Press.

Jackson, P. (1986). *The practice of teaching*. New York: Teachers College Press.

Shulman, L. S. (1987). Knowledge and teaching: Foundations of the new reform. *Harvard Educational Review, 57*(1), 1–22.

Smith, B. O. (1983). Some comments on educational research in the twentieth century. *Elementary School Journal, 83*(4), 488–492.

Squires, G. (1999). *Teaching as a professional discipline*. London: Falmer Press.

Stergiou, D. (2004). *Knowledge and teaching: An investigation on what makes good teaching in tourism higher education*. Unpublished doctoral dissertation, University of Surrey, Guildford.

Stergiou, D., Airey, D., & Riley, M. (2002). The development of constructs for the evaluation of academics teaching tourism: An exploratory study using Q-methodology. In: B. Vukonić & N. Čavlek (Eds), *Rethinking of education and training for tourism* (pp. 149–166). Zagreb: University of Zagreb, Graduate School of Economics & Business.

Stergiou, D., Airey, D., & Riley, M. (2003). The evaluation of the teaching of individual academics in UK's tourism higher education: Developing a construct for teaching profiles. *International Journal of Tourism Research, 5*(1), 62–67.

Stergiou, D., Airey, D., & Riley, M. (2004). Is tourism teaching higher education? *Proceedings of the CAUTHE 2004: Creating tourism knowledge conference* (pp. 749–760). Brisbane: The University of Queensland.

Tough, A. (1971). *The adult's learning projects*. Toronto: Ontario Institute for Studies in Education.

Tribe, J. (1997). The indiscipline of tourism. *Annals of Tourism Research, 24*(3), 638–657.

Tribe, J. (1999). *The philosophic practitioner: Tourism knowledge and the curriculum*. Unpublished doctoral dissertation, University of London, London.

Tribe, J. (2000). Balancing the vocational: The theory and practice of liberal education in tourism. *Tourism and Hospitality Research, 2*(1), 9–25.

Tribe, J. (2002a). Research trends and imperatives in tourism education. *Acta Turistica, 14*(1), 61–81.

Tribe, J. (2002b). The philosophic practitioner. *Annals of Tourism Research, 29*(2), 338–357.

Tribe, J. (2002c). Education for ethical tourism action. *Journal of Sustainable Tourism, 10*(4), 309–324.

Wilson, S. M., Shulman, L. S., & Richert, A. E. (1987). "150 Different ways of knowing": Representations of knowledge in teaching. In: J. Calderhead (Ed.), *Exploring teachers' thinking* (pp. 104–124). London: Cassell.

Winne, P. H., & Marx, R. W. (1977). Reconceptualising research on teaching. *Journal of Educational Psychology, 69*(6), 668–678.

Chapter 21

The Student Experience

Eugenia Wickens and Alastair Forbes

Introduction

Researchers have long been interested in issues concerning access to Higher Education and students' experiences (e.g. Smithers & Robinson, 1995). What is also interesting to note is that there exists a large body of international research and theory exploring students' experiences of Higher Educations (e.g. Bourdieu & Passeron, 1977; Tinto, 1993). Much of this work focuses on the institutional practices, which impact on student retention rates and performance. Recent contributions suggest that financial hardship is one of the primary reasons that students drop out of university.

Studies of students experiences of Higher Education Institutions (HEIs) have also found finance and part-time employment to be contributory factors to a student's decision to withdraw (Medway, Rhodes, Macrae, Maguire, & Gewirtz, 2003). Much has been written on student recruitment, retention and progression, and on university support services, as well as the academic difficulties faced by students in general. What is often neglected, however, is the challenges faced by first-year tourism undergraduates. What motivates them to succeed has received limited attention by tourism researchers. Furthermore, studies have paid insufficient attention to the changing context of Higher Education and the effect that this has on students' experiences of Higher Education support and provision.

In order to understand the student experience it is also important to consider some of the major changes which are currently shaping Higher Education provision. This chapter, therefore, commences with a brief discussion of the growth of mass Higher Education with particular reference to Britain. It then proceeds with an examination of the main theoretical approaches to student learning, followed by a review of studies concerning tourism students' retention and progression. Engagement with the literature on the factors influencing students' success or failure is supported by evidence from a case study of one Institution of Higher Education in the UK. A key finding of the study was that students' peer-group networks are vitally important, so much so that many students seek help from their friends much more readily than from academic tutors or other academic staff members.

An International Handbook of Tourism Education
Copyright © 2005 by Elsevier Ltd.
All rights of reproduction in any form reserved
ISBN: 0-08-044667-1

The Role of Higher Education

The rapid move from an elite to a mass system of Higher Education in advanced societies (e.g. USA, Australia and UK) is well documented in several studies (Scott, 1995; Barnett, 1994, Lewis, 2002). Studies show that the change from elite to mass Higher Education is mainly the result of socio-economic changes in advanced societies, which require closer integration of Higher Education and the economy. In the field of tourism, the links between Higher Education and the tourism industry have been explored and discussed in several works (e.g. Airey, 1997).

There is a broad range of opinions regarding Higher Education, the rapid expansion of student numbers and student learning. In the minds of some analysts, the emergence of mass Higher Education is consonant with the demands of the economy in the developed world (e.g. Newby, 1999). The heterogeneity of the student body, the modularity of knowledge, the learning outcomes of a course, as well as the provision of new subject areas such as Travel and Tourism are some of the distinctive features defining mass Higher Education. Writing about the emergence of this phenomenon in Britain, Newby (1999) observes that students should graduate not only with the knowledge and understanding of the subject studied at the university, but also with 'transferable skills' essential for gaining employability in the knowledge-based economy. This perspective justifies pedagogical changes by pointing to the needs of the knowledge-based economy for a graduate labour force with the right transferable skills for employability. Higher education reforms are presented as part of the modernisation process on grounds that they enhance flexibility and efficiency.

Opponents of mass Higher Education, whilst acknowledge that changed socio-economic circumstances are shaping HEIs, point to the marketisation agendas of Governments in many countries including Britain. Opponents argue that Government policies in countries such as Britain, Australia and USA are underpinned by 'neo-liberalism', an ideology which justifies the commoditisation of all institutional arrangements including those of HEIs. It is argued that, as a result of Government policies, universities have been forced to compete amongst themselves for a bigger slice of the student market. Higher Education courses including Tourism are packaged and sold like any other product. The commoditisation of 'educational services' is clearly echoed in the business terminology employed by the academic community — such as public–private partnerships, cost–benefit analysis, performance indicators, inputs/outputs and human investment (Aronowitz, 2000). Lamenting the lost golden age of higher learning, critics argue that the marketisation of Higher Education has led to the transformation of universities into 'knowledge factories' (Aronowitz, 2000). Critics of mass Higher Education bemoan the lack of higher learning at universities and the perceived 'vocationalisation' of Higher Education. It is argued that the continuing under resourcing of teaching from the public purse is unsustainable because it undermines university standards.

The debate concerning the transformation of Higher Education is still ongoing with some analysts raising serious questions about student learning. In the minds of some academics, the idea of falling standards is fixed. Moreover, questioning the role of higher education, critics make the claim that mass university education has now undermined the authority of 'pure' knowledge. Supporters of mass expansion argue that more students should go to university because it is an individual's 'right', and a passport to a career. It is, indeed, a right enshrined in the International Covenant on Economic, Social and Cultural Rights, which specifically states that "higher education shall be made equally accessible to all, on the basis of capacity, by every appropriate means, and in particular by the progressive introduction of free education" (UN, 1967, Article 13). Other commentators argue that the traditional role of the university as the pursuit of knowledge for its own sake has now been replaced by the pursuit of useful knowledge.

In the field of tourism, the growth of students interested in the pursuit of 'useful knowledge' is well documented in several studies (e.g. Airey, 1997). There is also research which shows that the composition of the tourism student body has been changing significantly over the last 10 years. Common explanations offered by commentators include widening participation, the changing nature of prior qualifications, a rise in student part-time employment, a fall in Higher Education per capita spending and changes in student subcultures. Furthermore, in the UK the introduction of fees for a degree is also affecting the make up of the student body (Crosling & Webb, 2002). Some observers claim that, because of the introduction of fees, fewer students from the working class are attending university in general. Voices are now being raised against tuition fees paid by students. Consequently, new universities in Britain, for instance, are experiencing some difficulties in attracting high calibre students who tend to enrol on courses offered in universities positioned higher up the league tables.

Departments offering tourism-related subjects in many universities faced by these developments see it as imperative to recruit greater numbers of students from home and overseas in order to ensure course viability. The trend to look for students overseas has also been facilitated by the provision of distance education in the last few years. Higher Education providers in countries such as the USA, Britain and Australia supply courses to tourism students based overseas (e.g. India, China and South Africa) by distance education. The promise of the 'virtual university' is that a student can study how, when, where, and to a certain extent what he or she judges appropriate and useful for enhancement of career prospects.

The trend, therefore, is towards large enrolments with diverse student populations. This, coupled with the lowering of entrance requirements for tourism-related courses, has significant implications for all aspects of learning, teaching, progression and support in tourism-related subjects. Some commentators have been questioning the ongoing expansion of Higher Education, drawing our attention to the correlation between student early withdrawal and wider participation as evidenced by research into student retention and motivation. Furthermore, there are those commentators who blame the individual student, and in the minds of others the blame is placed squarely on institutional practices. This ongoing debate concerning higher learning and student success is the central theme of the following section.

The Literature: Some Generalisations

Early studies on the nature of student learning asserted that the most obvious explanation for differences in educational attainment is the ability of the individual student. Critics of such 'deterministic' explanations (e.g. Bourdieu & Passeron, 1977) argue that it is class stratification that is directly linked to individual educational success or failure. Strongly influenced by Marxism, they argue that working class failure is the fault of the education system which is biased towards the 'culture' of the 'dominant' social class, i.e. the upper class. Students with upper-class background are said to have a built in advantage, because they have been socialised into the dominant culture. From this perspective, a student's success depends fundamentally on the education received in the earliest years of life and his or her social background. There are several empirical studies which show that the child's early years' socialisation forms the basis for success or failure in the educational system (e.g. Low & Cook, 2003). Behaviour patterns laid down in childhood are said to have important and lasting effects. Such explanations draw our attention to the importance of early socialisation in shaping an individual's personality and motivation to succeed. From this perspective, children learn to have high expectations for success.

The themes of the home environment, parental support and the manner in which young children are prepared in school are also found in studies pertinent to student retention and progression in Higher Education (Clark & Ramsey, 1990). Lack of preparation for the demands of Higher Education is seen as being a key contributing factor to student dropout and underperformance. It is claimed that many first-year undergraduates, having little idea of what to expect and little understanding of how the university environment can affect their lives, are ill prepared for higher learning. The demands can be overwhelming for them and lack of understanding on the part of many tutors compounds the problem (Yorke, 1999).

The relationship between student and tutor, and the ways in which tutors make sense of and respond to the student's behaviour have also been examined and are well documented in writings concerning student success or failure. It is argued that good interpersonal relationships between tutors and students are important to sustaining student progression (Medway et al. 2003; Yorke & Thomas, 2003). The conclusion drawn from this work is that students should be closely monitored by their personal tutors and any warning signs of a student experiencing difficulties should be acted upon immediately. From this perspective, tutorial support is crucial (Jones & Thomas, 2002).

In addition, study skills tutors at departmental level are also recognised by analysts as being central in addressing students' problems. This argument is based on the observation that given governments' commitment to 'widening participation' in countries such as Britain and elsewhere, students from non-traditional background should be given a 'helping hand'. It is important to note here that the label non-traditional is applied to students from under-represented groups including mature students (i.e. adults over the age of 21), students with disabilities and those from low socio-economic family backgrounds. It is these groups which are targeted by government widening participation policies in countries such as Britain (Scott, 1995; Lewis, 2002; Yorke, 1999; Yorke & Thomas, 2003).

Clearly from the above analysis, it can be seen that reasons for academic underachievement in Britain and elsewhere tend to fall in two broad categories namely 'the personal' and 'institutional' (Thomas, 2002). Personal reasons for dropout, most commonly cited in literature, include lack of academic preparedness, student difficulties of managing pressures of combining studying with employment, financial costs of participation and student debt (Ozga & Sukhnandan, 1998; Sinclair & Dale, 2000; Lowe & Cook, 2003). Evidence from recent studies shows that after the introduction of tuition fees, an increasing number of students were working part-time and that introduction of this policy has directly contributed to non-completion (Thomas, 2002).

Institutional reasons frequently cited in the literature include concerns about the quality of teaching, poor student support and lack of opportunities for students to interact with staff (Tinto, 1993; Thomas, 2002). As Tinto (1993, p. 48) explains, the absence of suffi-cient contact with staff is the most "important predictor of eventual departure even after taking into account the independent effects of background, personality and academic per-formance". Fieldwork from one University College in England, UK provides further evi-dence in support of Tinto's observation that encounters between students and tutors, as well as students are crucial to student retention and progression.

Study Methods

The context of the research project was one of six constituent faculties of one Institution of Higher Education which is committed to wider participation and the success of its students. The faculty has in excess of 1000 full-time undergraduate students studying a range of voca-tionally focused programmes, mainly honours degrees but also Higher National Diplomas and Foundation Degrees. Postgraduate students in the faculty were excluded from the study.

The research aimed to investigate the reasons for failure or success in first-year Leisure and Tourism students in their own terms. A qualitative approach was adopted for under-standing the student perspective of university life. Fieldwork, in the form of focus groups and one-to-one semi-structured interviews was undertaken in the academic year 2003–2004. Qualitative data was collected through initial focus groups. A total of 70 stu-dents were involved. This fieldwork prepared the ground for the second round of fieldwork in the form of one-to-one in-depth interviews. Data from the focus groups was analysed and the broad issues that emerged from the first-stage of data collection informed the con-struction of an interview guide. The interview guide was piloted and the revised version was utilised with first-year undergraduate students. A convenient and, wherever possible, 'theory-driven' sample of 18 students was chosen. As Strauss and Corbin (1990) have pointed out, our choice of respondents should be driven primarily by our conceptual ques-tions and concerns and not simply by a concern for 'representativeness'. The selection strategy is common amongst researchers in the field (Burgess, 1984; Veal, 1997).

Interviews were taped with the consent of the participants, and subsequently transcribed. The analysis followed the 'grounded theory' approach advocated by Strauss and Corbin (1990). It started with the organisation of the material in some kind of order. The mass of qualitative data was condensed, organised and coded. This involved a discriminatory process of selecting data, which appeared important and meaningful for the study. When looking for differences and similarities in participants' responses to a given question, care was taken that responses to a specific question were analysed with due regard to the con-text and the conditions which produced them. Significant statements were then selected and coded in terms of theoretical concepts and themes found in literature (such as family sup-port and commitments and institutional support and student lifestyles). Drawing upon qual-itative data, the following section presents and discusses the key findings of the study.

Discussion

The most striking theme emerging from the study is that of students' reliance on their peer group. Many stated that the most enjoyable aspect of university life was meeting people and making friends, which is perhaps unsurprising. However, what is more significant is the extent to which students rely on each other for support, assistance and even motivation. Support from fellow students is seen as vital to students' success, partly because they are the only ones who are seen as having the same experience, and can therefore understand them fully. Worryingly for the institution, when asked to whom they would go if they had a problem while on campus, many students said that they would talk to a friend in preference to an Academic Tutor, or any of the support services provided by the university college or the students' union. Some felt it was beneficial to share a house (or a flat in a university hall of residence) with other students on the same course, as only they would understand the requirements of the programme (such as its assessment). Students support each other by discussing academic work, sharing resources such as library books and in some cases working on assessments together.

This finding, on the vital importance of students' peer-group networks, supports the work of Thomas (2000) who also found that social networks were of immense significance in the lives of students. It is interesting to note, however, that the majority of the students interviewed were first-generation undergraduates. Most reported that their parents were supportive, morally and financially, but that they could not be expected to know what their sons and daughters were going through, as they had not been to university themselves. In particular, students felt that their parents did not see the importance of a university social life: "they don't understand like the social life as well, like, going out, and you need to go out in order to make new friends, and they're like 'you're just spending loads of money' ", as one interviewee expressed it. This perceived lack of understanding on the part of parents may account for a greater reliance on students peer groups for support on academic matters than has been reported in some other studies (e.g. Tinto, 1975, 1993; Thomas, 2002). On the other hand, several students reported that their parents were proud of them, and that it was important not to let them down by failing the course.

The success of the university college in recruiting students from non-traditional backgrounds may also account for some of the students' difficulties in approaching their Academic Tutors for support. Although these tutors have a pastoral role, and are amenable to approaches from students with concerns of many kinds, some interviewees reported that their Academic Tutors were unfriendly or not approachable, even rude, or in one case 'scary'. Some students simply did not get on with their designated Academic Tutor and preferred to seek advice from other members of staff. The general lack of success of the Academic Tutors at establishing good working relationships with the students may have something to do with class. While the tutors, unlike many of the students' parents, have experienced student life themselves, it may be that they have difficulty communicating with students who are from a very different background to them, socially and sometimes ethnically. The tutors are part of the dominant social class (Bernstein, 2000) and are unable to relate to the students who do not share their culture (Bourdieu & Passeron, 1977). This lack of understanding by tutors has been noted in other studies (e.g. Clark & Ramsey, 1990; Thomas, 2000, 2002).

Despite their reluctance to seek assistance from Academic Tutors, students felt that tutors in general held the key to success in university study. Their definitions of what makes a good lecturer were interesting. Positive traits in lecturers included enthusiasm for the subject, a willingness to listen to the students, friendliness, approachability, propensity to give students handouts and willingness to explain exactly what was wanted in assessed work. Several interviewees thought the assistance offered by the lecturers fell short of the level of support they were accustomed to in further education. This comment is typical: "It was really hard coming from College to University in terms of type of work we were doing; assignments were just given out to us and it was not really explained how to do them. It was hard at first". Rather than the traditional idea of reading for a degree, many of today's students apparently expect their tutors to tell them exactly what they need to know in order to pass the assessments. There is clearly a mismatch between the expectations of lecturers and those of students with regard to the level of explanation required for assessed work.

While the institution is committed to helping students develop into progressively more independent learners, it is probable that tutors are guilty of assuming that students are further along that road when they begin degree studies than is actually the case. On the other hand, just as Clark and Ramsey (1990) found, first-year undergraduates are ill prepared for higher learning, having little idea what to expect from the university or its tutors. Many find the work demanding, sometimes perplexing and they consider the lecturers are not supportive enough.

The importance for students of making friends, and the reliance they place on support from their peer group, has already been discussed. The concept of freedom is another recurring motif in the interview transcripts. Students equate coming to university with freedom, particularly those who have moved away from their parents. Interviewees valued the fact that they were no longer under scrutiny from, or answerable to, their parents and other relations. Even those who relied on their parents for financial support felt independent. While a tendency to consume unreasonable quantities of alcohol has always been associated with student life, the study provides some evidence that students coming from strict families (particularly Asian ones) are particularly prone to alcohol problems when let 'off the leash' for the first time. One interviewee said: "… some people do come to university to get away from home… if people at home haven't had the freedom to go out, they think university is a chance to get away from parents… some people who haven't been out ever, they come here and they just go wild… They go out all the time and drink ridiculous amounts, and get drunk every night…".

Conclusions

Several conclusions emerge from the study of first-year university college leisure and tourism undergraduates. The first is that there is some evidence that students drawn from lower social groups may be disadvantaged in the Higher Education context. Despite the widening participation agenda, the system may still be biased in favour of middle-class students, who are better prepared for degree study, know what to expect and enter Higher Education having already been initiated into the dominant culture of the university (Bourdieu & Passeron, 1977; Bernstein, 2000). Students who were subjects of the research certainly felt unprepared by their previous educational and social experience for what was to come in Higher Education. This unpreparedness often manifested itself as an unreasonable expectation of direct instruction by tutors on exactly what should be learned, read and reproduced in order to succeed in assessments.

Although many of the students reported that they were the first members of their families to enter Higher Education, almost all stated that they were supported by their parents, morally, financially and otherwise. There was a feeling that parents were proud of their offspring and wanted them to do well, while students did not want to let their parents down. Parental support was significant for the students, but many also reported that they were enjoying the freedom of being away from their closest relations. While this unaccustomed measure of independence sometimes led to alcohol abuse and poor self-discipline, it was generally thought to be important. Students did not believe, however, that their parents understood the academic pressures of university life, nor indeed the importance of students' social lives and peer-group networks.

These peer-group networks are perceived by students to be of vital importance. Students who fail to make friends are unlikely to attend their courses, and they typically rely very heavily on their friends for support of all kinds. This includes working together on assignments, sharing resources, comparing notes, discussing academic concepts and so on, but students also rely on friends for emotional and moral support and guidance. Their perception is that only their friends are in a position to understand them, by virtue of their background and the shared experience of being on the Higher Education programme.

Students' relationships with tutors are important, but there is a significant difference between their relationships with Academic Tutors, whose role includes pastoral support, and module tutors who deliver the academic programmes. In many cases, students do not seek help or advice from Academic Tutors, as they feel that these people do not understand them, or have time for them. Some students do not like the Academic Tutor allocated to them, and when they have a problem they are far more likely to seek help from their friends. Poor interpersonal relationships with tutors can be problematic — as Medway et al. (2003) noted, these relationships are crucial to sustaining student progression. Students' relationships with module tutors were generally better, as long as tutors were prepared to give students the support they felt they needed, which was generally more directive than is traditional in Higher Education. Although this area is complex, the study can be seen to support the findings set out by Tinto (1993), who noted that students' contact with academic staff is of crucial importance in determining their progression and ultimate success.

References

Airey, D. (1997). *Exploring the links between industry and education*. Conference paper given at the ATTT/Tourism Education Exchange conference, University of Westminster, 5th February.

Aronowitz, S. (2000). *The knowledge factory: Dismantling the corporate university and creating true higher learning*. Boston: Beacon.

Barnett, R. (1994). *The limits of competence: Knowledge, higher education and society*. Buckingham: Society for Research into Higher Education, Open University Press.

Bernstein, B. (2000). *Pedagogy, symbolic control and identity* (Revised edition). Lanham/Oxford: Rowman and Littlefield.

Bourdieu, P., & Passeron, J. C. (1977). *Reproduction in education, society and culture*. London and Beverly Hills: Sage.

Burgess, R. G. (1984). *In the field: An introduction to field research*. London: Allen and Unwin.

Clark, E., & Ramsey, W. (1990). Problems of retention in tertiary education. *Education Research and Perspectives*, *17*, 47–59.

Crosling, G., & Webb, G. (Eds) (2002). *Supporting student learning: Case studies, experience and practice from higher education.* London: Kogan Page Ltd.

Jones, R., & Thomas, L. (2002). Not 'Just Passing Through': Making retention work for present and future learners. *Journal of Widening Participation and Lifelong Learning*, *4*, 2–4.

Lewis, B. (2002). Widening participation in higher education: The HEFCE perspective on policy and progress. *Higher Education Quarterly*, *56*, 204–219.

Lowe, H., & Cook, A. (2003). Mind the gap: Are students prepared for higher education? *Journal of Further and Higher Education*, *27*, 69–76.

Medway, P., Rhodes, V., Macrae, S., Maguire, M., & Gewirtz, S. (2003). *Widening participation through supporting undergraduates – what is being done and what can be done to support student progression at King's?* Unpublished report, King's College, Department of Education and Professional Studies, London.

Newby, H. (1999). *Some possible futures for higher education.* London: DfEE.

Ozga, J., & Sukhnandan, L. (1998). Undergraduate non-completion: Developing an explanatory model. *Higher Education Quarterly*, *52*, 316–333.

Scott, P. (1995). *The meanings of mass higher education.* Buckingham: Society for Research into Higher Education, Buckingham: Open University Press.

Sinclair, H., & Dale, L. (2000). The effect of student tuition fees on the diversity of intake within a Scottish new University. Paper presented at British Educational Research Association Annual Conference, Cardiff University, 7–9 September 2000.

Smithers, R., & Robinson, P. (1995). *Post-18 education: Growth change and prospect* (p. 2). London: Council for Industry and Higher Education (Executive Briefing).

Strauss, A., & Corbin, J. (1990). *Basics of qualitative research: Grounded theory procedures and techniques.* London: Sage.

Thomas, L. (2002). Student retention in higher education: The role of institutional habitus. *Journal of Education Policy*, *17*, 423–442.

Thomas, S. L. (2000). Ties that bind: A social network approach to understanding student integration and persistence. *The Journal of Higher Education*, *71*, 591–615.

Tinto, V. (1975). Dropout from higher education: A theoretical synthesis of recent research. *Review of Educational Research*, *45*, 89–125.

Tinto, V. (1993). *Leaving college: Rethinking the causes and cures of student attrition* (2nd ed.). Chicago: University of Chicago Press.

UN. (1967). *International covenant on economic, social and cultural rights: International covenants on human rights.* New York: United Nations Organisation.

Veal, A. J. (1997). *Research methods for leisure and tourism* (2nd ed.). London: Pitman Publishing.

Yorke, M. (1999) *Leaving early: Undergraduate non-completion in higher education.* London: Falmer Press.

Yorke, M., & Thomas, L. (2003). Improving the retention of students from lower socio-economic groups. *Journal of Higher Education Policy and Management*, *25*, 63–74.

Chapter 22

Issues in Teaching and Learning

Brian Wheeller

Fancy the concept of a philosophical hotel? Try the Manhattan, Pretoria. Arriving there recently, I was greeted by a poster in the main lift with the hotel's very own "thought for the day" embezzled across — "The mediocre teacher tells. The good teacher explains. The superior teacher demonstrates. The great teacher inspires". Fine words of wisdom. Except, looking at it (and assuming the same maxim applies to lecturing in general, and, in this case, to lecturing tourism in higher education in particular) personally I was sorely tempted to scrawl at the bottom. "And the sensible lecturer abandons teaching and concentrates on research".

The quotation was anonymous. But enquiry a little later reveals the source (culprit?) to be one William Arthur Ward. The fact that he was monikered The Christian Optimist might very well account for his somewhat rosy, hybrid Mr. Chips/Miss Jean Brodie meets Dead Poets Society perspective. Apposite in his day … but how times change. Such idealism has, at least for many embroiled in the machinations of higher education in the UK, been replaced by a far more prosaic necessity … namely, that of survival (and promotion) via publication and income generation: not, it must be emphasised and despite protestations from some quarters, through ability demonstrated in the lecture theatre. Witness "Brunel University Council will meet next week to approve plans to replace 60 academics with new 'research stars'… it is clear that research and publication levels will be the key factors in selecting staff" (Mitchell, 2004, p. 1). And the result of this trend? Well, at least to my way of thinking — and again notwithstanding spin to the contrary — teaching suffers, rather than benefits, irrecoverably as a consequence of the inevitable changing emphasis on priorities imposed by this perverse 'meritocracy'.

Cynicism born of (and borne by) experience? Well, yes I guess so. And yet, despite my dark, jaundiced view of much that is happening in higher education — and my initial, though fortunately suppressed, jet-lagged desire to deface the poster — there may, surprisingly, be some glimmer of hope in what the good W.A. Ward proclaimed. For, even against ever mounting odds, perhaps there is still sufficient room for the inspirational lecturer to manoeuvre and escape… if only temporally… the ever tightening vice of conformity that is gripping education. As such, Ward's words provide the flimsy, deliberately ambiguous platform from which to launch this chapter.

A couple of riders by way of further introduction. Although I have tried to incorporate some wider international dimensions, this is essentially a white, middle-aged British perspective drawn from 33 years teaching, researching and working in UK tourism … initially for a short period in hotels, holiday camps and local authority, then in the old polytechnic and subsequently (and primarily) the red-brick university sector before moving, in the last couple of years, into a professional education university in The Netherlands. Secondly, there are undoubtedly difficulties in trying to cover, in a single chapter, such broad issues as teaching and learning. When it comes to exploring our approaches to them we are faced with situations that superficially appear reasonably simplistic but which of course, on closer inspection, are not. Rather than being straightforward, on the contrary, the topic is complex and multi-layered. No longer restricted to education (encompassing as they do political, social, cultural, racial and gender issues) approaches differ with, and are often determined by, both the environment and parameters within which the lecturers and students are operating. These circumstances are, to a degree, fluid in the sense that they fluctuate at varying rates, sometimes in opposite directions, and at different times. As such, generalisations can be too vague: yet specific examples restricted in their wider relevance. Aware of the difficulties, and running the danger of falling between two stools, the attempt here then is to marry these stances by drawing on examples gleaned from personal experience to elaborate on generalisations — before concluding with a couple of considered "recommendations" that might have universal appeal.

Teaching and learning are obviously integral to the education experience. As such, they do not stand alone, isolated. Rather they dovetail into and, to varying degrees, inter-relate with, the wide range of issues that constitute the educative spectrum.

In particular, it is argued here that in the current climate they are inextricably linked with the twin issues of "research" and the drive for "assessment" — both of which dominate much debate in UK higher education. Significantly, for instance, in the last Quality Assessment Audit in the UK, teaching, learning *and* assessment were reviewed under one banner. Although assessment is dealt with in some detail elsewhere in this text, I do strongly believe that assessment clearly — or, perversely, to be more precise, "unclearly" — has a crucial, determining influence on approaches to both teaching and learning. And, of course, it is not just assessment of the students that is pertinent here … it is also the assessment and league tabling of individual lecturers, teams within departments, schools and institutions themselves. In this respect, these assessment criteria, and procedures, impact not only on the actual choices of approaches to teaching and learning available but effectively are instrumental in determining who actually decides which of these approaches are undertaken/imposed. The freedom of the individual lecturer to determine his/her approach is, it is suggested here, being continually eroded — squeezed by the pressure from "above" to conform. Increasingly, the role played by "management" is taking on ominous importance: institutional and national policies have become critical in influencing, indeed to a large extent determining, individual approaches. Under the "control" of management/national bodies, these approaches become ever more restricted, tied as they are to the albatross of assessment.

Assuming we should, then how do we measure the success, or otherwise, of teaching and learning? And whom? Or what? And, significantly, when? Temporal analysis is, quite rightly, an important feature in many tourism programmes, for example, in tourism planning and sustainability. But is sufficient attention given to the passing of time when actually assessing the teaching and learning outcomes? In the teaching arena too surely more attention should be given to the dichotomy of short versus long term. With the onslaught of sustainability, so-called sustainable tourism and the drive to include the S word in tourism courses (see, for example, Eber, 2003), isn't it strange that sustainable courses, the subject matter of what is so ostensibly concerned with the long-run, are themselves inevitably judged by end of term/semester course work or examination? What sweet irony there is in stressing to the students the importance of the long term while, when actually assessing their ability to understand/appreciate/comprehend sustainable tourism, they themselves, of logistic necessity, are always assessed in the short term.

It is not, therefore, simply the type of assessment that primarily concerns me here. It is, in this context of teaching and learning, as much about the time horizons over which our efforts to educate are actually judged. True, we may debate about the type/appropriateness of the assessment, but as far as I am aware very little attention is given as to the time period in which the student is judged. It has to be completed by the end of the month, end of year etc....i.e. over a relatively short time period. In other words, something that is essentially concerned with the long run is assessed in the "immediate". And both tourism lecturer and tourism student "cut their cloth" accordingly.

And so too with education in general. It is all very well institutions having snappy logos like "Courses for Careers. Learning for Life", but just how is the latter measured? If we are trying to achieve an "education" for life, isn't confining the measuring of success or otherwise of these efforts to the immediate somewhat perverse? Shouldn't we also be judged in the long run? Unfortunately this does not seem to be either what current forms of assessment dictate: nor, concomitantly, what students want.

Yet, it seems crucial in determining approaches to teaching. If educating for the long term isn't assessed in the long term ... and if assessment criteria is short term orientated well there is the obvious danger that the more obtuse, longer term, but surely profound, "benefits" are, in the age of instant/immediate assessment, the first to be jettisoned by the lecturer and the student. Even if lecturers persevere, students are reluctant to embrace things that do not have an immediate, measurable return. Students want tangible, quick, short-term, specific returns... a degree/diploma certificate takes precedence over any far more abstract benefits infused by that idealistic dream of "educating for life".

Assessment also plays a key role in the interplay between teaching, learning and research — links that also need to be addressed here. Though it is certainly risky to go against the accepted notion that the research-led approach to teaching is automatically the best, conventional wisdom needs to be questioned. What sounds, and on paper looks, good does not — at least from the student perspective — always automatically translate as well into practice. Not only are individuals themselves rewarded for research but so too are institutions for research active lecturers ... raising, as this does, the ugly head of the funding agenda.

The "accepted" approach seems to be that research-led teaching is the panacea to stimulating, up-to-date teaching. Active researchers, by feeding their current work into their lectures, are the dream ticket. This, however, not only assumes that the researchers do introduce their research material into their lectures. But, fundamentally, that they do, in fact (willingly and enthusiastically), actually embrace classes, and students, in the first place.

Undoubtedly such published stars are (initially, at least) attractive to students ... be it directly as "names", or indirectly through the undoubted influence they have on research-led league tables so crucial to attracting overseas markets. While they certainly play a key role as part of an institute's recruitment drive, do the students actually see much of the researcher either as personal tutor, lecturer or undergraduate/ postgraduate supervisor? And in terms of net contribution to the students' learning surely there is a (strong) case to be made for the argument that had the time and effort invested by the lecturer in research instead been put directly into their preparation and actual teaching/contact time with students then wouldn't that … again from the student perspective … have proved more rewarding?

The relationships between teaching, learning and research (and, crucially, funding) are also, again, far too complex to be comprehensively covered here and partial debate immediately raises anomalies and contradictions. For example, while I am advocating more emphasis (and reward?) be given to teaching the students, on the downside, departments which are not scoring highly in the research assessment exercise do so at their peril, finding themselves threatened with closure (Barkham, 2004) … even though they are maintaining high levels of student satisfaction with regard to their teaching (and learning?) capabilities. Nevertheless, this does not detract from questioning the mantra that research active staff automatically makes for the best lecturers. It does, though, again highlight the pivotal, and vexed, role that assessment (via determining vital funding flows) plays at the heart of higher education.

One direct way in which assessment affects learning manifests itself in the worrying "if it isn't assessed, why bother?" trait. We need only look at attendance on non-assessed modules; or selective attendance as students focus exclusively on the lectures related to those aspects of their own coursework topics that they are assessed on; or how lectures are abandoned when assessment deadlines (often for other modules) loom. Initially the preserve of the student, this truculent attitude has spread to many — by their own definition — beleaguered-lecturing staff as well, and effort tailored accordingly.

In a refinement of the same malaise, we have the situation where if the lecturer introduces something related, yet tangential, to the main subject, the more able, willing, adventurous student will pay attention while the weaker, narrower student cannot/will not see the immediate relevance and, as a result, probably may not want to know. (Of course, it will only tend to be the "different" lecturer that will try to introduce, and then persevere with original, unusual material.) The craving for the safety blanket of the "familiar", of planned lectures, hand-in dates, regimentation of structure, etc., while worthy in its own right, inevitably militates against the flexibility of the spontaneous.

The danger is, usually the weaker the student the greater the need for a safety blanket. Actually, the word "weaker" could be misleading. And perhaps I'm being a little hard here. Maybe lacking confidence in their own ability/circumstances might, in many cases, be fairer. In particular, there is the tendency for some foreign students, understandably, to be particularly vulnerable in this respect. Not only are they struggling with language difficulties but also with an alien culture in general … and often a totally different educational experience. Many Southeast Asian students in the UK initially fall, headlong, into this category … to, later emerge, having admirably worked incredibly hard to overcome their disadvantages.

According to Utley, "Anyone currently working in higher education cannot fail to have noticed that with the introduction of fees students are becoming ever more exacting customers. The significance of this shift should not be underestimated. With 'top-up' fees just around the corner in the UK, it looks likely that students' expectations will continue to rise at an unprecedented rate" (Utley, 2004, p. 1). So, somewhere along the line, students have metamorphosed into customers — demanding ones at that. And — at the risk of getting slandered, libelled and hearing words we've never heard in the Bible — we all know that, as Simon and Garfunkel informed us long ago, we have to keep the customer satisfied. At all costs.

While expectations may well rise, unfortunately, with the much vaunted drive for widening access/social inclusion some would argue that ability, inevitably, might well move in the opposite direction. So, the rather worryingly reasoning goes, we end up, overall, with more demanding, less able "customers". A recent article in the *Times Higher* "argues" as such. Candid, forthright and very much to the (or rather his) point, Day provocatively and vehemently exhorts we " … keep the tasteless working class away from our universities… If after years of literacy, they still can't spell whatever words they tattoo on themselves, then what on earth do they hope to achieve at university? (Day, 2004, p. 13).

Although this and the rest of his article might well be regarded, and dismissed, as repugnant bigotry, Day does, at least, beg one pertinent question with his lament "What happened to the idea that knowledge should be valued for its own sake?" (Day, 2004, p. 13). This may have particular resonance in the field of tourism "education", where there is often conflict between the "educative" as opposed to "training" schools of thought. Some might see this as the "vacational/vocational divide". While this may appear to be a flippant perspective, perhaps there is an element of truth in it. Indeed, possibly tourism to an extent bucks the trend in that some (of us) involved in tourism teaching during the eighties and nineties tried increasingly to move the subject away from a narrow training base.

We should, I believe, be concerned more with educating rather than training — certainly at postgraduate level. Whether this is the case in practice is a moot point. Indeed, whether this should be the "correct" approach is still, in some circles, open to dispute. But to my way of thinking we should be "educating" not "training"… unless, that is, we are training students to think for themselves. We should be discussing tourism education, not tourism training, here. However, again things aren't that straightforward.

In tourism debates we have, for years, automatically distinguished between tourism education and the tourism industry … separating, and often bemoaning, the lack of cooperation between the two. However, haven't the differences between education and business become blurred? Hasn't (tourism) education become as much a business as the tourism industry itself? Isn't higher education now driven by the same forces that power big business? And doesn't this affect our approaches to teaching and learning? [The scramble for high fee paying overseas students; strategic policies to secure research funding; 'common' lectures and group work to reap economies of scale; 2 years Master programmes concertinaed into 12 months … in the interests of education or economics?]. Foundations once set in rock are now in shifting sand.

Tracing the history of the campus novel gives some indication of the evolving atmosphere of university life in that changes in the mood and tone of the genre reflect changing attitudes on the campus. [Regardless, they make for entertaining and informative reading.] David Lodge, a past master of the genre, remarked, "The high ideals of the university as an institution — the pursuit of knowledge and truth — are set against the actual behaviour and motivations of the people who work in them, who are only human and subject to the same ignoble desires and selfish ambitions as anybody else". (Edemariam, 2004, p. 12). Fiction mirroring fact.

As financial reality bites and the rigours of corporate business take a stranglehold on the more liberal educative ideals, these human frailties that Lodge refers to come to the fore and our foibles are increasingly exposed. Some academics are student orientated: many unfortunately are not, preferring to pursue their own careers through research … often, it is suggested here, at someone else's expense … that 'someone' being the students, or another member of staff, or both. Then there is our own hypocrisy. How many of us while not being too enamoured by the inequities afforded by exclusive public school, private education, are desperate to attract fee-paying students to our postgraduate courses? None too proud to feed from, rather than bite off, the hand that feeds us.

In approaches to teaching there are the conflicts and tensions between the individual and the institutional perspectives … or rather the individual aspirations operating within, and usually confined by, institutional demands. This brings, simultaneously, both spatial and temporal analysis into the frame. The institution and the environs, where the teaching and learning is actually taking place inevitably have some bearing on the proceedings. Approaches are adapted, and adopted accordingly. And temporally, it is not just the level at which the students are being taught, but also, and risking death by political correctness, the age (or rather, the number of years service) of the lecturer. Rightly or wrongly, this probably brings some influence to bear, too. If enthusiasm is crucial, after a point, doesn't this too diminish with age? Obviously, experience brings with it plus factors, but, perceptively according to the Herd "Experience has dulled my eyes, with repetition wonder dies" (Howard & Blaikley, 1967). And this brings me to my own particular favourite campus novel character Sefton Goldberg, Jacobsen's protagonist in his eighties novel *Coming from Behind*. Trapped teaching at Wrottesley Polytechnic College, Goldberg's plight is best encapsulated in his musing following a salutary conversation with one of his colleagues … "Sefton didn't envy Arthur his fervour, but he did sometimes look back, in a melancholy sort of way, to the days before the demise of his own. But age had dampened his fire and the students at the Polytechnic had extinguished it completely". (Jacobsen, 2003, p. 46).

So much, of course, depends on the attitude and ability — particularly the vision and imagination — of both the lecturer and the students. On the downside we have … "Most educators would continue to lecture on navigation while the ship is going down" (Boren, 1980, p. 490) and "For every person wishing to teach there are thirty not wanting to be taught" (Sellar & Yeatman, 1980, p. 480). On the other hand, and somewhat more encouragingly, there's the re-assuring adage "You can teach a student for a day; but if you can teach him (sic) to learn by creating curiosity, he (sic) will continue the learning process as long as he lives". (Bedford, 1980, p. 481). Reminiscent of Ward.

And it is here where I see that glimmer of hope through the gathering gloom of conformity. But how might we create this curiosity and assist discovery in today's restrictive, pressurised climate?

Much has been written on making the learning process more desirable, more enjoyable. Gower, hyperventilating in a recent article in the *Jakarta Post*, oscillates between the ecstatic and the euphoric. The classroom, he eulogises, is "an avenue for a near endless rendezvous of hearts and minds that can open up the wonderful world of learning for both teachers and students". (Gower, 2004, p. 6). And arguing, only a tad less flamboyantly, that while too regimented a regime quashes curiosity and creativity…"The teacher alone can create an atmosphere that is positive and appealing just by being receptive, responsive and attentive to students' human needs".

But even here we are again blighted by limitations imposed by restrictive assessment. It is all very well professing to be creative, injecting "curiosity" into one's lectures, but if that isn't part of the (short-term assessment) then there's trouble. Big trouble. Recent research into the effectiveness of "the video" in teaching postgraduate tourism cohorts supported this particularly disturbing conclusion. A respondent perceptively, but depressingly, noted "… you said postgraduate studies are about thinking in depth and out of line. About instilling curiosity and generating creativity. However, that is not what is used in classes to give us grades" (Wheeller, forthcoming).

Utilitarianism prevails. And averaging and mediocrity become the order of the day. "Since variety is the spice of life, it is bizarre that some of those who work in higher education should be hell-bent on destroying it". (Birkhead, 2004, p. 23). The "it" in this context could refer equally well to either "variety" or "higher education". Or both. Birkhead continues damningly to suggest that " … the powers that be would prefer all academics to be clones, giving uniform lectures in a uniform style, with a uniform structure to feed the uniform notebooks of uniform undergraduates to justify their uniformly good marks" (Birkhead, 2004, p. 23). His erudite assault on the "obsession with uniformity" is welcomed here … echoing as it does the poignant, sardonic but prophetic lyrics of *Flowers are Red*, Chapin's (1979) incisive warning as to the dangers of conditioning emanating from restrictive, blinkered teaching. Personally, I too regale against this compulsive drive for regulated, assessed conformity … a blunt, dumbing down cudgel, if ever there was one. What about 'differentiation', accommodating individual learning styles? But is the plea for creativity futile? Well, to a large degree I'm afraid it is. Even so, the clarion call here is nevertheless for the original, the quirky, the maverick.

It was pointed out earlier that the heterogeneity of the teaching and learning "experience" does make generalisation difficult — and prone to oversights. Something suitable to one set of circumstances may well be inappropriate, or impossible, in another. Sometimes this is obvious. What suits students at Master degree level may be lost on undergraduates. (Or, disconcertingly, in some cases, *vice versa*.) Elsewhere, the differences are far more subtle … difficult to discern, complicated to decipher. This is an acknowledged pitfall that presents inevitable difficulties. So, bearing this danger in mind, there are, I believe, two specific, related, but as yet relatively underdeveloped, themes that have further fruitful potential, and universal appeal, to the teaching of, and learning in, tourism. And, as such, I strongly believe they should be embraced, on a widespread basis, in all approaches to teaching and learning … assuming, that is, that we do still have some influence on how we, individually, approach our teaching. (If not, then maybe another dictate?)

Tourism we argue is part of the modern world … but how much of contemporary culture — be they positive or negative aspects — do we integrate into our teaching? Surely, then of paramount importance is the need to ensure our teaching contextualises tourism in the "real" world. But, as with most things, this again is easier said than done. The problem here is not just how to achieve this noble aim but rather in ascertaining what the "real" world actually is. We should, I believe, engage more with popular culture to contextualise tourism … ideally within contemporary events. Here, I strongly believe television, film, music, newspapers and (unfortunately, to an ever diminishing degree) literature can, and should, have a vital role to play in our teaching. In addition, obviously, to referring to academic texts students should be encouraged to reference from a far broader, eclectic range of material — drawn more widely from their own popular culture. However, based on considerable experience of external examining/auditing/and being a member of review (revue?) panels, etc. to me this practice is not in vogue. Nor does it seem to have been encouraged. Which is a shame. But if, as I suggest, we introduce contemporary issues into our teaching, whose "reality" are we considering? To what extent is the student world … and their representative cultural signifiers … the real world? Are our contemporary issues the same as the students? There is the disturbing, but real, danger here of trying in a vain, vain attempt to identify with the students … of playing Peter Pan in a Walter Mitty world. However, though the specific examples differ with generations, the underlying parallels drawn from one's own examples may transcend time. Hard to believe, but while *The Beach* may have resonance with today's students, surprising parallels can be drawn with yesteryear's *Summer Holiday*. The doors of imagination should never close.

The second suggestion is that far more prominence be given to the use of "the visual" in our work. The visual is, of course, already used in practice, but it is so far woefully underemployed as a teaching medium in tourism. While there are technical, and copyright, limitations on the use of imagery, I contend the real barriers are our own blinkers — our own reluctance to be more imaginative in the material we employ. Not only does it require vision on the part of the lecturer, it also takes considerable time and effort in preparation. And our resources are already stretched. However, what I strongly advocate is greater emphasis on the use of images — at all levels of lecturing tourism. And I don't just mean the traditional video or ubiquitous power-point display. In this respect too, our horizons should not be limited. There must be scope for something more inventive than that currently seen as the norm. While Rice's (2001) brief look at tourism and television is, perhaps, a small step in, roughly, the right direction, I do, however, envisage something far more "personal" in approach … one that encourages and fosters the opportunity for individual expression to prosper. Having assembled a vast array of eclectic slides and images, which always seem to go down well with the students, I have, over the years, practised what I preached and concentrated heavily on the use of the visual in my own teaching. International students especially often find it easier to respond to the visual image rather than the spoken word. (Wheeller, forthcoming).

There are examples where these two approaches are effectively combined — of the visual being employed effectively to contextualise tourism in the student world. Although some lecturers may regard aspects of the book as elementary and pedantic, Bertram's *Using Media in Teaching* is worth a quick read. In her review of the text de Villiers (2004, p. 14) claims, with justification, "One of the most obvious features of our times is that we live in the information age. It will enable teachers to assist their students to navigate critically through an information-saturated world. Furthermore, the new South Africa requires that teachers teach in ways that actively link learning to students' own lives and experiences. The popular media in particular provide a host of opportunities that could be harnessed to achieve this". Robinson and Dale (2004, p. 13), in their research, endorse this, concluding — not too surprisingly — that "using visual imagery is an effective way of stimulating interest in the subject matter". With particular reference to teaching tourism, they provide examples that "tap into the students' immediate understanding of the subject matter by contextualising research methods to examples they can empathise with".

Feighey (2003) makes a convincing argument for greater use of the visual in tourism at research level. Here, I make a claim for it to play a far greater role in our teaching. It is also an accessible way of visually contextualising tourism in the contemporary. Adopting these dual approaches of "contextualising imagery" could provide the scope to enable the individual, be that lecturer and/or student, to flourish within an overall framework.

On reflection, though, I suppose it all really depends where the heart lies. Personally, as something of a "Romantic (secular) Pessimist", I guess it is more about how you teach rather than what you teach. Besides the obvious qualities of enthusiasm and passion for the subject, together with commitment to the students, there is the need to engage. But while some in higher education are student-orientated, others are not. And never will be. This must cast a shadow on the preaching of such luminaries as Barnett (2004) who seem either to be unaware of, or choose to ignore, this situation. Certainly a positive, it is suggested here idealistic, approach was adopted by Barnett (2004) in his keynote address at the *Critical Issues in Tourism Education Conference* in December 2004. Almost evangelical in delivery, it appeared to be based on the assumptions that all those engaged in lecturing actually want to teach; that their top priority lies with getting the best out of their students; and that they are prepared to invest all their time and effort to this end. And that students want to "learn".

Despite having considerable sympathy, indeed empathy, with Barnett's laudable ideals… I'm afraid, though it saddens me to say so, in reality that is all they amount to — ideals. Unfortunately, these are totally out of kilter with the cutthroat, day-to-day shenanigans of contemporary higher education. As with the concept of sustainability, there is an ever-widening chasm between what should be and what actually is. While a necessary crutch for the theorist, idealism doesn't provide the prerequisite edifice for practitioners to bridge that alarming gap. Returning to Ward's world, idealism is, after all, a somewhat flimsy fabric when it comes to re-enforcing his platform, the chapter's initial springboard. What is needed in today's higher education is an antidote to the straightjacket of restrictive assessment and the ethos of uniform conformity. Something, positive, practical but flexible: an environment to give the inspirational lecturer room in which to nurture curiosity: one that enables the student to thrive.

But aren't these also nebulous, hypocritical ideals? Well, yes I'm afraid they are. That there is a degree of ambiguity, indeed apparent contradiction, in some aspects of this chapter is not regarded, at least by the author, as a problem. After all, isn't the fundamental purpose of a lecture (and chapter?) often to confuse, to provoke debate, to stimulate and encourage independent thought? To enhance "learning"?

But even that might not be enough. On checking out of the Manhattan – this time on the wall, behind the desk – was the dictum 'Do not confine your children to your own learning, for they were born in another time.' Now, there's a thought. And a lesson in itself.

References

Barkham, P. (2004). Architects attack 'philistine' move by Cambridge. *Guardian* (30 November), 2, Weekly newspaper, London.

Barnett, R. (2004). *Keynote address critical issues in tourism education.* A joint international conference organised by Association for Tourism in Higher Education, Leisure and Tourism

Education Research Network of Buckinghamshire Chilterns University College, Learning and Teaching Support Network for Hospitality, Leisure, Sport and Tourism, Association for Tourism and Leisure Education. Buckinghamshire Chilterns University College, 2–3 December.

Bedford, C. (1980). In: L. Peter (Ed.), *Quotations for our time.* London: Magnum.

Bertram, C. (2004). *Using media in teaching.* Oxford: Oxford University Press.

Birkhead, T. (2004). Why the best academics are just like sperm. *The Times Higher,* (3 September), 23, Weekly newspaper, London.

Boren, J. (1980). In: L. Peter (Ed.), *Quotations for our time.* London: Magnum.

Chapin, H. (1979). *Flowers are red.* Los Angeles: Elektra Records, British Lion Music.

Day, G. (2004). Intellectuals should speak out against social inclusion… *The Times Higher,* (8 September), 13, Weekly newspaper, London.

de Villiers, F. (2004). *The Teacher.* (August), 14, Weekly newspaper, Johannesburg.

Eber, S. (2003). *Integrating sustainability into the undergraduate curriculum: Leisure and tourism. Guidelines No 10.* Guildford: ATHE.

Edemariam, A. (2004). Who's afraid of the campus novel? *The Guardian Review,* (2 October), 12, Daily newspaper, London.

Feighey, W. (2003). Negative image? Developing the visual in tourism research. *Current Issues in Tourism, 6*(1), 76–85.

Gower, S. (2004). Schools must be able to stimulate their students to love learning. *Jakarta Post,* (13 March), 7.

Howard, K., & Blaikley, A. (1967). *Paradise lost.* London: Fontana, Carlin Music.

Jacobsen, H. (2003). *Coming from behind.* London: Vintage.

Mitchell, P. (2004). In: A. Fazackerley (Ed.), 'Jobs cull gathering pace'. *The Times Higher,* (10 December), 1.

Peter, L. (1980). *Quotations for our time.* London: Magnum.

Rice, A. (2001). *Tourism on television.* London: Tourism Concern.

Robinson, N., & Dale, C. (2004). *Watching the detectives: Using contextualisation Link 9.* Oxford: LTSN.

Sellar, W., & Yeatman, R. (1980). In: L. Peter, (Ed.), *Quotations for our time.* London: Magnum.

Wheeller, B. (2005). We'll go somewhere where there's cheese. Wallace and Gromit's Grand Day Out. *Critical Issues in Tourism Education. Conference Proceedings.* Buckingham Chilterns, High Wycombe.

Utley, A. (2004). A new agenda. Advertisement feature. *The Times Higher,* (15 October), Weekly newspaper, London.

Chapter 23

Assessment

Nina Becket

Assessment

> Sometimes we have great ideas; sometimes we seem in a mental rut. Is it
> any wonder, then, that assessment — finding out what our students have
> learned — is such a challenge? (Suskie, 2000).

This chapter provides an introduction to assessment practice in tourism higher education
(HE). As such it concentrates on the ways in which the setting, marking and reviewing of
assignments and examinations are undertaken, and so will not include for example, the evaluation of courses. Following an introduction to assessment, the chapter concentrates on key
issues and challenges in tourism HE, and concludes with an example assessment to illustrate the concepts discussed. Tourism academics are required to work within their institutional, and possibly their departmental learning teaching and assessment strategies, so the
aspects covered here concentrate on what is broadly within the control of the individual
tourism academic and the issues they face within their subject and institutional context.

   Assessment is defined as:

> The process by which one attempts to measure the quality and quantity of
> learning and teaching using various assessment techniques, e.g. assign-
> ments, projects, continuous assessment, objective-type tests, final examina-
> tions and standardised tests (Page & Thomas, 1979, p. 26).

Whilst this draws attention to various assessment methods, perhaps most important is the
idea that assessment is a process by which attempts to measure the quality and quantity of
learning are made, assessment is not scientific with predictable outcomes, rather it is
crafted by lecturers, often through trial and error.

   In contrast, the Northbrook College (UK) assessment policy states that:

> Assessment is at the heart of the learning experience of students.
> Assessment motivates students and drives their learning. It determines their

An International Handbook of Tourism Education
Copyright © 2005 by Elsevier Ltd.
All rights of reproduction in any form reserved
ISBN: 0-08-044667-1

progression through their programmes and validates their success or failure in meeting programme objectives. It is assessment that provides the main basis of public recognition of achievement and gives it its value and marketability (HEFCE, 2003, p. 50).

This captures a fundamental dimension, assessment is at the heart of the student learning experience and drives their learning, progress and achievement. Furthermore, Gibbs (1995) advises that the way in which assessment is used is likely to have more of an effect on student learning than any other aspect of curriculum design. There are various objectives and purposes in assessment, when brought together these include those summarised in Table 1.

In tourism there has been a shift in patterns of HE teaching towards more student-centred learning. This is in line with other subjects at an international level and is based on the premise that:

> Learning takes place through the active behaviour of the student: it is what he does that he learns, not what the teacher does (Tyler, 1949, p. 63 in Biggs, 2002, p. 1).

This move has demanded changes in assessment practice towards more student-centred methods such as enquiry and problem-based learning, and more use of coursework, peer and self assessment, groupwork and portfolios etc.

Table 1: Purposes of assessment.

Learning	Provide feedback to students to improve their learning
	Motivate students
	Diagnose a student's strengths and weaknesses
	Help students develop their self-assessment skills
	Provide a profile of what a student has learnt
Certification	Pass or fail, grade or rank a student
	Licence to proceed or practice
	Select for or predict success in future courses
	Select for or predict success in future employment
Quality assurance	Provide feedback to lecturers on student learning
	Improve teaching
	Evaluate a course's strengths and weaknesses
	Assess the extent to which a course has achieved its aims
	Judge the effectiveness of the learning environment
	Ensure the course is credit worthy to other institutions and employers
	Monitor standards over time

Mutch and Brown (2001, p. 2).

Various sources (e.g. HEFCE, 2003; Brown, 2001) provide listings of potential assessment methods. In tourism these are most effectively grouped into written and oral assessments as described in Table 2.

> The most effective learning (i.e. the quickest and most long lasting!) occurs when students are engaged with their study material. This means relating it to their existing knowledge and prior experience, evaluating, considering its limitations and, most importantly, using the learning. This is what Entwistle (1992) calls 'deep learning' (Hills et al., 2003, p. 24).

Good examples of these types of learning experiences are reports on fieldwork trips or placements which are individual to the student, and as the students are personally involved, they are more likely to be motivated and engage with the assessment. Whilst there is certainly a greater variety in assessment methods today (Rust, 2002), in tourism courses, despite assessment innovations, it is fair to say that essays and experiential learning still dominate assessment methods. While there has been general acceptance that in order to effectively support student learning, coursework may be preferable to examinations, the increase in student numbers and a consequent rise in plagiarism (discussed later) has led many staff to reconsider the pros and cons of examinations and coursework, and has resulted in a renewed use of examinations. Brown (2001) discusses the pros and cons of both methods, and suggests that if examinations are to be used then it is worthwhile to consider whether students could be given the topics to be examined prior to the examination, or indeed be allowed to take their texts and notes into examinations. This is likely not to change the overall rank order of students' performance in examinations. He does warn however, that if it is sought to measure student performance against course outcomes, then 'a variety of assessment tasks' (p. 20) is vital. Essays and experiential learning as tourism assessment methods are now discussed.

Table 2: Written and oral assessment methods.

Written assessments	Essay, report, examination (open book, seen, unseen), short answer/multiple choice questions, case studies, critiques, problems, electronic presentations (e.g. videos, CDs or web pages), fieldwork reports, in-class tests, synoptic assignments/examinations, analytical bibliographies, projects (group or individual), dissertations, computer aided assessment, and experiential/reflective practice assignments (e.g. portfolios, learning diaries, placement reports, or learning contracts)
Oral/presentation assessments	Exhibitions, posters, student-led seminars, presentations, simulated interviews, role plays, observation, peer and self assessment, and vivas/orals

Essays

In tourism there is likely to be an emphasis on the use of essays, whether as coursework or within examinations. Banister (2004) suggests that essays as an assessment tool have a number of advantages, which include: that they are relatively easy for staff to set, they encourage students to search the literature, demonstrate their knowledge acquisition, and potentially innovation and initiative. In terms of skills, essays may also support the development of criticality, material selection and comprehension, working to deadlines, writing style and constructing a cogent argument. They also have disadvantages in that they are prone to plagiarism, and may arguably be outmoded when considered against necessary employability skills, such as producing a report or article. From a staff perspective, essays cannot be marked quickly and it is generally difficult to achieve reliability in marking. Using essays with large student groups does however enable the lecturer to gain an indication of the general level of group learning, and to overcome potential plagiarism Miller, Imrie, and Cox (1998) suggest that smaller tutor groups could be given different questions.

Individual essay questions used in tourism coursework or examinations will have specific learning outcomes, for example, they may require students to select evidence to support an argument or demonstrate analysis and evaluation, for example,

> Critically evaluate:
>
> the role that market research has to play in the development of successful tourism firms, or, the extent to which measurements of customer satisfaction are facile or academic, using examples from the literature and the tourism sector,

or diagnose and suggest solutions to a problem, for example,

> You have a developed concept for a new tourism venture, and have identified a site, and now need the finance to develop the concept. Explain what options might be open to you to fund the project, and the information that potential backers would need in order to be convinced to invest their money in the venture.

In order to add variety to the use of essays within programmes, alternatives to longer type essays are short answer essays, which may require students to demonstrate their understanding of facts, principles or concepts, or essay outlines, which require students to demonstrate their ability to select and organise material and construct coherent arguments (Race, 1995). For example, either of the following examples could be used as short answer essay questions, or essay outline assignments:

> Justify the importance of effective human resource management practices to the tourism industry, identifying appropriate sources and examples, or Identify the potential benefits of an effective marketing plan in the support of tourism development and management.

Furthermore, in addition to summative assessments, either of these two approaches would also be useful for formative assessment tasks.

From the student perspective, perhaps the most important aspect of essay assessments is their need to understand the criteria used. As staff we can do much more to help them understand and interpret the criteria which we use. Price, O'Donovan, and Rust (2001) suggest that in order to achieve this understanding, it is necessary to actively engage students with the assessment criteria through, for example, marking exercises (see http://www.hlst.heacademy.ac.uk/resources/cases/case_studies.html).

Experiential Learning

In tourism curricula, experiential learning often forms an important part of the curriculum, for example, through experience of fieldwork and related activities, which are used to develop students' research skills in the 'real world'. This type of learning may increasingly include work-related learning, such as work placements, or live projects, fieldwork, case studies, simulations or role plays which may take place inside or outside the classroom. It is widely acknowledged that one of the roles of HE is to suitably equip graduates for the workplace (Yorke, 2004). In the current environment work-related learning is of increasing importance within the HE tourism curriculum. The development of student employability skills goes beyond the ability of a graduate to obtain a job, rather it is derived from the ways in which students learn from their experience, and is based on this 'good learning' (e.g. Yorke, 2004).

Much of the foundation of experiential learning relates to the work of Kolb (1984), who identified that lifelong and experiential learning is cyclical, moving from experience, through reflection and conceptualising, then on to further experience, and so on. For students, these types of learning experiences need to be accompanied by reflection, analysis and most importantly by putting the experience into an academic context. Therefore this process needs to be captured within the assessment. A good example of this is provided by the Global Practicum/Project at Rollings College (USA). This assignment provides an ideal opportunity for students to apply theoretical concepts and skills to a real problem, for example, the development of a meaningful tourism industry in Rio Preto, Brazil (Johnson, 2003). The course runs for one semester, during the first half, students gather secondary information, define the objectives of their trip, identify data they need to collect in country, and how it will be obtained. During their visit they make an interim presentation to the host country sponsors, and then return to compile a report. Assessment is completed by the academic tutor, the host country sponsor, and student peer evaluation.

In tourism fieldwork, assessment is often summative and required in the form of reports, but increasingly there are opportunities to use presentations, student conferences, web presentations, diaries, or logbooks. At Sheffield Hallam University (UK) for example, staff running a tourism fieldwork module have developed a course which uses Sheffield, the university city, as its locus. Students are required to add information to a database and then share and use this data for summative and formative assessments which include seminar activities and written and oral reports. (see http://www.hlst.heacademy.ac.uk/resources/cases/case23.html)

Main Issues and Challenges

Various authors have identified assessment issues in contemporary HE (e.g. Yorke, 2001; James, McInnis & Devlin, 2002; Miller et al., 1998). The key issues identified include the following, and these challenges form the basis of this section:

- Using formative assessment and feedback to improve learning;
- Pressure on staff and the assessment of large classes;
- Minimising plagiarism;
- Assessing groupwork;
- Improving the marking and grading of student work.

There is little information specific to assessment practice in tourism education. However within the UK, the Quality Assurance Agency (QAA), which has responsibility for reviewing the quality of HE, undertook a review of hospitality, leisure, recreation, sport and tourism courses in England and Northern Ireland between 2000 and 2001. Individual quantitative ratings and reports were generated for each department and an overview report was published (www.qaa.ac.uk). One of the six aspects of provision investigated was 'teaching, learning and assessment'. Regarding assessment, the overview report states that:

> While there is much exemplary practice in assessments, weaknesses were frequently evident in the relationship between learning outcomes, assessment criteria, marking and the written feedback provided for students. This led to inconsistencies that undermined the rigour and objectivity of assessment, as well as its formative function (QAA, 2001, p. 4).

This criticism largely relates to 'constructive alignment' within programmes. It is likely that these comments have resonance on an international level, so this aspect is also included here.

Constructive Alignment

'Constructive alignment' is an approach to curriculum design that optimises the conditions and opportunities for good learning, it is an integrated system where 'all aspects of teaching and assessment are tuned to support high level learning' (Biggs, 2002, p. 1).

'Constructive' is concerned with what the learner does in constructing meaning through relevant learning activities, and 'alignment' with what the teacher does in designing a learning environment that supports students in achieving the learning outcomes. So, for the teacher designing assessment, the process should be:

1. Definition of specific learning outcomes;
2. Selecting teaching/learning activities likely to lead to achievement of the learning outcomes;
3. Assessing the learning outcomes of students, to see how well they match what was intended;
4. Finally arriving at a grade representative of the extent to which the learning outcomes have been met (Biggs, 2002).

Problem-based-learning (PBL) is suggested to offer a good example of constructive alignment (Biggs, 2002). This is because the aim of PBL is to produce graduates able to solve professional problems, the main teaching method involves students in solving professional problems, and the assessment used judges how well these have been solved. It is not possible to give sufficient attention to PBL in this chapter. However, useful information can be found at http://www.samford.edu/pbl/index.html or http://www.hss.coventry.ac.uk/pbl/.

Using Formative Assessment and Feedback to Improve Learning

It is generally accepted that assessment is construed as being either, diagnostic, formative or summative:

> *diagnostic assessment* provides an indicator of a learner's aptitude and preparedness for a programme of study and identifies possible learning problems;

> *formative assessment* is designed to provide learners with feedback on progress and inform development, but does not contribute to the overall assessment;

> *summative assessment* provides a measure of achievement or failure made in respect of a learner's performance in relation to the intended learning outcomes of the programme of study (QAA, 2000, p. 3).

A single assessment can often include one or more of these elements. For example, a piece of coursework which is assessed summatively may also include a formative aspect where students receive feedback on their performance. Alternatively a diagnostic assessment, used at the beginning of a course, may be used for a summative judgement about student progression.

The main purpose of formative assessment is to provide feedback to students to stimulate and help them judge the effectiveness of their learning. It also alerts tutors to aspects of a course where students may be having difficulties, and gives students practice in developing essential skills, such as essay writing or problem solving, arguably without the fear of failure (Miller et al., 1998).

As well as students learning through their assessment tasks, they should also be in a position to learn from the feedback they receive from their tutors. Race (1995) suggests it is important for students to be able to learn from their mistakes as well as their triumphs. In the QAA inspection of UK subject provision, feedback to students was identified as an aspect which required improvement:

> The quality of the written feedback given to students on their assessed work is varied. The best feedback seen gave detailed and constructive comment, and was clearly set in the context of learning outcomes and assessment criteria: this guided the students on how to improve their performance. In contrast, some feedback was found to be perfunctory, late or too general to be of value (QAA, 2001, p. 4).

The guidance in Table 3 (Rust, 2002, p. 153) is likely to be of interest to new staff, and can also act as a useful checklist for more experienced staff when providing feedback.

Table 3: Feedback to students.

- Be prompt
- Start with a positive encouraging comment
- Include a brief summary of your view of the assignment
- Relate specifically to the learning outcomes and assessment criteria
- Balance negative with positive comments and turn criticism into positive suggestions
- Make general suggestions on how to go about the next assignment
- Ask questions which encourage reflection about the work
- Use informal conversational language
- Explain all your comments
- Suggest follow-up work, references and specific ways to improve the assignment
- Explain the mark or grade, why it is not better (or worse)
- Offer help with specific problems, or to discuss the assignment

Further extensive resources on enhancing feedback can be found in the Student Enhanced Learning Through Effective Feedback (SENLEF) project (www.heacademy. ac.uk/senlef.htm).

A further consideration regarding formative feedback is the international political agenda to widen participation in HE. Yorke proposes 'that to increase first-year retention the first semester should be primarily formative' (in Rust 2002, p. 151), and that new assessment strategies are required to support non-traditional entry students who may be lacking in self belief and so are likely to need 'good and sensitive feedback', and perhaps staged assessments with interim feedback for longer pieces of work.

However, even if students receive excellent feedback as outlined, research suggests (Fritz, Morris, Bjork, Gelman, & Wickens, 2000) that due to the passive receipt of feedback as opposed to the activity of generating the work, they may not make significant use of it. Therefore staff may find it appropriate to experiment with various methods to encourage students to use their feedback from staff more effectively (e.g. Buswell & Matthews, 2004). An alternative method of increasing the feedback to students would be through making more extensive use of peer evaluation and feedback.

Pressure on Staff and Assessing Large Classes

A result of decreasing resources per student and increasing student/staff ratios is an increase in the pressure on staff and a potential detrimental effect on student learning, through for example larger class sizes, or a reduction in the amount of assessment. Newstead (2004) suggests that increasing academic workloads are resulting in higher stress levels, and that the assessment load on staff is almost certainly a contributing factor.

Brown and Glasner (1999, p. 202) suggest that 'Ensuring that assessment is fair, accurate and comprehensive – and yet manageable for those doing it – is a major challenge'. Therefore to deal with this scenario, staff need to employ more effective methods of teaching, learning and assessment. Rust (2001) suggests that any changes to assessment practice need particularly to maintain formative assessment elements and the quality of feedback to students. Whilst some solutions which reduce the pressure on staff may be allied to departmental or institutional decisions, others can be implemented by staff within individual modules. Rust (2001) identifies six ways in which the burden of assessment on academics could be reduced, without a reduction in the quality of the assessment:

- front-ending assessment;
- 'doing it in class';
- using self and peer assessment;
- assessing groups;
- mechanising the assessment; and
- making strategic reductions in the amount of assessment.

For example, instead of setting essays, students could set tasks and then present their findings as a poster or a presentation in class; tutors could be use statement banks for adding comments directly into text when marking on a PC; or objective tests could be used to test knowledge of specific material. Further examples relating to effective reductions in assessment can be found in Rust's (2001) Briefing on Assessment of Large Groups.

Minimising Plagiarism

Universities across the world are concerned with how to minimise and respond to student plagiarism and cheating. A survey at Monash and Swinburne Universities found that 80% of 700 students admitted that they had cheated at some stage in their study, the most common methods were collaborating on individual work and copying from the internet or textbooks (Szego, 2003). It is likely that institutions and/or departments will have policies to deal with plagiarism which staff need to be familiar with, however, there is also much that individual staff can do within the design of assessment tasks to minimise plagiarism. Miller et al. (1998, p. 242) state that:

> Academic honesty or integrity is the academic business of all members of the university – an individual as well as a collective responsibility.

Defining plagiarism is complex, but the following examples in Table 4 (James et al., 2002, p. 38) give a good indication of common forms of plagiarism.

Furthermore, all plagiarism is not 'equal', it depends on the intent of the student, whether it was done intentionally or by accident, due perhaps to a lack of understanding, and the actual extent of the plagiarism, for example, was a whole essay downloaded and submitted, or was it a misuse of quotes or referencing conventions? (James et al., 2002).

A briefing on plagiarism (Stefani & Carroll, 2001) concentrates on two aspects. First, the need to define plagiarism with students, ensuring they receive clear guidelines, and an opportunity to work with definitions and their meaning, and second, the potential for staff to lessen opportunities for plagiarism, through using assessment effectively. They suggest that information is now available to students on an unprecedented scale, therefore in student-centred learning, staff should put greater emphasis on the 'skills of analysing and

Table 4: Common forms of plagiarism.

- 'Submitting as one's own, an assignment that another person has completed
- Downloading information, text, computer code, artwork, graphics or other material from the Internet and presenting it as one's own without acknowledgement
- Quoting or paraphrasing material from a source without acknowledgement
- Preparing a correctly cited and referenced assignment from individual research and then handing part or all of that work in twice for separate subjects/marks
- Cheating in an exam either by copying from other students or using unauthorised notes or other aids
- There are also forms of plagiarism and cheating that relate directly to student participation in groupwork
- Copying from other members while working in a group
- Contributing less, little or nothing to a group assignment and claiming an equal contribution and share of the marks'

---

evaluating information rather than just finding it' (Breivik, 1997 in Stefani & Carroll, 2001, p. 9). James et al. (2002, p. 44) suggest a three-point plan to minimise plagiarism:

- Make expectations clear to students;
- Design assessment to minimise opportunities for plagiarism; and
- Visibly monitor, detect and respond to incidences of plagiarism.

In support of this they provide 36 strategies, many of which relate to designing out the potential for plagiarism within assessment, for example, by relating assignments to field work, designing mini assignments requiring students to demonstrate their skills in summarising and paraphrasing, or using assignments that can be done in class rather than as coursework. Although not discussed here, there are now various electronic plagiarism detection systems available. These systems act as a deterrent to students and are most likely to be effective when used in conjunction with a positive approach which starts with student learning and assessment.

Assessing Groupwork

As outlined, the design of courses begins with the constructive alignment of learning outcomes, learning activities and assessment methods. Therefore when considering whether to use groupwork, the first question must be, do the learning outcomes demand group or independent work by students? If assessed groupwork is to be used, then the assessment tasks are crucial in determining the success or otherwise of student learning. This is highlighted within the assessment policy of the University of Wollongong (Australia) (James et al., 2002 p. 47):

> Groupwork under proper conditions, encourages peer learning and peer support and many studies validate the efficacy of peer learning. Under less ideal conditions, groupwork can become the vehicle for acrimony, conflict and freeloading.

Potential opportunities for using groupwork include: enabling students to engage in larger scale projects not possible for an individual, better quality learning outcomes than an individual student could manage, the development and assessment of team working skills, for example, through personal reflection or peer evaluation activities, and the economical use of staff time through a potentially reduced assessment burden.

If assessed groupwork is to be used, then it is necessary to identify the purpose of the assessment, does this relate to the product of the groupwork, for example, a report or a presentation, or to the personal skills learning and development as a result of experiencing the process? In the light of current employer and government agendas, the development of personal and transferable skills by students is becoming increasingly important to employers and students alike (Yorke, 2004). In this respect, groupwork offers excellent opportunities to include personal development activities (for example, in team working, negotiation, organisation and cognitive skills) through assessment related to the groupworking process and reflective activities, otherwise not possible through independent working.

Whilst groupwork encourages collaborative and peer learning, and potentially deep learning through active engagement in the learning process, the link between groupwork and plagiarism is often cited as a problem by academics (Stefani & Carroll, 2001). James et al., indicate that students may be at particular risk of unintentional plagiarism in groupwork situations, when 'students are often uncertain about where co-operation and collaboration stops, or should stop, and where copying begins' (2002, p. 40). So it is vital that students are given detailed guidance, for example, regarding the precise requirements of individual reports produced from groupworking.

One of the most significant concerns when using assessed groupwork is the fairness of assessment practices for individuals. Gibbs (1995, p. 13) puts this into context stating:

> The main problem with group project work is that it is individuals who gain qualifications, not groups, and some way has to be found to allocate marks fairly to individuals.

In order to achieve fairness in assessment, its design is paramount. The criteria used for the assessment of groupwork needs to reflect the learning outcomes, and requires careful planning regarding who will set the criteria and how they will be applied, for example, by the tutor or peers, or self assessment. It is not possible to cover this in detail here, but a sensible starting point is the guidelines in Figure 1 from Lincoln University (New Zealand) (http://learn.lincoln.ac.nz/tls/groupwork/assessment/guidelines.htm): The 'First Words' on assessing groupwork (http://www.brookes.ac.uk/services/ocsd/firstwords/fw26.html) also provides guidance on aspects such as group selection and mark allocation.

Marking and Grading

Assessment needs to be:

> Valid – it assesses the stated learning outcomes, it does what it says it does
> Reliable – it can be reproduced by whoever marks the work or whenever it is done

---

'Ensure that the marking practices encourage and reinforce effective group work.

Give students a full explanation of the requirements for the assignment in writing. Include the usual assessment information (weighting, due date, penalties etc.); also include full details of procedures relating to:

- the task to be undertaken
- the basis for group membership
- rules that cover the operation of the group
- task allocation within the group
- the criteria for assessing the group report/presentation
- the procedure for assessing individual contribution, if such contribution is to be assessed
- who will carry out the assessment (e.g. examiner, peers, self etc.)
- the fall-back position if a group loses a member or in some way falls apart.

Use lecture time or tutorials as a basis for further clarifying requirements verbally. Develop a process for providing the group with detailed feedback to assist the ongoing work of the group and provide specific feedback on all aspects of the activity and its outcome upon completion.'

Figure 1: Guidelines for Assessment of Groupwork.

Transparent – everyone knows what is assessed, how it is assessed, where it is assessed, especially the students
Fair – free of favouritism and without bias
Affordable within the available budget, including staff time (Hills et al., 2003, p. 26).

It is perhaps surprising that despite the drives in HE towards measuring and enhancing quality, new staff are not likely to routinely receive training in marking student work, particularly when,'... the business of marking student scripts still remains as the most significant quality event in the lives of the students and the academics' (Fleming, 1999, p. 83).

Fleming (1999) identifies the potential sources of bias, which may have positive or negative effects on marks awarded, relating to: personal aspects (such as gender/ethnic factors), halo effects (resonance with the marker), standard of presentation, the contrast effect between the standard of the previous work reviewed, marker disposition, and the number of markers assessing one piece of work. In striving to reduce potential bias, Fleming (1999) suggests it is good practice for example; to evaluate all answers to one question before going on to the next, use numbers not names for students, use a marking schedule with clear criteria, use the whole marking scale, and shuffle the order of the papers after marking each question.

Atherton (2003) draws attention to the lack of validity of essay marking and indicates that this can be made more objective by using defined criteria. After deciding on the learning outcomes, it is then possible to identify the major factors which need to be included, for example: demonstration of knowledge, critical discussion, use of sources, argument, structure and expression. These five aspects can then be used to form the criteria for levels of achievement and weighted according to their relative importance. Atherton suggests this grid could then be given to students, used to form the basis of feedback to them and will also ensure that the marks awarded can be justified.

Assessment Example

In concluding this chapter and illustrating the aspects discussed, a specimen assessment is now given (Bibbings, 2004), although this is a fieldwork assignment, many of the principles are likely to be equally applicable to other assessment methods. The focus is the student experience of the fieldwork preparation, visit, analysis, groupwork and presentation of their findings. Therefore students are working from their personal experience which is likely to create interest for them. This minimises the opportunity for plagiarism, and clear guidance is given on what is, and is not, acceptable in this respect both in the module guide and by staff within a workshop.

The task requires students to investigate the tourism development process, impact, problems and opportunities of a newly established visitor attraction which has significantly enhanced the local economy. Working as individuals and as a member of a group, students are required to undertake substantial secondary research prior to the fieldwork visit, and on their return: to prepare an individual report concerning the tourism development process of the operation, and in groups of five or six, to complete a report on their overall conclusions and recommendations, and a poster exhibition which provides a detailed evaluation of a current issue faced by the operation.

The grading of the work is undertaken by the tutors in line with agreed departmental grade performance criteria, classified according to the extent to which students have achieved the learning outcomes. The grade performance criteria were devised by the staff and so have been jointly discussed and interpreted by those marking the student work.

Learning outcomes:

1. Analyse the problems and opportunities offered by tourism as an economic generator to sustain the economy of an area that preserves both nature and culture;
2. Evaluate the tourism development process as applied to the given operational context;
3. Undertake secondary and primary research adopting a reasoned methodology;
4. Select and apply appropriate theory to a current tourism context;
5. Effectively present the findings of an investigation using both written and oral communication;
6. Work effectively as a member of a group to analyse, evaluate, synthesise and present research data and findings.

Tables 5–7 show the links between the assessment criteria and the learning outcomes for the three assessments. On the feedback sheet given to students, feedback is provided in the relation to the specific learning outcomes and assessment criteria. Using a standardised form reduces the staff time required to provide feedback. If this was done on a PC and utilised a statement bank devised for the assignment, further time could also be saved, while maintaining the level of feedback to students. Here, the comments section explains the approaches used for the assessments.

Table 5: Individual element report (40% of total marks).

Assessment criteria	Learning outcomes assessed	Comments
Content Understanding of the tourism and development process Application of theory Clarity of argument Reasoned methodology Appropriate use and range of sources	Learning outcomes 2, 3 and 4	Originally the assessment required a group rather than an individual report. However, experience suggested that students were working independently to produce their own sections of the report and then together to join their individual pieces, and may not receive a fair mark as a result of the input of others. So the benefits of groupworking were not being achieved, and students potentially felt unfairly treated. Therefore the individual report was introduced (40% of the assessment). The learning outcomes test the ability of students to evaluate the operation from a theoretical perspective, adopting an appropriate methodology. A potential benefit of submitting this work as part of a group report is that individual students are likely to benefit from giving and receiving peer feedback prior to submission
Presentation Format, presentation and style (including spelling and grammar) Appropriate referencing method used	Learning outcome 5	This learning outcome requires students to effectively present their findings in a format which is similar to that required on a commercial basis

Finally

Some sensible advice:

> assessment shapes learning so if you want to change learning then change the assessment method;
> match the assessment tasks to the learning outcomes;
> match the criteria to the task and learning outcomes;
> keep the criteria simple;

Table 6: Group element report (20% of total marks).

Assessment criteria	Learning outcomes assessed	Comments
Team work		
Evidence of: meetings, appropriate allocation of work, reflection on how the group worked together, project planning, including a Gantt chart	Learning outcome 6	This aspect requires students to jointly analyse the performance of their group. They are encouraged to utilise Microsoft Project to support project planning, and reflect on the success or otherwise of their groupworking. All students in the department receive input in their first year on effective groupworking and the department has a groupwork policy which students work to. (The latter includes for example, processes for recording meetings)
Conclusions and recommendations		
Identification of tourism development potential Application of theory Clarity of argument Logical conclusions Appropriate recommendations	Learning outcomes 1, 4 and 6	This aspect is undertaken by a group of students. On their own they would not be able to get sufficient detailed data, so it would not be possible for individual students to compile this type of analysis, therefore students benefit from working collaboratively. In order to achieve the learning outcome they would need to work together as a group prior to the visit and afterwards in order to develop their conclusions and recommendations. They are required to present their recommendations in a form suitable to be presented to the operation, skills relevant to the world of work
Presentation		
Format, presentation and style (including spelling and grammar) Appropriate referencing method used	Learning outcome 5	As above, but with collective responsibility

be fair, reliable and valid in your marking;
provide meaningful, timely feedback (Brown, 2001, p. 6).

Assessment is a crucial part of our work and has a direct impact on the experience of our students. Therefore it is vital that we work together to share our experiences and improve

Table 7: Exhibition (40% of total marks).

Assessment criteria	Learning outcomes assessed	Comments
Issues chosen Appropriateness Depth of analysis Critical evaluation	Learning outcome 1	This requires students to jointly prepare a poster and present their ideas in a succinct way at an exhibition. As there are a number of student groups, this activity creates a buzz of excitement, and a variety in the assessment diet. Using the exhibition has significantly reduced staff assessment time and has enabled direct and immediate feedback to students
Presentation Creativity Clarity Suitability of display	Learning outcome 5	This aspect tests the creativity of the students in presenting their findings in a visual format and their ability to orally convey their learning by responding to staff questions
Group Work Each member participates, demonstrates knowledge and understanding Logical answers to questions	Learning outcome 6	This provides a forum for students to participate collectively in the assessment, it will also highlight any members of the group who may have been 'freeloading' If desired, it would be possible to introduce peer or self evaluation to extend the input by the students. As this is a final year module, student groups could also be required to design their own assessment criteria (see Gibbs, 1995)

assessment practice. Your tourism subject association is an excellent place to start this activity. In addition to the bibliography, further sources likely to be particularly useful are:

- The Higher Education Academy resources and examples relating to tourism from the Subject Network site at http://www.hlst.heacademy.ac.uk/, and generic guidance, including the assessment of key skills, using portfolios and effective feedback from the Higher Education Academy site at http://www.heacademy.ac.uk;
- Assessing Learning in Australian Universities is an extensive site compiled for the Australian Universities Teaching Committee at http://www.cshe.unimelb.edu.au/assessinglearning/.

References

Atherton, J. (2003). Learning and teaching: The problem of assessment. http://www.dmu.ac.uk/~jamesa/teaching/assess_problem.htm http://www.dmu.ac.uk/~jamesa/teaching/marking.htm.

Banister, P. (2004). Assessment as a tool for fostering key skills. *Psychology Learning and Teaching,* *3*(2), 109–113.

Bibbings, L. (2004). *Tourism development and management course handbook*. Oxford: Oxford Brookes University.

Biggs, J. (2002). Aligning the curriculum to promote good learning. *Constructive alignment in action: An imaginative curriculum symposium*, Monday, November 4th, London, http://www.heacademy.ac.uk/resources.asp?process=full_record&section=generic&id=167.

Breivik, P. S. (1997). *Student learning in the information age*. Oxford: Oryx Press.

Brown, G. (2001). *Assessment: A guide for lecturers, LTSN generic centre assessment series number 3.* York: Learning and Teaching Support Network.

Brown, S., & Glasner, A. (1999). *Assessment matters in higher education: Choosing and using diverse approaches*. Buckingham: The Society for Research in Higher Education and the Open University Press.

Buswell, J., & Matthews, N. (2004). Feedback on feedback! encouraging students to read feedback: A University of Gloucestershire case study.*Journal of Hospitality, Leisure, Sport and Tourism Education, 3*(1), 61–67.

Entwistle, A., & Entwistle, N. (1992). Experiences of understanding in revising for degree examinations. *Learning and Instruction, 2,* 1–22.

Fritz, C., Morris, P., Bjork, R., Gelman, R., & Wickens, T. (2000). When further learning fails: Stability and change following repeated presentation of text. *British Journal of Psychology, 91,* 493–511.

Fleming, N. (1999). Biases in marking students' written work: Quality? In: S. Brown & A. Glasner (Eds), *Assessment matters in higher education: Choosing and using diverse approaches* (pp. 83–92). Buckingham: The Society for Research in Higher Education and the Open University Press.

Gibbs, G. (1995). *Assessing student centred courses*. Oxford: The Oxford Centre for Staff and Learning Development.

Higher Education Funding Council for England. (2003). *Supporting higher education in further education colleges — A guide for tutors and lecturers*. Bristol: HEFCE.

Hills, J., Barron, E., Freeman, P., Adey, M., Robertson, G., & Murphy, R. (2003). *Dine out on work related learning*. Newcastle: University of Newcastle upon Tyne.

James, R., McInnis, C., & Devlin, M. (2002). *Assessing learning in Australian universities*. Victoria: Centre for the Study of Higher Education.

Johnson, J. (2003). Experiential learning in emerging markets: Leveraging the foreign experience. Conference paper at Emerging markets and business education: Trends and prospects conference, Atlanta, GA. November.

Kolb, D. A. (1984). *Experiential learning*. Englewood Cliffs, NJ: Prentice–Hall.

Miller, A., Imrie, B., & Cox, K. (1998). *Student assessment in higher education: A handbook for assessing performance*. London: Kogan Page Limited.

Mutch, A., & Brown, G. (2001). *Assessment: A guide for heads of department, LTSN generic centre assessment series number 2.* York: Learning and Teaching Support Network.

Newstead, S. (2004). The purposes of assessment. *Psychology Learning and Teaching, 3*(2), 97–101.

Page, T., Thomas, J., & Marshal, A. (1979). *International dictionary of education*. London: Kogan Page Limited.

Price, M., O'Donovan, B., & Rust, C. (2001). Strategies to develop students' understanding of assessment criteria and processes. In: C. Rust (Ed.), *Improving student learning: 8 improving student learning strategically*. Oxford: Oxford Centre for Staff and Learning Development.

Quality Assurance Agency. (2000). *Code of practice for the assurance of academic quality and standards in higher education. Section 6: Assessment of students*. Gloucester: Quality Assurance Agency.

Quality Assurance Agency. (2001). *Subject overview report: Hospitality, leisure, recreation, sport and tourism 2000 to 2001*. Gloucester: Quality Assurance Agency.

Race, P. (1995). The art of assessing 1. *The New Academic, 4,* 3. http://www.city.londonmet.ac.uk/deliberations/assessment/artof_fr.html.

Rust, C. (2001). *A briefing on assessment of large groups, LTSN generic centre assessment series number 12*. York: Learning and Teaching Support Network.

Rust, C. (2002). The impact of assessment on student learning — how can the research literature practically help to inform the development of departmental assessment strategies and learner-centred assessment practices? *Active Learning in Higher Education, 3*(2), 145–158.

Stefani, L., & Carroll, J. (2001). *A briefing on plagiarism. LTSN generic centre assessment series number 2*. York: Learning and Teaching Support Network.

Suskie, L. (2000). Fair assessment practices — giving students equitable opportunities to demonstrate learning, *AAHE Bulletin*, May.

Szego, J. (2003). Shock finding on Uni cheating. http://www.theage.com.au/articles/2003/01/06/1041566360939.html.

Yorke, M. (2001). *Assessment: A guide for senior managers, LTSN generic centre assessment series number 1*. York: Learning and Teaching Support Network.

Yorke, M. (2004). *Employability in higher education: What it is — what it is not. Learning and employability series number 1*. York: Learning and Teaching Support Network.

Chapter 24

Undergraduate Dissertations

Karen A. Smith

Introduction

The dissertation research project holds a revered place within the undergraduate curriculum. Taken in the final year, the dissertation is a student-centred course that encourages independent learning, supported by a supervisor. In tourism, it is normally a piece of academic research collecting and analysing primary and/or secondary data, although occasionally it may be an extended literature review. The dissertation course's main, and often only, summative assessment is a written thesis, varying in length between 5,000 and 15,000 words. The dissertation promotes a degree of freedom and independence not seen elsewhere in the curriculum. There is a more prolonged engagement with a topic, and the work is expected to be more 'in-depth'. Most students not only find the dissertation highly motivating and rewarding, but also challenging and a potential source of academic and practical concern. The dissertation is perceived by many students and academics, as well as potential employers, as a, or even *the*, defining element of an undergraduate degree. A dissertation is the distinguisher between an honours and an ordinary degree, and is frequently used as the discriminator for students on the borderline between degree classifications. The course exerts high demands on staff and student time, and is characterised by high student numbers, one-to-one contact, and a large assessing team. It highlights and exemplifies wider concerns across higher education (HE) over the reliability and consistency of course delivery and assessment. The dissertation course can also play an important role in developing and demonstrating the link between research and teaching.

This chapter will refer to some of the sources of assistance available for those undertaking dissertation research, but the purpose is not to provide a guide on 'how to' write, or supervise, a tourism dissertation, rather it aims to evaluate the key challenges that the dissertation assessment presents to students, educators, and institutions. The terminology of the student research project is potentially confusing with terms often used interchangeably, even within the same institution or school. In a British context, Clewes (1996) suggests 'project' to refer to first-degree research, 'dissertation' for masters degrees, reserving 'thesis' for higher research-only degrees. However, the terms may also be used differently

An International Handbook of Tourism Education
Copyright © 2005 by Elsevier Ltd.
All rights of reproduction in any form reserved
ISBN: 0-08-044667-1

internationally (Paltridge, 2002): in the USA the terms are reversed: master's students write theses and PhDs are dissertations. In Australia and New Zealand, 'thesis' is used for masters or doctoral level and 'dissertation' refers to research during the optional 'honours' year; the standard 3-year bachelors degree does not normally contain a research project component. This chapter focuses on undergraduate research projects and for consistency the term 'dissertation' is used throughout.

Research on the Dissertation

The majority of literature on student research projects is at the postgraduate level, particularly the doctoral thesis, but also within masters programmes. This chapter will draw on selected postgraduate texts as there are some commonalities between graduate and undergraduate dissertations: the research process, independent learning, and guidance from a supervisor. However, there are also significant differences in word length, the period of registration, and expected hours of study. In the sequential progress through bachelors–honours–masters–doctorate, research projects play a role in the progressive development of a deep learning cycle (James, 1998), but the undergraduate dissertation is often the first time a student is required to undertake an independent research study of this nature. The relative importance of the thesis component within the overall programme is different, forming a higher proportion of the overall classification as the qualification level increases. The undergraduate dissertation course is taken in tandem with other final year taught papers, presenting different challenges to the graduate student's exclusive focus on their research project. A supervisor is likely to have a larger number of undergraduate dissertations to supervise than at a higher degree level.

Most published research on the undergraduate dissertation is action-research by reflective HE practitioners, mainly in the UK, and is concerned with evaluating and improving pedagogical practices. The Learning, Teaching and Support Network (LTSN) Hospitality, Leisure, Sport and Tourism dissertation benchmarking project (2004) will provide data on current practice, but currently the only detailed research on undergraduate dissertations in these disciplines are in tourism (I'Anson & Smith, 2004) and sports science (Lane, Devonport, Milton, & Williams, 2003; also see Edwards & Thatcher, 2004, on research methods teaching). The LTSN also includes briefer case studies of dissertation practices in hospitality (Ball, 2004; Burgess, undated) and leisure and food (Lyons & Nield, 2004). Dissertations are widespread in undergraduate tourism programmes, although not universal. In Stuart-Hoyle's (2003) analysis of 30 UK tourism degrees, 22 included an individual research project as a core course; and in UK hospitality degrees the dissertation was compulsory in 13 out of 15 institutions (Ball, 2004).

Undergraduate dissertations are a feature across disciplines, and whilst projects may vary in scope and nature, there are key characteristics (Todd, Bannister, & Clegg, 2004) that enable tourism educators to learn from research in other disciplines, including: business and management (Clewes, 1996; Disney, 1998; Hand & Clewes, 2000; Sanderson, Clewes, & Hand, 1998; Saunders & Davis, 1998); social sciences and humanities (Hammick & Acker, 1998; Todd et al., 2004; Webster, Pepper, & Jenkins, 2000), including geography (Bell, 1997; Matthews, Limb, & Taylor, 1998; Pepper, Webster, & Jenkins, 2001) and environment-related courses (James, 1998); the arts (Ho, 2003); and the sciences (Heylings & Tariq, 2001; Stefani, Tariq, Heylings, & Butcher, 1997; Tariq, Stefani, Butcheer, Heylings, 1998; Zydney, Bennett, Shadid, & Bauer, 2002). Most research focuses on collecting data from faculty members on the supervision and marking processes; fewer studies include the students' perspective (Clewes, 1996; Heylings & Tariq, 2001; I'Anson & Smith, 2004; Stefani et al., 1997; Tariq et al., 1998; Todd et al., 2004), or other stakeholders (Clewes, 1996).

The Role of the Dissertation in the Undergraduate Curriculum

The purposes of the dissertation is multi-fold; objectives include developing and demonstrating analytical problem-solving skills, active learning through identification of a problem to be explored and completed, skills development for independent research, and application of academic knowledge (Hussey & Hussey, 1997). The role of the dissertation has evolved as HE has changed (Rowley & Slack, 2004): increased coursework assessment means that the dissertation is no longer the first, or only, time students are exposed to independent learning; the composition and learning styles of the student body is more diverse and students are subject to increasing pressures to balance work, study, and personal commitments; and the digitisation of information sources means literature is more accessible but students require more guidance on formulating research strategies and differentiating between both search mechanisms and the resulting sources. The dissertation is typically an expensive module to deliver (Lyons & Nield, 2004) and there have been pressures to abandon dissertations as being too costly in the context of providing mass undergraduate education (Todd et al., 2004). Nevertheless, its pedagogical value is still widely acknowledged. Clewes' research (1996) with heads of department, undergraduate course leaders, project supervisors, employers, and final year business studies students, both domestic and international, found that all groups indicated overwhelming support for the educational value of the project as an assessment method. All agreed that it was an extensive piece of work that promotes independence; and a majority of groups noted other benefits: it allows students choice and the opportunity to develop an area of interest in-depth; it has academic and practical value; and facilitates skills development including project planning, time management, stress management, and, for international students, language skills.

The dissertation course is normally weighted more heavily than other papers, and may be spread across more than one semester. The written component, the thesis itself, is commonly the main, or major, piece of summative assessment. This is likely to be substantially longer and more in-depth than any previous assignment; typically 10,000 words (Ball, 2004). Other elements may be incorporated into the assessment strategy for both formative and summative purposes. An initial research proposal enables the student to set out, and receive feedback on, the planned project; this is often the end-of-course assessment on a preparatory research methods paper. Given the length and complexity of the dissertation course, it is crucial to identify problems as early as possible and design appropriate intervention strategies to address them. Periodic interim reports are a common strategy (and may be included as a minor part of the final assessment), and the student's progress is also judged formatively through the ongoing supervisory process. An oral presentation, a *viva voce*, is rarely seen as desirable, or practical, at the undergraduate level.

The Students' Experience

Students see their responsibilities for the dissertation as being to complete a substantive piece of work, working largely independently, with reference to a supervisor when necessary (Stefani et al., 1997). They can find the dissertation highly motivating and satisfying; British social science students perceived the dissertation as rewarding and largely worthwhile in terms of:

- the subject knowledge acquired and skills developed (particularly in relation to working independently);
- its 'authenticity' as a vehicle for student learning and as a method of assessment…;
- its high intrinsic value, which extended beyond the degree course…; and
- the strong sense of ownership (and thus motivation) that it brought (Todd et al., 2004, p. 345).

The same students also articulated a range of concerns regarding the dissertation, including: difficulties in generating a workable research topic or question; uncertainty and worries over collecting primary research and gaining access to secondary materials; problems relating concepts and data to their research question; and time management and planning. Students generally find that the dissertation requires higher personal investment than other coursework and they put in more time than other courses of an equivalent credit value (Clewes, 1996). This may be because of personal interest and enthusiasm for their topic and the ownership they feel of the course, but the technical demands of the dissertation and the unfamiliarity with independent learning may also increase the input required (Todd et al., 2004).

The dissertation gives students the "responsibility for taking a research project all the way from conception to completion" (Lindsay, 1997, p. 14), and even with preparatory research methods training, students often feel they are 'working in the dark', with worries over getting started, difficulties with data collection, and problems writing-up (Hampson, 1994, cited in Clewes, 1996). As novice researchers, they may lack the ability or confidence to recognise, and respond to, the challenges and uncertainties of designing, conducting, and analysing research (I'Anson & Smith, 2004).

Easterby-Smith, Thorpe, and Lowe (1991, p. 18) articulate the difficult dilemma facing dissertation students: "It is very rare for students to have a clear focus from the outset of their research, and yet many find the lack of a clear focus is a major impediment to getting started". Students often find the freedom given to them to determine their own topic daunting. The topic has to be within the disciplinary framework and suitable for the course's learning outcomes, as well as sustaining the student's interest over the necessary period of time (Clark, Riley, Wilkie, & Wood, 1998). Table 1 illustrates popular topics for tourism dissertations, with examples; destination-based case studies are particularly prevalent, with common topics including tourism development, marketing, impacts, and sustainability. I'Anson and Smith (2004) established that motivations of tourism students for choosing a particular topic may be related to personal interest (including links to previous courses), career aspirations, ease of primary data collection (including contacts to provide access to data or organisations), and to a much lesser extent, ease of access to secondary data and/or the literature. Scale and manageability of topic is crucial; common problems with initial ideas are to be widely over-ambitious in scope (Bell,

Table 1: Analysis of BA (Hons) tourism management dissertation titles submitted at a UK university, 2000–2002 (n = 113).

Common Topics* (appearing two or more times), with examples of dissertations completed by University of Greenwich students	**No. of dissertations**
Tourism development An investigation into tourism development and community involvement in the Banda Islands, Eastern Indonesia	16
Marketing (including destination image, marketing communications) The use of Maori culture in the promotion of North Island, New Zealand	15
Impacts (socio-cultural, environmental, economic) Environmental impacts of adventure tourism: perceptions, attitudes and actions of adventure tour operators in Colorado An evaluation of local community views on the socio-cultural and economic impacts of all-inclusive tourism in the Dominican Republic	10
Sustainable tourism development The sustainable tourism development of Hiliadou Beach, Evia Island, Greece	8
Community involvement in tourism An analysis of the extent of local community involvement in tourism development in Canterbury	7
Human resource management and development Recruitment and selection processes for airline cabin crew	7
Visitor management Managing the balance between conservation management and visitor management in the New Forest	6
Information and Communications Technology UK travel insurance market — the internet opens new possibilities for smaller companies	5
Quality management An analysis of customer care practices in UK visitor attractions, with specific regard to training and development	4
Travel motivations and destination choice Attitudes and motivations of decision-makers within English secondary schools towards the purchase of team sports tours	3
Legislation impacts The impact of 1992 deregulation of air transport in Germany in terms of competition and price structure	3
Ethics and responsible tourism Ethics of tourism development — a case study of Tibet	3
Access/disability Disability and access in luxury hotels	3

Table 1: Continued.

Common Topics* (appearing two or more times), with examples of dissertations completed by University of Greenwich students	No. of dissertations
Common Research Contexts	
Destination-based case studies	60
Airlines (including five on 'low cost' airlines)	12
Visitor attractions	10
Hospitality industry	3
Travel agents	3
Tour operations	2
Other transport	2

*Topic areas are not discrete and, as the examples illustrate, many dissertation titles occur in multiple categories.

1997; Todd et al., 2004), focus on the latest 'hot' topic, or on contexts which are hard to access without the right work or life networks and experiences (Rowley & Slack, 2004).

Once an appropriate topic is chosen, there are a number of other barriers in the research process that students may experience. Access and ethical issues can arise due to the choice of topic (particularly sensitive topics, for example, sex tourism, Bell, 1997), the geographical and cultural location of the research (and access to that location for planning, research and follow-up work), the perceived status of the researchers as students, the type of respondents required for the research (for example, gaining access to organisations and dealing with confidential data; or undertaking research with vulnerable groups such as children, Matthews et al., 1998), and a lack of contacts or access to key gatekeepers. The analysis and writing up of the research is no less daunting. The growth of international students means many students find themselves writing their dissertation in a non-native language and potentially under different conventions and expectations of academic writing than they are used to (Ballard & Clanchy, 1997, cited in Paltridge, 2002).

With a heavy credit weighting on the dissertation course, and the thesis assessment, the pressure to perform well is high and can be a source of anxiety for students. Students undertaking sports science dissertations (Lane et al., 2003) identified six competencies needed for dissertation success and self-efficacy towards these factors was linked with subsequent performance. Confidence towards obtaining support and guidance from a dissertation supervisor, the ability to understand theory, and the ability to write the dissertation (including accurate referencing) were significantly correlated with positive performance in the assessment, whereas self-efficacy towards maintaining motivation, planning, and time management did not significantly correlate. Lane et al. suggest that a self-efficacy survey could identify those at risk of failing and enable the enactment of strategies to enhance performance.

Supporting the Dissertation Process

As an exercise in independent and deep learning, some of the challenges identified above are part of the "intellectual struggle [that] is an inherent part of the experience of autonomy"

(Todd et al., 2004, p. 346), and it is this different learning experience and the need to take responsibly for outcomes that is part of the perceived value of the dissertation. Nevertheless, students require a range of support to complete this major assessment. The introduction of independent and unstructured learning into earlier stages of the curriculum may help students cope with the autonomy required to successfully complete a dissertation (Todd et al., 2004). Other support includes research methods training, identification of useful resources, and supervision.

Research Methods Training

A detailed consideration of the development and teaching of research methods is beyond the scope of this chapter (see Brunt, 2003, for a resource guide); however, an important aim of these courses is to prepare students for their final year dissertation. Edwards and Thatcher (2004) propose a student-centred, tutor-led approach to teaching research methods, including providing opportunities for students to work through discipline-specific problems in seminars and encouraging students to identify dissertation topics early. A research proposal is an essential element in preparing students for the dissertation, providing the opportunity to evaluate and give feedback on a research idea early in the research process.

Dissertation Resources

For the student, and supervisor, there are a plethora of general research methods resources that can offer guidance on the research process and methodologies. There are also a number of handbooks and guides that deal with the design, development, and writing-up of a dissertation. Although the majority focus on higher degrees, particular doctoral thesis (Dedrick & Watson, 2002, provide a useful US-dominated reference list), there are a number of research texts (e.g. Clark et al., 1998; Finn, Elliott-White, & Walton, 2000; Jennings, 2001; Ryan, 1995; Veal, 1997) and dissertation guides (Foley, 1996; Poynter, 1993; Tourism Concern, 1996) targeted at tourism students. These texts are an invaluable resource to the novice researcher; usually ordered sequentially they lead the reader through the stages of the research process, identifying approaches, and evaluating strategies to successfully produce a dissertation in the required time period. However, guides tend to focus on the *process* of research with much less attention given to the writing itself or the content of individual chapters (Paltridge, 2002).

Supervision

> Undergraduate dissertation supervision is a highly demanding task, in which the supervisor plays a pivotal role in supporting students towards realising their potential. (Rowley & Slack, 2004, p. 180)

As a form of independent learning and assessment, the dissertation gives students unprecedented freedom of choice over the topic, research approach and design, and even the format of the written thesis. Conversely, students also get one-to-one contact with individual faculty members through the supervisory relationship. The supervision framework is expensive to operate; for example, between 6 and 20 hours of staff time is allocated to the supervision of each dissertation student in UK hospitality management degrees (Ball, 2004). Unlike graduate supervisory panels, undergraduates usually have no, or minimal, say over the allocation of their sole supervisor. Whilst matching dissertation topics and the supervisor's interests and expertise is desirable, achieving an even workload across the faculty is often a driving force (Hammick & Acker, 1998; Rowley & Slack, 2004). Training for undergraduate supervisors is uncommon and guidance difficult to access; the one-to-one nature of supervision sessions means they are often inaccessible for peer review, and whilst there is likely to be discussion over the assessment and marking of dissertations, the supervision process itself is rarely discussed (Rowley & Slack, 2004).

Rowley and Slack (2004, p. 179) identify seven roles that an undergraduate dissertation supervisor may potentially adopt:

- provider of subject expertise, and ready access to the literature on the subject;
- provider of access to research contexts (e.g. organisations);
- mentor, to support reflection on the process;
- director or project management to take the student through the steps in the process in a logical order, and to a time scale;
- advisor on research methodologies, both in relation to their selection, and appropriateness, and in relation to specific design issues;
- signpost or teacher assisting with access to the literature; and
- editor, supporting structuring and writing of the dissertation.

What students want most from a supervisor is guidance (Stefani et al., 1997), both on the subject area and managing the dissertation process, as well as motivation, encouragement, and constructive feedback on work and progress (Todd et al., 2004).

A range of factors will influence the nature, and success, of the student–supervisor relationship, including: institutional policies and frameworks; the supervisory style and the student's learning style; both parties' enthusiasm, interest and skills in the topic and research approach; and differences or similarities in primary dimensions of diversity such as gender, ethnicity, and cultural background. There is no one 'right' way to supervise and supervisors need to be flexible in their approach to reflect the individuality of the student, the topic, and themselves. There will be different beliefs, motivations, abilities and learning styles, and the direct one-to-one contact of the dissertation can provide the opportunity to tailor supervision to individual student's learning needs. However, identifying the diverse needs of students, and designing and implementing appropriate intervention strategies can be challenging within the truncated length of an undergraduate dissertation, particularly when supervising a large number of students. The independent nature of the dissertation places an onus on the student, and lack of engagement can be frustrating and concerning for a supervisor (Ho, 2003). The amount and structure of contacts with students will differ; some students are happy with low levels of direct contact (Todd et al., 2004) whilst others want more formality. Each student is likely to respond differently to similar direction, for example over time management strategies (Ho, 2003), and the supervisor has to adapt accordingly. Todd et al. (2004) found that key points in the dissertation process where students felt they benefited from supervisor intervention were: establishing the parameters of their proposed research enquiry; selecting an appropriate methodology; and practical advice on structuring and editing the final work to supplement written assessment guidelines.

Traditionally, dissertation supervisions have been on a one-to-one basis, however, dissatisfactions with this approach include: its inefficiency and cost implications, especially with increased student numbers; the repetition of the same information and guidance to each student individually (at least in the initial stages); and the potential for variation in the quality of supervision and consistency of advice. It also enhances the individualistic, and isolating, nature of the dissertation experience, giving little opportunity for support between students, or the chance to share experiences (Clewes, 1996). Increasingly, there are advocates for different approaches, for both pedagogical and practical reasons.

Encouraging, or requiring, students to form peer support groups or action learning sets involving a tutor can offer an alternative, or parallel approach, to traditional supervision. Learning sets can facilitate student learning about the technical content of the project, the process of doing research, and about themselves (Sanderson et al., 1998); students can learn from the supervisor and each other; and self-efficacy and confidence can be enhanced through observing others perform successfully (Lane et al., 2003). Issues for supervisors include (Sanderson et al., 1998): the life cycle and individuality of each learning set; the power and role of the tutor; the time input required (from tutors and students); the need to allocate time to learning about the sets and their operation (e.g. setting ground rules); and, not least, the personal satisfaction and empowerment it can bring, to both students and tutors. This approach does not suit the learning style of all students (Sanderson et al., 1998), and in Todd et al.'s study (2004) whilst most students had interacted informally with their peers regarding the dissertation, they found it was of limited help because of the individual nature of the task. Group seminars may work well at the beginning of the dissertation process, but as students advance with their research, one-to-one supervisions can give more individualised, focused support (Burgess, undated). Lyons and Nield (2004) suggest a 'health practice' approach, with each student having a named supervisor within a subject team of supervisors, but with the opportunity of being referred to other specialists for individual or group consultations.

IT and CMC (computer-mediated communication) are also able to support and enhance the student–supervisor relationship. At its most basic this may be email communication to supplement one-to-one meetings, but the potential is much greater, including the incorporation of an online dimension to learning sets (Edwards, 2002).

Assessing the Dissertation

The dissertation is an example of a summative assessment tool and good practice regarding assessment procedures are particularly relevant given the significance of the dissertation to the student's overall programme. As with supervision, there is little formal staff training for the dissertation marking process; Hand and Clewes (2000) found most staff learnt by 'doing it'. Their qualitative research with dissertation markers revealed three common criteria for assessing dissertations: content (namely the relation of theory to practice), research process (understanding of methodological issues and evidence of data collection), and presentation (including referencing and keeping a narrative thread). Webster et al. (2000) and Saunders and Davis (1998) each identify nine, broadly similar, assessment criteria (see Table 2).

Table 2: Comparison of common dissertation assessment criteria.

Areas of assessment	Subareas of assessment	Potential common dissertation assessment criteria
Saunders and Davis (1998, p. 163) *Department of Business and Finance (UK)*		**Webster, Pepper and Jenkins (2000, p. 75)** *Seven departments in a School of Social Science and Law (UK)*
Task definition and approach 25%	Objectives/rationale	Clearly define the problem studied and questions to be asked and investigated
	Approach/process	Use and show an understanding of appropriate methods
Literature review, findings and evaluation 50%	Literature review	Put into context by showing understanding of the disciplinary perspective and relevance of the study to the discipline
	Analysis of material	Show ability to analyse primary and/or secondary material
	Synthesis/evaluations	
	Conclusions/ recommendations	Draw conclusions based on understanding of evidence and material gathered
	Creativity/reflection	Show evidence of critical thinking about the problem, about underlying assumptions, about options and values encountered.
Communication of ideas and presentation 25%	Coherence of argument	Argue and discuss clearly and coherently (choosing a structure that helps to do this)
	Format and language	Write clearly and succinctly Properly cite sources and reference them

Assessment criteria need to be published, explained, and applied to ensure equity, consistency, and transparency. Saunders and Davis (1998) provide a detailed example of good practice for the dissertation procedure, and specific criteria, and grade descriptors, for their nine subareas of assessment. Worryingly, both Hand and Clewes (2000) and Webster et al. (2000) identified potentially serious problems concerning the use, meaning, and application of assessment criteria by staff. Published criteria were not used consistently by markers, terms used to describe criteria were often undefined (and could be interpreted differently by different assessors), the relative importance of different criteria was not necessarily communicated to students, indeed, markers often applied their own interpretations of which criteria were more, or less, important overall (Hand & Clewes, 2000), and some brought in additional criteria which they considered personally significant (Webster et al., 2000). Saunders and Davis's (1998) example includes specified marks for each of their three main assessment areas (see Table 2); within these, weightings for the subareas are left to the marker's discretion, meaning a degree of academic judgement is retained, different approaches can be accommodated (e.g. literature-based compared to investigative research), and creative and individualistic approaches by students can still be rewarded. As *independent* projects the range and variety of approaches and outputs are more diverse than most other forms of assessment and criteria need to be flexible enough not to penalise the unconventional or 'maverick' dissertation (Pepper et al., 2001).

The blind double-marking of dissertations is standard practice. The large number of markers brings logistical challenges for course co-ordinators and administrators, and submission at the end of the final year means staff are often working to tight deadlines with large workloads. The (unequal) power relationship between staff and student is reinforced as normally the supervisor is also one of the assessors (Hammick & Acker, 1998) and the student's previous performance can bring potential bias, in essence marking the supervisory process rather than the final piece of work (Hand & Clewes, 2000).

In a comparative marking experiment, Saunders and Davis (1998) found that the longer the time spent assessing a dissertation, the lower the grade it received; for fairness, they recommend that marking one dissertation should take between one and two hours. Overall, Hand and Clewes (2000) found a broad equivalence of grades between first and second markers, however, there was a natural tendency for convergence overall, sometimes influenced by the seniority of one staff member, or deferring to the supervisor who 'knows the student'. They, and their colleague Disney's research (1998), suggests that often the markers use the mean as compromise mark ('splitting the difference'), which satisfies no one. A third marker can be introduced, for example when the overall marks differ by more than 10% or the markers disagree (Saunders & Davis, 1998), and the external examiner plays an important role for both benchmarking and for dissertations on the borderline between two classes of degree. Disney (1998) recommends an independent marking procedure, completely removing the supervisor from the double-marking process; this gained general support from both staff and students who felt that supervisory debate over the academic and practical issues could be more open as both knew it would not affect the final grade.

Conclusions

The dissertation is an established form of assessment and there is still a great deal to recommend it. It offers students a unique opportunity to research a topic of their choice in-depth, it develops both academic and practical skills, and engenders independent and deep learning. It is in the dissertation and research methods courses where students are made particularly aware of staffs' research interests, and this enhances their learning experiences and research skills (Jordan, 2004). Given the student, and staff, input into the dissertation, its credit rating needs to reflect this, with enough weight to enable in-depth and rigorous research, and enough time to allow students to develop both intellectual and practical skills, not least, the ability to work independently.

As with other aspects of the curriculum and assessment, an increasingly diverse student body requires support from both supervisor and institution. For example, part-time students have to deal with different time management and planning issues than full-time students; students working in a non-native language have different expectations of the dissertation and require specific preparation and support (Paltridge, 1997); and students with disabilities again have specific needs which need to be accommodated in curriculum design and support (LTSN for Geography, Earth and Environmental Sciences, 2003). Supervision requires staff to adopt a range of roles to guide the student through the research process and dissertation production. Students exhibit a range of different learning styles and abilities to respond to the deep and independent learning required by the dissertation. Whilst some students desire greater levels of formality and structure (Todd et al., 2004), others will be happier completely embracing the autonomy of the dissertation, rarely seeking or wanting supervision. Supervisors need to be flexible enough to adapt and serve these differing demands, but also be alert for the student who is not engaged because of intellectual or personal problems. Either formally or unofficially, the supervisor is often the pastoral tutor for final year students, the dissertation giving the opportunity for ongoing support. For supervisory relationships that break down, including a mismatch of research areas or epistemologies, institutional procedures need to be in place to ensure the student has access to support elsewhere in the school or university.

Given the resources allocated to the dissertation, training for undergraduate supervisors is seriously under-developed. Whilst the closed nature of one-to-one sessions does not easily lend itself to peer observation, staff shadowing is an opportunity to share good practice of the supervision process, as well as the assessment and moderation of marks. Pedagogically and practically there are strong reasons for adopting a more flexible and varied approach to the format of supervision. Whilst the allocation of a named supervisor, ideally with subject-specific expertise, remains central, there is the opportunity to combine traditional one-to-one sessions with formal learning sets, or more informal peer support groups, didactic teaching through lectures or seminars on particular methodological or practical elements, and online support through CMC.

Whilst the written thesis is likely to remain the cornerstone of the undergraduate dissertation course, other elements of its assessment schedule could include a research proposal (ideally linked to research methods training), interim reports, notes from supervisory meetings, a reflective log or diary, and, though often less practical, an oral presentation. Lyons and Nield (2004) suggest the varied needs and interests of students can be captured by adapting the dissertation to encompass different processes and outputs, for example: a traditional dissertation, a consultancy report, or publishable articles for specified refereed journals. Requiring periodic progress reports is one strategy to help students cope with the daunting task of researching and writing the dissertation, and the dangers of delaying getting started. Ongoing monitoring of progress and requiring submission of reports or drafts of work is also important in combating plagiarism.

The understanding and application of assessment criteria by supervisors is often variable, and can change as their level of experience, and the role of the dissertation, develops. Students themselves are also likely to interpret criteria differently. Periodic revisiting of assessment criteria enhances fairness and quality standards, and involving staff in the development of criteria fosters ownership, confidence, and understanding, helping to ensure that they are interpreted and applied consistently (Saunders & Davis, 1998).

To retain a quality dissertation experience and outcome for students, supervisors, and institutions there needs to be awareness of the changing context within which the dissertation assessment operates. Increased demands on both students and faculty are challenging the existence of the dissertation, however by thinking creatively about approaches to dissertation preparation, support and assessment, the strengths of the dissertation can be retained and it can be a highlight of the undergraduate degree for all involved.

References

Ball, S. (2004). Research and teaching connections in hospitality management education. *LINK 9*, 5–6. Available: http://www.hlst.ltsn.ac.uk/resources/publications.html.

Bell, D. (1997). Sex lives and audiotape: Geography, sexuality and undergraduate dissertations. *Journal of Geography in Higher Education*, *21*(3), 411–418.

Brunt, P. (2003). *Teaching research methods in hospitality and tourism*. LTSN HLST Resource Guide. Available: http://www.hlst.ltsn.ac.uk/projects/specialists/brunt.html.

Burgess, C. (undated) *Managing undergraduate dissertations*. LTSN HLST Case Study. Available: http://www.hlst.ltsn.ac.uk/resources/cases/case4.html.

Clark, M. A., Riley, M., Wilkie, E., & Wood, R. C. (1998). *Researching and writing dissertations in hospitality and tourism*. London: International Thomson Business Press.

Clewes, D. (1996). Multiple perspectives on the undergraduate project experience. *Innovations — The Learning and Teaching Journal of Nottingham Trent University*, *1*, 27–35.

Dedrick, R. F., & Watson, F. (2002). Mentoring needs of female, minority and international graduate students: A content analysis of academic research guides and related printed material. *Mentoring and Tutoring*, *10*(3), 275–289.

Disney, J. (1998). Independent dissertation marking. *Innovations — The Learning and Teaching Journal of Nottingham Trent University*, *3*, 89–93.

Easterby-Smith, M., Thorpe, R., & Lowe, A. (1991). *Management research: An introduction*. London: Sage Publications.

Edwards, D. F., & Thatcher, J. (2004). A student-centred tutor-led approach to teaching research methods. *Journal of Further and Higher Education*, *28*(2), 195–206.

Edwards, R. (2002). Enhancing learning support for masters dissertation students: A role for action learning online? *BEST conference 2002*, Edinburgh. Available: http://www.business.ltsn.ac.uk/publications.

Finn, M., Elliott-White, M., & Walton, M. (2000). *Tourism and leisure research methods: Data collection, analysis, and interpretation*. London: Pearson Education Limited.

Foley, M. (1996). *Doing your dissertation: A guide for students in tourism, leisure and hospitality management*. London: Chapman & Hall.

Hammick, M., & Acker, S. (1998). Undergraduate research supervision: A gendered analysis. *Studies in Higher Education*, *23*(3), 335–347.

Hand, L., & Clewes, D. (2000). Making the difference: An investigation of the criteria used for assessing undergraduate dissertations in a business school. *Assessment and Evaluation in Higher Education*, *25*(1), 5–21.

Heylings, D. J. A., & Tariq, V. N. (2001). Reflections and feedback on learning: A strategy for undergraduate project work. *Assessment and Evaluation in Higher Education*, *26*(2), 153–164.

Ho, B. (2003). Time management of final year undergraduate English projects: Supervisees' and the supervisor's coping strategies. *System*, *31*, 231–245.

Hussey, J., & Hussey, R. (1997). *Business research: A practical guide for undergraduate and postgraduate students*. London: Macmillan Press.

I'Anson, R. A., & Smith, K. A. (2004). Undergraduate research projects and dissertations: Issues of topic selection, access and data collection amongst tourism management students. *Journal of Hospitality, Leisure, Sport and Tourism Education*, *3*(1), 19–32.

James, P. (1998). Progressive development of deep learning skills through undergraduate and post-graduate dissertations. *Educational Studies, 24*(1), 95–105.

Jennings, G. (2001). *Tourism research.* Sydney: John Wiley and Sons.

Jordan, F. (2004). Linking teaching and research in hospitality, leisure, sport and tourism: Exploring the student perspective. *LINK 9,* 20–22. Available: http://www.hlst.ltsn.ac.uk/resources/publications.html.

Lane, A. M., Devonport, T. J., Milton, K. E., & Williams, L. C. (2003). Self-efficacy and dissertation performance amongst sport students. *Journal of Hospitality, Leisure, Sport and Tourism Education, 2*(2), 59–66.

Lindsay, J. M. (1997). *Techniques in human geography.* London: Routledge.

LTSN Geography, Earth and Environmental Sciences (2003). *Learning support for disabled students undertaking fieldwork and related activities.* Available: http://www2.glos.ac.uk/gdn/publ.htm.

LTSN Hospitality, Leisure, Sport and Tourism (2004). *Learning, teaching and assessment benchmarking project — dissertations.* Results available from: http://www.hlst.ltsn.ac.uk/projects/benchmarking.html.

Lyons, H., & Nield, K. (2004). New approaches to embedding investigation and research in the curriculum at Sheffield Hallam University. *LINK 9,* 5–6. Available http://www.hlst.ltsn.ac.uk/resources/publications.html.

Matthews, H., Limb, M., & Taylor, M. (1998). The geography of children: Some ethical and methodological considerations for project and dissertation work. *Journal of Geography in Higher Education, 22*(3), 311–325.

Paltridge, B. (1997). Thesis and dissertation writing: Preparing ESL students for research. *English for Specific Purposes, 16*(1), 61–70.

Paltridge, B. (2002). Thesis and dissertation writing: An examination of published advice and actual practice. *English for Specific Purposes, 21,* 125–143.

Pepper, D., Webster, F., & Jenkins, A. (2001). Benchmarking in Geography: Some implications for assessing dissertations in the undergraduate curriculum. *Journal of Geography in Higher Education, 25*(1), 23–35.

Poynter, J. M. (1993). *How to research and write a thesis in hospitality and tourism: A step-by-step guide for college students.* New York: Wiley.

Rowley, J., & Slack, F. (2004). What is the future for undergraduate dissertations? *Education and Training, 46*(4), 176–181.

Ryan, C. (1995). *Researching tourist satisfaction: Issues, concepts, problems.* London: Routledge.

Sanderson, P., Clewes, D., & Hand, L. (1998). Action learning with business school undergraduates: Three tutors use learning sets for project support. *Assessment and Evaluation in Higher Education, 23*(1), 33–42.

Saunders, M. N. K., & Davis, S. M. (1998). The use of assessment criteria to ensure consistency of marking: Some implications for good practice. *Quality Assurance in Education, 6*(3), 162–171.

Stefani, L. A., Tariq, V. N., Heylings, D. J. A., & Butcher, A. C. (1997). A comparison of tutor and student conceptions of undergraduate research project work. *Assessment and Evaluation in Higher Education, 22*(3), 271–288.

Stuart-Hoyle, M. (2003). The purpose of undergraduate tourism programmes in the United Kingdom. *Journal of Hospitality, Leisure, Sport and Tourism Education, 2*(1), 49–74.

Tariq, V. N., Stefani, L. A. J., Butcher, A. C., & Heylings, D. J. A. (1998). Developing a new approach to the assessment of project work. *Assessment and Evaluation in Higher Education, 23*(3), 221–240.

Todd, M., Bannister, P., & Clegg, S. (2004). Independent inquiry and the undergraduate dissertation: Perceptions and experiences of final-year Social Science students. *Assessment and Evaluation in Higher Education, 29*(3), 335–355.

Tourism Concern (1996). *Writing your dissertation on sustainable tourism*. London, Tourism Concern.

Veal, A. J. (1997). *Research methods for leisure and tourism: A practical guide*. Second edition. London: Pitman Publishing.

Webster, F., Pepper, D., & Jenkins, A. (2000). Assessing the undergraduate dissertation. *Assessment and Evaluation in Higher Education*, *25*(1), 71–80.

Zydney, A. L., Bennett, J. S., Shadid, A., & Bauer, K. W. (2002). Faculty perspectives regarding the undergraduate experience in science and engineering. *Journal of Engineering Education*, *July*, 291–297.

Chapter 25

Cultural Issues in Learning

Paul Barron

Introduction

The education of full fee paying international students has increased in popularity and importance in the university sector of most Western nations. Indeed, international education is one of Australia's largest industries, and the fees generated by international students are becoming increasingly important to the budgetary health of most Australian universities. While the student body is becoming more diverse, traditionally, many international students that study for a qualification from one of the major English speaking destination (MESD) countries originate from Asia and a majority of these students are of Chinese nationality or ethnicity, or share a common Confucian culture heritage. While there is a growing body of literature that explores learning issues of international, particularly Asian, students involved in western style higher education, there are examples in the literature that promote stereotypical views of the strengths and weaknesses of such students. Indeed, previous research has highlighted that these students have unique needs and requirements and experience a range of learning issues and problems associated with the move to a western education environment. This chapter reports on significant research undertaken in Australia that examined the learning style preferences and associated issues and problems of international students studying hospitality and tourism management. This research analysed the preferred learning style of 514 international students, examined such students' learning experiences, identified differences in educational approaches and highlighted specific problems and issues regarding such students learning experiences. Particular attention is paid to those students who are of a Confucian Heritage Culture (CHC) and this chapter compares the preferred learning style of such students with other international students studying hospitality and tourism management in Australia.

   While the author recognises the danger of highlighting, concentrating on and potentially adding to the often misleading stereotypical image of this group of students, such concentration is felt necessary as this group often forms the majority of international students studying in MESD universities. Indeed, the fact that most, if not all, MESD universities who attract international students provide some form of specific or specialised

An International Handbook of Tourism Education
Copyright © 2005 by Elsevier Ltd.
All rights of reproduction in any form reserved
ISBN: 0-08-044667-1

orientation (see for example, the University of Queensland International Students Orientation, 2005) to academic life at the start of the student's university career would suggest that universities themselves recognise that such students come from very different academic backgrounds. It might therefore be concluded that in order to succeed, some form of academic adjustment is required on the part of the student (Barron, 2002a). However, regardless of the provision of specific orientation sessions and an understanding on the part of the university, it is suggested that it is the international student who is required to fit into and cope with the alien teaching methods common in MESD university classrooms. The attitude of 'our way' being best appears to prevail even in the increasingly multi-cultural and multi-national classroom. It is therefore the aim of this research to further highlight the specific learning problems and issues of an important subsector of international students and to present strategy whereby the educational experience of such students might be approached in a more empathetic manner by western universities.

International Students Studying in Australia

During the past decade, education has developed to be Australia's eighth largest export industry, earning AUD$3.149 billion in export income in session 1998/1999 (Davis, Olsen, & Bohm, 2000) and contributing AUD$4.2 billion to the Australian economy in 2001 (Bohm, Davies, Meares, & Pearce, 2002). In comparison to domestic students who pay tuition fees through a combination of government subsidy and personal contribution, invariably international students pay full tuition fees (roughly double the domestic student fee) to the educational institution. As a whole, in 2000, these international students contributed an estimated AUD$900 million annually to university budgets in Australia (Davis et al., 2000).

Considering the potential income opportunities for Australian universities, it is not surprising that they are keen to attract and retain international students. Many are often explicit in their desire to increase their proportion of full fee paying international students. Consequently, higher education institutions in Australia are adopting strategies that will result in international students undertaking tertiary study at that particular university. Indeed, the drive to attract international students is often quantified and translated to university, faculty and school strategic objectives.

The recruitment strategies adopted by many Australian universities appear to be successful as international student enrolment at Australian higher education institutions has grown significantly over the past decade. Australia now ranks third behind the United States and the United Kingdom as the destination of choice for international students (Meares, 2003; IDP Education Australia, 2000). The number of international students studying Australian programs in Australia more than doubled from 46,600 to 108,600 students in the period 1992–2000 (Maslen, 1999; IDP Education Australia, 2000). This figure has continued to rise with some 115,365 international students studying for Australian higher education qualifications in semester one 2003 (IDP Australia, 2003). While Australia trails both the UK and the USA in terms of international student enrolments, the annual growth rate of international students studying in Australian higher education institutions at 15.3% outstripped the growth rate of both the USA and the UK, at 4.9% and

3.5%, respectively, during the period 1997–2003 (Meares, 2003). Currently, more than 13% of the total student enrolment in Australia originates overseas (IDP Australia, 2003).

Future demand for Australian education appears strong with the International Development Program (IDP Australia, 2003) considering the forecasted 7.6 million students who will be studying overseas by 2025, almost 1 million will be studying for Australian qualifications, either onshore in Australia, by distance learning, or at an offshore campus of an Australian institution (Bohm et al., 2002).

Traditionally, the majority of international students who study for an Australian qualification originate from Asia with Malaysia, Singapore, Hong Kong, Indonesia and more recently China, contributing two thirds in excess of the total overseas student enrolment (Davis et al., 2000; IDP Australia, 2003). Asia is forecast to continue to represent the major source countries for international students in the future and it is forecast that students from Asia will represent 92% of the total number of international students studying in Australia by 2025 (IDP Australia, 2003). Regardless of nationality, it has been found that the majority of Asian students who study in Australian higher education institutions are of Chinese nationality or Chinese ethnicity, or originate from countries that share a common Confucian tradition, such as Vietnam, Japan and Korea (Bohm et al., 2002). This group of students is commonly referred to as CHC students (Lee, 1999; Barron, 2004).

While generalizations about cultural orientation are rarely accurate in terms of the individual or in terms of subgroups within that culture, there are abundant examples in the cross-cultural educational literature which promote stereotypical views of the strengths and weaknesses of CHC students. Viewed positively, CHC students studying overseas are considered as being high achievers, diligent note takers, well disciplined, hard working, quiet, respectful of lecturing staff and good attendees (Barron, 2002a; Volet & Renshaw, 1999; Burns, 1991; Bradley & Bradley, 1984). This positive view is, however, tempered by a more negative perspective of CHC students; a view that continues to remain widespread among Australian academic staff (Volet & Renshaw, 1999). The main criticism focussed towards CHC students is a perceived propensity to rote learn (Samuelowicz, 1987; Kember & Gow, 1990) and an assumption that the CHC student does not understand material, but merely commits it to memory in order to access it at some later time. Further criticisms include viewing the teacher and/or text as the definitive source of knowledge and lacking in the skills of self-management, which results in an expectation and/or requirement of identifying specific reading for a subject (Burns, 1991; Ballard & Clanchy, 1994; Samuelowicz, 1987), being passive, quiet and non-participative in class (Kember & Gow, 1990; Ballard & Clanchy, 1991; Ramsay, Barker, & Jones, 1999).

The Unique Needs of International Students

In conjunction with the drive to attract the ever-increasing number of CHC students to study in Australia, universities invest substantial funds in a variety of recruitment methods. Such is the importance placed on this market that most universities have designated international departments responsible for marketing and recruitment, the administration associated with processing applications and the orientation and continued pastoral care of international students. Consequently, it would seem appropriate that once international students have been attracted to a university, initiatives would be undertaken to ensure that the student has an enjoyable and successful learning experience (Kennedy, 1995; Yanhong Li & Kaye, 1998). Indeed it has been suggested that institutions should provide "holistic support services for (international) students" (Jennings, 2001, p. 50). However, a criticism faced by western universities is that great emphasis is placed on the initial attracting of international students but that they are ignored thereafter (Niven, 1987; Kennedy, 1995). Recent studies have indicated students' frustration and disappointment regarding the level of support received by CHC students in comparison to the level of fees being paid (Moon, 2003).

The needs and requirements of CHC students have been identified as being concerned with two general areas. First, it is contended that CHC students will experience issues concerned with living in a foreign country, such as dislocation, culture shock, accommodation problems and homesickness (Ballard & Clanchy, 1991). Second, it has been suggested that CHC students have been identified as experiencing issues and problems concerning the overall learning experience. In particular, it has been found that such students appear to adopt a reflector learning style preference that is at odds with other international students who tend to adopt an activist learning style preference (Barron, 2004). Essentially, this means that CHC students prefer to learn in more passive situations where they have the opportunity to stand back from, and observe activities in order to make carefully considered decisions. Such students will react against situations where they are required to make quick decisions and are forced into the limelight. In addition, these students have been found to be lacking in certain study skills and display classroom behaviour that is very different to other students in western classrooms. Figure 1 presents results from data collected that aimed to determine international student's preferred learning styles. In all, some 514 international students from 52 different countries took part in this research, approximately half of whom identified themselves as being of Chinese nationality or ethnicity, or from Korea, Vietnam or Japan. It can be seen that both groups achieved very similar scores for theorist and pragmatist learning styles. However, as this chart brings together both groups of participants' results on the same scale, the level of difference between the critical reflector

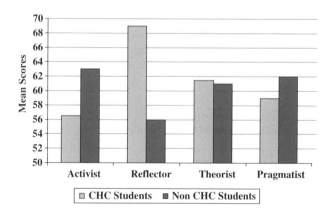

Figure 1: Comparison of learning style preferences of CHC and other international students studying hospitality and tourism management at a selection of universities in Australia.

learning style preferences and activist learning style preferences are brought into sharp relief. This figure clearly shows that CHC students have a preference for the reflector learning style and appear to least prefer the activist learning style preference. On the other hand, the other international students who took part in this research appear to prefer an activist learning style preference and least prefer to adopt a reflector learning style preference. Thus it might be stated that CHC students and other international students studying in Australia have opposite learning style preferences.

The situation concerning CHC student's learning style preferences is further complicated when the learning style preferences of Australian domestic students is considered. A variety of commentators have found that domestic students studying in western universities also tend to adopt an activist learning style preference (Barron, 2002b; Lashley, 1999). This would suggest that in a typically diverse Australian classroom, the learning style preferences of those students sharing a common Confucian heritage will be at odds with not only the domestic students in the classroom but also with their other international peers. Consequently, it has been suggested that CHC students' specific needs and concerns should be recognised and dealt with separately from the needs and concerns of other international students (Barron, 2004; Yanhong Li & Kaye, 1998).

Learning Issues and Problems of CHC Students Studying Overseas

It has been suggested that it is normal for the CHC student to experience stress throughout their home country education (Chan, 1999). This sensation is subsequently accentuated by gaining a position at an institution overseas and it would appear that CHC students who undertake university-level study in one of the MESD countries experience a range of issues and problems associated with their education. When compared to their domestic counterparts, CHC students themselves suggest that they feel incompetent across a range of study skills, including time management, revision, English language and examination skills (Burns, 1991). Such students have also reported themselves as experiencing extreme difficulty joining in classroom discussion and consequently experienced various physical and psychological stress symptoms as a result of their western education (Chan, 1999; Robertson, Line, Jones, & Thomas, 2000). Indeed, voluntary discussion in the classroom situation is alien to most CHC students (Choi, 1997). Consequently, it has been suggested that these feelings of stress are, in part, brought about by the different approach to learning that CHC students have to adopt when studying overseas (Chan, 1999) and it has been suggested that CHC students experience difficulty in employing a learning strategy other than memorising (Robertson et al., 2000). The concept of participating in group work and giving presentations to peers has been found to be a key concern for many CHC students (Barron, 2004).

CHC students also appear to experience issues regarding their relationship with the teacher. It has been suggested that, in Australia, CHC students are required to get used to a more casual student/teacher relationship where the student is required to take the initiative, for example, regarding meeting with academic staff as opposed to being told specifically when a member of staff will be available (Choi, 1997). Consequently, it has been found that many students decide not to communicate with the academic as such an action might be considered rude due to the perceived status of the academic and the excessive regard for authority held by the students (Moon, 2003).

When compared to local students CHC students experience additional concerns and problems at a more extreme level (Mullins, Quintrell, & Hancock, 1995), including worry and feeling scared (Ramsay et al., 1999). In order to combat these feelings and overcome difficulties in class, many international students adopt such coping strategies as working harder, undertaking additional reading and cooperating with other international students regarding note taking and study sessions.

The stressful situation in which these students find themselves has been found to be compounded by three issues. First, these students have to contend with the family pressure to succeed (Yee, 1989). Second, by the lack of understanding that western educators have regarding the behaviour of CHC students in the classroom and their overall approach to learning (Chan, 1999), and finally, that many students are involved in racist incidents both on and off campus (Robertson et al., 2000).

Lecturing staff responses tended to echo many of the concerns of students but with different emphases. The staff considered that CHC students were reluctant to become involved in, and contribute to, class discussion. In addition, the CHC students' difficulty with the concept of there not being one correct answer to a question was highlighted. Other concerns expressed by lecturers were the CHC students' reliance on books, not taking responsibility for their own learning and not understanding the concept of plagiarism (Robertson et al., 2000). The problem associated with CHC students not being aware of the requirement of acknowledging other people's intellectual property within their assignments and the concept of plagiarism has been identified in earlier Australian studies (Watson, 1999).

It is reasonable to expect that all students will experience an initial period of anxiety and stress associated with university study. However, it would appear that many CHC students' problems increased in both number and intensity as the students progressed through their program (Mullins et al., 1995). It might therefore be suggested that when a university expends resources attracting lucrative international students to study their programs, it would be appropriate that some responsibility for the overall experience of those students be shouldered by the host university. That the university provides a supportive atmosphere from both an academic and social perspective will go some way to ensuring that international students will continue to come to that university. It might be argued that a successful student will communicate their satisfaction concerning their educational experience to friends and relations who, in turn, may decide to pursue study in that particular university or country (Mullins et al., 1995; Huang & Brown, 1996). It would thus seem appropriate for Australian (and other MESD) universities to adopt strategies that would make an international student's learning experience as positive as possible.

In order to determine learning issues and problems specific to CHC students, focus group interviews were conducted at four tertiary education providers of hospitality and/or hospitality and tourism management in Australia. The decision to utilise focus groups as the main means of data collection was to encourage participants who might naturally be quiet to naturally react to one another (Priest, 1996). Indeed, the research objectives and the group of participants chosen were deemed entirely suited to the synergistic and dynamic nature of focus groups (Morgan, 1997). In addition, Ticehurst and Veal (1999) suggested that it is most appropriate to use focus groups when a particular group is important to a study, but is so small in number that members of that group would not be adequately represented in a general survey, for example, in the case when people of a specific culture or ethnic group form the focus of a study.

The focus group interviews were recorded and transcribed and the data were analysed *via* content analysis which is described by Neuman (1997, p. 272) as "a technique for gathering and analysing the content of text". Content analysis allowed the researcher to probe into and discover content in a meaningful way and allows the researcher the opportunity to compare content across a variety of texts. In this instance, content analysis allowed the researcher to compare content across the four focus groups conducted in this study. The content was then analysed using quantitative techniques and the data were able to be displayed *via* charts. In order to develop a more sophisticated data set, the results were weighted thus allowing the researcher to identify the overall importance of the participants' comments.

Results and Discussion

Participants were asked to reflect on what different study approaches they have had to adopt in order to successfully complete subjects at their Australian institution. Figure 2 gives an overview of participants' responses. Respondents made comments regarding the change of emphasis from memorising to understanding. Indeed, the most common response concerned the students' new found focus on understanding the material

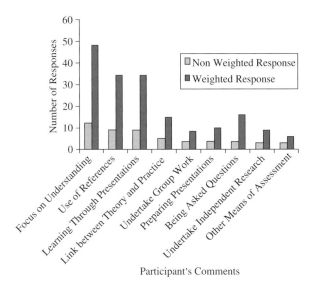

Figure 2: Non-weighted and weighted responses to question: What different study approaches have you had to adopt in order to successfully complete subjects/courses here in Australia?

presented. One participant stated that "I've had to change because well, usually I just study and memorise things but now I have to digest (the material) myself and not just memorise but make it more clear".

In addition to a realisation regarding the need to understand the material presented, this comment would also suggest that there has been a perceptible shift in the responsibility for learning, with this respondent clearly understanding his requirement for recognising the material. This shift towards understanding the material presented in class also appeared to be important with participants in all four groups making comments concerning this point. In addition, several participants commented that their requirement to understand the material resulted in a clearer link between theory taught in the classroom and practice in industry. One participant suggested that "it's not just memorising, it is connected with the real world experience".

Respondents appeared to understand that a change in classroom behaviour was required in order to be successful. Respondents commented that the focus was no longer on the individual student and that group work and presentations were now commonplace. Several respondents made the clear link between presentations and their increased level of understanding with one participant stating that "because you are standing there you have to fully understand the material you are presenting and so you can answer questions about the material".

Focus group participants were then asked to specify what issues or problems had affected their learning experience in Australia. It can be seen from Figure 3 that the most common response to this question concerned students' participation in class. This aspect appeared to be very important as members of each focus group commented that participation in class was a major issue or problem concerning their educational experience in Australia thus far.

Group work and presentations were again mentioned as a significant difficulty and several comments regarding the issue of students of particular nationalities working together

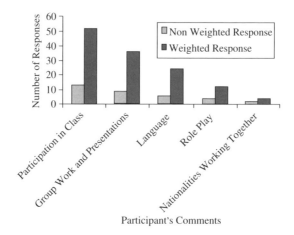

Figure 3: Non-weighted and weighted responses to question: What learning issues or problems have you experienced here in Australia?

were raised. This last comment was raised both from an exclusion and an excluded perspective. First, respondents considered that Australian students tended to stick together when forming groups and preparing presentations and the accusation was made that Australian students considered that international students would not make a valuable contribution to the group project, with one participant commenting that:

> There is also a problem I've encountered when I'd join the Aussies. Then (sic) what it turned out to be was they don't really appreciate my participating because they all think that you know nothing. You're not from an English background country. Sometimes I would try and participate but they may reject and at the end of the whole assignment they would go up to the tutor and say that I didn't participate and so I don't deserve the mark.

Focus group participants were asked to reflect on their learning experience in Australia so far. Generally, the majority of comments were very positive with the most frequently mentioned response suggesting that participants' educational experience thus far had been good. However, it must be noted that on the negative side, several participants mentioned that their Australian educational experience had been stressful. Comments made by participants suggest that the stress they were experiencing was founded in the recognition of the serious consequences that would be associated with them failing their program. This feeling of stress was reasonably commonly felt as members from three focus groups made such comments.

Respondents also made comments concerning the overall approach to learning and it was noted that respondents appeared to enjoy the learning methods common on their Australian program. When asked this question, one enthusiastic respondent stated:

> Good, good, because here things are very interesting and after you have finished studying your subject, you still remember things. You still remember the things you were studying in your previous semester.

In addition, respondents stated that they enjoyed sourcing information and relished the opportunity to debate, discuss and ask questions. Many participants recognised the direct link between their studies and their future careers and commented that the focus on understanding and the information sourcing and debating skills would be relevant and of use in the future. Several respondents also made comments regarding the positive relationships that existed between students and lecturers and complimented the good standard of teaching.

Towards the end of the focus group interview, participants were asked what recommendations they could suggest that would improve their learning experience in Australia. Details concerning participants' responses is contained in Figure 4. However, broadly speaking, respondents' comments fell into three categories. The first and most frequently mentioned response to this question concerned students' classroom behaviour. Responses to this question suggest that the respondents considered that responsibility for encouraging CHC student classroom involvement needs to become the responsibility of the institution. It was suggested that the lecturer in charge should take a more active role in managing

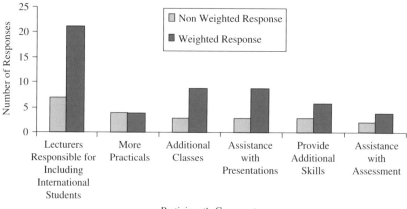

Figure 4: Non-weighted and weighted responses to question: What recommendations would you suggest that would improve your learning experience?

the class interaction, ensuring that international students be included in class discussions and that group composition for presentations be controlled to ensure that there was a mix of nationalities in the groups.

Respondents also considered that the university could provide additional classes after formal lectures that were specific for international students. It was suggested that these classes would be an opportunity for international students to question the lecturer, seek clarification regarding the content of the lecture and have the opportunity to more fully reflect and digest the material presented in the preceding lecture. Similarly, respondents also considered that the development of study skills and more assistance with assessments, particularly presentations would improve their learning experience.

Conclusion

From this research, it is evident that the CHC students are required to make a paradigm shift in their approach to education. They are expected to fit into a system that is very different to their home country. These results would suggest that their level of learning has progressed from describing and replicating to understanding, evaluation and analysis. In addition, there is a recognition of an assumption of responsibility for learning through debate and disagreement and the substantiating of discussion and submitted work. These students are exposed to classroom dynamics that are very different to their previous experience and are expected to treat their once revered lecturers with what some feel is disrespect. In addition, students are introduced to a range of new methods of assessment for which they are ill prepared and find extremely difficult and uncomfortable.

While this research has focussed on student experiences, it is possible to make several comments regarding the institutions that these students attend. It would appear that students consider that many of these institutions treat students well. However, it might be suggested that these students would appreciate and benefit from additional institutional support and consequently, it is suggested that more could be done in terms of the development of practical study skills and the support that such students receive as part of their study program.

Finally, it might be possible to make several comments regarding the lecturing staff with whom these students have to deal on a daily basis. It is reasonable to conclude that students appreciated the high quality of teaching they had received and enjoyed the more relaxed and informal student/teacher relationship. However, it was noted that many students considered that lecturers might take a more proactive role in the management of classroom activities, most notably regarding the composition of groups. It would appear from comments made that while students recognise that there has been a shift in the responsibility for learning, students do feel that the lecturer does have some responsibility for classroom management, which appears to be lacking.

It has been found that the majority of CHC students academically outperform their western counterparts and most students successfully complete their western education (Biggs, 1998). However, this research has highlighted that a CHC student who studies and eventually graduates from a western university will have to contend with a variety of learning issues and problems throughout their period of study. That such students succeed is testimony to their hard work, diligence and flexibility. This research has highlighted several proactive strategies that might be adopted by universities and academics in order to make this learning experience less stressful and ultimately more enjoyable.

References

Ballard, B., & Clanchy, J. (1991). *Teaching students from overseas: A brief guide for lecturers and supervisors*. Melbourne: Longman Cheshire.

Ballard, B., & Clanchy, J. (1994). *Study abroad: A manual for Asian students*. Melbourne: Longman.

Barron, P. E. (2002a). Providing a more successful education experience for Asian hospitality management students studying in Australia: A focus on teaching and learning styles. *Journal of Teaching in Travel and Tourism, 2*(2), 63–88.

Barron, P. E. (2002b). Hospitality management students' preferred learning styles: A preliminary study. Presented at the 12th international research conference of CAUTHE Fremantle, Western Australia, February 2002.

Barron, P. E. (2004). *An evaluation of learning styles, learning issues and learning problems of Confucian heritage culture students studying hospitality and tourism management in Australia*. Unpublished Ph.D. Thesis. The University of Queensland, Brisbane, Australia.

Biggs, J. B. (1998). Learning from the Confucian heritage: So size doesn't matter? *International Journal of Educational Research, 29*, 723–738.

Bohm, A., Davies, D., Meares, G., & Pearce, H. (2002). *Global student mobility 2025: Forecasts of the global demand for international higher education*. IDP Education Australia, September 2002.

Bradley, D., & Bradley, M. (1984). *Problems of Asian students in Australia: Language, culture and education*. Department of Education and Youth Affairs, Canberra.

Burns, R. B. (1991). Study and stress among first year overseas students in an Australian university. *Higher Education Research and Development, 10*(1), 61–77.

Chan, S. (1999). The Chinese learner: A question of style. *Education and Training, 41*(6/7), 294–304.

Choi, M. (1997). Korean students in Australian universities: Intercultural issues. *Higher Education Research and Development, 16*(3), 263–282.

Davis, D., Olsen, A., & Bohm, A. (2000). Transnational education providers, partners and policy: Challenges for Australian institutions offshore: A research study. Presented at the 14th Australian international education conference. Brisbane.

Huang, S. E., & Brown, N. E. (1996). First year international graduate students in hospitality programs: School choice, career expectations and academic adjustment. *Hospitality Research Journal, 20*(1), 109–117.

IDP Education Australia. (2000). *Survey of international students at Australian universities*. IDP, Canberra.

IDP Education Australia. (2003). *International students in Australian universities — Semester 1, 2003 national overview*. IDP Education, Australia.

Jennings, G. R. (2001). Do I or don't I teach them? — Benefits and challenges as well as pedagogical and ethical issues of educating tourism students in English when English is not their first language. *The Journal of Teaching in Travel and Tourism, 1*(4), 35–52.

Kember, D., & Gow, L. (1990). Cultural specificity of approaches to study. *British Journal of Educational Psychology, 60,* 356–363.

Kennedy, K. (1995). Developing a curriculum guarantee for overseas students. *Higher Education Research and Development, 14*(1), 35–46.

Lashley, C. (1999). On making silk purses: Developing reflective practitioners in hospitality management education. *International Journal of Contemporary Hospitality Management, 11*(4), 180–185.

Lee, W. O. (1999). The cultural context for Chinese learners: Conceptions of learning in the Confucian tradition. In: D. D. Watkins & J. B. Biggs (Eds), *The Chinese learner: Cultural, psychological and contextual influences* (pp. 25–41). Centre for Comparative Research in Education, Hong Kong. Australian Council for Educational Research, Camberwell, Victoria.

Maslen, G. (1999). Australian universities set records in foreign enrolments. *The Chronicle of Higher Education.* 14th May, Washington, USA.

Meares, D. (2003). Global student mobility 2025: The supply challenge — Meeting and managing demand for international education. Paper presented at the 17th IDP Australia international education conference. Melbourne.

Moon, S. H. (2003). Managing international education: Korean students and student support staff perspectives at the University of New South Wales. Paper presented at the 17th IDP Australia international education conference. Melbourne, Australia.

Morgan, D. L. (1997). *Focus groups as qualitative research* (2nd ed.). Thousand Oaks, CA: Sage Publications.

Mullins, G., Quintrell, N., & Hancock, L. (1995). The experiences of international and local students at three Australian universities. *Higher Education Research and Development, 14*(2), 201–231.

Neuman, W. L. (1997). *Social research methods: Qualitative and quantitative approaches* (3rd ed.). Sydney: Allyn and Bacon.

Niven, A. (1987). Salad days without the dressing? What British higher and further education institutions can do for their overseas students. *Higher Education Quarterly, 41*(2), 144–161.

Priest, S. H. (1996). *Doing media research: An introduction.* London: Sage.

Ramsay, S., Barker, M., & Jones, E. (1999). Academic adjustment and learning processes: A comparison of international and local students in first year university. *Higher Education Research and Development, 18*(1), 129–144.

Robertson, M., Line, M., Jones, S., & Thomas, S. (2000). International students' learning environments and perceptions: A case study using the Delphi technique. *Higher Education Research and Development, 19*(1), 89–102.

Samuelowicz, K. (1987). Learning problems of overseas students: Two sides of a story. *Higher Education Research and Development, 6*(2), 121–133.

Ticehurst, G. W., & Veal, A. J. (1999). *Business research methods: A managerial approach.* Australia: Longman.

Volet, S.E., & Renshaw, P. (1999). Chinese students at an Australian university: Adaptability and continuity. In: D. A. Watkins & J. B. Biggs (Eds), *The Chinese learner: Cultural, psychological and contextual influences* (pp. 205–220). Centre for Comparative Research in Education, Hong Kong, Australian Council for Educational Research, Camberwell, Victoria.

Watson, D. I. (1999). 'Loss of face' in Australian classrooms. *Teaching in Higher Education, 4*(3), 355–361.

Yanhong Li, R., & Kaye, M. (1998). Understanding overseas students' concerns and problems. *Journal of Higher Education Policy and Management, 20*(1), 41–50.

Yee, A. (1989). Cross cultural perspectives on higher education in East Asia: Psychological effects upon Asian students. *Journal of Multilingual and Multicultural Development, 10*(3), 213–232.

Chapter 26

e-Learning and e-Assessment

Marianna Sigala

Introduction: e-Learning in Tourism and Hospitality

Internet advances enable students to receive and interact with educational materials and to engage with teachers and peers in ways that previously may have been impossible. Indeed, because of its three unique features namely, interactivity, connectivity and technological convergence, the Internet has irrevocably altered how people access information and how much information anyone can access, while local and wide-area networks release the Internet as a learning resource with software tools that enable interactive communication. e-Learning or Internet-based learning, therefore, offers significant opportunities for those in the tourism sector to up-grade skills and knowledge, as its flexibility matches the specific conditions of work within the sector (Sigala, 2002). Moreover, good e-learning can foster collaborative learning by drawing on the expertise of leading subject authorities in all key subject areas, which in turn also allows students to experience multicultural diversity and teamwork by interacting online with people of different social and cultural background. The acquisition of social, multicultural and communication skills are of a crucial importance for tourism graduates (Christou, 1999), because the inherently multinational and cultural tourism workplace requires a knowledgeable workforce that can work collaboratively irrespective of their spatial, time and cultural differences. e-Learning also acclimatizes graduates to the changes occurring in the tourism workplace, e.g. growth of e-business applications and increasing alliances and merges among tourism companies.

However, although e-learning is widely being adopted for enhancing and complementing tourism and hospitality instruction (Sigala & Christou, 2003) and its advantages for tourism and hospitality education are extensively argued (Sigala, 2002; Cho, Schmelzer, & McMahon, 2002; Clements, Buergermeister, Holland, & Monteiro, 2001; Christou & Sigala, 2000), little is still known on how to design and implement effective e-learning platforms. Moreover, although an increasing number of tourism and hospitality educators are adopting and incorporating Internet tools in their instruction, only very few of them are fully exploiting the Internet's capabilities to transform and extend their pedagogical models (Sigala & Christou, 2002). On the other hand, it is generally agreed that the reimplementation of conventional models borrowed from classroom based or distance education that are focused on passive transmission would permit only marginal improvements. Thus, there is a need to: examine how knowledge is acquired and how online learning occurs and so, illustrate how e-learning pedagogy should be designed; investigate the e-assessment pedagogies that can support and foster the former; and identify the factors influencing the effectiveness of e-learning experiences. This chapter aims to achieve these objectives by reviewing the literature and current practices as well as by providing insights from research studies and best practices. Finally, future trends and developments are also discussed.

Theoretical Underpinnings and e-Learning Pedagogy

The internet's capabilities imply a different type of thinking in terms of how to make full use of its learning-enhancing features and pedagogical potential. In particular, the internet's affordance for enhanced communication provides great opportunities for combining collaborative techniques with technology to dramatically enhance the learning process and learning outcomes (Sigala, 2002; Cho et al., 2002). Harasim (2000) also advocated that the asynchronous, hypertext and multimedia-based nature of the technology represents cognitive advantages — such as flexibility with regard to the nature of interaction, reflection on stored communication or reduction of discriminatory communication patterns based on physical features and social clues — that provide an augmented domain for collaborative learning. The electronic implementation of collaborative learning often results in the development of a virtual classroom, whereby tools such as electronic bulletin boards, mail, grade books, quizzes and lectures are used to provide feedback, distribute material and develop a learning community similar to a traditional classroom. The general effectiveness of collaborative learning in traditional classrooms is supported by decades of research (e.g. McKeackie, 1980; Palloff & Pratt, 1999), while recent studies (McConnel, 1994; McConnel, Hardy, & Hodgson, 1996; Campos, Laferriere, & Harasim, 2001) point to Online Collaborative Learning (OCL) as an effective learning method within electronic environments. Thus, e-learning platforms are increasingly adapting a pedagogical approach of OCL that is based on the theoretical underpinnings of constructivism (critical thinking skills) and collaboratism (detailed literature review in Sigala, 2002, 2004b).

Briefly, constructivism argues that knowledge is created by searching for complexity and ambiguity, looking for and making connections among aspects of a situation and speculation. So, when learners are exposed to new information, each learner evaluates and analyses it, sees the relationships between the new information and his/her existing knowledge and makes inferences and judgments for new knowledge (Kafai & Resnick, 1996). In other words, to enhance learning, students should think critically, have the ability of analysing situations, search for evidence and seek links between a particular situation and their prior knowledge and experience (Sigala, 2002). In such learning environments, instructors should act as facilitators, while students should actively participate in the learning process and control their learning pace.

Collaborative learning evolved from the work of psychologists (e.g. Johnson & Johnson, 1975) and involves social (interpersonal) processes by which a small group of students work together to complete a task designed to promote learning. Thus, collaborative learning involves the creation and interpretation of communications among persons/groups that might have different understandings and opinions (Sigala, 2002), which in turn enhance learning by allowing individuals to exercise, verify, solidify, and improve their mental models. Dillenbourg and Schneider (1995) identified three collaborative learning mechanisms directly affecting cognitive processes. First, conflict/disagreement, because it forces learners to seek information and find a solution. Moreover, internalization of interactions with more knowledgeable peers, explanations from more advanced peers as well as self-explanations (self-explanation effect) can also enhance learners' learning processes. In collaborative learning, group processes are a part of the individual learning activity — individual and collective activities are mutually dependent on each other. This is because the learner actively constructs knowledge by formulating ideas into words, and these ideas are built upon through reactions and responses of peers. In other words, individual learning is a result of group processes and so, learning is not only active but also interactive. Thus, collaborativism may also be seen as a variation of constructivism that stresses the cooperative efforts among students and instructors in the learning process (Sigala, 2002).

e-Learning Models and Practice

Sigala (2002) identified and analysed in detail the different e-learning models and their developmental stages. In her model she identified three major stages of e-learning environments that educators can implement. *The transfer of traditional instruction on the Internet* is the earliest and most extensive category of online instruction. e-Learning models under this category do not fully exploit Internet capabilities for transforming and enhancing instruction, but they rather imply and demonstrate a simple transfer of traditional practices on the Internet, e.g. information distribution and publishing. According to Sigala and Christou's (2002) findings, this simple webification of learning processes is evident in the electronic distribution of learning material (e.g. lecturers' websites with lectures' notes, presentations, learning material, references, etc.), in electronic student-to-tutor and student-to-student interactions (synchronous and/or asynchronous electronic communications overcome place and times boundaries and are of great support to students conducting their industrial placements in international settings) as well as in electronic assessment procedures. Analytically, Internet tools are used for communicating with students, simulating discussions found in traditional classrooms and extending them beyond the classroom walls, e.g. McDonnell (2000) described how they used Internet and computer simulations for simulating classroom discussions. However, while the technology tends to support a certain degree of egalitarian participation, and does allow users the freedom to input messages at their convenience, the conditions which are needed to produce good educational discussions are far more complex, more people-dependent and more educationally determined than mere technology will ever influence very significantly. Sigala (2004a) reported that students' negative perceptions towards the internet's features and their learning style significantly inhibited them in participating in online forums. As concerns assessment, the Internet and web-in-a-box software is used for disseminating traditional evaluation practices, e.g. multiple choice tests, without changing or even enhancing their form and content. Mason (1998) advocated that existing assessment practices are ill suited to the digital age in which using information is more important than remembering it, and where reusing and applying material should be viewed as a skill to be encouraged, not as a plagiarism to be despised. Overall, as in this e-learning model the principles and aims of instruction do not change, the roles and tasks that students and tutors should assume and undertake also remain the same. Consequently, such practices result in computer-based learning environments that can be characterized as "page turning devices" of learning material that is a simple digital photocopy of current texts and so, which fall short of the interactive, user-centred features originally made for them.

The second wave of e-learning pedagogy models, online collaborative and constructive learning models, illustrates a more educational than technology determined approach to e-learning. The internet capabilities imply a different type of thinking in terms of how to make full use of its learning-enhancing features and pedagogical potential. Because one of the key affordances of the Internet is for communication (e.g. through email, bulletin boards, chats, electronic conferencing), the combination of collaborative and constructivist (or critical thinking) techniques with technology are argued to significantly enhance the learning process and learning outcomes dramatically. The electronic implementation of collaborative learning often results in the development of a virtual classroom, whereby tools such as electronic bulletin boards, chat rooms, e-mails, grade books and quizzes are used in order to provide feedback, distribute material and develop a learning community similar to a traditional classroom (Hammond, 2000; Wachter, Gupta, & Quaddus, 2000; McConnell et al., 1996; Cho and Schmelzer, 2000). Constructivism is an epistemology of how people learn and assimilate new knowledge asserting that knowledge is acquired by a process of mental construction. Both Harasim (2000) and Akyalcin (1997) (see literature review in Sigala, 2002) analysed and illustrated with several examples, how internet tools can support the four following processes of knowledge construction as initially presented by Piaget (1977):

1. Assimilation: associate new events with prior knowledge and conceptions;
2. Accommodation: change existing structures to new information;
3. Equilibrium: balance internal understanding with external "reality" (e.g. other's understanding);
4. Disequilibrium: experience of a new invent without achieving a state of equilibrium.

Koschmann, Meyers, Feltovich, and Barrows (1996) also considered discourse and interactions as a fundamental aspect of learning by arguing that "learning is enhanced by articulation, abstraction and commitment on the part of the learner: instruction should provide opportunities for learners to articulate their newly acquired knowledge". Articulation is a cognitive act in which the student presents, defends, develops and refines ideas. Thus, in order to articulate their ideas, students must organize their thoughts and information into knowledge structures. Ultimately, active learners' participation in online discourses leads to multiple perspectives on issues, a divergence of ideas and positions that students must sort through to find meaning and convergence. However, it is the conflict and collision of adverse opinions that lead to cognitive growth and development of problem-solving skills. Thus, in collaborative learning settings, online discourses are the "heart and the soul" of online education enabling interaction, conceptual exchange and collaborative convergence across differences of knowledge, skills and attitudes. Indeed, collaborative learning should thrive on these differences. Overall, computer conferencing and network capabilities of the internet tools enable communication and discourses that are best described as a form of discourse-in-writing. The unique attributes of communication in e-learning environments and the cognitive activities that they enhance for augmenting the online learning experience are summarized by Harasim (2000) as follows:

- *Many-to-many* (*group communication*) enables: motivational (socio-affective) benefits of working through problems with peers; active exchange: rich information environment; identification of new perspectives, multiplicity; opportunity to compare, discuss, modify and/or replace concepts (conceptual exchange); encouragement to work through differences and arrive at intellectual convergence;
- *Time independence* supports: 24 h access, users can respond immediately or reflect and compose a response at their convenience; ongoing, continuous knowledge building; participation by users at their best learning readiness time;
- *Place independence* allows: access to the wealth of Web resources (as well as peers and experts); shared interests, not just shared locations among participants;
- *Text-based/media-enriched messaging* encourages and contributes to: verbalization and articulation of ideas; focus on message rather than on the messenger (reduced socio-physical discrimination); clear expression of ideas; rich database/web of ideas;
- *Computer-mediated environments* enable: searchable, transmissible and modifiable archived database; multiple passes through conference (discourse) transcript; building tools to exchange and organize ideas and support collaborative learning; building templates, scaffolds and educational supports.

Salmon (2002) provides several examples and cases on how to develop collaborative-constructivism e-learning platforms and activities, while in the context of tourism and hospitality education examples and suggestions are given in Sigala (2004a, b) and Cho and Schmelzer (2000). Constructivism online communications are also helpful and valuable to researchers conducting doctoral and research studies, as online discussions and communications can be used for several purposes such as idea generation, concepts debates, material identification and exchange, collaborative research projects etc. Nowadays, a similar and widely known and used application is the communications and interactions found in tourism e-mail lists and servers. Overall, the specific nature and features of tourism education and industry (such as multi- and inter disciplinary, international, dynamic and changing, multicultural, people-centred) enhance the applicability, appropriateness and value of constructive communications in tourism e-learning environments. For instance, the integration of online communications and debates can be designed in order to foster and include in discussions opinions from different disciplines, from the professional circles and from the international community in an ad hoc basis, i.e. when it is required. This creates as Cho and Schmelzer (2000) called it "just in time" tourism education environments allowing learning to be continuously updated and developed according to industry needs and changes.

Nowadays, researchers and designers are seeking more sophisticated learning theories based on proven research showing how brains works, e.g. recent neuroscience research reveals how the brain's emotional system influence and how individuals learn and memorize facts. Such developments reflect research (e.g. Martinez, 1999; Martinez & Bunderson, 2000) based on a learning orientation approach, which attempts to reveal the dominant power of emotions and intentions on guiding and managing cognitive processes (no longer demoted to a secondary role). Moreover, by understanding the structure and nature of the complex relationships between learning orientations and interactions, the learning orientation research aims at developing instructions that do not fit the average person but fit groups of students with particular aptitude patterns. Here, Sigala (2002) predicted the development of personalized and adaptive (mass customization) e-learning models that would be customized to individual learners based on an individual's emotions, intentions and intentions' about why, when and how to use learning and how it can accomplish personal goals. These models are very useful because effective e-learning instruction should provide multiple ways to provide instruction and e-learning environments so that all learners will want to learn on the Web and continue to have opportunities for success. In this way, the benefits of personalized e-learning to individual differences would be the ability to address important human issues previously managed by instructors in the classroom (e.g. lack of confidence, impatience, mistakes, boredom).

Overall, Table 1 provides some examples of how e-learning models can and could be applied in tourism education.

Table 1: Examples of e-learning models in tourism education.

e-Learning model	Examples
The transfer of traditional instruction on the Internet	Module websites including lectures notes, presentations, learning material, multiple choice tests, examples of examinations' questions, case studies, videos, multimedia and other learning material
Online collaborative and constructive learning models	Collaborative-constructivism communications can be used for: • Moral, technical and administrative support to students in industrial placement; • Doctoral and research projects; • Inclusion of the professional community in the learning process; • Simulation-games, (team-based): e.g. airline management; games, hotel management games, revenue optimization games, menu engineering and restaurant management games, tourism destination model software. (http://www.datapathsystems.net/TourismDestination/pct.html)
Personalised and adaptive (mass customization) e-learning models	Multiple-choice tests that adapt to individual needs, e.g. tests that depending on student' performance customize on real time the question databank e-learning platforms that adapt learning material to student progress and performance

Factors Determining e-Learning Effectiveness

Webster and Hackley (1997) remarked that although students' performance represents a key aspect of teaching effectiveness, they highlighted that the following dimensions also capture the concept of effectiveness: student participation and involvement; cognitive engagement; technology self-efficacy (i.e. ones belief on his capacity to interact with a given technology); perceived usefulness of the technology; and the relative advantages/disadvantages of online delivery. Bernard, Rubalcava, and Pierre (2000) also argued that e-learning should be evaluated on its three dimensions namely commitment, coordination and communication by measuring variables such as group cohesion and productivity, use of resources and level of communication. Moreover, because e-learning requires learners to be active participants of their own learning, other learner's variables should also be considered. However, previous studies investigating the learning quality/effectiveness have generally used students' grades, attitude surveys and observational data (Porras-Hernadez, 2000). Other studies revealed the impact of affective aspects such as confidence in learning abilities and expectations (Brosnan, 1998; Schlechter, 1990). More recent studies evaluating e-learning are also focusing on specific abilities and attitudes needed in e-learning by including student's perceptions of themselves (Bernard et al., 2000; Martinez, 1999) rather than only looking at students' perceptions of technology, tasks and their ability with technology. Porras-Hernadez (2000) also stressed the need to include learners' capability for educational achievement in general, while Hammond's (2000) findings revealed that two learners' factors determine learning effectiveness namely cognitive aspects (e.g. previous experience in mediated education and computer skills) and affective variables (e.g. expectations, self-efficacy for self-regulated learning, perceptions of instructors and their efforts, feelings of anxiety and success). Overall, students' factors determining e-learning effectiveness include: prior experience with technology; country of origin and native tongue; educational skills and self-discipline; perceptions of the self and self-regulatory processes. The latter can crucially determine students' participation and e-learning effectiveness, since e-learning emphasizes and requires learners' ability and responsibility of their own learning. Sigala (2004a) also found that students' perceptions on the electronic medium significantly affected their participation in OCL. Online discussions have four major characteristics: messages are permanent; messages are public; communication is asynchronous; and messages can be edited before sending. Depending on the way students perceive these attributes, students' participation on online forums varies considerably. For example, the permanency of messages may encourage learners to contribute as they can easily access and refer to past debates. However, this can also discourage communication as writers know that their texts are open for scrutiny and that they cannot easily retract anything they would write.

The following technology issues were also found to affect e-learning effectiveness (Dillon & Gunawardena, 1995; Laurel, 1990; Blattner & Dannenberg, 1992; Martinez, 1999): (a) the medium's reliability, quality and richness; (b) capability for both synchronous and asynchronous communication; (c) quality of interface, e.g. factors regarding: ease of use, navigation, screen design, information presentation, aesthetics and overall functionality; (d) the perceived richness (synchronous, asynchronous and multimedia communication tools) of the used technology.

However, it is not the technology but rather its instructional implementation that determines learning effectiveness. Thus, the role of the instructor becomes central and instrumental in the effectiveness of e-learning. Actually, the following instructor factors can influence learning outcomes (Salmon, 2002): attitude towards technology, control of technology and teaching style, e.g. the way he/she facilitates/mediates e-learning platforms. In particular, the instructors' facilitating and mediating capabilities and roles are crucially important because unless these are effectively achieved, serious problems may arise. For example, an online conference may turn into a monologue of lecture type material to which very few responses are made or to a disorganized mountain of information that is confusing and overwhelming for the participants. To avoid such situations, Harasim (2000) stressed that instructors should adapt an online instruction teaching paradigm that is away from the traditional lecture format as well as become active e-moderators. Actually, instructors must assume three crucial tasks namely contextualizing, monitoring and meta-communication functions (Sigala, 2004b), which Salmon (2002) summarized into the concept of weaving. The first two functions aim to compensate for the absence of physical cues found in traditional classrooms, while meta functions aim to resolve problems in communication that are addressed in classrooms by body language and to summarize the state of a discussion to provide the sense of accomplishment and direction.

In investigating the factors affecting e-learning effectiveness in hospitality, Sigala (2004a) identified three major factors while also discussing several ways in addressing them: (a) instructor factors: instructor attitudes towards learners; instructor technical competence; and instructor efforts for facilitating/mediating forums and interactions; (b) technology factors: easy access and navigation; interface; and interaction both with peers and instructors; and (c) student factors: students' ability of controlling learning processes; students' effort in searching and understanding learning material; and students' ability to participate in collaborative processes. Sigala's (2003) findings also revealed that students' cultural background and gender can crucially affect their level and type of contribution in e-learning activities and communities. However, Sigala (2004a) concluded that future research should aim to assess e-learning effectiveness also in terms of the communication, social, interpersonal and technology skills that it aims to enhance.

e-Assessment Pedagogy

e-Learning activities and processes are not complete and may not lead to the desirable learning outcomes, unless they are integrated and aligned with appropriate assessment strategies. This is because it is common that assessment related tasks attract students' attention at the expense of non-assessed tasks. Thus, assessment criteria and processes can significantly direct, motivate and guide students' learning processes. In this light, interest in the evaluation of e-learning and online discussion forums is continuously increasing and demonstrated in the great number of tools applied for teasing out key aspects of the interaction that can lead to improvements in online learning environments (Pittman, Gosper, & Rich, 1999). However, the appropriateness and impact of such tools on reliably assessing e-learning processes and outcomes as well as on fostering and supporting skills' development are not always effective neither do they support student-centred learning. In general, e-assessment methods are classified into two categories namely quantitative and qualitative assessment tools.

Quantitative methods aiming at assessing the amount, frequency and direction/interaction of online discussions have pushed instructors to calculate statistics such as number of online users, frequency of access, number of messages per student, number of threads/messages per thread (Harasim, 1989) or to develop "message maps" for reflecting the flow of communication within the group (Levin, Kim, & Riel, 1990). Although such metrics are good at identifying the level of students' adoption and engagement in e-learning processes, there is a danger of implying that the level of online participation reflects the level of learning. Moreover, such assessment metrics are limited in their ability to assess and motivate students towards skills' development, simply because they ignore messages' content. Instead, assessing students solely based on their level of online participation may lead to: information/messages overload that have nothing to do with the learning task; limited student guidance and direction as to what and how has to be achieved; increased students' stress for catching up and reading messages that in turn leaves limited time for reading, reflection, concepts' internalization and assessment.

Qualitative assessment methods aim to address the limitations of previous metrics by exploiting the transparency of online discussions (i.e. the fact that all communication is easily organized, stored and retrieved) and analysing text-based archives/transcripts for understanding and evaluating e-learning processes. This is achieved by first breaking the transcript down into small units and then classifying these units according to the content. Different approaches have been developed and applied for identifying units' categories. Categories may be defined either retrospectively in order to capture the flavour of a particular forum (e.g. McLoughlin, 2002; Mowrer, 1996) or *a priori* based on the learning processes and tasks in which theory implies that students should be engaged for enhancing their learning. However, it is the second level of analysis that is needed to evaluate e-learning and guide the use of online discussion environments. This is because of two major reasons. First, students are assessed based on evidence of the learning processes that they have been engaged. Secondly, by making students aware of the assessment criteria (i.e. the predefined units' categories) in advance, instructors can get students acquainted to the learning processes while also directing and motivating their efforts towards the tasks they need to engage.

For developing unit categories, a number of theoretical models of e-learning processes exist in the literature (see literature review in Sigala, 2004b), but the most effective is argued to be that developed by Gunawardena, Lowe, and Anderson (1997) as it reflects the "gestalt" of the entire online discussion rather than focusing on links between specific messages. A gestaltist approach to analysing the interaction of the entire online conference was central to Gunawardena et al.'s (1997) purpose to evaluate evidence for the social construction of knowledge. Their own preferred method of content analysis was developed to capture the whole progression of ideas as they were reflected at following different phases of the debate:

- *Sharing/comparing information*: this phase may include an observation, opinion, agreement, corroborating example, clarification and/or identification of a problem;
- *Discovery and exploration of dissonance or inconsistency among the ideas/concepts or statements advanced by other participants*: this is defined as an inconsistency between a new observation and the learners' existing knowledge and thinking skills, e.g. identification of differences of terms/concepts/schema and questions to clarify the extent of disagreement;

- *Negotiating meaning and co-construction of knowledge*: e.g. negotiation/clarification of the meaning of terms, detection of areas of agreement, proposal of a compromise/ co-construction;
- *Testing and modification of proposed synthesis*: testing against an existing cognitive schema, personal experience, formal data experimentation, contradictory data from the literature;
- *Agreement, statements and application of newly constructed meaning*: including summarizing agreements/metacognitive statements showing new knowledge construction and application.

Overall, it becomes evident that assessment of online collaborative learning should not focus solely on metrics reflecting the quantity of students' interaction but also on assessment criteria that simultaneously consider the quality and learning ability of students' interactions/communications. Assessing students based on both the quantity but also the quality of their interactions should direct and motivate them towards the online and constructivism creation of knowledge and skills. Sigala (2004b) described how Gunawardena et al.'s (1997) constructivist model of online assessment has been applied for designing collaborative e-assessment strategies and integrating/aligning them with e-learning strategies that can overall motivate and foster the development of constructivism students' learning processes and outcomes. Moreover, some additional insights and lessons learned from this case study are presented below.

The e-assessment strategy (as presented in Table 2) was gradually guiding students' into the development of cognitive skills, as it included assessment tasks that evaluated not only the quality of final individual achieved *learning outcomes* (e.g. essay), but also the team-based *learning processes* used for achieving the former, which in turn supported the development of a positive and team-socially, friendly e-learning environment. Analytically, students' contribution to the learning processes was assessed both in terms of students' performance in isolated learning tasks (e.g. five individual messages) as well as students' ability to use, reflect, assess and exploit others' contributions in the learning processes. So, students' reading and internalization of knowledge, ability to express themselves on a topic, ability to engage with, negotiate meaning, respond to other students' contributions while concentrating on their own line of thought were assessed through assessment 1 (Table 1). Students' ability to synthesize and present arguments was assessed through assessments 2 and 3. Assessment 3 also focused on evaluating students' metacognitive skills, while assessment 4 aimed at making students think about, reflect and evaluate their individual and group learning strategies. In other words, assessment 4 was designed for enabling students to better learn how to learn, while also illustrating them how they could also possibly transfer and develop more effective learning strategies in other modules.

Overall, students are judged on both their individual and team contributions. The aim was to achieve a good balance and interdependence between individual and team/community assessment tasks and marks in order to foster and support the development of the spirit and culture of an online virtual learning community. Indeed, students could not get marks by relying only on their own contributions, as the latter had to be supported by and related with interactions of other students. In other words, one cannot achieve marks alone. Instead, he/she has to respond to communities' interactions, while his/her contributions

Table 2: e-Assessment strategy: aligning assessment tasks with learning outcomes and processes.

Assessment task	Description of assessment	Level of learning Process addressed	Allocated marks (%)
1 (Learning process)	Student submission and selection of his/her five best messages contributed to the online debate Each message supported by another message to illustrate an ability to interact and build on other contributions.	Identify and read, internalize, express, respond and engage in debates, negotiate meaning	10
2 (Learning process)	One summary of a weekly debate among two groups	Synthesize, contextualize	20
3 (Learning product and process)	Individual essay on a topic directly related to the online discussion, i.e. "Analyse how a five star hotel operator can effectively exploit and implement Information and Communication Technologies for enhancing the quality of the customer service provided" online messages are expected to be incorporated into the essay as an evidence of understanding of online debates. Quotation, comments and assessment of other comments accounted for 5% of the essay mark.	Assessment, synthesize, metacognitive skills	20
4 (Learning product)	Learning diary: reflection and assessment of group's and individuals' learning strategy and suggestions for future improvement	Reflect and assess on learning processes and development of learning strategies: learn how to learn, transferable skills	10
5 (Learning product)	Examination	Various skills	50

will in turn consist the basis of another student assessment. In other words, assignments were designed so that they would support the group coherence and cohesion, as students worked together and learnt to respond to each others' comments and arguments. Thus, assignments were important and instrumental in developing the culture of the online learning community.

Moreover, assignment 2 was designed and implemented for several reasons: to introduce a formative type of assessment in order to provide student feedback in intervals, which would in turn appraise and motivate students' good performance, guide them to the appropriate directions, while also avoiding disappointing results at the end of the module; to help the instructor in moderating online discussions (reading of summaries not all messages) and guiding/keeping them in the correct directions; to enable students to catch up with online debates and exchange views among groups; to help students contextualize arguments; to enhance students' synthesizing skills; to enhance students' (electronic) communication and negotiation skills; and to facilitate students in writing their essay.

Concerning assignment 4, a number of reasons also justified its development and use. Previous findings (Sigala, 2004b; McDonald, 2003) have shown that students needed time and practice if they were to become effective online collaborators. The reflective exercise was thus devised in order to encourage students to reflect on and assess the process of online collaboration that was used as well as then produce a strategy for future collaboration. In this way, the exercise aimed at incrementally developing students' skills for online collaboration for subsequent years and modules. Indeed, in his e-assessment practices, McDonald (2003) reported that many students had found the forward planning very helpful as it was an opportunity to reflect on their experiences of online collaboration as well as a forum for discussing procedures and working practices. Finally, this reflective log was also useful for gathering students' feedback regarding the effectiveness of the e-learning platform and strategy as well as identifying the good and bad practices. This feedback was found as extremely useful in further designing, implementing and improving e-learning strategies for the following years. Some of the feedback and lessons learned are reported below.

However, the biggest challenge for educators is the assessment of online lurkers, an issue, which also needs future consideration and examination. As passive e-learning participation may not entail that students do not learn (as happens in traditional classes whereby students may remain silent but they do learn by just listening to debates), online lurkers should not be penalized in grading, because this may not be fair. To overcome this dilemma, Gunawardena's model can have a dual role: it can be used for rewarding students based on the quality of their online performance: or it can offer a diagnostic, formative type of assessment identifying students that cannot or do not want to contribute so that tutors can take corrective action well in advance. Finally, the practical and industry importance of developing effective, motivational and e-learning constructive e-assessment strategies is highlighted by the Loreal case study (www.e-strat.loreal.com). Loreal has developed an online simulation game of its company and products, in which it invites all business graduates to participate in teams. Based on teams' and individuals' performance, Loreal then recruits the best skilled candidates that also match its culture and company. This type of e-assessment serves as a "cheap" and highly effective tool for recruiting from an international market and it is increasingly being adopted by several firms and from which tourism and hospitality companies will not be an exception. Thus, educators' responsibility is to train and experience tourism graduates with such simulation games before students go out to the marketplace.

Conclusions

Despite the wide adoption of e-learning in tourism and hospitality, little knowledge and practice still exists regarding how to develop effective technological and human e-learning platforms. This chapter aimed to fill in this gap by reviewing previous literature, studies and e-learning practices in e-learning and e-assessment pedagogies. The chapter also provides stimulus and directions for further research as it identifies critical and important research areas for future research. Of particular interest and importance is the identification of any specific factors related to learners' cultural and/or learning disabilities that could impact on e-learning and the investigation of effective ways for addressing them. The tourism and hospitality literature and practice can and has a lot to learn from generic literature and studies, however, tourism educators should continually try to assess, critically apply and adapt tools developed for other disciplines. In this vein, the development of tourism-specific e-learning platforms should be the future challenge for both academics and technology suppliers.

References

Akyalcin, J. (1997). Constructivism–an epistemological journey from Piaget to Papet, www. kilvington.schnet.edu.au/construct.htm[accessed 20/04/2000].

Bernard, R., Rubalcava, B., & Pierre, D. (2000). Collaborative online distance learning: Issues for future practice and research. *Distance Education, 21*, 260–277.

Blattner, M., & Dannenberg, R. (1992). *Multimedia interface design*. New York: ACM.

Brosnan, M. (1998). The impact of computer anxiety and self-efficacy upon performance. *Journal of Computer Assisted Learning, 14*, 223–234.

Campos, M., Laferriere, T., & Harasim, L. (2001). The post-secondary networked classroom; renewal of teaching practices and social interaction. *Journal of Asynchronous Learning Networks, 5*(2), 36–52.

Cho, W., Schmelzer, C. D., & McMahon, P. S. (2002). Preparing hospitality managers for the 21st century: The merging of just-in-time education, critical thinking, and collaborative learning. *Journal of Hospitality & Tourism Research, 26*(1), 23–37.

Cho, W., & Schmelzer, D. (2000). Just-in-time education: Tools for hospitality managers of the futures? *International Journal of Contemporary Hospitality Management, 12*(1), 31–36.

Christou, E. (1999). Hospitality management education in Greece: An exploratory study. *Tourism Management, 20*(6), 683–692.

Christou, E., & Sigala, M. (2000). Exploiting multimedia for effective hospitality education. *EuroCHRIE spring conference proceedings*. Ireland: Dublin Institute of Technology, 18–20 May, 2000.

Clements, C., Buergermeister, J., Holland, J., & Monteiro, P. (2001). Creating virtual learning community. *Journal of Teaching in Travel and Tourism, 1*(2/3), 73–89.

Dillenbourg, P., & Schneider, D. (1995). *Collaborative learning and the Internet*. http://tecfa. unige.ch/tecfa/research/CMC/colla/iccai95_1.html [Accessed 2001, 18 July].

Dillon, L., & Gunawardena, C. (1995). *Evaluation of telecommunications-based distance education*. Open University report. Milton Keynes: Open University.

Gunawardena, L., Lowe, C., & Anderson, T. (1997). Interaction analysis of a global online debate and the development of a constructivist interaction analysis model for computer conferencing. *Journal of Educational Computing Research, 17*(4), 395–429.

Hammond, M. (2000). Communication within online forums: The opportunities, the constraints and the value of a communicative approach. *Computers & Education, 35*, 251–262.

Harasim, L. (1989). Online education: A new domain. In: R. Mason & A. Kaye (Eds), *Midweave: Communication, computers and distance education* (pp. 50–57). Oxford: Pergamon Press.

Harasim, L. (2000). Shift happens: Online education as a new paradigm in learning. *The Internet and Higher Education, 3*(1–2), 41–61.

Johnson, D., & Johnson, R. (1975). Learning together and alone: cooperation, competition, and individualization. Englewood Cliffs: Prentice Hall.

Kafai, Y., & Resnick, M. (1996). *Constructionism in practice: Designing, thinking and learning in a digital word.* Hillsdale: Lawrence Erlbaum.

Koschmann, T., Myers, A., Feltovich, P., & Barrows, H. (1994). Using technology to assist realising learning and instruction: A principled approach to the use of computers in collaborative learning. *Journal of the Learning Sciences, 3*(3), 227–264.

Laurel, B. (1990). *The art of human computer interface design.* Reading, MA: Addison-Wesley.

Levin, J., Kim, H., & Riel, M. (1990). Analysing interactions on e-message networks. In: L. Harasim (Ed.), *Online education: perspectives on a environment* (pp. 185–213). New York: Praeger.

Martinez, M. (1999). Research design, models, and methodologies for examining how individuals successfully learn on the web. *Special Research in Technical communication, 46*(4), 470–487.

Martinez, M., & Bunderson, C. V. (2000). Building interactive web learning environments to match and support individual learning differences. *Journal of Interactive Learning Research, 11*(2), 77–93.

Mason, R. (1998). Models of online courses. *Asynchronous learning networks magazine, 2*(2), 9–19.

McConnell, P. (1994) *Implementing computer co-operative learning.* London: Kogan Page.

McConnell, D., Hardy, V., & Hodgson, M. (1996). Groupwork in educational computer conferences. ESRC end of award report. University of Lancaster.

McDonald, J. (2003). Assessing online collaborative learning: Process and product. *Computers & Education, 40*, 377–391.

McDonnell (2000). An electronic tutorial: a teaching innovation for tourism management studies. *International Journal of Tourism Research, 2*, 367–374.

McKeackie, W. (1980). *Learning, cognition and college teaching.* San Francisco: Jossey-Bass.

McLoughlin, C. (2002). Computer supported teamwork: An integrative approach to evaluating cooperative online learning. *Australian Journal of Educational Technology, 18*(2), 227–254.

Mowrer, D. E. (1996). A content analysis of student/instructor communication via computer conferencing. *Higher Education, 32*, 217–241.

Palloff, R., & Pratt, K. (1999). *Building learning communities in cyberspace: Effective strategies for the online classroom.* San Francisco: Jossey Bass.

Piaget, J. (1977). *The origin of intelligence in the child.* Neuchatel-Paris: Delachaux et Niestle.

Pittman, A., Gosper, M., & Rich, D. (1999). Internet based teaching in geography at Macquarie University. *Australian Journal of Educational Technology, 15*(2), 167–187.

Porras-Hernadez, H. (2000). Student variables in the evaluation of mediated learning. *Distance Education, 21*, 385–403.

Salmon, G. (2002). *E-tivities. The key to active online learning.* London: Kogan Page.

Schlechter, T. M. (1990). The relative instructional efficiency of small group computer based training. *Journal of Education Computing Research, 6*, 329–341.

Sigala, M. (2002). The evolution of Internet Pedagogy: Benefits for tourism and hospitality education. *Journal of Hospitality, Leisure, Sports and Tourism Education, 1*(2), 29–45.

Sigala, M. (2003). Internationalising hospitality & tourism education in Virtual Learning Environments (VLE): Exploring critical student factors. *Annual EuroCHRIE (European Council for Hotel, Restaurant and Institutional Education) Conference: The Internationalisation of Future*

Hospitality, Tourism and Aviation Management Education, Bad Honnef – Bonn, 22–25 October. Bonn, Germany: International University of Applied Sciences.

Sigala, M. (2004a). Investigating the factors determining e-learning effectiveness in tourism and hospitality education. *Journal of Hospitality & Tourism Education, 16*(2), 11–21.

Sigala, M. (2004b). Developing and Implementing a Model for Assessing Collaborative e-Learning Processes and Products. In: P. Comeaux (Ed.), *Assessing online teaching and learning* (pp. 88–98). Bolton, MA, USA: Anker Publishing NG Company, Inc.

Sigala, M., & Christou, E. (2002). Using the Internet for complementing and enhancing the teaching of tourism and hospitality education: Evidence from Europe. In: K. W. Wober, A. F. Frew & M. Hitz (Eds), *Information and communication technologies in tourism 2002*. Wien: Springer.

Sigala, M., & Christou, E. (2003). Enhancing and complementing the instruction of tourism and hospitality courses through the use of on-line educational tools. *Journal of Hospitality & Tourism Education, 15*(1), 6–16.

Wachter, R., Gupta, J., & Quaddus, M. (2000). IT takes a village: Village communities in support of education. *International Journal of Information Management, 20*, 473–489.

Webster, J., & Hackley, P. (1997). Teaching effectiveness in technology mediated learning. *Academy of Management Journal, 40*, 1282–1309.

Chapter 27

Teaching and Research

Fiona Jordan

Introduction

This chapter deals with what Jenkins et al. (2003) describe as 'perhaps one of the most significant developments in thinking about teaching and learning in higher education in recent
years' (2003, p. ix), the inter-relationship between teaching and research. The intention of
the chapter is to analyse the connections between teaching and research and to suggest
mechanisms that may assist in linking these activities for the benefit of undergraduate and
postgraduate student learning (Willis & Harper, 2000). Given that the curricula of international tourism programmes vary widely, and that research in tourism covers a very diverse
range of issues, the purpose of this chapter is not to provide a single definitive account of
how 'effective' links may be made. Instead, the aim is to discuss a range of factors that
influence what Neumann (1994) has termed the 'teaching/research nexus', to review literature on this topic and to present examples of good practice in the integration of tourism
research into teaching and learning activities. The chapter will end with consideration of
key issues and challenges for the future.

For a number of years there has been a wide-ranging, international debate (see for
instance Boyer, 1990; Brew & Boud, 1995; Fox, 1992; Jenkins et al., 2003; Woodhouse,
1998) concerning 'the vital but vexed relationship between teaching and research' (Jenkins
et al., 1998, p. 127). As far back as 1963, the Robbins Report in the UK (NCEHE, 1963)
argued that able students should be encouraged throughout their studies to aspire to postgraduate activities and to access their full academic potential. The Dearing Report of 1997
(NCEHE, 1997) similarly reinforced the importance of scholarship and research in underpinning teaching in higher education. A number of studies undertaken in the late 1990s and
early 2000s (see, for example, Elton, 2001; Healey et al., 2003a; Lindsay et al., 2002;
Jenkins et al., 1998; Zamorski, 2000, 2002, 2004) suggest that there is evidence both that
linkages between teaching and research do exist, and that they have the potential to be beneficial to student learning. There are, however, those who argue that the benefits of linking
teaching and research are at the very least unproven. Ramsden and Moses (1992), for
instance, found little or no evidence of a positive link between teaching and research.

An International Handbook of Tourism Education
Copyright © 2005 by Elsevier Ltd.
All rights of reproduction in any form reserved
ISBN: 0-08-044667-1

Similarly, Hattie and Marsh, state that 'the common belief that research and teaching are inextricably entwined is an enduring myth. At best, research and teaching are very loosely coupled' (1996, p. 529). Thus, as Willis and Harper (2000) comment the linkage between teaching and research is more widely assumed to exist than proven to do so. Even where such an inter-relationship has been found to exist its exact nature may not be fully understood (Brew & Boud, 1995). More recently, the Department for Education and Skills in the UK has stated controversially that:

> it is clear that good scholarship, in the sense of being aware of the latest research and thinking within a subject, is essential to good teaching, but not that it is necessary to be active in cutting edge research to be an excellent teacher (DfES, 2003).

It has also been suggested that from the 1990s onwards there has been a gradual, often structural, separation between research and teaching in higher education (McNay, 1998) exacerbated in the UK, according to Brown (2002), by the Research Assessment Exercise (RAE). In the RAE, the quality of submitted university research over a given time period (in the last RAE this was 1996–2001) is graded (a scale of 1–7 was used in the RAE, 2001), to determine the selective allocation of research funds in different subject-related Units of Assessment (Tribe, 2003b). In 1990, the Boyer Commission in the US commented that despite the fact that many academics had entered the profession to teach, the route to academic status and success was now widely viewed as being inextricably linked to publishing (Boyer, 1990). Similarly a study by Drennan and Beck (2000) concluded that many academic staff viewed research as the primary route to career advancement creating a need for institutions to do more to motivate and reward excellent teachers. These anxieties have given rise to renewed efforts to explore the ways in which the teaching/research nexus can be developed to overcome potential problems caused by separation of research and teaching.

In relation to the position of tourism research and its perceived strengths and values within the UK, Tribe suggests that:

> from the cosy world of the inside, tourism research seems to be developing quite nicely. It seems to be expanding (2003b, p. 225).

This, he argues, is evidenced by the fact that there are more than 37 journals publishing over 500 tourism-related articles per annum. It would appear that tourism research is flourishing and is therefore in a good position to influence curriculum and teaching on tourism programmes. This notion is supported by Botterill and Haven (2003) who highlight the impressive growth of tourism research in UK universities. This was exemplified by the fact that during the RAE (2001) there were over 354 tourism-related outputs submitted by 146 staff across 7 Units of Assessment (Botterill & Haven, 2003, p. 6). As Stuart points out, this proliferation of research has the potential to strengthen 'the Tourism academic community's case for academic respectability for their subject ...' (2002, p. 15).

There are, however, concerns that the UK's RAE has presented particular challenges for tourism researchers. According to Botterill and Haven (2003) the structure of the RAE assessment panels has tended to 'invisibilise' tourism submissions potentially impacting negatively upon future funding of work in this area. This state of affairs seems likely to continue, with government plans for the future of research funding in the UK failing to address these concerns (Tribe, 2003a). The Government proposals (DfES, 2003) have given rise to concern that 'divorcing the processes of knowledge creation and knowledge dissemination would [could] lead to a weakening of academic standards, a stifling of the teaching of research methods and a dilution of the breadth of knowledge and expertise within disciplines' (Johnes, 2004, p. 47). An increasingly competitive culture within higher education in the UK (Stuart-Hoyle, 2004) has intensified the pressures placed on academic staff teaching on tourism programmes. Such external factors have a significant influence on the extent to which staff teaching tourism have the opportunity to incorporate research into their teaching.

Defining the Terms: Teaching, Research and Scholarship

Research by Brew (1999) has revealed important differences in the way in which 'research' is defined by staff and confusion concerning which activities constitute relevant scholarship for the purposes of supporting teaching. When considering the linkages between 'teaching' and 'research' it is thus useful to reflect briefly on what is actually meant by these terms. While there is always a danger of over-simplification in adopting concise definitions, it is important to distinguish what is meant by these concepts if we are to examine the links between them. For the purposes of this chapter 'research' is taken to refer to those activities that involve elements of primary investigation (Jenkins et al., 2003) and the term 'teaching' to encompass the range of activities involved in engaging students in learning and in the sharing of knowledge with students.

There is, additionally, a third concept that is assuming an increasingly central role in discussions of the links between teaching and learning — that of 'scholarship'. Jenkins et al. define 'scholarship' as 'careful reflection on practice and review of the literature and research evidence' (2003, p. 9). According to the Boyer Commission (1990) recognising the value of 'scholarship', may assist in highlighting the synergies between teaching and research. Boyer (1990) offered a now widely adopted typology of scholarships as: the scholarship of discovery (advancing knowledge); the scholarship of integration (synthesizing knowledge); the scholarship of service (advancing and applying knowledge); the scholarship of teaching (advancing and applying knowledge about how to teach and promote learning). These forms of scholarship should not be viewed hierarchically but as interlinked and complementary. Some or all of these scholarships may be used in teaching and learning.

Griffiths (2003, cited in Healey et al., 2003b) suggests that there are a variety of ways in which research can be integrated into teaching and curriculum design. Teaching can be: 'research-led' as characterised by a one-way transfer of research findings from staff to students; 'research-oriented' in that the processes of undertaking research and producing knowledge inform the curricula rather than just the outputs; 'research-based' through the adoption of inquiry-based learning designed to enhance the interaction between staff and student; and finally 'research-informed' through pedagogy. Within her studies of the student perspective of linking teaching and research, Zamorski (2000, 2004) identifies five principal 'modes of research-led and research-based teaching and learning' (2004, p. 3). These are categorised as:

- those teaching activities where students on taught courses are provided with knowledge based on research carried out by their lecturers or others;
- those where students gain greater understanding of the complex inter-relationship between knowledge and its production through research;
- those in which students are encouraged to acquire or develop their own research skills throughout their courses;
- specific modules, such as Research Methods, in which students focus on these issues;
- the opportunity for students to undertake their own research project within a course or particular module.

Many of us teaching on tourism courses will recognise a number of these activities as already embedded within our programmes etc. Teaching and learning strategies involving the use of group working, problem-solving and reflective practice have traditionally been linked with the delivery of vocationally and/or professionally oriented programmes of study. For this subject area in particular then, a broad definition of research, encompassing key elements of scholarship, is likely to be beneficial in terms of any exploration of the links between teaching and research. The ideas put forward by both Zamorski and Griffiths demonstrate that there is unlikely to be one single 'right approach' to link teaching and research. Thus good practice in this complex task will necessarily encompass a variety of strategies aimed at enhancing both students' knowledge of research outputs and developing their research skills.

Studying the Teaching/Research Nexus in Higher Education

A number of studies have analysed various facets of the teaching/research nexus as it is perceived by undergraduate, postgraduate and doctoral students in Australia (Neumann, 1994), the UK (Healey et al., 2003a; Jenkins et al., 1998; Lindsay et al., 2002; Thomas & Harris, 2000, 2001; Zamorski, 2000, 2002, 2004) and in New Zealand (Willis & Harper, 2000). Such studies have identified many advantages to student learning from the integration of research into teaching activities. Benefits perceived by students to accrue from staff research include:

- stimulating interest in learning about a subject because a particular member of staff is more interested in teaching it;
- courses informed by research are seen to be up-to-date and therefore of particular value in preparing students for employment;
- students may feel more empathy with staff whom they get to know as researchers rather than simply disseminators of knowledge;
- research-active staff are perceived as talking more authoritatively about the processes of doing research, thereby increasing student awareness of methodological issues;
- the prestige linked to staff research and consultancy may extend beyond the individual to enhance the status of the university in the eyes of students and their peers at other universities;
- students may be more motivated to undertake their own research and go on to postgraduate study by staff who are themselves researchers.

Research into student perceptions of the teaching/research nexus indicates that the most positive experiences of research enhancing the learning experience occur when students themselves are actively involved either through undertaking their own projects or where tutors utilise their research as a basis for lectures (Elton, 2001). Brew, for instance, identifies benefits of 'using research and scholarship as models for university teaching' in terms of: student development of problem-solving skills; encouraging students to be 'open to changing their conceptions of the world'; encouraging collaboration in learning, for instance through use of peer review processes; inclusion of personal issues within studies; and encouraging students to adopt a professional approach to their work (1999, p. 1).

In concurrent studies by Healey et al. (2003a) and Jordan (2003, 2004) students on vocational courses such as tourism expressed particular interest in staff links with industry whether or not these might constitute 'research' as defined in academic terms. Student participants in these studies believed that an up-to-date knowledge of industry trends and business practices was very appropriate given the vocational nature of the subject. Lecturers undertaking industry-based research and consultancy projects were perceived as keeping in touch with the 'real world' and this was viewed as having potential benefits for students' employability.

Studies of student perceptions of the teaching/research nexus have also identified problematic issues in relation to the impact of staff research on student learning. Some students point to a tension between the benefits they themselves acknowledge as accruing from staff involvement in research/consultancy and their frustration in feeling that staff research may take priority over their learning experiences. Jenkins et al. (1998) highlight four potential difficulties associated with staff research as perceived by students. These are: lack of staff availability to students; staff preoccupation with research to the detriment of teaching; staff research steering curriculum content; and a lack of involvement of students in staff research. In research by Healey et al. (2003a) students themselves suggested a number of practical strategies for minimising such detrimental impacts, including:

- enhancing electronic contact between staff and students;
- giving students as much information as possible about why staff are not available to see them;
- ensuring that students are warned in advance of prolonged staff absences for research purposes and provided with other means of support during these times.

These relatively simple strategies can help to ensure that students are clear about exactly when and how their learning needs are being addressed by research-active staff and may also assist in enhancing communications between staff and students more generally.

In addition to exploring student perspectives of the teaching/research nexus, a number of studies have examined the views of academic staff on this topic. In the US Colbeck (1998) studied departmental working practices, cultures and policies for integrating teaching and research at two universities. She concluded that structural and cultural factors were significant in shaping staff perceptions of the teaching/research nexus. Smeby (1998) studied staff perceptions of the relationship between teaching and research at universities in Norway, concluding that staff are more likely to have their postgraduate teaching influenced by research than their teaching at 'lower' levels. Studies undertaken in the UK (see for instance Ball, 2003; Botterill, 2003; Rowland, 1996; Thomas & Harris, 2000, 2001) have suggested that staff view the linkages between teaching and research as valuable in terms of both teaching quality and university status. Academic staff in some studies have, however, expressed concern that external pressures such as funding and expanding student numbers can impinge on their abilities to make these links effectively.

Overall, investigation of the teaching/research nexus has tended to suggest that these links are regarded by both staff and students as potentially beneficial in terms of the student learning experience, university prestige and the development of academic staff themselves. However such research also shows that the linkages require active management if these benefits are to be achieved and potential drawbacks avoided. The next section outlines some examples of good practice in how these links may be developed in tourism.

Practical Strategies for Linking Teaching and Research

Jenkins et al. (2003) suggest that strategies designed to enhance the linkages between learning, teaching and research should be adopted at all levels of higher education from national policy-making, through institutional missions, at a departmental level, on an individual staff basis and through curriculum design. The examples of practice presented here primarily focus on strategies adopted at the level of the individual member of staff and curriculum design. As Jenkins et al., point out however:

> … one has to be careful in taking research from one national context and applying it to another…[in] that there may be important differences in how teaching and research are funded and audited, and how institutions and academics see their roles (Jenkins et al., 2003, p. 24).

A number of the examples of good practice identified here have been drawn from resources available through the UK's Learning and Teaching Support Network (LTSN) Subject Centre in Hospitality, Leisure, Sport and Tourism now the Higher Education Academy Subject Network for Hospitality, Leisure, Sport and Tourism and can be accessed at www.hlst.heacademy.ac.uk. The Subject Centre's newsletter LINK no. 9 contains further information and examples of linking teaching and research and can be accessed at via the website address shown above. It should also be noted that the examples referred to here often have application beyond the subject of tourism.

The first task facing academics in linking teaching and research is simply to make students aware of who is undertaking what research and where it can be found. Practical suggestions offered by students to help increase their awareness of research (Healey et al., 2003a; Jordan, 2003) include:

- use of departmental notice boards as a means of publicising research events and outputs;
- lecturers using their own publications (for instance texts, articles or industry reports) as a basis for examples in lectures;
- introducing staff research interests as early as induction so that students become used to the idea of staff as researchers rather than simply teachers;
- compiling staff research and consultancy CVs and making these available as an easily accessible electronic resource publicised in module guides or other student documents;
- circulation of a student-friendly newsletter detailing the most recent research/consultancy/scholarship activities of staff and relevant forthcoming events.

The most effective strategies for integrating research into teaching are those that move students from passive consumption of research concepts to active engagement in research-related activities. One example of how to integrate research directly into the curriculum is provided by Altinay (2003), who has devised a tutorial and resource-based module in which Masters level students select their own topic but based on current staff research expertise. Staff members set questions and tasks related to their particular area of interest and students are required to write an academic article conforming to publishing conventions for the subject. In this way, students are both made aware of staff research and also provided with the opportunity to develop their own research and academic writing skills. When encouraging students to develop their research skills through such project work it is essential to ensure that sufficient support is available to them. Robinson and Kay (2003) have created an online resource called the Research Gateway (http://www.hlst.ltsn.ac.uk/ gateway). This tool supports students through all phases of a research project including topic selection, reviewing literature, collecting data and analysing and presenting findings.

In research by Healey et al. (2003a) students suggested that they tended to become more aware of research towards the end of their studies rather than regarding it as an integral element of their course from the beginning. In addressing this issue, Lyons and Nield (2003) advocate developing research or 'investigation' as a strand running through all levels of a student's programme so that it is seen as a natural part of studying. This process is under-pinned by an 'investigation skills' module that runs throughout the first year and is designed to provide students with an introduction to literature and academic writing. It may also be useful early in programmes of study to raise the question of how research contributes to tourism generally and to explore different types of research used in various tourism contexts. This could be combined with a practical exercise on resource selectivity requiring students to produce work using a minimum number of academic resources of different types (for instance conference papers and journal articles rather than electronic resources). This may also be an appropriate time to introduce students to the ethics of the research process and the guidelines that they need to follow. Encouraging students to regard research skills as a natural part of learning may assist in overcoming any fear of research that they may have.

Zamorski (2004) highlights the potential of problem-based learning and evidence-based learning for enhancing students' research skills. Wellings and Tongue (LTSN case study available at http://www.hlst.ltsn.ac.uk/projects/linktr.html) adopt such an approach in devising, for first year students, a consultancy brief based on a live project with industry providers. Local leisure and tourism businesses are invited to submit topics and/or problems to be researched by groups of three or four students. Students must then design and undertake relevant research to complete their task and are responsible for liasing with their industry contacts. Such an approach provides a useful example of how the vocational orientation of tourism programmes can constitute a vehicle for integrating industry-linked teaching and research.

Similarly, Snelgrove et al. (2003) demonstrate how enquiry-based learning (EBL) can be utilised in a first year research methods module. Groups of three or four students undertake projects based on staff research and teaching. The groups must 'progress the research project along a predefined path, each task along that path suggesting a course of action, but leaving the group to explore their particular circumstances' (2003, p. 8). The module is supported with lectures, seminars, electronic resources and tutorials. The assessment comprises of a research poster for which each group member takes responsibility for a specific element. Groups must then present and 'defend' their poster as a group. This approach can assist in overcoming the tendency for some students to be passive recipients of information, particularly at the beginning of their studies. Placing emphasis on problem- and enquiry-based learning, and the adoption of assessment criteria that explicitly assess reflective and analytical skills, is not only useful in developing research skills but is also appropriate for the vocational nature of many tourism programmes. Strategies that actively encourage students to be researchers can also act as a springboard for students to develop their own research agendas within their undergraduate programmes and beyond.

Key Issues and Future Challenges in Linking Teaching and Research in Tourism

The final section of this chapter will highlight some of the key issues and future challenges facing tourism educators in seeking to enhance the links between teaching and research. While a number of these are common to higher education providers in many countries, others are more specific to the UK. Healey and Jenkins (2003) identify one of the most significant challenges in linking teaching and research as stemming from rapid global progress in information technology. While the Internet has undoubtedly proved a very valuable resource for students and academic staff alike, it also constitutes a potential impediment to students developing research and investigative skills. Increasingly students are becoming reliant on instant downloading of information in order to complete assessed work rather than the more time-consuming task of reading around published research outputs. Students thus need to be taught both to discriminate between the many available sources of information in terms of academic quality and to be critical and selective in their use of sources.

According to Zamorski (2004) the rising costs of higher education in a number of countries may result in students focusing almost exclusively on the assessed elements of curriculum required to successfully complete their programme of studies rather than exploring their educational potential more broadly. If research-led curricula are perceived as less time-efficient than those that are more assessment-driven students may opt for less research-intensive programmes. Zamorski (2004) also argues that the move towards students as paying customers of universities coupled with more litigious societies (for instance, the US and increasingly the UK) may serve to stifle innovations in research-based teaching as educators become more cautious in their approaches.

The nature of tourism as a subject area presents its own challenges in terms of both research and teaching and correspondingly the linkages between the two. Key issues related to researching and/or teaching in tourism include: the multi-disciplinary nature of many tourism courses spanning a wide variety of management and social sciences perspectives and topics; the vocational and industry-oriented nature of many tourism management courses; the rapid expansion of tourism programmes and the shift towards modularity (Airey & Johnson, 1998; Stergiou et al., 2003); pressures on individual teaching staff (Stuart, 2002); the over-reliance of tourism research and corresponding curriculum development on a scientific positivist epistemology (Botterill, 2001; Tribe, 2001); a lack of pedagogic research in tourism (Stergiou et al., 2003; Tribe, 2002) the underdeveloped and/or marginalised position of tourism research in the UK (as discussed earlier); and debates centring on the status of tourism as a distinct discipline or subject area (see for instance Echter & Jamal, 1997; Tribe, 1997, 2000).

Despite these contentious issues, and the more general challenges faced by many higher education providers, it is suggested that there are significant benefits to be realised by both staff and students from linking teaching and research. These benefits centre on staff enthusiasm and on their contribution of up-to-date, industry-related knowledge in the context of these vocational and/or professional programmes. The key to managing the research/teaching nexus appears to lie in adopting a broad definition of research (possibly to further incorporate notions of scholarship as suggested by Boyer) and in encouraging staff to further integrate their own research interests into their curriculum design. In addition, further strategies aimed at making information about the research and scholarship activities of staff more freely available to students (for instance through staff talking at lectures and/or circulation of newsletters) may assist in limiting negative outcomes and in developing greater empathy between students and staff as both learners and producers of knowledge.

References

Airey, D., & Johnson, S. (1998). The profile of tourism studies degree courses in the UK: 1997/98. *The Association of Tourism in Higher Education Guidelines, No. 7*. Surrey: ATHE.

Altinay, L. (2003). Linking teaching and research in practice at masters level. *LINK 9*, (Spring), 28–29.

Ball, S. (2003). Research and teaching connections in hospitality management education. *LINK 9*, (Spring), 26–27.

Botterill, D. (2001). The epistemology of a set of tourism studies. *Leisure Studies, 20*, 199–214.

Botterill, D. (2003). *Staff perceptions of linking teaching and research*. LTSN for hospitality, leisure, sport and tourism. Available at http://www.hlst.ltsn.ac.uk/projects/linking_staff.pdf.

Botterill, D., & Haven, C. (2003). Tourism studies and the research assessment exercise 2001. *The association of tourism in higher education guidelines No. 11*, Surrey: ATHE.

Boyer, E. (1990). *Scholarship reconsidered: Priorities of the professoriate*. Princeton, NJ: Carnegie Foundation for the Advancement of Teaching.

Brew, A. (1999). Research and scholarship as models for university teaching. Paper presented at the conference of the European association for research in education, Gothenburg, Sweden, August.

Brew, A., & Boud, D. (1995). Teaching and research: Establishing the vital link with learning. *Higher Education, 29*, 261–273.

Brown, R. (2002). Research and teaching – repairing the damage. *Exchange, 3*, Autumn, 29–30.

Colbeck, C. C. (1998). Merging in a seamless blend. *Journal of Higher Education, 69*(6), 647–671.

DfES (Department for Education and Skills). (2003). *The future for higher education*. Norwich: HMSO. Available at: www.dfes.gov.uk/highereducation/hestrategy/

Drennan, L.T., & Beck, M. (2000). Teaching quality performance indicators: Key influences on the UK universities' Scores. *Quality Assurance in Education, 9*(2), 92–102.

Echter, C., & Jamal, T. (1997). The disciplinary dilemma of tourism studies. *Annals of Tourism Research, 24*, 868–883.

Elton, L. (2001). Research and teaching: Conditions for a positive link. *Teaching in Higher Education, 6*(1), 43–56.

Fox, M. F. (1992). Research, teaching and publication productivity: Mutuality versus competition in academia. *Sociology of Education, 65*(4), 293–305.

Hartley, H. (2003). Staff perspectives on the links between research and teaching: A Pilot Study. *LINK 9*, (Spring), 23–25.

Hattie, J., & Marsh, H. W. (1996). The relationship between research and teaching: A meta-analysis. *Review of Educational Research, 66*(4), 507–542.

Healey, M., Jordan, F., Pell, B., & Short, C. (2003a). The student experience of research and consultancy in a new university. Paper presented at SEDA/SHRE joint conference, the Scholarship of Academic and Staff Development: Research, evaluation and changing practice, University of Bristol, 9–11 April.

Healey, M., Blumhof, J., & Thomas, N. (2003b). *Linking teaching and research in geography, earth and environmental sciences*. Available at http://www.gees.ac.uk/linktr.

Healey, M., & Jenkins, A. (2003). *Linking teaching and research: The benefits for student learning*. Workshop presented at University of Calgary, Canada, 11 August.

Jenkins, A., Blackman, T., Lindsay, R., & Paton-Saltzberg, R. (1998). Teaching and research: Student perspectives and policy implications. *Studies in Higher Education, 23*(2), 127–141.

Jenkins, A., Breen, R., Lindsay, R., & Brew, A. (2003). *Reshaping teaching in higher education: Linking teaching and research*. London: Kogan page and the staff and educational development association.

Johnes, M. (2004). The teaching – research nexus in a sports history module. *Journal of Hospitality, Leisure, Sport and Tourism Education, 3*(1), 47–52.

Jordan, F. (2003). Linking teaching and research: Managing the student experience. *Workshop presented at progress through partnership, 2nd Annual conference of the LTSN for hospitality, leisure, sport and tourism*, Oxford, September.

Jordan, F. (2004). Linking teaching and research in hospitality, leisure, sport and tourism. *LINK 9*, (Spring), 20–22.

Lindsay, R., Breen, R., & Jenkins, A. (2002). Academic research and teaching quality: The Views of undergraduate and postgraduate students. *Studies in Higher Education, 27*(3), 309–327.

Lyons, H., & Nield, K. (2003). New approaches to embedding investigation and research in the curriculum at sheffield hallam university. *LINK 9*, (Spring), 5–6.

McNay, I. (1998). The paradoxes of research assessment and funding. In: M. Henkel & B. Little (Eds), *Changing relationships between higher education and the state*. London: Jessica Kingsley.

NCEHE (National Committee of Enquiry into Higher Education). (1963). *Committee on Higher Education* (the Robbins Report). London: HMSO.

NCEHE (National Committee of Enquiry into Higher Education). (1997). *Higher education in the learning society: Report of the National Committee of Enquiry into higher education* (the Dearing Report). London: HMSO.

Neumann, R. (1994). The teaching–research Nexus: applying a framework to university students' learning experiences. *European Journal of Education, 29*(3), 323–339.

Ramsden, P., & Moses, I. (1992). Associations between research and teaching in australian higher education. *Higher Education, 23*(3), 273–295.

Robinson, L., & Kay, T. (2003). The research gateway. *LINK 9*, (Spring), 9–11.

Rowland, S. (1996). Relationships between teaching and research. *Teaching in Higher Education, 1*(1), 7–20.

Smeby, J. -C. (1998). Knowledge production and knowledge transmission: The interaction between research and teaching at universities. *Teaching in Higher Education, 3*(1), 7–20.

Snelgrove, M., Dainty, G., & Botterill, D. (2003). Making learning cool — A case study intervention in enquiry-based learning. *LINK 9*, (Spring), 7–9.

Stergiou, D., Airey, D., & Riley, M. (2003). The evaluation of the teaching of individual academics in UK's tourism higher education: Developing a construct for teaching profiles. *International Journal of Tourism Research, 5,* 59–67.

Stuart, M. (2002). Critical influences on tourism as a subject in UK higher education. *Journal of Hospitality, Leisure, Sport and Tourism Education, 1*(1), 5–18.

Stuart-Hoyle, M. (2004). Critical incidents: Tourism in higher education. *Association of Tourism in Higher Education Guidelines, No. 12,* Surrey: ATHE.

Thomas, R., & Harris, V. (2000). Teaching quality and staff research: Are there connections? A case study of a metropolitan university department. *Quality Assurance in Education, 8*(3), 139–146.

Thomas, R., & Harris, V. (2001). Exploring the connections between teaching and research in hospitality management. *Hospitality Management, 20,* 245–257.

Tribe, J. (1997). The indiscipline of tourism. *Annals of Tourism Research, 24*(3), 638–657.

Tribe, J. (2000). Indisciplined and unsubstantiated. *Annals of Tourism Research, 27*(3), 809–813.

Tribe, J. (2001). Research paradigms and the tourism curriculum. *Journal of Travel Research, 39* (May), 442–448.

Tribe, J. (2002). Editorial. *Journal of Hospitality, Leisure, Sport and Tourism, 1*(1), 1–4.

Tribe, J. (2003a). Editorial. *Journal of Hospitality, Leisure, Sport and Tourism, 2*(2), 1–3.

Tribe, J. (2003b). The RAE-ification of tourism research in the UK. *International Journal of Tourism Research, 5,* 225–234.

Wellings, C., & Tongue, N. *Tourism management live project/leisure management live project.* Available at http://www.hlst.ltsn.ac.uk/projects/linktr.html. Accessed 24-08-04.

Willis, D., & Harper, J. (2000). Looking for learning: Postgraduate experiences of the teaching-research nexus. *Proceedings of the symposium on teaching and learning in higher education,* National University of Singapore, 6–7 July.

Woodhouse, D. (1998). Auditing research and the research/teaching nexus. *New Zealand Journal of Educational Studies, 33*(1), 39–53.

Zamorski, B. (2000). *Research-led teaching and learning in higher education.* Centre for applied research in education, Norwich: University of East Anglia.

Zamorski, B. (2002). Research-led teaching and learning in higher education: A case study. *Teaching in Higher Education, 7*(4), 411–427.

Zamorski, B. (2004). The impact of student learning/the student experience. Paper presented at research and teaching: closing the divide? An international colloquium, 17–19 March.

Chapter 28

Community Education

Stroma Cole

Introduction

Residents or villagers in less developed parts of the world, often referred to as hosts, interact with tourists on a daily basis. They are in the front line of tourism and are frequently
part of the product that is sold. Many have received minimal formal education and few
have had the opportunity to experience tourism as a tourist. This chapter is about the education of this stakeholder group, so vital in cultural tourism in less developed countries,
but so often ignored in the tourism education literature.

   This chapter firstly outlines the rationale for a more thorough discussion of the educational needs of host communities. This is followed by some examples of actions that have
been taken, and questions the ethics behind some of the educational programmes to date.
The third part of the chapter provides a case study that highlights some of the issues raised,
and the chapter then goes on to suggest some areas of curriculum and teaching methods
that would be useful in this and many other communities that seek non-formal community
tourism education.

Non-Formal Community Tourism Education: Rationale

There are two fundamental reasons that we should turn our attention to the education of
host communities:

(a) Service provision; and
(b) Sustainability.

Service Provision

Tourism is a competitive industry. A destination's attractiveness needs to be maintained,
and the service sector must meet visitor expectations. Increasing numbers of tourists are

An International Handbook of Tourism Education
Copyright © 2005 by Elsevier Ltd.
ISBN: 0-08-044667-1

drawn to places to experience different cultures, and new tourists increasingly want some level of social interaction with people in local communities. These cultural tourists want to feel welcomed and safe and they appreciate quality service. However, this welcome is not limited to their experiences in their hotels. It extends to a range of encounter situations, often with villagers in and around their homes. While Robinson and Yee (1996) discuss the education of "front-line workers: the people who interact with tourists" (p. 345), they are discussing the educational needs of front-line *workers* and are ignoring the educational needs of the communities with whom tourists interact, but who do not have a formal tourism job. As Mafati (2002) explains, those people in Caprivi, Namibia who have set up enterprises have received training but "it needs to extend beyond the people who run the enterprises to involve the community as a whole, this way there will be full understanding and cooperation" (p. 10).

Virtually, all tourist surveys show that "friendliness of local people" rates highly on the list of positive features about a tourist destination (Sweeney & Wanhill, 1996). Furthermore, holiday satisfaction and repeat visitation are in part determined by tourists' interpersonal experiences with their hosts. In less developed countries where cultural differences are great, the potential for misunderstanding, distrust, confusion, tension and conflict is greatest. Tourists often report interactional difficulties and suffer culture shock due to not understanding the rules of engagement (Pearce, Kim, & Lussa 1998) — while the hosts feel un-respected, belittled, and exploited. As Reisinger and Turner (2003) discuss, these problems result from a lack of knowledge of each other's culture. "The more cultural knowledge people have, the more they know about other cultural groups, the better they can predict their behaviour. Consequently the easier it is to enter social relationships" (p. 51).

As Ross (2004) discusses, trust between hosts and guests can be fostered where both parties have basic information about each other. The tourists can read about their hosts or pay a guide to provide the necessary information but how does the resident learn about the tourists' tastes, customs and expectations? While tourists can build up knowledge about tourism through their experiences, how do villagers in remote marginal communities, without the resources to travel or be tourists themselves, develop an understanding of the tourism phenomena? As Lipscomb (1998) discusses, "unlike most other economic activities in which indigenous technical knowledge (ITK) has some relevance to a more commercially orientated operation there is little ITK in most villages of direct relevance to tourism operations" (p. 193).

Sustainability

Local community participation is a widely accepted criterion of sustainable tourism. The reasons for community participation in tourism development are well rehearsed in the tourism literature. Not only does community participation need to be seen in development proposals but it is often essential to secure funding (Mowforth & Munt, 1998; Kadir Din, 1997). Involvement in planning is likely to result in more appropriate decisions and greater motivation on the part of the local people (Hitchcock, King, & Parnwell, 1993); and the protection of the environment, tourism's resource, will be supported (Tourism Concern,

1992). Community participation is considered necessary to get community support and acceptance of tourism development projects, and to ensure that benefits relate to the local community needs. As a service industry, tourism is highly dependent on the goodwill and co-operation of host communities. Service is the key to the hospitality atmosphere (Murphy, 1985, p. 120). Villagers' support and pride in their tourism is especially important in the case of remote village cultural tourism, where "meeting the people" is often sort by the tourists. Tosun and Timothy (2003) further argue that the local community is more likely to know what will work and what will not in local conditions; and that community participation can add to the democratisation process and often encourages various forms of equity and empowerment.

As has been identified by Arnstein (1969) and Pretty (1995), a ladder of participation exists ranging from "being consulted" (often only being informed of a *fait accompli*) to being able to determine every aspect of the development process. While it can be argued that all communities participate to a certain degree — sharing a despoiled environment, receiving menial jobs or getting a percentage of gate fees to a national park — community participation is about active participation and empowerment. As Warburton (1998) points out, the need for participation is not doubted but the empowerment end of the ladder has received little attention in the tourism development literature.

There are a number of reasons why active community participation is hard to achieve in practise. Frequently a lack of ownership, capital, skills, knowledge and resources all constrain the ability of communities to fully control their participation in tourism development (Scheyvens, 2003). In remote areas of less developed countries, a number of further barriers exist: the concept is new; decisions are taken by bureaucrats in a highly centralised system; planners believe that local people are uneducated and too ignorant to be involved, and lack the experience and training to facilitate participation (cf. Timothy, 1999, for example). Importantly, the local people do not have the knowledge to participate (Cole, 1997; Ashley, Roe, & Goodwin, 2001). As Abram (1998) suggests, "the difficulty for ordinary people in accessing technical discourse is often identified as a major barrier to full participation" (p. 6). Many communities lack any real understanding of what it is they are supposed to be making decisions about (Sofield, 2003). Kadir Din (1997) considers ignorance as the greatest barrier to participation but that the ignorance is not restricted to residents but "also affects the planning machinery and bureaucracy vested with implementation" (p. 79).

Active participation is then frequently constrained by a community's lack of information and knowledge. Knowledge of the decision-making process and the tourism system are essential if residents are to take an active part in tourism planning and management, and if participation is to move from the bottom rungs of the participation ladder to empowerment.

Communities need access to a wide range of information about tourism. Information provision is an essential first step; since meaningful participation cannot take place before a community understands what they are to make decisions about (Cole, 1999; Sofield, 2003). In addition to the need for information is the need for confidence to take part in the decision-making process. In many marginal communities, especially where there has been a long history of colonisation and/or authoritarian rule communities lack the confidence to take part in the decision-making (Cole, 1997; Timothy, 1999).

In order to bring about the confidence for meaningful participation and empowerment, many researchers have recognised the need for and value of considerable public education (for example Simmons, 1994; Connell, 1997; Pearce, 1994). As Ashley et al. (2001) have examined, the poor have a weak capacity in the general understanding of tourists and how the industry works. An understanding of tourists and tourism is the first stage of empowering the local communities to make informed and appropriate decisions about their tourism development.

Tourism Awareness Programmes: In Whose Interest?

While the need for public education in tourism is well documented, few studies discuss the philosophy and practice of such programmes. One programme aimed at generating awareness and understanding about tourism within the community is the Welcome Host Programme in Wales. Sweeney and Wanhill (1996) discuss the success of the programme in changing behaviour through training and altering attitudes by generating awareness in the host population. The programme aimed at changing local attitudes towards tourists and improving the quality of the visitors' experience, not only for those working in tourism but in any encounter situation, whether a chance meeting, polite enquiry or the service relationship. Based on *Superhost*, a similar programme in Canada, Welcome Host was promoted on the premise that "if we leave a good impression with customers, the chances are that our business will grow, they will stay longer, spend more money in our communities and return to visit us again" (Sweeney & Wanhill, 1996, p. 154).

The Indonesian Minister of Tourism launched a similar Tourism Awareness Program (*sadar wisata*) in 1989–1990. The public education campaign involved various media including the television, newspapers and brochures. At the heart of the programme was a seven-point formula for successful tourism (*sapta persona*) disseminated through government departments, community groups and youth organisations (Joop Ave, no date). The seven-point formula consisted of security, cleanliness, cool comfort, natural beauty, friendly people and memories. According to the minister, the objectives were "to form a strong, sturdy identity and to maintain national discipline" (Departemen Parawisata, Pos, & Telekomunikasi, 1990, p. 36). As Adams (1997) discusses, it promoted even the remotest villages in outer Indonesia to consider their touristic charms and attracting powers. In some places where tourism was already established, courses were offered to community members who were most likely to be involved with tourists (e.g. taxi and pedi-cab drivers, guest house and restaurant owners and street vendors) (Timothy, 2000).

While such public education schemes may seem laudable, they raise an ethical question. As Robinson and Yee (1996) ask, is preparing hosts to receive visitors in fact educating them? (p. 348) Is preparing hosts to provide quality service in fact training them for quality subservience? Similar questions need to be asked about other training programmes. As Gurung, Simmons, and Delvin (1996) suggested, many guide-training programmes are about meeting the needs of the clients while issues of sustainability are neglected. Many community eco-tourism training programmes have either the implicit or explicit aim of protecting wildlife resources (e.g. Rainforest Alliance, 2004). While this is an important educational objective in its own right, it does not necessarily develop the political skills of local people to actively take part in decisions about tourism development, the primary function of training for local participation (Goodwin, 1995).

The Case Study

The case study is based on research that took place in two villages, Wogo and Bena, in Ngadha, an area that approximates to the Southwest third of the Ngada regency, on the island of Flores, Indonesia. The study was carried between 1989 and 2003, during which time my position as researcher changed. Between 1989 and 1994, as a tour operator, I took groups of 12 tourists at a time to stay in Ngadha villages. In 1996, a Rapid Rural Appraisal was carried out. Then, between August 1998 and February 1999, ethnographic fieldwork was undertaken. I returned to the field in 2001 and 2003.

The Catholic villagers are largely peasants, eking out a hand-to-mouth existence on poor soils. The rugged mountainous area began to be visited by 'drifters' in the 1980s and has seen increasing numbers of tourists ever since. The most popular village, Bena, received 9000 tourists in 1997 (Regency Department of Education and Culture, 1998). The area is one of the poorest in Indonesia, and tourism is considered the area's best option for economic development (Umbu Peku Djawang, 1991).

The majority of villagers in Ngadha are passively participating in tourism. Tourists visit the heart of the villages (*nua*), consisting of between 20 and 40 traditional wooden houses, with high-thatched roofs, built around a rectangle, for between 20 minutes and 2 hours. They wander around the villages, look at the houses and 'totems to the ancestors'; take photographs and leave again. In one of the villages, Bena, there is an indigenous weaving industry, which provides additional interest for tourists and an opportunity for the villagers to gain financial benefit from tourism. However, in the majority of villages the local people have the inconvenience of tourism without economic advantage. They are passive participants, unpaid actors on a stage, gazed at by an affluent audience. However, tourism has brought non-economic benefits to the villages: convenient water supplies, pride in their cultural heritage, "friends" all over the world, and the villagers are happy to be visited.

Alongside the villagers positive view of tourism is a feeling of bemusement. Frequently, I was asked by villagers in Wogo, "Why do they come?" "What do they want?" "They don't ask anything; they don't learn anything; that one didn't even take any photographs". "They just look and take photographs; they do not understand the meanings". Villagers thought I should know why tourists came, looked, took photographs and departed. Similarly, villagers in Bena expressed their lack of understanding of tourists. They are unclear why tourists visit and what they want. Villagers in both Bena and Wogo bemoaned their lack of understanding of what tourists really want.

The villagers' knowledge of tourism comes from experience, guides and the government's Tourism Awareness Program (*sadar wisata*). Contact with tourists has enabled the villagers to distinguish between "young, low spending, dirty tourists"; "older, fatter, high spenders"; and "tourists who want to understand". From the guides villagers have learnt that tourists are impatient or at least do not like waiting for events; that tourists become anxious if villagers crowd around them and that tourists require personal space; and that tourist do not like 'begging children'.

The regency tourist office followed a provincial instruction to "develop the villagers"[1] through the Tourism Awareness Campaign. The villagers of Bena were invited to attend a presentation in 1996. The material presented[2] (Dinas Parawisata Ngada, 1995) included an explanation of what tourism is, how it benefits the area and its potential negative impacts,[3] how far tourism had come in the last national Five Year Plan, and the above seven point formula for successful tourism. The presentation was open to all the villagers, but initially was so badly attended that people had to be persuaded to attend. The programme provided an overview of the reasons why tourists visit their village and why preservation of both material and non-material culture would serve to develop economic rewards. The villagers considered the presentation too long especially as it was in Indonesian, which is not their first language. They thought it was boring and unhelpful. They felt patronised to be told, by townsfolk, to preserve their culture, which they had done for centuries with no thought of economic benefit. Furthermore, there was no opportunity for the villagers to ask questions or raise any of their issues about tourists or tourism development.

In 2000, another training programme was organised. Three members from each of the four villages were invited to attend one and half days training in Bajawa, the regency town. Each was paid expenses. Three villagers from Bena attended. "The same again, just like what they said last time, protection of culture, preservation of our material assets, be good hosts. Nothing new, no help, we did not learn anything" is how one villager described it to me. This programme was an attempt by the government to gain villagers' support for tourism development. It represents the bottom rung of Pretty's (1995) participation ladder. It was not designed to empower the villagers to develop indigenous plans. The essence of the programme was that tourists are the nation's guests, so the villagers should be good hosts to them.

The Department of Tourism has built three home-stays, a viewing point and toilet facilities in Bena. The majority of villagers did not know what a home-stay was for. They asked me, "What are home-stays?" "What are they for?" The terminology is clearly confusing. These were not anyone's homes for guests to stay in; they are dwellings built in traditional style for use by tourists. No individuals or groups were trained or made responsible for the upkeep and day-to-day management of the home-stays and thus they have become a "white elephant", and are not used to accommodate tourists. The provincial Tourism Department had organised the building of home-stays without educating the people as to their purpose, or providing any training on how to manage them.

The villages lacked knowledge about issues of carrying capacity. Several villagers suggested that each of the home-stays could accommodate 30 tourists. This was based on their own houses accommodating in excess of 30 members at major rituals. However, it is unlikely any tourist would be prepared to sleep in such cramped conditions. Although each home-stay could reasonably accommodate eight tourists, only one toilet was provided for all three houses, seriously restricting potential occupancy levels.

The villagers of Ngadha are unable to participate in the planning and management of tourism due to their lack of understanding. They are unable to access the "technical discourse"

---

[1] *Membina masyrakat.*
[2] Which was lent to me for analysis.
[3] dampak negatif.

of tourism, so often in English, as epitomised by the Tourism Department's "home-stays". The villagers' lack of tourism understanding is linked to the unfilled potential for further tourism development. The villagers were not short of ideas about potential future developments but did not have the confidence, knowledge or skills to put them into practice.

Curriculum

Ideally, the content of any training programme should be negotiated at the local level and provide for the specific needs of each community group. However, there are a number of recurring themes in the literature about tourism development in less developed countries and capacity building needs: (a) esteem, (b) cross-cultural understanding, (c) what tourists want and (d) tourism development. These areas, I would argue, are important for the entire community to appreciate, while a range of further topics would be more relevant to certain sectors of the community who want specific types of training: (e) product development, (f) marketing, (g) financial management, (h) food services and hygiene.

Esteem

One of the successes of the Indonesian Tourism Awareness Program was that villages all over the archipelago began to examine what they had that could attract tourists. However, as the case study illustrated they did not have the confidence to act on their ideas. As Timothy (2002) suggests "a sense of inadequacy appears to permeate developing societies" (p. 161). Many have negative self-images and downgrade all things local (cf. Lipscomb, 1998 with reference to the Solomon Islands). As Victurine (2000) discusses, with reference to Uganda, the villagers look outward "assigning lower value to local products and ways of doing things. They believe that they had to acquire goods from the outside and adopt practises, designs and styles from the cities…" (p. 224). The need for communities to appreciate that what they have locally is important, and is linked to "what tourists want" and "product development" (see below). Esteem is probably one of the most important aspects of any community training or capacity building for many communities. Where knowledge, ideas and entrepreneurial spirit do exist, it is often a lack of confidence that prevents active participation.

Cross-Cultural Understanding

As discussed, many of the problems, and lost opportunities, in tourism result from a lack of cross-cultural understanding between tourists and residents. Work has been conducted on teaching tourists the habits, rules of behaviour and interaction and customs of hosts. The "Cultural Assimilator" or cultural sensitizer programmes appear useful to provide cross-cultural understanding to tourists (Pearce et al., 1998). However, the methods, involving a lot of readings that were considered too complicated and overly long by Australian tourists, would clearly be inappropriate for villagers in remote marginal communities.

A dearth of literature exists on the curriculum needed to provide hosts with the social skills to understand the rules of western cultures to prevent them from feeling inadequate and embarrassed, and to reduce the chance of misunderstanding and hostility. A curriculum that included a basic understanding of the differences in patterns of greetings; showing emotions and expressing dissatisfaction; joking and asking personal questions; body language and touching and the use of time and space; would go a long way to reduce confusion and negative interactions.

What Tourists Want

As many villagers in less developed countries have never been tourists themselves, they have little understanding of why tourists travel or what it is they want. As Lipscomb (1998) discusses, villagers want to attract tourists but they have trouble understanding why foreigners want to visit their villages and what activities they would like to do. Many activities that are everyday life for villagers are a fascination to tourists. In Ngadha, for example, tourists' visits are nearly entirely limited to the central residential compound (*nua*) where tourists can observe the villagers moving in and out of their homes, the villagers totems[4] and megaliths. The tourist product could be diversified if tourists were taken to see (and try out) a variety of village activities. For example, seeing local people climb hairy palms, bleed the tree and attach long bamboo tubes to collect palm toddy is an activity that fascinates tourists. Furthermore, they are prepared to pay for the privilege of tasting the sweet mildly alcoholic liquid that is collected.

Understanding what tourists want is linked to having confidence in local products. In Ngadha the only food and drink on sale for tourists are items in the local roadside shop. They consist of bottled water, Coca Cola, Sprite and biscuits. Sales of the drinks are limited as there is no way of keeping them cold. On a number of occasions, I observed tourists order a bottled drink and give it back, as one tourist commented "We can't stand warm Sprite, we will wait till we get back to Bajawa". The idea that tourists would appreciate locally produced fruit juices or palm toddy did not occur to the villagers.

The villagers in Ngadha considered that electricity was a necessary addition to the home-stays. They found it hard to believe that for a couple of nights the tourists would enjoy the experience of being without. In contrast they did not realise the importance that western tourists place on cleanliness and hygiene.

Tourism Development

Destination residents need knowledge of the tourism industry and its potential effects (Kadir Din, 1993). Local communities cannot take part in decisions about tourism development if they do not understand the industry. They need to understand the pros and cons and how tourism could impact on their lives (Scheyvens, 2003). They need knowledge of the different forms that tourism can take and the advantages and disadvantages of the different types. They need to understand about carrying capacities and the limits to growth. Knowledge of leakages and linkages is linked both to tourists' desire for local products and maximising the economic gains from tourism — it is therefore crucial information to provide.

---

[4] A gloss for the sacrificial posts or shrines belonging to the clans that make up the villages.

In terms of tourism development, local ownership of all facilities will maximise the retention of profits and maintain control in local hands. It is imperative that residents are made aware of this. Maintaining ownership of the resource base is critical to the long-term success of any community-based tourism. Unfortunately, there are too many cases where villagers have been forced to give up their land. As Johnston (2003) discusses, an important aspect of community education is about human rights, how they are defined and the best avenues and tools for protecting them. It is imperative that villagers are made aware that selling their land to outsiders represents a loss of their potential to control the development tourism in the future. However, as many analysts have suggested, a lack of finance is a major limiting factor for many community tourism initiatives and therefore joint ventures need to be given consideration (Scheyvens, 2003).

Product Development

In order to gain some economic benefit to offset the inconvenience of having tourists in their midst, local communities need to be furnished with an understanding of what tourists will spend their money on and how local skills and crafts can be turned to economic advantage. There are two general areas where linkages can frequently be made: agriculture/food and crafts/souvenirs. A number of lessons could be shared as part of community education: sales are greater when tourists get an opportunity to see the production process. Tourists often want smaller, "taster" versions of local products. Crafts can be made more appealing to tourists if they act as a memento through being a tangible representation (Graburn, 1987).

Marketing

If a community wants to develop tourism then some training and capacity building in marketing will be essential. Even high-profile community development initiatives such as CAMPFIRE have low occupancy rates due to poor marketing (Scheyvens, 2003). As Ashley et al. (2001) discuss, access to markets is a crucial factor limiting many pro-poor tourism initiatives. An understanding of the tourism system will help communities understand the need to make links with tour operators. As tourism develops, increasing numbers of tourists travel to remote regions with intermediaries. Tour operators wield considerable power over tourist itineraries and activities. It is therefore necessary to make links with domestic and international tour operators so that they can channel their clients and market the villages' tourism potential on the villagers' behalf. One of the failures of the home-stay developments in Bena was the lack of link with operators that would bring their tourists to stay in them. Developed by the Provincial Tourism Department, their lack of use is testimony to the futility of developing infrastructure without markets.

Finance

Both cash flow and reinvestment are areas that frequently need skills development. Many organizations in Uganda were keen to take profits immediately and not reinvest profits

(Victurine, 2000). In poor communities the temptation not to reinvest is great but the importance of longer-term financial planning is essential if projects are to be sustainable in the long term. Further areas of training that are needed are in basic book keeping, charging realistic prices, and in inventory planning so that tourists' requests can be catered for.

Food Services and Hygiene

In order for tourists to stay for more than a day or so in a community tourism project, consideration needs to be given to the types of meals provided. As Lipscomb (1998) suggests tourists soon tire of the typical Solomon Island meal of boiled white rice with some slippery cabbage on top. Similarly, in Ngadha tourists will not put up with rice and instant noodle for very many days. Victurine (2000) reports that in Uganda the standard of the food was the cause of tourists departing early. Consideration needs to be given to menu variety, the use of local products, balanced meals including plenty of fresh fruits and vegetables. Many villagers will provide high protein, expensive to produce meals for tourists, as these represent "giving your guests the best". However, these meals are frequently not appreciated by tourists, some because they are vegetarians, and others because the meat is tough, too fatty, or full of bones, in other words the meat does not live up to tourists' expectations. Food provision is linked to cross-cultural (mis)-understanding, for example, in Indonesia it is normal to use the feet of chicken (with claws clipped and cleaned) in soup. Tourists have been observed pushing their soup away in disgust on seeing a chicken foot, and thus offending their host by refusing food offered (Cole, 2004a). Tourists are often appalled by food preparation and kitchen hygiene standards in other cultures. While basic hygiene lessons are important, strategies to put a distance between tourists and food preparation are also necessary.

Teaching Methods

Very little literature exists on the delivery of training programmes designed to encourage further participation. Marien and Pizam (1997) provide an in-depth analysis of citizen participation in the planning process. However, many of the techniques are not suitable for remote marginal communities, for example, they suggest television, e-mail and the internet to send and gather information — clearly not appropriate for villages without access to electricity. Similarly, newspapers and bulletin boards would exclude many who lack literacy skills. Although many studies refer to the need for capacity building for rural/pro-poor/community-based tourism, methods of delivery of such support has received little, if any, discussion. Villagers in remote marginal communities frequently cannot leave their homes for long training sessions and do not have the academic qualifications to attend courses in established educational institutions. Support needs to be of a high quality and on going nature. As Scheyvens (2003): suggests, "sending a few members on various one-week training courses and expecting them to return home and become skilled marketers or business managers virtually overnight, is simply unrealistic" (p. 244).

With reference to ecotourism training, the World Wildlife Fund suggests that short, technical courses have little impact. Longer courses, including learning by doing and on the job training, have proved more successful. However, such methods would not be best suited to some aspects of the curriculum discussed earlier. Learning by observing other projects and places in action can be very fruitful, it would give the villagers an opportunity to be tourists themselves and appreciate some of the successes and pitfalls of tourism (Cole, 2003).

Focus groups can also be a useful method to transfer knowledge into a community. Ngadha villagers used focus groups, which I set up for my research, to probe my knowledge and experience. During the research, villagers frequently complained about culturally insensitive behaviour by tourists. The focus groups allowed a discussion on this and possible solutions to the problems. The villagers were able to learn from me what is done about similar problems in other regions (with a longer history of tourism or greater numbers of tourists) and discuss whether these solutions would be appropriate in their own setting. Furthermore, the villagers used the focus groups to glean information about tourism development and to clarify issues and positions held by officialdom (as they knew I had interviewed tourism officials at the regency and provincial levels) (Cole, 2004b).

Conclusions

Increasing numbers of villagers in remote marginal communities of less developed countries are in the tourism front line. They lack experience of tourism and frequently are unable to access any formal education and training. While there is an extensive debate on the curriculum and teaching methods for tourism workers and undergraduate programmes, there is a dearth of literature about the content and methods of community education programmes.

To date, government programmes have emphasised quality service provision, i.e. providing for the needs of the tourists. Such programmes are an attempt to get support for tourism and represent the bottom end of the participation ladder. They do not educate residents about tourism development issues or develop confidence and skills for empowerment.

Using the case study of villagers in Ngadha, this chapter has illustrated the need for community-wide esteem building, cross-cultural understanding as well as education about tourism development and what tourists want. It also suggests that education about product development, marketing, finance and food and hygiene would aid communities that aspire to develop a tourism initiative. Further research and dissemination of best practise is required about methods appropriate to deliver informal community tourism education to build on the suggestions that field trips and focus groups are useful. Short courses appear unsuccessful and the process needs to be long term and ongoing.

References

Abram, S. (1998). Introduction. In: S. Abram & J. Waldren (Eds), *Anthropological perspectives on local development* (pp. 1–17). London: Routledge.

Adams, K. (1997). Touting touristic "primadonas": Tourism, ethnicity and national integration in Sulawesi, Indonesia. In: M. Picard & R. Wood (Eds), *Tourism, ethnicity and the state in Asian and Pacific societies* (pp. 155–180). Honolulu: University of Hawaii Press.

Arnstein, S. (1969). Eight rungs in the ladder of citizen participation. In: E. Cahn & A. Passett (Eds), *Citizen participation: Effecting community change*. London: Preager Publishers.

Ashley, C., Roe, D., & Goodwin, H. (2001). *Pro-poor tourism strategies: making tourism work for the poor. A review of experience*. London: Overseas Development Institute.

Cole, S. (1997). Anthropologists, local communities and sustainable tourism development. In: M. Stabler (Ed.), *Tourism and sustainability* (pp. 219–230). Oxford: CABI publishing.

Cole, S. (1999). Education for participation: The villagers' perspective. Case Study from Ngada, Flores, Indonesia. In: K. Bras, H. Dahles, M. Gunawan & G. Richards (Eds), *Entrepreneurship and education in Tourism ATLAS Asia conference proceedings*, Bandung, Indonesia (pp. 173–184).

Cole, S. (2003). *Cultural tourism development in Ngadha Indonesia*. London Metropolitan University: Unpublished Ph.D. thesis.

Cole, S. (2004a). Cultural values in conflict: Case study from Ngadha Flores, Indonesia. *Tourism — an Interdisciplinary Journal, 52*(1), 91–101.

Cole, S. (2004b). Shared benefits? Longitudinal research in Eastern Indonesia. In: J. Phillimore & L. Goodson (Eds), *Qualitative research in tourism: Epistemologies, ontologies and methodologies* (pp. 292–310). London: Routledge.

Connell, D. (1997). Participatory development: An approach sensitive to class and gender. *Development in Practice, 7*(3), 249–259.

Departemen Parawisata, Pos, & Telekomunikasi (1990). *Annual Report*, Jakarta.

Dinas Parawisata Ngada (1995). *Meteri penyuluhan sadar wisata* Kabupaten daerah tingkat II, Ngada.

Goodwin, H. (1995). Training for local participation. *In Focus, 16*, 6.

Graburn, N. (1987). Tourism: The sacred journey. In: V. Smith (Ed.), *Host and guests. The anthropology of tourism* (pp. 21–36). Philadelphia: University of Pennsylvania Press.

Gurung, G., Simmons, D., & Delvin, P. (1996). The evolving role of the tourist guides: The Napali experience. In: R. Butler & T. Hinch (Eds), *Tourism and Indigenous peoples* (pp. 107–128). London: International Thomson Business Press.

Hitchcock, M., King, V., & Parnwell, M. (1993). Tourism in South East Asia: Introduction. In: M. Hitchcock, V. King & M. Parnwell (Eds), *Tourism in South East Asia* (pp. 1–31). London: Routledge.

Johnston, A. M. (2003). Self-determination: Exercising indigenous rights in tourism In: S. Singh, D. Timothy & R. Dowling (Eds), *Tourism in destination communities* (pp. 115–134). Oxon: CABI.

Joop Ave (no date). *Indonesia tourism gearing up for the nineties*. Jakarta: Directorate general of tourism.

Kadir Din (1993). Dialogue with the hosts. In: M. Hitchcock, V. King & M. Parnwell (Eds), *Tourism in Southeast Asia* (pp. 327–336). London: Routledge.

Kadir Din (1997). Tourism development: Still in search of an equitable mode of local Involvement. In: C. Cooper & S. Wanhill (Eds), *Tourism development environment and community issues* (pp. 153–162). Chichester: Wiley.

Lipscomb, A. (1998). Village based tourism in the Solomon Islands: impediments and impacts. In: E. Laws, B. Falkner & G. Moscardo (Eds), *Embracing and managing change in tourism: International case studies* (pp. 185–201). London: Routledge.

Mafati, R. (2002). Nambia: The community worker. *In Focus, 45*, 10.

Marein, C., & Pizam, A. (1997). Implementing sustainable tourism development through citizen participation in the planning process. In: S. Wahab & J. Pigram (Eds), *Tourism, development and growth: The challenge of sustainability* (pp. 164–178). London: Routledge.

Mowforth, M., & Munt, I. (1998). *Tourism and sustainability: New tourism in the third world*. London and New York: Routledge.

Murphy, P. (1985). *Tourism: A community approach*. London and New York: Routledge.

Pearce, P. (1994). Tourism-resident impacts: Examples, explanations and emerging solutions. In: W. Theobald (Ed.), *Global tourism* (pp. 103–123). Oxford: Butterworth-Heinemann.

Pearce, P., Kim, & E., Lussa, S. (1998). Facilitating tourist — Host social interaction. In: E. Laws, B. Falkner & G. Moscardo (Eds), *Embracing and managing change in tourism: International case studies* (pp. 347–365). London: Routledge.

Pretty, J. (1995). The many interpretations of participation. *In Focus, 16*, 4–5.

Rainforest Alliance (2004). www.rainforest-alliance.org/programs/cce/indonesia.html (accessed 16/09/2004).

Regency Department of Education and Culture (1998). Ngada, NTT, Indonesia. Unpublished tourism statistics.

Reisinger, Y., & Turner, L. (2003). *Cross-cultural behaviour in tourism: Concepts and analysis.* Oxford: Butterworth Heinemann.

Robinson, C., & Yee, J. (1996). Education and indigenisation. In: C. Cooper, R. Shepard & J. Westlake (Eds), *Educating the educators in tourism* (pp. 338–366). Madrid: World Tourism Organisation.

Ross, G. (2004). The value of trust within visitor — host community interactions. *E-Review of Tourism Research, 2*(2), 27–32.

Scheyvens, R. (2003). Local involvement in managing tourism. In: S. Singh, D. Timothy & R. Dowling (Eds), *Tourism in destination communities* (pp. 229–252). Oxon: CABI.

Simmons, D. (1994). Community participation in tourism planning. *Tourism Management, 15*(2), 98–108.

Sofield, T. H. B. (2003). Enpowerment of Sustainable Tourism Development: Pergamon.

Sweeney, A. & Wanhill, S. (1996). Hosting the guest: Changing local attitudes and behaviour. In: C. Cooper, R. Shepard & J. Westlake (Eds), *Educating the educators in tourism* (pp. 148–159). Madrid: World Tourism Organisation.

Timothy, D. (1999). Participatory planning: A view of tourism in Indonesia. *Annals of Tourism Research, 26*(2), 371–391.

Timothy, D. (2000). Building community awareness of tourism in a developing country destination. *Tourism Recreation Research, 25*(2), 111–116.

Timothy, D. (2002). Tourism and community development issues. In: R. Sharpely & D. Telfer (Eds), *Tourism and development: Concepts and issues* (pp. 149–164). Clevedon: Channel View Publications.

Tosun, C., & Timothy, D. (2003). Arguments for community participation in tourism development. *The Journal of Tourism Studies, 14*(2), 2–11.

Tourism Concern (1992). *Beyond the green horizon.* Surrey, UK: World Wildlife Fund.

Umbu Peku Djawang. (1991). The role of tourism in NTT development. In: C. Barlow, A. Bellis & K. Andrews (Eds), *Nusa Tenggara Timor: The challenge of development political and social change* (pp. 155–164). Monograph 12, ANU University: Canberra.

Victurine, R. (2000). Building Tourism Excellence at the community level: Capacity building for community-based entrepreneurs in Uganda. *Journal of Travel Research, 38*, 221–229.

Warburton, D. (1998). A passive dialogue: Community and sustainable development. In: D. Warburton (Ed.), *Community and sustainable development* (pp. 2–19). London: Earthscan.

RESOURCES, PROGRESSION AND QUALITY

Chapter 29

Teachers

Marion Stuart-Hoyle

Background

Tourism's most valuable asset in Higher Education (HE) is arguably the Tourism teacher. This is, perhaps, ironic when faced with the fact that those who teach Tourism in HE have yet to be the subject themselves of any significant body of research. In the mid-1990s Middleton and Ladkin (1996) estimated that there were approximately 375 full time lecturers in Tourism in the UK (compared to 200 in 1993) with an additional 950 full- or part-time lecturers who contributed in some way to the 'conduct' of Tourism courses. There have been no published attempts since to establish the number of Tourism lecturers in UK institutions of higher education (IHE). In addition, Snaith and Miller (1999) noted very high levels of movement within the Tourism academic community and little awareness of newly departed/arriving lecturers by institutions and departments, a fact that probably accounts for the lack of accurate data regarding the size and scope of the Tourism-teaching community.

It is the Tourism teacher who, faced with the pressures of the desire and need to carry out research and the apprehensions surrounding Quality Assurance audits, has been the driving force behind the growing profile of the subject within the HE arena. It is all too easy to become so caught up in the intricacies and contentions surrounding the next Research Assessment Exercise (RAE) or in the perhaps now subsiding debate surrounding the evolving Tourism curriculum. While it would be unwise and even naïve to assume that these are not critical issues that the subject community would ignore at its peril, there is a strong argument for focusing some attention upon those individuals who are the 'bread and butter' of Tourism provision in HE.

Much of the research carried out about Tourism in HE to date is by those who have been immersed in its teaching over the last 20 years. It has focused upon the study of Tourism as a subject with reference to the existence of, and need for, a minimum core curriculum. Research in the 1990s also concentrated on the growth of provision and concerns of over-provision of Tourism graduates due to the proliferation of Tourism programmes since the first two programmes at undergraduate level were introduced at Dorset Institute and Newcastle Polytechnic in 1986. Research has also been focusing on invisibility of Tourism in the last two RAE (Botterill et al., 2002; Tribe, 2003). However, this author's research concentrates on why Tourism has developed in the manner it has, and what factors have contributed towards that development. A significant gap in research offered the opportunity to evaluate Tourism lecturer perceptions of the key factors influencing the development of Tourism undergraduate programmes, based upon depth interviews, which are more fully documented in Stuart (2002) and Stuart-Hoyle (2003). This chapter draws from key aspects of this research and places it in the context of some of the considerations that Tourism teachers have to make and the pressures under which they must work in the early part of the 21st century.

The key aim of the chapter is twofold. Firstly, the aim is to explore the nature of the Tourism 'teacher' in HE in terms of characteristics and traits, motivations and 'defining features'. Secondly, mindful of these 'defining features', observations are made about the current pressured environment within which Tourism teachers are expected to operate and survive with notable reference to the increasingly competitive HE job market. This chapter focuses solely upon Tourism teachers in the UK; however, conclusions can be drawn as to their future development and survival that could have implications for the global supply and satisfaction of Tourism teachers worldwide.

Literature Review

There are a number of concepts that require brief exploration in order that the full extent of Tourism teachers' nature, defining characteristics and activity can be evaluated. These focus on the motivational factors associated with lecturing in HE, with particular reference to the research–teaching link, disciplinary backgrounds of teachers and the nature and strength of academic community or 'tribes'.

In addition to recognising the number of Tourism teachers in HE, it is important to recognise the importance that motivation has had on the type of individuals who find themselves teaching this relatively new subject in UK HEIs. At a time when reports over the last few years have focused on demotivation of academic staff (see Panel 1), if the profession is associated with high stress levels and perceived 'poor career' status, what is it that motivates Tourism teachers to enter and stay within the profession?

More than 15 years ago, Becher (1989, p. 118) emphasised the importance of avoiding the 'closed shop' approach, recognising the value of accepting 'new blood' into an academic community which could be the source of innovative conceptual approaches and teaching practice.

Panel 1: Demotivation in HE.

(Of HE lecturers in the UK) 'underpaid, stressed and de-motivated' (BBC, 2000); 'low pay and job insecurity are discouraging young people from becoming academics' (BBC, 2003)

'Too few of our best young people are attracted to academic careers. And they are right. It is now a poor career' (David Triesman, AUT gen sec. (BBC, 2000)

> Career mobility…is amongst the most potent sources of innovation and development within a discipline. Immigrants bring fresh ways of looking at familiar issues, and perhaps relevant but hitherto unfamiliar techniques as well.

If 'immigrants' or new blood (from different disciplinary backgrounds or even from non-teaching backgrounds) are put off from entering the Tourism-teaching profession because of broader pressures placed upon lecturers in HE, then this is an issue for the future teaching of a subject that has already struggled to prove its claim for 'respectability' (Leiper, 2000; Stuart, 2002; Tribe, 1997, 2000). The latter stages of this chapter look at what is expected of new/young lecturers in general terms and more specifically, the requirements of individuals looking for Tourism teaching posts in HE, whether at the junior 'Lecturer' level or more-experienced Senior or Principal Lecturer level.

It would be reasonable to assume that the key motivation for teaching Tourism is the desire to impart subject knowledge, whether it be derived from an individual's industry experience, from their study, research or consultancy in the field or a combination of all these activities. Job satisfaction is a complex concept in HE and according to Busch et al. (1998), can be described in terms of a single aspect or facet of the job (global satisfaction) or in multi-dimensional terms, capturing different aspects of a job situation that can vary from one individual to another. Factors that contribute towards motivation or demotivation could in fact, be related directly to the subject 'Tourism' (teaching and research) or they could be more general issues relating to administrative and pastoral responsibilities.

One of the key 'measures' or indicators of motivation is to investigate the ways in which individuals respond to change in the environment in which they work. Continual change in the nature and structure of the HE system has meant that the higher education institution (HEI) has had to take on the 'characteristics of a post-Fordist organisation, in which the structures are more fluid and uncertain' (Barnett, 1997, p. 51). HEIs are no exception to the trend where organisations have to deal with recurring change, while always having to respond to an unpredictable HE environment and of consequently 'living in a state of permanent uncertainty' (Winter, 1996, p. 72).

In his analysis of a single site new university and its academic responses to change in curriculum policy and structures in that environment, Trowler (1997) saw academics taking on one (or more) of four approaches to dealing with change as seen in Figure 1.

Academics who 'sink', faced with change in this context, are typified by intensified workloads, suffer as a result of declining resources and increasing student numbers, and display demotivation and disillusionment. Administration pressures are also a feature of the academic who sinks under the pressure of change. 'Coping' strategies include using previous years' teaching notes to reduce preparation time, unofficial working to rule, making themselves unapproachable to students and making their assignments very difficult. Attending meetings and taking on extra projects are out of the question and teaching becomes either very student-centred in its approach or at the other end of the spectrum, purely didactic. The third approach involves actually 'reconstructing' and reinterpreting policy. This might include the design of courses and programmes which move away from the idea of flexibility and back to the idea of a more traditional style, with fewer option courses and tighter rules regarding prerequisites, leading to constrained student choice. The final approach is that of

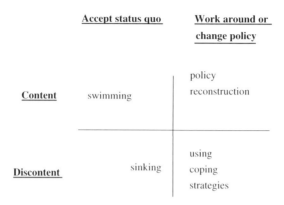

Figure 1: Academic responses to change (Trowler, 1997, p. 306).

'swimming' and is most appropriate for those academics who thrive in the face of continual change within their institution of HE (Trowler, 1997). Tourism teachers in HE can be recognised quite clearly within this framework as a result of interviews with a range of Tourism teachers in UK universities and are detailed later in this chapter.

Another factor which characterises the experience of Tourism teachers is the extent to which any research carried out by individuals or groups, whether RAE focused or not, can be fed into the teaching of Tourism. Jenkins (2003, p. 1), however, warns that although research plays an integral role in motivating individuals in HE, it is not always possible to see the 'research feeding teaching' scenario through to fruition:

> For many of us the links between teaching and research are what distinguishes higher education. For staff their identity and their motivations are profoundly shaped by their commitment to research in their discipline …
> The research evidence cautions us that positive teaching/research links are not automatic.

Rather, it has been suggested that

> there is little evidence to suggest that synergies between teaching and research (were) managed or promoted at departmental or institutional level …
> there (were) some attempts to manage teaching and research workloads in departments, partly to allow more time for research (JM Consulting, 2000).

The importance of lecturers being able to develop their own personal areas of interest and integrate them into their teaching should not be underestimated. Smeby (1998) noted the fact that it is much more likely for teaching to benefit from an individual's research if the teaching is at a specialist, or postgraduate level.

The ensuing demotivation that could be experienced as a result of an inability to let research feed teaching at any level, could be a critical factor in the development of a committed workforce. However, the literature does not appear to consider this possibility specifically; Brew (1999) highlighted the importance of the time dimension in the changing nature of the relationship between teaching and research; Rowley (1996) concluded that there is little evidence to suggest that a lecturer's involvement in research means positive outcomes for the student, while Rowland (1996, p. 7) offered evidence to support a view that 'closer relationships between the two (research and teaching) can provide the basis for a programme to improve the quality of university teaching'.

The final concept that requires some clarification before the characteristics of Tourism teachers are evaluated is that of the nature of academic communities and the sense to which they are, in fact, communities or 'tribes' rather than a collection of disparate individuals. Across the HE system there exist 'tribes' which operate as 'communities', whether convergent or divergent by nature (Becher, 1994, p. 151). While it is recognised that the 'tribe' of individuals which has had responsibility for developing and delivering Tourism is quite young in comparison with other, more established academic communities, research has revealed that it is as yet unclear as to whether it is convergent or divergent by nature. It could also be that 'Tourism lecturers' are, unlike the Business Studies community, an academic body with recognisable similarities and common disciplinary backgrounds (Stuart, 2001).

According to Becher (1989, p. 37) 'disciplinary communities which are convergent and tightly knit in terms of their fundamental ideologies, their common values, their shared judgements of quality, their awareness of belonging to a unique tradition. In short, their fraternal sense of nationhood, are likely to occupy intellectual territories with well defined external boundaries, e.g. economics'. Tourism does borrow freely yet heavily from a wide range of disciplines and other subject areas, and at first glance it would be difficult to claim a well-defined external boundary.

A divergent community, on the other hand, is described as one where 'the constituent members lack a clear sense of mutual cohesion and identity...the cognitive border zones with other subject fields are liable to be ragged and ill-defined, and hence not so easy to defend' (Becher, 1989, p. 37). The Business Studies academic community appears to be regarded as a divergent community 'populated by a large number of refugees, nomads and tourists' (Macfarlane, 1998, p. 42). Both the Business Studies and Tourism academic communities are made up of a number of other disciplines and subject areas. The extent to which the Tourism community is convergent or divergent by nature may have some bearing on the future strength, motivation and ability to shoulder both the pressures facing HE lecturers in general and those which are specific to this subject.

Many of the issues explored here would be common to most lecturers in HE but research amongst the Tourism teaching community reveals the particular relevance of these concepts to the characteristics and motivations driving the 'Teacher' of Tourism in the UK which are the focus of the next section of this chapter.

Tourism Teachers — Practice

Before looking at evidence of Tourism teachers' emerging characteristics, as evidenced by the author's field research, it might be useful to set this against the backdrop of the formal findings of the Quality Assurance Agency (QAA) during the last Subject Review 1999–2000.

The QAA Subject Overview Report for Hospitality, Leisure, Sport and Tourism in its summary of Teaching, Learning and Assessment (QAA, 2001, p. 4) commented upon 'a dynamic teaching and learning environment that displays a rich diversity of methods to meet the learning needs of students'. In addition, the report highlighted the value of 'industry-supported consultancy projects' and noted the fact that:

> (teaching) sessions were characterised by good planning, clear learning objectives and the effective use of relevant technology. The enthusiasm and commitment of staff, many of whom bring personal professional and scholarly activity to their teaching, was consistently praised.

It would be naïve to assume that this is proof of undisputable quality in all Tourism teachers. Equally, however, it would be unfair to ignore these positive words in the process of evaluating the nature and characteristics of this body of teachers.

This chapter has so far briefly considered factors that might, to a greater or lesser extent, motivate HE teachers. Clearly in the light of the evidence presented by the QAA, it is fair to say that motivation levels must be sufficiently high to result in 'quality teaching', but what exactly have individuals been bringing to the profession to allow this to be the case?

This author's review of 20 of the 50 HEIs offering Tourism undergraduate programmes in 2001 found that teaching teams range from two to fifteen full-time members of staff, although the mean number of staff was five. All 20 institutions had at least one member of the team who was qualified at Masters level in Tourism or a Tourism-related field, and in the majority of cases more than one. Sixteen institutions had at least one member with a PhD. The latter were for the most part in the Tourism field, including Tourist Attraction Management, Tourist Motivations, Transport Planning, Tourism Education, Tourism Economics and Tourism in the Developing World. Other PhD disciplines included Sociology and Geography, both of which have obvious contributions to make to the Tourism curriculum. MA/MSc qualifications were, for the most part, in Tourism or subjects allied to Tourism. These included (Outdoor) Recreation Management, Tourism and Leisure and Tourism Marketing. Some team members held Masters degrees on non-tourism-related subjects, such as Politics, Geography, Marketing and Anthropology, but again these disciplinary areas all contribute towards the wider study and delivery of Tourism at undergraduate level.

With regard to research profiles and activity, all 20 teaching teams were research-active at the time and were able to offer areas of particular interest or ongoing research. What is perhaps of most interest is the fact that there did not seem to be a link between the number of core teaching staff and the range of research being undertaken. Some of the smaller teaching teams (for example, a new university with four members in the core teaching team) were carrying out research in a number of areas and arguably could be described as at least as research active as some of the larger teams. Experience in the Tourism or other industries also appeared to be considerable, irrelevant of the size of the core teaching team, although not all members of every team had industry experience. It would be difficult to conclude a 'common' industry background for Tourism lecturers, although local government, small business management, marketing, hospitality/hotel management, attractions, planning, tour operations, airline industry and heritage all appeared with a degree of frequency within the core team profiles.

However varied and numerous the qualifications, research activity and industry experience, the critical factor in terms of the nature of the Tourism curriculum is how those factors are reflected in the courses taught. Table 1 offers a range of examples which demonstrate the links between some of the core teaching teams' profile and courses delivered.

Table 1: Qualifications, research and industry experience links to courses delivered.

Institution	Qualification (Q), Research (R) or industry experience (I)	Courses*
University College	**R** – Development in Poland/Azerbaijan **I** – Marketing for an NTO **I** – Environment Consultancy	Level 3 Destination Management Level 2 Marketing. Level 4 Rural Tourism.
College of Higher Education	**Q** – Msc Outdoor Recreation Management and **R** – Recreation Conflict Management. **I** – Event/conference management.	Level 2 Countryside as a Leisure and Recreation Resource. Level 4 HRM 2 for Leisure.
Old University	**Q** – PhD Tourist Motivation **I** – Heritage Attractions **R** – Tourism in developing Countries.	Level 2 Tourism Behaviour Level 2 Heritae and Interpretation. Level 4 Tourism in developing Countries
University College	**R** – Destination image and advertising. **I** – Practising Law	Level 3 Destination Marketing and Advertising Tourism and Leisure. Level 3 Legal Issues in Tourism.
New University	**R** – National Lottery/ Millennium Projects **I** – Heritage	**Level 2 Public Policy of Leisure and Tourism** and Level 4 Museums and Heritage. Level 4 Museums and Heritage.
University College	**R** – Rural tourism **Q** – PhD Tourism Marketing	**Level 2 Tourism and Leisure Environments and Level 3 Countryside: Conservation and Recreation Management.** **Level 3 Tourism Marketing.**

* Courses in bold are cores.

It is clear from the 'snapshot' provided in Table 1 that the majority of courses which potentially benefited from the core teaching teams' qualifications, research and industry experience were option courses. In addition, there was a greater propensity for these courses to be delivered in the later stages of a degree programme, in the majority of cases in Levels/Years 3 and 4.

In summarising the characteristics of lecturers who made up core Tourism-teaching teams, they could be described as well-qualified at appropriate levels and in relevant fields. It would also appear that even the smaller teaching teams found time to carry out a wide range of research, despite the fact that they were responsible for the teaching of a significant number of courses. Industry experience appeared to be present in all teaching teams, although was not common to all members and there was some evidence of commonality in the type of industry experience. Links between qualifications, research and industry experience were visible in all institutions surveyed, and were particularly evident with reference to the option courses, which would support the earlier observation that it is often the option courses which allowed staff to utilise their specialist knowledge and experience (Smeby, 1998), which in turn reflect a programme's Unique Selling Proposition (USP).

There was evidence then of links between teachers' specialisms and courses offered, but were Teachers actually given responsibility, by their departments or faculties, to deliver the courses which match their interests? Many of the individual lecturers interviewed did actually feel quite aggrieved about the fact that they were not in a position to make the desired links between their research and their teaching, as Jenkins (2003) has observed. In extreme cases, concerns were emerging for the appropriate matching of lecturer to course, extended in some cases to a concern that lecturers from other departments or schools had been drafted in to cover courses that require the knowledge and experience of other disciplinary areas. Full-time Tourism lecturers interviewed expressed considerable concern over the fact that non-Tourism specialists were delivering generic Business courses to Tourism undergraduates, who were left to take responsibility themselves for providing the necessary contextualisation. The existence and quality of Tourism-specific knowledge among non-Tourism specialists appeared then to be of more concern to Tourism lecturers who have been defending 'their own patches of intellectual ground' (Becher, 1994, p. 24) in their attempts to ensure some level of influence over who was recruited from outside the specialism to deliver courses that contribute towards Tourism degree programmes.

This takes us to a related issue which has influenced the motivation of Tourism teachers in recent years, that of the perceived respectability of the subject. The disciplinary debates are now well-rehearsed and need no further airing. However, the fact that the teaching community has concerns over who is teaching Tourism (especially regarding 'who' is poaching their carefully researched/qualification-based specialisms) means that there is a real threat associated with 'inappropriate' individuals delivering Tourism in HE. Whether or not these concerns are well founded is hardly the issue. The fact that there is such a defensive approach to newcomers could signal a bigger threat for Tourism teachers. If they fail to develop a positive view of 'immigrants' and 'new blood' to the subject then given the negativity surrounding the teaching profession in HE in general, they will be ignoring opportunities to enrich the breadth and enthusiasm of a seemingly jaded, negative teaching community.

These concerns should, however, be countered with the view that according to the majority of lecturers interviewed, a career in teaching Tourism in HE was regarded as a job for life and most would not leave it, even if they had 'fallen upon' teaching Tourism in the first instance, a common characteristic of the Tourism teaching community.

While the sense of identity for the Tourism academic community might not have become as apparent (linked to a perceived lack of respectability) or consistent as one might have expected after nearly 20 years of the subject's existence at an undergraduate level and over 30 years at postgraduate level, the commitment of individuals to the teaching of courses cannot be doubted in the light of the evidence to date. The author's research revealed that Tourism teachers are characterised by individuals' expectations, personal goals and values that have been critical in offering quality teaching. Trowler (1997) has emphasised the importance of individuals in HE and the potential impact that their aspirations and values can have on HE, and this evidence would lend support to this view. The fact that Tourism lecturers appear to cope, and even swim, in the face of considerable teaching pressures (Trowler, 1997) could also reflect, on the part of institutions' management, a soft approach to managing people (Truss et al., 1997) where a committed group of individuals is developed by allowing Tourism lecturers a considerable amount of academic freedom regarding what they teach and how they teach it.

Is it, in fact, possible to describe Tourism teachers in HE as a convergent or a divergent community (Becher, 1989)? This is discussed in further detail in Stuart (2002). In the context of what motivates Tourism teachers, it would perhaps, based upon the limited evidence to date, be fairer to talk about the subject being taught by Tourism teachers who are committed to offering a 'quality learning experience'. However, there is a sense that many are not given the opportunity to capitalise on their research and industry experience in the preparation and execution of teaching. There is a real concern that the demotivation that has emerged as a result could signal problems for the subject in keeping Tourism teachers in post.

Trends and Developments in Teaching Tourism in HE

The final section of the chapter focuses on the Tourism teacher in 2005, what the academic community expects of the 'Teacher' and what support is available to them in order that they can deliver high-quality teaching. The key question is whether or not Tourism teachers will continue to 'cope' and 'swim' against the tide (Trowler, 1997). It might be that many of the systems recently launched to aid the teaching process are actually hindering the teaching, due to their complexity and demands upon the individual.

'PROSPECTS', the UK's official graduate careers website offers details of the typical 'work activities' of an HE Lecturer as follows (see Panel 2):

Added to the considerable list of activities, a starting salary of as little as £18,265 (teaching HE in Further Education Institutions — FEI) and such enticing statements as 'working hours are not generally stipulated as lecturers are expected to work the necessary hours to fulfil their duties and responsibilities' and the combination of research commitments with teaching, administrative and pastoral responsibilities can make the role very pressurised' (www.prospects.co.uk, Prospects, 2004) and it becomes easy to see why a career in lecturing is one to be considered carefully in the 21st century.

Panel 2: Typical work activities of an HE Lecturer.

Developing and implementing new methods of teaching to reflect changes in research

Designing, preparing and developing teaching materials

Delivering lectures, seminars and tutorials

Assessing students' coursework

Setting and marking examinations

Supporting students through a pastoral advisory role

Undertaking personal research projects and actively contributing to the institution's research profile

Supervising students' research activities

Undertaking continuous professional development (CPD) and participating in staff training activities

Undertaking administrative tasks relating to the department, such as student admissions, induction and involvement in committees and boards

Managing and supervising staff — at a senior level this may include the role of head of department

Representing the university/colleagues/discipline at professional conferences and seminars and contributing to these as necessary

Establishing collaborative links outside the university with industrial, commercial and public organisations

Liaising with colleagues across the university on administrative and student support matters

---

Source: www.prospects.co.uk The UKs official graduate careers website provided by AGCAS.

Universities UK, the Standing Conference of Principals (SCOP) and the HE Funding Councils concluded the initial consultation stage of its Professional Teaching Standards paper in the Summer of 2004 and the Higher Education Academy (HEA) has since been charged with the responsibility of progressing the development of national professional standards in teaching and learning in HE. The welfare of teachers in HE will, however, also depend upon the expectations that are placed upon the 'young blood' and 'rising stars'[1] within the profession.

A review of Tourism teaching posts in UK universities, as advertised in the Times Higher Education Supplement (THES) between July 2003 and July 2004, revealed 15 full-time posts as Lecturer or Lecturer/Senior Lecturer and one 0.5 post; no posts as Principal Lecturer were advertised during this 12-month period. The Lecturer/Senior Lecturer post might reasonably be expected to carry with it significant teaching responsibilities with some expectation of developing a research profile whilst individuals successful in these posts move up the 'career ladder'. There has been a trend in recent years for the post of Principal Lecturer to carry with it significant administrative responsibilities, on a temporary or (less

---

[1] 'Rising stars' is one of the three categories used by the National Teaching Fellowship Awards for the first time this year to describe those lecturers who have up to 6 years experience in HE.

common) permanent basis, and/or a significantly well-developed research record. Consequently these posts could, in view of the absence of posts advertised at this level, be ones that are designated as a result of institutions' internal promotion procedures. Of the 16 posts two required applicants to hold PhDs and a further two expected them to be 'near completion'. Arguably, this is not an unreasonable expectation, given the increase in the number of PhDs awarded in Tourism in recent years. According to Botterill et al. (2002) there were approximately 149 PhDs awarded in Tourism between 1990 and 1999. A further five institutions would expect applicants to have a relevant higher degree, but the majority of institutions seven expected a first degree 'in Tourism or a relevant/related subject'.

Analysis of institutions' expectations of potential Lecturers/Senior Lecturers in Tourism reveal the following quite exacting expectations and demands being placed upon those wishing to develop their career as a teacher of Tourism in the UK's HEIs with regards to their previous relevant experience in research and/or consultancy involvement. Five institutions required a 'proven track record' and extensive experience in publishing in appropriate academic journals. This could be perceived as potentially demoralising for those candidates for lecturing posts whose desire to publish is real but as yet, unrealised. A further eight institutions saw a current research profile and or consultancy experience as 'highly desirable' or 'offering a distinct advantage' to the candidate. Clearly employment/vocational experience is not regarded as highly as only two posts made such experience mandatory and a further five described it as 'preferable'. This is perhaps is evidence of misplaced priorities from those employing Tourism teachers in the light of the White Paper's emphasis of the importance of 'building key employability skills into courses … (and) supplying students with skills and knowledge they need for jobs' (DFES, 2002, p. 46). Surely those with experience of the Tourism industry are best placed to ensure that the Tourism curriculum and skills development is appropriate, not those with well developed academic research profiles?

A number of the relatively junior posts (Lecturer scale) required 'significant track records and expertise in undergraduate and postgraduate teaching' in named specialisms (10 posts) of which 6 expected applicants to be involved in (and in two cases, in charge of) curriculum development in stated specialist subjects. This does beg the question 'Where are the posts for those embarking upon a career in teaching Tourism in HE that do not require such a breadth of experience to date?'

'Many universities now require new lecturers without prior HE teaching experience to undertake a teacher training programme' (Bailey & Robson, 2002, p. 326), something which has to be 'completed alongside a lecturer's normal working duties … these courses cover theories of learning, practical skills and principles of learning within an HE context' (www.prospects.co.uk, Prospects, 2004). Is it possible that attracting young people into teaching Tourism in HE could become an impossible task as expectations of the 'new blood' soar? With salaries starting as low as £22,191 at the bottom of the Lecturer pay scale in universities and university colleges, many of the expectations outlined here in this brief review are unrealistic. Are we preparing the 'young blood' the profession needs to keep the subject afloat in HE for the levels of stress and discontent already prevalent in the HE teaching (see Panel 1)? In summary, it is unlikely that Tourism teachers will be able to maintain professional standards at any level when faced with such high expectations at such an early stage in their career.

Conclusions

This chapter has offered a glimpse into the pressured environment in which Tourism teachers must operate in the 21st century in the UK. Clearly there is evidence to suggest that the challenge of ensuring that this all-important human resource remains in good spirit and, indeed, in good supply, is not an easy one. While on the one hand, it is a fact of life that demands placed upon HE teachers are increasing, there is on the other, a palpable sense that some 'reigning in' may need to take place on the part of some institutions that perhaps have unrealistic expectations of the junior teachers, those who in the future will be responsible for the future of the subject in HE. Tourism teachers may well 'swim' and 'cope' faced with the range of administrative, teaching and research pressures placed upon them, but this relatively content community may not remain so if institutions fail to take the necessary steps to ensure that new appointees and existing teachers are given every opportunity to benefit from seeing see their study, research and industry experience feature, at least to some extent, in their everyday teaching activities. This author's research in 2001 indicated that a career in teaching Tourism was perceived to be a 'job for life' and that most would not want to leave the profession. Those who have been involved in teaching Tourism for a number of years and have witnessed the increasing pressures to account for student failures, the need to produce RAE-worthy publications and to manage the day-to-day running of a large cohort of demanding undergraduate students (while of course keeping up with the latest quality audit exercises) might be feeling a little less confident about the 'lot' of a Tourism teacher in 2005.

Dewar (2002) in his study of HE teachers in New Zealand, highlighted three key traits of a good teacher in HE — empathy, accessibility and good presentation. He added the importance of the existence of teaching awards, training courses and organisational commitment. These are in place in the UK but might require further development and promotion if the Tourism lecturing community is to thrive.

Another chapter highlights some of the resources and support mechanisms that are now becoming available to the Tourism teacher which hopefully will make their job a little more manageable and even stimulating in the years ahead, for example, the wealth of support material and directions to teaching research funds available though the UK HEA Support Networks.

References

Bailey, B., & Robson, J. (2002). Changing teachers: A critical review of recent policies affecting the professional training and qualifications of teachers in schools, colleges and universities in England. *Journal of Vocational Education and Training*, *54*(3), 325–341.

Barnett, R. (1977). *Higher Education: A critical Business.*Buckingham: SRHE/OUP.

Becher, T. (1989). *Academic tribes and territories: Intellectual enquiry and the cultures of disciplines.* Buckingham: SRHE/OUP.

Becher, T. (1994). The significance of disciplinary differences. *Studies in Higher Education*, *19*(2), 151–161.

Botterill, D., Haven, C., & Gale, T. (2002). A survey of doctoral theses accepted by universities in the UK and Ireland for Studies Related to Tourism, 1990–1999. *Tourist Studies*, *2*(3), 283–311.

Brew, A. (1999). Research and teaching: Changing relationships in a changing context. *Studies in Higher Education*, *24*(3), 291–301.

Busch, T., Fallan, L., & Petterson, A. (1998). Disciplinary differences in job satisfaction, self-efficacy, goal commitment and organisational commitment among faculty employees in Norwegian colleges: An empirical assessment of indicators of performance. *Quality in Higher Education, 4*(2), 137–157.

Department for Further Education and Skills. (2002). *The future of higher education*. London: The Stationery Office Ltd.

Dewar, K. (2002). On being a good teacher. *Journal of Hospitality, Leisure, Sport and Tourism Education, 1*,1. www.hlst.heacademy.ac.uk/johlste.

Jenkins, A. (2003). Designing a curriculum that values a research-based approach to student learning. In: *Link 9 — Linking research and teaching* (LTSN–HLST) (pp. 1–4). Oxford: Oxford Brookes University.

J. M. Consulting. (2000). Interactions between research, Teaching and other academic activities report for HEFCE as part of the fundamental review of research. In: *Linking Research and Teaching in Departments* LTSN Generic Centre — February 2003.

Leiper, N. (2000). An emerging discipline. *Annals of Tourism Research, 27*(3), 805–809.

Macfarlane, B. (1998). Refugees, nomads and tourists: An anatomy of business and management lecturers in higher education. *Journal of European Business Education, 7*(2), 37–44.

Middleton, V. T. C., & Ladkin, A. (1996). *The profile of tourism studies degree courses in the UK: 1995/6*. Summary of a report undertaken by the National Liaison Group. Guideline Number 4. London: Tourism Society.

Quality Assurance Agency (2001). *QAA subject overview report for hospitality, leisure, sport and tourism*. www.qaa.ac.uk/reviews/reports/subjIndex.asp.

Rowland, S. (1996). Relationships between research and teaching. *Teaching in Higher Education, 1*(1), 7–14.

Rowley, J. (1996). Making the tension between research and teaching creative in business and management: A pilot study. *Journal of Further and Higher Education, 20*(1), 74–92.

Smeby, J. C. (1998). Knowledge production and knowledge transmission. The interaction between research and teaching in universities. *Teaching in Higher Education, 3*(1), 5–16.

Snaith, T., & Miller, G. (1999). The evolution of the tourism academic: Missing links raise questions regarding sustainability and development of the profession. *Tourism Management, 20*(4), 387–388.

Stuart, M. (2001). *Degrees of difference: Influences of the development of tourism as a subject in UK higher education*. Unpublished doctoral dissertation. University of Kent, Canterbury.

Stuart, M. (2002). Critical influences on tourism as a subject in UK higher education: Lecturer perspectives. *Journal of Hospitality, Leisure, Sport and Tourism Education, 1*,1. www.hlst.heacademy.ac.uk/johlste.

Stuart-Hoyle, M. (2003). The purpose of undergraduate tourism programmes in the United Kingdom. *Journal of Hospitality, Leisure, Sport and Tourism Education, 2*,1. www.hlst.heacademy.ac.uk/johlste.

Tribe, J. (1997). The indiscipline of tourism. *Annals of Tourism Research, 24*(3), 638–657.

Tribe, J. (2000). Indisciplined and unsubstantiated. *Annals of Tourism Research, 27*(3), 809–813.

Tribe, J. (2003). The RAE-ification of tourism research in the UK. *International Journal of Tourism Research, 5*(3), 225–234.

Trowler, P. (1997). Beyond the Robbins trap: Reconceptualising academic responses to change in higher education (or…Quiet Flows the Don?). *Studies in Higher Education, 22*, 301–319.

Truss, C., Gratton, L., Hope-Hailey, V., McGovern, P., & Stiles, P. (1997). Soft and hard models of human resource management: A reappraisal. *Journal of Management Studies, 34*(1), 53–73.

Winter, R. (1996). New liberty, new discipline: Academic work in the new higher education. In: R. Cuthbert (Ed.), *Working in higher education* (pp. 71–83). Buckingham: SRHE/OUP.

www.prospects.co.uk. The UKs official graduate careers website provided by AgCAS.

Chapter 30

Learning Resources

Lyn Bibbings

Background, Dimensions and Profile

In the last 25 years higher education in the UK has changed considerably: the number of students has more than doubled, with a much wider and more mixed profile of age and background. While public funding has increased in real terms (although stayed about the same as a percentage of GDP) the unit of funding per student has dramatically fallen. After a very rapid increase in student numbers between 1988 and 1993, the Government capped the number of publicly funded undergraduate students and withdrew almost all funding for capital expenditure (The National Committee of Inquiry into Higher Education, 1997). This increase in diversity of students with less money to teach them has inevitably led to changes in the way students are taught, where they are taught and how they learn. There has been a shift from an instructional approach (where the teacher essentially supplies information and "facts" for students) to a constructivist approach where the teacher supplies the "scaffold" for learning, but the learner is expected to be active and to take responsibility for their own learning; a student-centred rather than a teacher-centred learning paradigm. In this approach the student needs to be able to access learning resources, either that are generally available in libraries through books, journals etc. or material specifically generated for the course by tutors, which may be made available to the student electronically via virtual learning spaces — for example WebCT or Blackboard. Additionally, of course, there is also now a huge amount of unvalidated material available via the world wide web (Armitage et al., 2002).

Changes in legislation such as the Disability Discrimination Act Part IV, which requires that students with disabilities (such as hearing, sight or mobility impairments, dyslexia, diabetes or epilepsy) are not disadvantaged in the learning process, and the UK government agenda to increase participation in post-compulsory education to 50% (DfES, 2003), has also led to pressure and motivation to change and develop new, more effective, methods of teaching and learning. Rapid developments in technology have also influenced both the skills that students need to develop during their studies and the way that higher education is, and can be, delivered. The challenge for lecturers has been, and still is, to deliver a high-quality learning experience for students under these conditions, while also satisfying the other demands of scholarship and research in an internationally competitive environment.

This chapter will focus on the changes that have been made in the last 5 years in particular, following the recommendations of the National Committee of Inquiry into Higher Education (1997), which have led to growth in learning resources to support both student learning and staff development in teaching and learning methods. While these changes have affected every subject in higher education, there are particular characteristics of the study of tourism which need separate consideration, such as its essentially international nature, participation in field work and in work placements.

In the UK since 1992, many Polytechnics have applied for University status under the Further and Higher Education Act. Although Polytechnics had been very successful in allowing access to higher education, and in offering innovative and responsive courses to suit changing student and employer needs (Pratt, 1997), they found it difficult to compete in the marketplace for students without becoming 'new Universities' with their own degree awarding powers. The Polytechnics tended to have a more regional focus and to teach more applied and vocational subjects (MacLeod, 2002), including Tourism — the first courses appearing in the mid to late 1980s. The teaching of tourism still largely resides within 'new Universities' and Further Education Colleges that deliver higher education courses. There has been a massive growth in both the number of institutions offering courses in tourism and the types of course offered at both undergraduate and postgraduate levels (Airey & Johnson, 1998). The amount of research undertaken in the subject has also dramatically increased as institutions teaching tourism take part in the Research Assessment Exercise — discussed elsewhere in this book.

This growth inevitably means that not only are more students involved in the subject, but also more staff who create both a demand and supply for and of, learning resources. These are in three main categories — learning resources for staff to enable them to become better teachers and facilitators of student learning leading to improved learning experiences within particular subject areas; subject-based learning resources for use by both staff and students; and learning resources designed to be used by students independently to complement the taught component of their course, or even to be used as an alternative to any face-to-face teaching.

The Dearing Committee

The National Committee of Inquiry into Higher Education, known as the Dearing Committee Report after its Chair, Sir Ron Dearing, has been extremely influential in changes that have taken place in teaching and learning in the UK since 1997. It was set up in 1996 to make recommendations for the development and funding of higher education over the following 20 years within a vision of a society committed to learning throughout life. For this to be achieved there needs to be a national policy objective to be world class in both learning at all levels and in research of different kinds, but the committee recognised that:

> "*there are some concerns that current arrangements for quality assurance are not sufficient to ensure comparability in an enlarged sector*" and that

> *"competition between institutions may have hindered beneficial collabora-*
> *tion, and that funding arrangements which reward high quality research*
> *have diverted attention from the delivery of high quality teaching"* (National
> Committee of Enquiry into Higher Education, 1997: Summary Report 5.)

The report sought to specifically address these issues by recognising a need to change the value system in higher education where research expertise, rather than teaching expertise, had been the main basis for professional advancement. It recommended that teaching in Universities should be professionalised through the establishment of an Institute for Learning and Teaching in Higher Education that would not only accredit professional achievement in learning and teaching, but also commission research into pedagogy, stimulate the development of innovative learning materials and assist institutions in exploiting the use of communications and information technology in learning and teaching.

Learning Resources and Organisations to Support Higher Education Staff

There are a number of organisations and agencies that have developed over the last 10 years or so in order to improve the quality of teaching and learning, and to co-ordinate the development of projects to research and develop good practice. Some of these projects address subject-based issues while others are thematic in nature, and can be used and adapted by a range of subjects. In February 2002, The Teaching Quality Enhancement Committee was established by the Higher Education Funding Council for England (HEFCE), and the two main associations of higher education institutions — Universities UK and the Standing Conference of Principals (SCOP), to review support for the enhancement of quality in learning and teaching in higher education. The final report, published in January 2003 proposed that a single central body should be formed, and in May 2004 a new Higher Education Academy was created through merging three organisations — the National Co-ordination Team, the Institute for Learning and Teaching in Higher Education and the Learning and Teaching Support Network. These bodies had previously been working separately, but alongside one another, to fund developments in learning and teaching, reward excellence and produce and disseminate resources. Although these are now part of one organisation, it is useful to review the origins and purpose of these initiatives.

The Higher Education Academy's mission is to *"work with the higher education community to enhance all aspects of the student experience"* (www.heacademy.ac.uk) and a key aim is to deliver *"a co-ordinated and coherent UK-wide approach to: curriculum and pedagogic development across the spectrum of higher education activity; professional development and increasing the professional development and recognition of all staff in HE; disseminating and embedding policies and practices that enhance the student experience"* (www.heacademy.ac.uk) and is therefore a key provider of learning resources for staff. The development of resources is encouraged through the funding of specific research and development projects linked to national priorities. Some projects are generic in nature and have relevance and application across a broad range of subject areas, for example employability; sustainable development, while others relate national priorities to subject-specific impacts, for example entrepreneurship.

National Co-ordination Team

The National Co-ordination Team co-ordinates projects that have been funded under the Fund for Development of Teaching and Learning (FDTL), and the Teaching and Learning Technology Programme (TLTP). The TLTP was set up in 1992 to work collaboratively to explore new technologies and how these can be exploited to improve quality in higher education. The FDTL, set up in 1995, was designed to stimulate developments in teaching and learning and the dissemination of good practice. In order to be eligible for funding, project leaders must have been judged as "excellent" when subject review was carried out in their institution by the Quality Assurance Agency (which is the main UK body for this work), although collaboration with institutions with lower grading is encouraged. The subject of tourism became eligible to apply for funding in 2004 and seven projects in Hospitality, Leisure, Sport and Tourism have been awarded funds to develop various aspects of teaching and learning specific to the subject areas. Most of the projects are collaborations between one or more institution. These projects aim to develop good practice and disseminate findings and resources in order that individuals, course teams and institutions can benefit. Access to websites for all the projects which include information and resources, arranged by subject and theme is available through the Higher Education Academy website (www.heacademy.ac.uk). Examples of projects specifically relevant to tourism are: image enriched learning in tourism; effective learning and teaching enhancement through peer review; developing creative assessment methods; enhancing graduate employability and supporting student assessment through an institutional portal.

Dissemination is a key aspect of the projects, and while this is likely to include making learning resources available for the subject community, often via the internet, dissemination for use is also key. This implies that there is unlikely to be an impact on the quality of teaching and learning or the quality of the student experience simply by making resources available; staff and students need to know how and why they can use these resources to improve their learning. The NCT was incorporated into the Higher Education Academy in May 2004.

The Institute for Learning and Teaching in Higher Education

The Institute for Learning and Teaching in Higher Education was set up in June 1999 as a direct response to the Dearing Committee recommendations, and initial funding was provided by the Higher Education Funding Councils for England, Scotland and Wales and by the Department of Higher and Further Education in Northern Ireland, although it was intended that it should eventually become self supporting through membership subscriptions and from its membership and accreditation services. The Institute worked collaboratively with individuals, institutions, partner organisations, other professional bodies and the higher education trade unions to generate a community of those involved in learning and teaching in higher education where ideas and best practice are developed and shared (www.heacademy.ac.uk).

The Institute (now part of the Higher Education Academy) worked with individuals to provide professional recognition through membership and with institutions through the provision of accredited courses for teachers in higher education. Partner organisations include the Higher Education Staff Development Agency and the Learning and Teaching Support Network (LTSN) to take forward the proposals of the Teaching Quality Enhancement Committee. The Institute also runs the National Teaching Fellowship Scheme, which is a key part of an agenda for recognising and rewarding excellence in teaching in higher education. This scheme recognises and rewards teachers or learning support staff for their excellence in teaching and provides a £50,000 award for research or development projects. While the emphasis of the scheme is a celebration of individual excellence, there is an expectation that this will raise the standards of teaching more generally. Sally Brown, as Director of ILT noted that the international experience — in Canada, Australia and the US, as well as in the UK, of bringing together groups of outstanding teachers and enabling them to work together collaboratively to share practice and ideas, maximises their impact on the academic community. As she went on to say *"First-rate teachers can, and do, work in isolation, but surely part of the purpose of marking them out as superlative is to enable others to learn from them so as to raise the overall standards of teaching"* (Brown, 2003, p. 5). In 2004, the scheme was expanded from 20 awards to fifty per year, with recognition offered in three categories: for experienced staff; for learning support staff and for "rising stars" — those that have fewer than six years experience. Outputs and resources from projects that National Teaching Fellows have carried out are available from http://www.ntfs.ac.uk/ or from the project finder facility at www.connect.ac.uk. However, to date there have been no National Teaching Fellow awards in the tourism subject area and there has been only one nomination. Nevertheless, resources from other subject areas or resources that address generic issues in learning and teaching may be useful to teachers of tourism.

The UK scheme draws on a number of international examples, notably the Carnegie Scheme in the US (http://www.carnegiefoundation.org) the 3M Teaching Fellowship in Canada (http://www.3m.com/intl/ca/english/about_us/whats_new_stories/news032.html) and the Australian Awards for University Teaching (http://www.autc.gov.au/aaut.htm). More recently a scheme has been introduced in New Zealand where particular emphasis is placed upon the sharing of good practice among award holders and the wider academic community (http://www.nzqa.govt.nz/for-providers/awards/ttea/index.html). In Sweden, a large-scale pedagogical development project, The Breakthrough, also includes a system for rewarding professionalism in teaching (http://www.lth.se/genombrottet/pedacademy. pdf). All of these schemes have, as a basic premise, that others should be able to benefit from the expertise and excellence in practice that these teachers have demonstrated, through the provision of resources to aid the development and improvement of teaching standards overall. This has resulted in a huge expansion of both pedagogical research and of the dissemination of knowledge and techniques to enhance learning.

The Higher Education Academy Subject Network — Formerly the LTSN

The support network for Hospitality, Leisure, Sport and Tourism is the single most important agency for the development and provision of learning resources for the subject of tourism in the UK.

The complete subject support network comprises 24 subject centres based in higher education institutions throughout the UK, which offer subject-specific expertise, advice, information and resources to support their subject community. The network was established in May 2000 as the Learning and Teaching Support Network (LTSN) but was incorporated into the Higher Education Academy in May 2004. The Higher Education Academy and the subject support network is funded by the HEFCE. One of the subject centres specifically represents the interests of the Hospitality, Leisure, Sport and Tourism subject areas, an alignment initiated by the Quality Audit Agency for the purposes of subject benchmarking and subject review. This support network has served to raise the profile of the subject areas and given them visibility where previously there was little. The provision of a network for these subjects has enabled the development of a much stronger liaison between subject associations (Association for Tourism in Higher Education (ATHE); Leisure Studies Association (LSA); Council for Hospitality Management Education (CHME); UK Standing Conference for Sport; British Association of Sport and Exercise Science (BASES) and, more recently, the Association of Events Management Education (AEME)) institutions, and individuals involved in the teaching, learning and research of tourism.
The three broad aims of the network are:

- *to create and support a vigorous educational practitioner network*;
- *to identify and disseminate best practice in learning, teaching and assessment in the Hospitality, Leisure, Sport, and Tourism areas*;
- *to encourage pedagogic research and the dissemination of outcomes* (www.hlst.heacademy.ac.uk/about/aboutus.html).

Most importantly, the network is about sharing practice and ideas to improve teaching and learning in the subject areas. This is primarily done through web-based materials although these are supported by some paper-based publications, workshops, conferences and projects. This allows free access to up-to-date information and materials to enable lecturers to respond to a changing higher education environment, characterised by a broader range of students with differing backgrounds and learning experiences and to engage with innovative practice; to collaborate on projects, and to share ideas within the subject community, something that was a very limited possibility 5 years ago before the creation of the network. This level of collaboration is, perhaps, all the more remarkable in a highly competitive market where there is, possibly, an over-supply of university places on tourism courses (Airey & Johnson, 1998; UCAS, 2005). Differentiation of courses is therefore one strategic response to this situation, but even so, lecturers have proved willing to produce and share teaching and learning resources that can be used by others in the sector.

Resources Available On-line from the Higher Education Academy Subject Network

The website for the Higher Education Academy Subject network for Hospitality, Leisure, Sport and Tourism (www.hlst.heacademy.ac.uk) provides access to a range of publications which meet different learning and teaching needs. These resources are largely provided by and for the subject community, and have served to raise the profile of learning and teaching practices and the specific issues generated by the demands of the subject areas, such as work placement and the use of field trips in tourism studies. The subject centre also helps users to be aware of national priorities and agendas for change and how these impact on the subject, such as assessment, widening participation through foundation degrees and employability.

Resources are primarily designed for lecturers working in higher education (whether they are in further or higher education institutions) and cover a range of approaches — the guide to current practice, for example, offers specific guidance on curriculum design; learning and teaching practice; assessment; managing quality; references and other resources.

The newsletter, Learning through Innovations, Networks and Knowledge (LINK) which is published three times per year, both paper-based and electronically, focuses each issue on a different topic relevant to learning, teaching and assessment in the subject areas. Examples are: employability; diversity; e-learning; linking teaching and research; assessment; higher education in further education institutions. National and generic priorities and agendas, for example, employability; diversity; assessment, are discussed and examined in the context of the subject area.

Other material published on the site includes: **resource guides** which provide a compact, but essential guide to texts, journals, websites and other resources for specific areas of study within programmes, for example, resources guides are available for Events Management, Rural Leisure and Tourism and the Strategic Management of Tourism. These are designed to be used by both staff and students and have been prepared by staff experienced in these areas of study.

Case studies are evidence-based examples of learning, teaching and assessment practice generated by teachers in the subject areas and include topics such as work placement, field work, group work, key skills, personal development planning, vocational relevance and linking teaching and research. There is a **catalogue of new publications** categorised by subject and topic e.g. Tourism and sustainable development, tourism marketing, tourism studies, which lists new books with date of publication and gives links to further information via the publishers' website. JoHLSTE is the **electronic peer-reviewed international journal** of Hospitality, Leisure, Sport and Tourism Education. It is published twice a year on the website and is one of very few journals specifically concerned with tourism education, and includes both academic and practice papers.

Other Agencies and On-line Services for Staff and Students

Joint Information Systems Committee (**JISC**) is a service funded by the UK Further and Higher Education Funding Councils and provides advice and guidance for the use of Information and Communications Technology (ICT) to support teaching, learning and research. The resource guide for Hospitality, Leisure, Sport and Tourism (www.jisc.ac.uk/rg_hosp_cat_learn.html) gives access to a number of different on-line resource services: BUFVC **Television and Radio Index** for Learning and Teaching (www.trilt.ac.uk) which gives extensive television and radio listings covering more than 300 UK channels. Resources are enhanced with additional information, and users can receive alerts for forthcoming programmes.

Biz/ed (www.bized.ac.uk/) provides resources for leisure and recreation and tourism as well as business and economics. Materials include study skills advice as worksheets as well as content-based material. Information and worksheets for the Advanced Certificate of Vocational Education (AVCE) in tourism is included.

Internet Detective (www.sosig.ac.uk/desire/internet-detective.html) is a web-based tutorial designed to raise awareness of the quality of internet resources and to help users to think critically about the source of information found on the internet that may be used for education or research.

RDN Virtual Training Suite (www.vts.rdn.ac.uk) is a suite of online tutorials for both lecturers and students to improve internet skills and to learn what the internet can offer in the subject areas of leisure, travel and tourism, sport and recreation and hospitality.

SPRIG (www.sprig.org.uk/) is an organisation that promotes information sources in leisure, tourism, sport and hospitality. It provides a general guide on "How to Find Out About Tourism" aimed at tourism students at undergraduate level and above. This provides an introduction to the literature of tourism (although is not comprehensive) organised by encyclopaedias and dictionaries; books; reference sources, for example tourism statistics; journals listing, including journals from the UK, USA and Australia; abstracts and indexes which are searchable databases of journals which include tourism articles such as Ingenta (www.ingentaconnect.com); Free Reference Lists from the University of Connecticut (http://playlab.uconn.edu/frl.htm) which has a bibliography for tourism books and articles. CAB International provide a subscription online service (leisure-tourism.com) which also contains new academic research, industry reports, books, book reviews and news from the leisure, recreation, sport, hospitality, tourism and culture sectors. The SPRIG site also offers links to subject gateways, organisations, libraries and publishers.

Other Portals of Information on Tourism

One of the most comprehensive portals of information to tourism resources and links for tourism educators and students is **Tourism Education** (www.tourismeducation.org). The main areas it provides are: books, through links to publishers; to key libraries and abstracting services; a specialist bibliography on tourism education; links to tourism organisations; providers of market research; jobs; courses; access to discussion groups and links to other similar pages including both research and educational providers.

Another portal developed by a tourism academic is John Beech's Travel and Tourism Information Gateway (http://www.stile.coventry.ac.uk/cbs/staff/beech/tourism/index.htm). The site is designed to be a starting point for British university students (although may also be relevant for other users) who wish to search the Web for data sources relevant to coursework for travel and tourism modules on Bachelor and Master degree programmes, and also for tourism staff undertaking desk research. There are currently 900 links from the Tourism Information Gateway and more from the Leisure and Sport Gateways.

ALTIS is a service which is part of the Resource Discovery Network and is also funded by JISC. The service aims to provide a trusted source of selected, high-quality Internet information for students, lecturers, researchers and practitioners in the areas of hospitality, leisure, sport and tourism. However, the number of resources included are relatively few.

Google (www.google.com) is a powerful search engine that can locate many useful tourism resources, and which has additional services such as advanced searching, searching for images and alerts for new information on particular topics. In November 2004, a new service was introduced — **Google Scholar** (http://scholar.google.com/) which allows searches for keywords in theses, technical reports, university websites and books. It is a free service and results are ranked by order of relevance, including the number of citations by other authors, rather than by the number of hits.

Discussion Lists

JISC also offers a mailing list service — **JISC mail** — (www.jiscmail.ac.uk/) to enable further and higher education communities to establish networks and to share information via e-mail or the web. JISC mail lists are organised by topics and several lists are relevant for those interested in tourism — tourism; tourfor, sustainable co-development of tourism and forestry; tourism-marketing, for academics and practitioners; tourism anthropology; small-tourism-firms for management of small tourism and hospitality businesses and heritage. These lists are open to subscribers all over the world and can therefore prove a rich source of information, events and networks of interested academics and practitioners.

Another key international discussion list is offered by **TRINET** (TRINET@ uhmtravel.tim.hawaii.edu) which is a moderated list of academics in the tourism field.

TechDis (www.techdis.ac.uk/) is a UK educational advisory service working in the fields of accessibility and inclusion and aims to enhance provision for disabled staff and students in further and higher education through the use of technology. This is a useful resource when developing teaching and learning materials, virtual learning environments or working with students with particular impairments who need to access to electronic resources.

Other Subject-Based Resources for Use by Staff and Students

There are a number of developing **video and film** resources which are available on-line, either to view or to download. Educational Media OnLine (www.emol.ac.uk/) is another JISC funded service hosted by Edina, still under development, which provides to subscribing institutions, downloadable digitised film which can be used for learning, teaching and research purposes. There are a number of film collections with those most relevant to tourism being from **Amber Films** — a collection of documentaries and feature films on the social history of the late 20th and early 21st centuries.

Moving History is a developing resource provided by the Centre for British Film and Television Studies (www.movinghistory.ac.uk) which has film from the UK's 12 public sector moving image archives and which documents social history in the UK. The **BBC** also hosts two projects which provide film and oral history archive material that would be of value to those studying tourism. The first — **Nation on Film** is a joint BBC and Open-University series which can be searched by topic or location. The collection on family and community (www.bbc.co.uk/nationonfilm/topics/family-and-community/) has film clips on outings, events and holidays at home which date from the 1930s to the 1970s. The site also allows for visitors to view clips and add their own memories and reminiscences. Oral histories are available through the **Twentieth Century Vox** (www.bbc.co.uk/education/20cvox/) website which archives material from BBC programmes on oral history since 1997. The area of the site on lifestyles is of particular relevance to UK tourism, with oral histories about British holidays, including working holidays.

Learner Autonomy

The availability of all these resources in tourism, whether paper-based books and journals or web-based written, film or audio material supposes that learners will know how to be independent learners and to be able to use these resources in a way which will allow them to construct their own meanings and achieve their own learning objectives. However, as students come from increasingly diverse backgrounds and previous learning experience it cannot be assumed that this will always be so. It is therefore important for teachers to consider carefully the curriculum design they adopt, and the skills that learners need in order to be able to make effective use of the resources provided. This may include technological skills, skills of critical thinking, analysis and evaluation or the organisation of resources, perhaps via a virtual learning space where the staff retain control of availability of resources or where a core of resources are centralised with others being freely available but not under the control of the teacher.

Resource-based learning may be considered an attractive approach when trying to teach large numbers of students with less resource, and the use of virtual learning environments (VLEs) can provide access to material as a substitute or in addition to face-to-face teaching. This can be approached in an incremental way (Gibbs & Parson, 1994) but normally requires the teacher to organise material, or at least provide access to material.

Issues for the Future

In January 2005 it was announced that substantial funding was to be awarded to 74 Centres for Excellence in Teaching and Learning (CETL) in UK universities. The CETL initiative has two main aims: to reward excellent teaching practice, and to invest further in that practice so that CETLs funding delivers substantial benefits to students, teachers and institutions. This will inevitably generate further resources and further developments in pedagogy so that these resources may be used more effectively both by teachers in curriculum design, and by students in the ways that they learn.

The Higher Education Academy has also had government funding secured over a longer period with the aim of further embedding professional practice in teaching. In recognising the need to find more effective and efficient ways of helping students learn, the future agenda for subject centres emphasises the sharing and transfer of knowledge and practice between disciplines as well as developing innovations. Subject centres will be working to include further education teachers who teach at higher education levels, an area of particular importance to tourism, with the aim of making resources freely available to this sector and to generate new materials to meet specific needs. The ultimate aim is to enhance the experience of students in higher education despite continuing change in the environment and pressure on resources.

References

Airey, D., & Johnson, S. (1998). *The profile of tourism studies degree courses in the UK: 1997/98. NLG Guideline* No 7. London: NLG.

Armitage, A. et al. (2002). *Teaching and training in post-compulsory education.* Buckingham: Open University Press.

Brown, S. (2003). Recognising and rewarding excellence. *Exchange.* Issue 5, Autumn.

Department for Education and Science (DfES). (2003). *The future of higher education.* London: DfES.

Gibbs, G., & Parsons, C. (1994). *Course design for resource based learning.* Oxford: Oxford Centre for Staff Development.

MacLeod, D. (2002). Poly genesis. *The Guardian.* September 3.

Pratt, J. (1997). *The polytechnic experiment 1965–1992.* London: Open University Press.

The National Committee of Inquiry into Higher Education. (1997). *Higher education in the learning society.* Summary Report. London: Stationery Office.

UCAS (2005) in LINK 12, *The Future of Hospitality: Leisure and Tourism in Higher Education,* Oxford: The Higher Education Academy Network for Hospitality, Leisure, Sport and Tourism.

Chapter 31

Careers and Employment

Adele Ladkin

Background

As tourism is an important sector of the service economy and is a creator of jobs, there is a need to examine tourism education in relation to careers and employment. This is not to detract from the value of tourism as an area of academic study in its own right, but the vocational element of tourism education necessitates that it is considered in the wider labour market context. It is not sufficient to examine tourism education without considering the progression of individuals that undertake tourism studies with a possible view to entering employment and developing their careers in the industry. Furthermore, given the amount of employment opportunities available in the various tourism sectors and the ability of tourism development to generate jobs, tourism education is often the starting point in the training and development of human capital to undertake these occupations. Therefore, tourism education is closely related to employment and careers in the industry from both an individual perspective in terms of their personal career development and opportunities, and an organisational perspective in terms of the supply of labour available for the industry.

Dimensions and Profile

In order to explore and understand careers and occupations in tourism, three key areas that warrant discussion. The characteristics of tourism labour markets, the nature of tourism employment and the dimensions of the tourism industry in employment terms. These aspects are linked, and they provide a picture of the magnitude of tourism employment along with the characteristics of the labour market that tourism jobs and careers operate within.

An International Handbook of Tourism Education
Copyright © 2005 by Elsevier Ltd.
All rights of reproduction in any form reserved
ISBN: 0-08-044667-1

Tourism Labour Markets

Labour markets comprise individuals in any given population who are considered to be of working age. Labour markets can be defined in a number of ways including their size, skill level and the nature of skills, cost of labour, geographical location and mobility patterns. Any analysis of tourism labour markets is problematic, due to the sheer size and diversity of the tourism industry. The difficulties begin with trying to define tourism, followed by attempts to define tourism employment. Even when a sector is identified, there are considerable levels of organisational and job diversity (Riley, Ladkin, & Szivas, 2002). Tourism labour markets are dynamic, with many sectors being characterised by occupational diversity, relatively low pay, a high percentage of young people in the occupations, high levels of mobility and low specificity of skills (Riley et al., 2002).

Despite the diversity of occupations, a number of characteristics of jobs in the industry can be identified. Andriotis and Vaughan (2004) reviewed a number of characteristics of the tourism workforce. These are seasonal, part-time, female, expatriate/migrant, pluriactivity, and existing in the informal economy. Many jobs in tourism are seasonal, with hotels and facilities either scaling down activities or closing after the main season. Part-time jobs and a high percentage of female workers are also widespread across the tourism industry, and often surplus jobs are filled by a migrant or expatriate workforce. These in turn can have a downward effect on pay. Tourism may also create multiple employment, whereby someone may have a main job in a different sector during the day, but then be employed part time in a tourism job at night. Finally, the informal sector of tourism is characterised by such activities as beach vendors (Andriotis & Vaughan, 2004). These job characteristics may give a negative perception of employment in tourism, which affects the dimension and qualities of tourism labour markets.

Tourism Employment

Although employment as a concept is relatively easy to define as either the act of employing or the state of employed, or a person's work or occupation, defining tourism employment fraught with difficulties. The overriding problem with a definition of tourism employment is tied to the difficulties of defining tourism and the dynamics and complexity of the industry. Issues such as the overlap and strong linkages of sectors, the problems of categorising tourists, the mixing of tourists and locals using the same facilities, the informal economy and the lack of statistics that hamper the definition of tourism can be equally applied to the problems of defining tourism employment. Tourism is not recognised as a single entity in the Standard Industrial Classification, but exists in a number of different areas. For estimating tourism employment in the UK the Department of Culture, Media and Sport use the following S.I.C codes; 551/552 (hotels and other tourist accommodations), 553 (restaurants, cafes, etc.), 554 (bars, public houses and nightclubs), 663 (travel agencies and tour operators), 935 (libraries, museums and other cultural activities), and 926/927 (sport and other recreation).

Despite the difficulties of definitions, any discussion on tourism employment does at least need to outline the dimensions of the industry. One framework that offers a simplified view is to identify the different sectors of tourism, the different occupational levels and the different tourism jobs.

In addition to the hospitality sector (accommodation, restaurants and catering) the various sectors that are commonly agreed as being part of the tourism industry have been defined by Riley et al. (2002) as

- transport;
- tour operators and travel agencies;
- tourist attractions;
- conference businesses;
- tour guides;
- tourist information services;
- souvenir shops;
- relevant government offices;
- NGOs;
- educational establishments.

This illustrates the scope and diversity of the industry at the supply level, and essentially defines the areas of tourism employers. Key areas of tourism employment as identified by the Association of Graduate Careers Advisory Services (AGCAS) are defined as tour operators, travel agents (retail and business) ground handlers, tourist boards (national and regional) local authorities, tourism information centres and tourism consultancies.

Occupational levels have been broadly defined by Cooper (1991) as operative, craft, supervisory and management, with the skill levels as unskilled, semiskilled and skilled. There is a dominance of the operative, craft and supervisory levels in many tourism occupations that often hampers career development (Cooper, Fletcher, Gilbert, Shepherd, & Wanhill, 1998).

The classification and identification of occupational classifications is a complex activity in general terms (Jones & McMillan, 2001). In relation to tourism, the list of occupations is seemingly endless. Two early classifications of tourism jobs are provided by Airey and Nightingale (1981), and examples of occupations given by Gunn (1998). Airey and Frontistis (1997) identify a comprehensive list of tourism jobs which includes hotel manager, hotel receptionist, chef, restaurant owner, airline pilot, airline stewards, coach driver, taxi driver, tourist information officer, travel agent, and tour guide. There are inherent problems in classifying jobs that go beyond the remit of the discussion here, but can be found in Riley et al. (2002). What is important in the context of tourism education is that the relationship between jobs and education is central to the development of human capital.

The Scale of Tourism Employment

According to the World Travel and Tourism Council (WTTC), the world travel and tourism industry is expected to generate 73,692,500 jobs and 3.8% of GDP in 2004. This is forecast to increase in 2014 to 87,450,300 jobs or 2.9% of GDP. On a broader scale, in 2004 world travel and tourism economy employment is estimated to be 241,697,000 jobs, representing 8.1% of total world employment, or one in every 12.3 jobs. Estimates for 2014 are that the total number of jobs will be 259,930,000 representing 8.6% of total world employment or one in every 11.6 jobs (WTTC, 2004).

Table 1: Travel and tourism industry employment 2004 ('000 of jobs).

Rank	Country	Number
1	China	14,787.0
2	India	11,404.0
3	United States	6,561.6
4	Indonesia	3,176.7
5	Japan	2,638.8
6	Brazil	2,263.6
7	Egypt	1,600.4
8	France	1,549.6
9	Spain	1,475.3
10	Thailand	1,453.9

Source: World Travel and Tourism Council (2004).

On a country basis there are differences in the number of people employed in the travel and tourism industry. The top 10 countries with regard to generating the largest amount (absolute) terms of travel and tourism industry employment in 2004 are shown in Table 1.

In Britain, in June 2002 there were an estimated 2,127,200 employees (including the self-employed) in tourism-related industries, representing 7% of all people in employment. (Department for Culture, Media and Sport, 2003).

Statistics for tourism employment are usually drawn from data using Tourism Satellite Accounts (TSA), and guidelines are provided by the World Tourism Organisation (WTO) for the development of National Tourism Statistics (STSs) and the TSA. Depending on the employment issues to be described or analysed and on the statistics available, statistics on employment topics may be organised in the context of TSA or they may be organised independently. Employment and labour statistics may be linked to TSA by co-ordinating and linking the statistical classification, definitions, scopes and reference periods (WTO, 2001).

While improvements in the ways in which tourism employment data are collected through the implementation of TSA are evident, the statistics on employment are not without criticism, and have been accused of being misleading (Leiper, 1999). A discussion of the ways in which tourism employment data is collected and interpreted is beyond the scope of this chapter, but TSA methods are fully outlined by the WTO (WTO, 2001).

Tourism Careers and Employment Literature

Despite the rapid growth of the tourism industry, the subsequent increase in the number of tourism jobs and the growth in educational courses, surprisingly little is known about careers and employment in the tourism industry. Information and research in this area comes from two main sources. The first is career information and guidance literature produced by governments, industry organisations and career and employment assistance services. Typically this type of information provides a description of the occupation, expected educational requirements, training and skill development, salaries and career progression, and in some instances, job vacancies.

The second source is research by the academic community who investigate a variety of different areas related to careers and employment in the tourism industry. For example, Ross (1992, 1993, 1997a) explores a range of issues relating to interest in tourism and hospitality employment, including work motivation, success perception and job acquisition strategies. Specific to one sector, travel agency employment perceptions have also been explored by Ross (1997b). The attitudes to careers in tourism from a UK and Greek perspective has been examined by Airey and Frontistis (1997). Related to the theme of perceptions, Hjalager and Andersen (2001) explore professionalism in tourism employment, and Hjalager (2003) investigates the educational opportunities and dilemmas that higher education faces in considering global tourism careers. Petrova and Mason (2004) assess the value of tourism degrees as perceived by a group of UK undergraduate students. Employment in tourism in times of economic transition has been examined by Szivas and Riley (1999), and exploration of the movement of labour into tourism in terms of attraction to and satisfaction with the industry is further outlined by Szivas, Riley, and Airey (2003). Seasonality issues are identified as being problematic in terms of labour supply (Jolliffe & Farnsworth, 2003). A recent research area focuses on vocational identities and careers in the tourism sector (Marhuenda, Martinez, & Navas, 2004). Characteristics of the tourism workforce have been identified by Andriotis and Vaughan (2004), who also provide an overview of previous research in this area. Finally, new ways of recording tourism employment as a means of reducing exaggerated statistics about tourism jobs is put forward by Leiper (1999), and developing human resources for the tourism industry have been discussed with reference to India by Singh (1997).

Apart from research by McKercher, Williams, and Coghlan (1995) who report on the career progress of tourism graduates from Charles Stuart University in Australia, little is known about what happens to tourism graduates after they leave education. Increasingly, with universities keeping data and alumni and undertaking first destination exits surveys a greater understanding of what happens to tourism graduates might emerge. Tracking the careers of those engaged in the industry gives important information on labour market behaviour and labour mobility.

A greater understanding of career progression is evident in the hospitality area, specifically in relation to hotel managers' careers (Guerrier, 1987; Riley & Turam, 1989; Baum, 1988, 1989; Tanke, 1990; Ruddy, 1989, 1990; Williams & Hunter, 1992). Ladkin and Riley (1996) examine mobility and structure in the career patterns of UK hotel managers, using a labour market hybrid of the bureaucratic model. There are two possible reasons why research into the careers of hotel managers is more advanced than for other occupations. The first is the importance of the hotel manager job as a profession in the industry, and the second is that as a target job it is easy to identify and monitor over time. The route to becoming a hotel manager often has clearly identified stages. Furthermore, evidence by Ladkin (2002) and Ladkin and Riley (1996) demonstrates that hotel managers are committed to the industry and their movements in the internal and external labour markets can be easily identified. Further research in the tourism area would address the imbalance.

Career Theory and Concepts

Career theory is a broad term, which refers to a set of exploratory and investigative approaches used to measure and analyse the phenomenon (Riley & Ladkin, 1994). The study of careers draws from a wide range of disciplines including economics in the form of job search processes, organisational behaviour for the structure of jobs, personality psychology which links careers to jobs, and motivation theory in terms of job choices and motivations (Riley & Ladkin, 1994). Although a career can be seen in a very simple form as a set of jobs that take place over time, this hides the complexity of a career that contains direction, time, pace, motivations, barriers, the development of human capital and goals. Furthermore, careers take place within the internal and external labour markets and are related to the cost and mobility of labour, all of which makes them a complex entity to understand. A comprehensive review and explanation of career theory has been given by Arthur, Hall, and Lawrence (1989). This review sparked the beginnings of a debate as to whether or not careers are a separate and distinctive area of study, with accepted identifiable theoretical perspectives and methodologies. Clearly, career theory, as with careers in general, does not remain static over time (Swanson, 1992). Emergent themes include the interaction of work and non-work, work and well-being, dual career issues and changing labour needs, and the changing nature of careers. Recently, Iellatcchitch, Mayrhofer, and Meyer (2003) argue for examining careers in terms of career fields as a means towards understanding overall career theory. Managing careers from both a theoretical and practical approach is further explored by both Swanson (1999) and Yehuda (2003).

However, regardless of any debate on the theoretical perspectives of careers, one certainty however is the importance of careers and occupations to individuals. They contain both an objective element relating to career structures and a subjective element that links careers to the self. Furthermore, jobs and careers contain an economic and structural element which links them to the wider aspects of societies and economic development. These reasons provide a case for continuing to develop an understanding of career theory and processes.

Practical Aspects of Career Theory

All careers contain a practical element. Riley and Ladkin (1994) identify three elements of career theory that can be related to the practical aspects of careers. These are career development, career planning and career choice. Career development refers to the outcomes for individuals and organisations and covers mobility, job transitions, career stages, career compromise and withdrawal, and economics. Career planning is concerned at the organisational level with the needs of organisations and human resource planning and at the individual level with the relationship between individual planning and career outcomes. Career choice explores a person's choice of job and organisation, and includes the career decision process, career anchors and career paths (Riley & Ladkin, 1994).

Career development is an umbrella term for personal or organisational career planning. Much of the research in this area relates to measurements of career development constructs (Chartrand & Camp, 1991), career development techniques (Luzzo, 1993), career stages (Erickson, 1963; Super, 1957; Levinson, 1978), career plateaus (Veiga, 1981) and career mobility and career paths (Driver, 1988; Gunz, 1988; Rosenbaum, 1979; Walker, 1992). The career planning literature either explores organisational needs in terms of planning (Bennison & Casson, 1984), and labour market analysis (Psacharopoulos, 1991; Adams, Middleton, & Ziderman, 1992), or individual career planning. This includes comment on the need for planning (Jennings, 1971; Hall, 1976; Edmond, 1989), success and satisfaction (Hall, 1976; Granrose & Portwood, 1987; Gould, 1979), variables that influence career planning (Korman, 1971; Greenhaus & Simon, 1976; Gould, 1979). The literature surrounding career choice is extensive (Lichtenberg, Shaffer, & Mariner-Arachtingi, 1993; Ben-shem & Avi-Itzhak, 1991; Osipow, 1990). Two of the most influential authors are Holland (1985) who explores personality types and their relationship to career choice, and Schein (1975) who developed the concept of career anchors, which are a set of criteria that you would not give up in your choice of career. Recently, Schein (1995) has explored career survival strategies through strategic job and role planning.

Given the variety of information available on the study of careers, a useful way forward would be to develop a framework for the analysis of careers in tourism. This has already been attempted by Riley and Ladkin (1994) who put forward a structural–technical framework for the analysis of careers that examines both the structural variables of a career and the behaviour elements.

Practical Elements of Tourism Careers

Set against the theoretical aspects of careers, as with any other industry there is a practical element to how people choose and develop their careers in the tourism industry. Three main issues with particular relevance to tourism education can be identified.

The first is in terms of taking a career decision to work in the tourism industry and searching for a job. The decision to seek employment in the tourism industry depends largely on whether or not there are perceived opportunities in the industry, and the attractiveness of jobs in the industry. Aside from the issue of the quality and level of the jobs, there is often no shortage of tourism employment opportunities in any given labour market. This is particularly the case in areas where tourism is developing as an industry (Cooper et al., 1998). Although little is known about the attractiveness of jobs in tourism, evidence provided by Hjalager (2003) and Szivas et al. (2003) indicates that certain tourism jobs remain attractive. Clearly, the willingness of people to consider jobs in the industry is dependent on other opportunities available in a given labour market.

The decision to work in the tourism industry is assisted by the range of information available to help individuals understand the nature of jobs and where the main sectors of employment can be found. The information sources include organisations devoted to helping people search for jobs such as educational career services, government employment centres and industry bodies such as the Association of British Travel Agencies (ABTA). In the UK, one of the main sources of information for graduates seeking jobs is the AGCAS. The tourism sector briefing includes an introduction to the tourism industry, the size, structure and current issues affecting the industry, who the key employers are, key roles for graduates and case studies of jobs (AGCAS, 2003). Books on careers in the industry are also available. For example, *Careers and jobs in travel and tourism* (Reily Collins, 2004). Increasingly, information on jobs and employers is provided by electronic sources. The on-line service provided by

AGCAS, www.prospects.ac.uk, provides services for a targeted career search, and for each type of job lists information on job activities, salary and conditions, entry requirements, training, career development, related jobs, case studies, contacts and resources, and vacancy sources. With many sources of information, the Internet is becoming the main place where individuals will search for career information and job opportunities.

The second career issue involves the decision to undertake tourism education prior to entering the labour force. The debate concerning whether or not a vocational education is required for employment in tourism is beyond the scope of this chapter and is discussed elsewhere (Cooper et al., 1994). However, it is possible to study tourism subjects at a range of different levels, some with a more practical skills-based element and others with a more academic focus. In England, the range of tourism education includes General National Vocational Qualifications (GNVQ), National Vocational Qualifications (NVQ), City and Guilds, General Certificate of Secondary Education (GCSE), General Certificate of Education (GCE) A levels, BTEC (Edexcel Foundation) Higher National Diplomas, Degrees and Postgraduate courses. Many universities also offer the opportunity to study for a research degree in the tourism area at MPhil, PhD and Professional Doctorate level. The prolific growth of tourism courses and course content in the UK has been outlined by Airey and Johnson (1999).

The third element is the issue of career development. Little is known about the routes that people take in order to develop careers in the tourism industry, as has been previously discussed. However, some organisations do have fixed career development routes that take place within their own internal labour markets. Graduate training schemes are becoming increasingly scarce, and on many instances only exist within large tour operator companies, hotels or airlines. For example, British Airways has the "Leaders for Business Programme", which is designed to train employees for a complete range of management capabilities they can apply across the business. This is a programme lasting between two and a half and three years, based on an introduction and placements.

An alternative career route might be to specialise in a particular role, for example, Information Technology or Marketing. Many tourism company training schemes are involved in "Investors in People" schemes. Often people gain experience in such functions in jobs not related to tourism. What is clear is that in order to succeed in many of the large companies in tourism is that a degree of mobility is required, using both the internal and external labour market. It is often this lack of perceived career development that dissuades people from entering the tourism professions.

Global Aspects of Careers and Employment

Tourism as an industry is characterised by international and domestic travel and is global in nature. Therefore it is important to consider career and employment in a global context. Central issues relevant to careers and employment in the tourism industry at the global scale are the importance of tourism employment, the movement of labour internationally, and job losses.

There is little doubt that tourism is a labour-intensive industry. The tourism industry provides a mechanism for generating employment opportunities for both developing countries with surplus labour and for industrialised countries with high levels of unemployment

(Cooper et al., 1998). The potential for job creation identifies tourism as a positive agent for change, resulting in governments using tourism as a development and regeneration strategy (Andriotis & Vaughan, 2004). Furthermore, in areas where other sectors of employment have declined, for example, in agriculture or heavy industry, tourism often becomes the main source of employment. As has previously been identified, the quality of these jobs is questionable, with a lack of higher level jobs resulting in a lack of career development. However, one feature of tourism employment is that while some jobs are directly related to travel and tourism and may suffer from the above characteristics, other jobs are produced as a result of the indirect effects of tourism. These jobs often do not suffer from the same characteristics (Cooper et al., 1998). Whatever the merits or problems of tourism jobs, and the difficulties in gaining accurate statistics on employment notwithstanding, it is clearly an important source of employment on a global-scale.

Linked to increasing globalisation is the issue labour mobility. Evidence on labour mobility from other employment sectors into tourism is provided by Szivas et al. (2003). Areas that are developing for tourism have to draw labour from somewhere, and depending on unemployment levels and the availability of skills, labour into tourism will either come from other areas or from other sectors of the labour market. With the move towards more liberalised employment opportunities particularly within the European Union, and with many global organisations such as hotels and airlines hiring from a global labour market, there are career and employment opportunities available in tourism that cross international boundaries. One of the problems with this movement of labour on an international scale is the recognition of tourism qualifications. Tourism qualifications that can be recognised internationally is an issue currently being addressed by the Education Council of the WTO. One certainty is the importance of language abilities for employees in tourism, and the ability to speak at least three major languages is often a requirement for employment in global tourism corporations.

A recent threat to the travel and tourism industry on a global scale is the issue of job losses. Belau (2003) from the International Labour Organisation (ILO) has identified that a combination of economic stagnation, safety concerns in view of recent security events, the effects of Severe Acute Respiratory Syndrome (SARS) and hostilities in the Middle East has resulted in a downturn in the travel and tourism industry that began in March 2003. Without significant improvements, the ILO predicts that 5 million jobs, representing 6% of the industry's total employment will be lost. The effects would not be the same in all regions, but countries experiencing the direct effects of the above would be the most seriously affected. The ILO also identify additional factors that could further affect job losses. These are that reductions in labour made in the short term tend to become permanent, as existing staff cope with the demand using new working methods and flexibility, and the modernisation of working methods. In Germany, TUI the world leader in tour operating, recently announced a US$280 million cost-cutting programme for 2004, with the possible loss of 2000 jobs (Belau, 2003). As with many other industry sectors, downturns and job losses are always a possibility.

Tourism Careers and Employment: Issues and Challenges

There are two main challenges for the industry in terms of developing careers and employment opportunities in tourism.

The first is part of an ongoing debate about the relationship between tourism education and tourism employment. The fact that the number of tourism courses and the number of tourism graduates searching for jobs in the industry is increasing is without doubt (Airey & Johnson, 1999; Kusluvan & Kusluvan, 2000; Petrova & Mason, 2004). The oversupply of tourism graduates is further compounded by the industry, which too often does not rate or recognise tourism education. Evidence provided by Hjalager and Andersen (2001) and Ladkin and Riley (1996) indicates that employees with a dedicated vocational tourism training do not necessarily have more rapid career progression than those with less relevant qualifications. Furthermore, industry has criticised tourism education for not adequately preparing people for employment in the industry (Airey, 1998; Petrova & Mason, 2004), and employers are confused about what educational courses are on offer due to the rapid expansion (Evans, 1993). On a more positive note however, there is evidence that employers are keen to work with tourism educators in order to improve the situation (Peacock & Ladkin, 2002). A recent UK government paper on *The future of higher education* (Department for Education and Skills, 2003) indicates the wish to build stronger partnerships between higher education institutions and the Regional Development Agencies (Tribe, 2003). If tourism education is to provide a valuable starting point for the development of human capital, then greater dialogue between industry and education would be useful.

The second challenge for tourism employment is the perception and attractiveness of jobs in the industry. The positive aspects have been identified by Szivas et al. (2003) as glamour, the opportunity to travel, meeting people, foreign language use and task variety. However, Thomas and Townsend (2001) identify that tourism jobs often compare unfavourably with jobs in other sectors in terms of employment relations, seasonality, and part time characteristics. Low pay, long hours, low skills, and minimal training can be added to this list (Szivas et al., 2003). This reliance on untrained labour leads to poor quality of service, but the benefit for the industry is cheap and plentiful labour supply (Cooper et al., 1998). One of the consequences of a poor perception of jobs in tourism is the loss of tourism professionals to other sectors (Hjalager, 2003). The attitudes and motivations for choosing a career in tourism and the aspirations of those entering the industry is a research area that has received increasing amounts of attention (Petrova & Mason, 2004; Hjalager, 2003; Ross, 1997a, b; Airey & Frontistis, 1997), which adds to an understanding of what drives people to work in the tourism industry.

Conclusion

The subject area of careers and employment in the tourism industry is extensive, and the above discussion concentrates on those issues relevant to tourism education. Tourism education, at whatever level, forms the starting point for the development of human capital and for providing a trained workforce with appropriate skills to undertake the wide range of tourism jobs and professions. The popularity of tourism courses is undisputed, and those involved in the provision of tourism education have come a long way to raise the profile of the topic as an area of study, and to prove it is credible as an educational qualification. Of less certainty is what happens to individuals who enter the tourism workforce, and how their skills are used and valued by the tourism industry. While there are enormous opportunities for employment in tourism, a lack of career development and the unattractiveness of some occupations remain a problem for those who choose tourism as a career route. Often the result is that many well educated and skilled individuals leave tourism for another sector. Furthermore, the tourism industry may also employ people with a variety of educational backgrounds, often completely un-related to tourism. This transferability of generic skills results in a difficulty to read tourism labour market signals. The tourism industry lacks distinct career paths and shares its labour markets with other segments. However, tourism as a service industry relies on the quality of its labour to develop and enhance the quality of the tourism product. An improved understanding of how best to educate and develop human capital would bring benefits to both individuals who wish to develop a career in tourism, and the tourism industry as a whole.

References

Adams, A. V., Middleton, J., & Ziderman, A. (1992). Market-based manpower planning with labour market signals. *International Labour Review, 131*(3), 261–279.

Airey, A. (1998). Academic papers: Education for tourism — East meets West. *International Journal of Tourism and Hospitality Research, 9,* 7–18.

Airey, D., & Frontistis, A. (1997). Attitudes to careers in tourism: An Anglo Greek comparison. *Tourism Management, 18*(3), 149–158.

Airey, D., & Johnson, S. (1999). The content of tourism degree course in the UK. *Tourism Management, 20*(2), 229–235.

Airey, D., & Nightingale, M. A. (1981). Tourism occupations, career profiles and knowledge. *Annals of Tourism Research, 8*(1), 52–68.

Andriotis, K., Vaughan, D. R. (2004). The tourism workforce and policy: Exploring the assumptions using Crete as the case study. *Current Issues in Tourism, 7*(1), 66–87.

Arthur, M. B., Hall, D. T., & Lawrence, B. S. (1989). *Handbook of career theory.* Cambridge: Cambridge University Press.

Association of Graduate Careers Advisory Services. (2003). *Sector briefings 2003: Tourism sector.* Sheffield: AGCAS.

Baum, T. (1988). Toward a new definition of hotel management. *The Cornell Hotel and Restaurant Administration Quarterly, 29*(2), 36–40.

Baum, T. (1989). Managing hotels in Ireland: Research and development for change. *International Journal of Hospitality Management, 8*(2), 131–144.

Belau, D. (2003). *New threats to employment in the travel and tourism industry 2003.* Geneva: International Labour Organisation.

Bennison, M., & Casson, J. (1984). *The manpower planning handbook.* Maidenhead: McGraw-Hill.

Ben-Shem, T., & Avi-Itzhak, E. (1991). Work values and career choice in freshmen students: The case of helping verses other professions. *Journal of Vocational Behaviour, 39*(3), 369–371.

Chartrand, J. M., & Camp, C. C. (1991). Advances in the measurement of career development constructs: A twenty year review. *Journal of Vocational Behaviour, 39*(1), 1–39.

Cooper, C. (1991). *Progress in tourism, recreation and hospitality management.* London: Belhaven Press.

Cooper, C., & Shepherd, R. (1994). Dimensions of the education-industry interface for tourism. *Industry and Higher Education, 8*(1), 36–45.

Cooper, C., Fletcher, J., Gilbert, D., Shepherd, R., & Wanhill, S. (1998). *Tourism principles and practice*. Harlow: Longman.

Department for Culture, Media and Sport. (2003). Available on-line at www.staruk.org.uk.

Department for Education and skills. (2003). *He future of Higher Education*. Norwich: The stationary office.

Driver, M. J. (1988). Careers: A review of personal and organizational research. In: C. L. Cooper & I. T. Robertson (Eds), *International review of industrial and organizational psychology* (pp. 245–227). London: Wiley.

Edmond, A. Jr. (1989). Building a bridge to a new career. *Black Enterprise, 19*(10), 96–100.

Erikson, E. H. (1963). *Childhood and society*. Harmondsworth: Penguin.

Evans, J. (1993). The tourism graduates: A case of overproduction. *Tourism Management, 14*(4), 243–246.

Gould, S. (1979). Characteristics of career planners in upwardly mobile occupations. *Academy of Management Journal, 22*(3), 539–550.

Granrose, C. S., & Portwood, J. D. (1987). Matching individual career plans and organisational career management. *Academy of Management Journal, 30*(4), 669–720.

Greenhaus, J. H., & Simon, W. E. (1976). Self-esteem, career salience, and the choice of an ideal occupation. *Journal of Vocational Behaviour, 8*(1), 51–58.

Gunn, C. A. (1998). Issues in tourism curricula. *Journal of Travel Research, 36*, 74–77.

Gunz, H. (1988). Organizational logics of managerial careers. *Organizational Studies, 9*(4), 529–554.

Guerrier, Y. (1987). Hotel managers' careers and their impact on hotels in Britain. *International Journal of Hospitality Management, 6*(3), 121–130.

Guerrier, Y. (1986). Hotel manager — an unsuitable job for a woman? *Service Industries Journal, 6*(2), 227–240.

Hall, D. T. (1976). *Careers in organizations*. Pacific Palisades: Goodyear Publishing Company.

Hjalager, A. (2003). Global tourism careers? Opportunities and dilemmas facing higher education in tourism. *Journal of Hospitality, Leisure, Sport and Tourism Education, 2*(2), 1–12.

Hjalager, A., & Andersen, S. (2001). Tourism employment: Contingent work or professional career? *Employee Relations, 23*(2), 115–129.

Holland, J. L. (1985). *Making vocational choices*. New Jersey: Prentice-Hall.

Iellatcchitch, A., Mayrhofer, W., & Meyer, M. (2003). Career fields: A small step towards a grand career theory? *International Journal of Human Resources Management, 14*(5), 728–750.

Jennings, E. E. (1971). *Routes to the executive suite*. New York: Macmillan.

Jolliffe, L., & Farnsworth, R. (2003). Seasonality in tourism employment: Human resource challenges. *International Journal of Contemporary Hospitality, 15*(6), 312–316.

Jones, F. L., & McMillan, J. (2001). Scoring occupational categories for social research: A review of current practice with Australian examples. *Work, Employment and Society, 15*(3), 539–563.

Korman, A. K. (1971). *Industrial and organizational psychology*. Englewood Cliffs: Prentice-Hall.

Kusluvan, S., & Kusluvan, Z. (2000). Perceptions and attitudes of undergraduate tourism students towards working in the tourism industry in Turkey. *Tourism Management, 21*(3), 251–269.

Ladkin, A. (2002). Career analysis: A case study of hotel general managers in Australia. *Tourism Management, 23*(4), 379–388.

Ladkin, A., & Riley, M. (1996). Mobility and structure in the career patterns of UK hotel managers: A labour market hybrid of the bureaucratic model. *Tourism Management, 17*(6), 443–452.

Leiper, N. (1999). A conceptual analysis of tourism-supported employment which reduces the incidence of exaggerated, misleading statistics about jobs. *Tourism Management, 20*, 605–613.

Levinson, D. J. (1978). *The seasons of a mans life*. New York: Knopf.

Lichtenberg, J. W., Shaffer, M., & Mariner-Arachtingi, B. M. (1993). Expected utility and sequential examination models of career decision making. *Journal of Vocational Behaviour, 42*(2), 237–252.

Luzzo, D. A. (1993). A multi-trait, multi-method analysis of three career development measurers. *Career Development Quarterly, 41*(4), 367–374.

Marhuenda, F., Martinez, I. M., & Navas, A. (2004). Conflicting vocational identities and careers in the sector of tourism. *Career Development International, 9*(3), 224–244.

McKercher, B., Williams, A., & Coghlan, I. (1995). Career progress of recent tourism graduates. *Tourism Management, 16*(7), 541–549.

Osipow, S.H. (1990). Convergence in theories of career choice and development: Review and prospect. *Journal of Vocational Behaviour, 36*(2), 122–131.

Peacock, N., & Ladkin, A. (2002). Exploring relationships between higher education and industry: A case study of a university and the local tourism industry. *Industry and Higher Education, 16*(6), 393–401.

Petrova, P., & Mason, P. (2004). The value of tourism degrees: A Luton-based case study. *Education and Training, 46*(3), 153–161.

Psacharopoulos, G. (1991). From manpower planning to labour market analysis. *International Labour Review, 130*(4), 459–474.

Reily Collins, V. (2004). *Careers and jobs in travel and tourism*. London: Kogan Page.

Riley, M., & Ladkin, A. (1994). Career theory and tourism: The development of a basic analytical framework. *Progress in Tourism Recreation and Hospitality Management, 6*, 225–237.

Riley, M., Ladkin, A., & Szivas, E. (2002). *Tourism employment, analysis and planning*. Clevedon: Channel View Publications.

Riley, M., & Turam, K. (1989). The career paths of UK hotel managers: A developmental approach. *Signet Quarterly, 1*(1), 1–13.

Rosenbaum, J. E. (1979). Tournament mobility: Career patterns in a corporation. *Administrative Science Quarterly, 24*(2), 220–241.

Ross, G. F. (1992). Working at leisure: Secondary school students' occupational and training preferences for tourism and hospitality industry work. *Australian Journal of Leisure and Recreation, 1*(3), 21–22.

Ross, G. F. (1993). Management and life values as predictors of tourism/hospitality industry employment interest levels among potential employees. *Asia-Pacific Journal of Human Recourses, 31*(2), 104–117.

Ross, G. F. (1997a). Tourism/hospitality industry employment acquisition strategies, higher education preferences and the work ethic among Australian secondary school graduates. *Managing Leisure, 2*, 82–93.

Ross, G. F. (1997b). Travel agency employment perceptions. *Tourism Management, 18*(1), 9–18.

Ruddy, J. (1989). Career development of hotel managers in Hong Kong. *International Journal of Hospitality Management, 8*(3), 215–225.

Ruddy, J. (1990). Patterns of hotel management development in South East Asia. *Hospitality Research Journal, 14*(2), 349–361.

Schein, E. H. (1975). How career anchors hold executives to their career paths. *Personnel, 52*(3), 11–24.

Schein, E. (1995). *Career survival: Strategic job and role planning*. Amsterdam: Pfeiffer & Co.

Schein, E. H. (1978). *Career dynamics: Matching individual and organizational needs*. London: Addison-Wesley Publishing Company.

Singh, S. (1997). Developing human resources for the tourism industry with reference to India. *Tourism Management, 18*(5), 299–306.

Super, D. E. (1957). *The psychology of careers*. New York: Harper.

Swanson, J. L. (1992). Vocational behavior, 1989–1991: Life span career development and reciprocal interaction of work and nonwork. *Journal of Vocational Behaviour, 41*(2), 101–161.

Swanson, J. L. (1999). *Career theory and practice: Learning through case studies*. London: Sage.

Szivas, E., & Riley, M. (1999). Tourism employment during economic transition. *Annals of Tourism Research, 26*(4), 747–771.

Szivas, E., Riley, M., & Airey, D. (2003). Labor mobility into tourism. *Annals of Tourism Research, 30*(1), 64–76.

Tanke, M. (1990). *Human resource management for the hospitality industry.* Albany: Delmar.

Thomas, B., & Townsend, A. (2001). New trends in the growth of tourism employment in the UK in the 1990's. *Tourism Economics, 7*(3), 295–310.

Tribe, J. (2003). Editorial: The future of higher education in hospitality, leisure, sport and tourism. *Journal of Hospitality, Leisure, Sport and Tourism Education, 2*(1).

Veiga, J. F. (1981). Plateaued versus non plateaued managers: Career patterns, attitudes and path potential. *Academy of Management Journal, 24*(3), 566–578.

Walker, J. W. (1992). Career paths in flexible organizations. In: D. H. Montross & C. J. Shinkman (Eds), *Career development: Theory and practice.* IL: Charles C. Thomas.

Williams, P. W., & Hunter, M. (1992). Supervisory hotel employee perceptions of management careers and professional development requirements. *International Journal of Hospitality Management, 11*(4), 359–372.

World Travel and Tourism Council. (2004). *Executive summary: Travel and tourism forging ahead.* London: WTTC.

World Tourism Organisation. (2001). *Tourism satellite account (TSA). Measuring the economic significance of tourism volume one.* Madrid: WTO.

Yehuda, B. (2003). Managing careers: Theory and practice. Harlow: Prentice-Hall.

Chapter 32

Quality Assurance

Derek Robbins

Introduction

A major issue facing higher education (HE) is how to ensure quality and equity. How is the appropriate level of awards and equivalence of standards achieved to ensure that a degree awarded at any university is both worthy of the title and comparable to an award made elsewhere? This chapter examines quality assurance systems for HE. It focuses on the experience of the UK, but the issues of how to measure, safeguard and enhance quality apply to HE systems around the world.

Background

There are over 180 universities and colleges of HE in the UK (QAA, 2003). There is also provision of HE programmes at some 230 further education (FE) colleges and this is growing.

The designation of university title and the power to award degrees is strictly controlled by UK law. Within this control, the universities and colleges are largely autonomous, self-governing institutions. They are not state-owned although they do receive significant levels of government funding. "Each is responsible for the standards and quality of its academic awards and programmes" (QAA, 2003, p. 2). How does one ensure that appropriate and equivalent standards are being consistently applied? Overseeing the internal monitoring of standards is the Quality Assurance Agency for Higher Education (QAA). Established in 1997 it has responsibility to assess independently the quality of HE provision in the UK. The Agency is partially funded by contracts with The Higher Education Funding Council for England (HEFCE) and other funding agencies, which have a statutory obligation to review the quality of the HE that they fund.

It is difficult to overestimate the influence of QAA. As Tribe (2003) points out, QAA has developed a specialised language of quality and the importance placed by institutions on QAA judgements has meant that "to survive, institutions have had to subscribe to a particular set of rules and formalities" (Tribe, 2003, p. 30). He goes on to argue that dissent

An International Handbook of Tourism Education
Copyright © 2005 by Elsevier Ltd.
All rights of reproduction in any form reserved
ISBN: 0-08-044667-1

to the QAA approach has largely disappeared, driven by self-discipline rather than any draconian enforcement (Tribe, 2003).

Stakeholders

The ability to measure, judge, confirm and enhance the quality of HE provision is important to four key stakeholders.

Government

Government requires reassurance on quality to justify the granting of degree-awarding powers and to ensure that public funding of HE teaching is supporting education of an acceptable quality.

The Public and Potential Students

Both the tax-paying public and the fee-paying student require confidence in the quality of provision, especially the latter, many of whom make significant financial sacrifices to undertake their studies. Current UK government plans for a substantial increase in the level of the tuition fee paid by students from the academic year 2006/7 will increase this emphasis. A university's reputation for high standards will increasingly influence student choice as to where, and possibly even whether, to study.

Employers

Employers have expectations when recruiting newly qualified graduates as to what they know and what they can do. The need for clear guidelines for employers was highlighted by the National Committee of Enquiry into Higher Education (1997) (the so-called Dearing Report) which called for "greater explicitness and clarity about the standards and the levels of achievement required for different awards" (National Committee, 1997, para 41, recommendation 21).

Universities

Last, but by no means least, the HE institutions themselves need to be able to measure, monitor, confirm and enhance their academic standards. Their most important asset is their "academic reputation" which they must guard zealously.

External Assessment or Free Market?

The influence exerted by QAA begs the question should independent bodies monitor and assess quality? The arguments for regulation versus deregulation so prominent in many areas of economic activity can be argued in the case of HE. Institutions that fail to maintain quality will gain a poor academic reputation which will impact both on recruitment and also upon employment rates for graduates. Ultimately if a free deregulated market were allowed to exist, institutions with a poor reputation over a prolonged period would fail and close.

Such a *laissez faire* approach is impractical in most instances, not least because of the time that it takes to come into effect and the danger of damage to existing students in the meantime. Government responsibilities to grant university title, degree-awarding powers and fund institutions also creates a duty to regulate them. Furthermore how will potential students or employers make an informed judgement about an institution's academic reputation? In reality, they rely on the information published by independent external bodies. QAA acknowledges one of its key roles is as "a major provider of public information about standards and quality in UK higher education" (QAA, 2004a, p. 3).

"Standards" and "Quality" in Higher Education

There are two key headings for quality assurance in the UK: Academic Standards and Academic Quality (QAA, 2003).

Academic Standards

Academic Standards describe the level of achievement that a student must attain to gain an award, gain a specific grade or classification of award, or progress from one level of an award to the next level. Standards can largely be measured or assessed by examining student output. Written assignments and examination scripts are evidence of the level of student attainment, available for either internal or external scrutiny. The role of the external examiner, explored in more detail below, is to undertake peer review on behalf of the university and comment upon whether the standards are appropriate and comparable to those of other HE institutions.

Some forms of assignment, most notably assessed verbal presentations, cannot be scrutinised so easily, so certain transferable skills such as verbal communication and presentation skills are possibly less likely to be included in the process of external peer review than written communication skills. Nevertheless evidence from presentations (summary reports, visual aids used, the marking criteria and internal mark sheets) can be made available. Although not yet common practice, presentations can be videotaped for subsequent scrutiny.

Academic Quality

Academic quality describes how well the learning opportunities made available to the students enable them to achieve their awards. It focuses on the quality of the student experience and assesses whether "appropriate and effective teaching, support, assessment and learning opportunities are provided" (QAA, 2003, p. 1). One might also add "learning resources". This can be partially assessed from documentary evidence including:

- student support materials (unit readers, lecture notes, reading lists, web pages, dissertation handbooks, student handbooks, etc.);
- the timetable, outlining contact hours;

- university and course regulations, incorporating turnaround time of marked coursework;
- examples of assignment briefs, incorporating assessment criteria;
- examples of marked assignments, showing the feedback;
- student-feedback from reports by elected student representatives to course committees and end of year questionnaires (Brookes, 2003).

Nevertheless, the objective measurement and assessment of the quality of the teaching and learning must incorporate an element of observation. Internal quality systems may include peer review of teaching with selected staff observing colleagues whereas external systems require some form of inspection regime.

What Constitutes "Academic Standards"?

In essence there are three elements in which the student must achieve an appropriate level of competence to attain an award: subject knowledge; intellectual skills; transferable skills.

Subject-Specific Content of a Degree

For many academic subjects, such as the natural sciences, there will be a core curriculum which all students on all courses will be required to study. Tourism does not fit into this model easily. It is not an academic discipline in itself but rather a subject area to which one applies a number of disciplines ranging from economics and business to sociology and environmental science. Nevertheless in the UK, there has been a certain amount on standardisation of syllabi requirements for degrees in all subject areas. The QAA has published 47 benchmark statements for different subjects to "make explicit the general academic characteristics and standards of honours degrees in the UK" (QAA, 2000c, p. 1). The statement for Hospitality, Leisure, Sport and Tourism (designated Unit 25) was published in April 2000 (QAA, 2000c). The purpose of subject benchmarks is complex. QAA states "they provide general guidance for articulating the learning outcomes associated with the programme but **are not a specification of a detailed curriculum in the subject**" (QAA, 2000c, p. 1). This allows variety and flexibility in programme design and encourages innovation (Stuart, 2002) whilst identifying key content which most tourism degrees will include, albeit with different emphases (see page 460). The Unit 25 benchmarking group has developed a set of generic statements which can be applied to all graduates from relevant programmes. This describes the conceptual framework, which gives coherence and identity (QAA, 2003). Additionally in recognition of the distinctive nature of each of the subject domains, sets of subject-specific guidelines have also been developed (QAA, 2000c). Development of tourism curricula is considered in more detail in Section 2 (Chapters 4–9).

Intellectual/cognitive skills   QAA published a framework for Qualification Descriptors in the UK (QAA, 2001b) to which all programmes receiving new student registrations must be aligned from the academic year 2003/4. The main purposes of the framework are:

- to enable key stakeholders to understand the achievements represented by the main qualification titles;
- to maintain international comparability of standards;

Table 1: UK National framework levels.

Level	Award	Equivalent examples
1. Certificate C	Certificate of Higher Education	HNC First year of degree
2. Intermediate I	Diploma of Higher Education Foundation Degree	HND Second year of degree
3. Honours H	Bachelors degrees Graduate Certificates Graduate Diplomas	
4. Masters M	Masters degrees Postgraduate Certificates Postgraduate Diplomas	
5. Doctoral D	Doctorates	

Source: Adapted from QAA (2001b, p. 4).

- to assist learners identify potential progression routes;
- to assist HE institutions, external examiners and QAA reviewers by providing important points of reference for setting and assessing standards (QAA, 2001b).

The framework has five levels (Table 1). The descriptors aim to describe and demonstrate progression of evaluative, problem solving, communication, research and interpretation skills and conceptual understanding as higher levels are achieved (Table 2). A full list of descriptors combined with a summary of what holders of the qualification can typically do is provided in Annex 1 of the framework (QAA, 2001b).

Transferable skills   The terms "key skills", "common skills", "core skills", "generic skills" and "transferable skills" have been developed by a range of institutions and awarding bodies and used interchangeably to characterise outcomes of learning that are common to most if not all subject areas. This concept is not limited to HE, although clearly there is an expectation for these skills to be refined and developed as one progresses through the various levels of study. Although the classifications of such skill sets vary there is much commonality. Broad headings are shown in Table 3.

The Quality Assurance Process

An institution's internal quality assurance procedures are not as independent as one might expect and have increasingly been influenced by, if not entirely driven by, the QAA. In response to the concerns first expressed in the "Dearing Report" (1997), QAA has developed a range of nationally agreed reference points, a benchmark of expected procedures and policies collectively termed "the academic infrastructure". There are three key components:

- the framework for HE qualifications (QAA, 2001b);
- subject benchmark statements (QAA, 2000c);

Table 2: Summary of descriptors.

Level C
Students will demonstrate:

(i)   knowledge of the underlying concepts and principles associated with their area of study, and an ability to evaluate and interpret these within the context of that area of study;
(ii) an ability to present, evaluate and interpret qualitative and quantitative data, to develop lines of argument and make sound judgements in accordance with basic theories and concepts of their subject of study.

Level I
Students will demonstrate:

(i)   knowledge and critical understanding of the well-established principles of their area of study, and the way in which these principles have developed;
(ii) ability to apply underlying concepts and principles outside the context in which they were first studied, including, where appropriate, the application of those principles in an employment context;
(iii) knowledge of the main methods of enquiry in their subject, and ability to evaluate critically the appropriateness of different approaches to solving problems in the field of study;
(iv) an understanding of the limits of their knowledge, and how this influences analyses and interpretations based on that knowledge.

Level H
Students will demonstrate:

(i)   a systematic understanding of key aspects of their field of study, including acquisition of coherent and detailed knowledge, at least some of which is at or informed by, the forefront of defined aspects of a discipline;
(ii) an ability to deploy accurately established techniques of analysis and enquiry within a discipline;
(iii) conceptual understanding that enables the student:

  • to devise and sustain arguments, and/or to solve problems, using ideas and techniques, some of which are at the forefront of a discipline;
  • to describe and comment upon particular aspects of current research, or equivalent advanced scholarship, in the discipline.

(iv) an appreciation of the uncertainty, ambiguity and limits of knowledge;
(v)   the ability to manage their own learning, and to make use of scholarly reviews and primary sources (e.g. refereed research articles and/or original materials appropriate to the discipline).

Source: Adapted from QAA (2001b).
For a fuller description of what students holding the award will be able to do see QAA (2001b, Annex 1).

Table 3: Indicative headings of transferable skills.

- Psycho-motor skills
- Self-appraisal and reflection
- Problem solving
- Communication skills
- Planning and managing one's own learning
- Interpersonal skills, working with and relating to others in a professional setting
- Career management personal skills
- Numerical skills
- IT skills

Source: Adapted from internal Bournemouth University guidelines, Academic Quality and Quality (ADQ) Guidance Note QA 19.

- Code of Practice for the Assurance of Academic Quality and Standards in Higher Education (QAA, 2000a). This has 10 sections of which this chapter will pay particular attention to the sections on: External Examining; Programme Approval, Monitoring and Review; Assessment of Students.

The Code of Practice identifies a comprehensive series of system-wide expectations relating to an institution's management of academic standards and quality. It is an authoritative reference point but "is not intended to be either prescriptive or exhaustive" allowing institutions "to use and adapt according to their own needs, traditions, cultures and decision-making processes" (QAA, 2000a, para 3, Section 4). However, the current QAA system of institutional audit, developed from June 2002 and discussed later, involves "scrutiny of internal quality assurance systems at institutional level, with a more detailed investigation at discipline level as to their effectiveness". (QAA, 2003, p. 5). Institutions are unlikely to stray far from the QAA reference point when they know that the new inspection regime involves a judgement of their internal systems by the QAA.

Internal Systems

Institutions have traditionally included an element of external participation in their internal quality assurance systems. This is now explicitly required by the QAA Code of Practice (QAA, 2000a). These complex systems are usually managed by a dedicated department within the institution. The main components of internal quality assurance are:

Annual Programme Monitoring

This is a process by which the programme team (i.e. those responsible for the development and delivery of a programme or course leading to an award) appraises its own performance. Traditionally, annual monitoring reports include a critical overview, an action plan and supporting evidence (often included as appendices) such as:

- external examiner's reports;
- student feedback (Brookes, 2003);

- statistical data on student entry levels, progression and achievement;
- staff monitoring of delivery of each individual unit/module;
- appropriate minutes from programme committees, teaching team meetings, etc.

Given that the role of quality assurance is to enhance the quality of provision, the overview should be objective, evaluative and candid. It should recognise the positive achievements of programmes as well as problems. The evaluation should refer to the previous action plan noting outcomes and identifying continuing issues. Other points of reference may include recommendations at evaluation panels, internal audit of the previous annual report and external reviews. In the case of tourism there is no national professional body which accredits qualifications, so the main source of external review will be the QAA. The recent TEDQUAL certification offered by the World Tourism Organization provides an international reference point for tourism programmes.

   To be effective, annual programme monitoring must be integrated into the institution's quality assurance system. It is formally reviewed, initially by the School, Faculty or Department responsible for delivery of the programme and then at an institutional level to provide the checks and safeguards to ensure that reports are acted upon.

Periodic Review

Periodic review of programmes typically takes place every 5 or 6 years to ensure that they remain current and valid in the light of developing knowledge and practice and that the intended outcomes of the programme remain appropriate. Documentation produced for this review will normally include:

- a self-evaluation document presenting a critical review of delivery over the past 5/6 years. Such documents can help form the basis of self-evaluation for QAA subject review at a later date (see institutional audit below);
- programme specifications that must provide details of teaching and learning methods, assessment, subsequent career opportunities and how the programme relates to the qualifications framework (QAA, 2000b, 2003);
- unit specifications incorporating unit learning outcomes, content and selected reading;
- resource documentation including statements of both physical and staff resources to support the programme.

Approval and review of programmes **must** involve appropriate persons who are external to the design and delivery of the programme (Precept 3, QAA, 2000a Code). Appropriate persons here include academic peers from other disciplines (and other departments) within the university and external advisors qualified to provide relevant information and guidance. These will most likely be academics from other institutions and practitioners from the industry. Potential outcomes from a validation or review panel are:

- the programme is approved without amendment;
- the programme is approved with conditions and/or recommendations;
- the programme is not approved.

A robust system of internal hurdles for programme proposals should make non-approval rare. Approval with conditions and recommendations is overwhelmingly the most common outcome. Conditions have to be met before the programme may enrol students whereas a recommendation by the review panel must be considered and responded to by the programme team, but not necessarily adopted. Programme design, approval and review should be linked to the process of annual programme monitoring (QAA, 2000a) and indeed the first annual report following the review will respond formally to the panel recommendations. The QAA also argues that "where practices for the initial approval of programmes are rigorous and effective, subsequent monitoring and review is likely to be relatively straightforward" (QAA, 2000a, para 10, Section 7).

External Examiners

"External examining provides one of the principal means for the maintenance of nationally comparable standards within autonomous HE institutions" (QAA, 2000a, para 6, Section 4). An expert seminar on external examining organised by the Subject Centre that includes Tourism argues that "the role of external examiner will vary between institutions and courses" (LTSN, 2004, p. 4). However, in the author's view the role is clear, namely: to assess, comment on and ideally confirm that the standards achieved by students are appropriate for the marks awarded and hence the degree awards made, as set out in the QAA Code of practice (Table 4). Significant variation does occur in the approach and practices adopted by institutions and some give external examiners additional responsibilities (QAA, 2000a).

The external examiner's responsibilities can be met by scrutinising an appropriate sample of student output. Clearly, the sample has to be representative and most institutions have established clear rules on this. It is common practice for a university to require all first class papers and all fail papers to be made available plus a selection of others. Practical arrangements vary, some deliver the sample of work to external examiners whilst others arrange for the external examiners to sample the papers at the institution, usually the day prior to the board that meets to consider examination results. External examiners may have relatively little interaction with the course itself. An annual visit for the examination board at the end

Table 4: Role of external examiner.

An institution should require its external examiners, in their expert judgement, to report on:

(i)   whether the standards are appropriate for its awards, or awards elements, by reference to published national subject benchmarks, the national qualifications frameworks, institutional programme specifications and other relevant information;

(ii) the standards of student performance in those programmes or parts of programmes which they have been appointed to examine, and on the comparability of the standards with those of similar programmes or parts of programmes in other UK higher education institutions;

(iii) the extent to which its processes for assessment, examination, and the determination of awards are sound and have been fairly conducted.

Source: QAA (2000a). Precept 1, Section 4.

of the academic year provides an opportunity for examiners to meet programme teams. There are criticisms of the system. Many examiners:

- do not have the opportunity to see delivery of the course. Their views on the quality of provision and the student experience can only be based on student output and supporting documentary evidence;
- do not have the opportunity to meet students. It is not uncommon for an external examiner to meet no students undertaking the programme during their whole term of office;
- have insufficient time to view the sample of work. There is scope to forward assessed coursework and possibly dissertations earlier but time scales between the examination period and the examination board leave limited time to review students' scripts;
- will find significant overlap in the timing of examination boards in different institutions, which means that external examiners have limited time for the work.

The external examiners are usually invited to provide a short verbal report to the examination board and to submit their written report some 4–6 weeks later. From 2005, summary reports from external examiners are publicly available.

Appointment of External Examiners

Institutions have criteria for nomination and appointment of external examiners. Usual procedures require the school or department to nominate an individual who is appointed on the basis of a number of criteria as follows: current post, employer and professional/teaching experience; subject knowledge including scholarly activity, publications, etc.; internal examining experience; external examining experience; and number of other external examiner posts currently held.

It may be self-evident, but all external examiners must at some stage have had a first appointment. So QAA stress that the criteria for appointment should be "sufficiently inclusive to allow for the nomination of external examiners with little or no prior experience of external examining" (QAA, 2000a, precept 4, Section 4). The majority of external examiners are academics from other institutions, but there are no formal criteria as to what constitutes appropriate expertise. Clearly, experience gained from internal marking is appropriate. The Subject Centre that includes tourism proposes course leadership or equivalent as an appropriate prerequisite for external examining as course leaders will have experience of subject standards, administration of examination boards and of periodic review and validation (LTSN, 2004). One approach adopted by many institutions is to appoint "first time" external examiners to larger courses where they can be mentored by more experienced external examiner colleagues.

A further issue is the desire for courses to appoint practitioners from industry as external examiners. There are clear benefits in this for a vocational degree programme, not least their experience of current industry practice and their ability to judge how effectively the programme is preparing graduates with appropriate skill and knowledge for careers in the industry. However, such practitioners may feel they have insufficient background knowledge of HE to judge academic work. Again practitioner examiners can be mentored by external examiner colleagues and many institutions also operate induction programmes. Notwithstanding this support, the time required often acts as a deterrent to accepting appointments.

The Code of Practice includes a number of safeguards to avoid conflicts of interest for external examiners. These include restrictions in length of appointment (usually 4 years), the number of external examiner posts held (usually a maximum of 2) and avoidance of reciprocal appointments between the school/department of two institutions (QAA, 2000a).

The financial reward for external examiners is fairly nominal. Current fees range from around £250 per year upwards with £300–£350 as the norm for undergraduate programmes. Whilst external examining can be valuable in career and personal development for academics which attracts applicants, this level of remuneration is not attractive to practitioners whose participation will be motivated by philanthropic considerations.

A combination of the increase in the number of undergraduate tourism programmes and the increasing development of niche degrees is resulting in a shortage of available examiners, especially in emerging subject areas (LTSN, 2004). In response the Subject Centre has developed a database of potential external examiners in tourism.

External Systems — Subject Review

The external quality assurance system has developed over time. On its formation in 1997, QAA inherited a system of *Subject Review*. The most comprehensive external review of Tourism HE in England was the universal *Subject Review* undertaken between September 2000 and April 2001. Tourism was included in the area of provision "Hospitality, Leisure, Recreation, Sport and Tourism". This was a major undertaking with visits to 61 HE institutions and 48 FE colleges over an 18-month period. Some 135 subject specialists were used to undertake these visits, all of whom had undertaken a rigorous residential training course.

The Process

The process, set out in the Subject Review Handbook (QAA, 2000d), involved a 4-day visit, (Monday lunchtime to Thursday afternoon) with the purpose of gathering and testing evidence of the quality of education. The central feature of review was the *Self-Assessment Document* (SAD) in which institutions set out their aims and objectives under six aspects of provision (Table 5). The outcome of the visit was a Subject Review Report that incorporated an overall judgement on the quality of the provision and a graded profile for each of the six aspects of provision based on the descriptors given in Table 6. Each aspect carried equal weight and a

Table 5: Aspects of provision.

1. Curriculum Design, Content and Organisation
2. Teaching Learning and Assessment
3. Student Progression and Achievement
4. Student Support and Guidance
5. Learning Resources
6. Quality Management and Enhancement

Source: QAA (2000d).

Table 6: QAA grade descriptors.

Scale points

1. The aims and/or objectives set by the provider are not met; there are major shortcomings that must be rectified.
2. This aspect makes an acceptable contribution to the attainment of the stated objectives, but significant improvement could be made. The aims set by the subject provider are broadly met.
3. This aspect makes a substantial contribution to the attainment of the stated objectives; however there is scope for improvement. The aims set by the provider are substantially met.
4. This aspect makes a full contribution to the attainment of the stated objectives. The aims set by the subject provider are met.

Source: QAA (2000d).

grade 2 or better meant that that aspect "makes at least an acceptable contribution to the attainment of the stated objectives" (QAA, 2000d, p. 8). Although a profile with all aspects graded 2 or better meant that the provision was "approved" in reality a grade 2 was interpreted as a poor result by institutions as it meant reviewers found more than one major shortcoming. Any profile with three or more grade 2s resulted in the call for an improvement plan from the QAA. A grade 1 constituted a failure with the provision subject to further review with 1 year.

The Results

QAA summarised the findings from the 109 visits in a Subject Overview Report (QAA, 2001a). This provides a largely positive picture as presented in Table 7. The subjects are achieving their main aims and objectives, although with a need to address a number of important "sector-wide issues" (QAA, 2001a, p. 2). Only three institutions were designated "quality not approved" although a further three were approved but had a profile of three grade 2s. Five institutions achieved the top grade of 4 in all six aspects of the provision. Two of these have significant tourism provision. High quality is reflected in the average grade of 3.4 awarded across all aspects and visits.

One very noticeable pattern was the higher grades awarded to the provision in the 61 HE institutions compared to that in the 48 FE institutions. All three of the providers where quality was not approved were FE institutions as were those with three grade 2s in their profile. This discrepancy was perhaps expected in some elements of the provision, such as in *Learning Resources* (LR). Libraries in HE institutions typically have a wider range of resources than those in FE institutions. But even in aspects where they might have been expected at least to match HE institutions, such as in *Student Support and Guidance* (SSG), where they could have benefited from small numbers of students, they also tended to achieve lower scores. One point that needs to be noted is that the 48 FE visits were all to colleges directly funded by the government funding agency, the HEFCE and operating courses independent of HE institutions. The FE colleges that offered university-validated awards under a franchise arrangement, usually with some type of associate college status,

Table 7: Summary of scores from subject review in hospitality leisure, recreation, sport and tourism 2000–2001 (%).

Aspect	1 (%)	2 (%)	3 (%)	4 (%)	Mean
CDCO	0	9	39	62	3.80
TLA	0	16	66	18	3.01
SPA	0	6	41	53	3.47
SSG	0	0	16	84	3.81
LR	0	4	28	68	3.65
QME	3	16	58	23	3.01
HE Institution					3.60
FE College					3.07
Overall					3.4

Source: Adapted from QAA (2001a).

were visited as an element of the provision of the HE institution and the judgements on such provision are included in the HE grade profile.

The strongest elements of provision were *Curriculum Design, Content and Organisation* (CDCO) and SSG. Under CDCO the overview report highlighted a range of positive elements including:

- multidisciplinary curricula with effective application of theory to practice;
- opportunities for work placement in around 70% of the provision;
- outward-looking and dynamic provision with good external links to industry.

One criticism to emerge was the need for staff to strengthen the underpinning of the curricula with enhanced research and scholarly activity. For SSG, the positive points highlighted clear information about the programmes, good academic guidance, effective tutorial support and the wide range of central welfare and support services in the institution.

LR were also highly rated with 88% of HE provision awarded a grade 4 (in contrast to 42% in FE colleges). Favourable comment was made on library provision including effective liaison between library and academic staff, IT resources and specialist facilities. *Student Progression and Achievement* (SPA) was also overall good with "high achievements in final awards attained when seen against modest student entry qualifications" (QAA, 2001a, p. 7) although reference was made to 25% of cases where there were concerns about low retention and progression rates. The biggest concerns emerged in the *Teaching, Learning and Assessment* (TLA) and *Quality Management and Enhancement* (QME) categories. Whilst "the quality of teaching observed was with few exceptions, judged to be of high quality" (QAA, 2001a, p. 5) with many examples of good practice, a significant number of providers dropped a grade because of weaknesses in assessment including:

- a mismatch between learning outcomes of the unit and the assessment criteria;
- a mismatch between the assessment criteria and the marking;
- variability of the quality of written feedback to students;
- variability in the length of time taken to give feedback.

QME displayed well-developed and comprehensive quality systems supported by good documentation, but the reviews revealed that "institutional arrangements are not always being applied consistently at the subject level" (QAA, 2001a, p. 9). Specific reference is made to the annual programme monitoring for which it is suggested that reports are "insufficiently evaluative in 20% of providers" (QAA, 2001a, p. 9) and there are deficiencies in the systems for the consideration of external examiners reports in 30% of providers (QAA, 2001a, p. 9). Given that the Institutional Audit arrangements, which have now replaced *Subject Review*, are based on the application of quality systems at subject level this is a serious point.

Assessment of Subject Review

The subject review process is not without its critics. The most commonly cited criticism is that the benefits were outweighed by the very high cost (Tribe, 2003; Macleod, 2001). In addition to the high cost of each visit (fees and expenses of the review chair plus subject reviewers) there are the preparation costs incurred by the institution. Many lecturers regarded the process as unnecessarily bureaucratic involving considerable time and paperwork which could have been spent more profitably on other activities (Tribe, 2003).

The real value of *Subject Review* was dependent on the extent to which it encouraged institutions to be reflective about their provision and prompt system improvements or whether it was an exercise in concealment. In brief, was it seen as an end in itself or the beginning of an ongoing process? There was scope for the subject review process to be used in a developmental way and although the paperwork required was significant, it did not have to be wasted effort. The QAA recognise the considerable demands they make on institutions but argue "that this is not wasted time or energy, and that the benefits to institutions, as well as to students and others are considerable" (QAA, 2004a, p. 2).

Another comment made by lecturers was that it focused on procedure rather than on the quality of teaching, research or even scholarship (Tribe, 2003). Such criticisms seem unfair. Teaching was observed, albeit during a short intensive visit, and documentary evidence to support claims for teaching was required and difficult for institutions to manufacture (external examiner reports, student feedback). Scholarship was discussed in many subject reviews and in the overview report and impacted on aspects of provision, most notably related to the CDCO and TLA categories. Whilst quality assurance procedures were central to the subject review process, it did try to measure how effectively institutions used them to deliver provision. The weakest aspect, the TLA category, was so identified because of what was delivered to the students. The criticisms identified under the QME category may reflect procedure but shortcomings in the application of quality assurance at subject level does impact directly on the student experience.

Perhaps the most significant criticism is that *Subject Review* did not use benchmark standards. Judgements were made against the aims and objectives set by the institution, making comparability between departments unfair if not impossible. Indeed departments making lesser claims may have achieved full marks by meeting them (Tribe, 2003; Macleod, 2001). However, these aims and objectives are published by QAA in the subject review report and institutions cannot afford to set claims and objectives of mediocrity. Nevertheless the overview did find that many SADs had been cautious in their construction and around 40%

Table 8: Lecturer perceptions of QAA score.

	% of responses
Was accurate reflection of quality at my institution	64
Overestimated the quality of provision	05
Underestimated the quality of provision	18
Don't know	05
Not applicable	08

Source: Tribe (2003).

were unduly descriptive rather than evaluative (QAA, 2001a, p. 7). Subject benchmarks were being developed and published around the time of the subject review process which made their use for subject review impractical.

Despite these criticisms, research by Tribe (2003) found that the majority of tourism lecturers regarded their subject review score as fair although rigorous as more felt it underestimated the quality of provision than overestimated it as shown in Table 8. Tribe found the largest discrepancies between lecturer perceptions and the subject review results in the TLA category, where 46% of lecturer respondents graded their institution at 4 (significantly more than subject review), and in LR and SSG where lecturers felt outcomes overscored their provision. The TLA result has already been discussed and despite many positive comments on teaching and on innovative assessment, collectively the subject review reports highlighted a quite specific weakness in assessment practice from which the sector would do well to learn. The lecturers' more pessimistic assessment of LR is partly explained by the nature of the category. A score of 4 does not reflect perfection, and in this aspect there is always scope to provide more. It is a fine judgement whether resources make a "full contribution" (hence 4) in an area where there is always "scope for improvement".

Academic Review

The universal *Subject Review* process has now been replaced by *Institutional Audit*. However, academic review of subjects is continuing in all FE colleges directly funded by HEFCE. The QAA claims that academic review at subject level helps build a record of review for these colleges but there seems little doubt that this more stringent regime is partly driven by the lower scores in the FE sector.

Foundation Degrees

QAA undertook a review of 33 foundation degrees (FDs) in 2003 representing around 33% of the total number of registered students. This included two programmes in Travel or Tourism and one in Hospitality Management. Overall, the review gave FD provision a positive review although 4 of the reviews resulted in judgements of no confidence. Key findings are summarised in Table 9.

Table 9: Summary of findings from overview of foundation degrees.

Strengths

- Well-designed curricula and teaching and learning;
- Contribution to widening participation in HE;
- Involvement of employers in the development and delivery.

However reviewers noted

- Clear articulation of progression routes to honours degrees in only around 30% of sample;
- Scope for the development and assessment of knowledge, understanding and skills. Reviewers found that many achieved practical and vocational skills but not the higher level, intellectual, analytical and reflective outcomes;
- Few cases where employers were full members of a consortium;
- Significant development of work-based learning practice.

Source: QAA (2004c).

Institutional Audit

The *Institutional Audit* process for England was launched in the summer of 2002 with the first visits taking place in January 2003. All English universities and colleges will be audited between 2003 and 2005 and from 2006 audits will be on a 6-year cycle. This involves "scrutiny of internal quality assurance systems at institutional level, with a more detailed investigation at discipline level of whether those systems are operating in the manner intended". (QAA, 2003, p. 5). These disciplinary audits are undertaken by subject review specialists included in the QAA team (rather like the specialists used for subject review) and are limited to around 10% of an institution's programmes. If significant weaknesses are found at the discipline level this may result in a recommendation for a separate full subject review under the process set out in the Academic Review Handbook (QAA, 2000e; Tribe, 2003). The new system can be seen to respond to a number of the criticisms of *Subject Review*.

Lighter Touch

The QAA have promoted the new institutional audit as a lighter touch for the process of external scrutiny. Certainly institutions will receive far fewer visits. It is also claimed there will be less duplication of effort preparing for an audit. The institution will prepare an SED for the visit but the underlying principle is to undertake an external peer review of the internal quality assurance systems and thus "deliver fair and secure judgements without undue burden" (QAA, 2004a, p. 1). Therefore much of the required documentation for the visit is that already produced for internal quality assurance.

Use of Authoritative External Reference Points

Reference has already been made to the lack of agreed benchmarks under subject review (Macleod, 2001). Institutional Audit judgements are made against the nationally agreed

Table 10: Summary of findings from overview of institutional audit.

Overall the report confirms:

- broad confidence can be reasonably placed in the management of quality and standards at all 8 institutions;
- none of the first 8 reports identify any area where there is good reason for a full review at discipline level;
- overall the institutions are engaging actively and appropriately with the academic infrastructure in the management of quality, the setting of academic standards and the use of external participation in internal procedures;
- some institutions are asked to give attention to their arrangements for participation of independent external persons in the internal periodic review of programmes;
- the majority of institutions lack systems for collecting and responding to feedback from employers.

Source: QAA (2004b).

benchmark standards developed by QAA over the last 4 years and discussed above (QAA, 2000a, c, 2001b).

Key Features and Findings of the First Audits

It is too early to review objectively the effectiveness of the new process. To date QAA have published one overview report covering the first eight audits, undertaken between January and July 2003 (Table 10).

Conclusions

The assessment of the quality of HE provision presents a number of difficulties. Some argue that a system of monitoring and evaluation impinges upon professional responsibility and discretion (Warrior, 2002) whilst others argue that a system of safeguards is required to protect the interests of the stakeholders. There is scope for debate on precisely what constitutes quality and therefore what should be measured. Whilst one can develop benchmarks outlining the expected outcomes at the various level of achievement (Table 2), there is subjectivity in the judgement of how well these are achieved.

The UK agenda is substantially set by the QAA to which institutions have, out of necessity, acquiesced. They have developed a "language" of quality which focuses on "standards" and "academic quality" placing the emphasis on student achievement and student experience, for which the QAA has developed techniques to judge and measure. Procedure has evolved to produce a substantive academic infrastructure with nationally recognised standards against which provision is judged. The progression from *Subject Review* to *Institutional Audit* involved much consultation with institutions and responds to two principal criticisms, the lack of nationally agreed criteria and the heavy demands placed on institutions. It is too early to judge the effectiveness of audit but lecturers' response to their institution's performance under *Subject Review* (Table 10) is as strong an endorsement as one could reasonably expect, despite their criticisms over the time, effort and stress that the process created. The overview report did highlight some sector-wide issues on assessment and on the application of quality systems, but whether this, combined with the overall finding that the quality of tourism education is good, justifies the cost of the whole process is another matter.

References

Brookes, M. (2003). Evaluating the 'student experience': An approach to managing and enhancing quality in higher education. *Journal of Hospitality, Leisure, Sport & Tourism Education*, 2(1), 17–26, www.hist.ltsn.ac.uk/johiste.

LTSN (2004). *External examining expert seminar*. Oxford Brookes University, www.brookes.ac.uk/ltsn/resources/eee_seminar.pdf!

Macleod, D. (2001). Trial by ordeal. *The Guardian*, January 30.

National Committee of Enquiry into Higher Education. (1997). *Higher education in the learning society*. London: Stationary Office (Dearing Report).

QAA. (2000a). *Code of practice for the assurance of academic quality and standards in higher education*. Gloucester: Quality Assurance Agency for Higher Education.

QAA. (2000b). *Guidelines for preparing programme specifications*. Gloucester: Quality Assurance Agency for Higher Education.

QAA. (2000c). *Subject benchmark statements: Hospitality, leisure, sport and tourism*. Gloucester: Quality Assurance Agency for Higher Education.

QAA. (2000d). *Subject review handbook — September 2000 to December 2001*. Gloucester: Quality Assurance Agency for Higher Education.

QAA. (2000e). *Handbook for academic review*. Gloucester: Quality Assurance Agency for Higher Education.

QAA. (2001a). *Subject overview report — hospitality, leisure, recreation, sport and tourism*. Gloucester: Quality Assurance Agency for Higher Education.

QAA. (2001b). *The framework for higher education qualifications in England, Wales and Northern Ireland*. Gloucester: Quality Assurance Agency for Higher Education.

QAA. (2003). *A brief guide to quality assurance in UK higher education*. Gloucester: Quality Assurance Agency for Higher Education.

QAA. (2004a). *Annual report and financial summary 2002–3*. Gloucester: Quality Assurance Agency for Higher Education.

QAA. (2004b). *Institutional audit: England. Key features and findings of the first audits*. Gloucester: Quality Assurance Agency for Higher Education.

QAA. (2004c). *Overview report on foundation degree reviews*. Gloucester: Quality Assurance Agency for Higher Education.

Stuart, M. (2002). Critical influences on tourism as a subject in UK higher education: Lecturers' perspectives. *Journal of Hospitality, Leisure, Sport & Tourism Education*, 1(1), 5–18, www.hist.ltsn.ac.uk/johlste.

Tribe, J. (2003). Delivering higher quality: A comparative study of lecturers' perceptions and QAA subject review in tourism. *Journal of Hospitality, Leisure, Sport & Tourism Education*, 2(1), 27–47, www.hist.ltsn.ac.uk/johlste.

Warrior, B. (2002). Reflections of an educational professional. *Journal of Hospitality, Leisure, Sport & Tourism Education*, 1(2), 1–9, www.hist.ltsn.ac.uk/johlste.

Chapter 33

Postgraduate and Ph.D. Education

David Botterill and Tim Gale

Introduction

The pursuit of a postgraduate higher education in tourism studies, particularly for students from developing nations, is largely achieved by studying in the countries of the developed world. This has, therefore, created patterns of temporary migration to, and an international marketplace for, higher education institutions in Europe, North America and Australasia that have developed expertise in tourism studies. In this chapter we are interested to explore the implications of this phenomenon for the form, content and context of postgraduate higher education in tourism. By the mid-1970s a small number of international postgraduate students began arriving in the UK to study tourism. Thirty years later we estimate that approximately 1000 postgraduate students are studying tourism in UK universities, the majority of whom are from outside of the European Union. International students now dominate postgraduate tourism studies at both levels and in all forms of postgraduate study; taught qualifications up to Master's level and research degrees leading to Master's and doctoral awards (Botterill & Platenkamp, 2004; Botterill, Haven, & Gale, 2002; Lengkeek & Platenkamp, 2004).

This chapter is in two parts. In the first part, we sketch out Dimensions and Profile and in the second, we identify the major Trends and Issues in postgraduate tourism studies, namely: growth and its consequences; status of the subject and the importance of tourism; and internationalisation.

Dimensions and Profile

Postgraduate Taught Master's Awards

A consideration of the current dimensions and profile of postgraduate taught Master's awards in the subject should explore the origins of subject studies in tourism and reflect the early disciplinary influences and the emergence of 'sister' subject areas such as leisure

An International Handbook of Tourism Education
Copyright © 2005 by Elsevier Ltd.
All rights of reproduction in any form reserved
ISBN: 0-08-044667-1

and recreation and to a lesser extent hospitality. The development of tourism studies occurred through the influences of a multidisciplinary set of social sciences. For example, in the Netherlands at universities in Wageningen, Groningen, Amsterdam and Tilburg the subject was particularly influenced by Geography, Economics, Sociology and in more recent times, Cultural Anthropology. In the UK the study of tourism at postgraduate level began in the late 1960s and early 1970s at different universities and in different academic contexts. At the University of Edinburgh in the late 1960s tourism became a topic of interest in Geography as a part of the growing interest in the leisure and recreational use of land in the UK. This was further stimulated by academics and students at the University of Hull. At the other end of the UK, De Kadt published his seminal work 'Tourism: Passport to Development' from the Institute for Development Studies at the University of Sussex and opened the debates about tourism's impacts on lesser-developed countries. At the University of Birmingham's Centre for Urban and Regional Studies, academics were interested in the public policy implications for leisure and tourism of changes taking place in the 1960s/early 1970s in UK national and local government structures, and at the Polytechnic of Central London (now the University of Westminster) the sociological analysis of leisure was extended to include tourism. Two of the earliest, dedicated postgraduate courses in tourism were created in the early 1970s at the Universities of Strathclyde and Surrey within departments concerned with hotel and catering management. It is noteworthy that the emergence of tourism higher education at postgraduate level began over 15 years before the establishment of the first named undergraduate degrees in tourism in UK higher education institutions (HEIs) at Bournemouth, Northumbria and South Glamorgan (Cardiff) Institute in 1986/1987. It was the subsequent growth in undergraduate students of tourism, however, and the formation of academic departments to support that provision that has enabled an increase in postgraduate provision.

The Western European tradition in leisure studies has largely followed a pattern across the nation states of Europe. Initially the labouring class was the main focus for research, from a political or cultural elitist point of view. The main aim in this research was to educate the people for and about their leisure time and moral panics about antisocial behaviour was a strong imperative. After the second world war, nation states embarked upon modernist projects in leisure that were predicated on a belief in creating a better society. This resulted in an increase in applied research and a serious interest in the planning process of leisure time. Aligned with these 'Welfarist' notions about leisure an expansion of higher education opened the academy to new subjects and enabled the introduction of leisure and tourism studies into higher education in Western Europe. More recently there has been a shift in emphasis away from issues of leisure as citizenship to embrace the questions associated with leisure consumption.

In the US, postgraduate study of leisure and recreation and subsequently of tourism emerged from a different mix of influences. The early 20th century concern for urban 'rational' recreation echoed the Western European tradition in leisure studies and combined with the emergence of physical education led to the creation of university departments of health, physical education and recreation (see, for example, Gitelson & Henkel, 1983 as cited in Botterill & Brown, 1985). A number of landmarks occurred during the 1930s with the development of a National Park management course at Colorado State College in 1934, a recreation and municipal forestry programme at Michigan State College in 1935 and both undergraduate and graduate courses in recreation education at New York University in 1936. In the 1960s the study of tourism did have a small foothold under academic programmes in travel at the Universities of Hawaii and Massachusetts. In Botterill and Brown's (1985) review of leisure studies in the USA there was little mention of the development of a 'tourism' studies dimension. Tourism or travel, sometimes the preferred subject label, had been taught since the late 1960s, usually as a stand alone or short series of optional modules, but awards in the subject were few and far between. Pioneers in the subject became influential figures beyond the borders of the USA through their publications. However, it wasn't until the early 1990s that many of the departments in which the teaching of tourism occurred, and which were created in this health/natural resource/recreation nexus referred to above, adopted the inclusion of tourism in their titles. (See, for example, Texas A&M University's Department of Recreation, Parks and Tourism Sciences.)

Specific documentation about the development of postgraduate taught Master's programmes in tourism across the main providing countries is in short supply in the public domain. It is likely that evidence exists in the numerous documents prepared by university departments as a part of the various approval processes used in starting a new academic programme but these are often regarded as university property and are not made available publicly. In the following section we rely heavily on generalisations that come from our own experiences of tourism postgraduate education in Western Europe and North America to supplement a very sparse number of published studies.

Further to the early developments at Strathclyde and Surrey the UK demand for postgraduate courses was stimulated in the late 1980s and early 1990s by the intervention of state agencies concerned with high levels of graduate unemployment. Postgraduate tourism study courses were perceived by government agencies as a route out of unemployment for graduates. Funding support was generous and many UK students were drawn to the study of tourism by the prospect of a subsidised postgraduate experience (this trend continues in recent times but with the influence of EU structural funds). The shift from domestic to overseas recruitment coincided with the withdrawal of UK government funding for postgraduate study as graduate unemployment became less of a national issue. It coincided with a fall in demand from 'home' students who began to accumulate significant debts during their undergraduate studies. The prospect of more borrowing to fund further study reduced the UK domestic demand for postgraduate study to a very small number of (wealthy or frugal) self-funded full-time students and local, often employer-supported, part-time students.

Postgraduate course provision in tourism really took off in the UK in the 1990s as a result of the following conditions. The establishment of academic units or departments in the 'new' university sector operating free from central planning constraints, considerable investment by those universities in the recruitment of academic staff to teach tourism and the development of learning resources for the study of tourism all contributed to the infrastructure for an argued 'natural' progression from undergraduate provision to include postgraduate courses up to Master's level. More recently, this progression has been further extended to include research degrees at Master's and Doctoral levels. For the reasons explained above, home student demand for postgraduate courses was weakening, however, and universities sought a new market place for their 'products'. The importance given to tourism in many countries' economic development plans was building across the developing world and UK universities found enthusiasm for the study of the phenomenon fuelled by individual career aspirations of postgraduate students.

Determining the extent of postgraduate tourism higher education is difficult as the following case of the UK illustrates. Airey (in press) estimates that in 1999 there were 48 postgraduate programmes and 685 new student enrolments. In a study of the role of sustainability in tourism postgraduate programmes, Flohr (2001) identifies 42 British universities offering 81 postgraduate courses in tourism in the academic year 1999/2000. The differences exposed here are compounded by the difficulties of collecting accurate statistics about higher education tourism studies. The multidisciplinary and interdisciplinary nature of the subject means that it sits uncomfortably with the subject classifications used by UK central government higher education agencies and data extracted from these sources are liable to under representation. On the other hand, studies that attempt to capture data at source, i.e. programme level, are subject to reliability and validity inconsistency.

Since 1999 it can safely be assumed that student enrolments have grown but as we have previously explained this growth predominantly comprises non-EU students. In this market, the location of the university, particularly its proximity to major urban centres, the international reputation of the department, and the university's international recruitment effectiveness become influential and the impact of these factors on the viability of programmes is unknown. Anecdotal evidence suggests that several postgraduate programmes in tourism identified by Flohr (2001) may have failed to recruit sufficient students because they could not easily meet these factors and, consequentially, may have been terminated. As the number of taught Master's programmes in tourism has grown so has the range of award titles. According to Flohr (2001) the most commonly used title is Tourism Management, accounting for approximately 20% . She identifies a further 32 titles many of which combine the words hospitality, tourism and leisure with management (20%), other awards incorporated the word international (5%) and a smaller proportion linked tourism with a specialist discipline or subject (e.g. Museums studies, Geography, Anthropology, Heritage). The titles convey several characteristics of postgraduate taught course provision. First, they convey the academic context or 'home' in which the programme is offered. Second, their diversity reflects the multidisciplinary nature of postgraduate tourism studies and third, they evidence the competitiveness of the market as universities attempt to carve out specialist 'niche' offerings.

Ph.D. Education

The earliest documented indication of doctoral output related to tourism occurred in the post-war period in North America. Jafari and Aaser (1988) refer to single doctoral submissions within geography for the years 1951, 1953, 1954, 1957 and 1958 before recording significant growth in 1971 (8 submissions) to 15 submissions in 1986. Three further contributions from the literature help to shape an understanding of doctoral studies relating to tourism. Mayer-Arendt (2000) confirms a 1951 start-point for submissions and plots the growth of interest in tourism geography in North American doctoral and Master's theses up to 1998. The growth of doctoral awards in British and Irish universities between 1990 and 1999 is reported by Botterill et al. (2002) and their analysis is updated in the following paragraphs. A contribution that extends the Anglophone emphasis in our analysis to include China is that of Bao (2002). In the article the author records a start for doctoral submissions in China, 1989, and a slow growth in submissions over the decade of the 1990s, peaking at seven submissions in 1999. The author comments on the enthusiasm for doctoral level studies in tourism geography among potential students and the constraints of the limited supervision available in Chinese universities for the study of tourism. The author concludes that this may encourage many students to study overseas.

In sketching out the dimensions and profile of Ph.D. education in tourism in the UK and Ireland, we have followed the lead of Botterill et al. (2002) in searching the online Index to Theses, www.theses.com, for relevant abstracts of Ph.D.s completed between 2000 and 2003 (using the same, salient keywords: 'holiday', 'holidaymaker', 'holidays', 'tourism', 'tourist', 'tourists', 'travel', 'visitor' and 'visitors'), which generated a further 90 hits to add to their original tally of 149. In doing so, we have extended their quantitative analysis of completions by institution into the present decade, and undertaken our own qualitative (cursory) analysis of topics, fieldwork locations and methods. Of course, this only relates to Ph.D.s awarded by universities in the UK and Ireland, and does not necessarily reflect the situation elsewhere in the world. We should mention the additional caveat that a significant proportion of Ph.D. students may fail for a variety of reasons to complete their studies, hence much work of potential interest and import is rendered invisible in an analysis such as this (including that which is awarded the 'lesser' qualification of M.Phil.).

The first thing to note is the continued growth in Ph.D. completions related to tourism beyond the year 2000. Having increased from 4 in 1990 to 22 in 1999, the number of completions reached an unprecedented high of 34 in 2002, although it remains too early to ascertain whether this upward trend can be sustained in 2003 (the data for this particular calendar year being incomplete at the time of going to press). On closer inspection, Figure 1 suggests a cyclical pattern to this growth with the number of completions peaking and then falling back slightly, roughly coinciding with previous Research Assessment Exercises

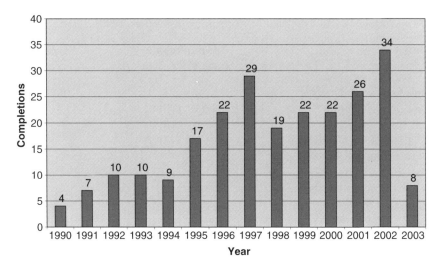

Figure 1: Ph.D. completions related to tourism, 1990–2003 (adapted from Botterill et al., 2002).

(RAEs) in 1992, 1997 and 2001. We might, therefore, infer that the prioritising of research by HEIs in the mid to late stages of each RAE cycle was responsible for a greater number of completions than might otherwise be expected, although this could also be down to other factors (e.g. the availability of trained supervisors).

Moving on, of the 239 completions recorded since 1990, almost a quarter (22.6%) were approved by the universities of Strathclyde and Surrey, with the University of Exeter running a distant third (5.9%), followed by a cluster of institutions with upwards of 5, but no more than 8, completions (between 2.1 and 3.3% of the total). Beyond that lay some 55 other institutions with a handful of, and more often than not a single, completion(s) to their name. The dominance of Strathclyde and Surrey is therefore confirmed, although it should be noted that their share has fallen marginally since 2000 and their productivity is rivalled by emergent HEIs in this field such as Sheffield Hallam University and the University of Nottingham. The presence of research units specialising in tourism within a number of these universities is noted (e.g. Exeter's Tourism Research Group and Sheffield Hallam's Centre for Tourism and Cultural Change), and is a lesson for those other institutions with aspirations to be in the 'top ten' (Table 1).

In the analysis of Ph.D.s completed since 2000, two topics stand out as the most popular by some distance: tourist behaviour, motivation and demand *per se*, and tourism impacts (predominantly negative and oriented towards the socio-cultural domain, host–guest interaction being a recurrent theme). Smaller concentrations were detected around tourism policy and planning, sustainable tourism and destination marketing/tourist imagery, whilst it is interesting to note that 'new' tourisms such as culture and adventure tourism featured more than once, yet ecotourism was conspicuous by its absence; likewise urban and rural (peripheral) areas outnumbered coastal and other purpose-built destinations (e.g. ski resorts, which did not figure at all). Certain segments, notably 'youth' and 'gay', and issues, such as sex tourism and tourism's crisis tendencies (which is likely to become a popular topic in this

Table 1: Ph.D. completions related to tourism, by institution, 1990–2003.

Institution	Completions since 1990 (2000)		% of total completions
1. University of Strathclyde	29	(7)	12.1
2. University of Surrey	25	(10)	10.5
3. University of Exeter	14	(6)	5.9
4. Sheffield Hallam University	8	(7)	3.3
5. University College, London	8	(2)	3.3
6. University of Cambridge	7	(1)	2.9
7. Oxford Brookes University	6	(2)	2.5
8. University of Birmingham	6	(1)	2.5
9. Cardiff University	6	(1)	2.5
10. University of Nottingham	5	(5)	2.1
All other HEIs	125	(48)	52.4
Total	239	(90)	100

Adapted from Botterill et al. (2002).

post-9/11 era), also attracted attention. In many respects these priorities are unsurprising, given their currency, although some of the discernable gaps in knowledge may constitute cause for concern (e.g. the dearth of work on postmature resorts). In addition, the research reported in these theses was more positive than normative in nature, although the notion of 'making tourism better' still pervades research at Level 'D'[1] in the subject area. Where the location of fieldwork was reported, the United Kingdom featured in a third of all studies (thus corroborating the findings of Botterill et al., 2002, who problematised the presumption of a stock of knowledge relating to tourism in the UK being constructed by its universities in reporting a marginally lower return of 29%), the remainder consolidating for the main part around clusters in north-west Europe, the (Eastern) Mediterranean Basin and less economically developed countries such as Brazil, Sri Lanka and Uganda. It is worth noting that, away from these various 'pleasure peripheries', a number of theses were dedicated to one or more points of the so-called 'Chinese Triangle' of China, Hong Kong and Taiwan, this being in all likelihood a product of China's emergence onto the global (tourism) stage, and the significant number of research degree students in British and Irish universities of Confucian origin (*cf.* the later discussion of tourism education in the 'international classroom'). Finally, with regards to data collection and analysis, several studies reported using two or more methods (usually one quantitative and one qualitative, and sometimes comprising a phased approach where the results of one informed the design of the other, though in no predominant order). Most stuck to a single method, however, notably questionnaires and interviews (thus confirming the enduring legacy of positivist and hermeneutic epistemologies). That said, the frequency with which these two, somewhat orthodox, methods were cited in the abstracts may conspire to draw attention away from the arguably more interesting studies located at the extremes of the 'methodological continuum', ranging from those employing mathematical modelling and econometrics on the one hand to auto-ethnographic narrative on the other. Pressingly, several abstracts made no mention of method, perhaps suggesting that the 'facts speak for themselves'. Correspondingly, though some may have engaged with epistemological debates in the Social Sciences, few made this explicit in the abstract with only the odd reference to the post-paradigmatic epistemologies of constructivism and critical realism (echoing Botterill et al., 2002).

Trends and Issues in Postgraduate Tourism Studies

Three clear trends emerge from the above section on dimensions and profile: growth of postgraduate studies; status of the subject and the importance of tourism; and internationalisation.

Growth and Its Consequences

The extant literature, without exception, points to the steady growth of postgraduate tourism studies in Anglophone regions of the developed world in the latter three decades of the 20th century. For example, using the reported data of Airey (2005) and Flohr (2001) we calculate

---

[1] Level 'D' refers to the doctorate level in the Framework of Higher Education Qualifications (FHEQ) in the UK.

that in the UK in 2005 the volume of taught Master's students can be estimated at 850. Additionally using a 4-year average of annual Ph.D. awards (26) and assuming a study period of 4 years and a 70% completion rate then it is possible to estimate that there are also approximately 135 concurrent doctoral candidates. Together these two cohorts of postgraduates amount to close on 1000 students of tourism studies in the UK alone.

The pace of growth raises many questions for the tourism subject academy not least the challenge of maintaining the quality and standards of the awards. Academic staff unfamiliar with Master's level work may find it difficult to 'pitch' their teaching, learning and assessment approaches at the correct level. In most departments, teaching at the postgraduate level has been achieved by staff who are themselves involved in professional development, often in the form of a doctoral research programme. The UK tourism academy has been through distinct phases of development with a gradual increase in individuals' qualifications at Master's and doctoral levels (Stuart-Hoyle, 2003). Consequentially the demand for postgraduate study threatened, on occasions, to outstrip the supply of qualified staff and this may have had a detrimental impact upon standards particularly as deregulation of the UK higher education sector in the late 1980s sought to release institutions from central control and encouraged greater entrepreneurial activity. A shortage of experienced postgraduate examiners in the subject has also stretched the capacity of the tourism academy to respond to the growth in provision.

Responsibility for quality assurance for postgraduate taught awards in the UK rests primarily, and almost exclusively, at institutional level. Quality Assurance Agency (QAA) benchmark statements developed at the undergraduate level have not been extended to incorporate postgraduate awards. Equivalence of standards of award across the sector are highly dependent, therefore, on a self-critical ethos within the tourism academy. To date there have been few attempts to co-ordinate professional development in postgraduate level education in the subject. Organisations such as the Higher Education Academy Subject Network for Hospitality, Leisure, Sport and Tourism have tended, thus far, to focus upon undergraduate learning, teaching and assessment and the UK subject association (ATHE) is insufficiently resourced to tackle this matter.

The position in research degrees has some parallels. Experience of supervision of doctoral studies is slow to accumulate given the average period of four years of study. International student demand for Ph.D. study is strong but is mediated by the 'high' costs (currently around £25,000 in fees alone) and for home students, demand is weaker and further constrained by the paucity of scholarship funding. Nevertheless current demands are placing strains on institutions' capacities to provide experienced supervision. Quality assurance for doctoral degrees is also located at the level of the awarding institution, although in the UK there is an increasing emphasis on asserting national standards around research degree programmes. This is largely due to increasing accountability placed upon the use of public funding to support some categories of research student. This has led the QAA, the body contracted by the four higher education funding councils of the UK to oversee quality in universities, to develop a code of practice for postgraduate research programmes against which institutions will be audited. The code covers all aspects of research degree work: the research environment; selection, admission and induction of students; supervision; progress and review arrangements; development of research and other skills; assessment and feedback; student representation, complaints and appeals. Although inspired by the audit culture surrounding public funding, the code will apply to all research degree work in UK higher education and all doctoral students of tourism will, therefore, be affected. There would, therefore, appear to be stronger safeguards for standards of postgraduate research awards than for taught awards, however there are some questions about the relevance of the code for 'typical' postgraduate research students of tourism. For example, a recent intervention in research programmes, and part of the QAA code, is to place an increased emphasis on generic research training and skill development, although such training is variable and largely dependent on institutional delivery. There is some concern that a centrally driven code of practice is predicated upon a particular 'model' of postgraduate student; typified as a young, recent graduate of a UK university of high academic standing in receipt of UK Research Council funding. Few postgraduate research students of tourism fit with this model (see, for example, Baum 1998 on mature doctoral candidates in hospitality studies). Consequentially, centrally inspired research training programmes may be inappropriate for the international, mature and professionally experienced candidates that dominate doctoral studies of tourism. Opportunities to facilitate more relevant, inter-institutional collaboration in tourism studies research training have been very limited to date.

At a time when increased attention is being given to the quality of research degree provision in UK universities, the doctoral level qualification is being opened to new routes and awards. The Ph.D. by publication route has become standard in most universities' award listings, remote learning or distance modes for Ph.D.'s by research are becoming more popular, and the numbers of subject specific 'new' or 'professional' doctorate awards are increasing. The impact of these new routes to a doctoral award relating to tourism studies has still to be assessed.

The Importance of the Global Tourism Phenomenon and the Status of the Subject

Growth in the postgraduate study of tourism is also a reaction to the importance of tourism as a global social and economic activity. Elsewhere arguments have been rehearsed on the struggle for tourism studies to gain any status in the wider academy. For example, Tribe (2003) and Haven and Botterill (2003) have addressed the invisibility of tourism studies in the UK government's most recent RAE. Part of the evidence for increased status within the academy is predicated upon the importance of tourism to economic and social life and it is this that has fuelled demand from postgraduate students and their sponsors. This has created opportunities for strengthening the status of the subject by building a postgraduate community but also poses some different dilemmas for the tourism academy in placing it squarely in the politics surrounding the knowledge economy.

Universities are increasingly understood by governments to be central to domestic knowledge economies through knowledge transfer and important in international economies as valuable exports; either as invisible export in the inflow of international students (as in international tourism) or as a visible export in the franchise or off-campus model. Knowledge in subjects such as tourism, which is also understood to be a key driver of a postmodern economy, is therefore seen as a valuable commodity. Higher education generally and tourism studies in particular become, therefore, increasingly politicised as a part of macro-economic policy and international relations. While this enhanced status for tourism studies might be perceived as good news for tutors, other agents, particularly institutional managers and the network of international recruitment staff they contract, seek to control access to the commodity. The pursuit of an intellectual basis for subject development becomes subject to increasing amounts of (distorting) commercial pressure. Locally, institutional economic reality drives a managerialist strategy; recruitment targets and income stream projections are set at the department level and tutors find themselves embroiled in achieving economic performance indicators and not intellectual projects. The spectre of competition appears and foregrounds the creation of 'competitive advantage' over other universities across the developed world. As a relatively enduring counter force, the academic community is founded upon strong collegiate values where cooperation, not competition, and the sharing of knowledge is paramount. This is embedded in the university system by the prominence of peer review as a quality system that can be found surrounding teaching (external examining, subject reviews, professional development and the idea of a Higher Education Academy in the UK) and research (research bid and publication refereeing, new researcher mentoring etc.). In this sense, tensions arising from competing value sets of 'managerialism' and 'collegiality' found in almost all higher education systems surround contemporary postgraduate tourism studies.

Internationalisation

The temporary migration of postgraduate students largely, but not exclusively, from developing countries to universities in the developed world is a well-documented phenomenon. The UK government has recently estimated that total global demand for international student places at the tertiary level could rise from 2.1 million to as much as 5.8 million between 2003 and 2020 (Tysome, 2004). Tourism studies, precisely because of the arguments made above in respect of tourism's importance to economic development in many nations, is an area of a university's portfolio where such expansion is likely to be felt. In this context the implications of further growth in postgraduate tourism studies is beginning to be assessed. Lengkeek and Platenkamp (2004) have coined the term the 'International Classroom of Tourism Studies" and Botterill and Platenkamp (2004) have developed the idea further in what they call Pandora's box of hope and despair. Pandora's box is chosen as an analogy for the practically adequate, critical realist account of the international classroom they have developed that exposes "the tensions at the intersections between structures and agency [that] create a dualism of emergent possibilities and dilemmas in the international classroom" (Botterill and Platenkamp, 2004, p. 3). Perhaps the most significant and hopeful possibility relates to a radical reform of the orthodoxy of tourism knowledge.

   The orthodoxy of tourism (and very often management) studies lies at the centre of the postgraduate curriculum. A community of mainly white, middle class, male, Anglophone, western academics, have been the architects of tourism knowledge. It is 'situated' knowledge but is rarely, if ever, acknowledged as such. In the international classroom it is laid out before an audience of students in which such characteristics are marginally represented. The possibility here is that tourism knowledge can be reformulated to encompass a more diverse 'situatedness' and that previously silent voices contribute to create 'new' tourism knowledge. The dilemma is that the student body largely expects to receive the orthodox, not to challenge it, exactly because it is the currency that has drawn them thousands of miles from their homes and supposedly will form the future of their professional careers and provide the pay back for their own, their families or even sponsoring government's investment.

The international classroom challenges the core processes that underlie postgraduate teaching, learning and assessment. The term postgraduate infers a simplistic coming after a graduate stage but the multitude of possible experiences of 'graduateness' that is imported into the international classroom confounds such simplicities. The complexity might be displayed in the differences of previous experience of what makes a 'good' student or tutor, what are acceptable conventions in assessment (i.e. citation and plagiarism), and discipline-informed or culturally founded learning styles (i.e. rote learning as contrasted against problem-based critical learning). The differences are not confined to the international dimension of our postgraduate classrooms particularly when 'graduateness' is substituted with relevant industry experience in our 'local' mature students but this complexity can create enormous tensions between possibility and dilemma. How should tutors 'be'? What should students 'do'? What outcomes are expected from teaching and learning? Whose standards should be applied to the outcomes to judge quality? This is a long list of pressing questions about the implications of the internationalisation of postgraduate tourism studies for the international students. To it we should add 'What are the implications for home students and the development of tourism studies worldwide'?

References

Airey, D. (2005). Scope and development. In: D. Airey & J. Tribe (Eds), *An international handbook of tourism education,* 2005 Oxford: Elsevier Science.

Bao, J. (2002). Tourism geography as the subject of doctoral dissertations in China, 1989–2000. *Tourism Geographies, 4*(2), 148–152.

Baum, T. (1998). Mature doctoral candidates: The case in hospitality education. *Tourism Management, 19*(5), 463–474.

Botterill, D., Haven, C., & Gale, T. (2002). A survey of doctoral theses accepted by universities in the UK and Ireland for studies related to tourism, 1990–1999. *Tourist Studies, 2*(3), 283–311.

Botterill, D., & Platenkamp, V. (2004). The international classroom of tourism studies: Opening Pandora's Box. Paper presented at the association of tourism in higher education annual conference, critical issues in tourism education. Buckinghamshire Chilterns University College, 1–3 December 2004.

Botterill, D., & Brown, G. (1985). Leisure studies in the United States: A British perspective. *Leisure Studies, 4*(3), 251–274.

De Kadt, E. (1979). *Tourism, passport to development?* Oxford: Oxford University Press.

Flohr, S. (2001). An analysis of British postgraduate courses in tourism: What role does sustainability play within higher education? *Journal of Sustainable Tourism, 9*(6), 505–513.

Haven, C., & Botterill, D. (2003). *Guideline 11: Tourism studies and the research assessment exercise 2001.* Guildford, Surrey: ATHE.

Jafari, J., & Aaser, D. (1988). Tourism as the subject of doctoral dissertations. *Annals of Tourism Research, 15,* 407–429.

Lengkeek, J., & Platenkamp, V. (2004). The international classroom of tourism studies. Paper presented at international sociological association interim symposium of the research committee on international tourism (RC 50) meeting 'understanding tourism — Theoretical advances'. University of the Aegean, 14–16 May 2004.

Mayer-Arendt, K. J. (2000). Tourism geography as the subject of North American doctoral dissertations and Master's theses, 1951–1998. *Tourism Geographies, 2*(2), 140–156.

Stuart-Hoyle, M. (2003). The purpose of undergraduate tourism programmes in the United Kingdom. *Journal of Hospitality, Leisure, Sport and Tourism, 2*(1), 49–74.

Tribe, J. (2003). The RAE-ification of tourism research in the UK. *International Journal of Tourism Research, 5*(3)*,* 225–234.

Tysome, T. (2004). UK drive to boost overseas numbers. *Times Higher Education Supplement,* (November 8th), 8.

POSTSCRIPT

Chapter 34

Practical Issues for Design, Delivery, Evaluation and Resourcing of Courses

Miriam Moir and Lisa Hodgkins

Part 1: Course Design, Delivery and Evaluation

Introduction

Safeguarding the academic standards and quality of tourism education institutions is reliant not only on high calibre and innovative teaching but also on rigorous and reliable processes and procedures. Institutions are responsible for managing and enhancing the teaching and learning environment through commitment to procedure which are designed to help achieve the institution's curriculum development, teaching and learning and evaluation strategies. These procedures also provide the information needed to ensure that the quality of the students' learning experience is monitored and enhanced.

  While procedures differ between tourism education institutions, the main principles remain the same:

- Ensuring that academic quality is assured within the development and design of the curriculum
- Maintaining the quality of the student experience at the point of delivery
- Monitoring the delivery and performance of courses through an evaluative review of provision

The following sections are designed to provide a planning framework for procedures for programme approval, running a module and the annual monitoring process. They are based on the Quality Assurance procedures followed at Buckinghamshire Chilterns University College, and are informed by the Quality Assurance Agency for Higher Education (2000) Codes of Practice.

An International Handbook of Tourism Education
Copyright © 2005 by Elsevier Ltd.
All rights of reproduction in any form reserved
ISBN: 0-08-044667-1

Table 1: Programme approval.

Stage	Activity
1	Proposal — initial discussions within the development team
2	Development — informed by current knowledge and best practice, and meeting the requirements of employers and students
3	Production of documents — proposal support, programme specification and module proformas
4	Programme approval event panel and document submission — identification of members of the Panel and forwarding of completed documentation to them
5	Programme approval event — examination of documents and discussion with the team
6	Institutional approval — the decision to endorse or reject the award

Section 1: Programme Approval

The approval of new programmes at institutional level is the end result of a lengthy process of curriculum design and development. Table 1 details the process from the initial idea through to endorsement.

Stage 1: Proposal

Purpose: Proposals need to be in line with institutional strategy.

Details: The course development team holds initial discussions regarding the proposal to develop a new programme/course/route. An initial proposal is produced giving details of the type and level of award, its duration and a working award title. The initial proposal is submitted to the appropriate institutional committee.

Outcome 1:

• Initial proposal approved — further development approved.

Outcome 2:

• Initial proposal rejected — no further development is permitted.

Once the initial proposal has been approved, the course development team produce a more detailed outline proposal for submission to the appropriate Faculty/School Committee. Here it is discussed in relation to several factors including the Faculty/School strategic plan: the institutional strategic plan: resource issues and evidence of demand.

Outcome 1:

• The outline proposal is approved

Outcome 2:

• The outline proposal is rejected. Further work on the proposal is then required to satisfy identified areas of concern. The proposal may be re-presented at a later date.

Once the outline proposal has been approved at Faculty/School level, it is forwarded to the appropriate institutional committee for consideration.

Outcome 1:

• The outline proposal is approved, and the title of the new award is received by the institutional governing body.

Outcome 2:

• The outline proposal is rejected and returned for amendment and re-presentation within the Faculty/School.

Stage 2: Development

Purpose: While under development, course teams should ensure that programmes meet with the requirements of both employers and students. Throughout the development process, the design of the curriculum should be influenced by current knowledge and best practice.

Details: The course development team plan and undertake the development of the programme paying particular attention to three considerations. First, appropriate external academic or professional advice should be sought. Second, external frames of reference (e.g. Subject Benchmarks) should be taken into account. Third, there should be evidence that a consultation process with externals (academics, professionals, industry experts) has taken place.

Stage 3: Production of documents

Purpose: A Programme Support document is a useful way to provide justification (and prove demand) for any proposed programme. It should record the development of the programme, the input of external academics and professionals and confirm that the requisite resources are in place. Programme Specifications should be published for use by all stakeholders including potential students, current students, staff and employers. Module specifications provide the information for the module leader when producing lectures and seminars, and when writing assessments.

Details: The development stage results in the production of the following documents for programme approval with the course development team ensuring that all specified areas are fully completed.

A Proposal Support Document including information on:

• Title/routes of the award
• Responsible Faculty/Schoolv
• Date of first intake
• Target numbers
• Reference to institutional plans
• Record of approval of the outline proposal
• Record of development meetings
• Consultation with externals
• Details of target entrants
• Overall justification for the programme
• Market research
• Provision elsewhere in the sector

- Staff responsibilities
- Resources

A Programme Specification detailing:

- Awarding/teaching institution
- Faculty/School
- Title of award
- Programme/course/route title
- Mode/length
- Date of production
- Reference to external frameworks — demonstrating how external reference points have been met
- Target group/entry profiles — details who the programme is aimed at, and the opportunities open to graduates of the award
- Educational aims
- Programme outcomes appropriate to the subject and level of the programme, and detailing anything distinctive about the programme
- Programme structure giving details of module title at each level and the type/weighting of assessment on each module
- Teaching and learning methods used, and how students will meet the programme outcomes through these
- Assessment strategies
- Special features detailing any distinctive features such as work placements

Module Specifications for each module in the programme structure including:

- Module title and type (undergraduate, postgraduate, etc)
- Module code
- Level
- Credit points
- Responsible Faculty/School
- Brief description and aim of the module
- Learning outcomes
- Assessment diet
- Indicative content
- Indicative teaching and learning strategy
- Indicative assessment strategy
- Skills development
- Specialist learning resources
- Sources (bibliography)

Once all the documents have been produced they are subjected to internal scrutiny to ensure that they are complete. This is an opportunity for comments to be made on the documents in advance of the Programme Approval event, and to ensure that they adhere to institutional regulations. Any identified amendments are made prior to finalisation of the draft documents.

Stage 4: Programme approval event panel and document submission
Purpose: The constitution of a panel to scrutinise the proposal ensures external academic and/or external professional input into the discussions with the development team.

Details: Members of the panel should be identified in advance of the programme approval event. The panel would typically include:

- Chair (senior member of the institution external to the submitting Faculty/School)
- Internal academic (internal to the institution, but external to the submitting Faculty/School)
- External members identified by the Faculty/School (academics/professionals, but not those involved in the development stage of the programme)

Completed draft documents need to be forwarded to members of the panel in advance of the approval event.

Stage 5: Programme approval event

Purpose: This event provides the opportunity for an in-depth consideration of the proposed programme regarding standards and quality, through examination of the documents and through dialogue with the development team.

Details: A meeting is convened of the programme approval panel and the course development team. The team presents the proposed programme and answers queries the panel may have. Typically, these might relate to appropriate standards, adherence to institutional regulations and requirements and the extent to which the curriculum design and programme structure support and deliver the intended learning outcomes.

Outcome 1:

- The programme is approved with no further amendments required. Definitive documents are then produced.

Outcome 2:

- The programme is approved subject to specific conditions/recommendations made by the Panel. These are addressed by the course development team, and the revised documents are forwarded to the Chair for signing off. Definitive documents are subsequently produced.

Outcome 3:

- The programme is not approved as the panel decides that it requires substantial revision. The team is asked to re-present revised documents at a new programme approval event, and repeats the process from Stage 2.

Stage 6: Institutional approval

Purpose: Programmes cannot run until official institutional endorsement has been obtained.

Details: The report of the programme approval event (plus the Faculty/School's response to any conditions/recommendations) is presented to the appropriate institutional committee where the final decision to endorse or reject the programme is taken.

Conclusion: Areas of good practice for consideration:

- Rigorous market research to establish demand for the programme
- Involvement of externals academics and professionals, both in the development and the approval stage
- Involvement of external peers to ensure consistency of programmes across the institution

Section 2: Running a Module

Guidance for running a module on a course is provided in Table 2, and is based on the guidelines used in the Faculty of Leisure & Tourism at Buckinghamshire Chilterns University College. Establishing procedures such as these helps to ensure that assessment is operated consistently and fairly across all courses, thereby providing parity of experience for students. The following procedures assume that the overall schedule and diet of assessment has been approved as appropriate for measuring student learning outcomes.

Stage 1: Preparation

Purpose: Assessment is the process by which to measure student learning outcomes, particularly understanding, knowledge and skills as detailed in the module documents.

Details: The module leader should produce a module plan, detailing week by week lectures, seminars, planned activities, hand out of assignment(s), submission of assignment(s) and examination dates. The module plan is given to each student taking the module at the first teaching session.

The module leader writes a draft assessment brief ensuring that it is consistent with the learning outcomes of the module and that it complies with the assessment strategy, type and weighting described in the module documents. The brief would typically include the following:

- module title
- learning outcomes being assessed
- assignment/examination text
- assessment criteria against which students will be assessed
- marking scheme
- format for submission

Table 2: Running a module.

Stage	Activity
1	Preparation of assessment — module plan and draft assessment briefs
2	Internal moderation of assessment — quality checking
3	External examining of assessment — quality checking for comparable standards
4	Student undertakes the assessment — assignments are completed and examinations undertaken
5	Marking and feedback — marks are awarded and supportive feedback provided
6	Internal moderation of student work — quality checking for consistency and fairness
7	External examining of student work — quality checking for comparable standards
8	Collection of student feedback — for evaluation of the module's performance
9	Completion of module report — record of the operation of a module

- submission date/ date and time of exam
- any special instructions for students

Stage 2: Internal moderation of assessment

Purpose: This quality assurance process ensures that the information given on the assessment is accurate and clear to the reader.

Details: Nominated teaching staff (e.g. course leaders) are given responsibility for the quality checking process as internal moderators. Their role is to check for academic appropriateness, 'levelness', content and completeness. They also ensure that the material and instructions make sense and are comprehensive and that grammar and spelling are checked.

The module leader gives the draft assessment with a Quality Control Checklist (see Example 1) to the appropriate internal moderator.

	Lecturer	Field Chair
ASSESSMENT QUALITY CONTROL CHECKLIST Please staple this to the top of the assessment and use ☑ or ☒ *No assessment may be forwarded to an external examiner, printed or distributed to students without the approval of the internal moderator* Module:　　　　　　　　Module Code:… Assignment type and no: Module leader:		
Module Plan		
Coursework/Examination Text (*delete as applicable*)		
Assessment Criteria – *clear assessment criteria are included for coursework assignments*		
Marking Scheme – *clear marking scheme included*		
Assessment type, weighting and timing are consistent with those specified on the module pro forma		
The assessment has been typed in the correct presentation style		
A hand-in date is given		
Grammar and spelling are correct		
The material makes sense		
The materials are complete		
Instructions for students are clear and comprehensive		
The assessment is related to the vocational focus of the degree/diploma		
Assessment is appropriate *at this level* in terms of:		
• 　Common/key skills		
• 　Knowledge and understanding		
• 　Cognitive skills		
• 　Subject specific skills including practical/professional skills		
The assessment is consistent with the learning outcomes of this module		
Final Internal Moderator approval (*Initials/date*)		
External Examiner approval (*Initials/date*)		

Example 1. Assessment quality control checklist.
Outcome 1:

- The internal moderator approves the draft assessment, signs off the checklist and returns the papers to the module leader.

Outcome 2:

- Changes are identified by the internal moderator and discussed with the module leader. Accepted changes are made to the draft assessment by the module leader, and the revised draft is returned to the internal moderator for final approval.

Once the internal quality control check has been successful, a version of the assessment and marking scheme can be prepared for forwarding to external examiners.

Stage 3: External examining of assessment

Purpose: External examiners are responsible for ensuring that standards of assessments are comparable to other institutions in the sector.

Details: The finalised and approved version of the assessment plus the module plan and the Quality Control Checklist should be sent to the external examiner, along with a deadline by which s/he should respond with any recommendations for amendments.

Outcome 1:

- The external examiner approves the assessment and signs the Quality Control Checklist.

Outcome 2:

- The external examiner makes recommendations for changes to the assessment. The module leader considers these, makes agreed amendments and returns the assessment to the external examiner again for final approval.

Once external approval has been obtained, it is conveyed to the module leader who then has the go-ahead to prepare and distribute the assignment or to proceed with an examination.

Stage 4: Student undertakes the assessment

Purpose: Assessment enables students to demonstrate that they have achieved the learning outcomes.

Details: Students complete coursework assignments or sit examinations for the assessment of the module. Student coursework should be recorded when it is submitted, so that late or non-submissions can be identified and tracked. Similarly, a register of students sitting examinations should be kept.

Stage 5: Marking and feedback

Purpose: Marking of assessments provides the measure by which students are classed, passed, failed and progressed. Feedback to students identifies deficiencies or commends achievement, thereby helping them to improve their performance.

Details: The module leader marks the student work against the assessment as detailed in the assignment brief or examination paper, using the marking scheme as guidance. Feedback sheets (see Example 2) are completed, with comments supporting the judgement

Example 2. Assessment feedback sheet.

Criteria	Excellent	Very Good	Good	Acceptable	Weak	Unacceptable
	☐	☐	☐	☐	☐	☐
	☐	☐	☐	☐	☐	☐
	☐	☐	☐	☐	☐	☐
	☐	☐	☐	☐	☐	☐
	☐	☐	☐	☐	☐	☐
	☐	☐	☐	☐	☐	☐
Addressing the question	☐	☐	☐	☐	☐	☐
Structure and flow/coherence	☐	☐	☐	☐	☐	☐
Appropriate use of language	☐	☐	☐	☐	☐	☐
Grammar	☐	☐	☐	☐	☐	☐
Spelling	☐	☐	☐	☐	☐	☐
Appropriate and varied reference sources	☐	☐	☐	☐	☐	☐
Correct use of referencing system	☐	☐	☐	☐	☐	☐

ASSIGNMENT FEEDBACK

Student :
Module Title:
Module Code:
Assignment Title:

Overall comment

Percentage Mark ....
NB All marks are provisional until confirmed by a formally constituted Board of Examiners

Signed:..................................... Date of marking:.......................................
For further help and guidance on any of the above please make an appointment to see me.

of the marker and the provisional mark given. Note that there are generic feedback items on this form as well as space to include subject or module specific items.

Marks for the whole module cohort are kept on a marking form, which should be forwarded to the administrative staff responsible for recording student marks. (A copy of this should always be kept!)

Stage 6: Internal moderation of student work
Purpose: Internal moderation ensures that assessment results conform to standards for the level, and that the marks awarded accurately reflect the marking scheme.

Details: Nominated members of the teaching staff are given responsibility for the quality checking process as internal moderators. A sample of the student work from across all grades is selected and, along with the assignment brief and marking scheme, is given to the appropriate internal moderator. The internal moderator checks that the marks awarded by the module leader correspond to the marking scheme, and that they are fair and consistent.

Outcome 1:

• The internal moderator agrees the marks, completes an internal moderation form (see Example 3) with supporting comments and returns the student work and internal moderation form to the module leader.

Example 3. Internal moderation form.

INTERNAL MODERATION FORM

Module title:
Module code:
Assessment element:

Module Leader/Ist Marker:

Internal Moderate:

Script seen by the Internal Moderate

() I agree the marks allocated for this assessment element

() I do not agree the marks allocated. The following action has been taken (eg. scaling of marks for the whole moduele)

() I am satisfied with the feedback given to students:

() I suggest that the following action be taken to improve the level of feedback to students:

General Comments on the scripts:

Signed: Date:

Outcome 2:

• The internal moderator disagrees with the marks awarded based on the marking scheme. The marks awarded are discussed with the module leader and scaling the marks may be suggested. Individual student marks should not be changed on the basis of a sample. If the internal moderator and the module leader cannot agree, then the sample of student work should be given to a second internal moderator. Once a compromise is reached, then any revised marks are recorded on the marking form.

The module leader makes copies of the student work and feedback in the internally moderated sample, and hands to staff responsible for forwarding student work to the external examiners, along with a copy of the assessment and marking form for the whole cohort. Student work and feedback with provisional marks is then returned to the students.

Stage 7: External examining of student work

Purpose: External examiners are responsible for ensuring that standards of student work are comparable with other institutions. They also confirm that the internal procedures for assessment of students have been followed.

   Details: The sample of student work and accompanying documentation should be sent to the external examiner.

   Outcome 1:

- The external examiner agrees the marks awarded.

   Outcome 2:

- The external examiner queries the marking and may discuss scaling. After discussions with the module leader, scaling of the whole cohort is either agreed or not agreed.

   Once agreed, the marks are forwarded for consideration at Boards of Examiners.

Stage 8: Collection of student feedback

Purpose: Feedback obtained from students contributes to the continuing evaluation of the quality of the module. It also informs the module report which in turn feeds into the annual monitoring process.

   Details: Towards the end of the teaching period a module leader should collect feedback from students on their opinion of the module. Questions could include whether the aims and objectives of the module were clear and whether they were achieved, the relevance of the module to the programme/course, the appropriateness of the teaching methods, the clarity of the lectures, the manageability of the assessment workload and the usefulness of the feedback received from the module leader.

Stage 9: Completion of module report

Purpose: The module report provides a record of the operation of a module, and in turn informs the annual monitoring process.

   Details: After completion of the module, a module report should be completed by the module leader giving details of the following:

- Student achievement
- Comments on results
- Comments on the module
- Student feedback
- External examiner comments if available

Conclusion: Areas of good practice for consideration:

- External examiners should be invited to visit and observe teaching and meet students
- External examiners should receive assessments sufficiently in advance of the hand-out date to allow for their comment and input
- The use of an internal moderation form provides evidence that standards of marking and feedback to students is taken seriously

Section 3: Annual Monitoring Process

Annual Monitoring enables institutions to evaluate their effectiveness, and demonstrate their concern for academic standards and quality of provision. The process facilitates the identification of good practice, whilst it also draws attention to areas of provision which may require improvement.

Table 3 details the annual monitoring process to be undertaken at Faculty or School level.

Stage 1: Collection of data at module level
Purpose: This enables the module leader to reflect on and evaluate the operation of a module.
Details: A Module Report should be produced (see Stage 9 of Running a Module above).

Stage 2: Programme/Course evaluation meeting
Purpose: A meeting of module leaders should be convened to encourage consultation and allow staff to have input into course reports.
Details: The programme teams should discuss, reflect on and evaluate the year's provision. Evidence to be considered should include:

- Module reports
- Student feedback
- Minutes of relevant meetings
- Progression and award statistics
- Reference to external frameworks

An external examiner's report for the programme/course should be prepared and considered, and a response constructed detailing any particular issues which need to be addressed and actions which need to be taken. Programme Specifications are examined to ascertain whether updating of information is required. The meeting may also involve annual monitoring auditors (appointed staff from different Faculties/Schools in the institution) enabling them to have the opportunity to observe the evaluation undertaken by those responsible for the provision.

Stage 3: Production of programme/course reports
Purpose: These reports demonstrate concern for academic standards of performance and quality of provision through critical self-evaluation. Production of reports also ensures that

Table 3: Annual monitoring process.

Stage	Activity
1	Collection of data at module level — evaluation of the module's performance
2	Programme/Course evaluation meeting — discussion between module leaders inputs into reports
3	Production of Programme/Course reports — texts of reports are written
4	Production of Faculty/School reports — text of report is written, informed by the Programme/Course reports
5	Consideration of reports — discussed at Faculty/School Board of Studies
6	Auditing of reports — examination of reports by academic peers

external examiners' reports are taken into consideration. Updating Programme Specifications ensures that information on the Programme/ Course remains current.

Details: Using information gathered at Stage 2, the text of each Report is written covering the following areas:

- Commentary on module performance
- Commentary on the course
- Teaching and learning approaches
- Impact of external frameworks
- Proposed changes to Programme/Course structure
- Programme/course statistics
- Feedback from students at Programme/Course level
- External examiner's report — issues and response
- Learning resources
- Status of key issues from previous year
- Key issues for forthcoming year

Programme Specifications are updated as necessary at this stage.

The reports should be considered at Programme/Course meetings and by annual monitoring process auditors and forwarded for consideration at the Board of Studies at School or Faculty level.

Stage 4: Production of faculty/school report

Purpose: This Report provides a record of activity in the Faculty/School for the academic year, and identifies issues affecting the quality of the educational provision and any actions taken to improve it. It also records and evaluates student achievement, student feedback and actions taken in response to issues raised.

Details: The text of the report is written, informed by issues raised in the Programme/ Course Reports, while also covering the following areas:

- Faculty/School overview
- Staffing including external activity
- Academic standards including impact of external referencing and overview of external examiners' reports
- Quality of the student experience as relating to the overall student learning environment
- Progression and achievement of students

The status of the previous year's action plan should be reviewed, and a new action plan identifying the main actions/issues for the forthcoming year constructed.

Stage 5: Consideration of reports

Purpose: A Faculty/School Board of Studies is responsible for ensuring it receives fully completed and considered Reports as it is the body responsible for maintaining and enhancing quality.

Details: Discussion of all the Reports should occur at a Faculty/School Board of Studies, which allows for additional information to be suggested for inclusion in the Reports, and also enables the sharing of good practice in their production. Any agreed changes are made to the

Reports, which are then approved at a subsequent meeting. Auditors should be present at the meetings to observe the transparency of discussion.

The final versions of the Reports are forwarded for consideration at institutional level.

Stage 6: Auditing of reports

Purpose: Auditing of the Reports ensures adherence to processes, identifies issues and confirms initiation of appropriate actions.

Details: Auditing involves the examination of the documents by peers external to the Faculty/School, plus discussions with the Programme/Course and Faculty/School teams. The auditors produce a report on their findings for consideration in due course at institutional level. Areas of good practice for consideration include inviting auditors to meetings where annual monitoring is discussed, ensuring auditors are sent the draft reports and sending copies of finalised reports to external examiners.

Conclusion

The practical issues around quality of curriculum design, delivery and evaluation are based around the plan–do–review cycle common to many quality systems. The key elements of a well-thought-out system are planning, transparency, evaluation and peer review. Planning should ensure that the curriculum is fit for its intended purpose. Transparency means that everyone involved — staff and students-know how the system works. Evaluation works at two levels. First, regular evaluation should ensure that the programme is delivered in the way it was planned. Second, evaluation should regularly review the programme for continued fitness for purpose. Finally, peer review should ensure that good ideas are shared, and that the process is undertaken thoroughly.

Part 2: Managing Learning Resources for Tourism Students

Introduction

In the current environment for teaching tourism, the learning resources available are numerous and diverse (see Chapter 30). They range from books, journals and other traditional print materials, to online sources of information in the form of websites, electronic journals and databases. Deciding which research tools to use, and finding specific information within these resources, offers a challenge to both students and educators.

Although universities still invest heavily in books and journals, electronic resources are increasingly taking up large portions of library budgets. In some cases electronic resources will replace print materials outright, but ideally, digital and print collections should complement each other and offer the widest possible scope for research. To maximise the benefit of both print and online materials, these collections should be well chosen and integrated.

Higher education institutions are trying a variety of means for making learning resources easily available. University library webpages and online catalogues often serve as starting points for finding resources both in-house and through the internet.

Virtual Learning Environments may provide direct access into specific educational materials. Departments within institutions and individual academic staff often provide 'useful internet links' from their own webpages. This multi-tiered approach may lead a student to valid information from whichever access point he/she is located. However, this method can also cause confusion if it means that learning resources are not organised in a coherent manner.

Even if the access to learning resources is straightforward, lack of training can hinder their use. In order to maximise the potential of learning resources, it is vital to provide basic information skills training along with user education for specific research tools. Effective training, along with strategic organisation and dissemination of learning resources, will not only assist students in finding high-quality and relevant information. It will also increase usage of learning resources — helping to ensure that an institution's investment in this area is well spent.

Collection Management

The majority of learning resources in higher education institutions are managed by the library, and each academic library should have its own collection management policy. Even a very basic collection management policy can be a useful tool for generating guidelines for the selection and management of learning resources and should address a few key considerations (Jenkins & Morley, 1999):

Allocation of budget: It will be necessary to make informed decisions regarding the funding and allocation of the learning resources budget. How the budget will be divided amongst individual subject areas may be influenced by factors such as student numbers, volume of courses or costs of discipline-specific resources.

Stock selection: Ideally, the library will purchase learning resources in consultation with academic staff. Factors influencing choice of material may include: relevance to teaching and/or research; currency; student demand for a particular resource; price and value for money. Table 4 details questions which can be posed when selecting specific types of learning resources.

Withdrawing stock: Considerations when withdrawing stock may include currency, actual use of the resource, physical condition, availability of electronic versions and space constraints.

Accessibility: Learning Resources should be located so that they will receive the highest possible use. Depending on the institution, this could mean housing a subject-specific collection at a separate site, or conversely, distributing resources across campuses. Decisions about which items are available for loan or for reference use, and what is available on and off campus will depend on costs and overall collection management policy, but can be influenced by the needs and expectations of both students and staff. Any access strategy should take into account distance learners and special needs users. The institution should also determine how it will assist students in accessing resources held elsewhere (for example, through inter-library loans or collaborative schemes).

Table 4: Stock selection.

Books (Core texts)	How many students require the book, and how many copies per group of students? (Are students expected to purchase their own copies or are they relying exclusively on library stock?)
Journals	How do new journals complement or duplicate existing subscriptions? Should a journal be available in print, electronically or both? Is it already available electronically via a database subscription?
Statistics, reports, conference proceedings	Are these reports required for specific reasons? How much use will they receive? Are they available elsewhere (for example, free via the internet)?
Background reading	How much background reading is required and how much can be found through existing electronic subscriptions (databases, electronic journals, etc.)?
Electronic resources	Which electronic databases are vital for tourism studies? Is there a duplication of content in database subscriptions, or between databases and electronic journals?
Multimedia	Are multimedia materials required for teaching, research, or both? How much use will they receive and do they offer something unique to the user?
Newspapers	Should newspapers be received in print, electronically, or both?
Theses	Where in the institution should theses be held and how will they be accessed?
Special collections	Where will special collections be housed, and who will manage them? Will there be a need to acquire more material for the special collection?

Integrating Learning Resources

Most academic institutions deliver electronic access to in-house learning resources via their library website. This approach means that all learning resources are available and managed at a central location, and therefore are easy to find. However, students are probably not concerned with the fact that learning resources are the 'domain' of the library. They simply want a convenient means of finding relevant information (Tenopir, Hitchcock, & Pillow, 2003). To ensure that students are taking full advantage of learning resources, there must be a straightforward access point (either through the library website or elsewhere) which clearly presents what is available, and allows easy navigation between resources regardless of format.

Although academic libraries still invest heavily in traditional print materials (Creaser, Maynard, & White, 2004), electronic resources are equally vital tools for research. Effectively integrating online and print collections is a challenge. The library catalogue will give students access to a full list of books and journals available in-house, and can also provide access to electronic versions of the same titles by including links into online subscriptions. However, although the catalogue can offer straightforward delivery of a mix of the institution's own learning resources, it may not be an appropriate means for accessing material elsewhere since it is, after all, a record of what is held in the library collection.

Some library catalogues also provide links into subscription databases. Yet, database access through the catalogue may cause confusion for students since a database is often used to find journal articles or book chapters, regardless of whether they are held by the institution. Databases can be treated as a unique type of research tool and grouped by subject on the library web page, and if the database provides full text, it can be used without reference to anything else. But in the area of tourism, the majority of databases provide only index records or abstracts, so after using the database, the student must then locate a copy of the actual book or journal to which the citation refers.

Databases, bibliographies and even internet search engines can lead students to resources which may not be available in their own academic institution. Union catalogue websites, usually sponsored by academic or local library networks, allow cross-institutional searching of library catalogues, so books or journals can be easily found in other collections. Any integration of in-house learning resources should take into account the facilities available for finding resources elsewhere, and there should also be information available about how these materials can be accessed.

Internet subject gateways and other relevant websites bring another dimension to the integration of tourism learning resources. Groups of useful websites are usually given to students in simple lists for the subject area, or are sometimes arranged by the type of resource (for example, 'statistics' or 'government reports'). This approach makes it easy for the student to find internet information sources for their area of interest, but there is the danger that by grouping websites in subject lists, others that may have tangential relevance will be missed. Regardless of how websites or other online resources are recommended, it is vitally important that they are checked regularly so students are not being directed to information sources that no longer exist.

Training

New students may receive an induction in the use of library resources, but this is often done in the first few weeks of term, and usually focuses on the basics of using the library facilities. At some point, they should also receive an introduction to learning resources for their subject area and training in the use of these resources — preferably before research for specific assignments begins. Because of demands on the time of both students and staff, this further training often is not provided. This is unfortunate since an awareness of available research tools and an understanding of their use will almost certainly save students' wasted research time in the long run. Once an institution has invested in learning resources, it makes sense to actively promote their use through training, rather than assume that students will be able to find and use learning resources without assistance.

Instead of overloading students with learning resources training at the beginning of the academic year, it may be more practical and useful to approach information skills as an ongoing part of their education. A checklist for learning resource training is given in Table 5. If user education sessions are strategically targeted to lectures or assignments, students are more likely to remember and immediately apply what they have learned. Printed guides which detail the use of particular learning resources should be on hand for students to refer

Table 5: Introducing students to learning resources — checklist.

- Have students had a library induction or training in the basic use of the library (i.e. borrowing books, finding journals, using the catalogue, etc.)?
- Are students familiar with the institution's library website and the resources available?
- Have students had the opportunity for training, or practice using specific electronic resources?
- Have students been given a list of relevant websites to explore?
- Do students know their options for sourcing material elsewhere?

to independently. The option for one-to-one training should be available along with the understanding that if a student tries a resource and it does not work, they can return for further advice. A librarian who understands the subject area as well as the application of learning resources will be able to recommend other in-house resources, or offer guidance on how to find resources elsewhere.

Academic staff can work with the library regarding the delivery of learning resources, but should also make sure they themselves have current knowledge of what is available. When actively using a variety of research tools, both students and staff can offer constructive feedback on what they find useful, and learning resources will become a dynamic part of the educational environment.

References

Buckinghamshire Chilterns University College, Formal Documents: *Q1 Validation and Review Process October 2003*; *Q6 Annual Review and Evaluation February 2004*; *Q26 Assessment Process September 2004*.

Creaser, C., Maynard, S., & White, S. (2004). *LISU annual library statistics 2004*. Leicester: Loughborough University.

Jenkins, C., & Morley, M. (1999). *Collection management in academic libraries* (2nd ed.). Aldershot: Gower.

Quality Assurance Agency for Higher Education. (2000). *Code of practice for the assurance of academic quality and standards in higher education — Section 6: Assessment of students — May 2000*.

Quality Assurance Agency for Higher Education. (2000). *Code of practice for the assurance of academic quality and standards in higher education —- Section 7: Programme approval, monitoring and review — April 2000*.

Tenopir, C., Hitchcock, D., & Pillow, A. (2003). *Use and users of electronic library resources: An overview and analysis of recent research studies*. Washington, DC: Council of Library and Information Resources.

Chapter 35

Issues for the Future

David Airey and John Tribe

As amply demonstrated in the chapters of this book, education for tourism has come a long way from its early beginnings in the 1960s. Tourism is now studied in virtually all parts of the world. Chapters 8–19 have examples from countries in all continents and there are many others, not covered here, which have thriving education for tourism. At the same time as the provision has extended across the world it has also been both deepened and strengthened. Depth has come from research and development of knowledge (as set out in Chapters 2–4), which has in turn allowed the curriculum to extend beyond its vocational origins. Strength has come from a range of developments in learning and teaching techniques. Indeed, as set out in Chapters 20–28, as a relatively new and growing subject of study, and with the challenge of bringing theory and practice together, tourism has often been in the lead in teaching developments. The organisation of work experience placements (Chapter 7), the use of dissertations (Chapter 24) and the inclusion of cultural issues (Chapter 25) provide examples. All this has been permitted by the massive development of resources, in academic staffing and staff qualifications (Chapter 29), in the range and quality of the literature (books, journals and e-materials) (Chapter 30), as well as in the number and size of organisations, conferences and other events focused on tourism in academia. More than a decade ago a study of tourism education at degree level in the UK suggested that the subject had "come of age" (Council for National Academic Awards, 1993). If that was true then it is even more so now.

Tourism education has indeed charted some significant successes in establishing itself as an important element in the education repertoire at virtually all levels for students, from about the age of 16 years. Certainly it has proved a popular field of study. Some of the early graduates are now among the leaders of tourism worldwide both in the commercial and non-commercial sectors. Some of tourism's journals rank with the best in the world. Bodies such as the Council for Australian University Tourism and Hospitality Education (CAUTHE), the Association for Tourism in Higher Education in the UK (ATHE) as well as The Association for Tourism and Leisure Education (ATLAS), with its international reach, have proved to be very effective in representing the views of tourism education and providing opportunities for the development of a community of scholars. But as noted in some country reports there is still scope for the development of such subject associations at the national level and beyond this to encourage co-operation between national associations at the global level.

Similarly, the internet contacts provided by TRINET were among the early developments in this form communication between scholars.

Over the time of its development, when tourism programmes have come in for scrutiny by national and international quality agencies they have been found to be providing good learning opportunities for their students. Chapter 32 provides a detailed look at this in the UK. At an international level the Tourism Education Quality (TEDQUAL) process of the World Tourism Organization has an increasing number of centres that have successfully passed its scrutiny. Indeed, it is some measure of the success of tourism education at an international level that the United Nations Specialist Agency for Tourism, the World Tourism Organization (WTO), has its own Education Council with its chair and representatives drawn from universities and colleges from around the world. Few other sectors of education have this kind of representation at the highest international level with opportunities to contribute to the meetings at the General Assembly and elsewhere (World Tourism Organization, 2004).

However, despite this apparent success, tourism as an area for study is still faced with uncertainties. In a keynote address to the annual conference of the Association for Tourism in Higher Education in the UK, Airey (2005) traced the seemingly ever-present uncertainties that have faced tourism educators over the past 40 years. These include simple misunderstandings about what the study of tourism is about, doubts about the seriousness of the subject, concern about the over-reliance on what Tribe has referred to as *extradisciplinary* knowledge (Chapter 4), worries about the proper balance between vocationalism and academicism, questions of whether there is a need for a core curriculum, the challenge of identifying a unique body of knowledge about tourism, concern about the best location for tourism programmes in institutional and organisational arrangements and the associated invisibility of tourism if it is spread and divided across a range of different subject areas and departments. In various ways these themes of uncertainty are reflected and given detail in many of the chapters here. It is notable in the country studies that all seem to be grappling with the same issues. As Airey (in press) has commented:

> In many ways, the issue is that tourism education is a victim of its own success. Its success in attracting students and scholars has created a thriving subject area that offers rich topics for research and study that can make a real difference to a major sector of human activity. Yet the very things that have made it successful, particularly its vocationalism and its multidisciplinarity are the very things that may stand in the way of its full development and recognition as a serious field of study. Vocationalism seems to have been good for attracting students but not for academic reputation and multidisciplinarity makes for stimulating programmes but fragmented research.

Similarly, in a recent study of UK lecturer perceptions of quality in tourism higher education Tribe also noted a mixture of strengths and challenges. Taking strengths first, he found that:

> The key strength that emerges from the survey is general lecturer confidence in quality … The high quality assessment of teaching is significant

… Specific areas that scored highly in the lecturer survey also included the level, coherence and knowledge content of the curriculum; moderation, marking and feedback; the use of module documents; assessment packages; academic guidance and tutorial support; pastoral and welfare support; and validation procedures (2003, p. 39).

Turning to challenges, Tribe found:

… the need to address the problem of the substantial group of lecturers who feel that they are falling behind in terms of scholarship…. Indeed the specific issue of scholarship appears to be part of a wider neglect of staff development in general, which the survey highlights as an area in need of improvement. Also perhaps related to these issues is the area of currency and innovation in the curriculum which many lecturers signal as a weakness. Interestingly, student scholarship is also seen as a particular problem. The oft-heard witticism that students no longer *read* for degrees is given clear credence by the findings of this survey… Then there are some specifics which achieved low scores in the lecturer survey. These include careers information and guidance; technical and administrative support; teaching accommodation; and quality management and enhancement (2003, p. 39).

Despite the uncertainties and challenges, as already noted and made clear in this book, many of the ingredients for success for tourism education are already in place. Success above all will now depend on a number of key factors. First among these will be the quality and development of the academic staff both as researchers and as teachers. All subject areas depend upon the creation and refreshment of knowledge and its effective dissemination. It is these that make the topic of interest and relevance to students, to employers and to the wider community. Tourism has certainly been effective in attracting some very talented scholars in recent years, the challenge now will be to retain them and ensure that they have opportunities for development.

In terms of research there are perhaps some interesting contrasts to be made here between the UK and Australia. In Chapter 8 of this book, King and Craig-Smith celebrate the fact that:

The tourism research environment in Australia has been transformed as a result of the establishment and development of the Sustainable Tourism Co-operative Research Centre (STCRC). The STCRC is the largest of the CRCs established by the Commonwealth Government to provide strategic research capacity as a result of partnerships between Government, the private sector and universities.

In the UK, however, tourism research does not appear to be well served by government policy. The research assessment exercise (RAE) is a key factor in assessing university research and distributing funding in the UK. But in its evidence to the consultation on the RAE planned for 2008, the ATHE included the following submission:

> The ATHE wishes to register a strong protest about the invisibility of Tourism Studies in the proposed Units of Assessment (UoAs) for RAE 2008. It contests the claim that RAE 2008 will 'recognise excellence … in new disciplines and in fields crossing traditional disciplinary boundaries' (http://www.rae.ac.uk/news/). For indeed, tourism studies seems to represent the epitome of a new field and one that crosses traditional disciplinary boundaries and yet is ill-served by the proposed UoA structure for RAE 2008. It therefore urges the funding councils to reconsider the current titles of UoAs and ensure that Tourism Studies is given the prominence it deserves (Tribe, 2004, p. 71).

This discussion demonstrates that in tourism education, as in most areas of international trade, a country's competitive advantage can be heavily influenced by government policy. Indeed this consideration led ATHE to warn that:

> Tourism research leadership will pass from the UK to our international competitors (Tribe, 2004, p. 73).

The other key research issue for tourism education is to combat the dichotomy that still persists between research and teaching. They are often seen as either/or, the latter is often given less status than the former, and the two are often able to exist in splendid isolation from each other. Research needs to inform teaching in two ways. First, lecturers must include their research methods and findings and those of others in their teaching as a matter of course rather than exception. Second, research into tourism education must be encouraged.

This latter research should contribute to the development of the pedagogy (including assessment) for tourism. Much of the debate about tourism education over its relatively short life has focused on the curriculum (Chapter 20). It is interesting to look back at the contents of one of the early contributions to tourism education, the special issue of the *Annals of Tourism Research* (Vol 8(1), 1981). Virtually all of the chapters deal with curricular issues and reflect the ongoing uncertainties about content, focus, cohesion and structure. If the subject has come of age, obsession with the curriculum should decline and in its place there needs to be a reconsideration of the pedagogy and the associated student experience. In this respect the issue of student reading mentioned above is an interesting one for our times. It is clear that there has been a monumental revolution in communications that separates the generation that teaches tourism from the generation that is now learning about it. Understanding the consequences, lessons and implication of this for contemporary pedagogy must surely be an urgent challenge for tourism lecturers.

Growth in higher education worldwide is leading all governments to re-examine the ways in which it is funded, and this almost inevitably will lead to some of the costs being passed to the student and their families and away from the general taxpayer. This is already the norm in many countries. When this happens the student experience becomes a central issue in attracting and retaining students and within this the learning experience and associated pedagogy become extremly important. As outlined in the chapters in the *Teaching, Learning and Assessment* section of this book, tourism is well placed to meet the challenges of this. Already tourism programmes provide excellent examples of adventurous and stimulating teaching and learning, but there is still a need to keep attention focused more on what makes a good teacher and a good teaching experience and less on revisiting the past debates on the curriculum.

But growth in higher education does not just herald a move towards self-financing students who thereby become more discerning and demanding customers. It also means that the student body changes. Here issues of widening participation will offer significant challenges for the future. While it was possible in an elite system of higher education to assume a common inheritance of educational capital among first year students this assumption is likely to be seriously challenged as the student body becomes more diverse.

One of the characteristics of education for tourism in many parts of the world is that it is highly international both in the student population and in the academic staff. However, all too often this internationalism has not been well developed, either to provide wider cultural dimensions to the study or to provide wider mobilities. The developments under the Bologna initiative in the countries of the European Union, (Chapters 13, 15 and 17) provide a beginning to increased internationalisation in that part of the world. But the significant number of students from other areas, particularly from China and South East Asia, suggest that there is scope for a much more adventurous approach to internationalism. In part, this is about ensuring that the development of tourism knowledge, the delivery of programmes and the production of resources do not pursue an exclusively "western" orientation, but it is equally about providing opportunities for mobility of staff and students. With the development of multi-national campuses and distance learning opportunities, including e-learning, this becomes even more urgent. Given its head-start with international contacts, tourism could well trail a path for other subject areas in becoming global in its approach to education.

The international aspects of tourism education also demonstrate another interesting dynamic. Just as in tourism we may distinguish between tourism generating countries and tourism destinations, a similar distinction can be applied to tourism education. Historically the UK, North America and Australasia have been significant tourism education destinations while the developing world has tended to represent the main sites for generating students. However the outcome of this process (more postgraduate and Ph.D. completions) has now led to greater capacity to provide tourism education in former generating countries. Thus, it is likely in the future that more students will be able to pursue tourism studies in their own regions — initially mainly at undergraduate level but increasingly at the postgraduate and research student level.

The over-supply of programmes and graduates has been a fairly constant strand of criticism of tourism education. Looked at in fairly narrow terms of programmes providing fairly specific training and education for specific entry positions in industry, the criticism may be justified. Indeed some of the early programmes may have had such a narrow orientation. However, today there is little excuse for programmes to be confined to narrow vocationalism. The knowledge base about tourism is extensive and provides a rich basis from which to develop programmes and in turn will provide a broad and demanding education at all levels.

From this graduates should be equipped for a range of career and personal development opportunities. The most important ingredient in this is that the education and the knowledge base on which it draws must do much more than reflect the immediate needs of the work place or the immediate demands of the entry employment positions. After an intense period of growth and development, tourism education is now in a good position to do this: to provide new insights to the operation and management of a major world activity; to contribute to the effective stewardship of scarce resources used by tourism; to ensure that those who leave their courses have a range of knowledge and skills for their career, whether it be in tourism or elsewhere. It is these features that will make tourism education relevant for the future.

As Craig-Smith, Cooper, and Ruhanen (2004, p. 17) have commented:

> Knowledge is increasingly seen as the key to strategic growth, sustainability and competitive advantage for both national economies and private enterprises, which has given rise to the concept of knowledge management. Knowledge management seeks to secure the viability and success of an organisation by maximising its knowledge assets... Knowledge management must be considered as an underpinning objective of future research agendas so that the increasing intellectual capital in tourism can be transformed into industry capabilities.

From the information provided by the contributors to this book the tourism education provision looks well placed to play a leading role in its contribution to knowledge and to tourism worldwide.

References

Airey. D. (in press). From here to uncertainty. *Critical issues in tourism education. Proceedings of association for tourism in higher education conference*, 1–3 December 2004. (forthcoming).

Council for National Academic Awards. (1993). *Review of tourism studies degree courses.* London: CNAA.

Craig-Smith, S., Cooper, C., & Ruhanen, L. (2004). Knowledge management and tourism in world tourism organization. *The role of education in quality destination management. Proceedings of the WTO education council conference in Beijing*, China, 23 October 2003. Madrid: WTO.

Tribe, J. (2003). Delivering higher quality: A comparative study of lecturers' perceptions and QAA subject review in tourism. *Journal of Hospitality, Leisure, Sport and Tourism Education, 2*(1), 27–47.

Tribe, J. (2004). Extracts from the ATHE response to the consultation document 'RAE 02/2004: Panel configuration and recruitment' for the UK research assessment exercise 2008. *Journal of Hospitality, Leisure, Sport and Tourism Education, 3*(1), 71–74.

World Tourism Organization. (2004). The role of education in quality destination management. Proceedings of the WTO education council conference in Beijing, China, 23 October 2003. Madrid: WTO.

Author Index

Subject Index